Career Development and Transition Services

A Functional Life Skills Approach

Fourth Edition

Donn E. Brolin

Late of University of Missouri–Columbia

Robert J. Loyd

Armstrong Atlantic State University

PEARSON

Merrill
Prentice Hall

Upper Saddle River, New Jersey
Columbus, Ohio

Vice President and Executive Publisher: Jeffrey W. Johnston
Acquisitions Editor: Allyson P. Sharp
Editorial Assistants: Penny Burleson and Kathleen S. Burk
Production Editor: Linda Hillis Bayma
Production Coordination and Text Design: D&G Limited, LLC
Design Coordinator: Diane C. Lorenzo
Photo Coordinator: Valerie Schultz
Cover Designer: Jason Moore
Cover art: SuperStock
Production Manager: Laura Messerly
Director of Marketing: Ann Castel Davis
Marketing Manager: Amy June
Marketing Coordinator: Tyra Poole

This book was set in Garamond by D&G Limited, LLC. It was printed and bound by R.R. Donnelley & Sons Company. The cover was printed by The Lehigh Press, Inc.

Photo Credits: Scott Cunningham/Merrill, pp. 1, 85, 94, 139, 166, 179, 221, 281, 306, 324, 328, 341, 419; Ken Karp/PH College, p. 282; Kathy Kirtland/Merrill, p. 59; Anthony Magnacca/Merrill, p. 35, 44, 117, 165, 195, 453; Anne Vega/Merrill, pp. 251, 299, 420; Tom Watson/Merrill, p. 2; Todd Yarrington/Merrill, pp. 93, 370.

Pearson Education Ltd.
Pearson Education Singapore Pte. Ltd.
Pearson Education Canada, Ltd.
Pearson Education—Japan

Pearson Education Australia Pty. Limited
Pearson Education North Asia Ltd.
Pearson Educación de Mexico, S.A. de C.V.
Pearson Education Malaysia Pte. Ltd.

10 9 8 7 6 5 4 3 2 1
ISBN: 0-13-048506-3

This book is dedicated to the late Dr. Donn Brolin, a wonderful person, teacher, researcher, writer, and visonary who, without his foresight, would not have provided all students with special learning and/or behavior needs the vehicle to have a better quality of life as adults. Donn was my friend, my mentor, and my hero. He has given my professional career real meaning and fulfillment. Donn's Life Centered Career Education (LCCE) curriculum has touched the lives of so many adults with disabilities, teachers, and other professionals and, more importantly, will continue to affect the lives of future consumers of the LCCE program.

I would also like to dedicate this book to Donna, who is my best friend, my soulmate, and my wife.

Foreword

Good ideas in education don't disappear. They come back again and again over time. Frequently, good ideas that are ahead of their times resurface as even better ideas when there is a readiness to accept them. Sometimes, the ideas are framed in different language, sometimes in different policy or delivery features. Certainly, this is the case for the long established idea that education should be useful and a means to multiple "ends" and not an end in itself.

Life skills instruction for students with special learning, behavior, sensory, or motor needs is a good idea that won't go away, even though the reform pendulum swings public and professional attention away from it in fairly regular cycles. Each generation of professionals has a need to respond to current educational challenges in its own way. Too often, this is done without much attention to what has been done or tried in the past. Our long-time friend and colleague, Donn Brolin, was an exception to this in his approach of looking ahead, but not losing sight of what had gone before.

The first time I met Donn was in response to his invitation in 1970 to come to his campus in Menomonie, Wisconsin (Wisconsin-Stout State University) to join a small group of people to help generate ideas related to research questions in his federally funded grant: What do students with mild mental retardation need to know or be able to do when they leave school? What do secondary special education teachers need to know and to do to prepare those stu-

dents for life after school? This early career project ultimately developed into the Life Centered Career Education (LCCE) model. Throughout his productive career, Donn held to enduring, valued ideas, but he adapted those ideas to the times and conditions of the educational community.

The succeeding editions of this book reflect the challenge of life skills education in the context of changing times. That is as it should be and this new edition extends the need for and power of life skills instruction in the language and perspective of transition services. The transition services provisions of the Individuals with Disabilities Act (IDEA) provided new conditions—the existence of legally mandated means of providing students the life skills instruction they need and the service linkages that are critical for their futures.

This edition is a tribute to the career contributions of Donn, Bob Loyd's continued refinements, and all those who worked closely with Donn to produce the LCCE model, LCCE curriculum, and the LCCE assessment battery. At the same time, it moves us forward and should breathe new life into the teachers, career development specialists, transition specialists, and administrators who believe in a useful education for all students.

Gary M. Clark, Ed.D.
Professor of Special Education
University of Kansas

About the Authors

Donn E. Brolin was a professor emeritus of educational and counseling psychology at the University of Missouri in Columbia. He received his Ph.D. in special education and rehabilitation psychology from the University of Wisconsin-Madison in 1969. Donn was the first president of the Division on Career Development and Transition (1976–1978) of The Council for Exceptional Children (CEC) and, in 1990, received CEC's prestigious J. E. Wallace Wallin Education of Handicapped Children Award which honors one professional each year who has made outstanding contributions to the education of children with disabilities. His professional activities and projects focused on educational consulting and writing with a major focus on validating, improving, and expanding the educational materials contained in his *Life Centered Career Education (LCCE) Curriculum* published by The Council for Exceptional Children.

Robert J. Loyd is an associate professor of special education at the Armstrong Atlantic State University in Savannah, Georgia. He received his Ph.D. from the University of Missouri-Columbia in 1987. Bob began working with Donn Brolin on the Life Centered Career Education Curriculum programs in 1983 and continues his work after Dr. Brolin's untimely passing. Bob's major contribution to Dr. Brolin's work has been the development of the Life Centered Career Education Curriculum for Students with Moderate Disabilities. His professional activities and projects focus on writing with a major focus on validating, improving, and expanding the educational and assessment materials for students with moderate disabilities. Dr. Loyd's major program materials include an LCCE Moderate Pictorial Knowledge Battery (PKB), LCCE Moderate Performance Assessment Batteries (PABs), 19 Competency Units, and Family Unit Notebooks (FUN).

Preface

· ·

Beginning in the 1970s, many professionals and parents envisioned and predicted that by the twenty-first century, schools would be preparing most students with disabilities with the skills to achieve successful adult outcomes. Nevertheless, as we progress through this first decade of the twenty-first century and after more than 30 years since the enactment of the Education for All Handicapped Children Act (P.L. 94-142) in 1975, we are still finding that many schools have not totally met this prognostication.

Ironically, it was during my first year of teaching special education that P.L. 94-142 was enacted. I remember that we neophytes, along with experienced special educators, spent many hours analyzing the law's novel provisions and had such hopes that the programs we were developing would be the remedy for preparing all students for successful community living and working.

I am not saying that schools haven't gotten better, because there have been significant improvements made to this landmark legislation. The law's reauthorizations have continually made strides toward the integration of students into general education and instillation of more equity between the general and special education systems. But still, after more than 30 years, I am still somewhat bewildered as to why we have not significantly (a) improved the personalized transitional outcomes of young adults with disabilities, (b) prepared students to become self-determined, (c) enhanced young adults' quality of life, and (d) developed systems of reliable alliances to provide follow-along suppor.

Maybe I am unrealistic and naive to expect that in this period of time the field could achieve such a goal. However, we currently do have many innovative and effective field-validated functional transitional curricular methods and materials available for preparing students with special learning and/or behavior needs for achieving this critical goal.

Have state and local educational agencies responded to the cry for reform to restructure their programs to better meet the personalized transitional needs of their students with special learning and/or behavior needs? Or, are most schools still providing, or emphasizing even more, the traditional standard academic-oriented curriculum that presents unwarranted stress, frustration, and failure experiences for the many students with special learning and/or behavior needs? If so, why don't schools make the changes to meet the personalized transitional needs of these students who have the potential to become independent, functioning members of their communities?

If the purpose of education is to prepare all students to realize their potential so they can function successfully in society, schools will need to provide flexible options for these students who need a modified curriculum to meet their special learning and/or behavior needs. If educators and others spend the time and effort to restructure their programs and attitudes appropriately, all students, including those requiring a modified curriculum, can become productive citizens.

Attitudes must change! Educators, family members, agency workers, employers, and most importantly the general public must believe that almost every student with serious academic learning and/or behavior difficulties can be prepared to function as productive citizens who can live and work successfully in their communities. They must believe that it is their joint responsibility to ensure that all students' potentials are realized. It is my firm belief that this goal is attainable *if all stakeholders/reliable alliances* develop and provide a more substantive systematic transitional program that emphasizes the appropriate blend of academic and functional skills instruction. Such a program must begin prior to the elementary years and requires the active involvement of the student's family along with many local support resources. The program must be built on the concepts of the career education movement of the 1970s and the transition approach of the 1980s that continued throughout the last part of twentieth century but which has not yet been widely adopted by the majority of schools. As the old adage goes, "Everyone is for change, unless it is they that have to do it!"

In this book, a comprehensive functional life skills curriculum model and framework is presented. This curricular approach—Life Centered Career Education (LCCE) Mild/Moderate Curriculum—has evolved over more than 25 years and has stood the test of time. LCCE provides the guidelines and specific information to interface with the academic curriculum, to form a comprehensive, functional K–12 life skills approach for students who need such an approach to become productive and independent members of their community. Numerous school districts throughout the country have adopted the model and are using its methods and materials to provide a more functional life skills approach that will eventually lead their students to a successful transition to community living and working. Examples of the efforts of several schools are presented. In addition to the LCCE Mild/Moderate Curriculum approach, several other models and curriculum materials and resources are covered so that readers may consider and secure information on them if they warrant further investigation.

ACKNOWLEDGMENTS

Special appreciation is expressed for Professor Gary N. Clark, University of Kansas, who is one of the most outstanding and highly respected visionaries in the area of transition, functional skills, and career development. Gary has supported Dr. Donn Brolin's efforts since 1970, when he first provided consultative services to his federal special education curriculum development project. He has never stopped providing support and advice on Donn's need to expand and improve LCCE Curriculum research and development activities while he has been contributing immensely himself to the transition career development literature and field.

Appreciation is also extended to the reviewers: Ruth M. C. Buehler, Millersville University; Patrick Grant, Slippery Rock University; Kathy Peca, Eastern New Mexico University; and James Yanok, Ohio University.

I am also particularly indebted to the late Bruno D'Alonzo, Rick Roessler, Mike Wehmeyer, Pat and Mike Burch, Iva Dean Cook, Sharon Field, Sharon Davis, Stephen Thomas, and to the other contributors to this book, especially my dear friend, Michael Bullis.

Robert J. Loyd

Discover the Companion Website Accompanying This Book

THE PRENTICE HALL COMPANION WEBSITE: A VIRTUAL LEARNING ENVIRONMENT

Technology is a constantly growing and changing aspect of our field that is creating a need for content and resources. To address this emerging need, Prentice Hall has developed an online learning environment for students and professors alike—Companion Websites—to support our textbooks.

In creating a Companion Website, our goal is to build on and enhance what the textbook already offers. For this reason, the content for each user-friendly website is organized by topic and provides the professor and student with a variety of meaningful resources. Common features of a Companion Website include:

For the Professor—

Every Companion Website integrates **Syllabus Manager**™, an online syllabus creation and management utility.

- **Syllabus Manager**™ provides you, the instructor, with an easy, step-by-step process to create and revise syllabi, with direct links into the Companion Website and other online content without having to learn HTML.

- Students may logon to your syllabus during any study session. All they need to know is the web address for the Companion Website and the password you've assigned to your syllabus.

- After you have created a syllabus using **Syllabus Manager**™, students may enter the syllabus for their course section from any point in the Companion Website.

- Clicking on a date, the student is shown the list of activities for the assignment. The activities for each assignment are linked directly to actual content, saving time for students.

- Adding assignments consists of clicking on the desired due date, then filling in the details of the assignment—name of the assignment, instructions, and whether it is a one-time or repeating assignment.

- In addition, links to other activities can be created easily. If the activity is online, a URL can be entered in the space provided, and it will be linked automatically in the final syllabus.

- Your completed syllabus is hosted on our servers, allowing convenient updates from any computer on the Internet. Changes you make to your syllabus are immediately available to your students at their next logon.

For the Student—

- **Overview and General Information**—General information about the topic and how it will be covered in the website.

- **Web Links**—A variety of websites related to topic areas.
- **Content Methods and Strategies**—Resources that help to put theories into practice in the special education classroom.
- **Reflective Questions and Case-Based Activities** —Put concepts into action, participate in activities, examine strategies, and more.
- **National and State Laws**—An online guide to how federal and state laws affect your special education classroom.

- **Behavior Management**—An online guide to help you manage behaviors in the special education classroom.
- **Message Board**—Virtual bulletin board to post and respond to questions and comments from a national audience.

To take advantage of these and other resources, please visit the *Career Development and Transition Services: A Functional Life Skills Approach*, Fourth Edition, Companion Website at

www.prenhall.com/brolin

Educator Learning Center:
An Invaluable Online Resource

Merrill Education and the Association for Supervision and Curriculum Development (ASCD) invite you to take advantage of a new online resource, one that provides access to the top research and proven strategies associated with ASCD and Merrill—the Educator Learning Center. At **www.EducatorLearningCenter.com** you will find resources that will enhance your students' understanding of course topics and of current educational issues, in addition to being invaluable for further research.

How the Educator Learning Center will help your students become better teachers
With the combined resources of Merrill Education and ASCD, you and your students will find a wealth of tools and materials to better prepare them for the classroom.

Research
- More than 600 articles from the ASCD journal *Educational Leadership* discuss everyday issues faced by practicing teachers.
- A direct link on the site to Research Navigator™ gives students access to many of the leading education journals, as well as extensive content detailing the research process.
- Excerpts from Merrill Education texts give your students insights on important topics of instructional methods, diverse populations, assessment, classroom management, technology, and refining classroom practice.

Classroom Practice
- Hundreds of lesson plans and teaching strategies are categorized by content area and age range.
- Case studies and classroom video footage provide virtual field experience for student reflection.
- Computer simulations and other electronic tools keep your students abreast of today's classrooms and current technologies.

Look into the value of Educator Learning Center yourself
Preview the value of this educational environment by visiting **www.EducatorLearningCenter.com** and clicking on "Demo." For a free 4-month subscription to the Educator Learning Center in conjunction with this text, simply contact your Merrill/Prentice Hall sales representative.

Brief Contents

Contents

● ●

Chapter 3

Life-Centered Career Education (LCCE) Mild/Moderate Curriculum Programs   59

PART 2

FAMILY AND COMMUNITY RESOURCES   93

Chapter 4

Family Support   94

Robert J. Loyd, Michael Wehmeyer, and Sharon Davis

Chapter 8

Transition Planning   195

*Robert J. Loyd, Iva Dean Cook, Carol Opperman,
and Melody Thurman-Urbanic*

Chapter Outlook: Jean N. Boston   197

Chapter 9

Functional Transition Materials and Resources   221

*Iva Dean Cook, Robert J. Loyd, Carol Opperman,
and Melody Thurman-Urbanic*

Chapter Outlook: Pat Burch   224

Chapter 10

Self-Determination   251

Robert J. Loyd and Michael Wehmeyer

Chapter Outlook: Mike Wehmeyer   253

PART 4

TRANSITION INSTRUCTIONAL DELIVERY   281

Chapter 11

Daily Living Skills   282

Chapter 12

Personal-Social Skills   328

Chapter 13

Occupational Guidance and Preparation Skills   370

PART 5

LCCE MILD/MODERATE CURRICULUM IMPLEMENTATION   419

Chapter 14

Developing LCCE Mild/ Moderate Curriculum Programs   420

Chapter 15

Critical Transition Issues and Future Directions   453

Appendix A

Cooperative Agreement Between the Department of Education and the Division of Rehabilitation Services, State of West Virginia   473

Appendix B

List of Professional Organizations   477

Appendix C

LCCE Performance Test 17   482

Appendix D

Functional Assessment Resources   492

Appendix E

LCCE Resources Available from the Council for Exceptional Children   493

Appendix F

Materials Correlated to the LCCE Competencies/Subcompetencies and List of Publishers   496

Appendix G

Blank Lesson Plan Outline   511

NOTE: Every effort has been made to provide accurate and current Internet information in this book. However, the Internet and information posted on it are constantly changing, and it is inevitable that some of the Internet addresses listed in this textbook will change.

LIFE SKILLS/
TRANSITION OVERVIEW

CHAPTER 1

Educating Students with Special Learning and/or Behavior Needs

PRELIMINARY QUESTIONS

1. What proportion of students with special learning and/or behavior needs drop out of school each year and fail to graduate from high school?
2. Approximately what proportion of American students have special learning and/or behavior needs?
3. What is the adult adjustment outcome of most students with special learning and/or behavior needs after leaving the school system?
4. Identify three major forces that effect positive educational change in American schools.
5. What have been the results of the more recent court cases that have addressed the rights of students with special learning and/or behavior needs to be educated in general education settings?
6. What major special education legislation has mandated that transition services be documented and provided to all students receiving special education services?
7. What federal legislation passed in the 1990s and 2001 reflects the growing national concern and need for more transition/career development efforts in our schools?
8. What is meant by "full inclusion" and how does it differ from the least restrictive environment (LRE) provision?
9. Overall, how would you characterize the present state of the art in America relative to the education of students with special learning and/or behavior needs, especially those with disabilities?

OVERVIEW

Approximately 30%, or 15 million, of the students in American schools have some type of special learning and/or behavior need. These students are generally described as those who are disabled or students who are disadvantaged. Each of these groups, in essence, is at risk of not having success in school. Approximately 6 million (12%) students are identified as having dis-

abilities, and 9 million (20%) students can be considered disadvantaged. *Students with disabilities* are those who are classified as having learning disabilities, communication disorders, mental retardation/developmental disabilities, serious emotional and behavioral disorders, deafness/hardness of hearing, visual impairments, autism, and traumatic brain injury. Over half of these students have specific learning disabilities (U.S. Department of Education, 1999). Students who are disadvantaged are those who are economically, socially, or academically disadvantaged; are unsuccessful learners; are substance abusers; are pregnant; or have a juvenile criminal record. These students with special learning and/or behavior needs have presented a formidable challenge to educators for many years. It is their responsibility to provide these students with an education that will appropriately meet their educational needs and preferred learning styles.

In the previous two decades, the nation has been involved in a reform movement to ensure that all students' educational needs were being met. Most education experts would agree that this restructuring movement was propelled from the negative criticisms of public education raised in the publication *A Nation at Risk* (National Commission on Excellence in Education, 1983), which warned that "the educational foundations of our society are presently being eroded by a rising tide of mediocrity that threatens our very future as a Nation and as a people" (p. 5). In response to this concern and that American education was contributing to poor student outcomes leading to poor quality in the American workforce (Murphy, 1990), the Bush administration proposed six National Education Goals envisioned to be met by year 2000:

1. Every child in America must start school prepared to learn, and be sound in body and sound in mind.
2. The high school graduation rate in the United States must increase to no less than 90%.
3. All students in grades 4, 8, and 12 will be tested for progress in critical subjects.
4. American students must rank first in the world in achievement in mathematics and science.
5. Every adult must be a skilled, literate worker and citizen, able to compete in a global economy.

6. Every school must be drug-free and offer a disciplined environment conducive to learning. (Bush, 1991)

The Clinton administration continued this effort and in 1994, Congress enacted a new legislation, Goals 2000: Educate America Act (P.L. 103-227), a U.S. Department of Education project to encourage and support grassroots, community-wide efforts to reach the National Education Goals. The Act added two additional goals:

7. The nation's teaching force will have access to quality professional preservice and inservice skill preparation to prepare all American students for the next century.
8. Schools will promote partnerships with parents to increase participation and involvement in their child's educational program.

This book devotes primary attention to individuals in need of special services and consideration to keep them in school to prepare them for successful adult community adjustment and good quality of life. In the opinion of many transition/career development experts and educators in American schools, many students who are at risk and students who have learning and/or behavioral difficulties need a more functional life-centered/outcome emphasis if they are going to complete their education and have the skills to become

successful college and vocational students, workers, family members, and citizens in their communities. These students must also have an opportunity to experience and meet the six national goals. This book addresses just how this can be accomplished.

This chapter begins with a discussion of expert opinion and research that supports those who believe there is a critical need to make significant changes in the educational system on behalf of students with special learning and/or behavioral needs. Some of the major forces that effect positive educational change in the United States are presented, followed by a discussion of some of the major recent legislation enacted to better meet the transition/career development and adult living needs of students with special learning and/or behavioral needs. The final section describes recent educational reforms to integrate students into general education classrooms. Final comments on the state of the field, along with suggestions for class activities, conclude the chapter.

MEETING THE NEED

Coming up with a definition of appropriate education continues to be an issue discussed by many educators, parents, and society. Since the passage of

CHAPTER OUTLOOK

Dr. Paul Beare is Dean, College of Education, at Fresno State University.

My thirty-two years as a special educator have included overlapping stints as a classroom teacher, crisis intervention specialist, due process hearing officer, head of an agency supplying day services for adults with severe disabilities, college profes-

sor, and university administrator. From this vantage point, I have seen oscillation in the concern for individuals with disabilities and progression and regression in effective programming and intervention with this group. The concerns when I entered the field in 1972 were much the same as those today. Individuals with disabilities were served in overly segregated programs. Special education showed little efficacy in terms of either lasting student achievement as measured by standardized tests and high school graduation rates, or adult adjustment as measured by gainful employment and independent living.

With enthusiasm, our profession has embraced a number of movements including facilitated communication, perceptual motor training, Orton-Gillingham, use of the developmental model, and most lastingly, mainstreaming and inclusion. Unfortunately, our profession has faced disappointment when these solutions are shown to be either quackery or less than definitive. Many advocates tout legislation as having the most promise for the future, starting with the Education of All Handicapped Children Act in the 1970s extending through IDEA (Individuals with Disabilities Education Act) in this new century. My experience as a hearing officer proved to me that a solely legalistic or bureaucratic approach shows little promise as an effective solution. Legal standards and state or district rules can be easily circumvented and due process to protect rights is so expensive that both parents and districts accept almost any compromise to avoid litigation. Even totally unreasonable demands, reflecting extremely poor practice, are routinely agreed upon to avoid the more unreasonable costs of a hearing.

Research and experience tell us certain special education practices are highly effective. Foremost among effective techniques may be applied behavior analysis and direct instruction. Their efficacy is verifiable across settings and age ranges.

In 1984, I began consulting with a day activity program for 47 adults with severe disabilities. All had been rejected by the sheltered workshop as being too "low functioning" for placement there. Programming was based on the developmental model. Persons with retardation were "developmentally delayed" and had to be helped to develop through the use of mental age equivalent tasks; thus, adults spent their days drawing in coloring books, watching Sesame Street, and learning to sort buttons. The idea was that they would

eventually develop to the point they could advance to the sheltered workshop. In the sheltered workshop, they could develop to the point of placement in community-based employment. As of 1984, no person in the county had ever moved from day activity to sheltered workshop and no person had ever moved from the workshop to community employment, despite the presence of a full-time employment placement specialist.

To change this situation, we read articles by Lou Brown, Paul Wehman, and Donn Brolin and tried to emulate what they advocated. Our day activity program began attempting supported employment placements with our clients, mainly using the two aforementioned techniques, applied behavior analysis and on-site direct instruction, in the skills needed for specific jobs. By 1991, our agency was serving 87 adults with disabilities, 100% of whom were placed full- or part-time in community-based employment. This program was the result of the natural evolution of the field, taking research on program efficacy into account. Eventually, the sheltered workshop followed suit and learned how to successfully place their clients as well.

The problems and issues of special education today mirror those of the last half of the previous century, although the potential for educating students with disabilities and helping transition them into the general community is greater today because of our broader base of knowledge, experience, and the evidence of data-based research. There are no easy answers, bromides, or quick cures; however, if teachers and professionals continue to care, explore, and research, there is reason for optimism. One of the brightest hopes and reasons for optimism is the functional life skills curriculum and Life-Centered Career Education. This approach provides direct instruction in the functional skills individuals with disabilities need to meet our socially defined criterion of success and to provide individuals with the means to happy and fulfilling lives.

Public Law 94-142 (Education of All Handicapped Children Act), many attempts and movements to definitively explain this concept have come and past. Unfortunately, as the debate continues, large numbers of students exit school without the skills to become successful and productive adults. Dropout rates have remained constant over the past thirty years, while discipline and drug abuse in schools are dramatically rising, the number of students who end up in our correctional facilities is rising, and underemployment and unemployment continues to be a problem for students with special learning and/or behavioral problems.

What should be the primary purpose of education?

A fundamental question or issue that must be resolved by educational policymakers and decision-makers is, what should be the primary purpose of education? Is it to teach basic core academic/literary standards along with expecting all students to acquire the other skills needed for living and working on their own? On the other hand, is it to purposely teach every student what they need to learn, while they are in school, to become a productive and responsible adult successfully living and working in their community? Inspection of most school districts' mission statements would probably more closely resemble the latter, although the curriculum content and the national movement is reflective of the former.

The eight National Education Goals clearly reflected a genuine effort by the federal educational system to ensure that all students would become productive members of society, especially goal 5, "Every adult must be a skilled, literate worker and citizen, able to compete in a global economy." Although these goals were intended to improve the educational achievement of all students and some schools have put into effect more rigorous standards, these changes are requiring special educators to significantly examine how these will be addressed with our students who have special needs.

The proportion of students who drop out of school is still very alarming.

The Dropout Challenge

One of the best measures of the impact of the educational system on its students is what happens when they leave school. A revealing indicator is the number of students who drop out of school and never graduate. Unfortunately, the news is tragic.

The National Center for Educational Statistics (NCES) in 1999 reported that nearly 20% of young adults, ages 18-24, are high school dropouts. These figures may be conservatively figured because no real standardized definition of "dropout" has been accepted and utilized in the current research on dropouts. This figure could be higher, depending on the definition utilized. Many of these students are the so-called at-risk students. It is commonly reported that in some cities dropout rates may exceed 40% (Hahn, Danzberger, & Lefkowitz, 1987).

The Twenty-third Annual Report to Congress on the Implementation of the Individuals with Disabilities Education Act (IDEA) (U.S. Department of Education, Office of Special Education Programs, 2001) noted that students with disabilities drop out of school at a significantly higher rate than other secondary students. In addition, for youth who at ages 14 to 20 left their secondary schools, the following was reported:

- Thirty percent of those with disabilities, including those who were expelled or suspended, became drop-outs. This compared with 20% in the general population.
- Dropouts were less likely to enroll in postsecondary vocational or academic programs.
- Only 14% of all vocational rehabilitation clients are transition-age youth.
- Nearly 2/3 of those who do receive specific vocational rehabilitation services (education or training services or diagnositic/evaluative services) had a greater likelihood of achieving a positive employment outcome and entering competitive employment.
- Significant relationships were found between aspects of students' school programs and students' outcomes. For example, linking school learning experiences to experiences outside the classroom can motivate students, help improve rates of grad-

uation, and improve the quality of life and post-school outcomes for students with disabilities.

Students diagnosed as having a serious emotional disturbance have particularly high dropout rates. The Twenty-third Annual Report to Congress noted a 51% rate. The commonly associated factors leading to these high dropout rates have been attributed to absenteeism, discipline problems, course failures, and out-of-school suspensions. Sinclair and colleagues (1998) recommended developing a procedure to systematically track these behaviors as a way to reduce dropouts among students with serious emotional disorders. Wehman (2001) stated that these students are often tense, unable to relax, and express fears about competency, embarrassment, and success, which all could contribute to higher rates of dropping out. He noted that these students could benefit from vocational counseling and transition planning.

Rylance (1997) tracked students with and without disabilities for 6 years following leaving school; he presented data indicating a great disparity in postsecondary planning and postsecondary outcomes between the groups. It has been reported that greater than 50% of young adults without disabilities obtain a 2- or 4-year degree and the others seek employment in the work force directly after high school. As might be expected, the significant number of young adults with disabilities who do drop out are less likely to enroll in postsecondary training or other academic training programs. Despite these outcomes, secondary programs continue to emphasize more academic curricula and place students with disabilities in programs that prepare students for college rather than for living and working in the community. It should be apparent that *the current educational system is not effectively meeting the needs of all students with disabilities through the standard curriculum.* With tremendous differences in learning styles, skills, and problems, students with disabilities will continue to experience a lack of success in becoming adults. The problem of dropping out may begin to increase again unless educators engage in providing more relevant functional curriculum approaches including vocational training and mean-

ingful work experiences. Kaufman, Kameenui, Birman, and Danielson noted,

> children with disabilities are not dropping out of special education; they are dropping out of school. Significant numbers are being arrested in their communities and, after leaving school, are not engaged in employment, education, or other productive activities. (1990, p. 109)

"Children with disabilities are not dropping out of special education; they are dropping out of school."
Kaufman et al. (1990)

Dropout rates and successful post-school training, employment, and community adjustment are clearly linked to what schools do with students with special learning and/or behavior needs in the classroom (Wehman, 2001). More specific and recent studies on the post-school adult adjustment of students with various disabilities and other learning and/or behavior needs are presented next.

Adult Adjustment Challenge

Of the approximately 65% of students who leave high school, only 30% will actually graduate from college. For the majority of students, the journey from school to work consists of a rough passage of several years of dead-end, low-paying jobs. Most employers want mature individuals with work experience, not someone just out of high school or who is a dropout. Thus, it is no wonder that one third of all young people fail to find stable employment by the time they reach the age of 30 (Winters, 1993).

Many follow-up studies of the post-school adult adjustment of former students receiving special education services have been conducted over several decades. In the 1980s and 1990s, a substantial number of studies were conducted with generally similar results. For the most part, the studies revealed an unsatisfactory outcome for the majority of former students who received special education services. Only about one third of these individuals could be considered as leading a relatively satisfactory life. These studies will not be identified or reviewed here, because they have been reported in numerous other publications and the 1980s studies are somewhat dated. Instead, reviews of some of the more recent and significant studies reported in the 1990s are described.

Research has found that most students with disabilities lack sufficient functional skills.

The National Longitudinal Transition Study (NLTS), conducted by SRI International, has provided the most comprehensive investigation of numerous aspects of student outcome (Wagner et al., 1991). SRI International studied 8,000 former special education students, ages 13 to 21, and secondary students receiving special education services in the 1985 to 1990 school years. The students were followed for a 5-year period to provide important information about their transition from school to early adulthood. Some of the most important findings of their research follow:

• The proportion of persons falling into 11 categories who were employed full-time 1 year or more out of school was 29.2%. Adults with learning disabilities were employed the most (37.9%); those with multiple disabilities, orthopedic impairments, and visual impairments were employed the least (1.3%, 1.3%, and 10%, respectively).

• The average wage of the former students was $4.35 per hour. Those employees with learning disabilities earned the most ($4.63); those with visual impairments and mental retardation (developmental disabilities) earned the least ($3.12 and $3.68, respectively); those classified as orthopedically impaired, health impaired, multidisabled, and deaf-blind accounted for too few cases to report.

• Although the former students' ability to perform self-care skills were rated very well by parents in 86.4% of the cases, only 40.4% of the entire group was rated able to adequately perform functional mental skills such as looking up telephone numbers, using a telephone, counting change, telling time, and reading common signs. Those who were particularly deficient in this area were classified as being deaf-blind, multidisabled, visually impaired, mentally retarded (developmentally disabled), and deaf.

• The social experiences of these young adults were also quite limited, becoming more so the longer they were limited and the longer they were out school.

These data do not present an impressive outcome for the majority of students who are receiving special education. For years, experts in the field have noted that, if students with special learning needs are properly trained, the vast majority can become independent, productive, and contributing members of their communities. Apparently, however, they have not yet been given this opportunity. SRI International data revealed that only approximately 27% had received any postsecondary education 3 to 5 years after leaving the secondary school, compared to 68% of those without disabilities.

"Although people with mental retardation (developmental disabilities) have successfully demonstrated their capacity for gainful employment, few are actually integrated into the work force with people who have no disability."
Sharon Davis (1993)

In 1993, The Arc, a national organization on mental retardation, issued "A Status Report to the Nation on Inclusion in Employment of People with Mental Retardation" (Davis, 1993). Based on her review of recent studies and other data, Davis concluded that although people with mental retardation have successfully demonstrated their capacities for gainful employment, few are actually integrated into the workforce with people who have no disability. She noted the emergence of some positive trends, in that many people with developmental disabilities who were employed in sheltered employment are now being employed in supported and competitive employment.

She attributed much of this improved state of affairs to federal legislation (i.e., the Rehabilitation Act Amendments of 1992, the Americans with Disabilities Act of 1990, and the Job Training Partnership Act) and greater awareness by employers of the capabilities of these individuals. However, Davis concluded that people with mental retardation (developmental disabilities) still face many barriers to successful adjustment: the failure of the public education system to adequately prepare them for work, the misconceptions about their inability to be employed in integrated settings held by many employers and families, and the work disincentives existing in federal entitlement programs.

Agran, Snow, and Swaner (1999) reported that even individuals with significant cognitive disabilities now have a greater opportunity to perform meaningful work in the community. Community-based programs have significantly increased this type of educational option in the schools for preparing students with disabilities to make the successful transition to community living and working. The transition mandates included in the ndividuals with Disabilities Education Act (IDEA) Amendments of 1997 (PL 105-17) have also contributed to changes in stakeholders' perceptions of the employment capabilities of individuals with developmental disabilities.

Sitlington and Frank (1998) conducted a number of statewide follow-up studies in Iowa to determine the adult adjustment of former students with disabilities 1 to 3 years after leaving school. Some major findings from these studies follow:

- Three years after graduation, only 19% of 322 persons with mental disabilities (developmental disabilities) interviewed met the low criteria of successful adult adjustment, and only 4% met the high criteria for success.
- Only 11% of students with learning disabilities met high standards of success and an additional 27% met the low criteria 3 years out of school.
- Dropouts experienced the least number of gains in adult adjustment.
- The longer individuals are out of school, the less we can attribute to the influence of the educational (transitional) program.
- Only 10% of individuals who were labeled either behaviorally disordered, learning disabled, or mentally disabled were successful by stringent criteria and 25% to 50% did not even meet minimal adult adjustment criteria.

These important findings in a state that is known for excellent educational and transitional programs reflect the continued challenge that still confronts us today.

Schools are experiencing a tremendous increase in students who are disruptive and dangerous to both students and teachers. "Youth with emotional disorders experience a high dropout rate; as a result, many of these students never have access to training designed to prepare them for meaningful careers" (Bullis & Gaylord-Ross, 1991). These experts in the field noted that very few follow-up studies have tracked these persons and documented their experiences.

> Transition services offered adolescents with emotional disorders during the secondary years are apt to be the last set of coordinated educational and social services they receive. If these programs are to affect these young people positively and improve their post-school transition outcomes, they must be offered in as powerful and focused a manner as possible. (Bullis et al., 2002)

Indications are, however, that these individuals have limited success and that a transition/career education (functional) curriculum focus is badly needed if they are to learn the social and vocational skills needed for the workplace.

DROPOUT PREVENTION

In summary, much has been reported regarding the importance of keeping students with special learning and/or behavior needs in schools, as well as reporting some of the more common factors related to dropping out. Figure 1.1 provides categories along with demographic factors associated with dropping out of school.

Schools need to address those factors that they can effect. Examples of how schools can address some of these fators are illustrated in Table 1.1.

REFORM CHALLENGE

The majority of students with special learning and/or behavior needs still encounter significant difficulties in achieving successful employment, independent living, and social relationships after leaving the educational system. Although their status will improve somewhat over time, and some will become successful, the

Category	Demographic Factor
Demographic	• Age/grade
	• Gender
	• Ethnicity/LEP status
	• Geographic region
	• Community type
Social & Family	• Parents' marital status
	• Parents' educational/occupational level
	• Family support received
	• Socioeconomic status
	• Peer group influence
	• Family size
	• Sibling dropout status
Personality	• Self-concept
	• Motivation level/attitude
Early Transition to Adulthood	• Pregnant
	• Children
	• Dating/marital status
	• Employment
Deviant Behavior in Society	• Discipline issues/suspension
	• School grades/academic achievement
	• Achievement test scores
	• Extracurricular participation
	• Absenteeism/tardiness
	• Special education status
	• Poor relationship with teachers

FIGURE 1.1   Categories and Demographic Factors Associated with Dropping Out of School
Source: Reprinted with permission from Deschamps (1992): 83–84.

majority will most likely become either unemployed or substantially underemployed and low-paid members of the secondary labor market. They will tend to be dependent on their families, many will get in trouble with the law, and they will have limited friendships and recreational outlets.

"External pressure exerted on an organization to change its basic structure will, for as long as that pressure is applied, cause the organization to bend and assume a new shape. Once that pressure is removed, the organization will reassume its original shape!"
Kenneth B. Hoyt (1976) speaking on
"The Marshmallow Principle"

Although our nation continues to be a nation at risk, greater recognition for the need to accomplish true educational reform is even stronger than it was in the 1980s and 1990s, when numerous reports were

TABLE 1.1   Activities schools can implement to resolve some of the major demographic dropout factors.

SOCIAL & FAMILY

1. School personnel can provide print materials regarding community and state resources to support families' economic, psychological, and transitional needs.
2. School personnel can provide informational meetings in the evenings and/or on weekends in which representatives from community and state resources to support families' economic, psychological, and transitional needs can describe services.

PERSONALITY

1. School personnel can provide print materials to students regarding the importance of staying in school.
2. Invite former students who dropped out but have received their GED to discuss the importance of staying in school.
3. Have former students attend school assemblies to discuss services available to help students believe in themselves or improve their self-perception.

EARLY TRANSITION TO ADULTHOOD

1. School personnel can provide print materials to students regarding the importance of staying in school.
2. Invite former students who dropped out to discuss the importance of staying in school for obtaining better employment opportunities.
3. Have former students attend school assemblies to discuss services available to help students who have children or want to have children to stay in school.

DEVIANT BEHAVIOR IN SOCIETY

1. Have former students attend school assemblies to discuss services available to students to assist in helping to break the abuse problems.

IN-SCHOOL VARIABLES

1. Provide students other opportunities to participate in extracurricular activities other than after school.
2. Provide before school, after school, and weekends for extra support to improve grades and achievement.

released by many prestigious professional groups concerned about the deteriorating nature of the educational system. Even though many professionals responsible for educational change and improvement were responsive to this need for change, others failed to heed the cry, believing they alone really understood what was best for their local school systems. Consequently, little substantive change occurred.

In many school districts, dedicated administrators, teachers, counselors, and others are trying to respond to the many needs of their students. Unfortunately, many of these dedicated educators are not always supported by the significant others (parents, other educators, agency personnel, and community resource people) on whom change is dependent. In several school districts, exemplary programs have evolved to demonstrate what can be done if the will is there. Much remains to be accomplished, however, if the majority of students in American schools are to get an education that will help them to realize their potential to achieve a satisfying life style and career that will benefit them and their community.

MAJOR FORCES AFFECTING EDUCATIONAL REFORM

How does change really happen? Who are the major constructors of significant and positive change for persons who have special learning and/or behavior needs? Certainly, many professionals working in the field are continually trying to improve the quality and quantity of services to children, youth, and adults. Major change, however, must come from society as a whole. Public awareness of the problems and their remedies are important stimulants. Education and other human service systems depend on taxpayers. Unfortunately, with numerous forces vying for government money (i.e., military, domestic programs, health care, and labor department), even the greatest needs often go relatively unheeded.

In the case of persons with special learning and/or behavior needs, three distinct forces have promoted change to enhance their educational, employment, and accessibility outcomes: parents and advocacy organizations, litigation, and legislation. Each of these forces interacts to bring about educational change.

Parents and Advocacy Organizations

It is appropriate to begin a discussion of major forces for educational change with a review of the numerous organizations that have been founded by the parents and advocacy groups for individuals with disabilities. Such organizations have a long history dating back to the founding of the National Society for Crippled Children in 1921. But the biggest surge of progress was made in 1949 to 1950, when the National Association for Retarded Children/Citizens (now The Arc) and the United Cerebral Palsy Association were organized within a few months of one another. Membership in such organizations is open to parents, stu-

dents, and professionals and now numbers in the hundreds of thousands.

These organizations were created by parents as a response to public inaction manifested by the absence of school programs, treatment centers, or even skilled personnel who were interested in working with children with more severe disabilities. A well-known example of the parents' efforts can be found in the story of the beginnings of the New York State Cerebral Palsy Association. A parent advertised daily in several local newspapers that those individuals interested in receiving help should call or write to her (Killilea, 1960). There are numerous examples of parents, guardians, and advocates who sought each other's support to receive and provide solace and receive answers to basic questions regarding their children's education and future options. Today, these organizations also function as viable representatives of individuals with disabilities in affecting political and social action.

The parent organizations had initial problems in working with professionals. Turnbull and Turnbull (2001) indicated that as recently as the late 1970s, professionals expected parents to comply completely and to be grateful for the decisions professionals were making regarding their child's service delivery and program content. Parents were forced into combined action because very little was being provided by agencies employing doctors, teachers, and psychologists. At first, these problems forced parents to rely on themselves for counsel and directions; in time, they learned to use the professionals' skills as the parents' organizations continued to expand their role and influence. Numerous parent groups now have professionals as consultants and members of their board of directors, although the parents still control the overall development of policy.

Parents' strongest drive and accomplishments have been to promote legislation from the local level through the statehouses and Congress. Several organizations have active legislation committees that monitor the progress of bills, organize attempts to lobby on behalf of favorable legislation, produce expert testimony during committee hearings, and function as information providers to its members, legislatures, and representatives of the media. These efforts have been rewarded. Repeated laws that support the rights of individuals with disabilities have been enacted at all levels of government.

Parent groups also have served individuals with disabilities by doing the following:

- Organizing educational facilities and services when the public schools or agencies were unable.
- Promoting public awareness and support for programs and efforts to assist individuals with disabilities.
- Supporting parents through counseling, guardianship plans, respite care, futures planning, and medical services.
- Promoting research into causes, treatment, education, training, and other aspects of the individual's quality of life.
- Sponsoring training for teachers, teacher aides, community leaders, physicians, and other individuals who may be in care, education, treatment, and training.
- Building and operating permanent structures for sheltered workshops, day schools, and diagnostic centers.
- Developing materials and programs for such necessary functions as daily care, orientation, mobility, recreation, leisure, and caring for a family.

Finally, parent groups have established themselves as advocates by representing individuals with disabilities as plaintiffs in litigation involving public agencies. One of the most prominent suits, *Pennsylvania Association for Retarded Children v. Commonwealth of Pennsylvania*, is reviewed later in the chapter. The case and decision have been termed landmark and instrumental, and it is appropriate that a parent organization was intimately involved in a decision that affirmed the constitutional right of every child to an education.

Since the 1980s, the federal government has funded state parent resource centers to work on behalf of persons with disabilities. Currently, there are approximately 70 parent training and information centers (PTI). Each state has at least one PTI whose primary purpose is to provide training and information to parents of infants, toddlers, children, and youth with disabilities and persons who work with parents. The PTI projects assist parents in the following:

- To better understand the nature and needs of the individual's disabling condition.
- To provide follow-up support for their child's educational program.
- To communicate more effectively with special and general educators, administrators, related service providers, and other relevant professionals.
- To participate fully in educational and training decision-making processes, including the development of the individualized education plan (IEP).
- To obtain information about the range of options, programs, services, and resources available at the local, state, and national level and to provid information about the appropriateness of these services for the individual.
- To understand the provisions for educating and training infants, toddlers, and youth under the Individuals with Disabilities Education Act (IDEA).

In addition to these federally funded programs, several additional avenues of family information, resources, and emotional support exist, including community resource programs, clearinghouses, family organizations, adults with special learning and/or behavior needs, books and magazines, media, and technology. (See Turnbull and Turnbull [2001] for a complete description of these information resources.)

Case Law

As important as the physician, teacher, or psychologist may be in the history of special education, the attorneys and judges should not be forgotten. Since 1960, legal suits and judicial decisions have had a direct effect on the education, training, care, and protection of individuals with disabilities.

The Supreme Court decision in *Brown v. Board of Education of Topeka Kansas* (1954) set a major precedent in litigation regarding every citizen's right to an education. The court ruled that state laws could not permit segregation of students on racial grounds and that the doctrine of "separate by equal" education facilities was unconstitutional. The court stated:

In these days, it is doubtful that any child may reasonably be expected to succeed in life if he is denied the opportunity for an education. Such an opportunity, where the state has undertaken to provide it, is a right which must be made available to all on equal terms.

Although racial discrimination was the prominent concern in the *Brown* case, the Supreme Court's ruling helped establish arguments used in later cases involving individuals with disabilities who were being denied education or equal education because of the unfounded belief that they would not be able to profit from it and contribute to society.

Hobson and Hansen (1968) was one of the first litigations that included special education within the broader context of segregation and labeling of children. Judge Skeley Wright ruled that the five-part track system used in grouping students was unconstitutional because it deprived students who were African American or those from lower socioeconomic families an opportunity to experience equal educational services. The school system was unable to demonstrate that the system allowed students to advance within and across the tracks or that instruction at the lower levels was meeting the needs of the students. The *Hobson* case established additional precedent for future right-to-education suits in the following ways:

1. It established that school districts had to provide evidence that programs yielded adequate results. It was not enough for school districts to *intend* to design adequate programs for students.
2. It indicated that placement of students into appropriate programs had to be substantiated by adequate procedures and supporting evidence. The courts would not accept procedures that violated the constitutional right of the child or tests that were inappropriate for the intended educational objectives.
3. It forced the field of special education to examine its unwilling partnership in de facto segregation and the practice of placing students into categories of disabilities.

The third landmark decision was reached in *Pennsylvania Association for Retarded Children (PARC) v. Commonwealth of Pennsylvania* (1971). On behalf of the parents of 13 children with mental retardation, The Arc filed a class action suit in the U.S. District Court against the state of Pennsylvania for failing to provide publicly supported education for all students with mental retardation. The class action suit was a strategic move by the plaintiff's lawyer, Thomas Gilhool, because the court decision would effect all children with mental retardation in the state. His second strategic move was to base the case on the right of every American child to education. Using expert witnesses before a panel of three judges, Mr. Gilhool elicited testimony establishing that individuals with mental retardation could profit from an education and contribute to society. After only two days of testimony, the parties mediated an agreement.

The court ordered the state to provide the necessary education and rejected the argument that lack of funding, personnel, and facilities were legitimate reasons for substandard education for students with mental retardation. The court maintained that if, in fact, the state did not have the resources to educate all the children, the children with disabilities must take a share of the burden with other children but that they should not have to bear the entire load of the state's financial difficulties. As a postscript to the decision, which further substantiated the plaintiff's contention that there was a general absence of programs, a survey of all eligible children with mental retardation and not enrolled in school was conducted by the state of Pennsylvania. The survey indicated that 14,267 children with mental retardation were being denied access to public schools (Gilhool, 1973).

The *PARC* case signaled the beginning of a succession of similar suits in other states for the following reasons:

1. It established that all children, both children who are nondisabled and those that are disabled, have a right to an appropriate educational program.
2. It established the precedent that every state has the obligation to provide the personnel and resources to meet the instructional needs of children with disabilities.

3. It outlined a due process procedure whereby students with disabilities and their parents can approve or challenge a school system's action on educational programming to the extent where a final decision can proceed to the courts, if necessary.

4. It established the necessity of fulfilling an individual with disability's rights (i.e., those to be immediately exercised and safeguarded).

The *PARC* case was a major advancement on behalf of individuals with disabilities' rights to receive both a free and an appropriate education. Previous related cases, *Diana v. State Board of Education of California* (1970) and *Mills v. Board of Education in the District of Columbia* (1972) also helped advance the cause. The *Diana* decision led to modifications in state codes related to testing, assessment, and assignment of individuals from minority groups to classes for students with disabilities. The *Mills* decision extended the results of the *PARC* case by affirming that all individuals with disabilities have the right to a public education. These cases also established judicial precedent for organizations working on behalf of individuals with disabilities by encouraging state legislatures to enact laws based on the *PARC* and aforementioned court decisions.

If those laws were not forthcoming, these same groups had the option to turn to the courts. Both of these alternatives required time, effort, and funding. Furthermore, states were inconsistent in supporting legislation for various groups of individuals with disabilities. What was needed? Simply a legislative act applying to all states mandating a funding base to support appropriate education for individuals with disabilities. That form of legislation was in its embryonic stage of being drawn up when the *PARC* case became widely known in the field of special education.

Davis (1993) reported more recent cases of litigation. She noted the case of an 8-year-old boy, Rafael, with severe intellectual and communication disabilities whose school system believed his low level of intellectual functioning precluded him from participating in the general education class and additional behavior concerns would be too disruptive to the general education teacher and students. The school system recommended placement in a self-contained classroom located in an out-of-district school for students with multiple disabilities. The chief judge in this case ruled that "Inclusion is a right, not a privilege" and ordered the school system to develop an inclusive education program for the boy. He provided the following statements regarding including students with disabilities into general education classrooms:

- "That segregated classrooms may harm Rafael and other students like him by keeping them away from friends and family and by being surrounded by inappropriate role models."
- "Will not be successful in special schools and special classes and is unlikely to lead to Rafael being able to function successfully in integrated school settings or in the community."
- "Like Rafael, schools need to provide these students with access to integrated experiences where they can learn to function effectively."
- "Correspondingly, individuals without disabilities need to learn to accept and function with individuals with disabilities through such integrated experiences."

(*Oberti v. Board of Education of the Borough of Clementon School District,* 1992)

Inclusion, the opportunity for all students to participate in the totality of the school experience (Davis, 1993), is discussed later in the chapter.

Another case law Davis (1993) reported involving the right to inclusive education and affirmed in the court is *Rachel Holland* in California. The judge ruled in this case that Rachel had the right to be educated in the general education classroom and noted that "placement in other than general education classes will be unsuccessful" (*Board of Education, Sacramento City Unified School District v. Rachel Holland, 1993*).

Legislation

The growing urgency for more appropriate education of individuals with disabilities can be documented by the increased number of laws passed in the states over the last 25 plus years. According to the Constitution, each state should assume the major responsibility of establishing school law, districts, procedures, and in some instances, financial support. In effect, there are 50 plus states and territories with plans and definitions of state and local partnership in the conduct and funding of education for all infants, toddlers, children, youths, and adults. Thus, states or territories in the United States differ in their support of individuals with disabilities, as well as medical facilities, research, and employment options.

In 1961, President John F. Kennedy appointed a panel of experts to prepare a "national plan to combat mental retardation." President Kennedy recognized that the office of the president could be a springboard to develop approaches to this problem that all states embraced, realizing that no state had the means to the solution. The report developed by the President's Panel on Mental Retardation (1963) established long-term goals in the following areas:

- Research and scientific manpower
- Prevention
- Clinical and social services
- Education and vocational rehabilitation and training
- Residential care
- The law
- Public awareness
- Planning and coordination of services

Although this think tank focused on mental retardation, findings from the report were applicable to other disabilities and, more importantly, were placed into law by Congress. These laws have generated more equal-opportunity legislation guaranteeing the rights of individuals with disabilities in the areas of using public facilities, receiving a free and appropriate education, and obtaining gainful employment.

As a result of the groundwork provided by this panel and Congress in the 1960s, significant landmark legislation was passed in the 1970s and 1980s. The laws that are particularly relevant can be divided into five major categories: vocational rehabilitation, special education, vocational education, mental retardation/developmental disabilities, and

employment services legislation. These are discussed in chronological order to give the consumer an appreciation of past efforts to improve education and other services for individuals with disabilities. The most recent significant legislation is then briefly described.

The first civil rights law for individuals with disabilities: The Rehabilitation Act of 1973

Vocational Rehabilitation

The Rehabilitation Act of 1973, Public Law 93-112, has been referred to as the civil rights law for individuals with disabilities. The greatest significance of PL 93-122 to schools is found in Section 503 and Section 504.

Section 503 requires employers to initiate "affirmative action" for all employment settings. It also addresses equal actions for employment of individuals with disabilities as it relates to areas of: upgrading, transfer, demotion, layoff, and termination. The most significant provision included in Section 503 for school systems is the importance of better preparation of graduates for the workplace; students still must be qualified for employer's jobs, to be given equal opportunity and to institute discriminatory objections, if necessary and justified. This section also addresses the collaboration process between schools and vocational rehabilitation to develop the Individualized Work Rehabilitation Plan (IWRP) that outlines the plan to provide job preparation skills and jobs for students with disabilities.

Section 504 mandates equal opportunities in education and training for students with disabilities. Students who do not qualify for special education services but demonstrate significant learning and/or behavior needs that affect their ability to be successful in school qualify for service provisions under Section 504 of PL 93-112. PL 93-112 does not provide funding, but mandates that these aforementioned students be provided a plan developed by school officials, the student, teachers, and the parents to help accommodate the special learning and/or behavior needs in the general education classroom. Figure 1.2 illustrates a

General Education Accommodation Plan

Name: Joshua Green   School / Grade: Platte Valley Elementary, 3rd

Date: 6/5/95   Teacher: Myrna Mae (lead teacher)

Participants in Development of Accommodation Plan

Mr. and Mrs. Walter Green   Julie Hartson   Myrna Mae, Teacher   Arlo Wachal, Teacher
parents(s)/guardian(s)   principal   teacher(s)

Joel Schaeffer, Counselor   Violette Schelldorf, Nurse

Building Person responsible for monitoring plan: Joel Schaeffer, Counselor   Follow-up Date: 6/5/96

Currently on Medication   X   Yes _____ No   Physician Eveard Ewing, M.D.   Type Ritalin   Dosage 15 mg. twice daily

Area of Concern	Intervention or Teaching Strategies	Person Responsible for Accommodation
1. Assignment Completion	1. Daily assignment sheet sent home with Josh 2. Contract system initiated for assignment completion in math and social studies	Myrna Mae Parents will initial daily, and Josh will return the form Myrna Mae, Arlo Wachal
2. Behavior / Distractibility	1. Preferential seating—study carrel or near teacher, as needed 2. Daily behavior card sent home with Josh	Myrna Mae, Arlo Wachal Parents will initial daily; and Josh will return the form
3. Consistency of Medication	1. Medication to be administered in private by school nurse daily at noon	Violette Schelldorf

Comments:

Josh will remain in the general education classroom with the accommodations noted above.

Mr. & Mrs. Walter Green

Parental Authorization for 504 Plan

I agree with the accommodations described   I do not agree with the accommodations described
in the 504 plan.   in the 504 plan. I understand I have the right to appeal.

FIGURE 1.2   Sample 504 Accommodation Plan.
Source: "Section 504 accomodation plans" by G. Conderman and A. Katsiyannis, 1995, *Intervention in School and Clinic*, 31, 44. Copyright 1995 by Pro-Ed, Inc. Reprinted by permission.

sample 504 plan of modifications for a student with special learning and/or behavior needs (who is not eligible to receive special education services).

Amendments were enacted in 1983 and in 1986 that provided financial funding for the purpose of developing and implementing state transition activities (plans) and for the training and placement of youths with disabilities into either competitive or supported employment. Thus, collaborative efforts between vocational rehabilitation and the school system for the benefit of transitioning of students with disabilities was an important intent of this law and its amendments.

The Bill of Rights for children with disabilities: The Education for All Handicapped Children Act of 1975

Special Education

As mentioned earlier, the *PARC* case and other case law set up the foundations for federal legislation passed to provide free and appropriate educational opportunities for students with disabilities. The Education for All Handicapped Children Act of 1975, Public Law 94-142, has been referred to as the "landmark legislative mandate" and the Bill of Rights for children with disabilities. The term "children" in PL 94-142 is used to describe all students with disabilities between the ages of 3 and 21.

> It is the purpose of this Act to assure that all children with handicaps have available to them, within the time periods specified ... a free appropriate public education which emphasizes special education and related services designed to meet their unique needs, to assure that the rights of the children with handicaps and their parents or guardians are protected, to assist States and localities, to provide for the education of all children with handicaps, and to assess and assure the effectiveness of efforts to educate children with handicaps. (Section 601 (c) of Public Law 94–142)

Some of the most critical provisions mandated by PL 94-142 include the following:

- *The right of all students with disabilities to a free and appropriate education (FAPE).*

    PL 94-142 was enacted to ensure that school systems would only receive federal funding if (when monitored) they are following the provisions to ensure that all students with disabilities are receiving an appropriate education.
- *The rights of students with disabilities and their parents to fully participate in the educational program decisions.*

    This provision was mandated to ensure that all decisions regarding testing, placements, and programming would include the participation of the most important stakeholders, the students with special learning and/or behavior needs, family members, and advocates in the provision of the FAPE.
- *The right of all students with disabilities to participate in the least restrictive environment (LRE).*

    This extremely important concept will be discussed in more detail later in this chapter.
- *The development of the annual Individualized Education Plan (IEP) that guides appropriate programming and review.*

    Public Law 94–142 specifically requires local educational agencies (LEAs) to establish a written IEP for each student who is receiving or is expected to receive special education. The law mandates that each state and LEA shall ensure policies and procedures for developing, implementing, reviewing, maintaining, and evaluating the IEP, regardless of which institution or agency provides special education for the student. The IEP should be developed, reviewed, and revised at the beginning of each school year. Although the program will contain references to services and goals to be obtained by the student, parents, and teachers, it should not be interpreted as a binding contract for the school system or agency. State and local educational agencies are responsible for establishing appropriate services so that the individual will achieve specified goals, but the agencies have not violated federal regulations if an individual falls short of the projected objectives. The list in Figure 1.3, derived from various state standards and federal regulations, describes several components of an IEP.
- *The overview of the basic elements and procedures of due process, a process outlined to settle a challenge among students with disabilities, school officials, agency personnel, and parents.*

    Due process is a course of legal proceedings in accordance with established rules and principles for enforcing and protecting individual rights. The basic elements of due process procedures are listed in Figure 1.4.
- *The right to receive a multidisciplinary and non-biased evaluation of abilities initially and every 3 years afterward.*
- *The right to have all information about the student with a disability confidential.*

- A statement of the student's present levels of educational performance, including academic achievement, social adaptation, prevocational and vocational skills, psychomotor skills, and self-help skills.

- A statement of annual goals describing the educational performance to be achieved by the end of the school year, according to the IEP. These goals would correspond to the areas of performance as identified in the above component and could include other domains.

- A statement of short-term instructional objectives, which are measurable, intermediate steps between the present level of educational performance and the annual goals.

- A statement of specific educational services needed by the student including all specific education and related services that are required to meet the unique needs of the student, including the type of physical education program in which he will participate, any special instructional media and materials that are needed, and the career education program in which the student may participate.

- The date when the above services will begin and end.

- A description of the extent to which the student will participate in regular education programs.

- A justification for the type of educational placement that the student will experience.

- A list of the individuals who are responsible for the implementation of the IEP.

- Objective criteria, evaluation procedures, and schedules for determining, on an annual basis, at least whether the short-term instructional objectives have been achieved.

- A statement of the needed transition services for students beginning no later than age 14, and including a statement of the interagency responsibilities or linkages or both before the student leaves the school setting.

FIGURE 1.3 Components of an Individualized Education Plan.

Much of the initial focus of PL 94-142 was with younger children. During the later part of the 1970s and the early 1980s, awareness grew regarding the lack of transitioning success of preschoolers to elementary school along with this same lack of success graduates were having in making the transition from school to post-secondary training, working, and community living. Readers interested in a copy of PL 94-142 provisions should write the U.S. Department of Education, Office of Special Education and Rehabilitation Services, 400 Maryland Ave., SW, Washington, DC 20202-2524.

The amendments of 1983 and 1986 were enacted to address the transition concerns regarding these two groups of students with disabilities. Funds were provided to assist in the development of early

childhood special education. Early childhood special education research indicated a great advantage to students who participated in these preschool experiences. There were funds also provided for the establishment of federal projects to meet the needs of preparing students with disabilities to successfully move into postsecondary/training programs, employment, and community living.

Vocational Education

The Education Amendments of 1976, Public Law 94-482, and the Vocational Education Section provisions, are built on the original Vocational Education Act of 1963 and its amendments of 1968. The 1968 amendments required that states spend at least 10% of the basic federal and state grant-in-aid funds to develop specific programs that meet the

- The child is represented by a parent surrogate when the parent or guardian is not known, the parents are unavailable, or the child is the ward of the state.
- The parents have the opportunity to participate in the evaluation and determination of the child's program.
- The parents receive written and oral notification in their native language before the child's status in the educational program becomes the subject of evaluation, hearings, or reviews.
- The educational agency establishes a specific period of time for the completion of each procedure.
- The parents receive written results of identified procedures and have the opportunity to respond to all notifications.
- Impartial hearings are conducted if parents disagree with decisions. In conjunction with hearings, parents can examine all relevant records, obtain independent educational evaluation, be represented by council, produce and examine witnesses, present evidence, receive records of hearings, and obtain written findings of fact and decision.
- Parents may appeal decisions to an appropriate civil court.
- The burden of proof for recommended action is on the educational agency.
- The educational agency conducts a periodic review of procedures.

FIGURE 1.4   Basic Elements of Due Process Procedures.

unique needs of students with disabilities. This provision was continued in the 1976 amendments. This prevented the practice of supplanting federal funds, substituting federal dollars for state funds in vocational education programs for students with disabilities to increase the total amount of fiscal support available for future efforts. This law was also consistent with the provisions of the Education of All Handicapped Children Act relative to vocational education and state plans.

The Carl D. Perkins Vocational Education Act of 1984, Public Law 98-524, which was also an amendment to the Vocational Education Act of 1963, was very important new legislation for students with disabilities and disadvantages to further their participation and success in vocational programs. Of particular importance was its mandate of the appropriate assessment of students' interests, abilities, and special needs; that students and parents must be notified about opportunities and options available to them by the ninth grade, and the inclusion of vocational services as a component of the IEP.

Developmental Disabilities and Mental Retardation

The Development Disabilities Assistance and Bill of Rights Act Amendments of 1987 and Public Law 100-146 were amendments to the original act of 1963. PL 100-146 enables youth with severe disabilities to pursue competitive employment goals by authorizing grants to support the planning, coordination, and delivery of specialized services to persons with developmental disabilities. The law mandates the development of plans and programs for transition from school to adult life. PL 100-146 also mandates a federal interagency committee to plan for and coordinate activities and for states to set up protection and advocacy systems for these individuals (Horne, 1991).

Employment Services

The Comprehensive Employment and Training Act (CETA) of 1973, Public Law 93-203, was passed to provide job training and employment opportunities for economically disadvantaged, unemployed, and underemployed persons. It required coordination of services with other employment and training-related programs such as vocational education and vocational rehabilitation. The federal funds provided communities with grants to design and administer comprehensive employment and training services to serve the needs of the community.

Amendments in 1978 provided mandates in giving more opportunities to individuals with disabilities, including the Job Corps. CETA was replaced by the Job Training and Partnership Act (JTPA) of 1982, Public Law 97-300, which is authorized to prepare unskilled adults and youth for productive employment. Provisions of JTPA require a State Job Training Coordinating Council, service-delivery areas appointed by the governor to receive federal funds, and Private Industry Councils (PICs) appointed by local elected officials to plan job training and employment service programs at the service-delivery area levels. Students with disabilities and disadvantages may be eligible for these programs, although the law does not specify them as potential recipients of the services.

It should be obvious now that many pieces of legislation were passed in the 1970s and 1980s in an attempt to address the needs of youth and adults with disabilities and disadvantages. These laws, and others not presented here, have benefited these individuals; many excellent programs were established; and some important changes and improvements did occur. As noted previously, however, much more remains to be accomplished if the majority of these individuals are to realize their potentials and lead satisfying, productive lives.

The next section presents more recent major legislation that has been enacted to further amend the various laws described above and to continue the efforts to better meet the needs of persons with disabilities and disadvantages.

LEGISLATION DURING 1990–2001

The legislation during the 1990s demonstrated a renewed commitment to better meeting the educa-

tional, vocational, social, accessibility, and other critical unmet needs of both children and adults with disabilities and those who are disadvantaged. These will be identified and described in this section.

Table 1.2 briefly illustrates the major legislation enacted to enhance the transition of persons with disabilities to a successful adjustment to adult living and to working. Because the laws are constantly being amended and reauthorized, readers interested in any changes to these and other legislative acts passed on behalf of persons with special learning and/or behavior needs should write the U.S. Department of Education, Office of Special Education and Rehabilitation Services, 400 Maryland Ave., SW, Washington, DC 20202-2524, for further information.

The Americans with Disabilities Act of 1990

The Americans with Disabilities Act (ADA), Public Law 101-336, is a further extension of the earlier federal legislation enacted to ensure the civil rights of persons with disabilities. It is intended to guarantee these individuals equal opportunity in employment, public accommodations, transportation, state and local government services, and telecommunications relay services. The employment provisions apply to private employers, state and local governments, employment agencies, and labor unions.

The ADA prohibits discrimination in all employment practices, including job applications procedures, hiring, firing, advancement, compensation, training, and other terms, conditions, and privileges of employment. It applies to recruitment, advertising, tenure, layoff, leave, fringe benefits, and all other employment-related activities.

Employers are still able to select the most qualified applicant available if the decision is made on essential skills needed for successful performance on the job. For example, if a job justifiably requires a certain level of manipulative skills and speed of work, and the person with a disability fails to meet those levels, all other factors being about even, the other applicant should be selected for the job.

TABLE 1.2   Major Legislation Important to the Career Development of Persons with Special Learning and/or Behavior Needs—1990–2001

Category	Legislation/Year
Civil rights	Americans with Disabilities Act (ADA), Public Law 101-336, 1990
Special education	Individuals with Disabilities Education Act (IDEA), Public Law 101-476, 1990
Vocational education	Carl D. Perkins Vocational and Applied Technology Amendments, Public Law 101-336, 1990
Vocational rehabilitation	Rehabilitation Act Amendments, Public Law 102-69, 1992
Employment	Job Training Reform Act Amendments, Public Law 102-367, 1992
	School-to-Work Opportunities Act, Public Law 103-239, 1994
Social services	Developmental Disabilities Assistance and Bill of Rights Act Amendments, Public Law 101-496, 1990, Public Law 103-230, 1994
Educational reform	Goals 2000: Educate America Act, Public Law 103-227, 1994
Special education	IDEA Amendments, Public Law 105-17, 1997
Vocational education	The Carl D. Perkins Vocational and Applied Technology Education Act Amendments, Public Law 105-332, 1998
Vocational rehabilitation	Rehabilitation Act Amendments, Public Law 105-220, (Title IV of the Workforce Investment Act), 1998
Employment	Workforce Investment Act, Public Law 105-220, 1998
Educational reform	No Child Left Behind (NCLB) Act, Public Law 107-110, 2001

Employers must also provide reasonable accommodations for the job and work environment so that otherwise qualified applicants with a disability can perform its essential functions. The accommodation, however, must not pose an undue hardship on the employer. Examples of reasonable accommodations are making existing facilities accessible to and usable by the individuals with a disability; restructuring a job environment; modifying work schedules; acquiring or modifying equipment/tools; providing qualified readers or interpreters; or appropriately modifying examinations, training, or other programs. The individual with a disability requiring the accommodation must otherwise be qualified, and the employer must know the disability. Additionally, an employer is not required to make an accommodation if it would impose an "undue hardship" on the operation of the employer's business.

Congress has enacted an ADA tax credit to assist small businesses in meeting the requirements of the law, that is, those with annual gross receipts less than $1 million who employ 30 or fewer full-time employees. An annual credit of up to $5,000 is available.

Persons interested in learning more about the ADA can readily obtain information from state agencies such as Vocational Rehabilitation and the Job Service. The employment provisions of the ADA are enforced under the same procedures applicable to race, sex, national origin, and religious discrimination under title VII of the Civil Rights Act of 1964. Complaints regarding actions that occur may be filed with the Equal Employment Opportunity Commission or designated state human rights agencies. Good reference sources are *The Americans With Disabilities Act at Work* (Arc, 1991) and an article written by Linthicum, Cole, and D'Alonzo (1991). Further discussion of the ADA is presented in Chapter 6.

The Individuals with Disabilities Education Act (IDEA) of 1990

The IDEA, Public Law 101-476, amended and changed the name of the Education of All Handicapped Children Act of 1975 (PL 94-142) and changed the use of the term *handicapped* to *disabled*. The major purpose of the this law is ensure that children with disabilities have available to them a "free and appropriate education (FAPE)" that includes special education and related services designed to meet their individualized needs. The legislation also ensures that the rights of children and youth with disabilities and their parents are protected. It assists states and local educational agencies to provide for these students' needs and assesses the effectiveness of efforts to appropriately educate these children.

The new legislation requires that no single procedure can be used to determine an appropriate educational program for the child. Children must be assessed in all areas related to the suspected disability. If a child's parents disagree with the results of the nondiscriminatory evaluation, they have the right to obtain an independent evaluation. The school district must also consider this outside evaluation when making any decisions about the child's educational program.

IDEA added an important provision related to this book's focus that mandated transition services. IEPs now are required to include "a statement of needed transition services" for students beginning no later than age 16 and annually thereafter. When determined appropriate, transition services may begin as early as age 14 or even younger, if deemed important. In fact, the U.S. House of Representatives Committee reporting on the law encouraged earlier services, stating

age 16 may be too late for many students, particularly those at risk for dropping out of school and those with the most severe disabilities. Even for those students who stay in school until age 18, many will need more than two years of transitional services. Students with disabilities are now dropping out of school before age 16, feeling that the educational system has little to offer them. Initiating services at a younger age will be critical. (U.S. House of Representatives Report No. 101-554, 10, 1990)

Transition services are defined as:

a coordinated set of activities for a student, designed within an outcome-oriented process, which promotes movement from school-to-post-school activities, including post-secondary education, vocational education, integrated employment (including supported employment), continuing and adult education, adult services, independent living, and community participation. The coordinated set of activities shall take into account the student's preferences and interests, and shall include instruction, community experiences, the development of employment and other post-school adult living objectives, and when appropriate acquisition of daily living skills and functional vocational evaluation.

The transition mandate focuses on *students' adult adjustment preparation needs* and requires the active participation of several cooperating agencies and services. It also highlights the need for the student with a disability to be more involved and self-determined in planning his/her transition services and goals at the annual IEP meeting.

Although many efforts have been made to establish interagency cooperation, much work still needs to be accomplished to establish a seamless process from school to post-secondary agencies services. Through a U.S. Office of Special Education Program initiative, federal funds have been made available to states to establish greater interagency cooperation between vocational rehabilitation and special education agencies. These funds have been used to develop state projects to improve secondary programs to enable secondary youth with disabilities to make a more successful transition from school to young adult adjustment in the areas of education, vocational training, and community living. Although no empirical data exists, many states have made significant improvement in their interagency collaboration efforts with vocational rehabilitation, which has improved transition programs for secondary youth with disabilities. More on transition is presented in the next section, discussing the 1997 amendments to IDEA and in later chapters throughout this book.

The Individuals with Disabilities Education Act Amendments of 1997

The first set of amendments to IDEA was enacted in 1997, when the 104th and 105th Congress reauthorized Public Law 105-17. These amendments to IDEA provided an expanded set of provisions to guide and improve the delivery of special education services to students with disabilities. Several key areas were addressed; these included the time-consuming nature of special education processes, the involvement of general education, the concerns of discipline policies, and the costly due process procedures. These major changes included:

- Streamline initial eligibility process for receiving special education services.
- Reduce time-consuming and costly redundant reevaluation procedures.
- Reduce redundant and unnecessary paperwork associated with the IEP process.
- Shift to a general education program emphasis that includes general educators participating in the IEP process.
- Establish new guidelines for disciplining students within a framework based on a relationship between behavior incidents and the disability.
- Introduce the mediation process as a measure to resolve disagreements without the use of costly due process procedures.

Most important to the focus of this book are the ways that IDEA 1997 broadened the scope of the transition language and provisions. A significant change in the policy related to when the transition planning must begin for students with disabilities. IDEA 1997 stated that the age of transition planning move from age 16 to age 14 and the IEP team, including the student with disabilities, focus on the child's course of study. Its intent was to focus on including students in secondary programs that prepare them to successfully transition to appropriate post-school environments. IDEA specifically stated that student transition planning should examine students' participation in the general education curriculum, advanced placement courses, vocational education, and applicable school-to-work programs. The IDEA 1997 amendments continued to mandate that each IEP include a statement of needed transition services, when appropriate, and a statement of interagency responsibilities and/or any needed linkages by age 16.

The IDEA 1997 amendments have enhanced the transition language to ensure that students are afforded earlier planning for preparing for and making appropriate post-school transitions. In addition, the transition provisions have strongly endorsed and succeeded in increasing the interagency planning and linkages at the secondary level. The next section highlights the recent changes in the rehabilitation legislation.

The Rehabilitation Act Amendments of 1992

The Rehabilitation Act Amendments of 1992, Public Law 102-69, the reauthorization of the Rehabilitation Act of 1973, contains a significant presumption of the potentials of persons with disabilities by noting that a *person with a disability, regardless of the severity of the disability, can achieve employment and other rehabilitation goals if the appropriate services and supports are made available.* This is a significant change in policy in that it previously required evidence that the person with a disability had potential for some type of gainful employment. With the passage of the legislation, rehabilitation agencies are responsible for working closely with other agencies and programs, including the local education agency, to better unify the service system. The amendments recognize that many students with disabilities will exit school in need of rehabilitation services. Thus, each state agency must develop a plan to ensure coordination of services with the state education agency so those students will be served immediately after exiting the school system. This will require IWRPs to be completed before the student leaves the school program (Revell, 1993).

These amendments helped shape the IDEA 1997 transition policy regarding interagency coordination. As Revell (1993) noted, now there is a consistent set of public legislation: the ADA, IDEA, and Rehabilitation Act Amendments of 1992. These three laws are now much more synchronized regarding philosophy, policy direction, and expectations (Gloeker, 1993). As a result of these legislative mandates, secondary programs should and probably have improved students with disabilities' transition from school to post-school adjustment areas of education, training, and community living.

The Carl D. Perkins Vocational and Applied Technology Education Act Amendments of 1990

The Carl D. Perkins Vocational and Applied Technology Education Act Amendments of 1990 (Perkins II), Public Law 101-336, is important vocational legislation for students with special learning and/or behavior needs. It is intended to assist in fulfilling the transition services provisions of the IDEA. A further extension of the earlier vocational education legislation described previously, this version requires that each local agency receiving federal funds adhere to the following list of assurances:

- Equal access to a full range of vocational programs
- Provisions of information no later than beginning of ninth grade
- Establishment of appeal procedures for parents, students, teachers, and area residents concerned with decisions affecting their interests
- Vocational education programs provided in the LRE
- Coordination among appropriate representatives from vocational education and vocational rehabilitation; progress toward vocational goals and objectives that will be monitored through the IEP for students with disabilities and the Individualized Vocational Education Plan (IVEP) for students who are disadvantaged
- Assistance in entering vocational programs and in receiving transitional services

- Provision of supplementary services (curriculum, equipment, classroom modifications, support personnel, and instructional aids and devices)
- Provision of guidance, counseling, and career development activities by professionally certified counselors and teachers
- Provision of counseling and instructional services to facilitate the transition from school-to-post-school employment and career opportunities (American Vocational Association, 1990)

The Perkins Act provides more federal funds to be expended for vocational education than previously. Students with disabilities and disadvantages fall under the category of "special populations" in this version of the law, which also includes individuals of limited English proficiency, those who participate in programs to eliminate sex bias, and those in correctional institutions. This version of the law constituted a major shift in the provision of vocational-technical education. Early provisions tended to separate and isolate vocational educators, students, and curriculum from the rest of the school community. This version now emphasizes academic as well as occupational skills preparation, is directed toward "all segments of the populations," and emphasizes closer linkages between school and work. The Act's technical preparation provision attempts to make high school more relevant for at-risk students by linking it with 2-year community or technical college curriculums to produce skilled technicians. This reform effort focuses on the "average" students who make up the middle 50% of the high school population (Hull, 1992).

The Carl D. Perkins Vocational and Applied Technology Education Act Amendments of 1998

The Carl D. Perkins Vocational and Applied Technology Education Act Amendments of 1998 (Perkins III), Public Law 105-332, although shortened considerably, still includes vocational education provisions for students with special learning and/or behavior needs (Sitlington, Clark, & Kolstoe, 2000). Still included in the Perkins Amendments of 1998 are individuals with disabilities, individuals who are from economically disadvantaged backgrounds, individuals preparing for nontraditional training and employment, single parents, displaced homemakers, and individuals who have limited English proficiency (LEP). Perkins III still includes the provision stating that, for state education agencies (SEA) to receive federal funds, each SEA must develop a state plan (Section 122). Included in the SEA's plan must be a description of each state's program strategies for serving the aforementioned special groups and a description of how individuals who are members of special populations will:

- Be provided equal access to vocational program options.
- Not be discriminated against.
- Be provided the same programs and opportunities designed to meet or exceed the state's standards, prepare for articulation to post-secondary options, and/or prepare high-skill, high-wage employment options.

For local vocational education agencies (LVEA) to receive Perkins III entitlements, they also must develop a plan outlining many of same components as requested in each SEA's plan. These components include:

- How LVEA will discriminate against the aforementioned special populations.
- How these aforementioned special populations; their parents; teachers; local business, industry, and labor groups; and special population advocates are involved in the development, implementation, and evaluation of the vocational programs.
- How these aforementioned special populations and their parents and/or advocates are informed and assisted in understanding the requirements of the LVEA program options.

Perkins III still includes funds for the development, implementation, and evaluation of tech-prep secondary programs. Tech-prep curriculum programs are designed for students in their last two years of high school in preparation usually for transitioning to a two-year postsecondary program leading to an associate's degree in a technical or health-related field of study (Smith & Rojewski, 1993). The advantage of the tech-prep program lies in the structured work component linked closely to the academic component. This program parallels vocational rehabilitation's work study program in that it progressively moves the student into large segments of work component. It is important for SEAs and LEAs to take full advantage of the benefits of this critically important transition-related legislation for students with special learning and/or behavior needs.

Job Training Reform Amendments of 1992

The Job Training Reform Amendments of 1992, Public Law 102–367, offer youth and adults with disabilities and youth who are economically disadvantaged a greater opportunity to participate in a variety of job training and employment programs relating to the JTPA. The amendments support a variety of transition programs and services such as supported employment, job coaches, internships, community-based training combined with educational services, entry employment experiences, postsecondary education transition services, apprenticeship training, and many other related services. Their intent also included earnings, thus decreasing the students with disabilities' dependency on welfare programs, improving the quality of the workforce, and enhancing the nation's productivity.

These amendments continued to support the funding of Adult and Summer Youth Employment Programs. An additional component, Title II-C Year Round Youth Training Programs were initiated to serve in-school and out-of-school economically disadvantaged youth in need of remedial education and/or job training.

The law also promotes interagency coordination to deliver appropriate employment and training programs that will prepare youth for the transition from school to work and community living. Educators should actively encourage JTPA program representatives to participate in interagency transition teams to pool resources so student needs can be most appropriately met. Individuals who participate in the JTPA programs must have a personalized plan outlining assessment services and the goals based on identified needs. The State Job Training Office or local service-delivery area representative should be contacted for specific information.

School-to-Work Opportunities Act of 1994

The School-to-Work Opportunities Act of 1994 (PL 103–239), signed into law on April 1, 1994, represents a cooperative effort between the Departments of Education and Labor. This act establishes a national network within which all states can create statewide school-to-work opportunities systems that are a part of comprehensive educational reform. It is intended to be integrated under the Goals 2000: Educate America Act (PL 103–227), so that all students, including those with special learning and/or behavior needs, can participate in a performance-based education and training program to learn the skills needed for "high-wage" employment and/or continuing education.

State and local applications for federal grants must show how programs will ensure the opportunity to participate is given to economically disadvantaged students, low-achieving students, students with disabilities, and dropouts.

The School-to-Work Opportunities Act is intended to improve the knowledge and skills of youths by integrating academic and occupational learning, integrating school-based and work-based learning, and building effective linkages between secondary and postsecondary institutions. Every school-to-work program must include the following:

- Work-based learning that provides a planned program of job training or experiences, paid work experience, workplace mentoring, and instruction in general workplace competencies and in a broad array of elements of an industry
- School-based learning that provides career exploration and counseling, instruction in a career major (selected no later than the 11th grade), a program of study that is based on high academic and skill standards as proposed in the Goals 2000: Educate America Act and typically involves at least 1 year of postsecondary education, and periodic evaluations to identify students' academic strengths and weaknesses
- Connecting activities that coordinate involvement of employers, schools, and students; matching students and work-based learning opportunities; and training teachers, mentors, and counselors

Partnerships between elementary, middle, and secondary schools and local businesses are promoted so students can be exposed to a vast array of career opportunities to help them select a career that is consistent with their interests, goals, strengths, and abilities.

"When President Clinton placed his signature on the Goals 2000: Educate America Act on March 31, 1994, he did more than just sign into law this innovative and comprehensive program to improve education. It was the day that America got serious about education."

U.S. Department of Education
informational flyer (April 1994)

Goals 2000: Educate America Act of 1994

The Goals 2000: Educate America Act (PL 103: 227) is intended to present voluntary national standards describing what all students should know and be able to do at certain grade levels. The national standards will provide a focus, not a national curriculum or federal mandates, so students can leave school with the skills and knowledge needed to succeed. This act set the following eight national goals in attempt to help students achieve these standards: (a) school readiness; (b) school completion; (c) student achievement and citizenship; (d) mathematics and science; (e) adult literacy and lifelong learning; (f) safe, disciplined, alcohol- and drug-free schools; (g) family participation; and (h) teacher education and professional development. Objectives were developed to further delineate the implementation of these major goals.

The Educate America Act supports a "bottom-up" grass-roots approach to school reform, with the federal government assisting states and local communities in the development and implementation of their own comprehensive and innovative reform programs. A broad-based leadership team, composed of policymakers, educators, business and civic leaders, parents, and others, will help create each reform plan. Federal funds will be provided to support state and local improvement efforts. By the second year of funding, 90% of the money will flow to local schools and districts to support their own plans. Parent information and resource centers also are being encouraged to help parents obtain the knowledge and skills they will need to be effective partners in their child's education.

The Educate America Act has established a National Skills Standards Board to promote the development of occupational skill standards that defines what workers will need to know and ensures that American workers are better trained. It also encourages the development of innovative student performance assessments to gauge progress in the core subjects. The first appropriation of $105 million was released in fiscal year 1994, with significant increases projected thereafter.

The preceding and other legislative amendments, such as the Developmental Disabilities Assistance and Bill of Rights Act Amendments of 1990 and 1994 and other laws passed in the early 1990s, reflect the continued social consciousness of the United States to be responsive to the career development needs of its citizenry, including those who have special learning and/or behavior needs.

No Child Left Behind (NCLB) Act of 2001

The first significant educational legislation introduced and passed in the twenty-first century was the No Child Left Behind (NCLB) Act of 2001. The NCLB Act of 2001 is the most sweeping reform to the Elementary and Secondary Education Act (ESEA) since the ESEA was first enacted in 1965.

On January 8, 2002, President Bush signed into law the NCLB Act of 2001. The NCLB Act emphasized the president's belief that "too many of the na-

tion's neediest children" were being left behind in their learning but being socially promoted. As a result, many at-risk children and students with special learning and/or behavior needs were entering high school unprepared to successfully complete the general education curriculum, and in some states, passing a graduation exit exam.

The NCLB Act, which reauthorized the ESEA, incorporated the principles and strategies of student accountability, choice, and flexibility in federal education programs nationally. These included increased accountability for states, school districts/local educational agencies (LEAs), and schools; greater choice for families and students, particularly those attending low-performing schools; more flexibility for states and LEAs in the use of federal education funding; and a stronger emphasis on reading, especially for our elementary students.

Increased statewide accountability will be demonstrated by the administration of annual statewide reading and mathmatics assessments, which are based on the state standards for Grades 3–8. Schools will report the assessment results, and those schools not meeting the proficiency goals toward adequate yearly progress (AYP) will be required to devise corrective actions to meet AYP.

LEAs must give families and students attending schools identified as not meeting the AYP the option to attend a better school, which may include a public charter school, within the school district. The districts must provide transportation to the new school.

New flexibility provisions in the NCLB Act include authority for states and LEAs to transfer up to 50% of the funding they receive under four major state grant programs to any one of the programs, or to Title 1. The covered programs include Teacher Quality State Grants, Educational Technology, Innovative Programs, and Safe and Drug-Free Schools.

The NCLB Act forces LEAs to ensure that every child can read by the end of the third grade. To accomplish this goal, a new Reading First initiative was introduced that significantly increases the federal investment in scientifically based reading instruction programs in the early grades.

These regulations, along with the previous commitments to lower class sizes and better teacher preparation programs, will serve as a critical roadmap for this decade's plan of record education funding and historic educational reforms to help every child learn and excel. The federal government is committed to working with states during this first decade to improve education and guarantee yearly progress.

INTEGRATING INSTRUCTIONAL SERVICES

In the 1960s, special classes for students with learning and/or behavior needs were the most prominent placement. However, much controversy reigned during this decade because of the watered-down curriculum that many of the students received; the high rate of dropouts, self-esteem, and social isolation problems; and the poor vocational/adult adjustment they experienced after leaving school. A myriad of studies was conducted, which are not identified here because of their vintage. However, Dr. Lloyd Dunn's (1968) famous article questioning the value of the special education approach during this period should be mentioned because it seemed to strike the conscience of the field and start the process of a more integrative approach for students with special learning and/or behavior needs.

A major reason for the ineffectiveness of many special education classes during the late 1960s was the lack of qualified teachers. Special education teacher-training programs were just getting underway during this decade, so trained specialists were not prevalent. However, the entire country was becoming more concerned about integration in the late 1960s, spurred by such emerging concepts as the normalization principle (Wolfensberger, 1972). Wolfensberger's normalization principle promoted that students with special learning and/or behavior needs be given opportunities to participate in the same environments as all other individuals. Thus, several other more normalized service-delivery op-

tions emerged: general education setting placement, consultant model in which a special educator works collaboratively with a general education teacher, itinerant teacher traveling to various schools to collaborate with general education teachers, and the resource room model where students spend part of their school day in a specialized services area. In the past 28 years, three major integrative and interrelated concepts or approaches surfaced with the goal of placing the student with special learning and/or behavior needs into general education settings: least restrictive environment (LRE), regular education initiative (REI), and inclusion. Each is discussed briefly in the following sections. However, more detailed explanations of these and other instructional delivery models and concepts are presented in several special education texts (e.g., Cronin & Patton, 1993; Langone, 1990; Mercer & Mercer, 1993; Polloway & Patton, 1993; Schloss, Smith, & Schloss, 1990).

Least Restrictive Environment (LRE)

Specifically mentioned in the Education for All Handicapped Children Act (PL 94–142) in 1975, the LRE approach encourages placement of students with special learning and/or behavior needs in general education settings whenever and wherever possible. The concept of LRE is that children have a right to, and can benefit from, participation in the general education program, if appropriate.

In April 1976, the delegate assembly at the 54th Annual International Convention of the Council for Exceptional Children (CEC) adopted the following definition of least restrictive environment: LRE is a process that involves placing students with special learning and/or behavioral problems in general education settings to the maximum extent possible as to appropriately educate the student. This concept recognizes that students with special learning and/or behavior needs have a wide range of special education needs, varying greatly in intensity and duration; that there is a recognized continuum of education settings which may, at any given time, be appropriate for an individual child's needs; that to the maximum extent appropriate, children with special learning and/or behavior needs should be educated with students without disabilities; and that special classes, separate schooling, or other exclusionary educational experiences from students without disabilities should occur only when the intensity of the student's special education and related needs is such that they cannot be satisfied in the general education setting, even with the provision of supplementary aids and services (Council for Exceptional Children, 1976).

One major problem with the institution of this approach has been the lack of training provided to general education teachers on how to effectively support students with special learning and/or behavior needs. Thus, considerable resentment toward the concept and approach resulted. Only when the LRE principle, which was specified in the Act, was adhered to by school personnel, did it become successfully implemented.

Regular Education Initiative (REI)

The Regular Education Initiative (REI) evolved in the 1980s because of the belief by certain reformers that the special education delivery system was inadequate (W. E. Davis, 1989). The basic message of the REI was that classroom teachers should be responsible for the education of all students in their charge and that principals should be authorized to distribute resources for children who have learning and/or behavior needs. The basic assumption of the REI is that general education teachers are charged with the following responsibilities: (a) Educate all students assigned to them, (b) Make and monitor major instructional decisions for all the students in their class, (c) Provide instruction that follows a normal developmental curriculum, (d) Manage instruction for diverse populations, and (e) Seek, use, and coordinate assistance for students who require more intense services than those provided to their peers (Jenkins, Pious, & Jewell, 1990).

The REI, like other proposed changes, was not without controversy. Semmel, Abernathy, Butera, and

Lesar (1991) surveyed 381 special and general education teachers about their perceptions and opinions of the REI and found that both general and special education teachers preferred the current special education delivery system. The teachers preferred pullout special education services rather than the consultant model in which students participate fully in general education settings and where the special education teacher has no direct instructional time with the students. Overall, the respondents felt the REI approach was not appropriate for most students.

Support for this survey was voiced by Banks (1992), a teacher who noted that her colleagues were very concerned about the general education of students who do not have the prerequisite skills and techniques to adjust in that setting. She noted that neither general education nor special education teachers wanted students dumped into general education settings without these students having the requisite skills. Byrnes (1990), a school administrator, suggested not too quickly jumping on the bandwagon. Rather, she recommended that all teachers appreciate diversity and keep all options open, because no single delivery system can be considered best for all students. As she noted, "the REI debate has been philosophical and theoretical. It needs to be augmented by practical and operational perspectives" (p. 345).

The plea for general education to become involved in special education concerns fell essentially on deaf ears, and now attention has turned to a new movement called *inclusive education* or *inclusive schools* (Fuchs & Fuchs, 1994).

Inclusion

Inclusive education is the most recent version of the integration of students with special learning and/or behavior needs into general education settings. Inclusion is a controversial concept. As Fuchs and Fuchs noted, "Like the REI, the newer term seems to defy straight forward interpretation. And like the REI, this is partly because 'inclusion' means different things to people who wish different things from it" (1994, p. 299).

Inclusion is based on an age-old philosophy that espouses bringing students, families, educators, and community members together to create schools and other social institutions based on acceptance, belonging, and community (Bloom, Perlmutter, & Burrell, 1999). Inclusive education seeks to establish a learning community that is supportive and nurturing and provides *all students* the services and accommodations they need to learn and appreciate the cultural or learning differences that all students bring into the general educational setting.

Many advocates of inclusion or full inclusion state that it requires all students with disabilities to receive their total education within the general education setting. Many professionals strongly believe this is the only alternative and are committed to this approach as the only option for these students. Others approach inclusion on a personalized student basis—where this option is based on the students' needs and capabilities to benefit from inclusion on an as-needed basis.

According to Schrag and Burnette,

> Inclusive schools do not just mainstream students—they include them. They maintain a continuum of educational options to provide choice and meet the needs of individual children. Inclusive schools forge strong ties with their communities, coordinating services with community agency personnel and embracing parents as equal partners. Students work in flexible learning environments, with flexible curricula and instruction that is accessible to all. All students work toward the same overall educational outcomes; what differs is the level at which these outcomes are achieved and the degree of emphasis placed on them. (1994, p. 64)

"The push to integrate all disabled kids in regular classes is destructive! Those demanding full inclusion are interested in only one thing—socialization ... but it is only one value and not the only reason taxpayers support the schools."

Albert Shanker, President, American
Federation of Teachers (1994)

The inclusion movement has stimulated considerable controversy and debate throughout the country and received a great deal of media attention. The American Federation of Teachers, for example, while noting the importance and right of all students to be in general education settings, questions the full inclusion being promoted by many special educators and parents. The federation noted that it is unreasonable to expect general education teachers to meet the needs of their nondisabled students if they are expected to teach anyone who is placed in their class; in January 1994, it called a halt to full inclusion. On the other hand, advocates of inclusive education believe that with proper support and teacher aides, almost every student with special learning and/or behavior needs can and should be in general education settings so as to experience a more normal environment with their age-appropriate peers. It remains to be seen as to the extent inclusive education will become pervasively immersed into our schools throughout the country.

A more moderate position on inclusion is taken by John Heskett, a state education agency coordinator of special education services and former president of the National Association of Special Education Administrators:

> The opportunity to be fully included in the regular classroom must be considered for any student with a disability. However, full inclusion may not be the required service for all students with disabilities. The process of individual determination must include, but not be limited to, the ability of the student to benefit from the integrative experience and the appropriateness of inclusive education relative to the goals, objectives, and services called for in the IEP.... Inclusion is a mechanism for achieving appropriate Least Restrictive Environment (LRE) decisions for individual students. (1993, pp. 2, 8)

The national special education association, the CEC, has taken a position that appears to be similar to Heskett's. Their policy on inclusion is presented in Figure 1.5.

The preceding discussion only touches on the major concepts and approaches to providing students with the most appropriate learning community. As can be noted, each approach seems to advocate flexi-

CEC POLICY ON INCLUSIVE SCHOOLS AND COMMUNITY SETTINGS

The Council for Exceptional Children (CEC) believes all children, youth, and young adults with disabilities are entitled to a free and appropriate education and/or services that lead to an adult life characterized by satisfying relations with others, independent living, producing engagement in the community, and participation in society at large. To achieve such outcomes, there must exist for all children, youth, and young adults a rich variety of early intervention, educational, and vocational program options and experiences. Access to these programs and experiences should be based on individual educational need and desired outcomes. Furthermore, students and their families or guardians, as members of the planning team, may recommend the placement, curriculum option, and the exit document to be pursued.

CEC believes that a continuum of services must be available for all children, youth, and young adults. The CEC also believes that the concept of inclusion is a meaningful goal to be pursued in our schools and communities. In addition, the CEC believes children, youth, and young adults with disabilities should be served whenever possible in general education classrooms in inclusive neighborhood schools and community settings. Such settings should be strengthened and supported by an infusion of specially trained personnel and other appropriate supportive practices according to the individual needs of the child.

POLICY IMPLICATIONS

Schools. In inclusive schools, the building administrator and staff with assistance from the special education administration should be primarily responsible for the education of children, youth, and young adults with disabilities. The administrator(s) and other school personnel must have available to them appropriate support and technical assistance to enable them to fulfill their responsibilities. Leaders in state/provincial and local governments must redefine rules and regulations as necessary, and grant school personnel greater authority to make decisions regarding curriculum, materials, instructional practice, and staffing patterns. In return for greater autonomy, the school administrator and staff should establish high standards for each child and youth and should be held accountable for his or her progress toward outcomes.

Communities. Inclusive schools must be located in inclusive communities; therefore, the CEC invites all educators, other professionals, and family members to work together to create early intervention, educational, and vocational programs and experiences that are collegial, inclusive, and responsive to the diversity of children, youth, and young adults. Policy makers at the highest levels of state/provincial and local government, as well as school administration, also must support inclusion in the educational reforms they espouse. Furthermore, the policy makers should fund programs in nutrition, early intervention, health care, parent education, and other social support programs that prepare all children, youth, and young adults to do well in school. There can be no meaningful school reform, nor inclusive schools, without funding these key prerequisites. As important, there also must be interagency agreements and collaboration with local governments and business to help prepare students to assume a constructive role in an inclusive community.

Professional Development. And finally, state/provincial departments of education, local educational districts, and colleges and universities must provide high-quality preservice and continuing professional development experiences that prepare all general educators to work effectively with children, youth, and young adults representing a wide range of abilities and disabilities, experiences, cultural and linguistic backgrounds, attitudes, and expectations. Moreover, special educators should be trained with an emphasis on their roles in inclusive schools and community settings. They also must learn the importance of establishing ambitious goals for their students and of using the appropriate means of monitoring the progress of children, youth, and young adults.

FIGURE 1.5   CEC Policy on Inclusive Schools and Community Settings.
Note. From *CEC Policy Manual, Section 3, Part 1* (p. 8) by The Council for Exceptional Children, 1994, Arlington, VA: The Council for Exceptional Children. Originally approved by the Delegate Assembly of the CEC in April 1993. Copyright 1994 by The Council for Exceptional Children. Reprinted by permission.

bility, options, and appropriate outcomes within each student's capabilities. However, Fuchs and Fuchs (1994) noted that REI opts for a cooperative effort between special and general education, but the full inclusionists opt for the elimination of special education. Their excellent article should be read for more detailed knowledge on this topic.

How well are students with special learning and/or behavior needs being integrated into the general education settings of the school community? Although much is currently appearing in professional literature and newsprint noting the implementation of inclusive education by many schools, a study by The Arc (S. Davis, 1992) found more than 75% of students with mental retardation were being educated in totally segregated settings with little interaction with their nondisabled peers, experiencing few opportunities for learning about career options and other postschool possibilities, and often receiving no vocational training, functional living skills training, or motivation for living and working in the community (Davis, 1992).

The TEC (1998) reported approximately 65% of students with mental retardation were being educated in segregated educational settings in public schools. Although this figure is somewhat lower, it further illustrates that for some students inclusive education is not always being offered. This same study reported that although students with learning disabilities are being included more in the general education class (40%), some 55% are either being educated in the resource room or separate class service alternatives. Wehmeyer (2002) indicated that this figure is holding steady in our schools.

Although these are only *two studies*, it appears that much remains to be accomplished for the inclusion concept to be implemented, at least in the case of students with mental retardation.

There is almost universal concurrence that students with special learning and/or behavior needs should be given every opportunity to participate and learn in general education settings like everyone else—*if this setting is the LRE for meeting their learning needs.* One other major reservation by many educators, particularly those with the functional skills/career education orientation, is whether or not the educational program

emphasis will include enough instruction in those areas to prepare each student to become a productive and functioning member of society with a good quality of life.

SELF-DETERMINATION

Teachers, parents, and agency personnel are beginning to realize that self-determination is an important component of the educational process. In addition, they also recognize that students with disabilities benefit from instruction in self-determination skills and opportunities to transfer these skills to other ecological environments. These skills have been deemed especially important for students with special learning and/or behavior needs who are preparing to make the transition from school-to-work and community living (Wehmeyer, Agran, & Hughes, 1998).

Professionals agree that if students with special learning and/or behavior needs are to become more self-reliant and prepared to successfully function as adults, self-determination must be a major integrated process of their personalized curriculums. More on self-determination programming will provided later in Chapter 10.

....

CHAPTER COMMENTARY

The appropriate educational focus in American schools has been a topic of great concern in this country for several decades. In the opinion of many experts, the entire educational system needs restructuring. The stage finally has been set for significant change. The recently passed Goals 2000: Educate America Act is designed to support fundamental, system-wide reform in all schools. Thus, it is an opportune time for professionals and advocates of all students, including those with special learning and/or behavior needs, to work closely with educational reformers in restructuring the educational system for all students. If this is not done, these individuals will suffer the consequences of trying to compete in this rapidly expanding global economy in which we now live.

The present developmental- and academic-oriented curriculum of most schools has not effectively prepared a large proportion of students for successful adult functioning. Most of these students simply do not respond positively or appropriately to a college-oriented delivery system that presents them with failure and embarrassment experiences. Many students with special learning needs come from such dire home and family situations that their learning and/or behaviors in the school situation need a different approach. Otherwise, the result is an increasing proportion of dropouts, school failure, school dissatisfaction, behavior problems, delinquency, and joblessness.

Many educational leaders would like to see one unified educational system rather than a number of separate categorical programs such as special education. Whether such an admirable goal can ever be achieved is yet to be seen. Some schools may claim to have accomplished such a goal. But, for the most part, too many schools continue to educate most of their special needs and disruptive students in a combination of regular classes, resource rooms, specialized programs, and/or special classes or alternative programs.

In spite of the enabling legislation, monies, increasingly professional personnel, and the creation of new concepts, approaches, strategies, and models for "fixing the system," not enough has changed on a broad scale because many personnel in the field do not want to change their policies, curriculum, and instructional methods. At the same time, many other professionals in the education system have worked diligently to continually improve their school systems. The dedication and effectiveness of numerous administrators, counselors, and teachers who provide their students with effective teaching and personal development opportunities is impressive. Many outstanding accomplishments have been made over the years; however, much remains to be done in most schools if the education of all students is to be satisfactory.

We must *quit reinventing the wheel* and instead face the arduous but meaningful task of restructuring and fine-tuning our curricula and collaborative efforts so that the educational efforts of the schools are effective for all students. In the following chapter, one effective solution that holds much promise for providing students with a more appropriate educational focus is presented.

. . . .

ACTIVITIES

1. Based on the student outcome data presented in this chapter, write a philosophical statement that clearly explains what you now believe should be the major purpose of education in your school district. Then, identify the educational goals that you would establish for your students who have learning and/or behavior difficulties.

2. Given the present legislative mandates and the present climate of inclusion, what curriculum areas do you believe must become part of the total curricular effort for the Goals 2000: Educate America Act to be achieved for all students, including those with special learning and/or behavior needs?

CHAPTER 2

A Functional Life Skills Curriculum Approach

PRELIMINARY QUESTIONS

1. Explain what exactly is meant by the terms functional life skills curriculum and functional curriculum approach.
2. Who should be taught functional life skills?
3. Identify and describe some of the major functional life skills curricula that are being advocated for students with special learning and/or behavior needs.
4. What is transition/career education, and what is its relationship to the functional life skills curriculum approach?
5. What is the difference between transition/career education and vocational education?
6. What are the most compelling reasons for implementing the education approach in the public schools?
7. What are transition services, and what is their relationship to the functional life skills curriculum approach?
8. When and by whom was the transition services concept introduced?
9. What are three major components that are needed for effective transition services?
10. What four areas of content must the Individualized Education Plan (IEP) contain for transition services?

OVERVIEW

The need to provide a more functional life skills curriculum for students with special learning and/or behavior needs and to address their transition service needs is not a new concept in American education. Special educators have recognized this need for decades, and there have been some notable efforts in many schools throughout the country. Terms such as *life skills, independent living skills, persisting life situations, occupational education, work-study, work experience, occupational adjustment, personal-social adjustment, social learning, vocational education, cooperative education, transition/career education,* and

career development are examples of descriptions from the past and present that have been used to reflect functional life skills curricula for students with special learning and/or behavior needs.

The first section of the chapter begins with a discussion of functional life skills and identifies some current functional skills curricula materials and guides. Two models of functional life skills curricula that are excellent contributions to the field are identified and described. Next, the transition approach is reintroduced.

Finally, the transition/career education approach is presented, including a historical account of the career education movement followed by an explanation of its basic concepts and approach. After reading this detailed section, the reader should understand career/transition education's close relationship to the functional life skills approach. An example of the well-conceived transition/career education curriculum model developed by Gary Clark concludes the chapter.

FUNCTIONAL LIFE SKILLS CURRICULUM

It is being more widely recognized that most, if not all, students need an appropriate blend of academic and functional life skills instruction, which should be taught not only in school but also in home and community settings. Functional skills are those that are academic and others that are critical for success in community/adult functioning. These include independent living, social, communication, leisure/recreation, and vocational skills.

"Functional curriculum is instructional content that focuses on the concepts and skills students need in the areas of personal-social, daily living, and occupational adjustment."

Gary Clark (1991)

The Division on Career Development and Transition (DCDT) of the Council for Exceptional Children (CEC) has published an excellent position paper

CHAPTER OUTLOOK

Frank R. Rusch is Professor of Special Education and Director, Transition Research Institute, at the University of Illinois, Champaign Urbana.

Janis Chadsey is Associate Professor of Special Education at the University of Illinois, Champaign Urbana.

Over the past 20 years, teachers and administrators, researchers, and state and federal policymakers have been concerned with transition practices. Yet, limited empirical research is available on what constitutes best transition practices. Thus, emerging practices are often labeled "best" without sufficient supporting research. The unfortunate consequence of this situation is the wholesale adoption of practices that may not be effective.

In a series of investigations, the Transition Research Institute at Illinois has identified studies for which evidence is available to support the claim that the practices they describe are effective (Kohler, in preparation, 1993; Kohler, DeStefano, Wermuth, Grayson, & McGinty, in press; Rusch, Kohler, & Hughes, 1992). Based on an analysis of over 60 studies contributed by researchers in career, vocational, special, and rehabilitation education, and the Institute's research (Kohler, in preparation), five categories of transition practices appear to warrant the label "best practices." These practices include student-focused systematic transition planning, family involvement, interagency and interdisciplinary teaming and collaboration, program structure and attributes, and student involvement.

Student-Focused Systematic Transition Planning

Post-school outcomes will vary by student, but typical areas addressed in the transition plan in-

clude residential, employment, social and interpersonal, medical, recreational and leisure, mobility, community access, and overall well-being. Planning should determine the outcomes desired by the student (with family input), and a plan should be formulated to achieve those outcomes. Students must be provided an opportunity to assert and advocate for themselves, make their needs known, self-evaluate progress toward meeting their goals, and solve problems.

Family Involvement in Planning, Education, and Service Delivery

Families need help to identify programs that will meet the needs and interests of their sons and daughters. Specifically, they need information about and access to the adult service system as well as other post-school options. They also need to be empowered to make decisions that enable them to facilitate their children's attainment of self-selected and valued outcomes after high school.

Interagency and Interdisciplinary Teaming, Collaboration, and Service Delivery

Because so many different people and agencies are often involved in facilitating the transition process, teaming and collaboration among the participants is critical. This includes interagency cooperation among state and local agencies. When personnel from different professions, advocacy groups, and agencies are collaborating in using a student- and family-centered approach, the result should be a reduction of duplicative services, elimination of turf issues, and delivery of services that ensure desired outcomes. In addition to the student and family and educational personnel, the team may also include individuals associated with vocational and rehabilitation personnel, employers, postsecondary representatives, friends, peers, and advocates.

Program Structure and Attributes

Practices that should be considered under the category of program structure and attributes include providing services within inclusive and integrated settings. Further, high schools should collect student follow-up data on which to base restructuring of existing practices to promote valued outcomes for all students.

Student Development

A critical component of the transition process involves teaching students skills and strategies that will enable them to reach their goals. Research conducted by the Transition Research Institute identified six student development categories, including assessment, accommodation and support, career and vocational curricula, work experience, employment skills training, and life skills training. Within each category, a number of practices have been identified and rated for importance. Within each of the six categories, the following transition practices were rated highest and lowest.

Categories

1. Assessment
   Highest: Ongoing assessment
   Lowest: Traditional vocational assessment
2. Accommodation and support
   Highest: Identification and development of natural supports
   Lowest: Peer mentorship
3. Career and vocational curricula
   Highest: Career and vocational curricula infused throughout academic subject areas
   Lowest: Technical preparation curriculum options
4. Work experience
   Highest: Matching students to jobs
   Lowest: Job shadowing
5. Employment skills training
   Highest: Community-based vocational skills training
   Lowest: Longitudinal vocational training
6. Life skills training
   Highest: Self-determination skills training
   Lowest: Leisure skills training

The knowledge is now available to change the course of today's youth with disabilities in preparing for the challenges facing them tomorrow. If the practices that currently are validated by research could be introduced in every high school in the near future, drastic improvements in secondary special education effectiveness would be realized.

Clearly, a youth's high school experiences provide one of the cornerstones to ensuring success throughout life. Our failure to provide an effective high school experience results in personal shortcomings, including failure to attain additional education and training to help mold a career of personal choice.

advocating the functional life skills curriculum approach as an important component in the provision of an appropriate education (Clark, Field, Patton, Brolin, & Sitlington, 1994). Some of the major tenets expressed in this paper follow:

- A functional life skills instruction approach should be a part of every school curriculum (i.e., included within existing course work) or a recognized and approved option (i.e., alternative course work) for all students at all grade levels.
- The first consideration for functional life skills education settings should be general education and the community.
- Least restrictive environment instructional alternatives must always be considered after the deci-

sion is made that the instruction in functional life skills content is not feasible or is inadequate in a general education setting.

- It is the responsibility of general educators at the elementary and middle school levels to ensure the applicability of basic skills education to the functional demands of independent living for students at school, at home, and in the community.

- Special educators should provide specialized or direct instruction in functional life skill areas at a level of such quality that there can be no question of commitment to meeting students' needs. (Council for Exceptional Children, DCDT, 1994).

The CEC noted that functional life skills, career development, and transition programming must begin in early childhood and continue throughout adulthood. As noted in that paper, a continually growing body of literature suggests that an appropriate education for students with special learning and/or behavior needs must be determined in terms of individual needs relative to the functional life skills demands of adulthood.

The Board of Directors of the CEC Division on Developmental Disabilities (formerly the Division of Mental Retardation and Developmental Disabilities) approved a position paper on April 15, 1992, advocating a de-emphasis of the general education track for a greater functional life skills approach. Although noting that the interaction of peers within the general education settings should be a first consideration, the CEC cautions that the needs of students in general education sometimes differ from those with mental retardation. Thus, many of these students may need specialized programs such as community-based instruction and an emphasis on functional life skills and vocational training (Smith & Hilton, 1994).

Unfortunately, the intent of functional life skills instruction is sometimes misinterpreted. The December 13, 1993, issue of *U.S. News and World Report* contained the following criticism of special education:

Special education classrooms become convenient places for teachers to send struggling students they don't want in their classrooms; academics, in such cases, takes a back seat. Indeed, special education instructors often do as much social work—sometimes known as life skills—as teaching. In one special education class in Ohio, students learned how to bake a frozen pizza in an oven. (Shapiro et al., p. 46)

Obviously, the writer of this article had little understanding of the many important benefits of such an activity to the students and jumped quickly to inappropriate conclusions without understanding the total situation and instructional goals established for these students for preparation for future adult living and working.

Basic Concepts

In many respects, special education has been teaching functional life skills to most of its students for a long time. As noted by G. M. Clark:

A functional curriculum approach is a way of delivering instructional content that focuses on the concepts and skills needed by all students with disabilities in the areas of personal-social, daily living, and occupational adjustment. What is considered a functional curriculum for any one student would be the content (concepts and skills) included in that student's curriculum or course of study that targets his or her current and future needs. These needs are (should be) based on a nondiscriminatory, functional assessment approach. (1994, p. 37)

"A 'functional life skills curriculum approach' has no restrictions regarding the type or location of instructional delivery."

Gary Clark (1994)

Functional life skills curriculums are often associated with students with more severe learning and/or behavior difficulties. However, there is greater recognition today that this approach is also important for a wide variety of students, not only those with special learning and/or behavior needs but also those for whom the general education curriculum holds limited value. As G. Clark noted, "Current functional curriculum models focus directly on knowledge and skills that need to be taught and leave the delivery procedures and instructional environment decisions to users" (1994, p. 37). Clark distinguishes between the terms *functional life skills curriculum* and *a functional life skills curriculum approach*. He describes the former as a document or written guide that is used for all students in a particular setting, whereas the latter has no restrictions regarding the type or location of instructional delivery. The functional life skills curriculum approach places considerable responsibility on both general and special educators to make sure functional life skills content prescribed on the IEP is delivered effectively.

Many educators and agency service providers are currently examining ways that academic and functional life skills can be offered together in integrated settings. With the current emphasis on inclusive education, instructional strategies such as personalized planning, curriculum mapping, cooperative learning, and team teaching are being instituted to facilitate the successful integration of students with special learning and/or behavior needs into general education settings (Field, LeRoy, & Rivera, 1994). Thus, functional life skills really do not need to be taught as a separate curriculum because they are important for all students to acquire for making successful transitions from school to postsecondary training and/or for other adult community living and working environments.

A functional life skills curriculum approach requires opportunities for community-based instructional experiences. As noted by Beck, Broers, Hogue, Shipstead, and Knowlton, commenting on the potential conflict between trying to integrate students in regular classes and provide learning experiences in the community, the functional curriculum approach "can present conflicts of time and instructional priorities, or it can present a golden opportunity for collaborative planning between general and special education teachers as well as for inclusive education" (1994, p. 44). Chapters 11 and 13 refer to these authors' program of functional life skills instruction for

kindergarten and other elementary students in inclusive settings.

TRANSITION/ CAREER EDUCATION

This book advocates a transition/career education curricular approach to meet the functional life skills and transition needs of students with special learning and/or behavior needs as well as students in general education, including students who are at-risk. Thus, in this section, it is important to provide the reader some background on the transition/career education approach and its close relationship to both the functional life skills and transition services approaches.

What Is Transition/ Career Education?

The term and concept of career education was first introduced in 1971 to the field as an educational reform by the U.S. Commissioner of Education, Dr. Sidney Marland, at a national educational convention to secondary school principals in Houston, Texas. Marland and other national leaders were extremely concerned about the high dropout rate in American schools and felt that one of the major reasons was the failure of the educational system to provide students with the knowledge and skills relevant to future adult community living and working.

Transition/career education can be conceived as an effort that begins no later than kindergarten and continues throughout the entire K–12 system for all students that aims to make *work—paid and/or unpaid—* a meaningful part of total lifestyle. Its emphasis, both on beginning at the kindergarten level and on using the concept of "work" as a basis for K–12 educational reforms, distinguishes "career education" from other currently popular "schooling to employment" program proposals (Hoyt, 1993, p. 36).

According to Hoyt, a major feature of career education is its emphasis on regarding the classroom as a workplace for both teachers and students. Thus, career development and the teaching-learning process are both emphasized.

Career education can be called a lifelong process that infuses a *careers emphasis* into all content areas, grades K-12, including job training, work study, job shadowing, apprenticeship programs, mentoring, career exploration, and the nonpaid work done as a family member, citizen, and leisure participant.

Transition/career education can be conceptualized as a progression of four interrelated stages: career awareness, career exploration, career preparation, and career assimilation.

- Career awareness begins at the elementary level and is intended to make students aware of the existence of work (paid and unpaid) and workers and how students will fit into the work-oriented society in the future. Career awareness relates to the self-awareness aspect of human development that is occurring during these years.

- Career exploration, the second stage, emphasized at the middle school/junior high level, is intended to help students explore their interests and abilities in relation to lifestyle and occupations. Students should learn to examine their own unique abilities and needs, be exposed to many hands-on experiences, and be given the opportunity to engage in several community-based experiences.

- Career preparation, emphasized at the high school level, is a period for career decision making and skills acquisition. Students should be able to identify their specific interests and aptitudes and the type of lifestyle that will meet these characteristics.

- Career assimilation is the transition of the student into postsecondary training and community living and working-adjustment environments. The student should be able to engage in satisfying avocational, family, and civic/volunteer work activities as well as gaining paid employment. Many students will need continuing education and follow-up services at this stage.

Sitlington, Nuebert, Begun, Lombard, and LeConte (1996) provide excellent examples of functional transitional skills (Figure 2.1) and questions (Figure 2.2) that transition service providers and parents can ask to determine students with special learn-

ing and/or behavior needs, functioning developmental career stage level.

Hoyt (1987) identified these seven major goals of career education: (a) to help persons in career awareness/exploration/decision-making; (b) to equip persons with general employability/adaptability/promotability skills; (c) to promote and implement private sector-education system partnerships; (d) to relate education and work so that better choices of both can be made; (e) to reform education by infusing a "careers" emphasis in classrooms; (f) to make work a meaningful part of the individual's total lifestyle; and (g) to reduce bias and stereotyping and thus protect freedom of choice. Some of these goals are similar to those advocated by the transition and school-to-work legislation.

One's career consists of many roles—occupational, avocational, family, and civic.

Central to understanding the concept of career education is the concept of *career roles.* An individual's career is multifaceted; that is, it consists of several work roles that one engages in during one's lifetime. Persons who are in school are engaged in the primary career role of a student. When they leave school and become permanently employed, a job is a primary part of their career, but they will also engage in the other career roles of family member (spouse, father/mother, etc.); a community member who engages in volunteer work and other citizenship activities; and as a participant in productive leisure, recreational, and other avocational activities such as hobbies. Thus, *one's career is more than a job;* it is all the important work activities one does in a lifetime. Retirees no longer may receive compensation for the work they do, but they engage in many productive work activities in their later life that contribute to the benefit of themselves and others.

An illustration of the many career roles comprising one's career is presented in Figure 2.3. Note that one's own personal determinants (e.g., intellectual and physical characteristics) and situational determinants (e.g., community and educational program) influence a career. Thus, educators are an important determinant in the type of career and successes their students will eventually experience.

Career Awareness

- Can identify parents' and other family members' jobs.
- Can describe what parents and others do on their jobs.
- Can name and describe at least 10 different occupations.
- Can describe how people get jobs.
- Can describe at least three jobs to investigate.
- Can discuss what happens if adults cannot or do not work.
- Can identify why people have to get along with each other to work.

Career Exploration

- Can discern the difference between a job and a career.
- Can identify three ways to find out about different occupations.
- Can state at least three things they want in a job.
- Can identify the steps in finding a job.
- Can identify at least three careers they want to explore.
- Can state preferences for indoor vs. outdoor work, solitary work versus working with others, and working with their hands and tools/machines versus working strictly with their minds.
- Can identify how to get applications and how to complete them.
- Can discuss why interviews are important.
- Can identify their strengths, abilities, skills, learning styles, and special needs regarding work or specific jobs.

Career Preparation

- Can identify career/vocational courses they want to take in school.
- Can describe the educational and work requirements of specific careers and jobs.
- Can identify where education and training can be obtained.
- Can explain steps in acquiring the skills necessary to enter a chosen field or job.
- Can describe entry level skills, course or job requirements, and exit level competencies to succeed in courses.
- Can identify community and educational options and alternatives to gaining education and employment in a chosen field.
- Can identify the worker characteristics and skills in working with others that are required in a chosen field or job.

Career Assimilation

- Can identify steps to take if they want to advance in their place of employment.
- Can identify educational benefits and ways of gaining additional training through their employment.
- Can explain fields that are related to their current work in which they could transfer.
- Can identify ways to change jobs without losing benefits or salary.
- Can describe appropriate ways of leaving or changing jobs and companies.
- Can relate their skills to other occupations or avocations.
- Can explain retirement benefits.
- Can identify and participate in leisure activities that they can pursue after they retire.

FIGURE 2.1 Career Development Checklist

Note: From *Assess for Success: Handbook on Transition Assessment* by Patricia L. Sitlington, Debra A. Neubert, Wynne Begun, Richard C. Lombard, and Pamela J. Leconte, 1996, Arlington, VA: The Council for Exceptional Children. Permission is granted to reproduce this page.

Awareness Phase

- What is work?
- What is a job?
- What are some jobs you know about?
- What kind of work do people do on these jobs?
- What have you dreamed of doing when you finish school?
- What kind of job do you want?
- Where do you want to live, and with whom, when you are grown up?
- Why do people work? Why do you want to work?
- What do you enjoy doing when you are not in school?
- What jobs do your mother, father, and other family members have?
- What types of things do they do on their jobs?
- What is college? Why do people go to college? What is vocational training?
- What is public transportation? How would you get where you want to go if your parents did not drive you?
- What is voting?

Exploration Phase

- What jobs are you interested in visiting?
- What exploratory courses would you like to take in school?
- What hobbies do you have?
- What activities do you do in your spare time?
- What volunteer or community service work do you do?
- Did you enjoy your summer job? What parts did you like best?
- Do you like being inside or outside better?
- Do you prefer being with other people, or do you enjoy being by yourself?
- Do you enjoy working with your hands and with tools, or do you prefer to solve problems in your head?
- Did you get along well with your classmates? If so, why did you? If not, why didn't you?
- What skills do you have that you can use in these or other courses?

Preparation Phase

- What courses do you need to achieve your career goals?
- What skills will you need to gain entry into those courses?
- How will you prepare to live on your own?
- Will you need to take courses during high school and after?
- Will these courses lead to college courses? Does the school have a tech prep program?
- Do you and your family plan for you to attend college?
- Will you gain the skills needed to succeed in college?
- Will you be able to get a job based on your high school and/or college coursework?
- Does the educational program provide job placement and support?
- Can you gain entry into an approved apprenticeship program?

Assimilation Phase

- Can you continue your training and education after you begin employment?
- Does the employer provide educational benefits?
- How can you advance within the company?
- Can you transfer between departments in the company?
- Does the employer offer a good retirement and benefits package?
- Do you have alternatives to pursue if your employer has to downsize or lay off workers?
- Do you have options for continuing education, even for leisure interests?
- Can you transfer your job skills and avocational skills to other employment?

FIGURE 2.2   Relevant Assessment Questions for Career Development

Note: From *Assess for Success: Handbook on Transition Assessment* by Patricia L. Sitlington, Debra A. Neubert, Wynne Begun, Richard C. Lombard, and Pamela J. Leconte, 1996, Reston, VA: The Council for Exceptional Children. Permission is granted to reproduce this page.

Community-based instruction assists in life skills development.

FIGURE 2.3   Illustration of the major work
roles that comprise one's career.

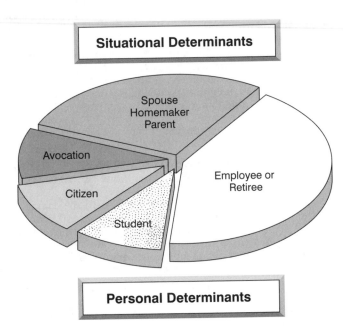

A historical account of some major events that occurred to promote the adoption and implementation of transition/career education throughout the country for both general and special education, which again is gaining momentum, is presented below.

Historical Aspects

During the 1970s and into the 1980s, transition/career education services progressed rapidly in most states. When Dr. Marland returned to Houston in 1976 to keynote the first National Commissioner's Conference on Career Education, he reported that "probably never in our educational history has there been such enormous movement toward a central concept of reform over such a brief span of time" (Neil, 1977). At the Helen Keller Centennial Conference, Hoyt (1980) noted that the career education concept had survived for a full decade—three times as long as the typical educational reform movement.

Some of the major historical events having direct implications for individuals with special learning and/or behavior needs follow:

- In 1972, the federal Special Education Agency (then the Bureau of Education for the Handicapped) endorsed career education. The bureau's director, Edwin Martin, declared career education a top priority and made funds available for a large number of curriculum and materials development projects, in-service and preservice training, and research studies.

- In 1973, a National Topical Conference on Career Education for Exceptional Children and Youth was held. This important conference, cosponsored by the CEC and the American Vocational Association (AVA), launched the concept of multidisciplinary career education, which received endorsement from professional teacher associations. The conference brought together legislators, lawyers, advocates, business and industry leaders, and an array of educators from various disciplines that presented service-delivery models, methods, and materials for providing career education.

- In 1974, the U.S. Office of Career Education was officially established within the Office of Education. Kenneth B. Hoyt was appointed the director of the U.S. Office of Career Education and established leadership for career education within the federal bureaucracy. The office wrote and disseminated important position papers and monographs, sponsored workshops and miniconferences with significant individuals and organizations, funded special projects, and promoted legislative and programmatic developments.

- In 1975, the Bureau of Education for the Handicapped (BEH) sponsored a conference for nationally recognized leaders, entitled "Research Needs Related to Career Education for the Handicapped." After several days of intensive group interactions and problem solving, members of the conference established priorities that set BEH funding patterns. In St. Louis later that year, a small band of concerned educators organized a committee to establish a new division within the CEC that would focus on and promote implementation of career education. The new division was entitled the Division on Career Development (DCD). A similar group formed within the AVA became known as the National Association of Vocational Education Special Needs Personnel (NAVESNP).

- In 1976, the Division on Career Development (DCD) was provisionally approved as the 12th division of the CEC by an overwhelming vote of its Board of Governors. The division elected its officers and became a significant branch of the CEC. In 1997, DCD was renamed the Division of Career Development and Transition (DCDT). Two other important events that occurred during 1976 were the first National Commissioner's Conference on Career Education and the passage of the Vocational Education Amendments. The Commissioner's Conference drew over 8,000 enthusiastic participants who exchanged ideas about providing career education to all age groups. The Vocational Amendments required that 10% of federal funds be allocated for students with disabilities, as outlined in Public Law (PL) 94-142.

- In 1977, the Career Education Implementation Incentive Act (PL 95-207) helped states infuse career education into school curricula so that it became part of ongoing local instruction and was not considered just vocational education. Congress declared, "A major purpose of education is to prepare every individual for a career suitable to that individual's preference . . . career education should be an integral part of the Nation's education process which serves as preparation for work."

- In 1978, the CEC issued a position paper supporting career education. Career education was described as the "Totality of experiences through which one learns to live a meaningful, satisfying work life . . . provides the opportunity for children to learn, in the least restrictive environment possible, the academic, daily living, personal-social and occupational knowledge, and specific vocational skills necessary to attain their highest levels of economic, personal, and social fulfillment. The individual can obtain this fulfillment through work (both paid or unpaid) and in a variety of other social roles and personal life styles . . . student, citizen, volunteer, family member, and participant in meaningful leisure time activities."

- In 1979, Special Institutes and the National Topical Conference on Career Education for Exceptional Individuals were held in conjunction with one another. This conference, sponsored by the CEC and the institutes, brought together a wide variety of professional workers who demonstrated that career education could be infused and implemented into a variety of settings by numerous methods. Approximately 1,000 people weathered the blizzard of 1979 in St. Louis and expressed enthusiasm for continuing the conferences on a more frequent basis.

- In 1980, the DCD started to form state DCD units. The division's membership became the fastest growing in the CEC, and states began to organize at the grass-roots level.

- In 1981, the DCD conducted an International Conference on Career Development. Despite severe nationwide financial constraints, the conference was highly successful and set into motion the planning of a similar conference that has been held every 2 years since. In addition, several states now conduct conferences at their state and local levels.

- In 1982, the Career Education Incentive Act was repealed on October 1 and the Office of Career Education began the process of phasing out. The Career Education Incentive Act was never intended to be renewed; instead, it was designed to provide federal incentive funds so that state and local districts could initiate career education and make it part of their educational effort. The Omnibus Budget Reconciliation Act of 1981 moved career education into the block grant program with the hope that most state departments of education and local school districts would make career education a priority and appropriate even more funds. Thus, the block grant approach could be a significant boon to the future of career education.

- In 1983, two important career education national conferences were held. The Second National Conference on Career Education was held June 13-16 in Louisville, Kentucky. Kenneth Hoyt, on leave from the federal government to serve as Distinguished Visiting Scholar at Embry-Riddle Aeronautical University, spearheaded its development. In polling career education proponents across the country, Hoyt found an overwhelming positive response to such a conference. The other important conference was sponsored by the CEC's DCD in cooperation with NAVESNP and the Special Needs Division of the AVA. It was held October 20-22 in Chicago. Both of these conferences demonstrated that interest and enthusiasm for career education were not waning but progressively growing (Brolin, 1983a, pp. 4-6).

Many other significant activities have had direct implications on the education of students and adults with disabilities. First, several early career education curriculum models were used successfully with special education students. These were the school-based model (G. M. Clark, 1979), experience-based model (Larson, 1981), career development model (Egelston-Dodd & DeCaro, 1982), and life-centered, competency-based model (Brolin, 1978). The reader is encouraged to review the models, curriculum, and in-service techniques discussed in these publications and other sources. Second, a substantial body of transition/career education literature has become available in the form of journals, textbooks, monographs, curriculum guides, and teacher and student materials. Third, over 20 states have transition/career education legislation, and most have transition/career education coordinators and resource centers. The transition/career education approach was endorsed by the Council of Chief State School Officers and many other influential groups (Hoyt, 1982).

In the decade of the 1990s, grass-roots support for transition/career education continued. Wickwire noted that there were many transition/career education-related programs and services in many schools, local and intermediate school districts, state departments of education, public and private community and state agencies, and by platforms and programs in professional and community associations such as the American Association for Career Education, National Career Education Leaders' Communication Network, National Association for Industry-Education Cooperation, California Career Education Association, Ohio Career Education Association, and Women's American ORT (1993, p. 20).

Transition/career education also continues to be a recognized need and viable approach for students with special learning and/or behavior needs. The DCD of the CEC, renamed the Division on Career Development and Transition (DCDT) in 1993, conducts biannual international conferences that include many presentations on the topic, and the DCDT's journal, *Career Development for Exceptional Individuals,* contains many articles reporting on transition/career education programs across the country. And, as noted earlier, much of what is being advocated today—namely, transition education, functional/life skills education, outcome-based education, and the like—closely approximate the basic tenets of transition/career education.

Why Embrace the Transition/ Career Education Approach?

There are many reasons why educators should seriously consider infusing the transition/career education concept and curriculum approach into their classrooms and school district programs. Some of these were noted earlier in this chapter (e.g., Hoyt's seven major goals. The following are some of the major benefits of a transition/career education approach, such as the one described later in this chapter, for enhancing the future adult adjustment of students with special learning and/or behavior needs and problems:

- It emphasizes teaching students all the important skills they will need in order to function as a productive family and community member and as a participant in meaningful leisure and recreational pursuits, and to secure entry-level employment on a job that is satisfying to the person.
- It addresses each individual's total lifestyle and the quality of life that every individual is entitled to achieve.
- It provides a mechanism by which all students can be educated together so that more normal relationships can be experienced and where all ability levels can learn to appreciate each other.
- It requires all teachers and other personnel to have a functional life skills focus and to learn more about the world of work, paid and unpaid.
- It opens the doors of the school to a wide variety of community representatives—employers, agencies, volunteers, and others.
- It encourages greater communication between school personnel and families and a more active partnership in teaching their children the skills they will need to become productive students, citizens, family members, and employees.
- It offers students a more interesting, motivating, and understandable purpose for their education because it directly relates the teaching-learning process to the real world and its requirements.
- It builds a greater sense of self-determination in the students by promoting each individual student's self-esteem and self-confidence.
- It enhances the learning of greater basic academic skills by infusing transition/career education concepts into various general education subjects.
- It provides an overall framework for the total curriculum by virtue of its developmental, sequenced, and competency-based approach.

An additional benefit for special educators to consider is that transition/career education is not specifically only a special education program; rather, it is an educational approach that many regular educators are implementing for general education students as well. Thus, transition/career education is not just for students with special learning and/or behavior needs, it is for all students.

Sabornie and deBettencourt (1997) have noted:

> Career education has an outcome-oriented focus that fits well into the mandate of P.L. 101-476, and it also mirrors the de-emphasis on regular academics tracks in which the large majority of adolescents with mild disabilities have failed over the years. We recommend its use in secondary and postsecondary programs as much as possible. (p.322)

It has commonly been reported that school districts that have developed and implemented transition/career education programs also have improved the transition from school to postsecondary education, to working and living in the community for many students at-risk in their schools as well as their quality of life.

The preceding is not a complete list of the benefits that result from instituting a transition/career education curriculum. More benefits, such as the requirement for substantial community involvement and a family involvement component, will become apparent throughout this book.

TRANSITION EDUCATION

During the late 1980s, the Assistant Secretary of the U.S. Office of Special Education and Rehabilitative Services (OSERS), Madeline Will, presented a keynote address, "Let Us Pause and Reflect—But Not Too Long," at the annual convention of the CEC. During her presentation, she recounted a speech she had heard from a state special education director, who proclaimed the need for a greater collaborative effort between special education, vocational education, and vocational rehabilitation. He highlighted in his speech a need for a greater focus on teaching students

more substantial independent living skills, social and interpersonal skills, and vocational skills. He felt this was absolutely necessary if they were to have a chance to become productive adults.

"Let us pause and reflect — but not too long!"
Madeline Will (1984a)

Will thought the special education director's speech was right on target with what needed to be done for the benefit of the students. The only problem was that the speech was given in 1969, and the needs he was talking about had still not been met in the 1984, the year of Will's speech. Currently, many schools still have not instituted a curriculum approach that will prepare students who have special learning and/or behavior needs to become productive, successful adults.

Will is given credit for introducing the transition movement. As noted previously, special education legislation in 1986, 1990, and 1997 established transition as an important component of the educational process for students with special learning and/or behavior needs. Much of what proponents of the "transition concept" advocate is not new. Rather, it is quite similar to much of what has been done by many special educators for years in work-study programs, life skills curriculums, vocational education, and the career education movement in the 1970s and thereafter.

Indeed, as Halpern (1992) noted in his article entitled "Transition: Old Wine in New Bottles," we have been trying to design programs to prepare young people with disabilities for adult adjustment for over 30 years. We developed cooperative/work study programs in the 1960s, career education in the 1970s, and transition in the 1980s and 1990s. Halpern noted that "in the area of curriculum and instruction, we are still frequently deficient in what we teach, how we teach, and where we teach. Curriculum content still tends to focus too much on remedial academics and not enough on functional skills" (p. 206).

Halpern's conceptualization of transition programming best illustrated the expanded components of OSERS first transition model (see Figure 2.4).

According to Halpern

transition programming is based on the outcome of students achieving successful adult community living and working (adjustment). Within this major domain reside three areas of residential environment, employment and social and interpersonal networks that are required in school programming to ensure a greater likelihood that students will successfully adjust in the community. (1985)

The Individuals with Disabilities Education Act (IDEA) of 1997 states that the IEP should contain statements of each public and participating agency's responsibilities or linkage before the student leaves school. A commitment by the participating agency regarding its financial commitment also should be included. The IEP must include a statement of the needed transition services by age 14 in four areas of content: instruction, community involvement, work/vocational skills, and daily living skills and functional assessment, if needed. Although originally the focus was

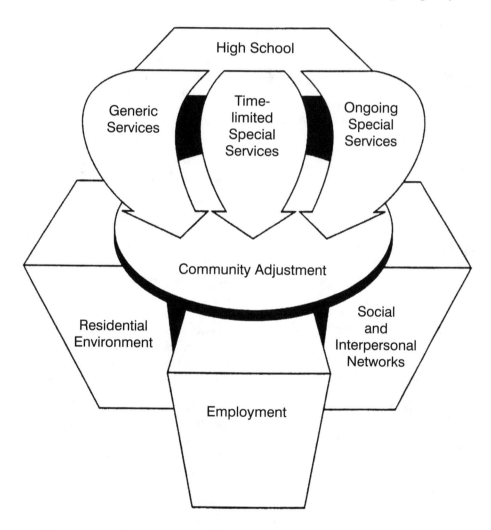

FIGURE 2.4   Halpern's transition model

Note. "Transition: A Look at the Foundations" by A.S. Halpern (1985), in *Exceptional Children*, 51(6), p. 481. Copyright 1985 by the Council for Exceptional Children. Used by permission.

on school-to-employment success, it soon changed to adult community adjustment.

"Transition planning requires a new way of looking at students and their educational programs. It demands that the IEP team create a vision of the student as an adult and plan for the adult environments the student will enter."

Arden Stephens (1992)

Transition programming is not simply developing cooperative relationships with community agencies and recommending additional services for students and their families to contact. Transition programming requires three major components to be an effective effort by the schools: (a) a functional/career development curriculum; (b) a collaborative effort with employers, agencies, and parents; and (c) a post-secondary support and follow-up/along system until successful community/job adjustment occurs.

Thus, transition programming requires active participation of many professionals working collaboratively in providing the following components: community-based instruction, support from both family members and agencies, follow-along services, and a substantial functional curriculum beginning at the elementary level. The school must do as much as possible to prepare the student for employment and community living. If further services are necessary, community agencies will provide additional training and placement assistance if they believe the school has done its part. In most respects, the transition concept is remarkably similar to the transition/career education concept—that is, a process that begins at the elementary level and continues into post-school services until the individual is successfully integrated into community life.

Readers interested in a greater knowledge base on all aspects of transition education are referred to two excellent textbooks: Rusch and Chadsey (1998), *Beyond Transition from School to Work* and G. M. Clark and Kolstoe (2000), *Transition Education & Services for Adolescents with Disabilities*. More on the transition concept is presented in Chapter 8.

Functional Life Skills Curriculum Models and Materials

Educators can draw on several functional life skills curriculum models and materials in adopting this approach. Table 2.1 lists some functional life skills curricula and guides that are but a few of those available from various publishers and other sources. In Chapter 12, "Teaching Personal-Social Skills," several social skills curricula are identified. The remainder of this section provides a brief description of three curriculum development models that are excellent models to provide functional curriculum programs. These three include: A Top-Down Model for Curriculum Development (Cronin & Patton, 1993); Taxonomy of Community Living Skills (Dever, 1988); and School-Based Career Development and Transition Model (1990).

A Top-Down Model for Curriculum Development

Cronin and Patton (1993) have conceptualized a four-stage model of curriculum development in the functional skills area. The four stages begin with: (a) an identification of the major adult domains and subdomains that students will need to learn to function in adulthood; (b) the identification of the major life demands or situations that most adults will encounter; (c) identification of specific life skills needed to meet each of the life demands; and (d) the organization of the instruction to successfully teach the functional life skills. Their model is presented in Figure 2.5. Each stage is briefly discussed next.

Stage 1: Adult Domains. The six domains of the model are employment/education; home and family; leisure pursuits; community involvement; physical/emotional health; and personal responsibility and relationships. Each of the domains is broken down further into 23 subdomains to better organize the 147 life demands. For example, the domain of employment/education consists of the subdomains of general job skills, general education/training considerations, employment setting, and transition/career refinement and re-evaluation.

TABLE 2.1   Examples of Functional Skills Curricula and Guides

Name	Publisher	Description
Adaptive Living Skills Curriculum (ALSC)	The Riverside Publishing Company	Used with the checklist of Adaptive Living Skills (ALS). 24 specific skill modules are organized into four domains: personal living skills, home living skills, community living skills, and employment skills.
The Life Skills Series I and II	PCI Educational Publishing	A fun-to-play board game format with blank draw cards, assessment booklets, and teacher's guide covering 16 areas such as eating skills, behavior skills, money skills, safety skills, survival skills, etc.
Functional Living Skills for Moderately and Severely Handicapped Individuals	Pro-Ed	Guidelines for teaching domestic skills, community mobility, social-interpersonal development, leisure skills, and functional academics.
Independent Living Skills Curriculum	University of Oregon	Covers such topics as budgeting and bill paying, nutrition and menu planning, grocery shopping, personal hygiene, cooking, and household management.
The Syracuse Community Referenced Curriculum Guide	Paul H. Brookes	Guide and manual for implementing the curriculum and teaching community living, academic, social, communication, and motor skills.
Tools for Transition	American Guidance Service	Comprehensive program including teacher's manual, a student workbook, script booklets, blackline masters, and videocassette.
Survival Skills System and Resource Guide for Transition Materials from School to Work	The Conover Company	Assessment and training programs for daily living covering such areas as vocational assessment, vocational exploration, career planning, social skills, and job-seeking skills.
Top-Down Approach for Curriculum Development	Pro-Ed	See description in text.
Taxonomy of Community Living Skills	American Association on Mental Retardation	See description in text.

Stage 2: Major Life Demands.   The 147 life demands represent the events or activities encountered in everyday life by most persons. For example, the life demands for the subdomain of general job skills are seeking and securing a job, learning job skills, main- taining one's job, and understanding fundamental and legal issues.

Stage 3: Specific Life Skills.   Each of the life demands can be broken down into specific life skills.

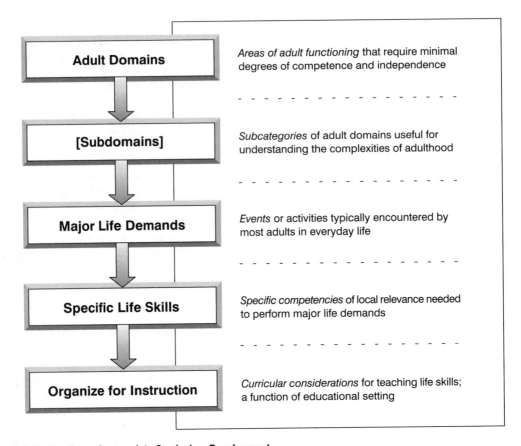

FIGURE 2.5   Top-Down Approach to Curriculum Development.
Note. From *Life Skills Instruction for All Students with Special Needs: A Practical Guide for Integrating Real-Life Content Into the Curriculum* (p. 10) by M. E. Cronin and J. R. Patton, 1993, Austin, TX: Pro-Ed. Copyright 1993 by Pro-Ed. Reprinted by permission.

For example, for seeking and securing a job, specific life skills could include identifying marketable job skills and interests, identifying sources of job possibilities, and locating the site of the prospective job on the map. The skills identified in the author's guide represent only a sample of the many possibilities that may need to be considered for various students. These skills are the ones that will become the instructional objectives in the student's IEP or individualized transition plan (ITP).

Stage 4: Organize for Instruction.   Cronin and Patton (1993) recommend a continuum of options for teaching life skills. They note that life skills instruction can be delivered as a comprehensive grouping of specific life skills courses; in select topical life skills courses; in a single generic life skills course; as a portion of exiting courses dedicated to life skills topics; and/or infused into the established content of existing courses. In essence, the options become an infusion approach, an augmentation approach, or a course work approach. Their guide provides many excellent examples of how instructional delivery can be achieved in both the classroom and in community-based settings, conducting assessment activities, selecting appropriate materials, and implementing a life skills approach.

Readers interested in learning more about this very well-conceived and organized approach are encouraged to refer to Cronin and Patton's publication entitled *Life Skills Instruction for All Students with Special Needs* (1993).

Taxonomy of Community Living Skills

Dever (1989) presents a list of all the things that people in the United States must be able to do to get through the day, the week, the month, the seasons, and the year. It lists every skill that people must perform in their daily lives, which range from obtaining a job to getting along with one's spouse to figuring out what to do when one is lost. It assumes that these are precisely the skills that people with mental retardation must acquire to take their places in the community. In other words, Dever's list is a taxonomy of the goals of instruction for persons with mental retardation, and its development constitutes the first step in the traditional concept of instruction: First, define the goals; and second, develop curricula leading to those goals. The taxonomy is most useful for those who develop curricula for persons with mental retardation (and perhaps for people with other disabilities as well).

Dever's taxonomy lists the skills in five domains: personal maintenance and development, homemaking and community life, vocational, leisure, and travel. These domains are shown in Figure 2.6, which depicts the individual in the center of the figure, with the community life domains surrounding the person. Connecting the person with the community is the travel domain.

The taxonomy is not a curriculum, but rather, a list of the end points for all curricula for persons with mental retardation. Traditionally, such curricula have included skills such as motor skills, communication skills, and academic skills. While these skills are important, they do not constitute end points for curricula, but rather, intermediate points that lie along the pathways to the ends. Therefore, these and other intermediate skills are not found in the taxonomy and must be derived by considering the goals and what a learner must do to attain them. This task must be carried out separately in each community because each community places unique performance demands on its residents. An example of the domain pertaining to homemaking and community life is illustrated in Figure 2.7.

Most of the goals listed in the taxonomy are not unique because most have been available in instructional circles for a long time. However, they have never been together in one list, and in this respect, the taxonomy is unique.

Dever's taxonomy also is unique in the fact that it includes glitches as an instructional thrust within each domain. *Glitches* are the transient problems with which everyone must deal on a daily basis. For example, we all must deal with events like breaking our shoelaces in the morning and missing our transportation to work. Experience indicates that such problems pose major obstacles for persons with mental retardation, and if they do not learn to deal with them, they will not be able to live without assistance (personal communication, R. B. Dever, February 15, 1994).

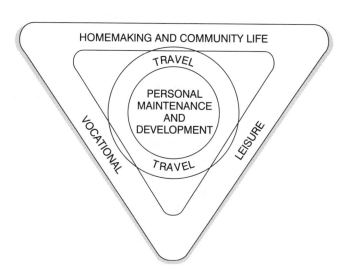

FIGURE 2.6   Organization of the Taxonomy of Instruction Goals for persons with mental retardation.
Note. From *Community Living Skills: A Taxonomy* by R. B. Dever, 1988, Washington, D. C.: American Association on Mental Retardation. Copyright 1988 by American Association on Mental Retardation. Reprinted by permission.

Domain H
Homemaking and Community Life

I. The learner will obtain living
    quarters

    A. Find appropriate living
    quarters

    B. Rent/buy living quarters

    C. Set up living quarters

II. The learner will follow community
    routines

    A. Keep living quarters neat and
    clean

    B. Keep fabrics neat and clean

    C. Maintain interior living quar-
    ters

    D. Maintain exterior of living
    quarters

    E. Respond to seasonal changes

    F. Follow home safety proce-
    dures

    G. Follow accident/emergency
    procedures

    H. Maintain foodstock

    I. Prepare and serve meals

    J. Budget money appropriately

    K. Pay bills

III. The learner will co-exist in a neigh-
    borhood and community

    A. Interact appropriately with
    community members

    B. Cope with inappropriate con-
    duct of others

    C. Observe requirements of the
    law

    D. Carry out civic duties

IV. The learner will handle "glitches"
    in the home

    A. Cope with equipment break-
    downs

    B. Cope with depletions of
    household supplies

    C. Cope with unexpected deple-
    tions of funds

    D. Cope with disruptions in rou-
    tine

    E. Cope with sudden changes in
    the weather

FIGURE 2.7   Example of a Domain From the Taxonomy of Instruction Goals for Persons with Mental Retardation.
Note. From *Community Living Skills: A Taxonomy* by R. B. Dever, 1988, Washington, D. C.: American Association on Mental Retardation. Copyright 1988 by American Association on Mental Retardation. Reprinted by permission.

Comprehensive Transition Education Model

Transition/career education is particularly important for persons with disabilities. Whether they are qualified for certain jobs or not, evidence exists that *over half of the adults with disabilities will not be employed at any point in time.* Because most people need to work, these individuals could be productively engaged in *unpaid work activities* such as volunteer and other com-

munity work, important home responsibilities, and constructive leisure and recreational activities that are of benefit to their general health and well-being. In this way, these individuals can experience and feel a sense of self-worth and dignity by contributing productively to their family, community, and themselves, even though they are unemployed. In the process, they can build further self-confidence, social, and functional skills that will enhance their chances for employment when the opportunity arises.

One career education and transition curriculum model that has focused on students with disabilities has been a school-based conceptualization developed by G. M. Clark, O. P. Kolstoe, & P. Sitlington (2000). The focus of this model, as illustrated in Figure 2.8, is on life-transition/career development beginning at the preschool level and continuing through adulthood. This model reflects an outcome-oriented set of performance domains that must be an integral part of the planning process. The current model shifts away from the perspective that the focus of student programs must address knowledge and skill outcomes, rather than knowledge and skill curriculum content. Nine domains make up this framework to address the Knowledge and Skills Outcomes: (1) communication and academic performance; (2) self-determination; (3) interpersonal relationships; (4) integrated community participation; (5) health and fitness; (6) independent/interdependent daily living; (7) leisure and recreation; (8) employment; and (9) further education and training. Each of these is discussed briefly next.

Communication and Academic Skills

The first component, communication and academic performance, represents the critical ability to understand and communicate ideas and thoughts with others. Academic skills refer to those content curriculum skills needed by students to be successful in the general education programs. Both communication and academic skills should be age- or grade-level appropriate to permit success in the current and future performance settings.

Self-Determination

The second component, self-determination, is the ability to make informed choices and to act upon those choices. Self-determination was an outgrowth of the need to prepare persons to be their own advocates as they prepare to live independently in their communities. The self-determination process evolves from understanding the performance of plans made to meet adult outcomes in the various ecological environments. These skills are teachable and are being included in the various curricula and materials discussed in Chapter 10.

Interpersonal Relationship Skills

The third component, interpersonal relationship skills, involves knowing and using prosocial skills with family members, in school, and in the community. Positive behavioral supports, those that are collaborative techniques used by all members of the student's support team, including family members and agencies, are now considered an important part of the child's educational/transitional program. Many believe that prosocial skills education is one of the most important of all of the educational components.

Integrated Community Participation Skills

The fourth component, integrated community participation skills, involves decision-making on many different levels. These decisions should, of course, involve the preferences and interests of the individual, but in some cases must involve other support personnel or advocates. Individual communities have their own set of activities specific to that area to be considered. Factors such as costs, safety, and personal choice all must be a part of the students with special learning and/or behavior needs taking part in area activities of living and working. Transition provisions now address the schools' responsibility of assessing students' preferences and interests beyond occupational or postsecondary options to also include identifying preferred community participation activities.

Health and Fitness Skills

The fifth component, health and fitness skills, is an area that is probably not being addressed as much as it should in transition planning and programming. Quality of life components include a knowledge of one's own health status and how to keep oneself healthy. This includes not only being aware of your own physical fitness and wellness but also understanding activities that are considered to be

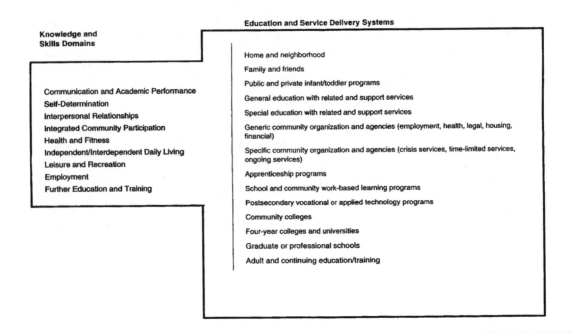

Education and Service Delivery Systems

Knowledge and
Skills Domains

Communication and Academic Performance
Self-Determination
Interpersonal Relationships
Integrated Community Participation
Health and Fitness
Independent/Interdependent Daily Living
Leisure and Recreation
Employment
Further Education and Training

Home and neighborhood

Family and friends

Public and private infant/toddler programs

General education with related and support services

Special education with related and support services

Generic community organization and agencies (employment, health, legal, housing, financial)

Specific community organization and agencies (crisis services, time-limited services, ongoing services)

Apprenticeship programs

School and community work-based learning programs

Postsecondary vocational or applied technology programs

Community colleges

Four-year colleges and universities

Graduate or professional schools

Adult and continuing education/training

Exit Points and Outcomes

Knowledge and
Skills Domains

Communication and Academic Performance
Self-Determination
Interpersonal Relationships
Integrated Community Participation
Health and Fitness
Independent/Interdependent Daily Living
Leisure and Recreation
Employment
Further Education and Training

Developmental /Life Phases	Exit Points
Infant/toddler and home training	Exit to preschool programs and integrated community participation
Preschool and home training	Exit to elementary school programs and integrated community participation
Elementary school	Exit to middle school/junior high school programs, age-appropriate self-determination, and integrated community participation
Middle school/junior high school	Exit to high school programs, entry-level employment, age-appropriate self-determination, and integrated community participation
High school	Exit to postsecondary education or entry-level employment, adult and continuing education, full-time homemaker, self-determined quality of life, and integrated community participation
Postsecondary education	Exit to specialized, technical, professional, or managerial employment, graduate or professional school programs, adult and continuing education, full-time homemaker, self-determined quality of life, and integrated community participation

FIGURE 2.8   A School-Based Career Development and Transition Education Model for Adolescents with Disabilities.
Note. From *Transition Education and Services for Adolescents with Disabilities*, Third Edition by P. Sitlington, G. M. Clark, & O. P. Kolstoe, Boston: Allyn & Bacon. Copyright © 2000 by Pearson Education. Reprinted by permission of the publisher.

preventative and understanding good nutrition. Schools who do not have good health education programs can still address this critical component by implementing one of the identified functional curriculum programs in this text.

Independent/Interdependent Daily Living Skills

The sixth component, independent/interdependent daily living skills, is the most common area addressed in the transition education of students with special learning and/or behavior needs. Many students with mild and moderate disabilities are provided training in the basic daily living skills that are necessary for current school and community functioning. Many young adults also leave secondary education with the basic daily living skills necessary to function as an adult in community living and working. Most special education teachers identify daily living skills as an area most often addressed in their special education programs. Although current functioning training in daily living skills are addressed, transition programming also must include training in skills of how to secure necessary support and skills needed for living and working as an adult in their communities.

Employment Skills

The seventh component, employment skills, needs to be addressed in the transitional planning whether or not occupational preparation involves postsecondary education or vocational training during secondary education. These skills address the general employability skills (following directions, producing quality work, working at an acceptable rate, and accepting and assimilating constructive criticism), occupational skills (seeking and maintaining a job, math, reading and communication skills, and adjustment to work changes), and vocational skills of a specific career cluster/occupational position.

Leisure and Recreational Skills

The eighth component, leisure and recreational skills, addresses an area of quality of life instruction

not always included in transition programming. Most individuals would include their avocational interests and hobbies as a critical component of their quality of life. Students need to know about their personal interests and how to participate in these activities. Even though it seems that participating in leisure activities is an instinctual behavior, many individuals with special learning and/or behavior needs require assistance in learning how to participate in leisure and recreational skills in current and future ecological environments.

Post-Secondary Education/Training Skills

The final component, further education and training skills, is the training that prepares individuals for the need for lifelong learning and/or job training. This area addresses the need to prepare persons leaving school with the knowledge that almost all employee and community living activities involve the need for additional education and training. Technology and societal changes move at a level that requires everyone involved in community living and working to keep up with the transitions.

The efficacy of the Comprehensive Transition Education Model lies in the fact these nine transitional areas need to be programmed to correspond to the natural exit points and to meet the outcomes in each of these specific knowledge and skill domains. Interested readers can secure detailed information on this approach by obtaining the following publications: G. M. Clark (1979), *Career Education for the Handicapped Child in the Elementary Classroom* (Love Publishing, Denver) or Sitlington, Clark, and Kolstoe (2000), *Transition Education and Services for Adolescents with Disabilities* (Allyn & Bacon).

The preceding approaches for functional curriculum implementation have many common components and relate very closely to the transition/career education approach, which was introduced in the 1970s, and the Life-Centered Career Education (LCCE) Curriculum Model for individuals with mild and moderate disabilities, presented in Chapter 3. The transition/career education approach, the framework from which the LCCE Mild/Moderate Curriculum Model was constructed upon, is presented next.

CHAPTER COMMENTARY

Students with special learning and/or behavior needs should receive an appropriate blend of academic and functional life skills content if they are to be prepared for a successful adult outcome. The transition/career education approach presents a viable method for meeting the functional skills and transition needs of students with special learning and/or behavior needs while helping to increase student motivation to learn the academic and enrichment subjects as well. The approach has evolved over almost 30 years and is important for all students to receive as a part of their total educational program. For students with special learning and/or behavior needs, it lends itself very well to the current focus on inclusive education. A functional skills/career education approach holds the promise of generating much acceptance and adoption by regular class teachers because they realize that it is an excellent mechanism for stimulating all students to learn practical information and skills.

It is not easy for anyone to successfully compete in today's modern and complex society. Almost everyone is worried about finding a good job, making enough money, living on their own, having meaningful friendships, being able to engage in leisure and recreational pursuits of interest, and other areas of life that affect a satisfying lifestyle. To achieve success in life, one must be a competent person—to have the skills to compete and assimilate into the fiber of the community. We must give all students such an opportunity. To do this, schools must offer a curriculum that meets the contemporary needs of its community in regard to productive paid and unpaid work, living, and leisure pursuits.

With the transition/career education approach, the emphasis is on the word *career*. Education focuses on what the student needs to learn to have a productive career as a family member, contributing citizen, employee, and as a participant in meaningful avocational activities such as hobbies, recreational endeavors, and other leisure-time activities. This is a "whole-person approach" to education.

In Chapter 3, a specific transition/career education curriculum is presented and described. Although this curriculum was developed initially for students with special education needs, it was built on the general transition/career education principles that have been developed for all students. Thus, its tenets and application are relevant for all students.

ACTIVITIES

1. In this chapter, four related curriculum approaches were presented. What is the possible contribution of each in helping you to conceptualize a functional curriculum effort that could result in preparing your students with special learning and/ or behavior needs for a more successful adult adjustment?

2. Identify all of the major skills or competencies you believe your students with special learning and/or behavior needs should be taught in a K–12 curricular effort so that by the time they leave the educational setting, they will be well equipped to secure satisfying employment and function independently and interpersonally in their home and community activities.

CHAPTER 3

Life-Centered Career Education (LCCE) Mild/ Moderate Curriculum Programs

PRELIMINARY QUESTIONS

1. What important components or conditions are needed for an effective transition curriculum model?

2. Under what learning conditions can most students, especially those with special learning and/or behavior needs, be most effectively taught?

3. Besides the basic academic subjects, what transition curriculum areas or domains should be included in a school's curriculum?

4. What are the three major instructional settings where students with special learning and/or behavior needs can be taught?

5. How long do most implemented educational innovations generally last?

6. What is meant by the term *work personality*, and when should educators give attention to its development in their students with special learning and/or behavior needs?

7. What are the four stages of development or learning that need to be addressed in organizing and delivering instruction in a career education/transition program?

8. What are the Life-Centered Career Education (LCCE) Mild/Moderate Curriculum approach for students with mild and moderate learning and/or behavior needs, respectively?

9. What is the correlation between the LCCE Mild/Moderate Curriculum and state standards?

10. What daily living skills are important for students with special learning and/or behavior needs to learn in their educational program?

11. What daily living skills are important for students with moderate learning and/or behavior needs?

12. What personal-social skills are critical for students with special learning and behavior needs to learn?

13. What personal-social skills are critical for students with moderate learning and/or behavior needs?

14. What occupational knowledge and skills should students with special learning and/or behavior needs learn before leaving the school program?

15. What occupational knowledge and skills should students with moderate learning and/or behavior needs have?

16. What transitional assessment and instruction materials are available for implementing the LCCE Mild/Moderate Curriculum approach?

OVERVIEW

Chapter 2 presented a strong case for infusing a substantial functional skills/career development component into the general education curriculum (K–12+) to better ensure that students with special learning and/or behavior needs make a successful transition from school to employment and to community living. But we can't just theorize about the need, we must have an organized, systematic framework on which such a curriculum thrust can be instituted. Such a framework, or educational system, must be flexible so that various methods and materials can be integrated into its design to meet the needs of a diverse group of students with special learning and/or behavior needs.

This chapter presents and explains the *Life-Centered Career Education (LCCE) Curriculum Programs (mild and moderate)*. The vast majority of educational innovations last only 3 to 5 years; the LCCE Mild/Moderate Curriculum Programs have evolved and expanded over a 25-year period. In fact, the LCCE Mild/Moderate Curriculum is more widely used throughout the country today than ever. LCCE is one curriculum that embraces current, progressive educational thinking, looking beyond the long-term tradition of the Carnegie Units and the narrow core curriculum concepts that have prevailed for decades.

In the following sections, the LCCE Mild/Moderate Curriculum model and its major program components, its curriculum and training materials, and its rationale for adoption are presented.

CHAPTER OUTLOOK

Richard McMullin is a former Superintendent in the North St. Francois County R-I School District, Bonne Terre-Desloge, Missouri.

Edward Garrigan is the Assistant Superintendent in the North St. Francois County R-I School District, Bonne Terre-Desloge, Missouri, and supervises the district's special education programs.

Public education continues to be thrust into the spotlight and scrutinized with regard to remediation and accountability. Often, as educators, we look beyond the immediate and grasp for new and well-intended solutions to redeem the perception of quality. Our mission, however, is to educate our youth with those qualities that lead to a successful, productive citizenry. Such concepts as applied education, academic integration, technical preparation, career awareness, and others give us some insight into the matrix of purposeful, functional skills. Therefore, any curricular attempt to focus on functional academics, coupled with enhancing the opportunity for students with special learning and/or behavior needs to enter adulthood with certain basic competencies, becomes a candidate for the illuminating spotlight.

A survey conducted on a local level disclosed that 80% of students with special learning and/or behavior needs with disabilities are unemployed 2 years after leaving high school. The potential for correcting this grim situation is certainly within our grasp. A partial solution resides in providing our children with a curriculum that will introduce them to a systematic program that focuses on the realities and responsibilities they will encounter during their transition from school into the working world. It is common knowledge among special educators that our graduates with disabilities tend to fail on the job primarily because they lack the skills related to job performance.

Exclusively addressing this single dimension will not, however, address the student's total needs. The nature of the problem is much broader and encompasses such areas as daily living skills, personal-social skills, as well as occupational guidance and preparation. If we are to truly provide our students with special learning and/or behavior needs an opportunity to gain meaningful employment and to attain meaningful levels of economic, social, and personal fulfillment, schools must incorporate career education programs. Such programs must involve the child's family, the school, and the community. For the program to be most effective, it must begin in elementary school and continue through middle and high school. Such programs must have the total support of the staff, administration, and local board of education. Without this commitment, any career education effort will be fragmented, and results will fall short of the school's expectations.

The LCCE program has far surpassed our expectations. We have incorporated it successfully into our total curricular program and find that it has important applications for all students with special learning and/or behavior needs. Through the joint efforts of our professional staff, administration, board of education, families, and community, our students with special learning and/or behavior needs are experiencing higher levels of independence and enjoying life to its fullest.

THE LCCE MILD/MODERATE CURRICULUM MODEL

Unlike the traditional educational approach in which students with special learning and/or behavior needs are taught knowledge for knowledge's sake through the academic content and enrichment subjects of reading, spelling, mathematics, history, art, chemistry, economics, and others, the LCCE Mild/Moderate Curriculum approaches focus on *the skills that the individual must know to become a more effective person.* In other words, the skills needed to *function* as a productive worker, family member, and citizen in their home and community. LCCE is a direct result of the career education movement and models of the 1970s. Considerable research and demonstration efforts in numerous school districts have contributed to its development and refinement over more than 25 years, resulting in a widely adopted and implemented curricular effort that mirrors the recognized need for an outcome-based, functional skills emphasis for students with special learning and/or behavior needs in American schools as well as abroad.

For years, it has been demonstrated that a large proportion of students, including those with special learning and/or behavior needs, learn best if the material presented is practical, familiar, hands-on, and meaningfully related to the real world. Esoteric, theoretical, and impractical instruction has proven not to be as effective with students with special learning and/or behavior needs. Most students with special learning and/or behavior needs who are given an appropriate blend of functional skills infused into general academic content instruction will be more motivated to learn the academic and functional skills they need for living and working in their communities. At least, this is the LCCE philosophy.

The LCCE model incorporates the basic tenets of the transition/career education approach, which were described in Chapter 2. In summary, these tenets are the broader view of the term *career,* the four stages of career development, the substantial involvement of the students with special learning and/or behavior needs' families and community resources, and major life skill competencies that are deemed critical for stu-

dents with special learning and/or behavior needs to learn by the time they leave school to succeed as adults. The LCCE Mild/Moderate Curriculum transition model is presented in Figure 3.1.

LCCE is a functional skills/transition curriculum built on the concepts of career development. Figure 3.1 illustrates how the LCCE competencies and the four stages of career development can be integrated into the scope and sequence of an academically based curriculum. The functional transitional model promotes the concept of infusion—that is, teaching the competencies in general education content classes, wherever possible. As Figure 3.1 shows, the emphasis on the LCCE functional skills (the gray area) should increase at the higher grade levels, although many career awareness and exploration activities (guest speakers, integrated career units, field trips, and other media presentation) should be taught at the elementary and middle school levels. The lower half of the graphic illustrates when parents, employers, and agencies should be involved with educators throughout the curriculum effort. Collaboration among all these groups is a key element of the LCCE approach.

The functional skills LCCE Mild/Moderate Curriculum approaches recognize the importance of general academic skills as the basic foundation for students' education. It also recognizes, as noted previously, the importance of infusing functional skills instruction in the areas of daily living, personal-social skills, and occupational guidance and preparation into the overall curriculum, K–12+, and into most academic content areas, to enhance the students with special learning and/or behavior needs' learning in all four areas. Figure 3.2 presents the three functional skills curriculum areas, 22 competencies, and the 97 subcompetencies comprising the LCCE Mild Curriculum for with special learning and/or behavior needs. Figure 3.3 presents the same three functional skill areas, but with 20 competencies and 75 subcompetencies comprising the LCCE Moderate Curriculum for students with moderate learning and/or behavior needs.

Figure 3.4 correlates the LCCE Mild Curriculum and the LCCE Moderate (LCCE-M) Curriculum competencies and subcompetencies.

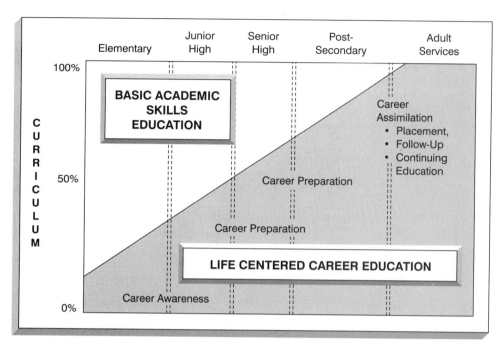

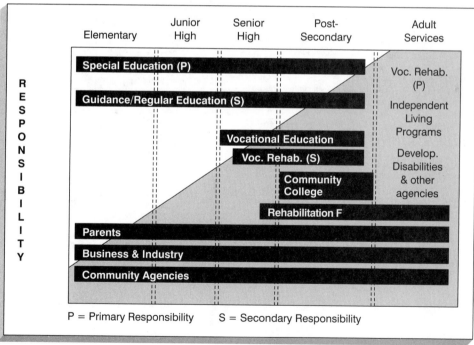

FIGURE 3.1   Curriculum/LCCE Transition Model.
Note. From *Life Centered Career Education: Professional Development Activity Book* (p. 43) by The Council for Exceptional Children, 1993.
Arlington, VA: The Council for Exceptional Children. Copyright 1993 by The Council for Exceptional Children. Reprinted by permission.

Curriculum Area	Competency	Subcompetency: The student will be able to:	
DAILY LIVING SKILLS	1. Managing Personal Finances	1. Count money & make correct change	2. Make responsible expenditures
	2. Selecting & Managing a Household	7. Maintain home exterior/interior	8. Use basic appliances and tools
	3. Caring for Personal Needs	12. Demonstrate knowledge of physical fitness, nutrition & weight	13. Exhibit proper grooming & hygiene
	4. Raising Children & Meeting Marriage Responsibilities	17. Demonstrate physical care for raising children	18. Know psychological aspects of raising children
	5. Buying, Preparing & Consuming Food	20. Purchase food	21. Clean food preparation areas
	6. Buying & Caring for Clothing	26. Wash/clean clothing	27. Purchase clothing
	7. Exhibiting Responsible Citizenship	29. Demonstrate knowledge of civil rights & responsibilities	30. Know nature of local, state & federal governments
	8. Utilizing Recreational Facilities & Engaging in Leisure	33. Demonstrate knowledge of available community resources	34. Choose & plan activities
	9. Getting Around the Community	38. Demonstrate knowledge of traffic rules & safety	39. Demonstrate knowledge & use of various means of transportation
PERSONAL-SOCIAL SKILLS	10. Achieving Self-Awareness	42. Identify physical & psychological needs	43. Identify interests & abilities
	11. Acquiring Self-Confidence	46. Express feelings of self-worth	47. Describe others' perception of self
	12. Achieving Socially Responsible Behavior— Community	51. Develop respect for the rights & properties of others	52. Recognize authority & follow instructions
	13. Maintaining Good Interpersonal Skills	56. Demonstrate listening & responding skills	57. Establish & maintain close relationships
	14. Achieving Independence	59. Strive toward self-actualization	60. Demonstrate self-organization
	15. Making Adequate Decisions	62. Locate & utilize sources of assistance	63. Anticipate consequences
	16. Communicating with Others	67. Recognize & respond to emergency situations	68. Communicate with understanding
OCCUPATIONAL GUIDANCE AND PREPARATION	17. Knowing & Exploring Occupational Possibilities	70. Identify remunerative aspects of work	71. Locate sources of occupational & training information
	18. Selecting & Planning Occupational Choices	76. Make realistic occupational choices	77. Identify requirements of appropriate & available jobs
	19. Exhibiting Appropriate Work Habits & Behaviors	81. Follow directions & observe regulations	82. Recognize importance of attendance & punctuality
	20. Seeking, Securing & Maintaining Employment	88. Search for a job	89. Apply for a job
	21. Exhibiting Sufficient Physical-Manual Skills	94. Demonstrate stamina & endurance	95. Demonstrate satisfactory balance & coordination
	22. Obtaining Specific Occupational Skills		

FIGURE 3.2   Life-Centered Career Education Competencies—Mild

Note. From *Life Centered Career Education: A Competency-Based Approach* (4th ed., pp. 12–13) by D. E. Brolin, 1993. Arlington, VA: The Council for Exceptional Children. Copyright 1993 by The Council for Exceptional Children. Reprinted by permission.

64

3. Keep basic financial records	4. Calculate & pay taxes	5. Use credit responsibly	6. Use banking services	
9. Select adequate housing	10. Set up household	11. Maintain home grounds		
14. Dress appropriately	15. Demonstrate knowledge of common illness, prevention & treatment	16. Practice personal safety		
19. Demonstrate marriage responsibilities				
22. Store food	23. Prepare meals	24. Demonstrate appropriate eating habits	25. Plan/eat balanced meals	
28. Iron, mend & store clothing				
31. Demonstrate knowledge of the law & ability to follow the law	32. Demonstrate knowledge of citizen rights & responsibilities			
35. Demonstrate knowledge of the value of recreation	36. Engage in group & individual activities	37. Plan vacation time		
40. Find way around the community	41. Drive a car			
44. Identify emotions	45. Demonstrate knowledge of physical self			
48. Accept and give praise	49. Accept & give criticism	50. Develop confidence in oneself		
53. Demonstrate appropriate behavior in public places	54. Know important character traits	55. Recognize personal roles		
58. Make & maintain friendships				
61. Demonstrate awareness of how one's behavior affects others				
64. Develop & evaluate alternatives	65. Recognize nature of a problem	66. Develop goal-seeking behavior		
69. Know subtleties of communication				
72. Identify personal values met through work	73. Identify societal values met through work	74. Classify jobs into occupational categories	75. Investigate local occupational & training opportunities	
78. Identify occupational aptitudes	79. Identify major occupational interests	80. Identify major occupaitonal needs		
83. Recognize importance of supervision	84. Demonstrate knowledge of occupational safety	85. Work with others	86. Meet demands for quality work	87. Work at a satisfactory rate
90. Interview for a job	91. Know know to maintain post-school occupational adjustment	92. Demonstrate knowledge of competitive standards	93. Know how to adjust to changes in employment	
96. Demonstrate manual dexterity	97. Demonstrate sensory discrimination			
There are no specific subcompetencies as they depend on skill being taught				

FIGURE 3.2   Continued

Curriculum Area	Competency	Subcompetency: The student will be able to:	
DAILY LIVING SKILLS	1. Managing Money	1. Count money	2. Make purchases
	2. Selecting & Maintaining Living Environments	6. Select appropriate community living environment	7. Maintain living environment
	3. Caring for Personal Health	10. Perform appropriate grooming and hygiene	11. Dress appropriately
	4. Developing and Maintaining Appropriate Intimate Relationships	16. Demonstrate knowledge of basic human sexuality	17. Demonstrate knowledge of appropriate dating behavior
	5. Eating at Home and in the Community	18. Plan balanced meals	19. Purchase food
	6. Cleaning and Purchasing Clothing	24. Wash/dry clothes	25. Buy clothes
	7. Participate in Leisure/Recreational Activities	26. Identify available community leisure/recreational activities	27. Select and plan leisure/recreational activities
	8. Getting Around in the Community	30. Follow traffic rules and safety procedures	31. Develop and follow community access routes
PERSONAL-SOCIAL SKILLS	9. Acquiring Self-Identity	33. Demonstrate knowledge of personal interests and abilities	34. Demonstrate appropriate responses to emotions
	10. Exhibiting Socially Responsible Behavior	37. Demonstrate appropriate behavior	38. Identify current and future personal roles
	11. Developing and Maintaining Appropriate Social Relationships	44. Develop friendships	45. Maintain friendships
	12. Exhibiting Independent Behavior	46. Set and reach personal goals	47. Demonstrate self-organization
	13. Making Informed Decisions	49. Identify problems/conflicts	50. Use appropriate resources to assist in problem-solving
	14. Communicating with Others	53. Demonstrate listening and responding skills	54. Demonstrate effective communication
OCCUPATIONAL GUIDANCE AND PREPARATION	15. Exploring and Locating Occupational Training and Job Placement Opportunities	56. Identify rewards of working	57. Locate occupational training and job placement possibilities
	16. Making Occupational and Job Placement Choices	58. Demonstrate knowledge of occupational interests	59. Demonstrate knowledge of occupational strengths and weaknesses
	17. Applying for and Maintaining Occupational Training and Job Placements	63. Apply for occupational training and job placements	64. Interview for occupational training and job placements
	18. Developing and Maintaining Appropriate Work Skills and Behavior	66. Perform work directions and requirements	67. Maintain good attendance and punctuality
	19. Matching Physical-Manual Skills to Occupational Training and Employment	72. Demonstrate fine motor dexterity in occupational training & job placements	73. Demonstrate gross motor dexterity in occupational training & job placements
	20. Training and Occupational Choices		

FIGURE 3.3   Life Centered Career Education—Moderate Curriculum (LCCE-M)

Note. From *Life Centered Career Education: Modified Curriculum for Individuals with Moderate Disabilities* (pp. 10–11) by R. J. Loyd and D. E. Brolin, 1997. Arlington, VA: The Council for Exceptional Children. Copyright 1997 by The Council for Exceptional Children. Reprinted by permission.

3. Keep basic financial records	4. Calculate & pay taxes	5. Use credit responsibly	6. Use banking services	
9. Select adequate housing	10. Set up household	11. Maintain home grounds		
14. Dress appropriately	15. Demonstrate knowledge of common illness prevention & treatment	16. Practice personal safety		
19. Demonstrate marriage responsibilities				
22. Store food	23. Prepare meals	24. Demonstrate appropriate eating habits	25. Plan/eat balanced meals	
28. Iron, mend & store clothing				
31. Demonstrate knowledge of the law & ability to follow the law	32. Demonstrate knowledge of citizen rights & responsibilities			
35. Demonstrate knowledge of the value of recreation	36. Engage in group & individual activities	37. Plan vacation time		
40. Find way around the community	41. Drive a car			
44. Identify emotions	45. Demonstrate knowledge of physical self			
48. Accept and give praise	49. Accept & give criticism	50. Develop confidence in oneself		
53. Demonstrate appropriate behavior in public places	54. Know important character traits	55. Recognize personal roles		
58. Make & maintain friendships				
61. Demonstrate awareness of how one's behavior affects others				
64. Develop & evaluate alternatives	65. Recognize nature of a problem	66. Develop goal-seeking behavior		
69. Know subtleties of communication				
72. Identify personal values met through work	73. Identify societal values met through work	74. Classify jobs into occupational categories	75. Investigate local occupational & training opportunities	
78. Identify occupational aptitudes	79. Identify major occupational interests	80. Identify major occupaitonal needs		
83. Recognize importance of supervision	84. Demonstrate knowledge of occupational safety	85. Work with others	86. Meet demands for quality work	87. Work at a satisfactory rate
90. Interview for a job	91. Know know to maintain post-school occupational adjustment	92. Demonstrate knowledge of competitive standards	93. Know how to adjust to changes in employment	
96. Demonstrate manual dexterity	97. Demonstrate sensory discrimination			
There are no specific subcompetencies as they depend on skill being taught				

FIGURE 3.3 Continued

**Correlation of Original Life Centered Career Education Curriculum
with the Modified Curriculum (LCCE-M) Competencies**

LCCE-Original   LCCE-Modified

Daily Living Skills

LCCE-Original	LCCE-Modified

1. Managing Personal Finances
   1. Count money and make correct change
   2. Make responsible expenditures
   3. Keep basic financial records
   4. Calculate and pay taxes
   5. Use credit responsibly
   6. Use banking services
	1. Managing Money
	   1. Count money
	   2. Make purchase
	   4. Budget money
	
	   5. Perform banking skills

2. Selecting and Managing a Household
   7. Maintain home exterior/interior
   8. Use basic appliances and tools
   9. Select adequate housing
  10. Set up a household
  11. Maintain home grounds
	2. Selecting and Maintaining Living Environments
	   7. Maintain living environment
	   8. Use basic appliances and tools
	   6. Select appropriate community living environment
	   9. Set up personal living space

3. Caring for Personal Needs
  12. Demonstrate knowledge of physical fitness, nutrition, and weight
  13. Exhibit proper grooming and hygiene
  14. Dress appropriately
  15. Demonstrate knowledge of common illness prevention and treatment
  16. Practice personal safety
	3. Caring for Personal Health
	  12. Maintain physical fitness
	
	  10. Perform appropriate grooming and hygiene
	  11. Dress appropriately
	  13. Recognize and seek help for illness
	
	  15. Practice personal safety

4. Raising Children and Meeting Marriage Responsibilities
  17. Demonstrate physical care for raising children
  18. Know psychological aspects of raising children
  19. Demonstrate marriage responsibilities
	4. Developing and Maintaining Appropriate Intimate Relationships
	
	  16. Demonstrate knowledge of basic human sexuality

5. Buying, Preparing, and Consuming Food
  20. Purchase food
  21. Clean food preparation areas
  22. Store food
  23. Prepare meals
  24. Demonstrate appropriate eating habits
  25. Plan/eat balanced meals
	5. Eating at Home and in the Community
	  19. Purchase food
	  22. Demonstrate meal clean-up and food storage
	  22. (See above)
	  20. Prepare meals
	  21. Demonstrate appropriate eating habits
	  18. Plan balanced meals

6. Buying and Caring for Clothing
  26. Wash/clean clothing
  27. Purchase clothing
  28. Iron, mend, and store clothing
	6. Cleaning and Purchasing Clothing
	  24. Wash/dry clothes
	  25. Buy clothes

7. Exhibiting Responsible Citizenship
  29. Demonstrate knowledge of civil rights and responsibilities
  30. Know nature of local, state, and federal governments
  31. Demonstrate knowledge of the law and ability to follow the law
  32. Demonstrate knowledge of citizen rights and responsibilities
	42. Demonstrate appropriate citizen rights and responsibilities

FIGURE 3.4   Correlation of Original Life Centered Career Education Curriculum with the Moderate Curriculum (LCCE-M) Competencies

Note. From Life Centered Career Education: Modified Curriculum for Individuals with Moderate Disabilities (pp. 5–7) by R. J. Loyd and D. E. Brolin, 1997. Arlington, VA: The Council for Exceptional Children. Copyright 1997 by The Council for Exceptional Children. Reprinted by permission.

8. Utilizing Recreational Facilities and Engaging in Leisure
   33. Demonstrate knowledge of available community leisure/recreational activities
   34. Choose and plan activities
   35. Demonstrate knowledge of the value of recreation.
   36. Engage in group and individual activities

   37. Plan vacation time

9. Getting Around the Community
   38. Demonstrate knowledge of traffic and safety
   39. Demonstrate knowledge and use of various means of transportation
   40. Find way around the community
   41. Drive a car

7. Participate in Leisure/Recreational Activities
   26. Identify available community leisure/recreational resources
   27. Select and plan leisure/recreational activities

   28. Participate in individual and group leisure/recreational activities
   29. Select and participate in group travel

8. Getting Around in the Community
   30. Follow traffic rules and safety procedures
   32. Access available transportation

   31. Develop and follow community access routes

Personal-Social Skills

10. Achieving Self-Awareness
   42. Identify physical and psychological needs
   43. Identify interests and abilities

   44. Identify emotions
   45. Demonstrate knowledge of physical self

11. Acquiring Self-Confidence
   46. Express feelings of self-worth
   47. Describe others' perception of self
   48. Accept and give praise
   49. Accept and give criticism
   50. Develop confidence in oneself

12. Achieving Socially Responsible Behavior
   51. Develop respect for the rights and property of others
   52. Recognize authority and follow instructions
   53. Demonstrate appropriate behavior in public places
   54. Know important character traits
   55. Recognize personal roles

13. Maintaining Good Interpersonal Skills

   56. Demonstrate listening and responding skills
   57. Establish and maintain close relationships
   58. Make and maintain friendships

14. Achieving Independence
   59. Strive toward self-actualization
   60. Demonstrate self-organization
   61. Demonstrate awareness of how one's behavior affects others

15. Making Adequate Decisions
   62. Locate and utilize sources of assistance
   63. Anticipate consequences
   64. Develop and evaluate alternatives
   65. Recognize nature of problems
   66. Develop goal-seeking behavior

9. Acquiring Self-Identity

   33. Demonstrate knowledge of personal interests and abilities
   34. Demonstrate appropriate responses to emotions

   35. Display self-confidence and self-worth

   36. Demonstrate giving and accepting praise and criticism
   35. (See above)

10. Exhibiting Socially Responsible Behavior
   39. Demonstrate respect for others' rights and property
   40. Demonstrate respect for authority
   37. Demonstrate appropriate behavior

   38. Identify current and future personal roles

11. Developing and Maintaining Appropriate Social Relationships
   53. Demonstrate listening and responding skills

   44. Develop friendships; 45. Maintain friendships

12. Exhibiting Independent Behavior

   47. Demonstrate self-organization

13. Making Informed Decisions
   50. Use appropriate resources to assist in problem solving
   52. Demonstrate decision making
   51. Develop and select best solution to problems/conflicts
   49. Identify problems/conflicts
   46. Set and reach personal goals

FIGURE 3.4   Continued

16. Communicating with Others
    67. Recognize and respond to emergency situations
    68. Communicate with understanding
    69. Know subtleties of communication

14. Communicating with Others
    55. Communicate in emergency situations
    54. Demonstrate effective communication

Occupational Guidance and Preparation

17. Knowing and Exploring Occupational Possibilities
    70. Identify remunerative aspects of work
    71. Locate sources of occupational and training information
    72. Identify personal values met through work
    73. Identify societal values met through work
    74. Classify jobs into occupational categories
    75. Investigate local occupational and training opportunities

15. Exploring and Locating Occupational Training and Job Placement Opportunities
    56. Identify rewards of working
    57. Locate available occupational training and job placement possibilities
    56. (See above)
    56. (See above)

18. Selecting and Planning Occupational Choices
    76. Make realistic occupational choices

    77. Identify requirements of appropriate and available jobs

    78. Identify occupational aptitudes

    79. Identify major occupational interests

16. Making Occupational and Job Placement Choices
    61. Plan and make realistic occupational training and job placement decisions
    60. Identify possible and available jobs matching interests and strengths
    59. Demonstrate knowledge of occupational strengths and weaknesses
    58. Demonstrate knowledge of occupational interests

19. Exhibiting Appropriate Work Habits and Behavior
    80. Identify major occupational needs
    81. Follow directions and observe regulations
    82. Recognize importance of attendance and punctuality
    83. Recognize importance of supervision
    84. Demonstrate knowledge of occupational safety
    85. Work with others
    86. Meet demands of quality work
    87. Work at a satisfactory rate

18. Developing and Maintaining Appropriate Work Skills and Behavior
    66. Perform work directions and meet requirements
    67. Maintain good attendance and punctuality
    68. Respond appropriately to supervision
    69. Demonstrate job safety
    70. Work cooperatively with others
    71. Meet quality and quantity work standards
    71. (See above)

20. Seeking, Securing, and Maintaining Employment
    88. Search for a Job
    89. Apply for a job
    90. Interview for a job
    91. Know how to maintain postschool occupational adjustment
    92. Demonstrate knowledge of competitive standards
    93. Know how to adjust to change in employment

17. Applying for and Maintaining Occupational Training and Job Placements
    63. Apply for occupational training and job placements
    64. Interview for occupational training and job placements

    65. Make adjustments to changes in employment status

21. Exhibiting Sufficient Physical/Manual Skills
    94. Demonstrate stamina and endurance
    95. Demonstrate satisfactory balance and coordination
    96. Demonstrate manual dexterity

    97. Demonstrate sensory discrimination

19. Matching Physical/Manual Skills to Occupational Training and Employment
    75. Demonstrate stamina and endurance

    72. Demonstrate fine motor dexterity in occupational training and job placements
    74. Demonstrate sensory discrimination in occupational training and job placements

22. Obtaining Specific Occupational Skills
    There are no specific subcompetencies listed here since they depend upon the specific occupational training selected.

FIGURE 3.4   Continued

As noted previously, the LCCE Mild/Moderate Curriculum approaches consists of four major components: (1) a focus on three curriculum areas (daily living skills, personal-social skills, and occupational skills), consisting of (a) 22 major competencies and 97 subcompetencies for students with mild learning and/or behavior needs and (b) 20 major competencies and 75 subcompetencies for students who have more moderate learning and/or behavior needs; (2) instruction that is provided in three settings—school, home, and community; (3) a K–12+ scope and sequence consisting of four stages of career development or learning; and (4) a focus on teaching the student all the important work roles that constitute a career—employee, family member, citizen/volunteer, and productive user of recreational and leisure time activities such as hobbies. Each of the four components is discussed in the next section.

Component 1a: The Competencies for the LCCE Mild Curriculum Model

All 22 competencies and the 97 subcompetencies of the LCCE Mild Curriculum have been subjected to rigorous review by hundreds of school personnel who have agreed that the competencies reflect major outcomes required for successful community living and working. The LCCE Mild/Moderate Curriculum model has been described as an *adult adjustment/outcomes approach* because it focuses on skills and competencies needed for a successful career (G. M. Clark & White, 1980). The following discussion briefly describes the three curriculum areas and the 22 competencies of the LCCE Mild Curriculum Model.

Daily Living Skills

The competencies under the daily living skills category include the following: (1) managing personal finances; (2) selecting and managing a household; (3) caring for personal needs; (4) raising children and meeting marriage responsibilities; (5) buying, preparing, and consuming food; (6) buying and caring for clothing; (7) exhibiting responsible citizenship; (8) using recreational facilities and managing leisure time; and (9) getting around the community. These competencies are directly related to the avocational, family, and civic roles that were mentioned earlier in the chapter. But the attainment of daily living skills can lead to the successful acquirement of many occupational and career path possibilities. The students with special learning and/or behavior needs must learn these competencies to survive in today's fast-moving society. Educators currently do not emphasize daily living skills enough because they assume that these competencies will be learned incidentally in the home and elsewhere. For most students with special learning and/or behavior needs, this typically does not happen. The school and family members therefore must make deliberate efforts to provide this instruction.

Daily living skills and interests lead to job possibilities in career paths such as clerk, stockperson, nursing aide, child-care worker, grocer, cook, maintenance worker, forklift operator, food service worker, housekeeper, press cleaner, laundry worker, furniture upholsterer, photographic finisher, and barber.

Personal-Social Skills

The competencies under the personal-social skills category include the following: (10) achieving self-awareness; (11) acquiring self-confidence; (12) achieving socially responsible behavior; (13) maintaining good interpersonal skills; (14) achieving independence; (15) achieving problem-solving skills; and (16) communicating with others. The lack of any of these personal-social skills contributes to the major demise of an individual's success in work, home, and other community settings—no matter how competent the individual may be in daily living and occupational skills. Curricular emphasis, instruction, and performance of these competencies are critical in all current and future adult outcome environments.

Personal-social skills are critical for successful performance on all jobs. Skills in this area include getting along with others, taking criticism, accepting supervision, giving praise, making vocational decisions, knowing proper behavior, respecting the rights of others, following directions, and being honest and loyal.

Occupational Skills

The competencies in occupational skills category include the following: (17) knowing and exploring occupational possibilities; (18) selecting and planning occupational choices; (19) exhibiting appropriate work habits and behaviors; (20) seeking, securing, and maintaining employment; (21) exhibiting physical and manual skills; and (22) obtaining a specific occupational skill. Occupational skills are most often associated with *career education/transition programming.* They deserve major curricular emphasis; however, because the occupational skills are subsumed under daily living and personal-social skills, the three curriculum areas are inextricably imbedded. The first two occupational competencies, awareness of occupational possibilities and making appropriate occupational choices, should be taught within a broad context; educators should not pressure students with special learning and/or behavior needs into making a premature occupational choice. Knowing and exploring occupational possibilities, exhibiting appropriate work habits and behavior, and developing physical and manual skills should be tackled almost immediately after the student enters school. Secondary education is the appropriate time for emphasizing the remaining three competencies.

Occupational skills development begins in the elementary school and depends on substantial career awareness and career exploration activities, experiences, instruction, and assessment. As students with special learning and/or behavior needs progress through the educational process, the need for exploring and narrowing down career path choices should be encouraged. The secondary education experiences should be focused on preparing for the transitioning to post secondary education, training, or employment.

Component 1b: The Competencies for the LCCE Moderate Curriculum Model

All 20 competencies and the 75 subcompetencies of the LCCE Moderate Curriculum for Students with

Moderate Disabilities (LCCE-M) have been subjected to rigorous review by hundreds of school personnel who have agreed that the competencies reflect major outcomes required for successful community living and working. The LCCE Moderate Curriculum model also has been described as an appropriate *adult adjustment/outcomes approach* because it focuses on the functional skills and competencies needed for individuals who have moderate learning and/or behavior needs to achieve successful adult living and working. The following discussion briefly describes the three curriculum areas and 20 competencies of the LCCE Moderate Curriculum Model.

Daily Living Skills

The competencies under the LCCE-M's daily living skills category include the following: (1) managing money; (2) selecting and maintaining living environments; (3) caring for personal health; (4) developing and maintaining appropriate intimate relationships; (5) eating at home and in the community; (6) cleaning and purchasing clothing; (7) participating in leisure/recreational activities; and (8) getting around in the community. These eight competencies are directly related to the avocational, family, and citizen roles that were mentioned earlier in the chapter. But, the attainment of daily living skills can help lead to the successful acquirement of many occupational and career path possibilities. The students must learn these competencies to survive in today's fast-moving society. Special educators and general educators in settings where students have been included into general education classrooms currently do not emphasize daily living skills enough because they assume that these competencies will be learned in other special education classes and incidentally at home. The acquisition of these skills for many students with moderate learning and/or behavior needs typically does not happen. The school and family members therefore must make deliberate efforts to provide this instruction.

Daily living skills and interests lead to job possibilities in the following career paths: clerk, stockperson, nursing aide, child-care worker, grocer, cook, maintenance worker, forklift operator, food service worker, housekeeper, press cleaner, laundry worker, furniture upholsterer, photographic finisher, and barber.

Personal-Social Skills

The LCCE Moderate Curriculum competencies under the personal-social skills category include the following: (9) acquiring self-identity; (10) exhibiting socially responsible behavior; (11) developing and maintaining appropriate social relationships; (12) exhibiting independent behavior; (13) making informed decisions; and (14) communicating with others. Lack of any of these personal-social skills contributes to the major demise of an individual's success in work, home, and other community settings—no matter how competent the individual may be in daily living and occupational skills. Curricular emphasis, instruction, and performance of these competencies are critical in all current and future adult outcome environments.

Personal-social skills are critical for successful performance on all jobs. Skills in this area include getting along with others, taking criticism, accepting supervision, giving praise, making vocational decisions, knowing proper behavior, respecting the rights of others, following directions, and being honest and loyal.

Occupational Skills

The LCCE Moderate Curriculum competencies in the occupational skills category include the following: (15) exploring and locating occupational training and job placement; (16) making occupational and job placement choices; (17) applying for and maintaining occupational training and job placements; (18) developing and maintaining appropriate work skills and behavior; (19) matching physical-manual skills to occupational training and employment; and (20) training and occupational choices. Occupational skills are most often associated with career education/transition programming in some secondary education classes for students with moderate learning and/or behavior needs. They deserve major curricular emphasis; however, because the occupational skills are subsumed under daily living and personal-social skills, the three curriculum areas are

inextricably interrelated. The first two LCCE Moderate Curriculum occupational competencies, exploring and locating occupational training and job placement opportunities and making occupational and job placement choices, should be taught within a broad context; special educators and general educators should not pressure students with moderate learning and/or behavior needs into making a premature occupational choice. All of these competencies need to be addressed almost immediately after the student enters school. Secondary education is the appropriate time for emphasizing training for and making occupational choices.

Occupational skills development begins in the elementary school and depends on substantial career awareness and career exploration activities, experiences, instruction, and assessment. As students progress through the educational process, the need for exploring and narrowing down career path choices should be encouraged. The secondary education experiences should be focused on preparing for the transitioning to postsecondary education, training, or employment.

In presenting these two competency-based approaches, it is not the intention of the developers for readers to assume that the emphasis and importance of basic academic content instruction is to be lessened. Students need intensive instruction in reading, mathematics, social studies, and science, but a specific purpose should underlie the traditional practice of bringing an individual to a certain grade level at the end of a year or teaching the student to master some kind of physical activity. In this instance, the specific purpose is the development of the 22 and/or 20 important life-functioning competencies, and every general education and special education teacher at every grade level has a stake in each student's career development and preparation for making the successful adjustment to adult living and working.

Component 2: School, Family, and Community Relationships

A competency-based curriculum involves changes in the roles of teacher and counselor and requires more involvement from family and community agencies, including the business and industrial sector. Students also should be allowed to express their opinions and must be given the opportunity to influence the direction of their personalized curriculum.

School Personnel

All members of the school community should share the responsibility for providing career/functional education and competency development for students. Unfortunately, little is done to ensure that this responsibility is applied systematically to prepare students with special learning and/or behavior needs for functioning successfully as adults. Many general and special educators wish to maintain their traditional mode of educating and imparting knowledge. They concentrate on grade-level content and manipulate the classroom environment for that purpose (Moore & Gysbers, 1972). Career/functional education responsibilities must be clearly delineated and assumed by various personnel. Many general education teachers oppose inclusion because they feel that students will be enrolled without their input. These teachers must be shown that they have important roles in teaching knowledge, information, and *skills* that will result in successful careers for all of their students during their adult years. The school administration must be advocates and provide support, additional resources for general education teachers, and in-service programs for those general education teachers who will educate students.

General education teachers are important in helping all students develop feelings of self-worth and competence by providing situations where each student can learn and be accepted by other class members. Almost every general education teacher can help students acquire at least one competency in the functional LCCE Mild/Moderate Curriculum approaches. Home economics, trade, and industrial technology teachers have always been instrumental in helping students acquire daily living, personal-social and occupational skills, while counselors also have been integral helpers in the personal-social and occupational guidance domains. Table 3.1 presents

examples of the types of school personnel who could assist the student in learning various competencies at the elementary, middle school/junior high, and secondary levels.

Special education teachers assume a different role within this competency-based career/functional education curriculum approach. The special educator becomes more of a consultant or advisor for all other school personnel, parents, and community agencies and industries by coordinating services and integrating the contributions that the school, community, and family can make in meeting each student's career and adult outcomes needs. They will become increasingly important as resource support personnel to general education teachers who will need in-service assistance; methods and materials consultation; modification, accommodations, and materials development assistance; and relevant information on the students' basic academic skills, values, and attitudes. Special classroom instruction may still be the least restrictive environment for many students who cannot always be appropriately educated full time in general education classes. The special educator should carefully monitor each student's progress and collaborate with the general education teachers to assist in providing the most appropriate education. They also should direct their energies in training the school staff on how to enure that their students acquire these critical career/functional competencies in as inclusive a setting as possible.

Family

The individual's family is extremely important in transition/career development. The family can provide meaningful assistance to school efforts by providing the child with hands-on experiences, positive reinforcement for achievements, a secure psychological environment, community experiences and involvement, participation in family decision making, specific job tasks around the house, an atmosphere encouraging meaningful leisure and recreational pursuits, and other transition/career development opportunities. The family must work closely with school personnel to coordinate efforts sequentially and consistently, to assist

TABLE 3.1 Possible LCCE Competency Instructional Subject Areas

Competency	Elementary	Middle School/ Junior High	Senior High
Daily Living Skills			
1. Managing personal finances	Math, language, reading	Business, math	Home economics, math
2. Selecting & managing a household	Language, social studies	Home economics, vocational	Home economics
3. Caring for personal needs	Science, health	Home economics, health	Home economics
4. Raising children & meeting marriage responsibilities	Health	Home economics	Home economics
5. Buying, preparing & consuming food	Reading, language	Home economics	Home economics
6. Buying & caring for clothing	Reading, language	Home economics	Home economics
7. Exhibiting responsible citizenship	Social studies	Social studies, music	Social studies, music
8. Utilizing recreational facilities & engaging in leisure	Health, physical education	Physical education, art, music, counselors	Physical education, art, music, counselors
9. Getting around the community	Health, science	Home economics	Driver's education
Personal-Social Skills			
10. Achieving self-awareness	Language, social studies	Music, physical education, counselors	Art, music, counselors
11. Acquiring self-confidence	Health, science	Art, music, physical education, home economics, counselors	Physical education, counselors, social studies, art, vocational education, music
12. Achieving socially responsible behavior— community	Social studies, language	Physical education, counselors	Social studies, music
13. Maintaining good interpersonal skills	Language, social studies	Counselors	Music, counselors
14. Achieving independence	Social studies, language	Counselors	Counselors

TABLE 3.1   Continued

Competency	Elementary	Middle School/ Junior High	Senior High
Personal-Social Skills (con't)			
15. Making adequate decisions	Language, social studies	Math, counselors	Science, counselors
16. Communicating with others	Language, reading	Language arts, music, speech, physical education	Language arts, speech, music, art
Occupational Skills			
17. Knowing and exploring occupational possibilities	Reading, social studies	Vocational education, home economics, counselors	Counselors
18. Selecting and planning occupational choices	Language, social studies	Business, vocational education, home economics	Counselors
19. Exhibiting appropriate work habits & behaviors	Science, art	Vocational education, math, home economics, art	Home economics, vocational education, music
20. Seeking, securing & maintaining employment	Language, social studies	Counselors	Counselors
21. Exhibiting sufficient physical–manual skills	Art, physical education	Vocational education, home economics	Vocational education, home economics
22. Obtaining specific occupational skills	Social studies, art, music	Vocational education, home economics	Vocational education, home economics

in the development of community resources, to assist as a volunteer or aide in school settings and functions, and to serve on advisory and action committees related to career education/transition programming. Family members can help schools in public relations, fund-raising, resource development, and other efforts needed to enhance school operations. Chapter 4 is devoted to family involvement and provides more information relating to these recommended practices.

Community Involvement

A wide array of agencies and organizations can assist school personnel and families help the student acquire the functional 22 LCCE Mild Curriculum and 20 LCCE Moderate Curriculum career education competencies. Agencies, organizations, and civic clubs such as the YMCA, Scottish Rite, Lion's Clubs, YWCA, Red Cross, League of Women Voters, Jaycees, Kiwanis, Rotary, Chamber of Commerce, Planned Parenthood, Parks and Recreation, Public Health, 4-H, Boy Scouts, churches, libraries, Girl Scouts, and Campfire, Inc., are all resources that can be used to help students acquire functional daily living skills and career education experiences. Groups that may help students acquire personal-social skills include many of the preceding organizations as well as state employment services and mental health, counseling, and university organizations. Occupational skills can be developed by using a wide variety of agencies and organizations including vocational rehabilitation and state employment services, community action programs, Veterans Administration, rehabilitation workshops, and the Governor's Committee on Employment of the People with Disabilities. Business, industry, and labor also offer a wealth of assistance in community-based experience opportunities. Businesses such as banks, grocery stores, department stores, factories, insurance companies, repair shops, gas stations, loan companies, and many other businesses can be used effectively in planning daily living, personal-social, and occupational learning activities. Chapters 5 and 6 will provide more detailed information and guidance in this area.

The interaction and interface of these three curriculum areas within the community for career development/transition programming cannot be over-emphasized. Sometimes it takes considerable time and effort to establish these relationships, but the benefits will be obvious in more fully realizing the career/functional education and development of students.

Component 3: Stages of Career Development and Learning

Career/functional education consists of several different stages or phases. As illustrated in Figure 3.5, the LCCE Mild/Moderate Curriculum model includes four stages of career development: career *awareness*, career *exploration*, career *preparation*, and career *assimilation*. Because students with severe disabilities need more time to develop the skills required for successful career development/transition programming,

adult functioning, these stages will begin earlier and last longer for these individuals.

Career Awareness

During the preschool and elementary years, *career awareness* should be emphasized. When learning daily living skills, students must become aware of how to manage and use money appropriately, how to manage and maintain a home, how to take care of personal needs properly, how to assume responsibility for raising children and living as a family, how to purchase and prepare food, and how to select and care for clothing. In addition, students will learn how to assume civic responsibilities and roles, how to fulfill interests and needs by becoming aware of recreation and leisure activities, and how to achieve greater mobility in the community.

Personal-social skills will help students develop a sense of self-worth and confidence as well as help them to become more aware of their feelings, values, and potentials. In addition, students will develop effective communication skills such as reading, writing, and speaking. They will become more aware of socially desirable behavior and learn how to interact appropriately with others. As students gain confidence, they will develop and maintain independent relationships. Finally, personal-social skills will enhance students with special learning and/or behavior needs' awareness of how to approach and solve problems and will teach them to think independently and make adequate decisions.

As they acquire occupational skills, students with special learning and/or behavior needs will begin to develop positive attitudes about work. They will begin seeing themselves as potential employees and explore different types of jobs and their requirements. As they become more aware of work habits and behaviors needed for success in work, they will develop a work personality based on their own unique set of needs, desires, and physical and manual skills.

Attitude, information, desires, and self-understanding are three main elements of career awareness. Attitudes are the foundation on which the career education/transition structure is built. Young

FIGURE 3.5   **Stages of career development**

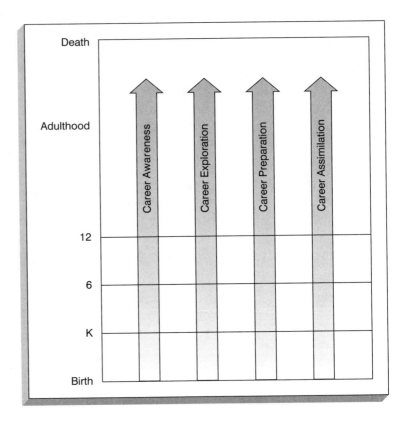

children with special learning and/or behavior needs must learn that people make many conscious efforts at producing some benefit for themselves and others, including working. They should learn and articulate that people work for many reasons: economic, psychological, and societal. They need to understand that work provides a major source of personal identification and satisfaction. Information helps the student learn the variety of ways people earn a living and how they use their time in avocational, leisure, and other community life pursuits. Self-understanding enhances the development of students with special learning and/or behavior needs' careers by making them more aware of their relationship to the world and by helping them identify their eventual adult living and working roles (Kolstoe, 1976).

Career awareness is not that difficult to infuse into a preschool or elementary curriculum. To a limited extent, most teachers already discuss various careers

such as police officers, fire fighters, mail carriers, doctors, nurses, waiters, chefs, and homemakers. But the career education/transition concept requires purposeful discussion of careers so that students with special learning and/or behavior needs become aware of their own career aptitudes, interests, and abilities. Like any other form of education, career education/transition programming must be designed sequentially, so that whatever happens at each grade level is built on and leads toward the attainment of all LCCE Mild/Moderate Curriculum competencies by the time students make the successful transition from school to postsecondary training, living, and working.

Career Exploration

Career exploration begins at the elementary level, but it should receive its greatest emphasis during the middle school/junior high school years. During this phase, students with special learning and/or behavior needs begin a more careful self-examination of their unique abilities, interests, and needs in relation to the working world, avocational interests, leisure and recreational pursuits, and all other adult roles related to transition/career development and community living. It is important for school personnel to design curriculum and instructional experiences so that self-exploration of the four aspects of career (employee, family member, citizen and active recreation, and leisure participant) can occur. This process should include the use of a variety of techniques, experiences, and settings relevant to each individual's personalized needs, strengths, and interests. The incorporation and involvement of community resources is crucial during the exploration stage of career development/transitional programming.

Daily living skills instruction should encourage students with special learning and/or behavior needs to explore various methods of managing personal finances, selecting and managing a home, caring for various personal needs, child-rearing and family living methods, buying and preparing nutritious food, buying and caring for clothing, engaging in civic activities, pursuing recreation and leisure activities, and trying various modes of community transportation. These explorations should be personalized to each individual student's emerging set of attitudes, values, interests, and needs by using various courses, field experiences, clubs and organizations, home activities, and community involvement such as part-time jobs, hobbies, reading, and social activities.

Personal-social skills exploration helps students with special learning and/or behavior needs to seriously begin questioning who they are and assisting them into leaving the child status they assumed during the elementary years as they move into adolescence. Transitional guidance and counseling help students with special learning and/or behavior needs identify their unique abilities, needs, and interests as they relate to career development/transitional programming. Individual and group counseling activities such as role playing, peer tutoring, cooperative learning, modeling, values clarification, and other inter- and intra-personal activities should be available to help students with special learning and/or behavior needs gain better understanding of themselves and others.

Occupational skills preparation helps students with special learning and/or behavior needs to carefully examine several career paths and engage in a variety of hands-on experiences, both in and out of school. To fully understand the characteristics of various occupational possibilities, students with special learning and/or behavior needs should observe and analyze jobs firsthand, try them out in simulated situations, participate in job shadowing, and talk to employers about various aspects of jobs and work. To select and begin planning tentative occupational choices, students with special learning and/or behavior needs will need assistance from transitional guidance personnel so they can receive a thorough career/transitional assessment of their vocational aptitudes, interests, and needs. At this time, occupational choices can be only generally related to any specific area, because the student's interest and needs may change during the secondary school experience. Students with special learning and/or behavior needs should be encouraged to try various work samples, simulated job tasks, and community jobs, and should begin analyzing and developing appropriate work habits and behaviors, physical and manual skills, and other competencies needed in the workplace. Prevocational classes such as trade and industrial technology and home economics will be beneficial during the middle/junior high school years.

Career exploration is the link between career awareness and career preparation. During the career preparation stage, young students with special learning and/or behavior needs begin to think seriously about their particular set of aptitudes, interests, and needs, and how these needs can be directed toward meaningful and successful adult roles. Sequential exploration activities and experiences should be planned so that by the time students with special learning and/or behavior needs are ready for high school, a more highly individualized educational/transitional plan can be designed, and a more relevant career development/transitional preparation program offered.

Career Preparation

Career preparation is not solely confined to one period of schooling. Like other stages of career development/transitional programming, it begins in the early grades and continues throughout life. But for most individuals, particularly for those who do not go on to postsecondary training, the high school years are critical for reaching the necessary level of competence in the three curriculum areas that compose the 22 and/or 20 life career development/transitional competencies for successful adult community living and working.

All educators, students with special learning and/or behavior needs, and family members should monitor and promote a functional curriculum that will help students with special learning and/or behavior needs master the nine (eight for LCCE Moderate Curriculum) competencies involved in daily living skills. Home economics, math, business, health, driver's education, social studies, trade and industrial technology, and physical education will help students with special learning and/or behavior needs attain these nine/eight competencies, respectively.

If development of personal-social skills has been satisfactory at the elementary and junior high levels, students with special learning and/or behavior needs are ready to learn and practice those personal-social skills needed for community living and working. The professional should identify any specific difficulties that students with special learning and/or behavior needs may have in learning these seven competencies (six competencies for LCCE Moderate Curriculum) and design procedures for their remediation. This may be accomplished by special education teachers/counselors consulting and providing general education teachers with procedures for remediating the difficulty, by altering classroom instruction to fit the needs of students with special learning and/or behavior needs, or by using individual and group counseling. Counseling, role-playing, modeling, values clarification, peer tutoring, and other techniques are effective with most students with special learning and/or behavior needs. Professionals should perceive each student with special learning and/or behavior needs as an independent and nearly adult-functioning individual who is to be listened to and respected. Their job is to help students with special learning and/or behavior needs identify specific interests and aptitudes and help them find an effective adult lifestyle.

Development of occupational skills can be more specifically directed toward the students with special learning and/or behavior needs' tentative career choices. Students with special learning and/or behavior needs should be able to select from a variety of vocational courses and community job experiences that fit the aptitudes, interests, and abilities comprising their unique work personality. If students with special learning and/or behavior needs have acquired work habits and behaviors, physical or manual skills, and work values and attitudes during the elementary and junior high years, they can begin to select an appropriate occupational area and develop specific occupational skills. However, this may be counterproductive if students with special learning and/or behavior needs are forced into making a premature occupational decision. Some students with special learning and/or behavior needs may choose to enter college or other postsecondary programs. In the process of learning specific occupational skills, students with special learning and/or behavior needs also acquire a much more positive self-concept, gain confidence in their ability to learn a specific skill, and master other personal-social skills. Guidance counselors and special education teachers are responsible for preparing students with special learning and/or behavior needs to seek, secure, and maintain employment. This competency should be emphasized throughout the entire secondary education program.

Because community experiences will be a major part of career preparation, students with special learning and/or behavior needs should be encouraged to use community resources and services. Intensive transitional and vocational assessment also is necessary to help students with special learning and/or behavior needs test the realism of their occupational choices and training needs. Finally, many students with special learning and/or behavior needs may need more than the traditional amount of time to prepare for a successful career and should be given additional time in either secondary or postsecondary settings.

Career Assimilation

Career assimilation may occur during the secondary or postsecondary years, depending on the students with special learning and/or behavior needs' readiness for this stage of career development/transitional programming. Work experience or job shadowing programs gives students with special learning and/or behavior needs opportunities to be placed in actual jobs as if they were being employed as regular employees. Work experience programs may be either full- or part-time and may last longer than one semester, depending on each student with special learning and/or behavior needs' ability level and needs.

Although career assimilation is usually associated with a job placement, students with special learning and/or behavior needs also should be given the opportunity to assume avocational, family, recreational, civic, and other nonpaying adult career roles so they can assess their abilities and needs in these areas, as well as in paid employment. School personnel should work closely with the family to support their child's participation in these endeavors. For example, the student with special learning and/or behavior needs should be given specific household responsibilities, which includes managing finances, managing a home, caring for personal needs, living as a member of a family unit, buying and preparing food, buying and caring for clothing, becoming involved in civic activities, engaging in self-planned recreation and leisure-time activities, getting around the community, and developing and maintaining satisfactory social relationships. Although school and family have probably worked on these critical functional competencies together before this stage, students with special learning and/or behavior needs should now be actively practicing these skills with and without assistance from the family.

Career assimilation pulls all previous stages together to enable the student with special learning and/or behavior needs to develop a personal career/transitional identity. During this stage, educators will identify whether the student with special learning and/or behavior needs still needs to refine any of the critical LCCE Mild/Moderate Curriculum competency skills. This is the most realistic stage of the career development/transitional program and may extend intermittently over several years for many students with special learning and/or behavior needs. Therefore, community resources and services are crucial to life career development and success and should

be included in this final stage. Most students with special learning and/or behavior needs will need important lifelong learning supports. Provisions must be made to account for these needs. Therefore, follow-up and supportive services are an important aspect of career assimilation and must be included in the students with special learning and/or behavior needs' transitional plan and future activities.

Component 4: The Career Roles

Another unique feature of the LCCE Mild/Moderate Curriculum design is its focus on not only future occupations but also on those many unpaid work roles necessary to adult life: (1) the many work tasks associated with living in a family, being married, and perhaps raising a family, and/or living by oneself in the community; (2) being a good citizen and neighbor, and engaging in such civic activities as volunteer work, voting, helping friends and neighbors, and the like; and (3) engaging in avocational activities such as hobbies, vacations, games, spectator sports, and other leisure time activities that are of benefit to oneself and others.

The career education/transition concept views people as having careers throughout their lifetime. Thus, when children are in school, their primary career is their work as a student, but they also need to learn proper behaviors and skills to function adequately as a family member, citizen, and participant in appropriate recreational and leisure time pursuits.

Figure 3.6 presents a three-dimensional model illustrating the interaction of the first three components of the LCCE approach: (1) competencies; (2) school, family, and community experiences; and (3) stages of career development. Although the model is not intended to be factorially or mathematically pure, it demonstrates that one or more resources available in the school, family, or community can be used to teach any of the competencies at each career development/transitional programming stage. For example, the LCCE Mild Curriculum for the mild competency 1 (managing personal finances) should be taught in a math class at the elementary, middle school/junior high, and secondary level. Before the competency is taught, the elementary teacher should

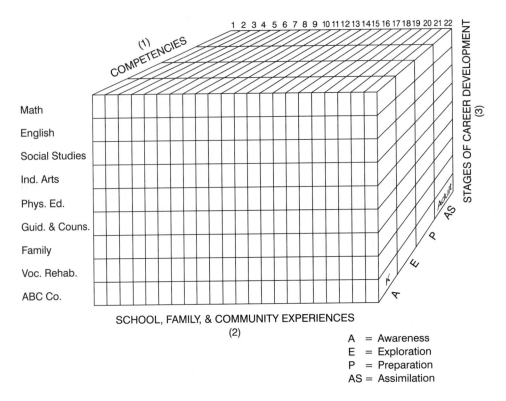

A = Awareness
E = Exploration
P = Preparation
AS = Assimilation

FIGURE 3.6   Competency-Based Model for Infusing Career Education into the Curriculum.

provide the student with special learning and/or behavior needs with a sufficient awareness of the importance of this skill, including how people acquire the skill, what kinds of things are involved in learning the skill, and what people can do with this skill (e.g., family responsibilities and job possibilities). With this background, the student with special learning and/or behavior needs becomes more aware of the importance of this competency in the real world and therefore becomes more receptive to learning the necessary skills. The student with special learning and/or behavior needs begins by learning how to identify money and make correct change. As upper-level elementary or middle school students with special learning and/or behavior needs learn basic skills, they should be provided with exploration experiences in and out of the school so they can observe how other people make wise expenditures, obtain

and use bank credit facilities, and so on. During late middle school/junior high and early secondary education, students with special learning and/or behavior needs should crystallize their skills in this competency area (preparation) with further complementary community and family experiences. Finally, during the assimilation stage, students with special learning and/or behavior needs have the opportunity to independently display their skill of managing personal finances. Students with special learning and/or behavior needs also will use this competency for family living and may have an interest in obtaining a job requiring this skill and to plan and participate in community recreational and leisure activities.

The preceding four components (the three curriculum areas with 22 and 20 competencies, three instructional settings, four stages of career development, and four major career/work roles) discussed in this section are the heart of the LCCE Mild and Moderate Curriculum approaches. Besides the conceptual framework, an extensive set of curriculum-based assessment and instructional materials has been developed with the assistance of hundreds of teachers and educational consultants for the LCCE Mild Curriculum and are being developed to accompany the LCCE Moderate Curriculum. School district personnel describe these in the next section, along with the recently developed staff development training materials for use.

LCCE MILD CURRICULUM MATERIALS

Many transition models and many types of transition curriculum materials are available to assist educators in instituting functional/transitional skills efforts in their schools. Some of these were identified and described in Chapter 2. One problem, however, is that many who have conceptualized a transitional model provide little or no transitional curriculum materials, and many who have developed transitional curriculum materials have no conceptualized model. Thus, it is up to the users to conceptualize and operationalize the transition model and/or to develop materials the best they can. Some educators prefer this approach and are able to do it well; others want a more organized and extensive set of established curriculum-based transition materials from which they can modify and expand their transitional instructional efforts as needed.

The LCCE Mild Curriculum model and its concepts are supported by both a variety of curriculum-based assessment measures and an extensive set of lesson plans that have been written to cover all 400 instructional objectives subsumed under the 22 competency/97 subcompetency matrix composing the system. In addition, an extensive staff training program with videotapes and other materials is available to school districts interested in learning to implement the complete transition system with students who have special learning and/or behavior needs. Parallel materials are currently being developed for the LCCE

Moderate Curriculum approach and will follow the discussion of the LCCE Mild Curriculum system. Each of the LCCE Mild Curriculum and training materials are briefly described next as well as the current and future materials for the LCCE Moderate Curriculum.

Basic LCCE Mild Curriculum Guide

The LCCE Mild Curriculum Guide, *Life Centered Career Education: A Competency-Based Approach* (Brolin, 1978, 1983b, 1989, 1993a, 1997, 2003), provides the framework for building a comprehensive and systematic effort for infusing/interfacing the 97 LCCE subcompetencies into academic content areas in general education classes. The guide provides the background on career education/transition concepts and the LCCE Mild Curriculum model and then presents a set of 97 subcompetency units with instructional objectives, suggested activities, and adult/peer instructional roles for supportive assistance. Teachers can develop their own specific lesson plans from the guidelines provided.

The guide also contains the Competency Rating Scale (CRS) covering each of the 97 subcompetencies and a suggested Individualized Education Plan (IEP) form with transition components (Brolin, 1993a). Many users of the guide find the CRS a valuable screening instrument to profile competency attainment among teachers, families, students with special learning and/or behavior needs, and agencies. The CRS also has been used as an alternative assessment instrument for those students with special learning and/or behavior needs not able to participate in the statewide assessment system or minimum competency testing.

LCCE Mild Knowledge Batteries Assessments

The *LCCE Knowledge Battery* (KB) (Brolin, 1992a) is primarily a screening instrument. It assesses the career education/transition skills knowledge of 7th- through

12th-grade students with special learning and/or behavior needs, although it can be used with younger age general education and at-risk students with special learning and/or behavior needs as well. The LCCE KB consists of two forms, each comprising 200 multiple-choice questions covering the first 20 competencies of the LCCE Mild Curriculum. The last two competencies do not lend themselves to assessment of transition skills knowledge concepts. Forms A and B contain questions addressing the 400 objectives in the total of 400 questions contained in the LCCE KB. This standardized instrument comes with a comprehensive administration manual. Questions have been matched with the competencies, subcompetencies, and objectives in the LCCE Mild Curriculum.

LCCE Mild Performance Batteries Assessments

The *LCCE Performance Battery* (PB) (Brolin, 1992a) covers all competency areas except competency 22 (obtaining specific occupational skills), which lends itself for vocational testing related to students with special learning and/or behavior needs' selected occupational training area. Each competency test consists of five questions that require the student to demonstrate application of a subcompetency area or to respond in writing or verbally to questions that reflect such competence. Each LCCE Mild PB provides examiners with information regarding specific materials used in the performance assessment, work sheets, score sheets, procedures, and specific guidelines for test administration.

LCCE Self-Determination Scale

The *LCCE Self-Determination Scale* (in preparation) is the most recent measure developed and assesses students with special learning and/or behavior needs on the concept of self-determination. The Arc staff, based on a federal research project, developed this 40-item self-reporting instrument. The study project identified four LCCE competencies and 17

subcompetencies as most nearly approximating the concept of self-determination. Items were then devised and field-tested to finalize a reliable and valid measure.

LCCE Mild Curriculum Competency/Instructional Units

This set of guides contains more than 1,000 lesson plans covering the objectives of the daily living, personal-social, and occupational guidance and preparation domains of the LCCE Mild Curriculum. These lesson plans have been developed and field-tested nationally with the assistance of school personnel and their students with special learning and/or behavior needs. The daily living skills area consists of 472 lesson plans; the personal-social area has 370 lesson plans; and the occupational area has 286 lesson plans.

The LCCE Mild Curriculum lesson plans address each of the 400 instructional objectives that comprise the 97 subcompetencies presented in the LCCE Mild Curriculum guide. The lesson plans are written to address the three levels of career education stages in the LCCE Mild Curriculum approach (i.e., career awareness, career exploration, and career preparation); to provide instruction in the three major instructional settings (home, community, and school); and to span the four major career roles that students with special learning and/or behavior needs will participate in as productive adults (family member, citizen/volunteer, employee, and leisure/recreation seeker). Thus, the lesson plans cover the entire range of 400 instructional objectives contained in the basic LCCE Mild Curriculum guide (Brolin, 1997). Users can modify them, add additional resources to them, and otherwise use them in conjunction with the assessment measures, to provide a comprehensive career education/transition program with a scope and sequence from the elementary through secondary and into post-secondary years.

Detailed descriptions of the LCCE instructional units and their lesson plans are covered in Chapters 11 to 13.

Personal-social skills development needs to begin early in students' education.

LCCE Mild Curriculum Staff Training Materials

An extensive set of staff training materials has been developed so that school districts can train their own personnel to implement the LCCE system. The training program consists of three major pieces: a trainer's manual, a set of videotapes, and a participant's activity book.

The *LCCE Trainer's Manual* (Loyd & Brolin, 2003) provides staff developers with step-by-step guidelines for organizing and conducting up to 30 1/2 hours of in-service training. The LCCE Trainer's Manual includes masters for trainees' handouts, transparencies, and support text for the trainer. The manual includes a 13-minute videocassette that presents an overview and discussion of the LCCE Mild/ Moderate Curriculum approach, which also can be presented to administrators, school boards, parents, and community groups. Guidelines for LCCE im-

plementation, sustainability and evaluation also are contained in this manual.

The second piece of the LCCE staff development package is a set of 10 videotapes that the trainer will intersperse throughout the training course (Brolin, 1993c). The tapes cover such topics as: the need to change and the law, the LCCE Mild Curriculum, assessing functional skills, teaching daily living skills, teaching personal-social skills, teaching occupational skills, instructional materials utilization, business and industry, parent involvement, interagency collaboration, curriculum modification and change, and individualized transition planning and implementation.

The third piece of the LCCE training package is the 458-page *Life Centered Career Education: Professional Development Activity Book* (Council for Exceptional Children, 1992), which is designed for use by all trainees along with the curriculum guide. The activity book, packaged in a three-ring notebook, is divided into 10 training sessions, corresponding to the videotapes described previously, and contains a series of activity sheets, resource materials, copies of all transparencies shown on the videotapes, and assignments to enhance the training effort.

The LCCE training program package can be used either in its entirety or in part, depending on the time constraints and needs of the school district. If school districts prefer to have outside consultants conduct the training, the Council for Exceptional Children (CEC) provides LCCE Mild Curriculum trainers who can implement the curriculum themselves.

LCCE MODERATE CURRICULUM MATERIALS

Few transition models and transition curriculum materials are available to assist educators in instituting functional/transitional skills efforts in their schools for students with moderate special learning and/or behavior needs. One problem is that few transitional models have been conceptualized for students with moderate learning and/or behavior needs. An additional problem is that little or no transitional curriculum materials have been developed for students with moderate learning and/or behavior needs. Thus, it has been up to users to conceptualize and operationalize a transition model and/or develop materials the best they can. Some educators prefer this approach and are able to do it well; others want a more organized and extensive set of established curriculum-based transition materials from which they can modify and expand their transitional instructional efforts as needed.

The LCCE Moderate Curriculum model and its concepts are and will be developed in the near future to support both a variety of curriculum-based assessment measures and an extensive set of lesson plans that will be written to cover all 200 instructional objectives subsumed under the 20 competency/75 subcompetency matrix composing the LCCE Moderate Curriculum system. In addition, an extensive staff training program with videotapes and other materials will soon be available to school districts interested in

learning to implement the complete transition system with students who have moderate learning and/or behavior needs. Each of the LCCE Moderate Curriculum and training materials that are available and are being developed are briefly described in this next section.

Basic LCCE Moderate Curriculum Guide

The LCCE Moderate Curriculum Guide, *Life Centered Career Education: Modified Curriculum for Individuals with Moderate Disabilities* (Loyd & Brolin, 1997), provides the framework for building a comprehensive and systematic effort for infusing/interfacing the 75 LCCE subcompetencies into functional academic areas in either general education classrooms, resource rooms, and/or community-based program. The guide provides the background on career education/transition concepts and the LCCE Moderate Curriculum model and then presents a set of 75 subcompetency units with instructional objectives, suggested activities, and community-based activities. Teachers can develop their own specific lesson plans from the guidelines provided.

The guide also contains the Competency Rating Scale (CRS) covering each of the 75 subcompetencies and a suggested Individualized Education Plan (IEP) form with transition components (Loyd & Brolin, 1997). Many users of the guide find the CRS a valuable screening instrument to profile competency attainment among teachers, families, students with special learning and/or behavior needs, and agencies. The CRS also has been used as an alternative assessment instrument for those students with special learning and/or behavior needs not able to participate in the statewide assessment system or minimum competency testing.

LCCE-M (Moderate) Pictorial Knowledge Batteries (PKBs)

The *LCCE-M (Moderate) Pictorial Knowledge Battery* (PKB) (Loyd & Brolin, in preparation) is a nonreading screening instrument. It assesses the career education/transitional skills knowledge of students with moderate learning and/or behavior needs at any age, although it can be used with younger age students who are at-risk or have special learning and/or behavior needs as well. The LCCE-M PKB consists of two forms, each comprising 150 multiple-choice questions covering the first 18 competencies of the LCCE Moderate Curriculum. The last two competencies do not lend themselves to the assessment of transition skills knowledge concepts. Forms A and B contain questions addressing the 200 objectives in the total of 300 questions contained in the LCCE-M PKB. This standardized instrument comes with a comprehensive administration manual. Questions have been matched with the competencies, subcompetencies, and objectives in the LCCE Moderate Curriculum.

LCCE-M (Moderate) Performance Assessment Batteries (PABs)

The *LCCE-M (Moderate) Performance Assessment Batteries* (PABs) (Loyd & Brolin, in preparation) covers all competency areas except competency 20 (training and occupational choices), which lends itself for vocational testing related to the students with moderate learning and/or behavior needs' selected occupational choice training area. Each nonreading LCCE-M PAB competency test consists of five questions requiring students with special learning and/or behavior needs to demonstrate or perform a related subcompetency area or to respond orally to questions that reflect such performance competence. Each LCCE-M PAB provides examiners with information regarding specific materials used in the performance assessment, work sheets, score sheets, procedures, and specific guidelines for test administration.

LCCE Moderate Competency/ Instructional Units

A set of guides containing more than 500 LCCE Moderate Curriculum lesson plans (Loyd & Brolin,

in preparation) covers the objectives of the daily living, personal-social, and occupational guidance and preparation domains of the LCCE Moderate Curriculum. These lesson plans will be developed and field-tested nationally with the assistance of school personnel and their students with special learning and/or behavior needs. There are approximately 200 lesson plans for daily living skills area and approximately 125 lesson plans for the personal-social area; the occupational area has 286 lesson plans.

The LCCE Moderate Curriculum lesson plans will address each of the 200 instructional objectives that comprise the 75 subcompetencies presented in the LCCE Moderate Curriculum guide. The lesson plans, like those written for the LCCE Mild Curriculum, will be written to address the three levels of career education stages in the LCCE Mild Curriculum approach (i.e., career awareness, career exploration, and career preparation); to provide instruction in the three major instructional settings (home, community, and school); and to span the four major career roles that students with special learning and/or behavior needs will participate in as productive adults (family member, citizen/volunteer, employee, and leisure/recreation seeker). Thus, the lesson plans will cover the entire range of 200 instructional objectives contained in the basic LCCE Moderate Curriculum guide (Loyd & Brolin, 1997). Users will be encouraged to modify them, add additional resources to them, and otherwise use them in conjunction with the assessment measures in preparation, to provide a comprehensive career education/transition program with a scope and sequence from the elementary through secondary and into postsecondary years.

LCCE Moderate Curriculum Training Materials

An extensive set of staff training materials will be developed so that school districts can train their own personnel to implement the LCCE Moderate Curriculum system. The training program will consists of three major pieces: a trainer's manual, a set of videotapes, and a participants' activity book.

The *LCCE Trainer's Manual* (Loyd & Brolin, in preparation) will provide staff developers with step-by-step guidelines for organizing and conducting up to 30 1/2 hours of in-service training. The LCCE-M Trainer's Manual will include masters for trainees' handouts, transparencies, and support text for the trainer. The manual will include a videocassette overview and discussion of the LCCE Moderate Curriculum approach, which also can be presented to administrators, school boards, parents, and community groups. Guidelines for LCCE implementation, sustainability, and evaluation also are contained in this manual.

The second piece of the LCCE-M training package will be a set of videotapes that the trainer will intersperse throughout the training course (Loyd & Brolin, in preparation). The tapes will cover such topics as: the LCCE Moderate Curriculum approach overview, assessing functional skills, teaching daily living skills, teaching personal-social skills, teaching occupational skills, instructional materials utilization, business and industry, parent involvement, interagency collaboration, curriculum modification and change, and individualized transition planning and implementation.

The LCCE-M training program package can be used either in its entirety or in part, depending on the time constraints and needs of the school district. If school districts prefer to have outside consultants conduct the training, the Council for Exceptional Children (CEC) provides LCCE Mild/Moderate Curriculum trainers who can implement the curriculum themselves.

RATIONALE FOR ADOPTING THE LCCE MILD/MODERATE CURRICULUM

The LCCE Mild/Moderate Curriculum offers educators a comprehensive framework for organizing an effective, functional curriculum that will prepare students with special learning and/or behavior needs to be productive adult members of their community and the labor market. It has been built on many proven transition/career education concepts pre-

sented in Chapter 2 and has been developed and field-tested in a large number of school districts throughout the country.

Students with special learning and/or behavior needs must develop a "work personality" beginning at the preschool and elementary levels.

The LCCE Mild/Moderate Curriculum models promote transitional programming beginning in preschool and at the latest in the elementary education level with purposeful and organized instruction directed at the development of a work personality and the important career/life skills needed for successful adult functioning in community living and working (Brolin, 1993a). The *work personality* is an individual's work habits, work behaviors, work values, work motivation, and positive work ethic—all the important positive characteristics one needs to be successfully employed. A work personality type is illustrated in Figure 3.7.

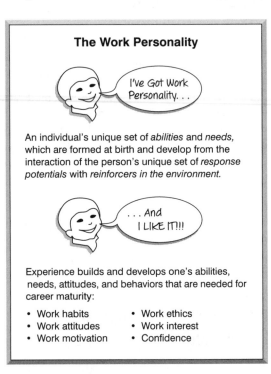

FIGURE 3.7   The work personality.

The state departments of North Dakota, South Carolina, Alabama, Florida, and others have advocated the use of the LCCE Mild Curriculum to educators throughout their states. In 1990, one of their guides provided a detailed explanation of how the curriculum could be used by school districts throughout the state. Figure 3.8 lists of some the major features of the LCCE Mild/Moderate Curriculum from their perspective and the compelling reasons for using this transitional approach.

According to Halpern, Benz, and Lindstrom (1991), four conditions are needed for a capacity-building curriculum model to work. Such a model must be (1) guided by a set of program standards, (2) implemented through a set of efficient and effective procedures, (3) supported by the provision of training

and materials, and (4) documented with concise and effective materials.

The LCCE Mild/Moderate Curriculum meets the four conditions needed for the capacity-building curriculum model. Figure 3.9 illustrates how each of these four conditions is addressed in the LCCE Mild/Moderate Curriculum system.

A brief explanation of each follows:

- *Set of Program Standards.* The LCCE Mild Curriculum Guide, *Life Centered Career Education: A Competency-Based Approach* (Brolin, 1978, 1983b, 1989, 1993a), provides the conceptual model and set of standards for the curriculum.
- *Concise and Effective Materials.* An extensive set of curriculum-based assessment instruments and

The LCCE curriculum lends itself well to the core curriculum concept . . . and is recommended as a guide for local curriculum review and development.

The 22 competencies can serve as a framework for infusing life-centered skills into all aspects of the curriculum by applying appropriate skills and knowledge of academic and content area subjects to everyday real life situations.

Each subject area is a vehicle for teaching life skills. LCCE is a way of tying curriculum content to the real world.

Unlike other curriculums, life-centered competencies apply to all students.

The concept of least restrictive environment and the life centered competency concept are closely interrelated.

Practice of these skills must occur as much as possible in the natural environment with nonhandicapped peers and other members of society.

Attending to the 22 LCCE competencies can aid the IEP team more than any other assessment information.

The student's present level of functioning in the LCCE competencies is basic to establishing goals and objectives, which will lead toward more successful overall functioning.

Core curriculum areas must be kept in the forefront during each IEP review . . . the 22 competencies may serve as a frame of reference in re-establishing priority areas.

FIGURE 3.8   Excerpts from the North Dakota State Department of Instruction guidebook.
Note. From *Special Education in North Dakato: Guide II: Educational Programming for Students with Mild to Moderate Mental Retardation.* 1990, Bismarck, ND: North Dakota Department of Public Instruction. Copyright 1990 by North Dakota Department of Public Instruction. Reprinted by permission.

FIGURE 3.9   LCCE Curriculum System.
Note. From *Life-Centered Career Education: Trainer's Manual* (3rd ed., p. 4) by D. E. Brolin, 1993, Arlington, VA: The Council for Exceptional Children. Copyright 1993 by The Council for Exceptional Children. Reprinted by permission.

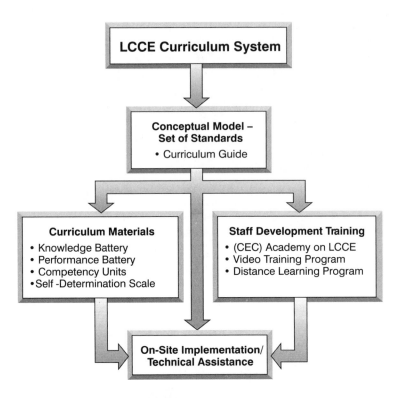

over 1,000 lesson plans have been developed and field tested, covering all 400 instructional objectives contained in the LCCE Mild Curriculum guide.

- *Professional/Staff Development Methods.* The LCCE staff have developed a videotape staff development training program with an accompanying *Trainer's Manual* (Loyd & Brolin, 2003) and trainee activity book (Loyd & Brolin, 2003) for school district staff to train their own people. In addition, the CEC's Professional Development section conducts regional conferences on LCCE Mild/Moderate Curriculum implementation training programs in communities and districts requesting in-service training programs.
- *Set of Effective and Efficient Implementation Procedures.* An implementation process has been developed and field tested and is outlined in detail in the *Trainer's Manual* (Loyd & Brolin, 2003) and other staff development materials.

The preceding materials and training programs are all available from the CEC at 1110 North Glebe Road, Suite 300, Arlington, VA 22201.

CHAPTER COMMENTARY

Students with special learning needs and others should be taught an appropriate blend of academic and functional life skills content if they are to be prepared for a successful adult outcome. Although the term *career education* is not as prominently used today as it was before the introduction of the transition movement, it continues to be used by many proponents of the approach because it more specifically focuses on the purpose of the educational efforts that need to be emphasized for all students with special learning and/or behavior needs of all types—career development. Many school districts are presently touting a new discovery called "Partnerships with Industry" or something similar. Students with special learning and/or behavior needs at all levels are spending more time with employers, their parents, and others learning about the world of employment so they can begin developing their career interests (and work personality) earlier.

The LCCE Mild/Moderate Curriculum competency-based approach does not advocate elimination of current courses or a significant change in the structure of education. Instead, it recommends that educators change the focus of instructional content to meet the transition/career development needs of students with special learning and/or behavior needs and for the family and community resources to become an integral part of this educational process. Each instructor must decide how the competencies can be delivered and integrated into the existing courses. With the movement toward an inclusive education for all students with special learning and/or behavior needs, the LCCE Mild/Moderate Curriculum approach provides a mechanism for making this important goal logical and successful.

Almost everyone wants to attain a satisfactory quality of life that includes satisfying employment, financial security, friendships, independence, leisure time, and for many, a family. All of these functional adult outcomes require individuals with learning and/or behavior needs to learn to work productively in their home, community, and on a job. A substantial transition/career education effort, incorporated into the ongoing curriculum of the school, can lead toward this end.

· · · · · · · · · · · · ·

ACTIVITIES

1. Prepare a presentation to give to your school board to convince them that a more substantive career education/functional skills approach, more specifically, the LCCE Mild/Moderate Curriculum, needs to be implemented in your district. Be prepared to explain the nature of the LCCE Mild/Moderate Curriculum and to give a strong argument in favor of its adoption.

2. Review the 22 competency/97 subcompetency matrix of the LCCE Mild Curriculum presented in Figure 3.2 . Then, conduct a curriculum analysis to determine in what general education subjects each of these functional skills could be taught to your students with special learning and/or behavior needs, if your school has a full inclusion policy.

3. Review the 20 competency/75 subcompetency matrix of the LCCE Moderate Curriculum presented in Figure 3.3. Then, conduct a curriculum analysis to determine in what general education subjects each of these functional skills could be taught to your students with special learning and/or behavior needs, if your school has a full inclusion policy.

PART 2

FAMILY AND COMMUNITY RESOURCES

CHAPTER 4

Family Support

**Robert J. Loyd,
Michael Wehmeyer,
and Sharon Davis**

PRELIMINARY QUESTIONS

1. How and why has family involvement in education changed in recent years?
2. What are some compelling reasons for educators to involve families in a substantial and meaningful way in their educational efforts?
3. How do you believe parents view the educational and decision-making process that they experience with professional educators?
4. What do you believe are the typical attitudes of the professional educator about parent involvement and child planning?
5. What is the dilemma that educators often find themselves in as they try to meet their responsibilities to the student and family while working within the constraints of their own system?
6. What are some of the major barriers that often preclude satisfactory school-parent relationships?
7. What strategies can be employed to encourage active and productive family involvement with the school?
8. How can families be advised to assist their child in preparing for the eventual transition from school to work and community living?
9. How would you advise families to become actively involved in the Life-Centered Career Education (LCCE) Mild/Moderate Curriculum approach?
10. As an educator, what would you do to encourage family involvement in the LCCE Mild/Moderate Curriculum approach and/or any other functional skills/transitional curriculum effort?

OVERVIEW

The Individuals with Disabilities Education Act (IDEA) of 1990 (P.L. 101-476) was written and structured to ensure parental and family involvement in the educational planning and decision-making process for their son, daughter, or family member. Cutler summarized IDEA 1990 as "a declaration of your child's *educational rights and of your rights as a parent to par-* *ticipate in the educational process"* (1993, p. 3, italics added) when describing the special education process to parents. According to IDEA 1990, parents and professionals are equal partners in the Individualized Education Plan (IEP) process. Although this does not mean that all participants hold equal knowledge of educational terms or procedures, it does mean that all are to share equal status in decision making. Additionally, students with special learning and/or behavior needs should have an active voice in decisions affecting their educational programs.

IDEA 1990 assigns numerous responsibilities to family members by providing procedural safeguards that protect their rights in the planning and decision-making process. The 1990 act uses the term *parent* when referring to the student's biological parent, guardian, surrogate parent (when the child is a ward of the state), or a person acting as the parent of a child, such as a grandparent. The law requires that parents be provided access to educational records regarding their family member and be notified in advance of planning, evaluation, and placement meetings, and it provides due process procedures when decisions are reached that violate these requirements or that do not adequately solicit the involvement of parents.

Resultant court decisions and additional authorized mandates have clarified and strengthened parents' rights and placed a greater emphasis on the importance of the involvement and collaboration with the whole family. The Individuals with Disabilities Education Act (IDEA) Amendments (P.L. 105-17) in 1997 brought many additional changes to P.L. 94-142 regarding a stronger mandate for parent participation in several old and new provisions. Additionally, Part H and Section 619 now use the term *families* rather than parents, which gives greater emphasis to the term *collaboration* among families, schools, and agencies. A new IDEA 1997 provision included the voluntary and more collaborative process of mediation. Mediation can be used to resolve parent-school controversies related to eligibility and placement decisions. IDEA 1997 strengthened the involvement of parents/families in all decision-making affecting students with special learning and/or behavior needs (National Information Center for Children and Youth with Disabilities, 1997).

These safeguards are in place to enable parents/ families to become equal partners in the education process. They are typically viewed as a list of rights, but rights and responsibilities go hand in hand. Parents should prepare for meetings by reviewing their child's past education records, developing goals and objectives based on what they see as needed, and talking with teachers and other personnel about the meeting (before, during, and after). Their participation in the meeting should be equally reciprocal, with all parties, professionals, family members, adult service providers, and the student working together collaboratively to design and implement the most appropriate educational program that best meets the unique learning and/or behavior needs of the student.

Unfortunately, the involvement of families in the educational planning process is too often limited by one or more parties, and the relationship among families/professionals sometimes becomes adversarial instead of collaborative, and possibly a problem instead of a partnership. This chapter discusses family involvement in educational planning, emphasizing the important role of families, particularly parents, to ensure a successful transition from adolescence to adulthood for students with special learning and/or behavior needs and students who are at risk for school failure. The discussion begins with a historical overview of perceptions society held for persons with special learning and/or behavior needs. This section will be followed by a review of twentieth century family involvement in education that addresses barriers to and strategies for effective communication between families and professionals. The chapter concludes with specific strategies for involving families through the LCCE Mild/Moderate Curriculum approaches.

HISTORICAL PERCEPTIONS OF PERSONS WITH SPECIAL LEARNING AND/OR BEHAVIOR NEEDS

Many professionals believe that the medical and educational models of disabilities have led to limited expectations for students with special learning and/or behavior needs. There have been other, equally debilitating, perceptions of people with special learning and/or behavior needs throughout history. In the late 1800s and early 1900s, people with special learning and/or behavior needs were viewed as menaces and linked with crime, poverty, promiscuity, and the decline of civilization or construed as objects to be feared or dreaded. They were seen as subhuman (e.g., vegetable or animal-like) and were objects of ridicule. This was reflected in the language used about people with mental retardation. For example, derogatory labels describing the levels of severity of mental retardation (idiot, imbecile, and moron) were used as insults.

As societal understanding of disability progressed, these negative stereotypes were replaced by fewer pejoratives but no less damaging perceptions. People and students with special learning and/or behavior needs were viewed as objects to be pitied, worthy of charity. Many people with special learning and/or behavior needs were perceived as "holy innocents" (e.g., special messengers, children of God, etc.) and thus incapable of sin and not responsible for their own actions. This perception was slowly edged out by the perception of people with special learning and/or behavior needs as "eternal children." Particularly for people with mental retardation, this perception was influenced by testing that deified "mental age." Many adults with special learning and/or behavior needs were excluded from adult roles because they were said to have "the mind of 3-year-olds." Educational classifications of disability also created unfair stereotypes. Students with mental retardation are labeled as trainable or educable. Society hardly expected a "trainable" student to hold adult roles such as spouse or employee or participant in community recreational/leisure experiences.

Most professionals now do not retain perceptions of disability that reflect beliefs held in earlier centuries. However, vestiges of the latter perceptions remain and impact how people interact with individuals with disabilities, what is expected of them, and what opportunities are made available. Adults with "the mind of a 3-year-old" are not expected to hold a job. "Holy innocents" cannot learn about human sexuality and social relationships. Recipients of pity and charity are to be helped and not accepted

CHAPTER OUTLOOK

Sharon Davis is the Director, Professional and Family Services at The Arc of the United States. Dr. Davis received her doctorate in Educational Administration from Cornell University after teaching in public schools in New York State. She has worked in areas of vocational education, students with disabilities, and in a variety of areas affecting people with intellectual and developmental disabilities and their families, including future planning for the person with a disablity.

As a parent of an adult daughter with a disability who has finally made a successful transition from school to employment and independent living in the community, and as a professional in a disability field, I have a dual perspective on issues faced by both parents and professionals as they consider the futures of individuals with disabilities. I am particularly concerned about the generally dismal employment picture for people with disabilities. We know that people with all levels of disability are capable of competitive employment when they obtain a job based on their abilities and are provided appropriate support to learn and maintain the job. Yet, the National Longitudinal Transition Study (Wagner et al., 1992) found that only 43% of youth with disabilities were employed full time three years after school. Few were earning wages sufficient to support themselves independently. Employment is the key to adults living fulfilling lives and being contributing citizens to their communities.

Professionals often blame parents for such high unemployment rates. Parents are said to have low expectations for their child's employment, to worry that if they go to work, their sons and daughters will lose government entitlements that provide subsistence and health coverage, and to prefer that their children work in a protected, sheltered envi-

ronment. On the other hand, some professionals believe that parents have unrealistic views of what their son or daughter can accomplish in the workplace and expect them to be happy with whatever menial job is provided.

I believe that, on the whole, parents are simply facing reality. In too many instances, their children are not provided the functional skills necessary to live and work in the community, such as those provided by the comprehensive LCCE. Many students with disabilities do not participate in vocational education to learn specific job skills and do not have opportunities to work in real jobs during their school years, experiences that lead to higher employment rates for youth after leaving school.

Youth with disabilities leave school, and families learn there is no entitlement to services. They may have difficulty finding an agency to guide them through the adult service system, as the school guided them through their child's education years. Parents may be totally unfamiliar with the vocational rehabilitation system. There may be no agency in their community to which they can turn to obtain help for their son or daughter in finding a job and to provide job support services. Parents are often left on their own. If the children manage to obtain the typical fast-food job, they find unpredictable, part-time hours, low wages, no benefits, and no public transportation. Even the paratransit system may not accommodate erratic work schedules, night and weekend hours. Parents provide the transportation if they can. Often, parents end up with two choices: Their sons or daughters sit at home with no meaningful activities, or they get in the van and go to the sheltered employment settings.

Schools can have a major influence on changing this situation. In fact, I believe the younger generation of parents will demand more of the schools. Many are requesting their children receive an inclusive education alongside children without disabilities. They need and want to be active partners with the school in planning and implementing their children's IEP. Educators need to help them create a vision for their children's future as citizens in their community, living, working, and participating in the community's leisure life. Transition planning should begin early for each student and should focus on the in-dividual's interests, abilities, and life choices. Schools must provide options for vocational education and real job experiences for students with disabilities before they leave school. Educators can play a major role in helping parents provide experiences to help their sons and daughters achieve independent lives in the future while being realistic in addressing barriers. The LCCE curriculum is a tool that can help schools reach this goal.

as colleagues, friends, or neighbors. In a very real sense, perhaps the most important change occurring is how educators, specifically, and the general public have a more positive view of persons with special learning and/or behavior needs.

People with special learning and/or behavior needs have emphasized one factor as critically important in changing attitudes and perceptions: People with disabilities are people first. By focusing on the person and not the condition, one can talk about hopes, dreams, abilities, and strengths. IDEA 1990, the 1992 Rehabilitation Act Amendments, and the 1993 Developmental Disabilities Act Amendments all contain language that embodies the way in which individuals with special learning and/or behavior needs must be perceived. All acts state that disability is a natural part of human experience and in no way diminishes the rights of individuals to live independently, enjoy self-determination, make choices, contribute to society, pursue meaningful careers, and enjoy full inclusion and integration in the economic, political, social, cultural, and educational mainstream of American society. [Sec. 2(a)(3)(A–F)]

Disability is seen not as aberrant, outside the norm, or pathological, but as a part of being human. All human abilities and experiences exist on a continuum, and disability is a part of that continuum, not off of it.

Viewing people with special learning and/or behavior needs inside this continuum allows us to apply new labels to people with special learning and/or behavior needs: neighbor, colleague, home owner, card collector, baseball fan, parent, dancer, dog owner, spouse, leader, role model, and friend. Not all people with special learning and/or behavior needs will, however, actually own a home; not all people without disabilities own homes. Some people with special learning and/or behavior needs will not be good leaders; some people without disabilities are poor leaders. The key is that people with special learning and/or behavior needs are people first, and they have the right to be valued and experience dignity and respect independent of any qualifier others might put on them.

FAMILY INVOLVEMENT IN EDUCATION

For much of the first half of the twentieth century, schools were responsible only for academic content instruction, while families were responsible for emotional and social development instruction (Flaxman & Inger, 1991). Social changes of the 1960s and 1970s, changes in the structure of the family and society, and changing demographics in America have significantly altered the role of schools in society and the role of families regarding school responsibilities (Flaxman & Inger, 1991). Parents/families no longer accept a passive role in educational planning and demand a voice in issues ranging from school budgeting and personnel decisions to curricular decisions and other educationally related areas that have traditionally been assigned to education professionals. Schools no longer teach only basic academic skills to a restricted population of students; now, schools must address complex topics such as prevention of acquired immune deficiency syndrome (AIDS) and human sexuality education or driver's education with students from diverse ethnic and socioeconomic backgrounds who possess widely different learning styles and abilities.

The contemporary notion of parental involvement dates back to the early 1960s, when the passage of federal legislation designed to address societal problems mandated parental involvement in planning and decision making about curriculum, instruction, and school improvement. The Head Start program was among the first to employ such a model, bringing educators and parents of young children together to address both child- and family-related issues (Flaxman & Inger, 1991). Similarly, the Education for All Handicapped Children Act of 1975 and subsequent special education legislative actions mandated such collaboration.

Such legislative intent typically emerges from an advocacy agenda targeting equal access and representation to ensure ongoing fairness and equality. This was the case, for example, for youth with special learning and/or behavior needs. As early as the 1940s, parents of children with special learning and/or behavior needs recognized that their sons and daughters were capable of much more than medical and educational professionals were attributing to them and, through grassroots organizing, began to demonstrate this and to advocate for equal access to appropriate educational services. Once access to educational services was mandated by legislation, families advocated for the provision of appropriate services, expanded opportunities to participate in school life, access to vocational and rehabilitation services, and mainstreaming and integration in all school environments.

Family involvement in this century will undoubtedly take on increased importance. One only has to examine today's headlines to realize that this is true. For example, school choice, where families are allowed to choose the educational setting for their son or daughter, will necessitate increased family involvement. By selecting which school their child will attend, families will wield increased control in determining the appropriateness of educational settings, materials, and instructional methodologies used by professionals. As in most free market systems, those educational settings and personnel that best meet the needs of the consumer and stakeholders (families and students as well as business and industry) will prosper, while those designed to meet the needs of the educational system alone and to perpetuate outdated or irrelevant practices will decline.

The concept of family empowerment is not unique to education. Many federally funded services, for example, vocational rehabilitation and family services, are placing greater emphasis on family and consumer/stakeholder empowerment and are implementing procedures to enable families and individuals with special learning and/or behavior needs to assume greater control in decision making and to advocate and choose services that more adequately meet their needs.

Several other factors suggest that family involvement in education will increase during this century. Flaxman and Inger (1991) identified several basic ways that parents can be involved in schooling. Families can be involved directly with decision making in the schools, as is the case for school choice. Recent trends in site-based management procedures in education essentially require that principals, teachers, and parents come together to manage the school and solve problems unique to that school and community, illustrating a second situation in which parental involvement might be direct.

Another way that parents will be involved in schooling is through parenting training programs and initiatives. Head Start is a good example of educational services that must incorporate parent training and parenting training to be successful. Exemplary early childhood education programs all use parent-training procedures to teach parents to assume responsibilities traditionally held by professionals. Families may essentially become paraprofessionals by receiving training to conduct some activities that would otherwise be school directed, such as limited physical or occupational therapy procedures, or by providing repetition and practice in activities important to language, motor, or cognitive development.

Finally, schools are becoming more of a focal point for community-focused activities that have not previously been the domain of education; families and schools will once again find themselves as partners who practice the eight obligations of reliable alliances (Turnbull & Turnbull, 2001). Although many educators disapprove of schools assuming broader responsibility in social issues, the reality is that many public schools have become providers of other direct services, including child care, health, counseling, and referral services. Once again, the face of education has had to change. Schools have undertaken such responsibility for a number of reasons, not the least of which is that research shows that they are educationally beneficial. Adequateness and availability of support services enable families to provide their child with special learning and/or behavior needs a stable home environment that encourages greater development and readiness for learning. As Flaxman and Inger pointed out, "children with fewer physical, emotional, and social problems are easier to teach and deal with in the classroom" (1991, p. 5).

Rationale for Family Involvement

Families must be involved in the educational planning process, and a parent-professional collaboration is established for a number of reasons. Some of these are pragmatic, others more ideological. Sinclair and Christenson (1992), noting that collaboration is an attitude integral to the success of students, speak to the latter when outlining the theoretical underpinnings of a partnership approach in education. These authors propose the following:

- Only through collaboration can real change occur. As illustrated in the prior discussion, schools and professionals alone cannot meet the complex, multiple needs of children in America today. According to Sinclair and Christenson: "The sheer number of at-risk children, problem situations and changing demographics of American society dictate a collaborative stance" (p. 12).
- Child development and learning do not occur in a single environment and without influence from multiple sources. "Children learn, grow, and de-velop both at home and at school. There is no clear-cut boundary between home and school experiences for children and youth. Rather, there is a mutually influencing quality between experiences in these two settings" (p. 12).
- The definition of education has expanded with advances in understanding about human learning and/or cognition. Again, according to Sinclair and Christenson, "a learning environment is educative when it enables the individual to learn and develop specialized skills; it is miseducative when it fails to encourage positive human development. The educative community is produced when learning environments of the home and school are linked together and carefully coordinated to serve the developmental needs of the individuals" (p. 12).

The theoretical validity of parent-professional collaborations is based on the recognition that learning and/or education occur each moment of the day and cannot be confined only to educational classrooms during school hours. The role of education is to prepare children and youth to succeed as adults. It is evident that to accomplish this, professionals in education must actively involve families and collaborate with parents to ensure learning opportunities throughout the student's day. In this sense, there must be a positive collaboration between home and school and there must be active family involvement for educators to achieve their stated goals and to succeed in their chosen vocation. This theoretical stance has been substantiated by research that documents that family participation in the educational process results in more positive educational outcomes for students with special learning and/or behavior needs, including better school attendance, reduced dropout rates, enhanced student self-esteem and confidence, and improved educational achievement scores (Flaxman & Inger, 1991). Sinclair and Christenson (1992) summarized the primary effects of family involvement as follows:

- "All forms of parent involvement strategies seem to be useful; however those that are meaningful, well-planned, comprehensive, and long lasting offer more options for parents to be involved and appear to be more effective. Student achievement is greater with meaningful and high levels of involvement.

- "Parent involvement affects noncognitive behavior; student attendance, attitudes about school, maturation, self-concept, and behavior improve when parents are involved.
- "There are benefits for parents, teachers, communities, and schools when parents are involved. In general, there are more successful educational programs and effective schools.
- "Student achievement gains are most significant and long lasting when parent involvement is begun at an early age" (p. 13).

There are pragmatic reasons to create strong family involvement/alliance in educational planning and decision making for youth with disabilities. Among the foremost is that IDEA 1997 requires this involvement. However, numerous other reasons illustrate why educators who are committed to providing the best possible education for learners at risk for school failure and students with special learning and/or behavior needs involve families in a meaningful manner and would do so even if there was no legal mandate.

As described earlier, human development and learning cannot be compartmentalized as occurring only in restricted environments. Children learn across multiple environments, and learning in one ecological environment has an impact on learning in all other ecological environments. For teachers to succeed, home environments and families must be conducive to learning and/or development. This recognition has driven the changing role of schools in our society, and it should be this factor that compels educators to establish effective, truly collaborative partnerships and alliances with families.

For students with special learning and/or behavior needs, there are other pragmatic reasons to involve families. Only two parties in any given IEP or transition planning meeting will be members of every meeting for the student: the student with special learning and/or behavior needs and family members. Teachers, administrators, related service personnel, and adult service providers all will change from year to year and school to school. In our increasingly mobile society, families can help maintain continuity by providing information about students with special learning and/or behavior needs' previous educational experiences and placements, their learning successes, and school failures. This is important even when educational records are available that document the same time span (which is frequently not the case). Examined alone, without the benefit of meeting with and talking to students and their families, educational documents such as diagnostic and placement information, family, medical and psychological histories, even past IEPs, become a litany of disability, disease, and disorder. They accentuate problems, focus on weaknesses, and set expectations for failure. Few educational records contain the families' hopes and aspirations for the student with special learning and/or behavior needs or the students with special learning and/or behavior needs' dreams and interests. Few educational records capture the "other" side of the story: the family's struggle to secure adequate services, to be recognized as an equal and participating partner, along with the student with special learning and/or behavior needs' participation.

Families are a repository of information about the student with special learning and/or behavior needs, his/her strengths and abilities, likes and dislikes, interests, limitations, and idiosyncrasies. They can tell you how a student with special learning and/or behavior needs spends his/her spare time, his/her hobbies and interests, and whether she/he has ever maintained a checkbook or has access to a computer at home. The student's sibling can tell you how many friends she/he has in the neighborhood. Parents and family members can tell you whether the student with special learning and/or behavior needs can cook a simple meal, has ever interviewed for a job, or reads the paper daily. There are not enough checklists available to encompass the amount of information to be gained from family members—information critical to education, and more importantly, adult success at living and working in the community.

This information becomes particularly important to the transition planning process. The 1997 amendments to Public Law (PL) 94-142 (IDEA) mandate that during the IEP meeting for students 14 and older, transition needs must be addressed and as appropriate that transition-related goals and objectives are included. Transition services are defined in the act as "a coordinated set of activities for a student, designed within an outcome-oriented process which promotes movement from school to post school activities" [Sec. 602(a)(19)]. Post-school activities are broadly defined and include postsecondary education, vocational training, integrated and supported employment, continuing and adult education, adult services, independent living, or community participation. The law also requires that the "coordinated set of activities shall be based upon the individual student's needs, taking into account the student's preferences and interests, and shall include instruction, community experiences, the development of employment and other post-school adult living objectives, and when appropriate, acquisition of daily living skills, and functional vocational evaluation" [Sec. 602(a)(19)].

These requirements take into account the critical importance of families and, when viewed in conjunction with language in the law mandating parental involvement, serve to broaden the focus on family involvement to include the student with special learning and/or behavior needs. To achieve outcome-oriented transition goals, educators need to tap resources available through families. Only the students with special learning and/or behavior needs and their families can, indeed have the right to, make decisions about where the students with special learning and/or behavior needs live and work as adults. Educators bring expertise on how to learn skills that lead to these outcomes. Adult service providers hold knowledge about systems that support these outcomes. It is, however, the right of all individuals in our society to make choices and decisions about their lives, and the presence of a disabling condition does not abrogate that right on an *a priori* basis.

Finally, families and students with special learning and/or behavior needs must be equal partners in decision-making because, quite frankly, they have the most to gain or lose from the educational process. When youth with special learning and/or behavior needs leave school to unemployment or jobs that do not provide sufficient wages to support independent living, it is the family that typically provides a home.

If youth with special learning and/or behavior needs leave school without a job and with no opportunity for postsecondary education, it is the family that finds them employment. Several studies examining adult outcomes for youth with special learning and/or behavior needs confirm that families become, in essence, the student's case manager. Sitlington, Frank, and Cooper (1989) found that of 648 graduates with learning disabilities, who were out of school for one year and employed, 43% found their jobs themselves and 40% identified families as having found their jobs for them. Only 5% found jobs through a community agency and 6% through school. Of 908 youth with learning disabilities out of school one year, 64% lived with their family. Sitlington, Frank, and Carson (1991) found that three years out of high school, 46% of youth with mental retardation lived with a family member and 31% relied primarily on parents for financial assistance and support. Wehmeyer, Kelchner, and Richards (1993) found that of 408 adults with mental retardation (mean age, 36 years), 35% lived with a parent or relative.

It is apparent that, legal requirements aside, the involvement of families in the educational planning and decision-making process is more than a good idea, it is essential to adult success and, in reality, the success of the educational process. However, there are significant problems in establishing a collaborative relationship between school and home. Parents/family members in attendance frequently feel alienated by the IEP planning process and rarely contribute as equal partners. Gilliam and Coleman (1981) asked IEP committee members to rank committee members on their relative influence during a meeting and their contribution to the meeting. Parents/family members were ranked 8th in influence (after special education teachers, psychologists, special education directors, supervisors and consultants, regular education teachers, and guidance counselors) and 10th in actual contributions (behind all of the above as well as principals and speech therapists).

Likewise, educators are often frustrated by the seeming lack of interest from family members. There are a number of reasons for the present circumstances, which are addressed next. There are also solutions to these problems, and these are highlighted subsequently.

Barriers to Effective Family Involvement

Sonnenschein (1981) characterized the parent-professional partnership as an "uneasy relationship," an apt decision in many cases. A partnership is a two-way street, and to understand breakdowns in collaborations between home and school, one needs to examine the actions and beliefs of both parties.

Professionals' Mishandling of Parents

You don't have to speak to many parents of children with disabilities to understand that, when it comes to the educational planning and decision-making process, families feel powerless, pressured, and put-upon. Truth is, the educational planning and decision-making process, historically, has been one in which families are *not* equal partners in planning, and their participation has often been marginalized and neglected. Some factors leading to this outcome are examined next.

Professionals bring to the table biases that influence every decision they make. These biases are often manifested in beliefs about others involved in planning and decision making. Too often, professionals' conceptualizations of parents lead to unequal partnerships. Sonnenschein (1981) identified several such conceptualizations.

Many professionals perceive parents as "vulnerable clients" and view their role in the school-home interaction as one of a helper. Relationships built on these assumptions typically have the professional as the expert, someone who has the answers and, essentially, the power and control to change outcomes for the family. Such relationships do not lend themselves to equal partnerships or collaborative efforts. A related perception, according to Sonnenschein (1981), is that of parents as "patients." Historically, the birth of a child with a disability has been viewed as an event precipitating a grieving and acceptance process, much as that described when coping with the death of a loved one. Parents are labeled as being at one point or another in this acceptance continuum and often are seen as not coping well or experiencing stress or anx-

iety as a result of their inability to come to terms with their child's special learning and/or behavior needs. This leads to perceptions that family members, themselves, need remediation and attention. Once again, a relationship based on these assumptions does not lend itself to effective collaboration. The truth of the matter, however, is that coping with the birth of a child with special learning and/or behavior needs differs widely from family to family and is best described by the individual family's coping strategies and abilities than by some global strategy.

Singer and Powers (1993) summarized the problems with these first two types of relationships when describing the tenets of traditional models of caring for families. One such tenet has been that family support is oriented toward professional control and the fitting of families into programs. The assumption is that special expertise is required to assist troubled families and that families should turn over decision making to professionals and program administrators. A second tenet is that "families are necessarily pathological because of the burden imposed by raising a child with a disability" (Singer & Powers, 1993, p. 4). Accordingly:

> This orientation stresses family problems and uses language derived from medicine in which pathology, treatment, cure, and prescription are common terms. It is assumed that parents require training, need assistance to learn how to raise their children and, invariably, are distressed. (Singer & Powers, 1993, p. 5)

Yet another common perception of families is one of blaming the family for the child's special learning and/or behavior condition. Turnbull and Turnbull experienced this, stating that professionals they were dealing with never "came right out and said, 'You caused it,' but everything they did was based on that premise" (1978, p. 42). Early theories regarding the cause of certain disabilities, most noticeably autism, explicitly blamed parents (usually mothers) for their child's condition. There is often an underlying assumption by professionals that the parent is somehow to blame for the student's special learning and/or behavior needs. Whether this perception is grounded in fact, and is indeed true, or simply part of the mythology of special education professionals, its impact on creating partnerships is devastating.

The perception that the parent is responsible for the child's special learning and/or behavior needs exists in part because many parents hold feelings of guilt and harbor questions about their own culpability in their child's developmental outcomes. If one is the birth mother of a child with fetal alcohol syndrome, this guilt is probably well founded. If one's child has Down syndrome, it is not. In either case, it is a short distance from parental feelings of guilt to professionals' assumptions of responsibility. In a similar manner, parents frequently are perceived as less observant, intelligent, and perceptive. Part of this emerges from inappropriate assumptions that, because the child with special learning and/or behavior needs has these characteristics, the family does also. Again, views of the parent as responsible or less able stigmatize parents and build barriers to collaboration and partnership. Myths about the family's inability to contribute to the planning and decision-making process are too widely accepted and often are misused to prevent effective collaboration and partnerships. Cutler (1993) lists several such myths:

- Parents are naive laypersons who cannot and should not teach.
- Parents are too emotionally involved to evaluate their children.
- Parents are still obedient school pupils who should be seen and not heard (p. 17).

The roots of the first myth lie in our stereotyped belief of the school's role in society. Many educators, indeed, many people in our society, continue to hold to the view that schools should only teach basic academics (the three R's) and that teaching should be done by experts. This belief, however, contradicts what we know about learning. As described previously, learning and/or development occur every minute of every day, and for education to be most effective, educators must capitalize on this fact. Parents/family members spend the most time with the child with special learning and/or behavior needs and in the long run are their only consistent teacher. Teach-

ers who can effectively involve parents and other family members as teachers (*not* parents as expert educators who replicate what occurs in the classroom) are effective and successful.

The second myth harkens back to perceptions about parents as victims, clients, or patients. The assumption is that until parents "work through" their grief and accept the child's special learning and/or behavior needs (acceptance is implicitly defined as viewing the child as the professional does), they cannot move past the emotional and mental barriers they have erected to contribute in a meaningful manner. Even now, this belief is inaccurate, yet pervasive in our society.

The final myth springs as much from the system as from any particular bias individual educators may hold. School systems are complex bureaucracies that often require "insider" knowledge to navigate. Educators themselves come to accept this as fact in a very short time, but because they are in the system, they can at least somewhat work their way through the maze. Parents/family members are viewed as outsiders to the system, and many educators soon portray parents/family members as naive about the "way things really work," and as such, believe that parents need to let them (the educator, administrator, etc.) work the system for them. Add to this the belief that professionals hold a key to teaching and learning, and it is obvious that parents/family members who try to become active and demand equal treatment are seen as naive and in some ways incapable.

When parents or family members enter the system and attempt to overcome the various barriers to equal partnership, they acquire a reputation and are sometimes seen as a problem and labeled as aggressive or unrealistic, creating yet another barrier to partnerships or reliable alliances. Some parents find that this occurs very early on in their interactions with schools and may adopt an equally strident position, digging in for trench warfare instead of trying to work with schools. The cycle repeats itself, and the home-school relationship is confrontational and, ultimately, destroyed. Although families may eventually obtain at least some of what they want, it is at great cost to the family, educators, and the student with special learning and/or behavior needs. There are no winners in this situation. Many parents come to the conclusion that this process is more harmful than helpful for their child with special learning and/or behavior needs and decide not to fight the system anymore. As a result, they are apt to not advocate for what they want for fear that the resulting environment will become more difficult or stressful for their child with special learning and/or behavior needs.

Not only do professional assumptions about parents and their role in education have an impact on family involvement, but beliefs about children with special learning and/or behavior needs, about their capabilities, and ultimately, about disability in society have an impact on family involvement. Families are frequently stereotyped as being unrealistic about their child with special learning and/or behavior needs' present or future capabilities based at least partially on professionals' beliefs about special learning and/or behavior needs and children with special learning and/or behavior needs. The well-known "self-fulfilling prophecy" is still alive and survives in many educational settings for students with special learning and/or behavior needs. Cutler lists several myths about students with disabilities that impact family involvement:

• These children's disabilities are the source of all problems.
• These children can learn only by rote.
• These children cannot handle a full day. (1993, p. 36)

This list could be expanded with little difficulty. Ultimately, what one expects of children with special learning and/or behavior needs reflects what one believes about disability. Historically, people with disabilities (special learning and/or behavior needs) have been viewed from either a medical model or an educational model. The medical model emphasizes disease and cure, placing the responsibility for treatment in the hands of highly skilled and trained professionals. The educational model places less emphasis on disease and treatment but replaces efforts to cure with efforts to fix disability. Both perspectives view disability as outside the norm. If the norm for society is walking on two legs, people who do not walk and in-

stead use a wheelchair are atypical and seen as needing to be cured or fixed so that they can experience the joy of being normative. In both cases, we lose sight of the person and emphasize the disability (special learning or behavior need). We attribute actions and behaviors to the disability and eventually expect less from people with special learning and/or behavior needs (disabilities). When our expectations are fulfilled, it reinforces our beliefs and compounds and even perpetuates the problem.

Parents' Mishandling of Professionals

Parents or family members raise an equal number of barriers to collaboration. Like educators, parents bring inaccurate perceptions and beliefs to the home-school relationship. Cutler identified three such false beliefs held by many parents:

• Educators are super experts in their field.
• Educators are totally objective.
• Educators are free agents. (1993, p. 29)

As Cutler noted, these myths are the mirror images of the myths about parents. They are, in many ways, as damaging to the family-school relationship/alliance as professionals' beliefs about parents. Specially trained educators have skills that enable them to work with students with special learning and/or behavior needs and to provide answers to difficult problems and situations. They also have a large number of student caseloads, limited planning time, and high demands on their nonteaching time. Many special educators have limited time to collaborate with general educators, which is attributable to the previously mentioned factors. Educators are as constrained by the system as parents are and often equally or more frustrated with the pressures and responsibilities associated with planning and teaching. However, the stereotype of the professional as the expert and holding all knowledge, perpetuated by schools and readily accepted by many parents, places undue burden on teachers and creates unrealistic expectations among parents and family members. These unrealistic expectations are often played out in unreasonable demands on the teachers' time and unfair criticism if the teacher is unable to deliver what parents/family members expect from the teachers.

If parents are viewed as too emotional or unobjective or unrealistic to be useful to the process, educators feel the need to be objective, or at least, educators feel the need to maintain this image. This has been reinforced by the fact that, during their training, almost all educators become familiar with the concept of "professional distance." Some professions, such as counseling, have emphasized distancing and the maintenance of absolute objectivity as necessary for success. In other cases, objectivity has been emphasized to prevent professional burnout or overinvolvement and internalization of the family's problems. In either case, it is unfair to characterize teachers as totally objective, just as it is to characterize parents as always being unobjective. Educators may strive to maintain credibility by distancing themselves from the family at least partially because it is expected of them. Needless to say, partnerships and reliable alliances cannot be formed under these circumstances.

Cutler describes the final false belief about educators held by many parents as the belief that educators are free agents. According to Cutler:

> Many parents ask why, if the school personnel know a program is needed, they don't just set it up. Because it is the school's job to educate all students with special learning and/or behavior needs, parents expect that school personnel will do what is necessary. (1993, pp. 35-36)

What these parents fail to take into account is that far from being a free agent or program developer, teachers and educators are bound to a system that is often slow and unresponsive to change and has limited time, budget, and/or personnel. Teachers are often caught between their empathy and agreement with the family member and the reality that advocating on behalf of the parent/family members may make them perceived as not team players and, in some circumstances, could lead to ostracism, limited career options, and possibly job loss. Additionally, educators may find themselves with conflicts between what they see as their responsibility to the students with special learning and/or behavior needs and their responsibility to the family. When these various responsibilities cause internal conflict, it is little wonder teachers distance themselves from developing effective family-professional partnerships.

Parents and families contribute to barriers to effective collaboration in other ways as well. Many professionals feel thwarted in their attempts to work with families because family members are searching for a professional who will tell them what they want to hear. Typically referred to as "shopping around" and associated with the diagnosis process, it is not unusual for family members (for both good and bad reasons) to disregard as valid one professional's advice or efforts to collaborate because they do not coincide with the family's expectations. This results in family members seeking another professional who more closely meets the family's wishes. If professionals are guilty of bringing biases and expectations to the table, so too are parents and family members likely to disagree with the information or advice provided.

The experience of having a child with special learning and/or behavior needs is one that is frequently associated with perceptions and beliefs that are not conducive to effective partnerships among the professionals and family members. While we eschew the traditional perceptions of parents as detailed previously, we do not wish to dismiss as invalid the range of emotions and feelings that accompany the birth of a child with special learning and/or behavior needs and the impact this experience has on the family system's functioning. The truth is many children with special learning and/or behavior needs require more time and energy on the part of parents and family members than do children without special learning and/or behavior needs. There are truths imbedded in the old notion of the cycle of acceptance of a child's special learning and/or behavior need. Parents feel at various stages of the educational process disillusioned, disappointed, frightened, frustrated, alone, vulnerable, guilty, and as if they have been treated unfairly. They also feel committed, joyful, excited, hopeful, confident, and proud of the accomplishments and achievements made by the student with special learning and/or behavior needs. It would be unfair for professionals to represent one without the other as family members support the family member with special learning and/or behavior needs.

For some parents and siblings, however, the experience of raising and living with a child with special learning and/or behavior needs can become overly stressful. Likewise, some parents and siblings may cope with the child's learning and/or behavior needs by creating unrealistic expectations (either too positive or too negative) or by denying certain limitations. These scenarios, however, are not uncommon to parents and siblings who have a family member with special learning and/or behavior needs. Stress and unrealistic expectations may lead to parents not being honest with themselves or professionals about their feelings and expectations. Parents who are overwhelmed at home may find it difficult to admit to a professional that they do not want or are not, at that time, capable of taking on additional responsibilities such as working with their child with special learning and/or behavior needs at home or participating in multidisciplinary team meetings or other meaningful activities (Cutler, 1993). Parents or family members may feel that their authority or integrity is threatened by professional advice and adopt a "no one is going to tell me what to do" attitude. Finally, parents who experience a great deal of stress may become overreliant on professionals, resulting in unreasonable demands for attention and time. This can cause undue hardships and damage to relationship, partnership, and alliance among family and professionals.

One frequent barrier to family involvement is that, too often, parents and educators approach a problem or an issue from different temporal orientations. Educators tend to be future oriented, looking at what may happen 1, 5, or 10 years later. Parents, often by necessity, must take one day at a time and are not able or willing to look at what is in store for their child. Many educators would like to discuss possible adult living and work options with family members with the notion that these ideas may be reviewed and revised during the annual IEP meeting. Many of us procrastinate when having to consider what may result in negative outcomes. Parents may be fearful of the future, misunderstand possibilities, and as such have little interest in long-term objectives, adopting an attitude that they can confront future issues at a later time. In far too many cases, medical professionals, and sometimes, educational personnel as well, have painted negative outcomes as the only possibilities for their child. Even during the late 1990s, parents were frequently told, at the time of the birth of their child with a special learning and/or behavior need, that institutionalization was the best option they could reasonably consider. This was predicated on the notion that it would be best for all family members. This doom-and-gloom prophecy understandably contributes to parental unwillingness to focus on future outcomes.

Other barriers that contribute to ineffective family involvement are not erected by either the educators or families but instead are legitimate differences. Parents and educators alike may feel certain competitiveness, probably unconsciously, in the collaborative alliance process. Family members feel that, because they know the child best, they are the most effective teachers. Professionals feel that their background and expertise make them the best teachers. Legitimate claims exist on both sides, which illustrates that there is little utility to placing blame or exerting the power play in the breakdown of the home-school collaboration process. It should be evident that home and school need to equally contribute in their collaborative efforts so that the child with special learning and/or behavior needs receives the most appropriate services.

STRATEGIES FOR PARENT-PROFESSIONAL PARTNERSHIPS

To overcome barriers to family involvement, professionals need to recognize that the role of the family in education has changed and will continue to change. The role of the educator must change to accommodate and take advantage of these shifts. McFadden and Burke (1991) identified a new paradigm for human services, including education for this century. This paradigm "envisions a social order wherein most important decisions are made at the local level ... and people are empowered to develop their own solutions to issues affecting their lives" (p. iii). Themes represented in this paradigm are empowerment, leadership, choice, and flexibility. Already, school reform proposals reflect these themes. Within this paradigm, it becomes the responsibility of the professional to increase the participation of family members in the decision-making process. McFadden and Burke stated:

> It is our belief that decisions that affect the quality of life experienced by people with developmental disabilities and their families are best made in consultation with and participation by the consumers themselves [people with disabilities and their families]. (1991, p. iv)

Educators rarely see students and their families as "consumers." The terms *teacher* and *student* connote a relationship far removed from that of a consumer, who dictates by his or her action what services are provided. The teacher-student relationship is more like a parent-child relationship. To move toward a truly collaborative relationship, educators need to incorporate into their multiple identities the role of enabler and to view as their responsibility the empowerment of families and students to assume greater control in educational planning and decision making. By so doing, they will set the stage for more positive adult outcomes for youth with disabilities and for greater success on their part.

Singer and Powers (1993) identified several basic principles of family support that can be applied to empower families to be involved in educational planning and decision making. Practices that empower seek to enhance a sense of community and reliable alliances for families (Turnbull & Turnbull, 2001). Special education has been and continues to be a process by which students and families become separated from the mainstream of the school community. We have set up a separate track for students with special learning and/or behavior needs and in the process have removed families from the mainstream and thereby lessened their involvement in the school community. For example, instead of becoming active with other parents through the Parent Teacher Associations, families of students with special learning and/or behavior needs join the Special Education Parent Teachers Associations (SEPTA). To enhance a sense of community alliance for families of youth with special learning and/or behavior needs, educa-

tors need to emphasize the common needs of all families and work to improve the family's link with the broader community and wider ranges of support. IDEA 1997 refers to this as "knowing families." Turnbull and Turnbull (2001) refer to this as "obligations"—requirements that can create reliable alliances among professionals and families. These reliable alliances can empower the opportunities for partnerships in all ecological environments (school, home, and the community). See Figure 4.1 for the components making up this reliable alliance.

A second tenet of family involvement is to focus more broadly on the family's needs, not just on child-centered personalized concerns. This recognizes that students with special learning and/or behavior needs' success is linked directly to family success. Schools are increasingly becoming the location for community-based family services. Even if such services do not exist, the schools can provide a referral service.

Third, educators must encourage shared responsibility and collaboration. Parents are equal partners by law and must be viewed as such by professionals. As Singer and Powers (1993) elaborated, all families have strengths, and when problems are identified in a family, members can learn to solve these problems if given the opportunity and resources. Practitioners must put aside assumptions and biases and enable family members to experience meaningful control and choice.

Attempts to empower families must recognize and protect the integrity of the family unit. Turnbull and Turnbull's (2001) concept "knowing families" is one approach to focusing on professionals and families that can help strengthen the partnerships in both the family and the school. America is a pluralistic, diverse society, and educators must respect cultural beliefs and differences within the family units of students with special learning and/or behavior needs. Singer and Powers (1993) also pointed out that professionals must respect family boundaries and privacy to the greatest degree possible. Many special educators at least imply that the home environment should replicate the school environment. For example, a teacher may have families give their child a work sheet. Instead, activities in the home must be configured

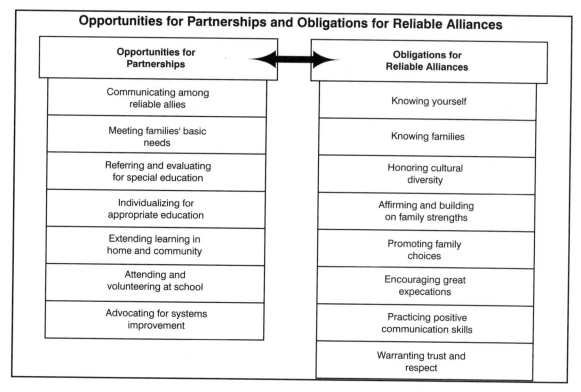

FIGURE 4.1   Opportunities for Partnerships and Obligations for Reliable Alliances
Source: From *Families, Professionals, and Exceptionality: Collaborating for Empowerment* (p. 34) by A. P. Turnbull & H. R. Turnbull, 2001, Upper Saddle River, NJ: Merrill/Prentice Hall. Copyright © 2001 by Pearson Education, Inc. Reprinted with permission.

within the flow of the natural routine. Many developmentally and educationally valuable opportunities are in the home, and families can be guided to use these as learning experiences (some specific to the LCCE Mild/Moderate Curriculum are provided later). Brolin (1997) reports that a key component of the LCCE Mild/Moderate Curriculum approach is the alliance between special educators and family. The LCCE Mild/Moderate Curriculum approach includes a major home component in the development of career education/transitional skills needed by students with special learning and/or behavior needs to transition into successful adult living and working in the community.

If educators act on the premise that their efforts are to empower families and place value on individuals with special learning and/or behavior needs as people first, it is likely that the battle is won. Such at-

titudes will manifest themselves in changes in behavior and action. Flaxman and Inger (1991) provided some pragmatic suggestions for school practices that encourage family involvement and reflect the orientation described:

• Increase the awareness and sensitivity of school staff to parents' time constraints; announce meetings long enough in advance to allow parents to arrange to attend.
• Give parents blanket permission to visit the school at all times—to visit the classroom, use the library, or talk to the teachers or administrators.
• Establish or support family learning centers in schools, storefronts, and churches and offer help to parents who want to help their children learn.
• Make the school facilities available to a variety of community activities.

- Facilitate teen-, single-, working- and custodial-parent peer support groups.
- Provide before-school childcare so that working parents can see teachers before going to work.
- Conduct evening meetings, with childcare, so that working parents can attend.
- Conduct evening assemblies to recognize students and parents for their contributions to the school.
- Establish bilingual hotlines for parents.
- Send messages in the family's language not only on routine notices but also on things parents can do at home to help educate their children.
- Do not make last-minute school cancellations.
- Print all signs in the languages spoken by school families (p. 6).

Sonnenschein (1981) pointed out that if educators assume that all parents have strengths and view parents as partners of the reliable alliance, they will quickly build a relationship based on mutual trust and respect. She identifies the following visible indicators of such a relationship:

- Information, impressions, and evaluations are promptly and openly shared.
- Collaborators are able to communicate their feelings, needs, and priorities without worrying about being labeled in a derogatory way.
- Collaborators can ask each other for help without being made to feel weak or incompetent and are able to say "I don't know" or "I don't understand" without fearing the loss of respect or credibility.
- Efforts are made to avoid the use of jargon or any practice that tends to make the other feel like an outsider. Careful attention is given to the implementation of procedures that encourage dialogue and equal sense of control (p. 65).

Sinclair and Christenson (1992) echo these indicators in identifying five key elements of effective and respectful parent-professional reliable alliances: (1) mutual respect for skills and knowledge; (2) honest and clear communication; (3) two-way sharing of information; (4) mutually agreed-upon goals; and (5) shared planning and decision making (p. 12). Like many others, these authors emphasize communication as the first step in collaboration.

FAMILY CONCERNS IN TRANSITION PLANNING

We have already identified that the families of students at risk for school failure or of students with special learning and/or behavior needs have (with the exception of the student) the most to gain and the most to lose from transition from school to adulthood. Although greater numbers of adult children are living at home with their parents than ever before, these rates for young adults with disabilities exceed national averages. Young adults with special learning and/or behavior needs generally remain unemployed or underemployed, dependent on family members for living expenses and arrangements, and are socially isolated. Most families share one primary concern in transition planning: that their child be enabled to live as independently as possible.

Many families may feel unsure about their role in transition planning. They are uncertain of the options available after their child leaves the public schools and, in many cases, have avoided thinking about this outcome. Previously, they had only educators to deal with in planning and decision making, now adult service providers, vocational rehabilitation counselors, and others must be involved in the transition planning process. The "insider" knowledge about how to work the educational system does not transfer directly to these other systems, and parents feel as if they must start again. They are frequently surprised to learn that, on graduation, no entitlement programs guarantee work or independent living. For these and many other reasons, the transition period may be more stressful and anxiety provoking, not to mention confusing, than when the adolescent was a young child with special learning and/or behavior needs.

Educators can do much to ease these concerns and facilitate effective parental and family involvement in transition. They can explain the concept of transition and transition services to parents, make them aware of mandates in IDEA 1990 and IDEA 1997, and provide families the knowledge to move forward into the planning process without stumbling over gaps in communication. Teachers can make parents aware of the transition and community-based activities that their child with special learning and/or behavior needs is experiencing in school. By presenting positive options and the image of the student with special learning and/or behavior needs as a capable employee or community participant, teachers can create a framework that allows parents to move beyond previously held stereotypes or expectations. Transition-related goals and objectives should be a part of students with special learning and/or behavior needs' educational programs from elementary school onward, but during adolescence, these become particularly important (and mandated by law). Families who have had experience with transition goal setting throughout their child with special learning and/or behavior needs educational program will be more willing and able to participate in transition planning during adolescence.

It is important to assist families to help their child with special learning and/or behavior needs develop positive work habits and behaviors, self-determination skills, and the self-confidence to succeed. Again, this is not something educators can do for families. Educators must be alliance enablers and must provide families the support and information necessary to accomplish this on their own. Davis and Wehmeyer (1991) suggested the following 10 steps for families to promote independence and self-determination, and educators could provide information such as this to parents:

1. Walk the tightrope between protection and independence. Allow your child to explore her/his world.
2. Children need to learn that what they say or do is important and can influence others. This involves allowing risk taking and exploration.
3. Self-worth and self-confidence are critical factors in the development of self-determination. Model your own sense of positive self-esteem to your child.
4. Don't run away from questions from your child about differences related to her/his disability. That does not mean, however, focusing on the negative side of the condition. Stress that everyone is an in-

dividual, encourage your child's unique abilities, and help him/her accept unavoidable limitations.
5. Recognize the process of reaching goals; don't just emphasize outcomes.
6. Schedule opportunities for interactions with children of different ages and backgrounds.
7. Set realistic but ambitious expectations.
8. Allow your child to take responsibility for his/her own actions—successes and failures.
9. Don't leave choice-making opportunities to chance.
10. Provide honest, positive feedback. Focus on the behavior or task that needs to be changed.

In some circumstances, it becomes difficult, if not impossible, for educators to provide information such as this without seeming judgmental or arrogant. In those circumstances, it is probably wise for the educator to serve as a referral agent and connect the family with support and advocacy groups. Most of these organizations consist of parents and family members who have experiences similar to that of the family and who can provide information without posing as an expert. The federal government funds Parent and Training Information Centers in every state that provide multiple information and support services. Disability-specific support and advocacy groups, such as the Arc, have state and local chapters around the country that run support groups and provide information and referral services. The transition period may consist of networking with other families, which provides valuable connections and information.

STRATEGIES FOR INVOLVING FAMILIES IN LCCE

The LCCE Mild/Moderate Curriculum was conceptualized to include the family as an integral part of the educational planning and decision-making process, as well as to include families in activities that augment school- and community-based lessons and activities. One of the features of the LCCE Mild/Moderate Curriculum is that it requires the school to work more closely with the family and community resources. The majority of learning occurs outside school. Career education/transitional programming promotes a partnership and alliance between parents and community resources whereby what is deemed important to learn about the world of work is taught beyond the confines of the school environment. In the process, parents and community members can become more aware and supportive of the school's program and objectives (Brolin, 1993a, p. 5).

Because the LCCE Mild/Moderate Curriculum focuses on career education/transitional programming and addresses the totality of the student's future and avocational needs, it is critically important that practitioners using the LCCE Mild/Moderate Curriculum secure active involvement from families based on a strong school-home partnership. Loyd and Brolin emphasized that:

> The LCCE Mild/Moderate Curriculum Program should encourage parents to get involved in the career development of their sons and daughters. Parents/family members are role models and provide an awareness of the responsibilities related to work. They can be responsible for teaching basic life skills and attitudes through both modeling and actual home and community training. They play the initial role in the career development process through the establishment of the life skills and attitudes. The collaborative efforts of the school and parents/family members should be directed toward maximizing the students' career development in school, home and community. (1989, p. 1)

Most of the LCCE Mild/Moderate Curriculum lesson plans for each of the LCCE competencies contain specific home activities that augment the school-based activity. These activities include detailed instructions and needed equipment to assist parents/families in their home-based actions. Additionally, however, the LCCE Mild/Moderate Curriculum process is most effective if practitioners go beyond implementing just the home activities. The LCCE competencies and subcompetencies address specific behavioral and attitudinal areas involved in career education that are critical for a successful transition from school to work and community living. These skills and competencies can serve as the

basis for establishing a dialogue between school and home. Families who understand that they are working on practical activities with their child with special learning and/or behavior needs that have practical, beneficial outcomes will be more likely to participate. As discussed earlier, however, this must be a two-way dialogue.

When family members understand the applicability of the home-based activities and feel empowered as part of the decision-making team, they can initiate activities that meet needs identified in the LCCE Mild/Moderate Curriculum but go beyond the scripted lesson plans by taking these critical objectives into other ecological environments. Teachers could provide families ideas such as the following as a starting point for how they can become actively involved in the LCCE Mild/Moderate Curriculum process:

- With younger children with special learning and/or behavior needs, encourage the development of gross and fine motor activities by providing frequent opportunities for physical exercise or motor-oriented activities around the house. This should include fine motor activities involved with preferred leisure and spare-time activities.
- Provide opportunities for students to engage in hands-on experiences with activities that give students a concept of certain work-related activities. This may include working with family members on household repair and maintenance activities that incorporate common tools. This also may include using a computer at home and participating in financial planning and decision-making activities.
- Assign specific jobs to the student. These duties should be completed to specifications and within a certain time frame. A second level of expectation is related to the student's development of a plan of action to complete the job. This plan may include following a routine, maintaining a schedule, and returning tools or utensils to specified locations.
- Identify jobs performed by various workers in the community. Visit job sites and discuss them in detail at home. Actively involve the student in these

discussions and observations. Such discussions help the student to express personal observations and ask questions about work. They also help build work values, interests, and long-term aspirations.

- Discuss the work of family members, necessary training, difficulties, and rewards. If possible, arrange a visit to the parents' work site or facility. This will add to the student's knowledge and perception of the family's role in the community.

- Provide a variety of family projects and activities, such as camping trips, sports events, travel, and church events so the student can build leisure, recreation, and social skills. These family projects and outings also provide students with disabilities with an opportunity to communicate ideas and feelings. These types of communications are important in helping students build positive concepts of themselves and their various roles in society.

- Insist that students make their own decisions. Reinforce the process of making decisions, including investigating alternatives and consequences. Problem-solving and decision-making abilities are essential to the development of self-determination and autonomy and emerge from experiences with choice and decision making in the home.

- Help students to feel psychologically secure by providing reinforcement for success and by providing opportunities to contribute in family decision making. Evaluation should be honest but not focused on the student; instead, on the task. If a student is unsuccessful, positive feedback regarding how to correct this and support to ensure success are effective learning tools.

- Work closely with school personnel to achieve educational goals and objectives that are tied to adult outcomes. Several classroom activities are richly supported by the cooperation of the family. For example, teachers often use classroom activities to teach students about their parents' occupations. The activities may include role-playing, child-parent interviews, and class field trips to the parents' workplace. The class functions also support the family's attempt to build personal skills such as communication and problem solving.

- Help school personnel develop community experiences that will expand curriculum opportunities, such as field trips, guest speakers, and work experience.

- Encourage part-time work experiences, community projects, and hobbies that expose the student to various people and their careers.

- Become involved in school advisory committees concerned with curriculum, development of resources, and other transition/career education matters.

What many teachers realize is that parents and family members can effect change in the schools when teachers cannot. Family members can serve as the teacher's greatest advocate to implement functional, community-referenced programs such as the LCCE Mild/Moderate Curriculum and to ensure that adequate resources are devoted to this effort. Likewise, home and school cooperation can make up for limitations in the teacher's activities. For example, because of financial constraints, schools may limit the number of community experiences per year. However, under the direction of the classroom teacher, parents can include their child in family outings to centers of work activity.

The use of the competencies in the IEP and for transition planning provides a sound basis on which professionals and parents/families can meet to exchange opinions and form plans/alliances. Parents may not be able to initiate measures within the home that prepare their child with special learning and/or behavior needs in all of the 22 competencies, but they should be able to better understand the direction of the school program and identify competency areas that can be implemented immediately within the home. The students with special learning and/or behavior needs' attainment of the 22 competencies can be a reference point for teacher-parent interactions related to transition planning. This enables teachers and families to begin the planning process with a common understanding of what skills are necessary for transition and what it will take to complete this process. Kokaska and Brolin (1985) listed several suggestions related to conducting, planning, and evaluating activities around the LCCE competencies:

- Evaluate the student's current status relative to the competencies to be achieved during the school year. This is standard practice in educational settings but is more difficult at home. Families cannot be expected to observe and record progress on activities in the same way teachers observe and record. Families can provide feedback to teachers regarding their child with special learning and/or behavior needs' progress on home activities related to the competencies. This might be accomplished through written notes or a daily log that is passed from the school to the home.

- Involve as many family members as possible in the planning and progress of activities designed to educate students with special learning and/or behavior needs in the competencies. Many of the experiences of students of with special learning and/or behavior needs' experiences with competencies in the daily living skills and personal social skills can involve peers and siblings or other relatives. This procedure ensures the greatest number of "teachers" available in the educational program. One must be cautious, however, not to unfairly place siblings, cousins, or other relatives and peers in a structured, systematized role of "teacher," taking away from the role of friend, playmate, and caretaker. Again, family involvement in instructional activities needs to follow the natural flow of the family's environment and not impose roles such as "teacher" on family members.

- Emphasize the importance of transition/career development as a process that extends from childhood through adult years. Parents of younger children will have difficulty visualizing farther down the road, nor should they be forced to do so. Few families of toddlers without disabilities have plans for their adult years. However, by continuing to focus on transition/career development with its stages of acquisition, families can move through similar stages of awareness related to their child with special learning and/or behavior needs.

- Encourage parents to ask questions, make suggestions, voice opinions, and contribute goals. The greater the parental involvement in LCCE Curriculum planning, the more the student with special learning and/or behavior needs will gain from the process.

- Be open and straightforward with families in the planning process. This does not mean being brutally honest or unfairly pessimistic. Educators need to recognize their biases and how they impact expectations for students with special learning and/or behavior needs within the LCCE Mild/Moderate Curriculum approach. Collaborations are built on trust and mutual respect, and these are only built when communication is open-ended.

- Develop a schedule of activities that parents can follow and that coincides with the classroom lessons. The schedule should be specific to the individual student with special learning and/or behavior needs and family situation. This does not mean that you have to send your lesson plans home with the student with special learning and/or behavior needs. The parents' schedule provides them with an estimation of those classroom lessons, daily assignments, or exercises that students with special learning and/or behavior needs should complete at home. It also allows families to plan ahead for home activities, identify resources, and prepare activities.

Finally, Loyd and Brolin (1989) provide a list of practical, day-to-day strategies teachers can use to encourage family involvement in LCCE:

- Schedule transition/career development conferences to meet with parents about the educational program. These should be as frequent as necessary, separate from the IEP or transition planning meeting, and can occur outside the school facility if appropriate. This provides parents a forum for providing input to the process that does not include the baggage that mandated planning and placement meetings include.

- Visit the home of students with special learning and/or behavior needs and, if possible, provide instruction in that setting to ensure generalization. At the very least, make it known that you are willing to visit the home and consider it important. Do not push the issue if families are not comfortable.

- Encourage families to make classroom observations and visits when LCCE Mild/Moderate Curriculum activities occur. Leave time following the observation to answer questions, explain teaching techniques, and reinforce the parents' efforts.
- Involve parents in district-wide discussions about transition and career development. Identify community discussions that focus on issues important to the transition process, and attend these with parents.
- Provide more structured workshops for families on the LCCE Curriculum process and program so that parents can get a more comprehensive look at the LCCE. Remember that this should be optional, and parents should not be expected to acquire the same sophistication about the LCCE that teachers hold.
- Host dinners during which child care is provided so that parents can relax and talk informally about the LCCE program, career development, and the transition from school to work and community living.

Loyd and Brolin (1989) also provided examples of parent-family contributions to the LCCE Mild/Moderate Curriculum competencies. The following examples show how the LCCE Mild/Moderate Curriculum competencies can be emphasized and practiced in the home.

Managing Personal Finances

One of the simplest ways the family can assist the student with special learning and/or behavior needs in this competency is to provide experience in identifying money correctly and to allow the student to make purchases and return with the correct change. Depending on the student with special learning and/or behavior needs' ability level, managing a weekly allowance is a possible ongoing activity. These skills and concepts coincide with the competency achieving independence.

Selecting and Managing a Household

Using basic appliances and tools is a subcompetency for which the family often provides direct instruction. Maintaining a home is usually a daily activity in which the student with special learning and/or behavior needs can participate. Modeling will be beneficial, but participation is helpful training for this competency and ultimately leads to the student with special learning and/or behavior needs' becoming self-sufficient.

Caring for Personal Needs

Dressing appropriately, a subcompetency of this competency, can be dealt with directly in the home. Teaching the child with special learning and/or behavior needs this skill does not mean picking out the clothes for him but rather assisting in clothing choices. This competency also encompasses basic hygiene and grooming, which can be fostered in a variety of ways in the home.

Raising Children and Meeting Marriage Responsibilities

These skills entail successfully modeling the responsibilities and life-style of marriage. Parents can emphasize the importance of carrying out these responsibilities.

Buying, Preparing, and Consuming Food

Because this competency encompasses the selection, purchase, and preparation of food, it can easily be demonstrated, explained, discussed, and practiced continually under direct parent supervision.

Engaging in Civic Activities

This competency includes informing the student with special learning and/or behavior needs of basic laws, rules, and regulations in the local community, taking the student with special learning and/or behavior needs to different organizations, and exposing her or him to a variety of activities in the community. Parental involvement can provide a strong motivation for the student with special learning and/or behavior needs to participate in civic activities.

Pursuing Recreation and Leisure

Parents can familiarize the student with special learning and/or behavior needs with recreational facilities and ways to spend leisure time, engage in recreational and leisure activities with the student with special learning and/or behavior needs, and encourage the student with special learning and/or behavior needs to choose recreation and leisure activities within her budget. Allowing the student with special learning and/or behavior needs to join in planning family vacations or outings can further develop the student's interest in recreation and leisure (Loyd & Brolin, 1989).

These are only a few of the ways families can be involved in providing their child/sibling with special learning and/or behavior needs in the LCCE Mild/Moderate Curriculum competencies and subcompetencies. The possibilities are limited only by the ability and willingness of educators and families to work together to achieve a common goal.

CHAPTER COMMENTARY

In this chapter, we have emphasized the importance of family involvement in educational planning and decision making, transition planning, and the LCCE Mild/Moderate Curriculum process for students at risk for failure and students with special learning and/or behavior needs. The family involvement must reflect changes in education and an understanding of learning in development that have occurred in the last few decades. Educators who want to succeed must empower families and students with special learning and/or behavior needs to take greater control in the educational process. They must work with families to develop collaborations in which family members are truly equal partners. In so doing, many educators will need to examine their beliefs about families and their role in education and about people with special learning and/or behavior needs and their role in society. By adjusting their practices to meet these changes, educators can ensure greater educational success for their students with special learning and/or behavior needs as well as greater vocational satisfaction and success for themselves.

ACTIVITIES

1. Develop a Parent/Family Involvement Plan, outlining the steps you would undertake to meaningfully involve your student with special learning and/or behavior needs' families in your functional curriculum efforts. Compose a compelling set of reasons that will convince most of the parents to become a substantial partner in your educational activities.
2. Assume that your parents are ready and willing to participate in your curricular efforts and that you are implementing LCCE Mild/Moderate Curriculum. Review the competencies in the personal-social or occupational domains, and develop a list of activities that the families could engage in to help their child to learn the competencies in the domain.

CHAPTER 5

Agencies, Organizations, and Informational Resources

PRELIMINARY QUESTIONS

1. Name three federal governmental agencies that are instrumental in promoting career development and transition services, and explain their particular contributions.
2. Identify six or more local community agencies and other resources that you would use to prepare your students for functional skills and transition services.
3. Explain the possible roles of the rehabilitation counselor in providing services to educators and students who are in school and those who have left.
4. How would you go about determining which agencies you need to be involved in with your students and how you would gain their cooperation?
5. What is a rehabilitation facility, and how can it be used by the educational program?
6. What is JTPA, and how can it help students with learning difficulties in their transition/career development?
7. What postsecondary services are available to teach the functional life skills that these students will need to secure satisfactory employment and function independently in their community?
8. What local and professional organizations can help provide information, guidance, and/or direct services for transition/career development needs?
9. Explain the composition of a Community Resource Directory and its use.
10. Identify three particularly useful national information systems or sources that will enhance your transition/career development and transition efforts.

OVERVIEW

One of the major contributions of the career education/transition concept has been the involvement of numerous community agencies and organizations in the career development/transition efforts of the school. In addition to drawing on considerable expertise not readily available in the school setting, there are several particularly significant reasons for involving community agencies and organizations. First, these agencies and organizations have funds, equipment, contacts, and a constituency far beyond the resources of the school. Second, the agencies and organizations can assist in the improvement of the school's curriculum and courses. Third, the agencies and organizations sometimes lend financial support for pressing needs the school encounters in implementing transition/career education. Fourth, the general public's negative attitudes and misconceptions toward individuals with special learning and/or behavior needs will be counteracted as these agencies and organizations become partners in transition/career development efforts.

Numerous civic, professional, and private non-profit organizations and government agencies are located in most middle-sized and large communities. Besides the many local avenues for transition/career development, there are several state and national resources that local personnel should use for additional information, literature, contacts, funding possibilities, and in some cases, direct services.

Educators in the schools cannot expect to teach all of their students with special learning and/or behavior needs all of the functional skills to the level that they will need for living and working successfully in their communities. In the previous chapter, the importance of the family involvement/alliance in the educational process was discussed. This chapter identifies and describes several important resources to assist educators in providing career development/transition experiences and other services for their students. The first section identifies and explains the key federal, state, and local agencies that are available to help educators. A section follows giving suggestions on how to access the agencies that need to be involved for career development/transitional services. The next section identifies and explains some important national, state, and local organizations for career development/transitional assistance. The final section describes some of the major informational systems for obtaining materials and references on career education, functional skills, and transition programming.

CHAPTER OUTLOOK

Dr. Arden Stephens is the Administrative Assistant of Columbia Area Vocational Center, Columbia, Missouri, Public Schools.

When beginning transition planning, the teacher's first and best resource is the student. The student's interests, aptitudes, and needs, translated into adult life goals, provide a vision of the future environment for the student. An understanding of the student and the future environment demands are the basis for determining the resources needed to obtain the goal. In transition planning, parents are the next best resource. When student and parent goals coincide, all involved in planning are working together for the same outcome. It is at this point that the transition planning team can identify the agencies, organizations, and instructional resources necessary for the student to become successful in his or her chosen future environment. Instructional resources include the entire community, of which the school is a part.

Teachers frequently do not have time to develop collaborative relationships with all the agencies and organizations available to students. Most often, these relationships are initiated through the needs of one student. The transition team creates the path to the future environment, and team members (including the student and parents) take responsibility for exploring the necessary resources.

As teachers make contact with agencies and organizations to meet the needs of one student, they build a directory of resources to use in the future. The resources are most often local, including local offices of state agencies such as Vocational Rehabilitation and Mental Health/Developmental Disabilities. As teachers search for resources, they also develop relationships with individuals in agencies and organizations. These relationships are essential to collaborative planning. Once developed, acquisition of the resource for the next student becomes easier. Some school districts publish their own local resource directory. This is helpful to teachers when explaining to students and parents what resources are available. However, to gain access to the service for a student, the relationship between teacher and individual in the agency or organization is instrumental in obtaining timely service.

Transition planning calls for an interdependence of schools, the home, the community, and local agencies and organizations. The search for appropriate services may include national databases, state or national organizations, and networking with experts in various fields. These searches are especially helpful when the transition planning team is unsure of what local resources exist to meet the student's needs. For most students, the transition plan will lead to relationships and a balanced interdependence with individuals in local businesses, agencies, and organizations.

GOVERNMENT AGENCIES

This section will identify and describe some of the major federal, state, and local government agencies that are responsible for the education, career development, and transitional programming of persons with special and learning needs and those who are disadvantaged. The first agencies to be discussed are those at the federal level. Readers should refer to Table 5.1 to get an overall picture of the agencies to be discussed.

TABLE 5.1   Federal Agencies Important to the Career Development of Individuals with Disabilities and Other Learning Difficulties

Agency	U.S. Department/Branch

Office of Special Education and Rehabilitative Services
    Office of Special Education Programs
    Rehabilitation Service Administration
    National Institute of Rehabilitation Research
	Education

Office of Adult and Vocational Education	Education

Administration for Children and Families
    Administration on Developmental Disabilities
    President's Committee on Mental Retardation
	Heath & Human Services

National Council on Disability	Independent Agency
Veterans Administration	Veterans Administration

Federal Agencies

The primary agencies in the U.S. Department of Education that are responsible for the delivery of education and rehabilitative services for persons with special and learning needs are the U.S. Office of Special Education Programs (OSEP) and the Rehabilitation Services Administration (RSA). Both agencies are divisions of the larger Office of Special Education and Rehabilitative Services (OSERS), which also includes the National Institute for Disability and Rehabilitation Research (NIDRR), which stimulates technology efforts and funds research and demonstration projects.

OSERS and its divisions are responsible for implementing the IDEA 1997 and Rehabilitation Act to ensure that special education programs and services are expressly designed to meet the needs and develop the full potentials of students with special and learning needs and that comprehensive rehabilitation service programs reduce human dependency, increase self-reliance, and fully use the productive capabilities of all persons with disabilities. Programs include support to universities for training of teachers, rehabilitation counselors, and other professional personnel; grants for research; financial aid to help state agencies

initiate, expand, and improve their resources; and media services such as captioned films for persons who are deaf or hard of hearing. RSA funds regional offices and state agencies on an established formula to carry out their program of services. One other Department of Education unit, the Office of Vocational and Adult Education (OVAE), administers the vocational education monies that are given to their respective state agencies to conduct programs for students, including those with special and learning needs and those who are disadvantaged.

The Administration on Developmental Disabilities (ADD), under the Administration for Children and Families of the U.S. Department of Health and Human Services, administers formula grants to states for use with individuals who incurred developmental disabilities before the age of 22. This includes about 3 million people with mental retardation, cerebral palsy, epilepsy, and autism. The agency awards grants to university-affiliated programs and to programs of national significance. It also has established state protection and advocacy services for these individuals. According to a report from the Committee on Energy and Commerce (U.S. House of Representatives, 1993), a substantial portion of individuals with developmental disabilities and their families do not have access to appropriate support and services from generic and specialized service systems and remain unserved or underserved. Another division of this agency is the President's Committee on Mental Retardation, which compiles information, conducts studies, promotes research, advises the Administration, and acts as a liaison among federal, state, local, and private agencies concerned with mental retardation.

The National Council on Disability spearheaded the development of the Americans with Disabilities Act (ADA) of 1990.

The National Council on Disability (NCD) is an independent federal agency composed of 15 members appointed by the president of the United States and confirmed by the U.S. Senate. It was established in 1978 as an advisory board within the Department of Education. The Rehabilitation Act Amendments of 1984 transformed the Council into an independent agency. The mission of the NCD is to provide leadership in the identification of emerging issues affecting people with disabilities and in the development and recommendation of disability policy to the president and Congress. Although many government agencies address issues and programs affecting people with special learning and/or behavior needs, the NCD is the only federal agency charged with addressing, analyzing, and making recommendations on issues of public policy that affect people with special learning and/or behavior needs regardless of age, disability type, perceived employment potential, economic need, specific functional ability, status as a veteran, or other individual circumstance.

Some recent examples of the NCD's activities are conducting hearings, forums, and conferences on such topics as assistive technology, ADA research, rural and Native American issues, health insurance, personal assistance services, minorities; testifying before Congress on various disability issues; providing guidance to the President's Committee on Employment of People with Disabilities; and disseminating information to persons with disabilities, their families, the administration, the Congress, and the public.

One final but important federal agency is the Veterans Administration (VA), which offers a broad range of programs, including medical care, rehabilitation, education and training, income support, and other benefits for eligible veterans with disabilities and their dependents. Their vocational rehabilitation service provides evaluation, counseling, training, employment, and other rehabilitation services to veterans with disabilities and many services to surviving dependents, including those with special learning and/or behavior needs. Veterans Administration regional offices and hospitals are situated throughout the country.

State Agencies

It is very important for educators to know about and use the various state agency resources that are available to most communities. Knowledge of these resources must be viewed as a major responsibility so that educators can better ensure the best possible preparation of their students with special learning and/or behavior needs for a successful transition from school to employment, community living, and participation. Because states have different bureaucratic organizational structures, it is impossible to illustrate exactly where and how these agencies are located and administered. This is something that will have to be discovered by the practitioners themselves.

In this section, several agencies that are felt to be the most important ones for educators to interface with while their students with special learning and/or behavior needs are still in school are identified and described. The agencies are Vocational Rehabilitation, including its Supported Employment component; the Bureau for the Blind; Developmental Disabilities; State Employment Services; and Job Training Partnership Act (JTPA) Programs. Although it takes some time to learn about and successfully involve the agencies and other organizations that are responsible for providing services to these individuals, the final result will be well worth the effort. Each of these is discussed next.

Vocational Rehabilitation

State vocational rehabilitation (VR) programs are a partnership between the federal and state governments. Approximately 80% of the funding for these programs comes from federal dollars. The state VR program's function is to provide a planned sequence of individualized services designed to assist persons with special learning and/or behavior needs to reach a vocational goal. To be eligible for these services, the individual (1) must have a physical and/or mental impairment that constitutes or results in a substantial impediment to employment, and (2) must be able to benefit from an employment outcome from vocational rehabilitation services. A list of services available through the VR program is presented in Figure 5.1.

Some of the services listed in Figure 5.1 are at no charge, whereas others depend on the needs and resources of the individual with special learning and/or behavior needs and the agency's policies. Educators need to become familiar with this agencies' resources

---

Vocational counseling and guidance

Vocational assessment

Vocational and other training services

Maintenance for additional costs incurred while participating in rehabilitation

Transportation in connection with the rendering of any vocational rehabilitation service

Services to family members of individuals with disabilities if necessary to the adjustment and rehabilitation of the individual

Interpreter services and note-taking services for individuals who are deaf, and tactile interpreting for individuals who are deaf-blind

Reader services, rehabilitation teaching services, note-taking services, and orientation and mobility services for individuals who are blind

Telecommunications, sensory, and other technological aids and devices

Work-related placement services, including job search assistance, placement assistance, job-retention services, and personal assistance services

Follow-up, follow-along, and specific postemployment services necessary to maintain services

Occupational licenses, tools, equipment, initial stocks, and supplies

Transition services that promote or facilitate the accomplishment of long-term rehabilitation goals and intermediate rehabilitation objectives

On-the-job or other related personal assistance services provided while an individual with a disability is receiving vocational rehabilitation services

Referral and other services designed to assist individuals with disabilities in securing needed services from other agencies through cooperative agreements

Supported employment services for individuals with severe disabilities and for whom competitive employment has not traditionally occurred

Rehabilitation technology services

Other goods and services necessary to render an individual with a disability employable

---

FIGURE 5.1   Services Available from State Vocational Rehabilitation Agencies.

and policies to use them appropriately and to advise their students with special learning and/or behavior needs and parents.

An important change in the 1992 Rehabilitation Act Amendments is that an individual with special learning and/or behavior needs is presumed to be capable of benefiting from VR services unless the state agency can demonstrate by "clear and convincing evidence" that the individual with special learning and/or behavior needs cannot. The state VR agency can no longer find individuals ineligible for their services without an extended evaluation proving the person is not employable. In addition, the phrase "assessment for determining eligibility and VR needs" replaced "evaluation of rehabilitation potential."

With the passage of the Individuals with Disabilities Education Act (IDEA), state VR agencies have an increased role in the transition of students from school to employment.

The need for better coordinated and collaborative services among agencies has been recognized as important to institute for decades. In 1977, a historic "memorandum of understanding" between the federal agency for VR and the then U.S. Office of Education was released as a commitment of the two agencies to pursue methods by which the two delivery systems could achieve greater cooperation and provide complementary services. The commissioners of the two agencies transmitted memorandums to their state directors, requesting them to seek a coordinated service delivery for persons with special learning and/or behavior needs.

In the years after the historic memorandum, some progress has been made in achieving a more cooperative effort. In some states, much closer working relationships evolved, and rehabilitation counselors have become important collaborators while the students with special learning and/or behavior needs are still in the educational program. Unfortunately, many state and/or local rehabilitation agencies, for various reasons, opted to wait to provide services at the time of graduation or thereafter, depending on the students' learning and/or behavior needs.

Rehabilitation counseling is now a related special education service.

The importance of rehabilitation counseling to the special education effort was enhanced in 1990 with the passage of the IDEA legislation, which included it as a related service for students with special learning and/or behavior needs, particularly in relation to transition services. The importance of this legislation is that it permits schools to hire rehabilitation counselors for their transition programs.

Rehabilitation counselors should be involved early in the students with special learning and/or behavior needs' program, as early as the elementary years, in those states where the agency is willing to become involved earlier. These professionals possess a wealth of knowledge about the labor market and the vocational potentials of persons with various disabilities. They can advise parents and educators on various skills and behaviors that should be emphasized during the early years so these children with special learning and/or behavior needs are prepared to benefit from higher-level functional skills and vocational instruction at the secondary level. The counselors are a valuable source of information about community training opportunities and can help unlock closed doors because of their many contacts with employers and other agencies and organizations such as the employment service and rehabilitation facilities. However, as one study in Alabama has uncovered in surveying rehabilitation counselors (Browning & Brechin, 1993), improved coordination, understanding, and cooperation between special education and rehabilitation are needed for students with special learning and/or behavior needs to receive better transition services.

"Supported employment" programs are a boon to the vocational preparation and employment of persons with severe disabilities.

Created in the 1986 Amendments to the Rehabilitation Act, supported employment has become an important thrust for school transition programs. The 1992 Amendments state that those eligible for services are individuals with the most severe disabilities and who, because of the nature and severity of their special learning and/or behavior needs, need intensive supported employment services to enter or retain competitive employment.

Supported employment services include "time-limited" ongoing support services and other appropriate services that the individual needs, such as the following:

- Placement in jobs in an integrated setting for the maximum number of hours possible for the individual with special learning and/or behavior needs
- Intensive on-site job skills training and other training provided by skilled job trainers, co-workers, and other qualified individuals with special learning and behavior needs
- Follow-up services, including regular contact with employers, trainees, parents, guardians, or other representatives of trainees to reinforce and stabilize the job placement

No specific number of hours per week is required for a successful supported employment placement, but rather, placements should be for the maximum number of hours possible based on the unique strengths, resources, interests, concerns, abilities, and capabilities of the individual with special learning and/ or behavior needs.

Bureaus or Commissions for the Blind

The bureaus or commissions for the blind are VR agencies that are either a unit of the larger state VR agency or a separate commission, as is the case in 25 states. The rehabilitation counselors are trained to assist their clients with special learning and/or behavior needs to learn daily living skills, mobility, complete job application forms, and to meet other needs. The agency also funds reader services for college students who are visually impaired.

Developmental Disabilities

Many students in special education can be classified as having developmental disabilities. The federal government has provided funds to cover medical assistance, job training, and social and other services, which are administered by a special state agency. In Missouri, for example, that agency is located in the Developmental Disabilities section of the Department of Mental Health. The state agency's role has changed dramatically over the years and now may include the coordination of Medicaid funding for institutions and community-based waivers and the coordination of state funds earmarked for persons with developmental disabilities, including adult day programs, group home services, sheltered work programs, and the provision of advocacy services. The services provided vary greatly from state to state and community to community. In North Dakota, for example, caseworkers from the agency have worked closely with school personnel providing services for the disabled from age 14 on to help long-range transition services.

The 1990 Amendments to the Developmental Disabilities Assistance and Bill of Rights Act defines a *developmental disability* as a severe, chronic disability of a person 5 years of age or older with the following characteristics:

- Is attributable to a mental or physical impairment or combination of mental and physical impairments
- Is manifested before the person attains age 22
- Is likely to continue indefinitely
- Results in substantial functional limitations in three or more of the following areas: self-care, receptive and expressive language, learning, mobility, self-direction, capacity for independent living, and economic self-sufficiency
- Reflects the person's need for individualized and coordinated special services

Infants from birth to age 5 who have substantial developmental delay or specific congenital or acquired conditions also qualify if there is a high probability of developmental disabilities resulting if services are not provided.

Each state has a Developmental Disabilities Council, which is mandated to promote, through systematic change, capacity building, advocacy, a consumer- and family-centered comprehensive system and a coordinated array of services, supports, and other assistance for individuals with developmental disabilities and their families. This council is often the leading edge in promoting the delivery and coordination of services between education, state agencies, private agencies, and communities.

The state employment service employs a specialist to work specifically with persons who have disabilities or who have special learning and/or behavior needs.

State Employment Services (Job Services)

There are more than 2,000 local employment service offices throughout the country to help employers find workers and to help workers find jobs. Each office is mandated by law to employ a specialist trained to work with persons with special learning and/or behavior needs. The state employment services agency can serve as a valuable information resource for students with special learning and/or behavior needs and also for those who are disadvantaged. The agency can provide school personnel with a wealth of information regarding the community's labor market needs and the skills their students with special learning and/or behavior needs must have to be considered for employment. Other services that the agency can offer many students with special learning and/or behavior needs are the following:

• Assessment to determine vocational aptitudes and interests
• Job search assistance workshops to develop job-seeking skills
• Youth programs to enhance students in transition
• Vocational guidance and counseling

The agency can assist employers who hire and train persons with special learning and/or behavior needs and certain others to obtain the Targeted Jobs Tax Credit (TJTC) for giving these individuals the opportunity to become stable employees.

An often-overlooked service of the employment service is its research program. One of the information databases available to students is the State Training Inventory (STI), a computerized inventory of state and local training resources that assists users in identifying local schools, colleges, training programs, and the training programs they offer. Each state publishes an STI through their Department of Labor, Manpower, or State Occupational Information Coordinating Committee (SOICC). The 1992 STI database includes 17,500 schools and 200,000 training programs. This information is available at little or no cost and is constantly being expanded and updated.

Each state also conducts an Occupational Employment Statistics survey on an ongoing basis, which is collected for over 750 occupations. This survey is conducted in every county in the state and includes:

• The typical or average staffing pattern of each industry in terms of occupational employment in each industry to total industry employment
• The industries in which people work and their employment
• Occupational employment projections

The Dictionary of Occupational Titles, Occupational Outlook Handbook, and Occupational Outlook Quarterly are important tools for transition/career education programs.

The U.S. Department of Labor integrates data from all states into national labor statistics and projections. The U.S. Government Printing Office publishes manuals that are very helpful to persons planning for the future. The *Dictionary of Occupational Titles* (DOT; 204.245.136.2/libdot.html/) was developed in response to the demand for standardized occupational information to support job placement activities. The use of this information has expanded from job-matching applications to various uses for employment counseling, occupational and career guidance, and labor market information services. The *Occupational Outlook Handbook* (stats.bls.gov/oco-home.html/) is updated every 2 years and describes about 250 occupations in detail. It covers approximately 87% of all jobs in the nation and is used as a reference book describing occupations in addition to what the work is like, what education and training are needed, advancement possibilities, earnings, job outlook, and employment projections. The *Occupational Outlook Quarterly* provides career updates every 3 months.

Educators' expectations about the future influence the decisions they make concerning the curriculum, their students with special learning and/or behavior needs' Individualized Education Plan (IEP), and their transition programs. Because work is such a vital part of each student's life, the information provided by the state and U.S. Department of Labor can be a very important part in making decisions.

Job Training Partnership Act Program

The JTPA program was created to prepare youth with special learning and/or behavior needs and unskilled adults for entry into the labor force and to afford job training to economically disadvantaged individuals and others facing serious barriers to employment who are in special need of training to obtain productive employment. Six primary services provided by JTPA are the following:

- Assessment of the individual's strengths and abilities
- Pre-employment training for job-seeking and job-keeping skills
- Try-out employment by paying the wages for first 125 hours for employers who provide the training and permanent employment
- On-the-job training where employers are reimbursed for 50% percent of the wages while the worker is being trained
- Institutional skills training at vocational technical schools and community colleges
- Summer youth employment and training programs so youth can get paid experience and develop work maturity (Steele, Burrows, Kiburz, & Sitlington, 1990)

Many individuals are eligible for JTPA services, and several school programs across the country are involving their students with special learning and/or behavior needs in JTPA programs. Interested readers should contact their local state employment service agency or the mayor's office to obtain specific information for programs in their area.

In addition to the preceding agencies that offer services at the local level, the departments or divisions of special education and vocational special needs also play extremely important roles in funding services in the schools. The state special education agency administers the state agency for the education of exceptional children; offers technical assistance to school districts and programs; conducts seminars and workshops; disseminates information; conducts student identification and needs studies; promotes the development of professional services; and promotes, writes, and enforces legislation.

The vocational education/special needs program administers the federal/state legislation that relates to vocational education for disadvantaged individuals and those with disabilities (called *special needs*); promotes the development and funds programs in secondary and postsecondary educational settings; and works closely with universities in developing personnel training programs, conducting special projects, developing and disseminating materials, and other activities of transition/career development.

The IDEA 1997 legislation states the IEP should contain statements of each public and participating agency's responsibilities or linkage (or both) before the student finishes school—including the agency's commitment.

Local Agencies and Programs

Each of the following state agencies described provides services at the local level. Regional and local offices are located in many cities throughout each state. People from rural areas will need to find out where the nearest office is located. In addition to these agencies, some other important programs and services are also available. Figure 5.2 shows the variety of community resources available in many communities. A description of some of these programs follows.

Community Rehabilitation Programs (Rehabilitation Facilities)

The 1992 Rehabilitation Act Amendments changed the previous term of "rehabilitation facility" to "community rehabilitation program." Each state VR agency is required to maintain a State Plan for community rehabilitation programs, which includes an inventory of those available in the state, a description of the use of each, a determination of needs for such programs, and a list of the projects they are conducting to achieve state goals.

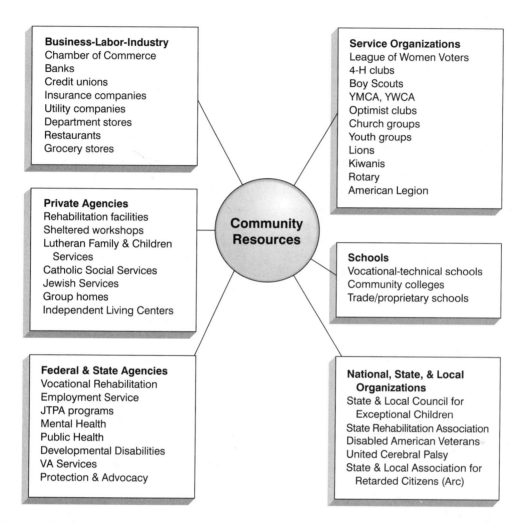

Business-Labor-Industry
Chamber of Commerce
Banks
Credit unions
Insurance companies
Utility companies
Department stores
Restaurants
Grocery stores

Service Organizations
League of Women Voters
4-H clubs
Boy Scouts
YMCA, YWCA
Optimist clubs
Church groups
Youth groups
Lions
Kiwanis
Rotary
American Legion

Private Agencies
Rehabilitation facilities
Sheltered workshops
Lutheran Family & Children
 Services
Catholic Social Services
Jewish Services
Group homes
Independent Living Centers

Community Resources

Schools
Vocational-technical schools
Community colleges
Trade/proprietary schools

Federal & State Agencies
Vocational Rehabilitation
Employment Service
JTPA programs
Mental Health
Public Health
Developmental Disabilities
VA Services
Protection & Advocacy

**National, State, & Local
 Organizations**
State & Local Council for
 Exceptional Children
State Rehabilitation Association
Disabled American Veterans
United Cerebral Palsy
State & Local Association for
 Retarded Citizens (Arc)

FIGURE 5.2   Some Community Resources Important to Transition/Career Development of Individuals with Disabilities and Those Who Are Disadvantaged.

Most community rehabilitation programs or rehabilitation facilities are private, nonprofit agencies that offer clients the opportunity to receive a comprehensive vocational assessment, work habits and work skills training, vocational guidance, independent living skills training, and job placement services. Progressive facilities use a considerable amount of community-based experiences rather than segregate their clients in one building, although the amount of this depends on the nature of the person being served.

Community rehabilitation programs and facilities employ evaluation specialists, instructors, work su-

pervisors and job trainers, counselors, case managers, job placement specialists, and other professionals, depending on the size and nature of the agency. These facilities are largely financed by the referrals they receive from the state vocational rehabilitation agency and others who pay for various services that lead to the individual's employment. The final job placement may be in supported employment for those individuals who are deemed in need of this type of supervised working arrangement.

Educators should involve rehabilitation facilities in providing career development/transition services to students who will need a more concentrated and specialized emphasis in functional skills. This involvement should begin at least during the sophomore year for those students with more severe learning and/or behavior needs. Facility personnel can be of substantial assistance in planning the career development/transition activities and services for students with special learning and/or behavior needs. Few rural areas will have ready access to such a service; however, near the end of the students' educational program or shortly thereafter, arrangements for post-school services may be financed by the vocational rehabilitation agency if it is deemed a feasible goal by that agency. This is another reason that the involvement of the vocational rehabilitation agency is so important while the students with special learning and/or behavior needs are still in school.

Vocational-Technical Education Schools and Community Colleges

In many states, postsecondary community colleges and vocational-technical schools provide selected opportunities for students with special learning and/or behavior needs and those who are considered disadvantaged to learn job and daily living skills. This is an area that has never been developed to meet the needs of the majority of students with special learning and/or behavior needs because of the resistance by some and lack of adequate skills by others who work in these settings. Admission to these schools has always been a controversial issue, despite the pressing needs of so many of these individuals with special learning and/or behavior needs when they are not prepared for community living and employment considerations after leaving the secondary school; and most of them are not prepared.

Some vocational schools and community colleges have accepted the responsibility for providing meaningful and quality post-school programs for students with special learning and/or behavior needs. They have established vocational assessment and job placement services to ensure the students with special learning and/or behavior needs' success. Specific instruction is provided in regular on-campus facilities and resources, in specially designed settings, or in community-based training settings with employers and others. Vocational education instructors are a very important resource because of their specific skill areas expertise and their contacts within the business community. Funding for these programs is generally contributed by the vocational education/special needs division and/or state special education agencies.

Other Agencies and Community Services

In each state, a protection and advocacy agency is available for people with developmental disabilities or their parents if they are having difficulty finding help in their communities. In some communities, private social service agencies such as Lutheran Family and Children Services, Catholic Family Services, and Jewish Services are available to help families and individuals resolve personal adjustment problems, interpersonal conflicts, and social and emotional difficulties. Trained social workers, using individual and group methods, help the student with special learning and/or behavior needs to find ways of fulfilling personal-social needs. Group homes and residential programs, with funding from state agencies, are another excellent resource in some communities. These facilities provide supervision while the residents receive vocational training and other career development/transition services. Some provide substantial training in daily living skills and personal-social development, particularly if they are not affiliated with another rehabilitation program. These agencies generally also provide a limited staff for individual and group counseling. Independent living centers/programs, funded in part from VR funds, are another resource in some communities. These facilities provide a wide array of services—such as advocacy and awareness, attendant care, counseling, information services, and referral—to people with physical and other special learning and/or behavior needs.

The number and type of agencies serving people with special learning and/or behavior needs in various communities in each state are substantial. Although most of these services are not located in small rural towns, they are available to residents if they are willing to be transported to them. Professional workers from agencies such as VR can be contacted to make the appropriate arrangements. With the current emphasis on planning for the transition of students from school to postsecondary services and eventual employment, co-operative planning among agencies is essential to ensure there are no gaps in services. More will be presented on interagency collaboration later.

ACCESSING THE AGENCIES

Many parents, advocate groups, professionals, and politicians have worked hard to achieve the legislation, funding, and personnel needed to provide important services to people with special learning and/or behavior needs and other disadvantages. Thus, it is the responsibility of professionals who are working with individuals with special learning and/or behavior needs to learn about these resources and how to access them for the benefit of their students or clients. In this section, some suggestions on approaching this challenge are presented.

Steps to Accessing Agencies

1. *Develop or secure a Community Resource Directory that identifies all possible sources of assistance in meeting student needs.*

   Besides reviewing information contained in this book on such resources and sending for more specific information relative to your state, a good source of information is the local telephone directory. In the Savannah, Georgia, telephone directory, for example, are five pages of resources listed under the category human services. The resources are divided into various categories, e.g., abuse-adult, abuse-child, alcohol and drug abuse/addition, child youth services, counseling services, crisis intervention, disabled services, employment services, health services, legal assistance, and volunteer services and opportunities. Telephone calls and/or correspondence to these agencies should result in relevant information on their services and appropriate contact persons. A sample community resource data form and work

sheet used by schools implementing the LCCE Mild/Moderate Curriculum are presented in Figure 5.3.

2. *Determine what needs of your students cannot be fully met by the school.*

   Examples of such needs might be vocational assessment, work adjustment training, vocational counseling and guidance, personal counseling, behavior modification, medical services, daily living skills training, social skills training, community work experience, family counseling/services, financial services, advocacy, interpreter, reader services, transportation, supported employment, special equipment, and job placement. The individual student's needs should be specified in the IEP and/or transition plan for that year. A rationale for why each of the identified needs cannot be met by the school program should be written so the agencies contacted will have clear justification for their involvement.

3. *Contact representatives from agencies that information from your resource directory indicates can provide for these needs.*

   In deciding which agencies to contact, be sure you have reviewed the eligibility requirements relative to disabilities and ages served, financial needs tests, and the like. The more familiar you are with the agencies' requirements and services, the greater the chance for success. It is suggested that you invite the agency caseworkers to the school to meet you and the students with special learning and/or behavior needs to become familiar with your needs. As you may recall, the IDEA regulations now require a transition plan that involves agencies, and most of them also are mandated to collaborate with schools in transition planning. Remember these agencies are charged by law to serve these individuals with special learning and/or behavior needs; thus, they will have to justify their reasons for denying any services that you believe are warranted. Obviously, you do not want to develop a threatening, aversive relationship with the agencies but rather, a cooperative, partnership in serving the students and their families.

Education Level: _____

LCCE Community Resource: _____

Related to LCCE Curriculum Domain(s):

_____ Daily Living Skills

_____ Personal–Social Skills

_____ Occupational Guidance and Preparation

Name of Resource Person: _____

Address: _____

_____

_____

Telephone: (   ) _____

Related Career Education Stage(s):

_____ Awareness

_____ Exploration

_____ Preparation

_____ Assimilation (Placement/Follow-up)

Type of Resource:

_____ Field Trip   _____ Speaker

_____ Classroom Consultant   _____ Student Tutor

_____ Instructional Materials   _____ Work Experience

_____ Training Site   _____ Other (Please List)

                                               _____

                                               _____

                                               _____

Detailed Description of Resource: _____

_____

_____

_____

_____

_____

_____

_____

_____

_____

_____

FIGURE 5.3   Community resource data form and work sheet.

	COMMUNITY RESOURCES WORKSHEET		Page _____ of _____
LCCE COMPETENCY	COMMUNITY RESOURCE	METHODOLOGY	NOTES

FIGURE 5.3 Continued.

4. *Additional suggestions.*
Some further suggestions or cautions in developing a collaborative relationship with community agencies are probably warranted. First, remember they are serving a wide array of persons with special learning and/or behavior needs, not only school-age children. Second, they do have limited funds, as you do, and must use their money judiciously and not duplicate what others can do. Third, most caseworkers are not always familiar with all the disabilities, characteristics, and learning problems associated with special education students. Thus, they need to become more knowledgeable and appreciative of these students with special learning and/or behavior needs. Fourth, professional jealousies and rivalries do exist and, unfortunately, protecting one's turf is almost a normal occurrence in the field of human services. Thus, considerable time may be needed to establish an atmosphere of trust and respect for each other's efforts. And, fifth, there will always be some hardheaded caseworkers who are unresponsive to the educator's needs. In these instances, the educator should contact the supervisor to achieve the needed assistance.

Interagency Agreements

Local interagency agreements initiated by the local educational agency provide one way to enhance the cooperation of community agencies to participate more actively in the career development/transition efforts of the school district. Written agreements are preferred, although they do not guarantee the expected collaborative effort from the agencies.

Several states, including Iowa, Kansas, and Minnesota, have instituted impressive interagency ventures to get various agencies to work more closely together to provide relevant transition services. As noted by Everson and McNulty (1992), the focus of interagency teams is to identify, create, and maintain services and supports needed by the students with special learning and/or behavior needs rather than matching them to existing slots or placements.

Minnesota has been a leader in initiating interagency cooperative agreements. In 1982, special education, vocational education, and vocational rehabilitation agencies developed their agreement. Shortly thereafter, a State Transition Interagency Committee was established, and then an Interagency Office on Transition Services. This latter agency provides information and technical assistance to local education agencies, assisting communities in establishing interagency agreements, and conducting workshops on interagency planning for transition (Minnesota Department of Education, no date).

Persons interested in developing more formalized interagency agreements at the local level should investigate what state-level agreements have been written between agencies at that level to gain some direction and leverage for their situation. An example of one state-level interagency/cooperative agreement is provided in Appendix A.

ORGANIZATIONS

Numerous private, nonprofit, volunteer, professional, and other organizations that are dedicated to providing transition support services to persons with special learning and/or behavior needs also are available in many small-to-large communities. Many of these were started by parent groups and other concerned citizens who felt those specific areas of need required special attention. Some cities will have local affiliates of the state and national organization, for example, The Arc (a national organization on mental retardation—formerly known as the Association for Retarded Citizens), United Cerebral Palsy, and the National Easter Seal Society. These parent/volunteer organizations receive considerable guidance and support from the state and national organizations to carry out their policies and objectives. They often support or operate day-care facilities, sheltered workshops, group homes, or other direct service programs at the local level.

The number of organizations that are committed to serving and enhancing the quality of life of persons with disabilities is impressive. One cannot help but wonder how anyone with special learning and/or behavior needs can be unserved or underserved with the vast amount of money and array of services that have been created over the past decades. Professional workers do have resources at their disposal if the effort is made to identify and use them. A list of some particularly important organizations for transition/career development services is provided for the reader's reference in Appendix B.

The Division of Career Development and Transition is an important professional organization for those involved in conducting career education and transition services.

Professional organizations also are very important resources and instigators of improving services to people with special learning and/or behavior needs and those who are disadvantaged. One organization that is particularly important to the career development effort is the Council for Exceptional Children's (CEC) Division on Career Development and Transition (DCDT). Several position papers prepared by the division were alluded to in earlier chapters. This organization, in existence since 1976, conducts an international convention every 2 years, and numerous sessions on transition/career education at the annual CEC convention, sponsors regional and state conferences, and keeps members informed of major legislative developments. The organization produces a professional journal *(Career Development for Exceptional Individuals)* to inform its members of the latest research activities, model programs, and issues in career development and transition planning. It also produces a newsletter with the latest information on legislation, projects, resources materials, and implementation strategies.

Another related organization that promotes career development/transition for persons with special learning and/or behavior needs, disadvantages, and limited English proficiency is the National Association of Vocational Education Special Needs Personnel (NAVESNP), which is affiliated with the Special Needs Division of the American Vocational Association (AVA). NAVESP publishes *The Journal for Vocational Special Needs Education* and a newsletter, holds conferences and workshops, and promotes legislation.

Two other organizations that focus on career education/transition programming for all students with special learning and/or behavior needs (the disadvantaged) are the American Association for Career Education (AACE) and the National Career Development Association (NCDA). Both of these professional groups also hold conferences, publish newsletters, and keep members informed of important developments in the field. These organizations have collaborated with DCDT in conducting important national conferences.

As indicated previously in Figure 5.2, many service organizations can help and have helped develop viable career education/transitional programs.

As indicated in Chapter 6, where those resources are described, industry, labor, and business resources can provide students with special learning and/or behavior needs with community work experiences and observations; help develop career-oriented curricula; assist in job placement efforts; provide volunteers for the school; and elicit support for career education/transition programming throughout the community. Many community resources such as banks, credit unions, insurance companies, utility companies, department stores, restaurants, and grocery stores can give students with special learning and/or behavior needs information and experiences in the daily living skills areas. These sources also are a powerful influence for obtaining additional and needed funds from the government and private sectors.

Service organizations and other civic groups can help develop viable career education/transitional programs. The League of Women Voters, church groups, youth groups, Lions International, and others generally look for projects that will benefit the community and persons with special and learning needs. These organizations also can provide schools and agencies with the talents of their members. *Rotary International Magazine* has featured a special section on the relationship between education and work. The American Legion adopted career education/transitional programming as a priority and has continued to emphasize ways in which members can assist schools in career development/transition efforts.

The list of community, state, and national resources for carrying out career development/transition efforts is almost endless. Space in this text does not permit identifying all the important resources. Persons interested in obtaining more detailed information on these and other national, state, and local organizations and services for persons with disabilities have several excellent resources at their disposal. These include the HEATH Resource Center, the National Center for Research in Vocational Education/TASPP, and the CEC Information Services, which will be described in the next section.

INFORMATION RESOURCES

Several national information centers are identified and described in this section so that educators can obtain additional information that will enhance their efforts with students with special learning and/or behavior needs. Once again, only a selected list of re-

sources is presented due to space restrictions. Each of these is listed in Table 5.2 for quick reference and is described in the following paragraphs.

National Clearinghouses

The first important resource presented is five clearinghouses that provide specialized information to teachers, students, counselors, policymakers, parents, disability advocates, and people with disabilities.

ERIC Clearinghouse on Disabilities and Gifted Education

The Clearinghouse on Disabilities and Gifted Education is one of the federally sponsored Educational Resources Information Centers (ERIC), and is operated by the CEC (Arlington, VA). The CEC produces the

TABLE 5.2   Information Systems for Materials on Career Development for Individuals with Special Learning Needs

Organization	Location
ERIC Clearinghouse on Disabilities and Gifted Education	CEC, Reston, VA
ERIC Clearinghouse on Adult, Career, and Vocational Education	Ohio State University
Heath Resource Center (National Clearinghouse on Postsecondary Education for Persons with Disabilities)	Washington, D.C.
National Clearinghouse of Rehabilitation Training Materials (NCHRTM)	Oklahoma State University
The Council for Exceptional Children Information Services	CEC, Arlington, VA
National Center to Improve Practice (NCIP)	Newton, MA
National Center for Youth with Disabilities	University of Minnesota
The Center for Education and Work	University of Wisconsin–Madison
Technical Assistance for Special Populations, The National Center for Research in Vocational Education, University of California	University of Illinois
Transition Institute	University of Illinois
President's Committee on Employment of People with Disabilities	Washington, D.C.

Exceptional Child Education Resources (ECER) database of more than 100,000 abstracts from the professional literature. Its quarterly journal, *Exceptional Child Education Resources,* provides abstracts and indexes of the most recent additions to the ECER database. The ECER's unique contribution is the inclusion of books, dissertations, and many journal articles not included in the ERIC collection. The CEC can provide either an ERIC-CEC product or a database search. Products include publications such as books, monographs, or reports; brief products such as summaries of current topics, digests, research briefs, and minibibliographies; and directories of research projects. Custom computer searches are complete CD-ROM or on-line searches of the ERIC, ECER, or related databases customized to meet specific user needs. Interested persons should call 1-800-328-0272.

ERIC/ACVE: Clearinghouse of Adult, Career, and Vocational Education

The ERIC/ACVE Clearinghouse is located at the Center for Education and Training for Employment, Ohio State University, 1900 Kenny Road, Columbus, OH 43210-1090 (1-800-848-4815). The focus of the ERIC Clearinghouse is formal and informal career education/transition at all levels that encompasses attitudes, self-knowledge, decision-making skills, general and occupational knowledge, and specific vocational and occupational skills; formal and informal adult and continuing education relating to occupational, family, leisure, citizen, organizational, and retirement roles; vocational and technical education that includes new entry level fields, industrial arts, and vocational rehabilitation for individuals with disabilities. The center has several bibliographies and information analysis papers on transition/career development.

HEATH Resource Center: National Clearinghouse on Postsecondary Education for Individuals with Disabilities

The HEATH Resource Center, a program of the American Council on Education, is located at One Dupont Circle, Suite 800, Washington, DC 20036-

1193 (1-800-544-3284). It operates under a congressional mandate to collect and disseminate information nationally about disability issues in postsecondary education. The center is funded by the U.S. Department of Education and is intended to increase the flow of information about educational support services, policies, and procedures related to educating or training people with special learning and/or behavior needs after they leave high school. More specifically, the HEATH Resource Center has the following functions:

- Identify and describe educational and training opportunities.
- Promote accommodations that enable full participation by people with disabilities in regular, as well as specialized, postsecondary programs.
- Recommend strategies that encourage participation in the least restrictive and most productive environments possible for each individual.

HEATH publishes a newsletter three times a year, free of charge to members. The newsletter provides information on campus programs and legislation and reviews new publications and media products. The center produces fact sheets, resource papers, guides, and directories related to disability issues as they occur on college campuses, vocational technical training schools, adult education programs, independent living centers, and other community-based training programs. The toll-free telephone number is 1-800-544-3284 (in the Washington, DC, area, it is 202-939-9320).

National Clearinghouse of Rehabilitation Training Materials

The National Clearinghouse of Rehabilitation Training Materials (NCHRTM) resources is funded by the Rehabilitation Services Administration and is located at Oklahoma State University, 816 West Sixth Street, Stillwater, OK 74078 (800-223-5219). NCHRTM disseminates information on vocational rehabilitation with its primary concentration on in-service training of personnel. Materials from special education are included, however, to respond to the transition needs of students with special learning and/or behavior needs in the period between the education and employment. Resources include print and media not found in traditional sources. An *NCHRTM Memorandum* is published quarterly, listing available materials and their cost.

Centers for Educational Information/Services

Several additional sources of information to the field that are not considered clearinghouses but provide valuable resource information that can be used for transition/career development programs are presented next.

The Council for Exceptional Children Information Services

As the major professional organization in the education of exceptional individuals, the CEC publishes materials in both print and nonprint formats that facilitate continued improvement in services. A list of the products includes the following:

- Exceptional Child Education Resources (ECER). This resource contains more than 80,000 abstracts of the published professional literature covering the education and development of individuals who have disabilities or who are gifted. ECER is available in print and CD-ROM formats.
- Topical bibliographies based on the references in ECER
- Professional books and nonprint media on instructional methods and materials, administrative procedures and programs, training of personnel, legislation and legal procedures, and projected changes in education and training of individuals with disabilities or those who are gifted
- Journals and newsletters published by CEC and its divisions. The two prominent journals are *Exceptional Children* and *TEACHING Exceptional Children*.
- Custom computer search of the ERIC and ECER databases on request

Information can be obtained by writing The CEC, 1110 North Glebe Road, Suite 300, Arlington, VA 22201.

The National Center to Improve Practice

The National Center to Improve Practice (NCIP) is a relatively new center located at the Education Development Center (EDC), Inc., 55 Chapel Street, Newton, MA 02158-1060 (800-225-44276). The NCIP is a joint endeavor between the EDC and WGBH Educational Foundation, Boston's public television station, to improve the outcomes of students with special learning and/or behavior needs by helping practitioners to effectively use technology, media, and materials to enhance instruction. Because knowledge alone does not promote change, the NCIP has designed a process for knowledge use called the *Dynamic Approach to Change*. Through this approach, the NCIP seeks to support change agents—those individuals in schools or districts who provide administrators, practitioners, and parents with the knowledge, resources, and training they need to embrace and implement innovative uses of technology, media, and materials. The NCIP's approach is dynamic because it integrates a variety of media, including newsletter packets, an electronic resource library and bulletin board, and video conferences; provides technical assistance to change agents through written guidelines, network support, and training institutes; encourages communication and sharing through electronic network conversations and video conferences; and expands the knowledge base through action research.

The National Center for Youth with Disabilities

The National Center for Youth with Disabilities is a project located at the University of Minnesota, Adolescent Health Program, D-124 Mayo Memorial Building, Box 721, Harvard Street at East River Road, Minneapolis, MN 55455 (800-333-NCYD). The center focuses on adolescents with chronic illness and disability and the issues surrounding their transition to adult life. Its goal is to foster coordination and collaboration among agencies, professionals, families, and youth in the planning and provision of services, and to promote awareness of and responsiveness to the student's health and social needs. The center offers a National Resource Library, which maintains a database containing separate bibliographic, program, training/education, and technical assistance files; it offers workshops and conferences at state and national levels supporting the design and implementation of state and community programs for youth and their families; it offers publications of monographs, bibliographies, and newsletters on vital issues regarding adolescence and disability; and it offers technical assistance.

The Center for Education and Work

The Center for Education and Work is located at the University of Wisconsin-Madison, 964 Educational Sciences Building, 1025 West Johnson Street, Madison, WI 53706-1796 (800-446-0399). National, state, and local contracts and grants support the center. Staff conduct research, develop instructional and in-service materials, provide technical assistance, and disseminate products worldwide. The center's expertise lies in vocational and technical education, education for employment, vocational equity, business and industry training needs, labor market information, transition/career development, students with special learning and/or behavior needs and at-risk students, program evaluation, corrections, and administration. Several products are available from the center on the following topics: curriculum development, exemplary secondary and postsecondary programs, best practices for the rehabilitation of learning disabled students, interagency linkages, technical preparation, ADA implementation, and replicating jobs with business and industry for persons with disabilities.

Technical Assistance for Special Populations Program

The Technical Assistance for Special Populations Program (TASPP) is a resource affiliated with the National Center for Research in Vocational Education at the University of California, Berkeley. It is located at the University of Illinois, Department of Vocational and Technical Education, 345 Education Building, 1310 S. Sixth Street, Champaign, IL 61820 (217-333-0807). The TASPP is a resource and referral source for practitioners, researchers, and policymakers working in vocational education with special needs populations at the secondary and postsecondary level. Other objectives are to initiate and support networks of professionals serving special needs students and to provide technical assistance on selected topics or problems crucial to improving the quality of vocational education programs provided to special populations. TASPP conducts workshops, publishes a quarterly newsletter on critical issues and policy options, and develops materials for national distribution.

Secondary Transition Intervention Effectiveness Institute

The Secondary Transition Intervention Effectiveness Institute is located at the University of Illinois, College of Education, 110 Education Building, 1310 S. Sixth Street, Champaign, IL 61820 (217-333-2325). The purpose of the institute is to operationalize a research model that will effect improvements in transition services. The institute addresses both the theoretical and practical problems associated with the transition needs of youth with special learning and/or behavior needs with the goal of seeking solutions through interventions, evaluation, technical assistance, and the development and implementation of more appropriate policy. The institute's staff, since its inception in 1985, has published an impressive array of research and technical reports.

President's Committee on Employment of People with Disabilities (PCEPD)

The President's Committee on Employment of People with Disabilities (PCEPD) is a resource located at 1111 20th Street, N.W., Suite 636, Washington, DC 20036 (202-653-5044). It serves as a national source of information and assistance on employment issues for persons with disabilities. It conducts an annual conference on the employment of people with disabilities, seminars, and workshops on a range of issues centered on employment. It publishes various publications and sponsors the Job Accommodation Network, an information system, developed by employers for employers, to exchange ideas about practical steps they have taken to accommodate persons with disabilities, located at the West Virginia University Rehabilitation Research and Training Center, Morgantown, WV. Each state has a Governor's Committee on Employment of People with Disabilities, which also is another excellent information source.

Some other important sources that will not be described but should be mentioned are the Apple Office of Special Education Programs at Apple Computer, the IBM National Support Center for Persons with Disabilities, and The National Rural Development Institute's Resource Center at Western Washington University. Again, the sources provided in the previous section should be contacted if further information is desired.

CHAPTER COMMENTARY

After reading this chapter, readers should be encouraged by the vast number of agencies, organizations, and informational sources that are available to help schools to provide a substantial transition/career development, functional skills component to their curricular efforts.

Community interest and involvement in career education/transitional programming is not new. As Hoyt stated many years ago, "It seems more legitimate to ask whether the education system will work with the broader community in transition/career education than to ask whether the community is willing to work with the formal education system" (1976, p. 25).

Those who have professed that career education/ transition programming lacks resources and community support are mistaken. The resources are there if the time and attention are given to developing the

necessary contacts, relationships, and methodologies for using them appropriately.

In communities with limited resources, state and national organizations may become more important. These organizations should be available to assist if they are contacted for relevant purposes. The amount of free technical assistance, materials, and referrals to other helpful sources by these associations and organizations is often overwhelming. A substantial number of different organizations serve as advocates for individuals with special needs and are extremely receptive to assisting community personnel.

Career education/transition programming requires school personnel to collaborate with those outside their internal structure. It requires certain individuals to assume a coordinating role if all the necessary resources are to be appropriately orchestrated. Although this is no easy task, it is indeed necessary if we are to offer the comprehensive and relevant curriculum that learners with special needs deserve.

It is encouraging to see the numerous articles, projects, books, reports, guides, and instructional materials that are available. Those of you who become familiar with the resources printed in this chapter and the appendixes should be able to identify and secure useful information and tools for your work.

ACTIVITIES

1. Conduct a community job survey of those agencies, organizations, and other resources in your community that could be important collaborators for a career education/transition program of services in your school. Secure names of appropriate contact persons, the contribution they could make, and the address and telephone number of the resource.
2. Refer to the LCCE Mild/Moderate Curriculum matrix in Figure 3.4 and determine which of the resources that you have identified can contribute to the instructional effort needed for each of the LCCE Mild Curriculum's 97 subcompetencies and the 75 subcompetencies of the LCCE Moderate Curriculum.

CHAPTER 6

Business and Industry Involvement

PRELIMINARY QUESTIONS

1. Why is this the best time in U.S. history for instituting more substantial transition, vocational training, and placement services for students with special behavior needs?

2. What are some of the key provisions of the Americans with Disabilities Act (ADA) that will help educators to expand transition/employment opportunities for their students with special behavior needs?

3. Identify ways in which employers can contribute to the career education/transitional curriculum of the school.

4. What are some of the commonly used sources of job leads?

5. What are some of the underused sources of job leads?

6. What considerations should go into providing students with special behavior needs with a work experience component in their educational/transitional program?

7. What are some meaningful ways that educational programs can involve business and industry personnel in their career education/transition program?

8. Identify some of the large corporations that have developed outstanding policies and procedures for providing persons with special needs training and employment opportunities.

9. What large corporation has been a leader in developing computer and other assistive technology and special training programs to enhance the employment and daily living skills potential of persons with special behavior needs and the disadvantaged?

10. What important considerations should be adhered to in conducting job placement efforts for persons with more severe disabilities?

OVERVIEW

In this new century, the American labor market has been changing quickly and dramatically. Large companies and corporations are downsizing their work forces to survive and become more efficient and productive. Companies are merging, and as a result they too are making adjustments that reduce their combined total number of employees. Large numbers of previously employed Americans are out of work, looking for new jobs or retraining, and settling for positions that often pay less than what they previously made. Although new federal employment legislation to provide training and employment opportunities for unemployed Americans was passed, well-paying jobs continue to be difficult to secure for those who lack the experience and technical skills needed in the current highly competitive and more technically sophisticated workplace.

What are the implications of employment possibilities for individuals with special behavior needs, for the disadvantaged, and for others who may have been one of the many school dropouts? Will they be shunted further into dead-end, low-paying, unstimulating jobs, which comprise the so-called "secondary/surplus labor market?" Will there be more unemployment among this group of citizens? Once again, only time will tell, but in the meantime, educators and rehabilitation personnel must rise to the occasion, dig in, and meet this next formidable challenge. This will require a much closer interface with business and industry than ever before. Otherwise, special education needs will not be addressed, and these individuals with special behavior needs will be left out in the periphery.

The career education/transition approach, with its focus on teaching productive work behaviors and other functional skills, provides a mechanism for bridging the gap between the schools and employers. A career education/transition curriculum makes sense to employers because of its emphasis on basic academic skills, general employability skills, work attitudes and behaviors, and personal-social areas such as building self-confidence and interpersonal skills. In fact, there is evidence that employers believe that an employee's self-confidence is perhaps the most important of a wide variety of skills that are needed for successful job functioning (O'Leary, 1989).

This chapter begins with a further discussion of the ADA, which was introduced in Chapter 1. This legislation is a good indicator that business and industry recognize the importance of using the potentials of persons with special behavior needs and that they will become more responsive to their employment needs from now on. The chapter then presents sections on education-industry partnerships; discusses specific contributions of business and industry to transitional programs; suggests ways in which educators can contact and involve members of the business and industrial community; and identifies some resources that both employers and educators can use to enhance the individual's employability. Guidelines for interviewing persons are given. The final section relates to important considerations in placing students with severe disabilities in the workplace.

THE AMERICANS WITH DISABILITIES ACT OF 1990

The United States Congress enacted numerous bills during the 1990s to help protect persons with disabilities against discrimination and other types of unjust practices. Most present-day educational reform proposals call for closer working relationships

CHAPTER OUTLOOK

Kenneth B. Hoyt is a University Distinguished Professor at Kansas State University and is the former and only director of the U.S. Office of Career Education. Dr. Hoyt is the nation's foremost expert and leader in the area of career education.

As our nation moves toward becoming an information-oriented high-technology occupational society, it will become increasingly necessary for all persons entering and participating in that society to acquire a number of kinds of occupational skills. For too long, many youth have left secondary school with few or no marketable occupational skills and have, as a result, spent up to 10–12 years in the secondary labor market, where more positive career development experiences are next to impossible to obtain.

It is now clear that, for almost all youth, the question on leaving high school is no longer "Should I go to college or should I seek employment?" Rather, the question today must be "Should I go to a four-year college, or should I attend some other type of postsecondary institution to acquire the skills necessary for participation in the emerging occupational society?"

If youth acquire these skills, it will be important to find employers willing to allow them to enter into the primary labor market in spite of their youth. Employer discrimination among youth in hiring practices has been very widespread for far too many years. It is hoped that this can be overcome. A second major responsibility of employers is continuing education of their employees. America has a lot of catching up to do to be in the same important position occupied by employers in other advanced industrial nations.

The Life-Centered Career Education (LCCE) approach is a natural and effective way of building the proper kinds of employer/education relationships. We must continue to develop these relationships and implement such an approach if we are to enhance the employability potential of all students, including those who have special learning needs. All students have the right to earn a decent living and achieve job satisfaction as a result of our educational system's efforts.

between education and the business and industry sector. The Carl D. Perkins Vocational and Applied Technology Education Act of 1990 (Public Law 101-392), for example, encourages but does not mandate the formation of business and education partnerships as a means to infuse more resources into schools and to enhance education programs.

The ADA of 1990 was enacted to pull everything together so that a truly comprehensive act of equality became a reality for persons with disabilities throughout the country. In regard to employment, Title I of the Act deals with discriminatory employment practices and specifies that *no covered entity shall discriminate against a qualified person with a disability relative to application procedures, hiring, advancement, discharge, employee compensation, job training, or other terms or conditions of employment.* "Qualified individuals with a disability" are defined as:

> an individual with a disability who, with or without reasonable accommodation, can perform the essential functions of the employment position.

The ADA definition of an individual with a disability is someone who has a physical or mental impairment that substantially limits one or more major life activities. Life activities include walking, speaking, breathing, working, performing manual tasks, seeing, hearing, learning, and caring for oneself. The definition of a mental impairment is any mental or psychological disorder, such as mental retardation, organic brain syndrome, emotional or mental illness, and specific learning disabilities. Physical impairments cover a range of physical and medical conditions and diseases.

It is necessary to identify the essential functions of a job to know whether the individual with a disability is qualified to do the job.

ADA regulations list several types of evidence to be considered in determining whether or not a function is essential:

- Employer's judgment
- Written job descriptions prepared before advertising or interviewing applicants for a job

- The amount of time spent performing the function
- The consequence of not requiring a person in this job to perform a function
- Work experience of people who have performed a job in the past and work experiences of people who currently perform similar jobs

The employer's judgment is an important consideration regarding a job's essential functions.

Other major terms to know about in addressing your client's job placement needs are "reasonable accommodation" and "undue hardship." An employer must provide a reasonable accommodation for the qualified applicant or employee with special behavior needs unless it can be shown that the accommodation would impose an undue hardship. A reasonable accommodation may include making existing facilities more readily accessible to and usable for these individuals by installing ramps and widening doorways and aisles to accommodate a wheelchair. It may also include restructuring a job, modifying work schedules, reassigning persons to vacant positions, moving the activity to an accessible area, purchasing special equipment or devices, or modifying existing equipment. The obligation to provide a reasonable accommodation applies to all aspects of employment and applies whenever a person's disability or job changes.

An employer cannot deny employment to qualified applicants or employees because of the need to provide reasonable accommodation, unless it would cause undue hardship. Undue hardship includes such factors as the nature and cost of the proposed accommodation, the overall financial resources of the organization, and the type of operation of the covered entity (U.S. Department of Education, Office of Special Education and Rehabilitative Services, 1992).

Organize an ADA Implementation Task Force like Herman Miller Corporation did.

The May/June 1992 and November/December 1993 issues of *Facility Management Journal* describe how one corporation, Herman Miller, a furniture manufacturer, put the ADA into action by going beyond the letter of the law to meet its spirit and provide equal access and equal opportunity for people with disabilities. It organized an ADA Implementation Task Force of 12 people representing the marketing, people services, research, corporate relations, operations, and facility management departments. One of its subcommittees revised job descriptions to include only "essential functions" and to use "more inclusive language." For example, a job description might state that a person have the ability to "move" rather than "lift" a box. They also established a formal and informal procedure for employees to request accommodations; the request is then processed through a rehabilitation services team leader and a disability management team if needed. A transitional work center is available to help employees get back to work. The subcommittee also educates work team leaders to look at an applicant's ability, not the disability. They refer to the nondisabled person as temporarily able-bodied (TAB). The company also formed groups to address making their facilities and products accessible and to develop a variety of communication tools, such as newsletter articles, video presentations, and resource persons, to educate their employees and others about the ADA and its requirements. The program has been highly successful in raising the awareness level and truly meeting the spirit of the ADA legislation (Hauser, 1993).

Another corporation that has been in the forefront of accommodating and employing persons with disabilities for many years, thanks in large part to the efforts of Bob Muller, is Steelcase, Inc., of Grand Rapids, MI. In their first edition of Workwell Magazine, they note

Since the passage of the Americans with Disabilities Act, reams of information have been published on ways to accommodate people with disabilities. Unfortunately, much of it doesn't get past the front door. (Steelcase, no date, p. 28)

They note that many office modifications for persons with special behavior needs are inexpensive (e.g., a footrest, a lowered telephone, or an adjustable-height work surface). Two related approaches to provide work stations that truly enable people with special behavior needs to do their job are presented in the article, which also notes that "businesses that embrace the spirit of the law gain access to needed human resources, while ensuring that millions of qualified individuals fully participate in the workforce" (Steelcase, no date, p. 29). Steelcase has become a leader in promoting the civil rights and employment of persons with disabilities. Their Employee Handbook provides information and direction to their employees relative to the ADA legislation. Figure 6.1 presents an example of some guidelines they provide their personnel in making reasonable accommodations for employees and potential employees.

"Together we have begun shifting disability policy in America from exclusion to inclusion; from dependence to independence; from paternalism to empowerment.... we do not have a single person to waste."
President Clinton (October 6, 1993, White House press release)

President Clinton stated:

Our Nation can ill afford to waste this vast and only partially tapped source of knowledge, skills, and talent ... this waste of human ability cannot be reconciled with our tradition of individual dignity, self-reliance, and empowerment. I congratulate the small business and industry leaders, labor leaders, and community leaders from all walks of life who are working together to implement the ADA and the Rehabilitation Act. Our ongoing progress attests to the fundamental vitality and openness of our free enterprise system and to our abiding commitment to civil rights for all. (October 6, 1993, White House press release)

It is obvious that the ADA has been a substantial force in stimulating even greater responsiveness to the employment needs of our citizens with special behavior needs. It has helped open the doors of business and industry even further to educators who are willing and able to develop effective partnership programs that will aid in the educational reform that most believe is badly needed in our schools.

REASONABLE ACCOMMODATION

That which can be adapted without undue hardship. If an individual with a disability is *qualified* to perform the essential functions of a job, you need to decide if accommodation is necessary for the individual to perform them.

Example	Accommodation
Making facilities accessible	Revising workspaces and restrooms; revising entry/doors to staff meeting rooms; rearranging employee lounge/lunch room; revising emergency procedures
Job restructuring	Reassigning non-essential job duties to another employee
Part-time or modified work schedule	Flexible or adjusted work schedules to allow for medical treatments, transportation schedule, and break periods
Reassignment to a vacant position	An employee who can no longer perform essential job functions (and another reasonable accommodation will not enable the employee to perform the job) should be offered an opportunity to move to a vacant position for which the individual can perform the essential job functions
Acquisition or modification of equipment or devices	Electronic visual aids; braille materials; talking calculators; high contrast computer screens; magnifiers; audio recording; telephone handset amplifier; telecommunications devices for deaf persons; mechanical page turner; raised or lowered furniture
Modifications of examinations, training materials, or policies	Removing the driver's license requirement for a job in which the essential job functions do not include driving; closed captioned video training materials
Qualified readers or interpreters	Allowing for readers, interpreters, or attendants on a part-time basis in cases where it does not cause undue hardship

COMMON ADA TERMINOLOGY

Term	ADA Definition
Accessible	A facility that can be approached, entered, and used by individuals with disabilities easily and conveniently.

FIGURE 6.1   Reasonable Accommodation.
Note. From *Employee Handbook* (p. 4) by Steelcase, Inc. Reprinted by permission.

PARTNERSHIPS WITH EDUCATION

Shortly after the introduction of Partnerships with Education in the early 1970s, the U.S. Chamber of Commerce, the National Alliance of Businessmen, General Motors Corporation, the Industry Education Council of California, General Electric Company, New York Life Insurance Company, the Bell System, and many other large national companies and associations developed career education/transition efforts to collaborate with school systems. Since those early efforts, many others have instituted collaborative partnerships with

Qualified individual	An individual with a disability who satisfies the requisite skills, experience, education and other job-related requirements of the employment positions such individual holds or desires, and who, with or without reasonable accommodation, can perform the essential functions of such a position.
Disability	Having any physical or mental impairment that substantially limits one or more major life activities; having a record of any such impairment; or being regarded by others as having such an impairment.
	The ADA specifically excludes as disabilities: homosexuality, bisexuality, transvestism, transsexualism, pedophilia, exhibition-ism, voyeurism, gender identity disorders not resulting from physical impairment, and other sexual behavior disorders; com-pulsive gambling, kleptomania or pyromania; and psychoactive substance use disorders resulting from *current* illegal use of drugs.
Essential job functions	Fundamental and not marginal job duties. Job descriptions should specify and can serve as evidence of the essential func-tions of a particular job.
Readily achievable	Easily accomplished without much difficulty or expense consider-ing: (1) the nature and costs involved in the action; (2) the resources of the facility or facilities involved (i.e., the bank), the number of persons employed at such facility, the effect on expenses and resources, or impact of the action on the operation of the facility; (3) the overall financial resources of the entity (i.e., the holding company); overall size of the business with respect to the number of employees; the number, type, and location of its facilities; and (4) types of operation(s) of the covered entity.
Reasonable accommodation	One that can be adapted without undue hardship.
Undue hardship	Action requiring difficulty or expense.

FIGURE 6.1   Continued.

their school districts, as their attempt to provide needed assistance to their communities and young people.

Despite the early efforts at partnerships between education and business and industry, graduates still are not prepared to meet employers' needs, and the discrepancy between the students' skills and the de-mands of the available jobs is growing (Tindall, 1992). As Tindall has noted, with the current move-ment to provide business and industry with more qualified workers,

> "Special educators need to be aware that school re-structuring and reform are inevitable . . . and that we must ensure that special education students are part of the planned revisions . . . it is imperative that plans include special education students." (1992, p. 333)

As Hoyt (1993) has noted, at a recent national conference, "Youth Apprenticeship-American Style," co-sponsored by 36 organizations, not one special education or vocational rehabilitation organization was represented. In addition, the conference publication lacked any references to special education students.

> "Our nation's 43 million people with disabilities want to participate and contribute like everyone else. I'm calling on CEOs of businesses, large and small, to join this dedicated group. It's good for America. It's good for business."
> James Brady, Vice Chairman, National Organization on Disability (National Organization on Disability, 1993)

The U.S. Department of Education's America 2000: An Education Strategy (1991) calls for each American business to become involved in reforming the schools in their communities (Phelps & Maddy-Bernstein, 1992). As noted by James Brady, the former Press Secretary for President Reagan who was disabled in an assassination attempt on the President, business and industry are being organized and becoming more committed to the national goal of expanding employment opportunities for people with disabilities. Several hundred companies have joined the Disability 2000-CEO Council, pledging their support to this important national goal.

The opportunity for education and business and industry to form even more meaningful and substantial partnerships has never been greater. The seeds have been planted for schools to initiate greater and more substantive collaborative partnerships to involve business and industry personnel in its curriculum efforts. As noted by Phelps and Maddy-Bernstein, "most of the current calls for reform speak eloquently and directly to the charge of uniting the education and business communities in such an endeavor" (1992, p. 33). They cite several effective partnerships that have become model business-education collaborative efforts for at-risk students. These include the California Peninsula Academies—where teachers work together to implement a coordinated curriculum in which academic and technical learning is integrated with mentors, summer em-

ployment, job shadowing, and the like—and the Portland Investment—using a multiagency planning team including representatives from business, schools, city government, and the Urban League.

It should also be noted that the National Alliance of Businessmen has promoted the development of effective school-business partnerships and has found it essential to building an effective coalition of many committed organizations and sectors. They have also found it important to establish an intermediary organization to manage day-to-day efforts and to manage progress (Phelps & Maddy-Bernstein, 1992).

D. H. Clark (1993) has reported another example of meeting the needs of students with special needs at the Center for High-Tech Training for the Disabled, Valencia Community College, in Orlando, FL. A Business Advisory Council, comprised of leaders from industry and representatives of collaborating agencies, directs the programs offered by the center in computer programming and computer-assisted design. This ensures training that is responsive to the needs of Central Florida businesses while meeting the training needs of the trainees with special behavior needs.

It should be apparent that mechanisms for building partnerships are being instituted across the country. Educators generally must take the initiative, and if they do, the business community will probably be quite responsive.

CONTRIBUTIONS OF EMPLOYERS

The resources and personnel within the sectors of business and industry are so extensive that educators must understand the objectives and means of collaboration. They should identify objectives and possible joint efforts before approaching members of business and industry. At the same time, they should be open to suggestions presented by these same members. In other words, educators should approach business and industry with an opening statement such as: "I have an idea on ways that we can work together in the career development/transition for individuals with special behavior needs. Do you have additional suggestions?" This is contrasted with the question: "What should we do?" which may only serve to alert businesspersons to the fact that the educator has not done his or her "homework."

This section includes discussions of several ways in which business and industry can assist educational programs. The following list provides suggestions for building a collaborative effort between major sectors in career development and transitional programming:

- Identify trends in the economy
- Further contacts with business and industry
- Become advocates
- Serve as a classroom resource
- Provide program consultation
- Provide work experiences
- Participate in conferences and workshops
- Provide instructional and resource materials

Trends in the Economy

Educators are always interested in trends that determine enrollments for years to come. Educators must be attentive to the overall condition of supply and demand in the labor market, as well as specific shortages within particular categories of employment that offer opportunities for their students with special behavior needs. Reports on employment by categories, age groups, and industries are available through several government agencies, although the Department of Labor is principally responsible for providing the public with continual assessment of the labor situation. For example, the Department of Labor projected a 38% growth in service-work jobs beginning in the year 2000. Job prospects for clerical workers, who are the largest part of the workforce in America, were projected to grow by 30%. Demand for craftsmen and skilled laborers such as carpenters, auto mechanics, and tool and die workers also increased. Sales jobs in retail stores, manufacturing, and wholesale firms grew by 32%. Categories that experienced slow growth or no growth include production workers (those on assembly lines), unskilled

laborers (e.g., freight and stock handlers), and farm workers. This type of information constantly appears in such government publications as the *Monthly Labor Review* and *Occupational Outlook Quarterly*. Special reports and reprints can be obtained from the regional office of the Department of Labor, Bureau of Labor Statistics.

Community members of business and industry can translate major trends in the economy and labor force into the potential effects of such movements on job development and training for individuals with special behavior needs. Businesspersons are often able to identify surges in demands for workers with particular skills, changes in job classifications and modifications of skill requirements that are due to the introduction of new machines or work routines, and growth or recession of the local economy. All of these factors affect the training, placement, and projected employment of various types of workers.

Teachers, counselors, placement personnel, and other educators associated with the several aspects of career development/transitional programming may not be expected to be familiar with every machine and routine in communication technology or the fast food industry. However, their familiarity with labor force data, general requirements for jobs within industries, and current conditions within the marketplace will improve communication between educators and local leaders in business and industry. This familiarity also provides a basic foundation for understanding the observations and recommendations from businesspeople relative to changes in procedures and practices within the educational community.

Contacts with Business and Industry

Self-reliance is a major part of the collective American personality. Most Americans believe that a person's efforts account for her success or failure, whether she falls into the white- or blue-collar categories. Such terms as clout, influence, and pull, to name a few, are used in a derogatory fashion to identify individuals who have advanced in the organization or achieved an objective based on means apart from their work skills.*

Educators would be fooling themselves if they did not imagine that meeting people in business and industry for the purpose of securing contacts was a necessary function associated with developing jobs for their students. American workers would like to believe that their success on a job is due to their own efforts and ability, but individuals with special behavior needs have stated that they would first like to have a chance at obtaining employment.

Individuals from one walk of life or profession (education and rehabilitation) need an entrée to another sector (business and industry) simply because the normal training and pursuit of professional goals does not bring members of one sector into frequent contact with those from the other. Bankers are more acquainted with other bankers than they are with teachers because most of their working day and, very often, their social life includes other bankers. Thus, it is a question of how an educator can meet individuals in business and industry who can help train or employ their students with special behavior needs. One answer is to utilize all possible leads and contacts within the business and industry sectors.

Educators can use the resources of vocational rehabilitation, employment services, rehabilitation facilities, youth training programs, and just about any organization that has contacts with business and industry. Such contacts are important because they:

1. Economize on the educator's time and energy, which are needed to complete other responsibilities.
2. Provide an element of support for the employer interview.

An educator can approach an employer independently and achieve favorable benefits for the program. However, the chances for success are enhanced if the placement personnel are recommended or endorsed by another businessperson.

---

*These terms, as well as the expression "It's who you know that counts, not what you know," are not confined to the world of work.

In their extensive review of rehabilitation and job placement of individuals with disabilities, Zadny and James (1976) distinguish between formal and informal sources of job leads. Contacts with members of business and industry (employers) fall in the category of informal sources and are also characterized by Zadny and James as "underused." These underused channels may provide better results simply because the commonly used sources support greater numbers of job seekers. The two categories of sources appear in Table 6.1.

Professionals can use the information in Table 6.1 to place clients or students with special behavior needs, or just plain job seekers. Underused sources of information can be categorized as personal contacts among professionals, workers, and businesspeople with prospective employers. As transition program personnel develop greater contacts with community organizations, advisory groups, and members of the business and industrial sector, they take advantage of underused channels of information and avoid excessive competition from other applicants for jobs.

Advocates for Persons with Disabilities

Many large corporations have enthusiastically publicized their belief in the capability of persons with special behavior needs to become outstanding and productive employees. Examples of some statements in various publications follow:

"Our experience with persons who have disabilities has been outstanding."

(Bruce Carswell, Sr. Vice-President, GTE Corporation)

"Hiring and training men and women who are disabled is clearly a plus —for companies, for those eager to help themselves, and for our economy."

(Colby H. Chandler, Chairman and CEO, Eastman Kodak Company)

TABLE 6.1 Used and Underused Sources of Job Leads

Commonly Cited Sources	Underused Sources
Newspaper want ads	Past employer
State employment service	Past clients
Private employment agencies	Counselor's acquaintances
Help wanted signs	Employers cited by employers who have
Yellow pages	hired clients
Trade publications	Counselor's co-workers
Unions	Service persons
Civil service bulletins	Client family and friends
Business pages of newspaper	Workers at business hiring clients
Employers who have hired clients	

Note. From "Another View on Placement: State of the Art 1976," *Studies in Placement Monograph No. 1* (p. 29) by J. J. Zadney and L. F. James, 1976, Portland: Portland Oregon School of Social Work, Portland State University. Copyright 1976 by Portland State University. Reprinted by permission.

"Success can be attained only by the full utilization of all resources, the most important being people."

(J. J. Albenze, Administrator,
Westinghouse Corporation)

These and many other similar statements in support of employing persons with disabilities are contained in the 1987 publication *Disabled Americans at Work* (The President's Committee on Employment of People with Disabilities, 1987), which is available from the U.S. Government Printing Office and developed by several corporations in cooperation with the Dole Foundation and the President's Committee on Employment of People with Disabilities. A list of the corporations that provided information about some of their employees with disabilities in that publication is presented in Table 6.2. It should be emphasized that this list of companies in Table 6.2 is just an example of some of the many large and small companies that have become strong advocates and employers of persons with disabilities and other disadvantages.

The momentum for employing persons with special behavior needs continues to grow in the 1990s, thanks in part to the ADA legislation. But many American businesses and industries have had a long history of being advocates for these individuals. No doubt, a survey of resources in one's own community would result in a larger number of businesses and industries that are engaged in many important advocacy activities on behalf of these individuals with special behavior needs.

Classroom Resource

Business and industry are providing schools with a myriad of teaching programs and materials to help teachers learn more about such important topics as ecology. In fact, some businesses even train teachers to use their programs. And, because most teachers don't have the time to look for information they could use to put corporate material in perspective for their students with special behavior needs, many corporations will assist teachers further in obtaining relevant information.

Members of business and industry also can help teachers select materials, training manuals, or instructional guides. For example, placement personnel may review application forms or provide suggestions on training students with special behavior needs for interviews. Plant supervisors can suggest training

TABLE 6.2   Examples of Corporations and Companies with Special Concern About Employing People with Disabilities

Sector	Company
Chemical industry	Dow Chemical Stauffer Chemical Company W. R. Grace & Co.
Communications industry	GTE AT&T IT&T New England Telephone
Computers and electronics	Honeywell Sperry
Consumer goods and services	Phillip Morris Miller Brewing Company Eastman Kodak Company Sears Continental Can Motion Designs Proctor & Gamble United Airlines General Mills
Energy and utilities	Washington Water Power Baltimore Gas & Electric Pennsylvania Power and Light Company Montana Power Company Texaco Duke Power Company Edison Electric Institute
Finance, banking, and insurance	Aetna Life and Casualty Allstate American Express Blue Cross, Blue Shield Mutual of Omaha The Prudential Insurance Company
Health and medical	Abbott Laboratories Merck & Co. Hospital Corporation of America

procedures that teachers can use in a school or workshop environment to prepare students with special behavior needs for the world of work. Although vocational educators are usually familiar with changes and modifications in selected industries, personnel from various companies should continue to advise them on changes in materials, machines, or routines that should be reflected in the training program.

Prepare your resource person is one rule that educators should keep in mind whenever they ask a representative from business or industry to act as a speaker, consultant, or tour guide to groups of students with

TABLE 6.2   Continued

Sector	Company
Heavy manufacturing	Westinghouse
	Rockwell International
	General Dynamics
	E.I.L. Instruments
	General Motors Corporation
	Innovative Concepts
	Phifer Wire Products, Inc.
	American Can
	Decc Company
	Steelcase
	Raytheon Company
Restaurant/hospitality	Burger King Corporation
	Valentino's Restaurant
	Refuge Restaurant
	The Marquette and the Northstar Hotels
	Marriott Corporation
	McDonald's

Note. From *Disabled Americans at Work* by the President's Committee on Employment of People with Disabilities, 1987, Washington, DC: U.S. Government Printing Office.

special behavior needs, faculty, or parents. Preparation should include an interview with program personnel and the presentation of printed or visual information about the resource person's role and importance in the development of the exceptional person's career. Preparation will give resource people an idea of what is expected of them and how they can use their time and resources more efficiently. This information will influence the resource person's decision regarding continued involvement with the school system.

Program Consultation

The scope of a career development/transition program, including vocational training and placement, requires several skills on the part of educators. These skills are essential to such program components as student evaluation, program evaluation, management of resources, and cost analysis. In addition, these skills may be used to resolve specific problems relative to minimum wage laws and work-study assignments, cooperative agreements between the school system and other agencies, and placement evaluation of former students with special behavior needs and their employers.

Opinions from members of the business and industrial sector may help educators find solutions to mutual problems. This collaboration will help in the development of more appropriate career development/transition program.

Representatives from business and industry also can advise program directors about the competencies required by teachers or other personnel to prepare students with special behavior needs for the job market. Jobs, skills, and work roles are in constant change and those people who prepare students with special behavior needs to enter such a fluid market must also command certain competencies.

Work Experience

If there is one ingredient that stands out as the prominent link between business and industry and the education system across the country, it is their co-operation in work experience or work-study programs for students with special behavior needs. Business and industry have been active in collaborative efforts to develop field experience, student internships, summer employment, and on-the-job training. These programs provide students with special behavior needs with hands-on experiences that test their interests in particular jobs; provide a source of evaluation for supervisory personnel; train students with special behavior needs to use tools and complete tasks; and reward them for the amount of energy that they have invested in the experience. Although it may be a cliché to say, "experience is the best teacher," almost every significant program for students normally involves work experience. Transition research indicates that structured work experience during the school years is the most significant factor for adults with special behavior needs' success in employment.

Program personnel should consider two significant points in establishing a series of structured work experiences for their students.

First, a sequence of experiences should be available so that individuals from elementary school through adult education can be involved in appropriate work positions, meeting their level of maturity, interest, and ability. Work experience is not the final stage of a training program. Ideally, work experience should be an integrated element of the training program and should be available at various points in the student's career development/transition program. Such a series of experiences provides the individual and program personnel with several forms of evaluation relative to intended and future occupational roles. It also allows the student with special behavior needs to experiment with work roles that may benefit him at later stages of all career roles development, as in the instance of a change of occupations.

Work experience is not the final stage of a training program.

Second, work experience is a training device for determining work adjustment of strengths and weaknesses. If program personnel permanently place a student with special behavior needs in a work-study position, they have lost that position as a work adjustment-training site for other students with special behavior needs. We are well aware of the temptation to place students in employment when the site supervisors indicate that they have openings, thus losing that position site for others to receive training. But the real value of work experience is that a number of students can be cycled through a series of work sites and work adjustments that allow the identification and evaluation of work skills by supervisors and educators. This knowledge becomes a standard by which other students can be measured and trained. Eliminating a training site or series of experiences forces educators to repeat the laborious effort of locating another cooperative businessperson, establishing communication with supervisors, and investing additional time setting up more sites that could be used to help more students find employment or provided work adjustment training.

One variation on work experience is the involvement of faculty members in similar on-the-job routines. For example, Kern High School District, Bakersfield, CA, financed the placement of its vocational instructors into the secured work-study sites in community businesses. Because these instructors trained students with special behavior needs before placing them in community work sites, the district made sure the teachers taught students with special behavior needs about the work routines and tasks that would enable them to be successful at the work experience sites. The in-service training of the faculty allowed them to work on jobs so that they then could structure their teaching to better prepare their students with special behavior needs for more work adjustment success during the work experience placement.

Most students with special behavior needs find employment during their high school years. These jobs are generally found by the student's family or friends, or by the students themselves. Whether or not students with special behavior needs are getting much educational benefit and adequate exposure to the real world of work, other than compensation, is something educators should be concerned about if they want to prepare these students for meaningful careers upon the transition from school to community training, living, and working. Halpern, Dorenz, and Benz (1993) suggest that educators consider encouraging students to decline or shorten some types of high school employment if it is not adequate for adjustment for more appropriate vocational learning. Schools need to improve their linkages to the business world so employers and school supervisors can structure the experience to be a more substantive career development experience for the students with special behavior needs. They note that new vocational training options should be considered, such as apprenticeship programs that are so prevalent in the European work adjustment system. These options are beginning in the United States now, as youth apprenticeship programs and work-based learning programs become more prominent for regular class students in our high schools. Hopefully, students in special behavior needs programs will also be given the same opportunity for these structured work adjustment experiences. As noted, these structured work experiences among business and school have proven to be of value in preparing the student with special behavior needs for successful adult employment.

Transition Conferences and Workshops

Transition conferences and workshops bring people together to discuss themes, problems, issues, or actions related to career development/transition for individuals with special behavior needs. These events can be used to explore such concerns as

- Partnership of business/industry and education
- Preparation to meet the changing job market
- Education's role in retaining the employee who is disabled while on the job
- Requirements imposed by legislation

Various professional organizations within the business world, as well as individual companies, have sponsored conferences and workshops in the broad area of career education/transition for American youth and workers. As long ago as 1977, the White House Conference on Handicapped Individuals made recommendations pertinent to extended cooperation by business and industry with education in career development/transitional programming of these individuals. Some of the delegates' recommendations also provided additional themes for joint conferences and workshops. The President's Committee on Employment of the Handicapped (now renamed The President's Committee on Employment of People with Disabilities) (1977) recommended:

- A national public awareness program should be developed to recognize employers who hire disabled people.
- Training for supervisors should emphasize the use of workers with disabilities.
- Transitional employment programs should be developed (e.g., psychosocial centers for mentally restored people and occupational training centers for individuals with intellectual deficiencies).
- Vocational schools, sheltered workshops, and other places of training should teach the skills that really meet the needs of local employers.

Instructional and Resource Materials

Business, industry, and education have collaborated for many years in the preparation of students with special behavior needs for work roles. In addition to providing inservice training and special conference meetings, they have provided informational resources for schools, students with special behavior needs, and their families.

An elaboration of the kinds of materials related to career education/transition to the world of work provided by organizations and companies is unnecessary; any description would soon be outdated as materials are changed or exhausted. The important thing to remember is that these transitions from school-to-work materials will exist as long as business/industry is involved in the career development/transition of American workers.

INVOLVING BUSINESS AND INDUSTRY

The previous section identified the potential contributions of members of business and industry to career development/transition programs from school-to-work postsecondary programs and employment. This section suggests how educators can contact and involve members of business and industry in career development/transition programs that benefit the entire community. The following list provides suggestions for establishing this support to the business and industry sectors:

- Invite business and industry to serve on a Community Advisory Committee.
- Give presentations to civic organizations.
- Issue publications about the program (e.g., brochures, reports, and news release items).
- Advertise in business publications.
- Conduct job fairs, workshops, and institutes.

Community Transition Advisory Committee

The role of a Community Transition Advisory Committee, such as the one described earlier by D. H. Clark (1993), can be a significant factor in the success of a school's career development/transition program. If school personnel anticipate that the community will accept the individual with special behavior needs and support school programs, the Transition Advisory Committee (TAC) must be more than a perfunctory group whose members' names enhance the program director's stationery. Campbell, Todd, and O'Rourke (1971) and Phelps (1976) stated that the TAC could provide valuable service by:

1. Reviewing transition program components, such as instructional materials, facilities, equipment, and cooperative training agreements
2. Identifying community transition contributions, resources, and effective measures of public relations

3. Developing evaluation designs that will be included in the transition Program

There is no hard and fast rule as to how many members should be on the TAC or for what length of time they should serve. TAC members would most likely include representatives from major industries that may employ graduates of the transition program. School personnel, however, should not assume or convey the impression that the TAC members are obligated to find jobs for students with special behavior needs or hire a certain number of graduates from the transition program. The members' principal role is to assist the transition program coordinator and function as community advocates for students with special behavior needs. The following list of suggested TAC members represents a cross section of the major groups of individuals who are interested in student success or who can directly influence training procedures:

1. Personnel or employment managers who would be able to advise educators about application forms, interview procedures, and employment trends
2. Supervisors who are in direct contact with employees with special behavior needs and can identify potential difficulties they may have in the work setting
3. Directors or managers of a firm that employs a number of workers with special behavior needs and who would speak to businesspeople about the company's successful experiences in employment or accommodation of students in the school's transition program
4. Members of parent organizations who are strongly interested in career development/transition efforts and could support school programs by forming coalitions of parents and workers with special behavior needs
5. Members of community agencies involved in the training and placement activities who could provide information on the challenges faced by the adult individual with special behavior needs
6. Members of an insurance firm acquainted with the practices and rates for industries that employ workers with special behavior needs

7. Individuals with special behavior needs who have succeeded in the work world and can provide unique insights into the program's training and placement components

Even though TAC members may have expertise in particular areas, educators should not assume that these members are familiar with the issues and problems involved in the career development/transition of individuals with special behavior needs. The members should attend a series of transition information sessions, informing them about the school's transition program, community efforts, and transition efforts nationally. At times, TAC members may conduct these sessions. But school personnel must initially plan the overall direction until the TAC members have had time to identify their interests and request information on specific transition areas where their expertise can best be served.

Civic Organizations

The term *civic organization* is used broadly to include all groups interested in improving the well-being of the members in their community. The organizations serve as fertile ground for contacts with members of the business community, simply because both the educator and businessperson share a desire to improve the quality of life for all members of the community. This mutual respect provides educators with an opportunity to present the benefits of the transition training and placement program and pursue possible leads for further involvement with business and industry. Several transition program directors have said that some of their strongest supporters or employment leads were established after they made a presentation to a civic group and were approached afterwards by interested community business leaders and representatives.

Transition coordinators should regard presentations to civic organizations as a major public relations project. The speaker should know the most appropriate technique to convey the message to the civic group using state of the art technology and publications to best inform and involve the audience.

1. The presentation should emphasize major points so that the audience will not get "lost" in too many figures and details.
2. The speaker should involve the audience by eliciting questions about transition from school-to-work, career development, training, and placement information, along with stories of job successes in local business and industry in the community.
3. Materials should be available to civic members who wish to read at their leisure or contact other sources of information.
4. Former or current students of the program should be included in the presentation to dispel the audience's possible misconceptions about the abilities of individuals with special behavior needs.

Transition Program Publications

The educator should always try to focus the community's attention on the students' goals and achievements. This can be accomplished through personal presentations, as described in the previous section, meetings with civic leaders, and interviews with businesses and parents. However, professionally developed publications can be used as a ready reference when the educator is unavailable and also can be distributed to the public as well as to members of business and industry to highlight transition program features and successes. The transition coordinator can use several kinds of publications to advertise transition programming/career development and to involve members of business and industry. These publications would include the following:

1. *An attractive brochure that provides an overview of the program, its intents, and the advantages that the program can offer to the reader:*
The brochure can help educators make contacts and obtain interviews with employers. Brochures may include pictures of students at work to convey the impression that one of the goals and accomplishments of career development is successful employment.

2. *Several types of reports that provide "hard data" about the program:*

This information is necessary to justify expenditures and is valuable to administrators, teachers, TAC members, and members of the community who wish to know how their tax dollars are spent wisely to prepare students with special behavior need in becoming productive and successful employees and tax paying citizens. The most frequent topics for these reports include successful placements by work titles; identification of business firms that have hired students; the amount of money that former students with special behavior needs have earned over a period of time; and the amount of tax dollars these students with special behavior needs returned to the community.

3. *News release items that can be used by the local media in direct reprints or broadcasts or that can provide the basis for a feature story:*

The news release can advertise the availability of qualified workers, such as a "work wanted" advertisement. The advertisement may include the unique accomplishments of the student, such as the completion of a training program for mechanics or computer operators.

Business publications also can be used to publicize the school's transition and career development efforts and involvement with business and industry. Several industries and companies publish their own materials. Anyone who has ever sat in a doctor's or dentist's office may have spent a long period of time paging through what are termed the trade journals. Articles about workers with special behavior needs have appeared in many of these publications. Transition personnel at the local and state level should be aware that such journals could help to advertise and inform potential employers about the school's transition/career development program.

Job Fairs, Workshops, and Institutes

Several organizations (parent groups, associations formed by individuals with special behavior needs, government agencies) have attempted to educate employers and other personnel in business and industry about the positive qualities of workers with special behavior needs. These organizations have combined their talents, contacts, and efforts to achieve the following:

1. Inform employers about ways they can meet recent changes in affirmative action laws to hire employees with special behavior needs.
2. Display the achievements of other employers who have hired workers with special behavior needs.
3. Provide a meeting place where employers can interview prospective employees with special behavior needs.
4. Provide a forum to discuss common problems experienced by both employers and employees with special behavior needs.
5. Discuss local or regional job openings and projected changes in the supply and demand of labor.
6. Increase employers' knowledge about the abilities and skills of the untapped segment of the labor force with special behavior needs.

These efforts may be presented over local or educational television and could be organized into the traditional conference or the increasingly popular job fair. The job fair is a central location at which representatives from business and industry interview applicants. It benefits individuals with special behavior needs by providing several interview possibilities within one location.

This section has focused on ways in which educators can contact and involve representatives of business and industry in career development/transition activities. The following are some important considerations permeating the numerous attempts:

• Involve members of business and industry as soon as possible in your transitional programs. There are several reasons for this recommendation. First, the active cooperation and commitment of members of business and industry may be stronger if they are approached in the formative stages of a program or project rather than serving as symbolic representatives. Second, they may be able to suggest important changes or ways of getting support while the transition program is in the developmental stages. This is especially crucial if the transition program includes provisions for cooperation with business and industry. Some transition coordinators have spent considerable time planning a project, preparing staff and students with special learning and behavior needs, identifying training experiences and appropriate industries, and then approaching business and industry with the expectation that employers, supervisors, managers, and businesspeople would just fit right into their plan. This course of action is not recommended.

- Maintain a continuity in communications with members of business and industry. Business executives are accustomed to a certain degree of punctuality, and supervisors want precision. Both are especially discouraged when they are approached by several representatives of the same program or project. Just imagine what your response might be if three of four salespersons for the same project called you on the telephone during your office hours. The continuity of communication is also important once individuals with special behavior needs are involved in the program, as emphasized in the discussion of the Transition Advisory Committee (TAC).

- Publicize the link between business and industry and education as much as possible. Of course, any efforts at publicity should be approved by the principal agents involved in the transition program. Once publicity has been approved, educators should use as many resources as possible within the community, area, state, region, and nation. Successive stages of information contain a corresponding vehicle for communication with the public. For example, the community may have a small, neighborhood, or local newspaper and radio station. A large-city newspaper may cover a larger area, television station, and several AM-FM radio channels. A state would be covered by official publications written by members of the legislature or speeches entered into the official proceedings. The region may be covered through professional publications that pertain to the particular industry. And the nation may release information through federal agencies that are concerned with the transition education and employment of individuals with special behavior needs. Publication of an existing collaboration between business and industry and education can

help to expand transition programs, as well as improve employment possibilities for individuals with special behavior needs, as discussed in the following section.

- Encourage the involvement of business and industry by using as many resources as possible. The previous discussions of publications and TAC members include references to the many agents within a community who can become advocates for transition training programs. These advocates, whether civic groups, parents' organizations, or influential citizens, will need the information and encouragement of special, vocational, and general educators. Furthermore, all educators must be aware of the potential for the involvement of the entire community and should coordinate activities with the goals of the career education/transition program.

EMPLOYER RESOURCES

Many employers may be reluctant to consider hiring persons with special learning and behavior needs because of their lack of knowledge or experience, misconceptions, fears, reservations, a poor previous experience, or for a myriad of other reasons that can be resolved by the professional willing to work closely with them. The potential employer needs to know that special educators and rehabilitation personnel are available to help both the trainee and employer in the transition phase with on-site training, counseling, and other services that will be required for the placement to succeed. One of the major ways the professionals can help employers is to provide them with information on available resources that may assist them in their efforts to accommodate their workers with special behavior needs. Some of these are identified and described briefly below:

- ABLEDATA is a consumer referral service that contains more than 18,000 listings of adaptive devices for all disabilities. It responds to requests for information from persons with special and learning needs and from employers. Address: 8455

Colesville Road, #935, Silver Springs, MD 20910 —Phone: (800) 227-0216, voice and Telecommunication Device for the Deaf (V/TDD).

- Disabled Access Credit (Section 44 of the IRS Code) encourages small business to comply with the ADA by providing a tax credit of up to $5,000 per year. The employer or small business can deduct 50% of "eligible access expenditures" between $250 and $10,000. More information is available from the local IRS office.
- The Targeted Jobs Tax Credit (TJTC, Section 51 of the IRS Code) provides a tax credit of 40% of the first $6,000 earned per employee, provided the individual with special behavior needs is employed at least 90 days or 120 hours. An employer may not claim TJTC and on-the-job training for the same wages. More information is available from IRS Publication 907 or from the State Job Service or Vocational Rehabilitation office.
- Architectural and Transportation Barrier Removal Tax Reduction (Section 190 of the IRS Code) provides a tax deduction to employers for up to $15,000 for making facilities and public transportation vehicles accessible to employees with special behavior needs. All alterations must meet the Department of Treasury Standards.
- Job Accommodation Network (JAN) is an information network for employers. Operated by the President's Committee on Employment of People with Disabilities, it is a database containing specific information about how individual tasks can be done by persons with special and learning limitations. It provides a free consulting service on the ADA and provides information on aids, devices, and methods for accommodating workers with special behavior needs. JAN enables employers to discuss with other employers accommodations that have proved successful. Phone: (800) ADA-WORD (V/TDD).
- The Arc National On-the-Job Training has been in operation for several decades. The U.S. Department of Labor funds the program. Funds are available for training persons with intellectual disabilities/developmental disabilities in business and industry; the employer will be reimbursed for training and employing the person with special

behavior needs for a specified length of time. Persons interested in more specific information should contact the project at Arc's national headquarters, 500 E. Border Street, Suite 300, Arlington, TX 76010. Phone: (817) 277-3491.

- The Industry-Labor Council's National Center on Employment and Disability, which acts as a consultant and technical assistant on employment of persons with special behavior needs, provides a clearinghouse for information on topics such as accessibility, outreach and recruiting, reasonable accommodation, legislation, and special behavior needs management. The center offers various forms of training to industry and maintains an extensive array of informational materials relative to employment of persons with behavior needs. Address: The Human Resources Center, 201 I.U. Willets Rd, W., Albertson, NY 11507-1599. Phone: (516) 747-6323.
- Projects with Industry is a program administered by private industry and rehabilitation agencies. The focus of the transition program is job placement, work adjustment, skills training, and/or linkage with business and industry so that rehabilitation services become more responsive to the needs of employers. Interested persons should contact their nearest vocational rehabilitation agency office.

A vast array of associations and other organizations can be of assistance to employers seeking information and advice on employing persons who have special behavior needs and the disadvantaged. A good resource for this information is the *Encyclopedia of Associations* (1992).

IBM makes many important contributions to the improved quality of life for persons with disabilities.

IBM has been a leader in enhancing the quality of life and the employability of persons with behavior needs through the use of their technology (assistive technology) for many decades. In 1985, they established their Special Needs Information and Referral Center (SNIRC). The SNIRC maintains a sizable database of available products, suppliers, and agencies. IBM supports a demonstration facility and conducts awareness seminars for executives inside and outside of IBM. The seminars increase awareness and knowledge about the employability of people with special behavior needs and current assistive technology.

In addition, IBM offers several other services to enhance the transition/career development of persons with special behavior needs and those who are disadvantaged. Through its Disabilities Assistance Network, IBM lends computers and software at no charge to federally funded disabilities support centers across the United States. IBM has helped establish 53 nationwide centers that train people with special behavior needs for careers in communication/information processing industries. In addition, IBM sponsors over 100 job-training centers for the economically disadvantaged, primarily in word processing, and a Basic Skills/Literacy Support Program for those who do not have the skills to enroll in job training. In 1993, IBM opened its Job Training and Competency Center in Arlington, VA, to demonstrate how the private sector can participate in successful partnerships with community-based organizations serving persons with special behavior needs and the disadvantaged and to provide management and staff development and training.

The center also exhibits the IBM Independence Series, which is a group of products designed to help people with visual, physical, and speech and hearing disabilities achieve greater personal and professional independence through technology. Eight products are currently available, five of them to increase accessibility to everyday activities:

- Screen Reader, for individuals with vision impairments, is a screen text-to-speech conversion tool that provides equal access to computer information.
- Phone Communicator, for persons who are hearing and/or speech impaired, provides telephone communications with another person via a touch-tone telephone and communicates with both Baudot and ASCII TDDs, displaying a full-screen view of the dialogue from both parties. Any telephone conversation can be saved and printed.
- VoiceType, for people with physical impairments, is a flexible speech-recognition program that pro-

vides an affordable keyboard alternative by speaking.
- AccessDOS is a utility to enhance keyboard access for IBM DOS users for each of the programs described previously.
- KeyGuard is a molded template to enhance keying accuracy so the keyboard can be positioned at any angle; the person with a mobility impairment can use it with a minimum of effort.

IBM has also developed a variety of input devices, readers, speech synthesizers, a Braille printer, and screen-enlargement software that interface with the previously mentioned systems. In addition, IBM has produced a program entitled SpeechViewer to increase the efficiency of speech therapy, SpeechViewer II, and THINKable to help clients practice thinking skills in four focus areas relating to communication and daily living skills. Information about IBM products can be obtained by calling 800-IBM-3333 for the number of the nearest branch office.

The preceding discussion reflects the considerably improving receptivity of business and industry to the employment of persons with disabilities and other learning difficulties. The President's Committee on Employment of People with Disabilities (1993) published, for employers, the following guidelines for conducting a job interview with individuals with special behavior needs:

- Make sure your company's employment offices and your interview location are accessible to applicants with mobility impairments, visual, hearing, or cognitive disabilities.
- Be willing to make appropriate and reasonable accommodations to enable job applicants with special behavior needs to present themselves in the best possible light. For example, offer assistance to applicants who are blind or have limited use of their hands in completing their job application forms; provide an interpreter for an applicant who is deaf; and offer detailed or specific instructions to persons with cognitive disabilities.
- Don't let a rehabilitation counselor, social worker, or other third party take an active part in or sit in on an interview unless the applicant requests it.

- Make sure you have in-depth knowledge of the essential job functions regarding the position for which the applicant is applying, as well as the details of why, how, where, when, and by whom each task or operation is performed. This will enable you to structure the interview better and ensure that all questions are job related.
- Relax and make the applicant feel relaxed. Don't be afraid of making mistakes. At the same time, remember that candidates (particularly those applying for professional positions) must be expected to assume an equal share of the responsibility for making your interaction with them comfortable.
- Don't speculate or try to imagine how you would perform a specific job if you had the applicant's special learning or behavior need. The person with special behavior needs hopefully has mastered alternative techniques and skills of living and working with her particular special behavior needs. You should ask an applicant to describe how she would perform a certain job function if it is an essential part of the position.
- Concentrate on the applicant with special behavior needs' technical and professional knowledge, skills, abilities, experiences, and interests, not on the special learning or behavior need. Remember, you can't interview a disability, hire a disability, or supervise a disability. You can interview a person, hire a person, and supervise a person.
- If the applicant is not technically or professionally qualified for the position in question, end the interview. If the applicant is qualified, feel free to discuss in an open, honest, and straightforward manner how the applicant plans to perform specific on-the-job duties and what he or she will need to get the job done. Remember, all questions should be job related and asked in an open-ended format.

Another set of guidelines is presented in Figure 6.2. These have been written by Steelcase, Inc., and portray the perspective of an employer.

The preceding guidelines and those in Figure 6.2 also have implications for those placing students with special behavior needs in work experience sites during their high school years. These guidelines should help the educator or transition specialist in preparing prospective employers for interviewing students with special behavior and learning needs and for integrating them into the work setting.

STUDENTS WITH SEVERE DISABILITIES

Unlike many individuals with mild special behavior needs, most individuals with substantial developmental disabilities will need the assistance/support of a job developer or placement person who contacts employers on behalf of the individual with severe disabilities (Hagner & Daning, 1993). The supported employment program has been extremely effective in preparing individuals with more severe disabilities for working in competitive working settings.

How can transition coordinators/job developers and others involved in the transition and placement process most appropriately approach employers? Hagner and Daning (1993) attempted to answer that question by interviewing 49 job developers from 26 organizations in one state. The investigators found that a considerable variety of techniques and methods were used but that they were generally quite successful after four or five employer contacts. Most important to attain jobs, employees needed personal contacts and a trusting relationship and the ability to work with employers, rather than responding to want-ad openings. Another important finding was the caution about mentioning the person's special behavior needs during the early stage of discussions.

Students with severe disabilities usually require considerably more accommodations than those with mild special learning and behavior needs. Employers will need to know that these individuals with more severe behavior needs, once successfully placed and accommodated, will make loyal and dependable workers. Some, not all, will be content to work on tasks that other employees find aversive or boring, although many others will be able to perform highly challenging and complex tasks, overcoming the imposition of a physical, sensory, behavioral, or learning disability.

GUIDELINES FOR INTERVIEWING AND HIRING INDIVIDUALS WITH DISABILITIES

Recruiting	Review the job description or any other documentation that delineates the essential job functions. If using an employment agency, be sure their recruiting and screening practices do not discriminate against a qualified individual with a disability. Look at alternative ways of advertising that will reach individuals with disabilities.
Pre-Interview	Be sure your tests, physical examinations, and application procedures, do not screen out people with disabilities who may, with reasonable accommodation, be able to perform the job. Make accommodations, if necessary, to testing procedures to allow for the person's disability. Review your selection criteria for screening candidates.
Interview	Treat the job candidate with a disability the same as any other job candidate. Make the person comfortable. Maintain eye contact. If the person requires any special assistance, offer to help. Maintain a professional environment. Focus on the job tasks and the candidate's ability to perform each of them.
Discussing the individual's disability	Provide opportunity for *individual* to initiate discussion on the effect his disability has on his capacity to perform job duties. Once the individual has *initiated* the discussion about his or her job duty limitations, maintain focus on performance of job duties. Pinpoint any barriers—physical or psychological. Decide which barriers can be overcome through reasonable accommodations. Look at reassigning non-essential job duties to another employee.
Integrating the individual with disability into the work force	Prepare co-workers to work with the disabled individual. Provide training, if necessary. Discuss openly any anxieties co-workers may have. Brainstorm ideas for overcoming barriers. Use a proactive approach to solving problems that might arise. Assign a partner to work closely with individual for the first few weeks.
Working with the new hire with disability	Welcome the new hire with disability as you would any new hire. Provide orientation. Make sure the new hire feels comfortable letting co-workers, as well as you, know about problems that arise. Focus on the person's abilities—the reason you hired the individual in the first place.

FIGURE 6.2 Guidelines for Interviewing and Hiring Individuals with Disabilities.
Note. From *Employee Handbook* (p. 6) by Steelcase, Inc. Reprinted by permission.

Transition coordinators working to place their students with more severe behavior needs in business and industry will need to follow several important principles. These include:

1. Placing students who are ready for such an experience. This requires adequate assessment of the student's vocational interests, abilities, and needs and matching them carefully to the community's resources. The student with more severe behavior needs must be a willing participant in the placement decision.

2. Assuring the employer that the student has the essential basic work habits, behaviors, interest, and ability for the placement. This requires the transitional program to provide its students with more severe behavior needs general employability skills training and adequate orientation to the world of work before placement, although further training in this area will also be a major objective of the experience.

3. Providing a job coach or support person who can orient employees to the student and be available to provide whatever training and supervision is needed. This will be especially critical during the initial period of training and will gradually fade in its intensity as the student becomes acclimated and able to function appropriately. The job coach or trainer will need to be available to return more frequently at various times in the training period when the student needs more extensive training, supervision, or problem resolution.

4. Keeping in frequent contact with the student's supervisor and employees regarding progress and needs. It is important for the student with more severe behavior needs to get as many work and interpersonal experiences as possible. The educator should ensure that the student with more severe behavior needs is treated as much as possible as any new employee would be and is expected to perform duties that the job coach/trainer deems reasonable and as an important training objective. A job performance rating form and a job task sheet should be used to gain frequent input from the supervisor and co-workers to determine the student with more severe learning and behavior needs' work performance and behavioral functioning and needs.

Many businesses and industries are providing persons with more severe behavior needs with the opportunity for vocational training and employment. Two Minneapolis hotels, The Marquette and The Northstar, have been recognized internationally for their pioneering program of hiring and training persons with more severe behavior needs. In their stewarding department, more than 100 of their 120 employees have more severe and learning needs, and they have reduced their annual turnover from an industry-wide average of 150% percent to 11%.

Marriott Corporation is another major employer of persons with special behavior needs, who account for about 5% of Marriott's work force nationwide. Marriott provides on-the-job training at many of its locations and works closely with many school systems and professional organizations to hire these individuals, including many with developmental disabilities/more severe behavior needs. Much joy and satisfaction can result, not only for the employee with more severe behavior needs, but also for the employer who provides these individuals with the opportunity to prove their ability to be productive and loyal workers.

"A diverse culture is our reality and our future."
McDonald's Corporation

McDonald's Corporation continues to be particularly responsive to the abilities of persons with more severe behavior needs. McDonald's has developed a comprehensive field training program to provide sensitivity training, including dispelling common myths and presenting facts about persons with more severe behavior needs, and exercises for its employees to heighten their appreciation of the inconvenience that a special behavior need presents. McDonald's has been a pioneer in the employment of people with special behavior needs for over 35 years and is an outstanding example of a major company that is giving persons with mild-to-severe special behavior needs a chance to become productive citizens and employees.

CHAPTER COMMENTARY

The opportunity for educators to form even more meaningful and substantial partnerships has never been greater. The ADA of 1990 has been a positive force in promoting this opportunity, and for the most part, business and industry have been responsive to the mandate to provide the accommodations necessary for individuals with special behavior needs to be successful and productive employees. Now, it is up to the educational/transitional system to respond accordingly by not only forming meaningful partnerships/alliances but also working together with community agencies in preparing their students with special behavior needs more adequately for the world of work and community living.

The methods and materials for providing a transitional program that meets the contemporary and complex needs of its community and its students have been developed. School districts now need to restructure their overall curriculums so these functional methods and materials are adequately incorporated. The preparation of students with special behavior needs for successful adult adjustment is a formidable task and realistic goal. The functional curriculum must institute a scope and sequence (K-12) that inculcates in these students a self-awareness, self-esteem, and work personality that will lead to the successful attainment of those adult life skills that are needed for a productive life of living and working in their community.

If the educational system does not prepare its students with special behavior needs with all of the important basic functional skills needed for training and placement in the labor market (i.e., academic, daily living, personal-social, and occupational), the result will be failure and continued rejection of these individuals with special behavior needs as worthy and productive citizens. Now that much of business and industry have accepted the challenge and responsibility to be transitional educators, it is up to the schools to become even more proactive in designing career development/ transitional/community-based experiences that will truly result in their students' successful transition from school-to-work/postsecondary training and community living.

ACTIVITIES

1. Conduct a survey of those businesses and industries in your community that could be potential work experience sites and future employers of your students with special behavior needs. Secure the names of appropriate contact persons, and interview some of these individuals to discern the level of awareness and receptivity toward working with the school in your career education/transition program.
2. Refer to the LCCE Mild/Moderate Curriculum Matrices in Figure 3.4 and determine which of the resources you have identified can contribute to the training needs of your students with either mild or more severe learning and behavior needs.

PART **3**

TRANSITIONAL EDUCATION

CHAPTER 7

Functional Transition Assessment

CHAPTER 8

Transition Planning

CHAPTER 9

Functional Materials and Resources

CHAPTER 10

Self-Determination

Functional Transition Assessment

Robert J. Loyd
and Stephen W. Thomas

PRELIMINARY QUESTIONS

1. What is the difference between norm-referenced and criterion-referenced tests?
2. What is meant by the terms functional transition assessment, career assessment, and vocational assessment?
3. What legal mandates presently exist that require educators to use functional transition assessment measures?
4. What are some important advantages and disadvantages of using a functional transition assessment approach?
5. What is a functional job analysis?
6. Identify several particularly useful functional transition assessment instruments for career development and transition planning.
7. What is curriculum-based vocational assessment (CBVA)?
8. Explain what is meant by the term functional transition assessment.
9. Identify and describe the Life-Centered Career Education (LCCE) Mild/Moderate curriculum-based instruments that have been developed for instructional and transitional planning.
10. List some of the organizations that can be contacted to obtain information about various functional transition assessment measures.

OVERVIEW

Assessment is a necessary and important component of the educational process that provides educators with information from numerous sources so informed personalized decisions can be made on behalf of their students with special learning and/or behavior needs. In the case of career education and transition planning, a functional transition assessment approach (career evaluation/assessment and vocational evaluation/assessment are terms that are used synonymously) is particularly critical in helping the student with special learning and/or behavior needs to identify strengths, weaknesses, and instructional

needs in those skills areas necessary for successful personal adult development and community living and employment.

Functional transition assessment involves two primary methods of measurement: norm-referenced testing and criterion-referenced testing. Norm-referenced tests compare an individual's performance on academics, dexterity, aptitude, interest, intelligence, and so on to those of other individuals. Criterion-referenced tests evaluate the individual's performance at some absolute standard that is independent of the performance of others. This type of assessment focuses on what the person knows and can do so that specific strengths and weaknesses can be discerned.

Although both assessment approaches are important in conducting functional transition assessments with individuals with special learning and/or behavior needs or the disadvantaged, many professionals believe the criterion-referenced approach yields the most relevant data for instructional planning, particularly transition planning for students with special learning and/or behavior needs (e.g., Brown, Browning, & Dunn, 1992; Halpern, Lehmann, Irvin, & Heiry, 1982). As noted by Browning, Dunn, and Brown, functional assessments need to be conducted throughout the entire transition period rather than serving as a databased resource for only a single point in time. The kinds of career/vocational assessment information needed will vary at different stages of the transition process (1993, p. 197).

There is no lack of tools/instruments to conduct functional transition assessments. A study by DeStefano, Linn, and Markward (1987) found 144 different functional transition assessment instruments are being used in various transition programs. This prompted Browning and Brechin (1993) to recommend that educators need to define functional transition assessment so they can use appropriate transition assessment measures. Those authors note that ecological functional transition assessments in community-based settings also are very important assessments to conduct during the secondary years, when students with special learning and/or behavior needs are provided more work and community living training experiences. Browning and Brechin also suggested that assessment endeavors be a cooperative, personalized program developed and approved by the students with special learning and/or behavior needs, their parents, and all significant stakeholders and service providers involved in the transition process.

This chapter begins with a discussion of the functional transition assessment approach. Next, more specific functional transition assessment measures, both norm-referenced and criterion-referenced, are identified and described. The following sections explain and illustrate the numerous LCCE Mild/Moderate Curriculum instruments that have been developed for this purpose. A case study is presented to depict the use of two LCCE Mild/Moderate Curriculum instruments.

FUNCTIONAL TRANSITION ASSESSMENT

Education and rehabilitation professionals have always sought efficient, comprehensive, and accurate ways to assess the strengths and needs of the persons with special learning and/or behavior needs they serve. However, because of widely differing settings, populations, and goals, practitioners have been hard pressed to find sound, standardized instruments that are quick and easy to use and can be broadly applied. Standardized tests and work samples associated with functional transition assessment are not always available, and when in the hands of inexperienced users may not always yield valid results. Curriculum-based assessments are often too time-consuming for some teachers, and the lack of standardization limits their accuracy.

As a result, numerous functional transition assessment inventories and rating forms have been developed for the purposes of initial transition screening and planning. The concept of "functional transition" assessment has grown from a desire for practical, concrete information on how well individuals learn and perform in a variety of situations and environments. The development and increased use of supported employment and community-based service-delivery models, transition mandates in special education and rehabilitation, and the Americans with Disabilities Act (ADA) have placed a growing emphasis on the "functional transition" aspects of independent (and interdependent) living and working in the community for adults with special learning and/or behavior needs.

Defining Functional Transition Assessment

Three key definitions of functional transition assessment that have value in career assessment/transition models are presented in this section. The first definition focuses on a theme in this text, lifelong transitions that embraces all ages, developmental levels, and all types and severity levels of individuals with special learning and/or behavior needs. Clark (1998) defines functional transition assessment as:

> Transitions assessment is a planned, continuous process of obtaining, organizing, and using information to assist individuals with disabilities of all ages and their families in making all critical transitions in students' lives both successful and satisfying. (p. 2)

Clark's definition focuses on a career development/life span development of persons with special learning and/or behavior needs. As indicated in this definition, there is a need for schools to address adulthood preparation and participation that involves two thirds of our current projected life span. Therefore, this definition endorses the school's responsibility for functional transition assessment beginning in the elementary years to address all of the critical transitions from school throughout the adult community living and working periods. This need is enormous for students with special learning and/or behavior needs.

A second component of this definition is the importance of involvement of the student with special learning and/or behavior needs and family in the transition planning process. Clark describes this functional transition assessment process to include an alliance with schools, students with special learning and/or behavior needs, and their families addressing the following functional transition assessment areas: interests; preferences; physical health and fitness;

CHAPTER OUTLOOK

Dr. Stephen W. Thomas *is professor and director of the Graduate Program in Vocational Evaluation, Department of Rehabilitation Studies, East Carolina University, Greenville, North Carolina.*

All effective education and transition planning requires a thorough assessment of student abilities, needs, and potential in relation to career and life goals. The development of these individual functional profiles involves the collection of performance-based information regarding abilities and limitations as well as the accommodations and services needed to overcome the identified limitations in a variety of settings. Accommodations are a key element not only for improved performance in the classroom but for ensuring successful employment under the Americans with Disabilities Act.

Profile information can be collected using a variety of instruments and techniques, including but not limited to norm-referenced and criterion-referenced tests, functional assessment inventories, work samples, vocational evaluation systems, curriculum-based assessments, situational assessments, and community-based assessments. Depending on the severity of the disability, any number of assessment instruments and techniques can be used in conjunction with staffing, file review, interviewing, and behavioral observation. Although one student might profit from the use of standardized tests and work samples, another would be more appropriately assessed through situational and community-based techniques. Differing abilities and goals require versatility in the assessment process.

In recent years, work samples have fallen out of favor in some education and rehabilitation settings. However, this has often resulted from a misunderstanding and misuse of the instruments. When creatively used, work samples can reduce bias (frequently associated with standardized tests),

enhance career exploration and decision-making, and provide opportunities to try out various accommodation methods that can improve learning and performance. When community-based strategies are unavailable, work samples can serve as excellent "hands-on" tasks to observe and address behavior and performance issues. This calls for flexibility in their use and in the interpretation of results for consumers and practitioners.

The vocational assessment process is no longer limited to evaluating the potential for vocational training and placement. It has been expanded to include a broader range of personal, social, and independent living factors that have an impact on inclusion and the quality of life outcomes. Generating useful transition information has challenged the creative talents of vocational evaluators and vocational assessment specialists. It also has provided opportunities for students and consumers to become involved in collecting assessment information and making decisions about planning directions. This process of involvement ensures ownership and provides the student with the information needed to make informed choices. The assessment of decision-making skills and the ability to learn how to make appropriate decisions (essential for self-determination) are becoming a more critical part of the assessment process.

The need for better planning to achieve transition goals requires the kind of information that can be collected through a versatile vocational evaluation and assessment process. Without thorough assessments, the accuracy of planning information will be reduced, students will not have the information necessary to make meaningful education and life decisions, and the sense of ownership required to optimize involvement will be diminished. Information collected through evaluation and assessment is empowering not only to rehabilitation and education professionals but also to students who live with the outcomes of transition plans.

motor skills; speech and language; cognitive development and performance; adaptive behavior; socialization skills; emotional development and mental health; independent and interdependent living skills; leisure skills; pre-employability, employability, and vocational skills; choice-making and self determination skills; community participation; needed skills or information for next vertical transition; needed family or other supports; and needed linkages with support services.

The second definition is from the *Functional Assessment Inventory Manual*: "In simplest terms, functional assessment is a systematic enumeration of vocationally relevant strengths and limitations" (Crewe, Athelstan, & University of Minnesota, 1984, p. 3).

This definition contains several key elements. The first is the reference to "systematic enumeration." To improve efficiency in administration and ensure thorough coverage of all functional transition areas, a systematic, well-organized process should be incorporated. This includes a systematic and uniform procedure for determining how each functional transition area can be reliably and validly rated. Once all functional transition areas have been assessed and rated, a functional transition profile of strengths and needs (weaknesses) can be established that will enumerate the various functional transition deficits that require attention. Resulting functional transition profiles then can be systematically matched to the functional transition requirements of courses, community training, jobs, and transition environments so that accommodation and successful placement can be planned and achieved.

The second important element in this definition, "vocationally relevant," defines the setting where the functional transition skills are to be assessed and applied. Although this definition stresses the vocational factors, Crewe et al. (1984) also refer to the "personalized" aspects to be covered in functional transition assessment that are needed beyond vocational situations. The Functional Assessment Inventory was designed primarily to assess vocationally relevant functional transition skills in vocational rehabilitation clientele, but the functional transition areas included in the instrument relate to a broader range of functioning.

The third and final element, "strengths and limitations," provides the basis for determining functional transition ability. Again, functional transition ability profiles specify the types of services or accommodations needed to minimize or overcome limitations. Transition profiles also can be used to match individual functional abilities to the functional transition requirements in a variety of community training, living, and work settings.

The third definition to be examined was developed by Halpern and Fuhrer:

Functional assessment is the measurement of purposeful behavior in interaction with the environment, which is interpreted according to the assessment's intended uses. (1984, p. 3)

This definition emphasizes the importance of environment and its influence on behavior and is not specific to any one setting or purpose. "It speaks to the diversity of information often sought through the administration of functional assessment procedures" (Thomas, 1992, pp. 4–5). Ecological assessment, often associated with supported and community-based employment, requires sensitivity to how individuals with special learning and/or behavior needs function in every environment they encounter (including the classroom).

Advantages and Disadvantages of Functional Assessment

Several key advantages have promoted the increased use of functional assessment. They are as follows:

- Functional assessment provides a quick yet thorough overview to individual functioning. It is often easy and inexpensive to administer and can be used by anyone, including the person being rated (i.e., self-rating process).
- Functional profiles can be developed for direct planning for service delivery. These profiles serve as a baseline of performance and behavior for comparison to the functional goals associated with a specified environment. Differences in the func-

tional levels will help tailor planning and service delivery to achieve success in the targeted environment.

- Standardized inventories, rating instruments, and tests can provide pre- and post-assessment opportunities to evaluate the degree and effectiveness of service delivery in achieving the functional goal.
- Functional assessments are easy to interpret, and because they relate to basic functional activities, they are easy to explain to participants and their families and to convert into plans.
- Resulting profiles readily can be matched to settings where the functional requirements are known.

Several key disadvantages have limited the effective use of functional assessment. They are as follows:

- Many inventories have not been standardized, so little is known about their utility and accuracy (i.e., reliability and validity).
- Rating bias or error may occur with untrained raters or with subjective rating processes.
- Possessing functional skills differs from the ability to perform a complex task or set of tasks composed of a combination or series of functions. Functional profiles only indicate an individual's potential abilities and do not ensure success in the classroom, the job site, or the community.
- When functions are assessed individually, there is limited understanding of how they can be applied when used in more complex and unrestricted situations where numerous functions are required.
- There is a lack of uniformity in the content, categories, and use of functional assessment instruments. Guidelines do not exist for the development, standardization, or use of such instruments. Because of the varied settings, populations, and goals, standardization will be difficult.
- It is difficult to determine on the continuum of functioning the precise cutoff between a strength and a limitation. This is often dictated by environmental requirements.

In spite of their shortcomings, functional transition assessment instruments serve an important purpose. They direct the systematic collection of information that can help determine if more comprehensive evaluations are needed or if planning can proceed. Although they provide a quick method of screening, they should not be considered to be the final word in assessment.

Mandates and Uses of Functional Assessment

Some of the early legislative mandates for functional assessment appeared in vocational rehabilitation. Many rehabilitation state agencies based eligibility on the number and degree of functional limitations (e.g., walking, standing, speaking, memory). The severity of a disability was often based on the documentation of two or more functional limitations. With the advent and expeditious use of supported employment and community-based service-delivery models, functional transition assessment inventories have rapidly grown in popularity.

Within the medical rehabilitation model, functional transition assessment—generally referred to as *functional capacity evaluation*—focuses on physical functioning activities such as strength, endurance, mobility, and range of motion. Occupational and physical therapists in rehabilitation hospitals and work-hardening centers usually provide these types of assessments to industrially injured workers to determine their potential to return to previous employment. This is a much more specialized application of functional transition assessment than is found in vocational rehabilitation, community-based education, or transition settings.

With the new transition language included in the Individuals with Disabilities Education Act (IDEA 1997), school personnel need a comprehensive and systematic way to assess functioning in the wide variety of transition environments available to students with special learning and/or behavior needs in and out of school. Transitional areas such as work, independent living, personal/social/family, and recreation involve combinations of functional skills that call for an in-depth assessment (often referred to in the legislation as a "functional vocational evaluation"). The movement toward outcome-based education has focused on the functional skills students with special learning and/or behavior needs most successfully enter and master, and the specific content domains and competencies for adult community living and working. Many state offices of education have developed competency guides that target specific functional requirements in all classes and provide a blueprint for developing functional transition assessment strategies.

The most recent and significant legislation mandating the assessment of functional transition skills is the ADA (Equal Employment Opportunity Commission, 1991). The employment provisions under Title I of the act define disability as "A physical or mental impairment that substantially limits one or more of the major life activities of such individual." Two important terms in this definition, "substantially limits" and "major life activities," have a direct relationship to the functional transition assessment process. *Major life activities* means "functions such as caring for oneself, performing manual tasks, walking, seeing, hearing, speaking, breathing, learning, and working." The term *substantially limits* means:

1. Unable to perform a major life activity that the average person in the general population can perform, or
2. Significantly restricted as to the condition, manner, or duration under which an individual can perform a particular major life activity as compared to the condition, manner, or duration under which the average person in the general population can perform that same major life activity.

With regard to the major life activities of working, "the term *substantially limits* means significantly restricted in the ability to perform either a class of jobs or a broad range of jobs in various classes as compared to the average person having comparable training, skills and abilities."

For individuals to qualify for employment under the ADA, they must possess a significant functional limitation to living or working. Reasonable accommodations must be provided to enable individuals with disabilities to perform the "essential functions" of a job. If vocational training is designed to prepare students to successfully perform the essential functions of targeted jobs, then schools also will be required to

make similar accommodations in the classroom. The key to a successful ADA-based vocational assessment is the accurate identification of functional strengths and limitations and the determination of reasonable accommodations that can minimize or eliminate the identified limitations (Thomas, 1992).

An interesting provision in the ADA employment regulations is the requirement that applicants be able to explain to potential employers how they would perform the essential functions of the job. It spells out a process whereby an employer can discuss accommodation needs with the prospective employee with special learning and/or behavior needs. The regulations state:

> To determine the appropriate reasonable accommodation it may be necessary for the covered entity to initiate an informal, interactive process with the qualified individual with a disability in need of the accommodation. The process should identify the precise limitations resulting from the disability and potential reasonable accommodations that could overcome those limitations.

Results of the functional transition assessment must be shared with consumers so they can effectively participate in this interview process. Information is empowering, and only when participants are provided with understandable assessment results will they be able to make well-informed decisions and become fully participating team members in planning their own transition objectives. One of the most beneficial skills we can teach the people we serve with special learning and/or behavior needs is how to successfully describe to employers their functional abilities and accommodations that can be used to competitively perform the essential functions of a particular job. Assessing this potential in students with special learning and/or behavior needs will help determine whether they possess sufficient decision-making skills to understand and verbalize the results clearly. Students with special learning and/or behavior needs who can articulate approaches to, and accommodations for, specific tasks may not require as much assistance as individuals with special learning and/or behavior needs who cannot understand or explain their functional transition strengths and needs. In this situation, someone will need to be empowered to represent the student with special learning and/or behavior needs. This process of empowerment involves sharing functional transition strengths and limitations profiles with students and discussing their understanding of and agreement with their profiles (Thomas, 1992).

Although functional transition assessment evolved from the need for a quick and easy technique to collect a broad range of information on an individual's strengths and limitations, the influence of legislation on its recognition and continued acceptance cannot be ignored. With increasing legal mandates for its use, there is greater importance for the standardization of functional transition assessment instruments.

Instrumentation in Functional Assessment

Functional transition assessment instruments have taken many forms, including rating scales, inventories, standardized tests, and test batteries. Rating scales and inventories are the most common functional transition assessment instruments. Such transition inventories can be purchased commercially or developed locally or may result from the modification of a commercially available scale. Information is collected through file review, staffing, interviewing, observation, test and work sample administration, situational assessment, and curriculum-based assessment, and is used to respond to the questions on the scale. These transition types of inventories are composed of a series of functional items (e.g., learning ability, vision, use of hands) that represent a comprehensive range of functional categories (e.g., physical, cognitive, personal, social). Each item contains a series of descriptive statements used to rate functional competence. For example, regarding the item of "making change," a rater could be asked to choose one of the following statements that best describe functional transition competence:

a. Can make change up to and above $20.00
b. Can make change up to $10.00
c. Can make change up to $5.00

d. Can make change up to $1.00
e. Cannot make change

These forms by themselves are not transition assessment tools in the strictest sense of the word, but simply provide the means for systematically recording, rating, and profiling functional transition information as it is collected. The accuracy of the ratings depends on the accuracy of the transition instruments and techniques used to collect the required transition information and to code it on the form.

Rating Scales/Inventories

The first example of a rating form is the Functional Assessment Inventory (Crewe, et al., 1984). It is composed of two rating forms with 30 functional items, each containing four descriptive choices. Examples of the functional items are learning ability, memory, hearing, use of hands, and speed. Items also are included that address support issues such as stability of condition, interest in working, financial incentives, and support from family and friends. Ten items that provide assessment in areas considered to be employment strengths (e.g., looks, personality, skill, motivation) conclude the Functional Assessment Inventory.

The first form, the Functional Assessment Inventory, is completed by the professional; while the second form, the Personal Capacities Questionnaire, is completed by the consumer. Items in this form are included in the following major functional areas: employment, daily living skills, self-determination, communication, and interpersonal relationships. Responses on the two forms can be compared and discussed with the participant and the participant's family, thus enhancing their involvement in the process. The Functional Assessment Inventory was originally designed for use with vocational rehabilitation clientele, and the manual contains reliability and validity studies based on this population.

The second example of a rating form is the Consumer Employment Screening Form (CESF) (Moon, Goodall, Barcus, & Brooke, 1986). Although somewhat similar in its rating procedure to the Functional

Assessment Inventory, the items on the CESF tend to be more basic (e.g., independent work rate, independent sequencing of job duties, adapting to change, time awareness, and independent street-crossing skills). The CESF does not have a form that can be completed by the consumer with special learning and/or behavior needs, but it does include a second form that can be used to conduct a functional job analysis. This enables the professional to match the functional requirements of a job or a specific vocational class. Like the Functional Assessment Inventory, the CESF contains rating areas that address support issues such as supervision needs, financial incentives, benefits needed, and family involvement. Space is provided after each item for comments. The inventory was designed for use in supported employment and is a part of a comprehensive training manual for supported employment service delivery. No standardization studies are reported in the manual containing the CESF.

The Supported Employment Technical Assistance Project (1989) modified the CESF for persons with traumatic brain injury. Items were added or revised to address functional transition issues common to head injury. The most noteworthy changes to the form were the inclusion of expanded items and space to document and describe the effects of attempted accommodations on functioning.

The Brigance® System offers two instruments that are particularly useful for assessing important functional academic skills and life skills. The Employability Skills Inventory (1999) covers the academic areas of reading/language arts, math, and study skills. The inventory contains approximately 1400 items across six subtests: career awareness and understanding; job seeking and knowledge; reading skills; speaking; speaking and listening skills; pre-employment writing; and math skills and concepts. Optional supplemental rating scale assessment scales include: self-concept; life skill assessments in the areas of food and clothing, money and finance, travel and transportation; and communication and telephone skills. Rating scales measure the applied skills of health and attitude, responsibility and self-discipline, job interview preparation, communication, and auto safety. Student record books indicate com-

petency levels and define instructional goals. The more recent Life Skills Inventory (1999), a criterion-referenced assessment tool, has been designed to assess listening, speaking, reading, writing, comprehending, and computing skills in nine life-skills sections: speaking and listening skills, functional writing skills, words on common signs and warning labels, telephone skills, money and finance, food, clothing, health, and travel and transportation. The instrument also is intended to serve as a curriculum guide by providing teaching sequences for functional life skills.

Standardized Rating Scales

A number of standardized behavior rating scales assess various functional skills. Examples include the Prevocational Assessment and Curriculum Guide, the Vocational Assessment and Curriculum Guide, the Vineland Adaptive Behavior Scales, the AAMD Adaptive Behavior Scale, and the Adaptive Behavior Evaluation Scale: School Version, Revised (1993). These instruments report reliability and validity studies and are norm-referenced.

The Prevocational Assessment and Curriculum Guide (PACG) (Mithaug, Mar, & Stewart, 1978) covers 46 specific school and workshop expectations arranged in nine areas: attendance/endurance, independence, production, learning, behavior communications skills, social skills, grooming/eating skills, and toileting skills. The inventory is supplemented by a curriculum guide to assist in setting transitional goals.

An extension of the PACG is the Vocational Assessment and Curriculum Guide (VACG) (Rusch, Schutz, Mithaug, Stewart, & Mar, 1982). Similar in its structure and use to the PACG, it was normed on service and industrial employees and geared to entry-level employment in light industry, food service, janitorial, and other service occupations. The VACG inventory and curriculum guide was designed primarily to address work adjustment functioning in vocational settings.

The Vineland Adaptive Behavior Scales (Sparrow, Balla, & Cicchetti, 1985) is available in three editions: the Interview Edition, Survey Form (297 items); the more comprehensive Interview Edition,

Expanded Form (577 items); and the Classroom Edition (a 244-item questionnaire). The interviews are administered to parents and care givers, and a teacher completes the Classroom Edition. The Vineland contains 11 subdomains organized into the four domains of communication, daily living skills, socialization, and motor skills.

Other standardized inventories such as the AAMD Adaptive Behavior Scale-School 2 (ABS-S2) (Nihira, Foster, Shellhaas, & Leland, 1993) provide software for scoring and profiling and provide an instructional planning manual. The ABS-S2 contains two parts measuring five major factors (personal self-sufficiency, community self-sufficiency, personal-social responsibility, social adjustment, and personal adjustment). These major factors assess the following 16 major domains (nine in Part I and seven in Part II): independent functioning, physical development, economic development, language development, number and time, prevocational/vocational activity, self-direction, responsibility, socialization, social behavior, conformity, trustworthiness, stereotyped and hyperactive behavior, self-abusive behavior, social engagement, and disturbing interpersonal behavior. The revised edition is considered a significant improvement over previous editions (Salvia & Ysseldyke, 1998). Norming is far more comprehensive and is more representative. Although the information on scale's reliability and validity seems to be more extensive, the ABS-S2 is most reliable with individuals with mental retardation.

A more recent addition to the adaptive behavior assessment is the Adaptive Behavior Evaluation Scale: School Version, Revised (ABE, S-R), (McCarney, 1995). The ABE, S-R is designed to assess adaptive behavior of individuals between the ages of 5 and 18 years of age. This instrument's 104 items are arranged in the same ten adaptive skill areas listed in the AAMR's 1992 Definition. This newer instrument appears to correlate with other adaptive measures and does discriminate between randomly sampled individuals in the population. Whatever type of standardized inventory is chosen, it should be comprehensive in its coverage of functional transition skills and behaviorally descriptive in the rating and interpretation process.

Basic Skills Assessment Through Standardized Testing

Because a number of functional assessment inventories lack standardization and objectivity, some professionals prefer to rely on standardized tests of functional skills. As with most untimed, standardized tests, the participant is asked to answer specific questions from knowledge domains, in this case, functional skills. Some of the shorter tests focus more on functional and transitional skills such as the Adaptive Behavior: The Street Survival Skills Questionnaire, the Social and Prevocational Inventory Battery (forms R & T), and the Tests for Everyday Living. Longer and more expensive performance-based assessment systems such as the Pre-Vocational Readiness Battery (VALPAR 17) provide opportunities for behavior observation, evaluation of learning styles, and exploration of accommodations.

The Adaptive Behavior: The Street Survival Skills Questionnaire (SSSQ) (Linkenhoker & McCarron, 1983) is an untimed, individually administered test containing nine subtests: basic concepts, functional signs, tools, domestics, health and safety, public services, time, monetary, and measurements. The administrator asks a question, and the respondent chooses the correct answer from a series of four pictures by pointing to the picture or saying the corresponding letter (A, B, C, or D). All nine scales do not need to be administered; however, a total functional score cannot be obtained from a prorated administration. Subtests from many of the functional assessment instruments reviewed can be administered and interpreted individually, but this practice limits the development of a complete transition profile. Each SSSQ subtest has 24 questions, and the results can be scored and profiled by hand or on a computer, and deficiencies can be matched to a curriculum guide.

The Social and Prevocational Information Battery (SPIB-R) (Halpern, Raffeld, Irvin, Link, & Munkres, 1986) is available in two forms: form "R" for students with mild intellectual deficiencies and form "T" for students with moderate intellectual deficiencies. This untimed, paper-and-pencil test can be orally administered to individuals or groups. Its 277 items provide assessment in these nine areas: job search skills, job-related behavior, banking, budgeting, purchasing, home management, physical health care, hygiene and grooming, and functional signs. A learning activities resource kit is available with the SPIB to address identified limitations.

The Tests for Everyday Living (TEL) (Halpern, Irvin, & Landman, 1979) is a transitional assessment measuring achievement in seven major functional areas, such as home management, purchasing habits, budgeting, banking, health care, job search skills, and job-related behavior. Although it was designed for use with average- or low-functioning junior high school students, it can be used with high school students with special learning and/or behavior needs.

Vocational/Transition Assessment Measures

Vocational/transition evaluation has been an important component to the transition/career education effort for many years and is another functional assessment approach. Many commercial evaluation systems have been developed over the past 20 or more years and used by several school systems. Some of the most noteworthy are the McCarron-Dial Work Evaluation System (P.O. Box 45628, Dallas, TX 75245); the Vocational Research Institute (VRI) assessment (Suite 1502, 1528 Walnut St., Philadelphia, PA 19102); particularly the APTICOM and Vocational Transit; and the TAP System and related instruments produced by Talent Assessment, Inc. (P.O. Box 5087, Jacksonville, FL 32207). Each of these systems offers computerized components to expedite and expand capacities to relate transition assessment findings to specific training and/or jobs that may be within the capabilities of the individual.

The TAP System, for example, is a "hands-on" assessment of several work samples or tasks that measure such functional skills as gross and fine motor dexterity, color and finger discrimination, spatial aptitude, and other aptitudes that are important on various jobs. The assessments can be given in just a few hours. Computer management reports to relate results to specific job possibilities are available for Mac or IBM personal computers. The TAP System is supported by several other assessment measures: the PIC,

which assesses vocational interests; the VIP, which assesses learning and/or personality styles; and the M.DOT, which is a job-matching system that provides information on jobs that match qualifications and interests.

The University of Arkansas Research and Training Center in Vocational Rehabilitation (P.O. Box 1328 Hot Springs Rehabilitation Center, Hot Springs, AR 71902) has developed its Employability Assessment Materials, a series of functional assessment measures that are being used successfully in many schools and rehabilitation settings. The Work Personality Profile (WPP) is a work behavior rating instrument that assesses 58 items that are essential to achieve and maintain suitable employment. The WPP takes 5 to 10 minutes to complete after an observation period of 1 week. A parallel self-report instrument, WPP-SR, also is available. The Work Performance Assessment (WPA) is a work-simulation procedure designed to assess an individual's response to typical on-the-job supervisory behaviors. The Employability Maturity Interview (EMI) is a 15-minute structured interview of 10 questions that measure individuals' readiness for vocational planning by focusing on their levels of self-knowledge and occupational information. The Job Seeking Skills Assessment (JSSA) assesses the individual's ability to complete job application forms and present oneself in an employment interview. These instruments, and others developed at the center, were extensively field tested, statistically analyzed, and well validated.

One example of a well-designed and standardized measure of vocational aptitudes and interests is the Occupational Aptitude Survey and Interest Schedule-2 (OASIS-2), developed by Professor Randy Parker (1991a, 1991b) of The University of Texas-Austin. This instrument is used to assist young adults to help them in their vocational self-exploration so they better achieve vocational self-understanding, decision making, and goal setting, and eventually attain a satisfying career. The OASIS-2 consists of two tests: the Aptitude Survey and the Interest Schedule, both of which are normed on a national sample of 1,505 8th- to 12th-grade students. The instrument can be administered by teachers, counselors, and other professionals to assist in the career development of all students, including those with special learning and/or behavior needs or who are disadvantaged. The Aptitude Survey consists of five subtests, which measure six aptitudes that are directly related to skills and abilities required in over 20,000 jobs listed in the *Dictionary of Occupational Titles* (1977). General ability, verbal, numerical, spatial, perceptual, and manual dexterity are tested. The Interest Schedule measures 12 interest factors directly related to the occupations listed in the *Guide to Occupational Exploration* (Harrington & O'Shea, 1984). Excellent reliability and validity data have been collected.

Another more recent development in this area is the concept of curriculum-based vocational assessment (CBVA), which is an ongoing process of collecting data while the student is engaged in vocational/transition education programs (Stodden, Ianacone, Boone, & Bisconer, 1987). Stodden and Ianacone are noteworthy leaders in developing this approach, which can be instituted at the middle school/junior high school level, as well as later.

Swisher and Clark (1991), who integrated the transition/career education concepts of career awareness and exploration into the basic concepts of CBVA, have described one example of a CBVA program. They contend that if students are exposed to sufficient middle school/junior high school awareness and exploration experiences that are monitored through a CBVA approach, then more appropriate vocational/transitional recommendations can be developed at age 14 years and beyond. To develop their exemplary curriculum-based assessment and exploration program, Swisher and Clark analyzed the nature of the business, home economics, and trade and industrial technology classes with the instructors to identify their generalizable and vocational skills. They then devised a series of 150 work sample activities that could be provided to the students over up to a 90-hour period. The result of this effort was a Practical Arts Evaluation System (PAES), which has become "an invaluable tool in the education and transition planning for students with special needs" (Swisher & Clark, 1991, p. 14).

The preceding examples of functional/transition assessment approaches and materials are only a sample of what is available. Although basic skills tests,

such as the ones cited, can assess transition skills, recent developments in the standardized testing of functional skills have focused on the information needs specific to transition planning. One major functional skills assessment package that falls into this category is the Life Centered Career Education (LCCE) Curriculum Assessment System for students with milder special learning and/or behavior needs (Brolin, 1992a). A companion system is currently in production for the LCCE Mild/Moderate Curriculum for students with more severe learning and/or behavior needs. When the LCCE Mild/Moderate Curriculum Assessment Batteries are used as a component of the LCCE Mild/Moderate Curriculum for both the mild and the moderate versions, continuity in transitional assessment, planning, and instruction can be optimized. The closer the relationship between the content of functional assessment and educational/transitional competencies, the greater the accuracy in targeting needs or interests with student with special learning and/or behavior needs, and achieving transitional outcomes needed for successful adult living and working. A detailed description of the LCCE Curriculum Assessment Systems is presented in the next section.

TRANSITION/CAREER ASSESSMENT AND THE LCCE CURRICULUM INSTRUMENTS
Transition/Career Assessment

Transition/career education is a broader concept than vocational education. Also, transition/career assessment is a more encompassing vocational evaluation because it focuses on the individual's interests, needs, aptitudes, and abilities that relate to all types of productive work activity that one does in the home and community—avocational and vocational activities.

Transition/career assessment is a developmental process beginning at the preschool level and continuing throughout adulthood. In a position paper on the topic, The Council for Exceptional Children's

Division on Career Development and Transition (DCDT) described the process as:

> related to all aspects of career education, including not only preparation for employment, but also preparation for the productive roles of a family member, citizen, and participant in leisure, recreational, and avocational activities. The career assessment process should be a foundation for individualized program planning and transition planning from kindergarten through adulthood. The goals of this process should be specifically geared to providing the information needed to make decisions in all areas of career education programming; these decisions may be related to developing an individualized program or determining what assistance the learner needs to succeed in an ongoing program. (Sitlington, Brolin, Clark, & Vacanti, 1985)

The transition/career assessment approach inherent in the LCCE Mild/Moderate Curriculum approaches is a curriculum-based assessment approach —that is, using the material to be learned (or similar material) as the basis for assessing the degree to which it has been learned or mastered. Within the field of transition/career education, the field of vocational education has a parallel term (introduced in the previous section), CBVA, to discern vocational instruction needs. Sitlington notes that, "to obtain maximum applicability of the two assessment concepts to the field of career education, we must do two things: 1.) define the curriculum as all experiences in which the learner is involved, including community-based experiences and 2.) define the career education curriculum" (1991, p. 2).

Sitlington believes the LCCE Mild/Moderate Curriculum meets the second criterion in that it:

> provides a series of competencies which can form the basis for an individual's transition/career education program, and which can be adapted to meet individual program and/or learner needs. The widely used LCCE Knowledge Battery and the accompanying LCCE Performance Battery provide the tools which professionals can use to apply the concepts of curriculum-based assessment and curriculum-based vocational assessment ... should not be used alone to determine the learner's

strengths, interests, and instructional needs, but they will provide a strong framework upon which an effective career/vocational assessment can be built. They will also allow professionals to broaden the application of curriculum-based assessment and curriculum-based vocational assessment to include transition/career education content. (1991, p. 2)

The LCCE Mild Curriculum Assessment System

Four LCCE Mild/Moderate Curriculum assessment measures are available to assess the transition/career education competencies contained in the LCCE Mild Curriculum for students with learning and/or behavior needs. Each of these measures provides a different range of assessment options, so educators can select from among these four measures, depending on the students' own situation and needs. In addition, educators are encouraged to use other measures such as those described previously to provide the most comprehensive and appropriate career/functional assessment for transition planning.

The four LCCE Mild Curriculum instruments, published by The Council for Exceptional Children (CEC), are described briefly next. Examples from each also are provided.

The LCCE Mild Curriculum Competency Rating Scale

The LCCE Mild Curriculum Competency Rating Scale (CRS) is built around the 22 competencies and 97 subcompetencies composing the LCCE Mild Curriculum. The subcompetencies and their objectives serve as the actual CRS items. A manual contained in the appendix of the LCCE Mild Curriculum Guide (*Life Centered Career Education: A Competency Based Approach*, Brolin, 1997), presents specific behavioral criteria or objectives on which to judge student mastery level for each subcompetency. These criteria approximate the behavioral/instructional objectives that are subsumed under each subcompetency unit in the LCCE Mild Curriculum Guide.

The CRS was developed with the philosophy that teachers who have worked closely with students can fairly accurately assess their competency levels, given helpful and appropriate guidelines. Another valuable use of this instrument is giving the student with special learning and/or behavior needs and/or their parents/guardians an opportunity to assess their own functional competence.

The CRS Manual provides these guidelines; identifies who should do the ratings and when they should be done; and provides criteria for the ratings, a rating key defining numerical rating values, a CRS Record Form for recording and summarizing ratings, and demographic information. CRS users rate their students, selves, or child on a three-point Likert Scale on each of the subcompetencies; as not competent (0), partially competent (1), or competent (2). Younger students will be too young and some lower functioning students may not be ready for rating on some of the subcompetencies; thus, a "Not Rated" (NR) response should be given. Raters should record the ratings and summarize them on a CRS Record Form so that a profile of the student's strengths and weaknesses is created: (a) the 97 subcompetencies; (b) the 22 competencies; and (c) a domain score obtained for each of the three curriculum areas: daily living, personal-social, and occupational guidance and preparation.

The CRS provides a quick and inexpensive method of curriculum-based assessment. It can be used at any grade level and with any type of student.

It is particularly useful at the elementary level, where a limited number of functional skills instruments related to the transition effort are available. An example of one page from the CRS is presented in Figure 7.1.

The LCCE Mild Curriculum Knowledge Battery

The second instrument, LCCE Mild Curriculum Knowledge Battery (KB), was developed to provide LCCE Mild Curriculum users with a more objective instrument for assessing students on their level of competency attainment. The KB is a functional transition criterion-referenced assessment that contains 200 multiple-choice questions covering the three LCCE Mild Curriculum domains. Ten questions cover the first 20 competencies of the LCCE Mild Curriculum. The last two competencies, covering physical-manual skills and specific occupational skills, do not lend themselves to knowledge assessment.

The over 400 functional instructional objectives of the LCCE Mild Curriculum were, like the CRS, used as the basis for developing KB test items because they define the important functional areas of the curriculum. Questions for each competency were divided among the subcompetencies composing the competency and their functional instructional objectives. The KB comprises two forms (A and B) and takes from 2 to 4 hours to administer, depending on the students.

LIFE CENTERED CAREER EDUCATION
Competency Rating Scale
Record Form
DAILY LIVING SKILLS

Student Name _____Susan_____ Date of Birth ____1–10____ Sex ____F____

School _____Progressive_____ City ____Columbia____ State ____MO____

Directions: Please rate the student according to his/her mastery of *each* item using the rating key below. Indicate the ratings in the column below the date for the rating period. Use the NR rating for items which cannot be rated. For subcompetencies rated 0 or 1 at the time of the final rating, place a check (✓) in the appropriate space in the *yes/no* column to indicate his/her ability to perform the subcompetency with assistance from the community. Please refer to the CRS manual for explanation of the rating key, description of the behavioral criteria for each subcompetency, and explanation of the *yes/no* column.

Rating Key: 0 = Not Competent   1 = Partially Competent   2 = Competent   NR = Not Rated

To what extent has the student mastered the following subcompetencies:

Subcompetencies	Rater(s)	JR	JR							Yes	No
	Grade Level	7	8								
	Date(s)	5/25/93	5/6/94								
DAILY LIVING SKILLS DOMAIN											
1. Managing Personal Finances											
1. Identify Money and Make Correct Change		2	2	—	—	—	—	—		—	—
2. Make Responsible Expenditures		1	1	—	—	—	—	—		—	—
3. Keep Basic Financial Records		0	*1	—	—	—	—	—		—	—
4. Calculate and Pay Taxes		0	0	—	—	—	—	—		—	—
5. Use Credit Responsibly		0	*1	—	—	—	—	—		—	—
6. Use Banking Services		0	*2	—	—	—	—	—		—	—
2. Selecting and Managing a Household											
7. Maintain Home Exterior/Interior		1	1	—	—	—	—	—		—	—
8. Use Basic Appliances and Tools		1	1	—	—	—	—	—		—	—
9. Select Adequate Housing		0	1	—	—	—	—	—		—	—
10. Set Up Household		0	1	—	—	—	—	—		—	—
11. Maintain Home Grounds		1	1	—	—	—	—	—		—	—
3. Caring for Personal Needs											
12. Demonstrate Knowledge of Physical Fitness, Nutrition, and Weight		1	1	—	—	—	—	—		—	—
13. Exhibit Proper Grooming and Hygiene		1	2	—	—	—	—	—		—	—
14. Dress Appropriately		1	2	—	—	—	—	—		—	—
15. Demonstrate Knowledge of Common Illness, Prevention, and Treatment		0	0	—	—	—	—	—		—	—
16. Practice Personal Safety		0	1	—	—	—	—	—		—	—

FIGURE 7.1   Curriculum-Based Assessment for Career Education: A One-Page Sample from the CRS.

Note: From *Life Centered Career Education: A Competency-Based Approach* (4th ed., p. 140) by D. E. Brolin, 1993, Arlington, VA: The Council for Exceptional Children. Copyright 1993 by The Council for Exceptional Children. Reprinted by permission.

The KB was developed over a period of several years with the assistance of several school personnel. A number of experienced special educators were involved in writing appropriate items, which were revised several times after the field testing of different versions with hundreds of students with special learning and/or behavior needs across the country. A detailed technical report is available to describe the extensive development and validation of the instrument.

Although the KB was developed originally for 7th-through 12th-grade students with mild intellectual and specific learning disabilities, many users will find the instrument useful with a variety of students with special learning and/or behavior needs. However, caution is advised in too quickly interpreting its results without keeping its development and validation in mind. It is important to remember that the LCCE Mild Curriculum KB, like any other assessment, is just a sample of basic knowledge. No measure should be considered to reveal every student's actual functional competence. Rather, such instruments are useful screening devices to assist special educators in instructional/transitional planning efforts.

An example of one page from one of the KB forms is presented in Figure 7.2.

The LCCE Mild Curriculum Performance Battery

The third instrument, the LCCE Mild Curriculum Performance Battery (PB), was developed to provide a more functional, real-life measure of the competencies in the LCCE Mild Curriculum. The first 21 LCCE Mild Curriculum competencies are addressed in this functional performance instrument. Competency 22 is not assessed, because its assessment depends on the specific occupational training area in which each student with special learning and/or behavior needs is being instructed.

The PB is a nonstandardized criterion-referenced instrument. It contains a combination of open-ended questions, role-playing scenarios, card sorts, and several hands-on activities that require the student with special learning and/or behavior needs, for example, to prepare a meal, use a telephone directory, and fill out a credit application. Because of the length of time required to assess actual performance in some of the LCCE Mild Curriculum competency areas, many advanced knowledge or cognitive items were used for some of the competency assessments. Three major types of items make up the battery: performance, simulated performance, and performance-related knowledge.

As with the CRS and KB, the subcompetencies and functional instructional objectives from *Life Centered Career Education: A Competency-Based Approach* (Brolin, 1997) were used in determining and developing test items. The PB presents a more realistic approach to assessing students with special learning and/or behavior needs' actual abilities and behaviors beyond what is gained from the more objective KB. Students with special learning and/or behavior needs must demonstrate a functional activity reflecting adequate command of the LCCE competencies and their subcompetencies. All subcompetencies are addressed in the PB tests. Each PB competency test has five questions. A PB Manual provides detailed directions for administering, scoring, and reporting the results. A special feature of the PB's approach is its flexibility in scoring, which allows examiners to use their discretion in deviating from the suggested correct responses based on regional and cultural differences. Some responses may not be listed but are correct for the ecological environment in which the student with special learning and/or behavior needs performs the LCCE Mild Curriculum functional objectives.

The PB has two forms, A and B. Because it would take more than 30 hours to administer the battery to small groups of students with special learning and/or behavior needs, users generally select one or more PB tests to administer at a time, based on the results of the CRS and/or KB assessments. Often, these tests are administered before and after students with special learning and/or behavior needs are instructed in one of the LCCE competency areas. Many teachers prefer the PB because it is the most natural and realistic measure of their students with special learning and/or behavior needs' functional/transitional skills.

PERSONAL-SOCIAL SKILLS QUESTIONS

Practice Multiple-Choice Item
When people are nice to you, it makes you
  a. **angry.**
  b. **disappointed.**
  c. **happy.**
  d. **sad.**

*Circle the LETTER of the **BEST** Answer*

91. Which physical need does your body require the MOST of to stay alive?
    a. clothing
    b. oxygen
    c. shelter
    d. sleep

92. An important part of feeling good about yourself is
    a. being happy with what you are doing.
    b. making money.
    c. telling others how good you are.
    d. wishing you were someone else.

93. Which of the following requires the MOST ability?
    a. playing a tape
    b. talking on the telephone
    c. typing a letter
    d. watching television

94. Your interests should be
    a. like other people's.
    b. like your friends'.
    c. like your parents'.
    d. what you like.

FIGURE 7.2   Objective Assessment of Competency in Career Education: A One-Page Sample of the LCCE Knowledge Battery.
Note. From *Life Centered Career Education: Competency Assessment Knowledge Battery* (p. 56) by D. E. Brolin, 1992, Arlington, VA: The Council for Exceptional Children. Copyright 1992 by The Council for Exceptional Children. Reprinted by permission.

The first two pages of one LCCE PB test (competency 17) are presented in Figure 7.3. The entire test for this competency—which includes the other questions, score sheet, and work sheets—is provided in Appendix C for readers interested in the entire nature of test construction.

LCCE PERFORMANCE TEST 17

Form A

KNOWING AND EXPLORING OCCUPATIONAL POSSIBILITIES (OCCUPATIONAL GUIDANCE AND PREPARATION)

MATERIALS FOR DUPLICATION

> Test Question 1: Occupational Remuneration
> Test Question 2: Job Information
> Test Question 3: Values from a Job
> Test Question 4: Job Categories
> Test Question 5: Investigate Job Opportunities
> Want Ads Sheet
> Score Sheet

MATERIALS NEEDED

> Telephone directories

DIRECTIONS

This test can be given in approximately one class period. Answers may be written or given orally, but care must be taken so other students do not overhear responses. Some directions and vocabulary used in this test may be too advanced for some students and may require further explanation. This test assesses the students' ability to:

1. identify remunerative aspects of work
2. locate sources of occupational and training information
3. identify personal values met through work
4. classify jobs into occupational categories
5. investigate local occupational and training opportunities

SCORING PROCEDURES

If the test has previously been administered to the student, circle the number of times on the score sheet.

Examples of appropriate responses are provided on the score sheet for items that may have several acceptable answers. Some questions may have only one acceptable response. For questions requiring demonstrations or role-playing, the examiner must make a judgement about scoring. Further guidelines are presented below.

Written Responses—On the score sheet, circle the example(s) the student has identified. If the student gives an example that seems appropriate but is not listed on the score sheet, record that response on the line provided. Then record the student's score.

Oral Responses—For test questions to which the student responded orally rather than in writing, record the student's response on the score sheet and score the response.

FIGURE 7.3   Sample Pages from the LCCE Performance Battery, Competency 17.

Note. From *Life Centered Career Education: Competency Assessment Knowledge Battery* (pp. 531–532) by D. E. Brolin, 1992, Arlington, VA: The Council for Exceptional Children. Copyright 1992 by The Council for Exceptional Children. Reprinted by permission.

Performance Test 17—Form A (cont.)

Observed Responses—For test questions requiring the student to perform by demonstrating or role-playing, record the response immediately after the response is made. If the task is not performed appropriately, note the reason for the point loss on the line provided.

Each question, including subquestions, is worth up to 2 points. A student must obtain a total score of 8–10 for mastery. Record the final score on the Student Competency Assessment Record (SCAR).

Allow students to respond to each request before reading the next task.

Question 1: Occupational Remuneration (Group Administration)

To the Examiner: Students are to provide explanations for differences in occupational remuneration and why people take lower paying jobs. Also, students are to answer a question concerning types of reductions to paychecks. Distribute Test Question 1.

Read to Students: Look at Test Question 1 and read along with me. People get paid different amounts of money depending on the kind of job they have. Lawyers and doctors make more money that dishwashers and food servers. (a) Give one reason why this is so. (b) Explain why people take lower paying jobs when others pay so much better. (c) When thinking of how much money you're going to make at a job, you must also consider what reductions will be made to your paycheck before you get it. An example of reduction is money taken out for your retirement plan. List two other possible reductions there may be to a person's paycheck.

Question 2: Job Information (Group Administration)

To the Examiner: Students are to use telephone directories to list four local sources (other than school) of occupational information. Distribute Test Question 2 and telephone directories.

Read to Students: Look at Test Question 2 and read along with me. There are many different places you can go to get information about jobs. Using the phone book, find four places in your town or area, other than school, where you could go to find information about jobs or careers and write the four places on the lines provided.

Question 3: Values from a Job (Group Administration)

To the Examiner: Students are to identify personal values met through work. Distribute Test Question 3.

Read to Students: Look at Test Question 3 and read along with me. There are many personal values, or rewards, that a person can get from a job. Why do you think bus drivers work as bus drivers? Besides money, what is another reward each of the following employees get from his or her work?

FIGURE 7.3   Continued.

The LCCE Self-Determination Scale

The most recent addition to the LCCE Mild Curriculum Assessment System, the LCCE Self-Determination Scale (SDS), was developed by the Arc (a national organization on mental retardation) from federal funding in cooperation with authors D. E. Brolin and M. L. Wehmeyer (1995). The instrument was published by the Council for Exceptional Children. The SDS is a 40-item self-report instrument in which students choose from one of three responses (no, maybe, yes) to their perceptions and beliefs relating to the concept of self-determination.

The Arc staff determined that four LCCE Mild Curriculum personal-social competencies closely approximate what experts believe to be inherent in the concept of self-determination: competency 10, self-awareness; 11, self-confidence; 14, independence; and 15, making adequate decisions. These competencies and their 17 subcompetencies were deemed representative of what the Arc considered to be the four domains of self-determination: self-awareness, self-confidence, choice and decision-making skills, and goal attainment behaviors.

The SDS was developed to augment the LCCE Mild Curriculum KB and PB assessments. Unlike the KB and PB, the SDS is a self-report measure. In addition, the scales differ: The KB provides information about the knowledge the students possess about the competency areas related to self-determination, whereas the PB assesses students' abilities to transfer that knowledge to practice, and the SDS assesses students' beliefs about themselves and their skills in this area. Thus, a complete picture of the student's abilities and attitudes related to self-determination can result. An example of several items contained in the SDS instrument is illustrated in Figure 7.4.

The four LCCE Mild Curriculum instruments, coupled with other measures and ecological assessments that provide other valuable assessment data for transition/career planning, can provide educators with a comprehensive armamentarium of instruments from which to make good, solid instructional decisions throughout each student's educational/transitional program. The next section presents a case study to illustrate the use of the LCCE Mild Curriculum assessment instruments.

Case Study

Sam is almost ready to begin his senior year in high school. Sam's LCCE KB and PB results, which are recorded on the Student Competency Assessment Record (SCAR), are presented in Figure 7.5. The scores are Sam's test results on these measures before 9th- and 12th-grade admission. The CRS was completed when Sam was in the fourth and seventh grades.

Inspection of Sam's KB results before beginning 9th grade reveal that Sam's knowledge base in three daily living skills areas, no personal-social skills areas, and one occupational area were at the mastery level (a score of 8 or above). He was administered PB tests in these four competency areas to further determine his ability to perform in these areas. Note that he scored at the mastery level in two of the four areas. Thus, with the cautions noted previously about tests in general, the LCCE Mild Curriculum assessment measures projected a basically satisfactory level of functioning in Sam's ability to take care of his personal needs and to engage in meaningful leisure and recreational pursuits. Thus, total mastery was checked in the far column on the right. Note that the SCAR ratings in this column include those for 12th grade as well; normally, a student completes several SCAR forms over time. Other measures may be used to confirm Sam's level of ability in these areas if needed.

Based on the assessment results, Sam's characteristics, the functional skill instructional effort instituted previously, and the available resources, the

---

Name _____

Circle the answer that best describes you. There are no right or wrong answers. Answer each question according to what you think is the best answer for you.

1.	I know I can do good work.	no	maybe	yes
2.	I am an important person.	no	maybe	yes
3.	I speak up for my own self.	no	maybe	yes
4.	I make decisions based on how I feel at the time.	no	maybe	yes
5.	I do the leisure activities I want.	no	maybe	yes

FIGURE 7.4 Five items from the LCCE Self-Determination Scale.
Note. From *Life Centered Career Education: Self-Determination Scale* (p. 1) by D. E. Brolin and M. L. Wehmeyer, 1995, Arlington, VA: The Council for Exceptional Children. Copyright 1995 by the Council for Exceptional Children. Reprinted by permission.

STUDENT COMPETENCY ASSESSMENT RECORD (SCAR)
LCCE INVENTORY

Student's Name **SAM** Age **18** Grade **12**

School **ANYTOWN** Examiner **Smith**

LCCE COMPETENCY	# ITEMS	FORM A SCORE	FORM B SCORE	# ITEMS	FORM A SCORE	FORM B SCORE	TOTAL	PARTIAL	NONE
KNOWLEDGE BATTERY				**PERFORMANCE BATTERY**			**MASTERY**		
I. DAILY LIVING SKILLS		DATE 4/92	DATE 4/95		DATE	DATE			
1. Personal Finances	10	3	(9)	10	/	6 4/95		✓	
2. Home Management	10	6	(8)	10	/	(8) 4/95	✓		
3. Personal Needs	10	(8)	(9)	10	(8) 5/92	/	✓		
4. Family Living	10	4	(8)	10	/	7 5/95		✓	
5. Foods	10	(9)	7	10	6 5/92	/			✓
6. Clothing	10	5	7	10	/	/			✓
7. Citizenship	10	7	(10)	10	/	5 5/95		✓	
8. Recreational/Leisure	10	(8)	(10)	10	(8) 5/92	7 5/95		✓	
9. Mobility in Community	10	6	(8)	10	/	(8) 5/95	✓		
TOTALS	90	56/62 %	76/84 %				3	4	2
II. PERSONAL-SOCIAL SKILLS		DATE 4/92	DATE 4/95		DATE	DATE			
10. Self-Awareness	10	7	(9)	10	/	(8) 4/95	✓		
11. Self-Confidence	10	6	1	10	/	/			✓
12. Responsible Behavior	10	6	5	10	/	/			✓
13. Interpersonal Skills	10	5	6	10	/	/			✓
14. Independence	10	7	6	10	/	/			✓
15. Decision Making	10	4	7	10	/	/			✓
16. Communicating	10	1	(8)	10	/	(8) 5/95	✓		
TOTALS	70	36/51 %	42/60 %				2	0	5
III. OCCUPATIONAL SKILLS		DATE 4/92	DATE 4/95		DATE	DATE			
17. Occ. Possibilities	10	7	(9)	10	/	6 4/95		✓	
18. Occ. Choices	10	(8)	(9)	10	5 5/92	(9) 5/95	✓		
19. Work Behavior	10	6	5	10	/	/			✓
20. Securing Employment	10	2	2	10	/	/			✓
21. Physical / Manual		–		10	2 5/92	(9) 5/95	✓		
22. Occ. Skills		–		10	/	/		✓	(CRS)
TOTALS	90	23/58 %	25/63 %				2	2	2
GRAND TOTAL	200	115/58 %	143/72 %				7	6	9

*Note: In the last column (Mastery), check *Total* for each competency the student has met or exceeded the criterion level of 8 (Knowledge Battery) and 8 (Performance Battery); check *Partial* if the criterion was met for only one Battery; check *None* if none were met

FIGURE 7.5 Sam's Student Competency Assessment Record (SCAR), Which Records His Results on the LCCE Knowledge Battery and Performance Battery.

Note. From *LCCE Professional Development Activity Book* (p. 398) by D. E. Brolin, 1993, Arlington, VA: The Council for Exceptional Children. Copyright 1993 by the Council for Exceptional Children. Reprinted by permission.

instructional team decided to focus on the following LCCE Mild Curriculum competencies during the 9th grade so appropriate career planning could be initiated by the 10th grade: personal finances (1), family living (4), interpersonal skills (13), decision making (15), communication skills (16), and occupational possibilities (17). Based on these results, other competencies needing to be learned better would be covered during 10th and 11th grade. During the 10th and 11th grades, the CRS was used to obtain teacher ratings of Sam's progress in the competency areas. (Note: More frequent KB administrations could be conducted if necessary.)

Before beginning his senior year, Sam was reassessed on the KB (Form B) and PB tests were administered and/or readministered in competency areas in which KB scores indicated a possible mastery level of knowledge. Inspection of his SCAR Profile reveals considerable progress in the competency areas of the daily living skills domain but not particularly significant gains in the other two domains. Sam achieved mastery scores on only two of the seven personal-social competencies on the KB. He also scored at the mastery level on both PB tests, so the instructional/transitional focus on learning communication skills was apparently quite successful. However, a serious drop in the self-confidence (11) competency resulted, as well as relatively low scores in the other personal-social competencies.

Sam's scores in the occupational domain reveal he gained knowledge partially well about the world of work (17) and that he learned even better the process of making occupational choices (18), scoring at a mastery level on both the KB and PB. In addition, his physical-manual skills (21) were assessed at a mastery level on the PB. His development of a specific occupational skill (22) was rated at a partially mastered level (this competency is not assessed by the KB and PB). However, work habits and behaviors (19) and the ability to seek, secure, and maintain employment (20) were poor.

It can be noted from Sam's profile that he has some serious deficiencies in several LCCE Mild Curriculum competency areas going into his final year of school. If a greater emphasis on some of these competency areas had begun earlier, perhaps Sam would not have so many deficiencies. The instructional/ transitional team

must make some hard decisions and focus on those competency areas in which Sam has good potential for learning in his last year. One other important piece of assessment information should be noted. Recall that Sam's score on the self-confidence competency (11) dropped dramatically on retest. He was administered the LCCE SDS, which further confirmed this area to be a real problem area for Sam. His self-report profile indicated a definite lack of self-confidence; thus, a special effort of counseling and success experiences will be important for him in instructional/transitional planning. In one study of LCCE Mild Curriculum, self-confidence (O'Leary, 1989) was found to be the most desired competency by employers who reviewed the LCCE Mild Curriculum competency matrix.

The LCCE Mild Curriculum assessment measures, along with other academic and functional skills instruments, can assist educators in focusing instruction on the greatest areas of need and help to avoid unnecessary efforts. This chapter can only introduce its readers to the topic. For additional information and a more extensive review of the entire range of assessment measures and methods, the reader is referred to Sitlington, Clark, and Kolstoe's *Transition Education and Services for Adolescents with Disabilities* (2000) and Cronin and Patton's publication on *Life Skills Instruction for All Students with Special Needs* (1993). Persons interested in more information or in reviewing the LCCE instruments should contact the Council for Exceptional Children, 1110 North Glebe Road, Suite 300, Arlington, VA 22201. In addition, a list of organizations that can be contacted regarding other functional assessment measures is presented in Appendix D.

The LCCE Moderate Curriculum Assessment System

Three LCCE Moderate Curriculum assessment measures are in preparation and will be available soon after this text is published. These instruments, such as those for the LCCE Mild Curriculum, are designed to assess the transition/career education competencies contained in the LCCE Moderate Curriculum for students with severe learning and/or behavior needs. Each of these measures provide a different range of assessment options, so educators can select from among these four measures, depending on the students' own situation and needs. In addition, educators are encouraged to use other measures, such as those described previously, to provide the most comprehensive and appropriate career/functional assessment for transition planning.

The three LCCE Moderate Curriculum instruments will be published by the Council for Exceptional Children (CEC), and are described briefly next. An example from each is provided.

The LCCE Moderate Curriculum Competency Rating Scale-M

The LCCE Moderate Curriculum Competency Rating Scale (CRS-M) (in press) is built around the 20 competencies and 75 subcompetencies that comprise the LCCE Moderate Curriculum. The subcompetencies and their objectives serve as the actual CRS items. A manual, contained in the appendix of the LCCE Moderate Curriculum Guide (*Life Centered Career Education: Modified Curriculum for Individuals with Moderate Disabilities*, Loyd & Brolin, 1997), presents specific behavioral criteria or objectives on which to judge student's mastery level for each subcompetency. These criteria approximate the behavioral/instructional objectives that are subsumed under each subcompetency unit in the LCCE Moderate Curriculum Guide.

The CRS-M was developed with the philosophy that teachers who have worked closely with students can fairly accurately assess their competency levels, given helpful and appropriate guidelines. Another valuable use of this instrument is giving the student with special learning and/or behavior needs and/or their parents/guardians an opportunity to address the student's functional competence.

The CRS-M Manual provides these guidelines; identifies who should do the ratings and when they should be done; and provides criteria for the ratings, a rating key defining numerical rating values, a CRS-M Record Form for recording and summarizing ratings, and demographic information. CRS-M users rate their students, selves, or child on a three-point Likert Scale on each of the subcompetencies as either not

competent (0), partially competent (1), or competent (2). Younger students will be too young and some lower functioning students may not be ready for rating for some of the subcompetencies; thus, a "Not Rated" (NR) response should be given. Raters should record the rating and summarize them on a CRS-M Record Form so that a profile can be created of the student's strengths and weaknesses in: (a) the 75 subcompetencies; (b) the 20 competencies; and (c) a domain score for each of the three curriculum areas: daily living, personal-social, and occupational guidance and preparation.

The CRS-M provides a quick and inexpensive method of curriculum-based assessment. It can be used at any grade level and with any type of student. It is particularly useful at the elementary level, where a limited number of functional skills instruments related to the transition effort are available. An example of one page from the CRS-M is presented in Figure 7.6.

The LCCE Moderate Pictorial Knowledge Battery

The second instrument, LCCE Moderate Pictorial Knowledge Battery (PKB) (in press), was developed to provide LCCE Mild Curriculum users with a more objective instrument for assessing students on their level of competency attainment. The PKB is a reading-free functional transition criterion-referenced assessment that contains 150 multiple-choice questions covering the three LCCE Moderate Curriculum domains. Questions cover the first 18 competencies of the LCCE Moderate Curriculum. The last two competencies, covering physical-manual skills and specific occupational skills, do not lend themselves to knowledge assessment.

The over 200 functional instructional objectives of the LCCE Moderate Curriculum were, like the CRS, used as the basis for developing PKB test items because they define the important functional areas of the curriculum. Questions for each competency were divided among the subcompetencies composing the competency and their functional instructional objectives. The PKB comprises two forms (A and B) and takes from 2 to 4 hours to administer, depending on the students.

LIFE CENTERED CAREER EDUCATION
Competency Rating Scale-Modified
Record Form
DAILY LIVING SKILLS

Student Name _____ Date of Birth _____ Sex _____

School _____ City _____ State _____

Directions: Please rate the student according to his/her mastery of *each* item using the rating key below. Indicate the ratings in the column below the date for the rating period. Use the NR rating for items which cannot be rated. For subcompetencies rated 0 or 1 at the time of the final rating, place a check (✔) in the appropriate space in the *yes/no* column to indicate his/her ability to perform the subcompetency with assistance from the community. Please refer to the CRS manual for explanation of the rating key, description of the behavioral criteria for each subcompetency, and explanation of the *yes/no* column.

Rating Key: 0 = Not Competent   1 = Partially Competent   2 = Competent   NR = Not Related

To what extent has the student mastered the following subcompetencies?

Subcompetencies	Rater(s)								Yes	No
	Grade Level									
	Date(s)									
DAILY LIVING SKILLS DOMAIN									Yes	No
1. Managing Money										
1. Count Money	—	—	—	—	—	—	—	—	—	—
2. Make Purchases	—	—	—	—	—	—	—	—	—	—
3. Use Vending Machines	—	—	—	—	—	—	—	—	—	—
4. Budget Money	—	—	—	—	—	—	—	—	—	—
5. Perform Banking Skills	—	—	—	—	—	—	—	—	—	—
2. Selecting and Maintaining Living Environments										
6. Select Appropriate Community Living Environments	—	—	—	—	—	—	—	—	—	—
7. Maintain Living Environment	—	—	—	—	—	—	—	—	—	—
8. Use Basic Appliances and Tools	—	—	—	—	—	—	—	—	—	—
9. Set Up Personal Living Space	—	—	—	—	—	—	—	—	—	—
3. Caring for Personal Health										
10. Perform Appropriate Grooming and Hygiene	—	—	—	—	—	—	—	—	—	—
11. Dress Appropriately	—	—	—	—	—	—	—	—	—	—
12. Maintain Physical Fitness	—	—	—	—	—	—	—	—	—	—
13. Recognize and Seek Help for Illness	—	—	—	—	—	—	—	—	—	—
14. Practice Basic First Aid	—	—	—	—	—	—	—	—	—	—
15. Practice Personal Safety	—	—	—	—	—	—	—	—	—	—

FIGURE 7.6   A Sample Competency Rating Form-Moderate

Note. From *Life Centered Career Education: Modified Curriculum for Individuals with Moderate Disabilities* (p. 83), by R. J. Loyd and D. E. Brolin, 1997, Arlington, VA: The Council for Exceptional Children. Copyright 1997 by the Council for Exceptional Children. Reprinted by permission.

The PKB was developed over a period of several years with the assistance of several school personnel. A number of experienced special educators were involved in writing appropriate items, which were revised several times after field testing different versions with hundreds of students with special learning and/or behavior needs across the country. A detailed technical report is available to describe the extensive development and validation of the instrument.

Although the PKB was developed originally for students with severe learning and/or behavior needs, many users find the instrument useful with a variety of younger students with little or no reading ability. However, caution is advised in too quickly interpreting its results without keeping its development and validation in mind. It is important to remember that the LCCE Moderate Curriculum PKB, like any other assessment, is just a sample of basic knowledge. No measure should be considered to reveal every student's actual functional competence. Rather, such instruments are useful screening devices to assist special educators in instructional/transitional planning efforts.

An example of one page from one of the PKB forms is presented in Figure 7.7.

The LCCE Moderate Curriculum Performance Assessment Battery

The third instrument, the LCCE Moderate Performance Assessment Battery (PAB) (in press), was developed to provide a more functional, real-life measure of the competencies in the LCCE Moderate Curriculum. The first 19 LCCE Moderate Curriculum competencies are addressed in this functional performance instrument. Competency 20 is not assessed, because its assessment depends on the specific occupational training area in which each student with special learning and/or behavior needs is being instructed.

The PAB is a nonstandardized, reading-free, criterion-referenced instrument. It contains a combination of open-ended questions, role-playing scenarios, card sorts, and several hands-on activities that require the student to prepare a meal, use a vending machine, and seek assistance when needed. Because of the length of time required to assess actual performance in some of the LCCE Moderate Curriculum

competency areas, many advanced knowledge or cognitive items were used for some of the competency assessments. Three major types of items make up the battery: performance, simulated performance, and performance-related knowledge.

As with the CRS-M and PKB, the subcompetencies and functional instructional objectives from *Life Centered Career Education: Modified Curriculum for Individuals with Moderate Disabilities* (Loyd & Brolin, 1997), were used in determining and developing test items. The PAB presents a more realistic approach to assessing students with special learning and/ or behavior needs' actual abilities and behaviors beyond what is gained from the more objective PKB. Students with more severe learning and/or behavior needs must demonstrate a functional activity reflecting adequate command of the LCCE competencies and their subcompetencies. All subcompetencies are addressed in the PAB tests. Each PAB competency test has five questions. A PAB Manual provides detailed directions for administering, scoring, and reporting the results. A special feature of the PAB approach is its flexibility in scoring, which allows examiners to use their discretion in deviating from the suggested correct responses based on regional and cultural differences. Some responses may not be listed but are correct for the ecological environment in which the student with special learning and/or behavior needs performs the LCCE Moderate Curriculum functional objectives.

The PAB has two forms, A and B. Because it would take more than 30 hours to administer the battery to small groups of students with severe learning and/or behavior needs, users generally select one or more PAB tests to administer at a time, based on the results of the CRS-M and/or PKB assessments. Often, these tests are administered before and after students with severe learning and/or behavior needs are instructed in one of the LCCE competency areas. Many teachers prefer the PAB because it is the most natural and realistic measure of their students with severe learning and/or behavior needs' functional/transitional skills.

The first two pages of one LCCE PAB test are presented in Figure 7.8. The entire test for this competency—which includes the other questions, score sheet, and work sheets—is provided in Appendix C for readers interested in the entire nature of test construction.

COMPETENCY #10

81.   Circle or point to the picture of an activity that you would do in your home after eating a meal or snack.

    a.   **Dropping Trash on Floor**   b.   **Dropping Clothes on Floor**   c.   **Washing Dishes**

82.   Circle or point to the picture of an activity that you should not do in your home.

    a.   **Dusting Furniture**   b.   **Dropping Clothes on Floor**   c.   **Hanging Up Clothes in Closet**

83.   Circle or point to the picture of an activity that you should do at your job.

    a.   **Clocking In**   b.   **Sleeping**   c.   **Talking To Coworkers**

FIGURE 7.7   Sample Page of the Pictorial Knowledge Battery (PKB)

Note. From *The LCCE Moderate Pictorial Knowledge Battery: LCCE-M PKB* by R. J. Loyd and D. E. Brolin, in press, Arlington, VA: The Council for Exceptional Children. Reprinted by permission of the Council for Exceptional Children.

. . . .

CHAPTER COMMENTARY

Assessment is more than testing. It is a systematic process of using information from a wide array of sources so that educators and significant others can make informed decisions about their students. It has become generally recognized in the field that there is a need to focus more instructional and assessment activities on the critical functional skills that students

LCCE PERFORMANCE COMPETENCY 1

Managing Money (Daily Living Skills)

Materials for Duplication

Test question 5 worksheet
Score Sheet

Materials Needed:

An assortment of pennies, nickels, dimes, quarters, and half dollars; magazines

Directions:

This test can be given in approximately one class period. Answers can be performed or given orally. Some directions and vocabulary used in this test may be too advanced for some students and may require further explanation. This PAB assesses the students ability to

1. Count Money
2. Make Purchases
3. Use Vending Machines
4. Budget Money
5. Perform Banking Skills

Scoring Procedures

If this test has previously been administered to the student, circle the number of administrations on the score sheet.

Examples of appropriate responses are provided on the score sheet for items that may have several acceptable answers. Some questions may have only one acceptable response. For questions requiring performances, role-plays, or demonstrations, the examiner must make a judgment about scoring. Further guidelines are presented as follows:

Written Responses—On the score sheet, circle the example(s) the student has identified. If the student gives an example that seems appropriate but is not listed on the score sheet, record that response on the line provided. Then record the student's score.

Oral Responses—For test questions to which the student responded orally, record the student's response on the score sheet and score.

Observed Responses—For test questions requiring the student to perform by demonstrating or role-playing, record the response immediately after the response is made. If the task is not performed appropriately, note the reason for the point loss on the line provided.

Each question, including subquestions, is worth up to 2 points. A student must attain a total score of 8 to 10 for mastery. Record the final score on the Student Competency Assessment Record

Question 1: Count Money

To the Examiner: Student will be able to identify a penny, nickel, dime, quarter, and half dollar from an assortment of coins.

FIGURE 7.8   Sample Pages from the Performance Assessment Battery (PAB)

Note. From *The LCCE Moderate Performance Assessment Battery: LCCE-M PAB* by R. J. Loyd and D. E. Brolin, in press, Arlington, VA: The Council for Exceptional Children. Reprinted by permission of the Council for Exceptional Children.

Read to Student: Look at the assortment of coins. Listen carefully as I state each coin. When I say a coin's name, you will point to the coin that I say. Point to the nickel. Point to the quarter. Point to the penny. Point to the half-dollar. Point to the dime.

Question 2: Make Purchases

To the Examiner: Student will be able to find pictures of items needed to be purchased, in magazines. A stack of magazine pictures of various purchasable items will be available to choose the appropriate item.

Read to Student: Look at the following pictures of items that can be purchased. Choose which one is shampoo. Choose which item is orange juice. Choose which item is paper towels. Choose which one is a tomato.

Question 3: Use Vending Machines

To the Examiner: Student will use "four quarters" method to buy a selected item from a vending machine. The student will put quarter(s) in the machine and push button after each quarter until item is received.

Read to Student: I would like you to pick a soda that you like and purchase it with the coins provided here.

Question 4: Budget Money

To the Examiner: Student will be able to identify his/her weekly personal income (assuming he/she has a job).

Read to Student: I am going to show you a list of personal incomes, and read each income to you. I want you to tell me which personal income is your personal income.

Question 5: Perform Banking Skills

To the Examiner: Student will be able to print his/her full name, address, birth date, telephone number, and names of references for use on an account application.

Read to Student: I am going to ask you to print the following information on this worksheet. Print your full name. Print your address. Print your birth date. Print your telephone number. Print the names of references.

FIGURE 7.8   Continued.

will need in order to compete in today's and tomorrow's rapidly changing and demanding society.

Criterion-referenced assessment is recommended over norm-referenced approaches because it is more useful in discerning students' proficiency level and in writing Individualized Education Plans (IEPs) and Individualized Written Rehabilitation Plans (IWRPs). Although there are a myriad of standardized and non-standardized assessment measures to choose from, most do not relate directly to the curriculum of the students. The adoption of criterion- and domain-referenced measures, such as the LCCE Mild and Moderate Curriculum instruments, will provide a more specific focus on the students' needs so that instructional needs for transition planning can be identified and tracked. These can be supplemented with other formal and informal transition assessment measures that the professional believes also are important.

In Chapter 8, some further reference to the use of assessment in the development of student IEPs and individualized transition plans is presented by Iva Dean Cook, Carol Opperman, and Melody Thurman-Urbanic.

. . . .

ACTIVITIES

1. Discuss how you would establish and conduct a functional career assessment program in your district from elementary through the secondary years. When would these assessments begin, what kind of assessment measures would you use, and when and how would they be administered?

2. Refer back to the case of Sam. Given his SCAR profile, what would you recommend as the focus of his instructional program for the senior year? What other assessment measures would you use to verify and establish his major instructional needs? What are some important considerations that would go into your instructional decision making?

CHAPTER 8

Transition Planning

Robert J. Loyd,
Iva Dean Cook,
Carol Opperman, and
Melody Thurman-Urbanic

PRELIMINARY QUESTIONS

1. How has the Individuals with Disabilities Education Act (IDEA) 1997 resulted in a major policy shift relative to providing students with special learning and/or behavior needs with functional curricula and transition services?
2. What are some of the key components that are essential for transition to be successfully conducted?
3. What barriers often impede the successful implementation of transition services and programs?
4. What exactly is the difference between the intent of the Individualized Education Plan (IEP) and the Individualized Transition Plan (ITP)?
5. Identify the categories of student needs that should be contained in the ITP.
6. What is meant by *interagency agreements,* and who is required to implement them?
7. What roles and responsibilities do you believe agencies, parents, and others must assume in the transition planning and preparation process?
8. What assessments should be conducted to provide direction for transition planning?
9. Why do the Life-Centered Career Education (LCCE) Mild/Moderate Curriculum developers believe it qualifies as a comprehensive transition model?
10. What changes do you believe need to be undertaken in most school districts to respond adequately to the transition needs of students with special learning and/or behavior needs?

OVERVIEW

Educators of students with special learning and/or behavior needs have become increasingly more aware in the past few years of the need to provide their students with career education and career information to facilitate successful transition from school to the adult environment. The IDEA of 1997, originally enacted as the Education for All Handicapped Children Act of 1975, mandated that transition services be made available to all students age 14 or younger. This has prompted school districts throughout the country to become even more responsive to the career development needs of their students than was accomplished during the career education movement of the 1970s and early 1980s, which preceded the newer federal mandate called transition.

It is both unfortunate and fortunate that it has taken a federal mandate for the career development and functional skills needs of our students with special learning and/or behavior needs to be more adequately addressed. Although it is still too early to determine the impact of the recent legislative mandates that give more attention to students' career development needs, it is significant that what was promulgated 25 to 30 years ago is finally being given the opportunity to be infused into the educational system. As noted by Halloran,

> the IDEA transition provisions represent a major policy shift from permissive to prescriptive, required services. This policy shift differentiates transition services from the movements of the 1960s, 1970s, and 1980s that encouraged improved services to achieve educational outcomes without a clear statement of entitlement for all youth with disabilities. (1993, p. 12)

This chapter focuses on individualized student transition planning. We discuss the transition concept, the IEP, and the ITP. We then attempt to describe how the LCCE Mild/Moderate Curriculum and its IEP form can be used to address the transition needs of students with special learning and/or behavior needs.

THE TRANSITION CONCEPT

Although the idea of carefully planning for the successful movement from school to postsecondary training and/or to work has been evident in the literature for many decades, it is only in the last few years that service providers have been required to seriously examine, expand, and develop collaborative efforts to facilitate the process called *transition* (Wehman, et al., 1989; Will, 1984b; Gemmel & Peterson, 1989).

CHAPTER OUTLOOK

Jean N. Boston is the former Director of Publications for The Council for Exceptional Children in Arlington, Virginia.

According to the mandates of the Individuals with Disabilities Education Act (IDEA) of 1997, every student with a disability must have an Individualized Education Program (IEP) that includes a transition plan to help students prepare for the demands of life beyond the school setting. Determining the skills most needed by individual students and then selecting an appropriate curriculum for teaching those skills are challenging tasks, indeed. Fortunately, help is available in the LCCE curriculum package and assessment batteries (Brolin, 1992a, 1992b) available from The Council for Exceptional Children (CEC). For over 25 years, teachers have been using Brolin's *Life-Centered Career Education: A Competency Based Approach* to provide the framework for selecting the daily living skills, personal social skills, and occupational skills needed by individual students. The expanded curriculum, published in 1992, offers teachers over 1,100 lesson plans, tested in the classroom and known to be effective in developing the functional skills identified in a student's IEP. Teachers who work with students with more severe learning and/or behavior needs now have Loyd and Brolin's modified LCCE Curriculum for providing functional skills preparation for this population.

Although the Life-Centered Career Education (LCCE) curriculum addresses 22 competency areas (mild) and 20 competency areas (moderate), individual students will always need special skills not included in the curriculum. The beauty of the LCCE approach is that it is very easy for a teacher to add new competencies using the LCCE lesson format. For example, each lesson plan includes an LCCE objective that identifies the specific competency that is being addressed; a lesson objective, which clearly states the student outcome; and a list of instructional resources that is needed to conduct the lesson. This is followed by a few lines introducing the lesson, a statement of where the lesson will take place (e.g., school, home, etc.), and the number of sessions it will take to complete the lesson. The steps involved in the actual instructional task are then presented; and finally, a lesson plan evaluation that describes an activity and performance criteria is available. Having a clear and simple framework for preparing instructional material is more than half the battle.

Teachers who need to develop lessons for competencies not presently covered in the LCCE curriculum can look to other publishers or to the Educational Resources Information Center (ERIC) database for additional ideas. ERIC is a federally funded information system that has been stockpiling educational information for almost 30 years. It contains more than 440,000 journal annotations and over 340,000 education-related document abstracts. The ERIC database may be accessed on CD-ROM in many libraries or on-line using your personal computer. On-line services are available through a number of database vendors including DIALOG (1-800-3DIALOG), Maxwell On-line (1-800-955-0906), and the Internet system. The ERIC database is easy to search, and it contains many excellent ideas for constructing lesson plans in a variety of skill areas. Many ERIC documents are research based, and the strategies described have been tested and analyzed for their effectiveness. For a fee, custom computer searches are available through the ERIC

Clearinghouse on Disabilities and Gifted Education. To initiate a search, call ERIC-CEC at 1-800-328-0727.

To get a really good understanding of how to use the LCCE system to serve students with disabilities, teachers and other members of the school-based team can attend one of the regional training workshops offered by CEC. Also available is a complete training package that includes 10 hours of videotapes, a Trainer's Manual, and Professional Development Activity Books for each trainee. To learn more about these materials, contact the Council for Exceptional Children, 703-620-3660.

Transition is an outcome-oriented process encompassing a broad array of quality services and experiences that lead to employment (and other life roles).

The original conceptualization of transition in 1984 by Assistant Secretary of the U.S. Office of Special Education and Rehabilitative Services Madelyn Will and her colleagues focuses on the movement of students from high school to employment, as depicted in Figure 8.1.

Since the introduction of the transition concept by Will and colleagues, the concept has expanded to include many other adult outcome objectives in addition to many community living outcomes. An expanded view of transition (Brolin, 1993a) that represents the thinking of many professionals in the field in using the familiar bridge model is presented in Figure 8.2. The model acknowledges elementary as well as secondary programs for transition efforts. And, as can be seen, the three bridges link elementary and secondary students not only to employment but also to community living, integration, and socialization.

Successful transition requires a number of key components to be successfully conducted:

- Interagency cooperation
- Individualized Transition Plans
- Employer incentives
- Supported employment (for some individuals)
- A functional career curriculum
- Collaborative efforts with employers, agencies, and parents
- A postsecondary support and follow-up system to ensure community and job adjustment

Transition seeks to maximize the productivity, community participation, and independence of students with special learning and/or behavior needs and to ensure that students receive the opportunities and services needed for adult adjustment to community living and working (Cook & Thurman-Urbanic, 1990).

FIGURE 8.1 Major Components of the Transition Process (OSERS Model). *Note.* From *OSERS Programming for Transition of Youth with Disabilities: Bridges from School to Working Life* by M. Will, 1984, Washington, DC: Office of Special Education and Rehabilitative Services, U.S. Department of Education, Office of Information for the Handicapped.

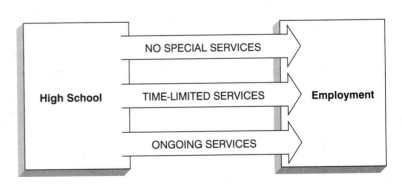

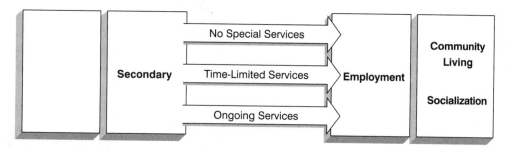

FIGURE 8.2 Expanded View of Transition

Note. From *LCCE Professional Development Activity Book* (p. 399) by D. E. Brolin, 1993, Arlington, VA: The Council for Exceptional Children. Copyright 1993 by The Council for Exceptional Children. Reprinted by permission.

Facilitators of Transition

Research has found consensus on several major facilitating factors in a successful transition effort (e.g., Halpern, 1985; Higgins, Fowler, & Chandler, 1988; D. Johnson, Bruininks, & Thurlow, 1987). These investigations seem to agree that the following are critical requirements for successful transition services:

- Team members explore all possible solutions to meet student needs
- Commitment
- Expanded interagency linkages
- The sharing of ideas and strategies among the agencies
- Favorable community atmosphere toward the students and their employment
- Decrease in duplicated and overlapping services
- A referral system that sends students to the most appropriate agencies

One study comparing successful and unsuccessful placement of secondary students with special learning and/or behavior needs found that more than 50% of the total influence in the training and placement process was due to the nature of the education program itself (Heal, Copher, DeStephano, & Rusch, 1989). The investigation found that many individuals with special learning and/or behavior needs are not encouraged to contribute to their own economic independence or to fulfill societal expectations for employment. The authors cite the 50% employment rate they found for special education graduates as a good

indicator that better transition services are needed. An important finding from the study was that the most important elements in the success of students are a strong transition team effort, employer support, employment supervision, and community acceptance.

Benefits of Transition

Wehman and his colleagues (1989) have reported the benefits of providing early transition planning and gainful employment for students before they leave school. They cite the following benefits to involving students in earlier transition programs:

- Institution of the necessary curricular changes (instructional and programmatic) to better facilitate the process
- Teachers who actually go into the community with their students and learn the specific needs and demands of various employers
- Teachers who can provide support and assistance to transitioning students while they are still in school
- Better continuity of service with agencies, employers, and parents
- Better case management from school to adult services
- Parent support

Wehman and colleagues advocate job placement before graduation to reduce the risk of not receiving services after graduation; to reduce the possibility of being put on long waiting lists for services; and to help offset the negative effect on high unemployment of students in special education by securing the job while they are still in high school.

Barriers to Successful Transition

Many barriers that impede the progress of transitional planning have been identified (Beck, 1988; Bellamy, 1985; Didley, 1987; Halpern, 1985; Naylor, 1985; Ward & Halloran, 1989). Those cited most often follow:

- Duplication of services by the education agency and service providers
- Lack of social integration of special education students into regular classes
- Inaccessibility to vocational education
- Poor planning linkages and lack of adequate adult services
- Poor data management and transfer between schools and agencies
- Lack of parental involvement
- Community prejudice and discrimination

One of the greatest barriers to transition seems to be the need for students to be better prepared to exhibit more appropriate prosocial skills (Beck, 1988; Neubert & Tilson, 1987; Rose, Friend, & Farnum, 1988; Wehman, 1981; Wehman & Hill, 1985). This research also has indicated that the majority of problems experienced by on-the-job transition participants relates to inappropriate work and prosocial behaviors rather than the task-related difficulty of work production on the job.

Developing the prosocial skills necessary for success in the world of work is one of the more challenging tasks of educational/transitional programs. Educators will need to give more emphasis to this area if community-based training and placement efforts are to succeed (Wehman & Hill, 1985).

Summary

All of the discussed recommendations for transition are readily accepted ideologically; in practice, however, their adoption is not expected to take place overnight.

Unfortunately, whereas administrators and policymakers struggle to make decisions on the future of transition in this country, many students, parents, educators, and employers will become frustrated with the inadequacy of transition program-delivery systems. A position statement by the Council for Exceptional Children's (CEC) Division on Career Development and Transition (CEC/DCDT) entitled "Career Development for Students with Disabilities in Elementary Schools," states the following:

> The Division of Career Development is composed of professionals who are committed to the aim that all children with disabilities have access to an instructional program which focuses on life/career development and transitional demands. (G. M. Clark, Carlson, Fisher, Cook, & D'Alonzo, 1991, p. 117)

"Transitions occur throughout one's lifetime and include both paid work and the work roles of students, homemakers, family members, volunteers, and retirees, as well as productive recreational, avocational, and leisure activities. Many people encounter problems when making various transitions. Adults in transition, especially many of those with disabilities, sometimes become confused and need special assistance to help them solve their problems and make wise decisions. The 'transition from school-to-work' concept is inextricably related to the career development concept that has been theorized and implemented in various education and agency settings for many years."

(Brolin & Schatzman, 1989, pp. 22-23)

INDIVIDUALIZED EDUCATION AND INDIVIDUALIZED TRANSITION PLANS

The IEP

The IEP is a written document that summarizes the educational program for the student. The IEP may be developed as early as elementary school. The contents of the stated goals are derived from an analysis of the student's strengths and weaknesses. The IEP not only establishes the goals, it also determines the services the local educational agency (LEA) must provide to assist in meeting those goals. The IEP also enhances the communication needed among parents and school personnel (Polloway, Patton, Payne, & Payne, 1989).

Traditionally, special educators have had the responsibility for those persons needing special education services as mandated by PL 94-142 (Education for All Handicapped Children Act of 1975). Figure 8.3 shows the general process used for identification and placement. The law mandates that the IEP be written for all students and contain the following components:

- Present level of performance
- Annual goals
- Short-term objectives
- Special education and related services
- Extent and participation out of general education classroom

- Dates and initiation of services and duration of services
- Objective criteria, evaluation procedures, and schedule for assessing short-term objectives

These required services were expanded with the passage of the IDEA of 1990 and 1997. As noted previously, the IDEA 1997 requires that the IEP incorporate a new provision: A statement of the needed transition services must be included, and a statement of interagency responsibilities or linkages must be included if these services are the responsibility of a state or local agency other than the school responsible for the student's education.

The IDEA 1997 expands the IEP team membership to encourage general education personnel's and other agencies' participation. In addition to the student, IDEA 1997 identifies the student's general education teacher, the student's special education teachers, parents, the LEA representative, and professionals

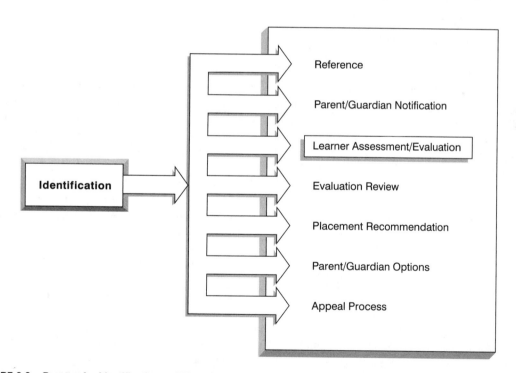

FIGURE 8.3   Process for Identification and Placement

Note. From *Transition Manual: TRIAD Telecommunications Project* (p. 39) by I. D. Cook and M. Thurman-Urbanic, 1990, Institute, WV: West Virginia Graduate College. Copyright 1990 by West Virginia Graduate College. Reprinted by permission.

from any other agency responsible for providing or paying for transition services to be present at the IEP meeting. Related legislation, for example, the Americans with Disabilities Act (ADA), Rehabilitation Act, and Carl Perkins Vocational Education Act, provide support and services for students in transition from school to the community and the world of work.

The IEP has traditionally been used as the foundation for each identified special education student's educational program. The heart of this foundation has been primarily academic; however, time and research have revealed a greater need—transition/career education. Therefore, more effective transitional services, as now mandated by federal law, are made available to the student. Legislative mandates have also introduced a partner component to the IEP—the Individualized Transition Plan (ITP).

The ITP Component

The ITP component is a written record of the student's long-range goals and needs for postsecondary training, employment, and other community living objectives that also specifies how they will be achieved. The ITP should outline the student's personalized transition programming interests, needs, and future opportunities; should contain precise objectives and activities; should have input from parents, general and special educators, and adult service providers; and should be longitudinal (Didley, 1987). Generally, the ITP becomes a component of the student's IEP by age 14 or younger, although some school districts have opted to have a separate document for this purpose.

As noted by Polloway and Patton (1993), the intent of the ITP differs from that of the IEP. The ITP is a plan for transition services, whereas the IEP is a plan for skill or knowledge acquisition. Like IEPs, ITPs have no set format, but unlike IEPs, ITPs have no required elements. Most address the following critical adult outcome functioning areas: postsecondary training, interpersonal relations, community and daily living, employment (training/ placement), leisure/recreational options, health and physical fitness needs, and self-determination and advocacy needs. School districts generally organize ITPs around transition areas that the team has determined to be critical to the successful movement from school to postsecondary, to community living, and to working.

The IEP/ITP is the educational map for students, kindergarten through graduation or leaving school. Other components included are a profile of the student's current level of performance, the curriculum options, needed support services, and ongoing functional assessment. During middle school and secondary education, transition plans are made to assist the student in achieving functional mastery of the major competencies needed for successful adult outcomes (i.e., attending postsecondary education or vocational training, securing and maintaining employment, participating as a family member, participating in recreational/ leisure options, participation as a productive citizen).

Although the student with special learning and/or behavior needs is the most important person in transition planning, it is also important to involve all other people who may be able to give valuable input into decision making regarding transition-related activities for the student with special learning and/or behavior needs. Participants may differ at the middle school, secondary education, and postsecondary training levels. Regardless of age and/or grade level, the student with special learning and/or behavior needs and the parents/guardians/primary caregivers must always be at the center of the planning process. Along with the student with special learning and/or behavior needs, someone such as a transition coordinator should collaborate in the transition planning to ensure that information flows smoothly among agencies. Figure 8.4 provides an example of possible participants for transition planning at the middle school, secondary education, and postsecondary training levels (Cook & Thurman-Urbanic, 1990).

The IEP/ITP must include a statement of the interagency responsibilities or linkages before the student with special learning and/or behavior needs leaves the secondary education experience. Thus, although it is the responsibility of the local educational agency to initiate transition planning, it must be done in cooperation with local adult service providers (i.e., Vocational Rehabilitation, postsecondary institutions,

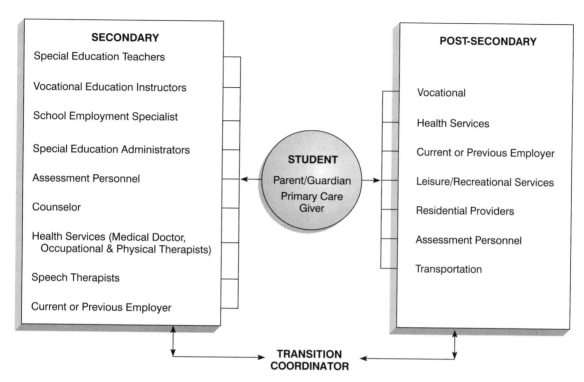

FIGURE 8.4 Participants in Transition Planning.
Note. From *Transition Manual: TRIAD Telecommunications Project* (p. 76) by I. D. Cook and M. Thurman-Urbanic, 1990, Institute, WV: West Virginia Graduate College. Copyright 1990 by West Virginia Graduate College. Reprinted by permission.

Social Security, Advocacy, and Adult Service agencies).

As the student with special learning and/or behavior needs enters the final years of schooling, the ITP provides the framework for planning the student's transition from school to postsecondary training, to community living, and to employment. The ITP reflects the student with special learning and/or behavior needs' changing interests and needs and then delineates major goals, including postsecondary training, vocational training, residential options, community service, health services, and financial support services. The IEP/ITP should include specific steps and activities the student with special learning and/or behavior needs must perform to attain the identified transition goals, a time frame for meeting the steps and activities, a time frame for completion of goals, and finally, the date when accomplished. It should outline logical steps that the student with special

learning and/or behavior needs, her family members, school personnel, and agencies must take in planning for the student with special learning and/or behavior needs' successful transition to achieving appropriate access to postsecondary training, adult services, and/or employment. Figure 8.5 presents a services referral checklist that can be used as a guide for selecting specific services for individual students with special learning and/or behavior needs.

IDEA 1997 reemphasizes the individualized/personalized nature of transition planning. It is important to note that "the services the student with special learning and/or behavior needs receives should be based on personal 'preferences and needs', *not* currently available programs or services. This wording encourages the development of new, restructured personalized service delivery models" (Whetstone, 1993). Instead of designing a student with special learning and/or behavior needs around an existing

Service Item	Date to Be Completed	Person Responsible	Date Completed
Referral to vocational rehabilitation			
Referral to MR/DD			
Referral to			
Referral to			
Social Security Card			
Medicaid application			
Medicare application			
SSI			
SSDI			
Guardianship			
Welfare			
Food stamps			
Medical exam			
Psychological exam			
Social history			
Educational summary			
Special transportation			
Residential services			
Group home			
Family support			
Foster care			
Respite services			
Counseling			
Waiver for minimum competency test			

FIGURE 8.5 Services Referral Checklist
Note. From *Transition from School to Work* (p. 94) by P. Wehman, S. Moon, J. M. Everson, & J. M. Barcus, 1988, Baltimore: Paul H. Brookes. Copyright 1988 by Paul H. Brookes. Reprinted by permission.

program/service, the student with special learning and/or behavior needs' transition program is developed to meet her personalized transition goals.

Interagency Agreements

Formal, written interagency agreements are needed for effective transition programs. Law requires individual states to have cooperative agreements between the State Departments of Education and Vocational Rehabilitation. These agreements provide a focus for the LEAs to ensure that each student with special learning and/or behavior needs is identified and provided with the appropriate services, including transition planning and programming. Some cooperative agreements clearly delineate at what age each agency becomes responsible for education and vocational training for students with special learning and/or behavior needs. As noted in Chapter 5, an example of a state-level (West Virginia) interagency agreement is presented in Appendix A.

A service responsibility chart may also be included with an interagency agreement to specify the activities provided. An example of such a chart is presented in Figure 8.6, developed by the West Virginia Department of Education and Division of Rehabilitation Services. The chart delineates responsibilities by preschool services, general and special education, vocational education, and the state rehabilitation agency.

Didley (1987) suggests that interagency agreements work only if the models developed for local school districts are based on local needs and services. He further suggests that these local school districts develop resource guides for transitional services facilitating collaboration and allowing the community, at large, to ensure quality transitional services. Didley perceives as a goal of the collaborative transition model the advocacy for public acceptance of and involvement with employing persons with special learning and/or behavior needs in the community. The involvement of both the student with special learning and/or behavior needs and her family members is viewed as integral in this collaborative activity (Cook & Thurman-Urbanic, 1990).

The identification of case managers or transition coordinators is an important consideration in transition planning and in implementing these collaborative interagency agreements. In Figure 8.7, we present our suggestions for the responsibilities of case managers from elementary to the postsecondary levels.

School administrators must recognize the need for staff flexibility to deliver appropriate functional curriculum and transition services in terms of timing and location. Research has shown that off-campus jobs are far more valuable to the transition of students with special learning and/or behavior needs than simulated work activities in the classroom (Cook & Thurman-Urbanic, 1990).

Transition/Career Assessment

Before the IEP and its ITP component are developed, a comprehensive career/vocational assessment should be completed as part of the total process of assessment and evaluation. As noted in Chapter 7, the CEC Division on Career Development and Transition (DCDT) describes career/transition assessment as embracing not only vocational areas but also the avocational and daily living skills areas as a necessary foundation for personalized program planning and transition planning from kindergarten through adulthood.

The components of a comprehensive transition/career assessment, from our perspective, are presented in Figure 8.8. Individuals who may be responsible for contributing to these data are also found in the graphic. The results of these transition/career assessments will provide the data from which the IEP/ITP can be developed (Cook & Thurman-Urbanic, 1990).

Summary

Four key elements of transition that must be addressed in transitional planning follow:

1. Systematic career/vocational training throughout the early, middle, and secondary school years
2. Effective work by cooperative and interagency teams

Services must be available and accessible to all students/clients with disabilities. The activities below can generally be provided by the specified agency. Where there is an overlapping or duplication of services, the question of WHO INITIATES SERVICES and WHO IMPLEMENTS SERVICES will be resolved at the local educational agency, preferably at the PAC/IEP conference.

Continuum of Services	Provided by Preschool	Provided by Spec. Ed. 5-21	Provided by Vocational Ed.	Provided by Rehabilitation Services
A. Referral	Awareness Child find Screening Referral to assessment	Awareness Child find Screening Referral to assessment	Awareness Referral to assessment Referral to assessment (intake process)	Awareness (case finding) Screening (referral development)
B. Assessment	(Formal/informal) Developmental data Psychological/ behavioral	(Formal/informal) Educational data Psychological/ behavioral	(Formal/informal) Prevocational exploration program Vocational and career development/special needs	(Formal) Current general health status and special examination Evaluation of vocation (Elig.) a. Preliminary diagnostic study (Elig.) b. Thorough diagnostic study to determine nature and scope of services (Vocational goals/strengths, functional limitations) Eligible students, ages 14 and above, in or out of school
C. Individualized program	Individualized education program (IEP)	Individualized education program (IEP) (Ages 5–21)	Instructional vocational plan (VIP) (secondary students only) 4-year education plan	Individualized written rehabilitation plan (IWRP) for all eligible students/clients. Developed jointly by client and counselor and if appropriate by guardian with participation in PAC and joint staffing with appropriate school personnel (The services, objectives, and goals included in the IWRP and IEP should be complimentary.) IEP/IWRP Individualized written rehabilitation program

FIGURE 8.6 Service Responsibility Chart.

Note. From *Cooperative Agreement by West Virginia Department of Education and the Division of Rehabilitation Services* in *Transition Manual: TRIAD Telecommunications Project* by I. D. Cook and M. Thurman-Urbanic, 1990, Institute, WV: West Virginia Graduate College, p. 39. Copyright 1990 by West Virginia Graduate College. Reprinted by permission.

Continuum of Services	Provided by Preschool	Provided by Spec. Ed. 5-21	Provided by Vocational Ed.	Provided by Rehabilitation Services
D. Program planning and implementation activities	Family consultation	Career education Prevocational education Formal vocational assessment Special (separate) vocational education College preparation curriculum	Career/prevocational education Regular vocational education Modified regular vocational education Special vocational education Adult programs	Regular vocational education/work adjustment (OJT, selective training experiences, co-op and related programs) Adaptive regular (specially designed vocational education/ work adjustment) Work experience Vocational assessment services as specified in Section B Special (separate) vocational education/work adjustment Vocational and other training including personal and vocational adj., books, tools, and other training materials. All on individual needs basis to eligible clients (client owned)
E. Service delivery system including related services	Special tools, devices, equipment (student loaned) Instructional modification Special support staff (aides, tutors, and paraprofessionals) Related services (OT, PT, and speech therapy) Curriculum modification and development Special transportation needs Monitoring services and student progress Parent training	Interpreter/notetaker Reader services for the blind Special tools, devices, equipment (student loaned) Instructional modifications Special support staff (aides, tutors, and paraprofessionals) Related services (OT, PT, and speech therapy) Curriculum modification and development Special transportation needs Monitoring services and student progress Vocational guidance and counseling	Interpreter/notetaker Reader services for the blind Special tools, devices, equipment (student loaned) Instructional modifications Special education instructor Special support staff (aides, tutors, and paraprofessionals) Related services Curriculum modification and development Monitoring services and student progress Vocational guidance and counseling Cooperative education programs (OJT) Prevocational exploration programs Job development and placement	Interpreter/notetaker Reader services for the blind Tools and/or materials for planned job placement (client owned) Special tools, devices, equipment (client owned) Technical assistance re: modifications or supportive services Monitoring of services and client progress Vocational guidance and counseling General medical-coordination of services if needed to vocationally prepare for job placement or supported employment a. Assist in location training stations

FIGURE 8.6 Continued.

Continuum of Services	Provided by Preschool	Provided by Spec. Ed. 5-21	Provided by Vocational Ed.	Provided by Rehabilitation Services
E. Service delivery system including related services (cont.)		Family consultation Work experience/ work study Formal vocational assessment Job development and placement Supportive employment Sheltered workshop	Work experience Supportive employment (task analysis)	b. Modify work environment c. Adaptive appliances d. Reimburse employers Physical and mental restoration Formal vocational assessment (work evaluation and functional assessment) Additional services provided as appropriate Supported employment Job placement
F. Access	Center-based accommodations	Public school accommodations Job training site accommodations	Vocational school accommodations Job training site accommodations	Individual/home accommodations Job training site accommodations
G. Exit	Transition	Transition	Transition	Transition

FIGURE 8.6   Continued.

3. Parent, consumer, and employer involvement in the transition planning process
4. Community and professional awareness and support of multiple employment options

Education for individuals with special learning and/or behavior needs should address these elements and prepare them for postsecondary training and competitive or supported employment. Thus, school systems cannot focus on transition programming alone and ignore the quality and content of foundation services, including elementary and secondary preparation, as well as vocational and postsecondary opportunities offered by community agencies.

Our major goal in the education and training of persons with special learning and/or behavior needs should be to prepare these individuals for independence and adult functioning. Obviously, transition/career education and training provide the important foundation for transitioning students from school to postsecondary training, to commu-

nity living, and to the world of work. The most compelling support for transitional services and the concept of service delivery through an interagency cooperative model may be drawn from the major pieces of federal legislation we discuss in this text.

"Collaboration is a key element in the transition process. Through collaboration, youth can receive planned, appropriate, and nonduplicated services. Many individuals are likely to participate in the transition process, including individuals charged with identifying persons in need of transition assistance, educators, clients, families, and service providers."

(Chadsey, Rusch, & Phelps, 1989, p. 232)

THE LCCE IEP AND ITP

The transition concept inextricably embraces the career development concept that has been theorized and implemented in various education and agency

Level 1: Elementary (K–8)

Transition Coordinator: Special Education Teacher

Responsibilities

- Conduct an ongoing evaluation of students' achievement performance in academics and career development.
- Use assessment data in program development and implementation.
- Write IEPs for students with a futuristic perspective.
- Develop basic academic skills with personal-social, daily living, and occupational guidance and preparation skills infused.
- Encourage parents to participate in planning and developing career education competencies.
- Keep an up-to-date profile on individual students.
- Form partnerships with regular educators, parents, adult service providers, and representatives of business and industry.
- Share student profiles (strengths, weaknesses, interests, etc.) with receiving environment (e.g., secondary education staff).

Level 2: Secondary (8–12)

Transition Coordinator: Secondary Special Education Teacher

Responsibilities

- Identify students for transition planning at the beginning of the school year.
- Collect and analyze assessment data and update student profiles.
- Coordinate the assessment and modification of curriculum as needed to prepare students for successful transition into adult life.
- Identify and become familiar with available post-school options, including vocational/educational, residential, community, health, and financial support services.
- Form partnerships with adults and representatives of business and industry.
- Organize and implement individual transitional planning meetings.
- Provide leadership in and for the development of the ITPs.
- Ensure that input is provided from students, teachers, parents, and as appropriate, adult service agencies and former or current employers.
- Advocate as needed, with administrators, for changes needed in the delivery from a classroom-based model to a community-based delivery system.
- Coordinate the implementation of transition plans.

FIGURE 8.7   Transition Preparation Responsibilities for Transition Coordinators/Case Managers.
Note: From *Transition Manual: TRIAD Telecommunications Project* (pp. 99–101) by I. D. Cook and M. Thurman-Urbanic, 1990, Institute, WV: West Virginia Graduate College. Copyright 1990 by West Virginia Graduate College. Reprinted by permission. (continues)

Level 3: (Final Year)

Transition Coordinator/Case Manager(s):
Secondary Special Education Teacher/Vocational Education

Responsibilities

Special Educator (Same as in Level 2)/Vocational Education.

- Attend ITP meeting and provide information on appropriate vocational goals.
- Ensure equal access vocational education for students with disabilities.
- Provide students and parents information on vocational education by the beginning of the ninth grade.
- Collect and analyze vocational evaluation data.
- Identify community cooperative agencies for job training and placement.
- Assist with job placement, job-site training or postsecondary vocational preparation for students during their last year in school.

Level 4: Post-school to Adulthood

Transition Coordinator(s):
Case Manager: Vocational Rehabilitation/Community Agency/Parents or Guardian

Responsibilities

- Continue to monitor and evaluate the progress of job training and placement activities.
- Ensure that support services (e.g. medical, psychological, therapeutic, financial management and residential options) are provided.
- Ensure the highest level of independence in job placement (e.g., movement from an enclave work site to supported or competitive employment).
- Address the needs for high quality of life (e.g., the rights and responsibilities of citizenship are ensured through full participation in the broad spectrum of leisure and community activities).

FIGURE 8.7   Continued.

settings for many years (Brolin & Schatzman, 1989). As noted by the CEC's DCDT position paper entitled "Career Development for Students with Disabilities in the Elementary Schools" (G. M. Clark et. al., 1991), successful transition will not take place without the adoption of a functional curriculum.

The LCCE Mild/Moderate Curriculum Programs and their functional skills lend themselves nicely to providing a comprehensive instructional program (kindergarten to postsecondary) to prepare students with special learning and/or behavior needs for a successful transition from school to successful post-secondary/vocational training, productive living, and working in their communities. An illustration of how LCCE Mild/Moderate Curriculum Programs can be used as a transition model was presented in Chapter 3. Figure 8.9 demonstrates how curriculum planning can be instituted in each of the three functional LCCE Mild/Moderate Curriculum/instructional domains (daily living, personal-social, and occupational skills) for the first three stages of career development/learning so a developmental and logical sequence of activities can be pro-

FIGURE 8.8 **Components of a Comprehensive Career/ Vocational Assessment.**
Note. From *Transition Manual: TRIAD Telecommunications Project* (p. 45) by I. D. Cook and M. Thurman-Urbanic, 1990, Institute, WV: West Virginia Graduate College. Copyright 1990 by West Virginia Graduate College. Reprinted by permission.

COMPREHENSIVE CAREER/ VOCATIONAL ASSESSMENT

Elementary Level:
• Health
• Psychological
• Social
• Daily Living
 Occupational Guidance & Preparation

Secondary Level:
• Cognitive Skills
• Manual Skills
• Interpersonal Skills
• Perceptual Skills
• Work Aptitudes
• Interests
• Previous Experience
• Job Exploration
• Social Adjustment

• Special Education Teacher/Specialist
• Vocational Education Teacher/Evaluator
• Vocational Rehabilitation Evaluator
• Parents
• Social Workers
• Psychologists/Guidance Counselors
• Speech/Hearing Clinicians
• Physical/Occupational Therapists

vided in each of the 22/20 competency areas, respectively.

An LCCE Mild/Moderate Curriculum Program IEP with an integrated ITP component has been constructed for educators who are using the LCCE Mild/Moderate Curriculum (Mild or Moderate) approach. The LCCE Mild/Moderate Curriculum IEP form contains 10 sections to meet the legislative requirements of PL 94-142 and IDEA 1997. Because their own local or state IEP forms bind most school districts, the LCCE Mild/Moderate Curriculum IEP may be used either as is or as an addendum to the district's mandated forms. The LCCE Mild/ Moderate Curriculum IEP form with its integrated ITP component is presented in Figure 8.10 with a hypothetical eighth-grade student named Susan as an example.

"In adopting a specific career model for developing the foundation for transition, it is helpful in carrying out the

continuous curriculum-based assessment if instruments such as those contained in the LCCE model do accompany the curriculum materials."

(Cook & Thurman-Urbanic, 1990)

The LCCE Program curriculum-based assessment instruments described in Chapter 7—LCCE Competency Rating Scales (CRS and CRS-M), the LCCE Knowledge Battery or PKB, the LCCE Performance Battery or PAB, and the LCCE Self-Determination Scale—are available to provide the necessary data for developing and evaluating the content of the IEP. Other measures may also be used, depending on the orientation and needs of the functional assessment team.

The LCCE Mild/Moderate Curriculum IEP form provides a document with functional skills and transition components that can be constructed from the LCCE Mild/Moderate Curriculum competencies and can be evaluated at least in part by the LCCE

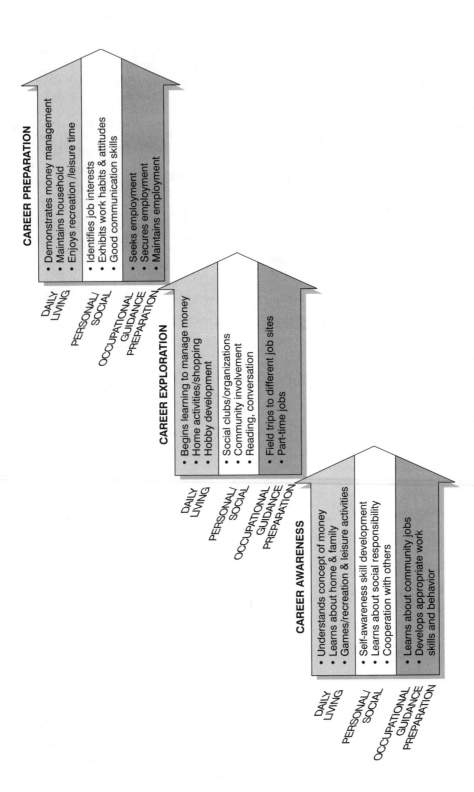

FIGURE 8.9 Overview of Curriculum Planning Based on LCCE and The Stages of Career Development.

Note. From *Transition Manual: TRIAD Telecommunications Project* (p. 49) by I. D. Cook and M. Thurman-Urbanic, 1990, Institute, WV: West Virginia Graduate College. Copyright 1990 by West Virginia Graduate College. Reprinted by permission. Originally adapted from *Life Centered Career Education* (3rd ed., pp. 10–12) by D. E. Brolin, 1989, Arlington, VA: The Council for Exceptional Children.

LIFE CENTERED CAREER EDUCATION
INDIVIDUALIZED EDUCATION PROGRAM FORM
(Use attachments as needed for each student)

Student's Name: ___Susan___   School: ___Progressive___   Grade: _8_   Date: __6/3/95__

SECTION I: Present Level of Educational Performance

Reading Level:	3.3 (CAT)	Math Level:	2.0 (CAT)
CRS Scores:	DLS (.59) PSS (.61)	OGP (.21)	(Maximum = 2.0)
KB Scores:	DLS (40%) PSS (43%)	OGP (25%)	TOT (38%)
PB Scores:	Mastery (Comp. 8)	No Mastery (Comps. 3, 5, 18, 21)	

SECTION II: Annual Goals

A. Academic Goals (see attachment)

B. LCCE Functional Skills for Transition Preparation (check those that apply)

This student will progress toward acquiring functional behaviors in the following competency areas. (Check the appropriate annual goals.)

_X_ 1. Managing Personal Finances
___ 2. Selecting and Managing a Household
___ 3. Caring for Personal Needs
_X_ 4. Raising Children and Meeting Marriage Responsibilities
___ 5. Buying, Preparing, and Consuming Food
___ 6. Buying and Caring for Clothing
___ 7. Exhibiting Responsible Citizenship
___ 8. Utilizing Recreational Facilities and Engaging in Leisure
___ 9. Getting Around the Community
___ 10. Achieving Self-Awareness
___ 11. Acquiring Self-Confidence

___ 12. Achieving Socially Responsible Behavior
___ 13. Maintaining Good Interpersonal Skills
___ 14. Achieving Independence
___ 15. Making Adequate Decisions
_X_ 16. Communicating with Others
_X_ 17. Knowing and Exploring Occupational Possibilities
___ 18. Selecting and Planning Occupational Choices
___ 19. Exhibiting Appropriate Work Habits and Behaviors
___ 20. Seeking, Securing, and Maintaining Employment
___ 21. Exhibiting Sufficient Physical–Manual Skills
___ 22. Obtaining Specific Occupational Skills

C. Other Transitional/Support Services Goals (check those that apply)

___ 1. Financial Assistance/Income Support
___ 2. Advocacy Legal Services
___ 3. Medical
___ 4. Insurance

___ 5. Transportation
___ 6. Other _____
___ 7. Other _____
___ 8. Other _____

SECTION III: Specific Educational Services Needed

Goal & Subcomp. Numbers	Special Services Needed	Special Media/Materials and Equipment	Individual Implementors
A	(See attachment)		
B 1 (3, 5, 6)	Job shadowing experience (banks, credit agencies), simulated business activities, speakers, home assignments	Credit banking & other forms, LCCE lesson plans, materials for setting up a model bank & store, transportation	Special education/math/business ed. teachers, bank & credit company employees, parents, peers
B 4 (17, 18)	Visits to public health department and day care centers, student role-play activities, community input	Varous health charts, thermometers, tub for bathing, medicine bottles, transportation	Special education/health teachers, school nurse, parents, public health nurse, nursery school personnel, child guidance center staff
B 16 (68, 69)	Group activities, role-playing (e.g., TV show)	Videotapes & films, telephones, audio recorders	Special education/speech/ language arts teachers, parents, peers, TV or radio interviewer
B 17 (71, 72, 73)	Field trips, role-play activities/ simulations, community input, home assignments	Bulletin boards, occupational literature, magazines, newspapers	Special education/work-study teachers, career counselors, employers, Chamber of Commerce, VR counselor

FIGURE 8.10   Form for Preparing Student's LCCE IEP.

Note: From *Life Centered Career Education: A Competency Based Approach* (4th ed., pp. 146–149) by D. E. Brolin, 1993, Arlington, VA: The Council for Exceptional Children. Copyright 1993 by The Council for Exceptional Children. Reprinted by permission. The attachments mentioned in Sections IIA, III, IVA, and ICV are not included here; they can be found in Brolin's (1993) text. (continues)

INDIVIDUALIZED EDUCATION PROGRAM FORM

SECTION IV: Short-Term Individual Objectives

A.   Academic Goals (see attachment)

B.   LCCE Functional Skills for Transition Preparation (check those that apply)

___ 1. Identify Money and Make Correct Change (1)

___ 2. Make Responsible Expenditures (1)

_X_ 3. Keep Basic Financial Records (1)

___ 4. Calculate and Pay Taxes (1)

_X_ 5. Use Credit Responsibly (1)

_X_ 6. Use Banking Services (1)

___ 7. Maintain Home Exterior/Interior (2)

___ 8. Use Basic Appliances and Tools (2)

___ 9. Select Adequate Housing (2)

___ 10. Set Up Household (2)

___ 11. Maintain Home Grounds (2)

___ 12. Demonstrate Knowledge of Physical Fitness, Nutrition, and Weight (3)

___ 13. Exhibit Proper Grooming and Hygiene (3)

___ 14. Dress Appropriately (3)

___ 15. Demonstrate Knowledge of Common Illness, Prevention, and Treatment (3)

___ 16. Practice Personal Safety (3)

_X_ 17. Demonstrate Physical Care for Raising Children (4)

_X_ 18. Know Psychological Aspects of Raising Children (4)

___ 19. Demonstrate Marriage Responsibilities (4)

___ 20. Purchase Food (5)

___ 21. Clean Food Preparation Areas (5)

___ 22. Store Food (5)

___ 23. Prepare Meals (5)

___ 24. Demonstrate Appropriate Eating Habits (5)

___ 25. Plan and Eat Balanced Meals (5)

___ 26. Wash/Clean Clothing (6)

___ 27. Purchase Clothing (6)

___ 28. Iron, Mend, and Store Clothing (6)

___ 29. Demonstrate Knowledge of Civil Rights and Responsibilities (7)

___ 30. Know Nature of Local, State, and Federal Governments (7)

___ 31. Demonstrate Knowledge of the Law and Ability to Follow the Law (7)

___ 32. Demonstrate Knowledge of Citizen Rights and Responsibilities (7)

___ 33. Demonstrate Knowledge of Available Community Resources (8)

___ 34. Choose and Plan Activities (8)

___ 35. Demonstrate Knowledge of the Value of Recreation (8)

___ 36. Engage in Group and Individual Activities (8)

___ 37. Plan Vacation Time (8)

___ 38. Demonstrate Knowledge of Traffic Rules and Safety (9)

___ 39. Demonstrate Knowledge and Use of Various Means of Transportation (9)

___ 40. Find Way Around the Community (9)

___ 41. Drive a Car (9)

___ 42. Identify Physical and Psychological Needs (10)

___ 43. Identify Interests and Abilities (10)

___ 44. Identify Emotions (10)

___ 45. Demonstrate Knowledge of Physical Self (10)

___ 46. Express Feelings of Self-Worth (11)

___ 47. Describe Others' Perception of Self (11)

___ 48. Accept and Give Praise (11)

___ 49. Accept and Give Criticism (11)

___ 50. Develop Confidence in Oneself (11)

___ 51. Demonstrate Respect for the Rights and Properties of Others (12)

___ 52. Recognize Authority and Follow Instructions (12)

___ 53. Demonstrate Appropriate Behavior in Public Places (12)

___ 54. Know Important Character Traits (12)

___ 55. Recognize Personal Roles (12)

___ 56. Demonstrate Listening and Responding Skills (13)

___ 57. Establish and Maintain Close Relationships (13)

___ 58. Make and Maintain Friendships (13)

___ 59. Strive Toward Self-Actualization (14)

___ 60. Demonstrate Self-Organization (14)

___ 61. Demonstrate Awareness of How One's Behavior Affects Others (14)

___ 62. Locate and Utilize Sources of Assistance (15)

___ 63. Anticipate Consequences (15)

___ 64. Develop and Evaluate Alternatives (15)

___ 65. Recognize Nature of a Problem (15)

___ 66. Develop Goal-Seeking Behavior (15)

___ 67. Recognize and Respond to Emergency Situations (16)

_X_ 68. Communicate with Understanding (16)

_X_ 69. Know Subtleties of Communication (16)

___ 70. Identify Remunerative Aspects of Work (17)

_X_ 71. Locate Sources of Occupational and Training Information (17)

_X_ 72. Identify Personal Values Met Through Work (17)

_X_ 73. Identify Societal Values Met Through Work (17)

___ 74. Classify Jobs into Occupational Categories (17)

FIGURE 8.10   Continued.

INDIVIDUALIZED EDUCATION PROGRAM FORM

___ 75. Investigate Local Occupational and Training Opportunities (17)
___ 76. Make Realistic Occupational Choices (18)
___ 77. Identify Requirements of Appropriate and Available Jobs (18)
___ 78. Identify Occupational Aptitudes (18)
___ 79. Identify Major Occupational Interests (18)
___ 80. Identify Major Occupational Needs (18)
___ 81. Follow Directions and Observe Regulations (19)
___ 82. Recognize Importance of Attendance and Punctuality (19)
___ 83. Recognize Importance of Supervision (19)
___ 84. Demonstrate Knowledge of Occupational Safety (19)
___ 85. Work with Others (19)
___ 86. Meet Demands for Quality Work (19)

___ 87. Work at a Satisfactory Rate (19)
___ 88. Search for a Job (20)
___ 89. Apply for a Job (20)
___ 90. Interview for a Job (20)
___ 91. Know How to Maintain Post-School Occupational Adjustment (20)
___ 92. Demonstrate Knowledge of Competitive Standards (20)
___ 93. Know How to Adjust to Changes in Employment (20)
___ 94. Demonstrate Stamina and Endurance (21)
___ 95. Demonstrate Satisfactory Balance and Coordination (21)
___ 96. Demonstrate Manual Dexterity (21)
___ 97. Demonstrate Sensory Discrimination (21)

C. **Other Transitional/Support Services Objectives (see attachment)**

SECTION V: Data and Length of Time relative to specific educational services needed for this student

Goal Number	Beginning Date	Ending Date	Goal Number	Beginning Date	Ending Date
B 1 (3, 5, 6)	9-1-95	12-15-95			
B 4 (17, 18)	9-1-95	12-15-95			
B 16 (68, 69)	1-10-96	5-20-96			
B 17 (71, 72, 73)	1-10-96	5-20-96			

SECTION VI: Description of Extent to which this student will participate in the regular educational program

	Percentage of Time	Narrative Description/Reaction
Language arts	15 %	Build greater communication skills
Math	10 %	Use practical, everyday situations and materials
Science	___ %	
Social science	___ %	
Vocational (Bus.) & Work Study	15 %	Limited typing & clerical skills—resource room needed
Physical education	5 %	No physical limitation
(other) Health	10 %	Provide supports and some co-teaching lessons
(other) Speech	5 %	Has problems expressing self; shy

FIGURE 8.10   Continued.

INDIVIDUALIZED EDUCATION PROGRAM FORM

SECTION VII: Justification for type of educational placement of this student

Narrative Description/Reaction

LCCE SCAR/KB/PB measures indicate these as primary needs and relate to student's interests and preferences at this time. Not enough instruction has been provided in these areas and it is felt she can benefit from this focus.

SECTION VIII: Individual Responsible for implementing the individualized education program and transitional services

Name	*Role/Responsibility*
Special education, vocational education, math, health, work-study, and language arts teachers	Participating in assisting Susan to learn the subcompetencies noted in Section IV B
Bank, credit company, nursery school, TV & radio interviewers, career counselors, Chamber of Commerce personnel, vocational rehabilitation, guidance center, & public health workers	
Parents/families, peers	

SECTION IX: Objective Criteria, Evaluation Procedures, and Schedule for assessing short-term objectives

Objective Criteria can be found in the LCCE Competency Rating Scale (CRS), and the LCCE Knowledge Battery (KB), and the LCCE Performance Battery (PB). Criteria listed reflect the short-term individual objectives checked in Section IV, Part B, of this form.

Evaluation Procedures can be determined by the IEP Committee reviewing the manuals for the Competency Rating Scale, Knowledge Battery, and Performance Battery.

Schedule for Assessment should include time, date, frequency, place, etc.

PB pretests to be administered prior to instruction and posttests upon completion. KB to be readministered in 1 year.

SECTION X: Estimated Date, Location, and Time for the next IEP Committee Review Conference

11/1/95   10: A.M.   Junior High School   Room 100

FIGURE 8.10   Continued.

Mild/Moderate Curriculum assessment instruments. In developing the LCCE Mild/Moderate Curriculum IEP form, it is suggested that annual goals be selected from the 22 or 20 competency areas of either the mild or moderate curriculums and that short-term objectives be selected from their 97 or 75 subcompetencies. Thus, the educator will be able to establish goals, success criteria, and a method of recording the necessary individualized plans and then evaluating their outcomes. Although they are designed to be used separately, the combination of the LCCE Mild/Moderate Curriculum IEP, the LCCE competency units (instructional lesson plans), the LCCE CRS (Mild or Moderate), the LCCE Knowledge Battery or LCCE PKB, LCCE Performance Batteries or LCCE PAB, and the Self-Determination Scale can be considered a complete transition planning, instructional, and evaluation package (Brolin, 1997; Loyd & Brolin, in press).

Muskegon (Michigan) Intermediate School District has developed a transition planning guide sheet using the first 21 competencies of the LCCE Mild Curriculum to identify planning options and agencies that can support their transition efforts in each of the competency areas. The occupational guidance and preparation component of the guide sheet is presented in Figure 8.11 to illustrate how one school district is organizing resources that can be involved in the total transition/career development of its students. In addition, the first page of Muskegon's individual transition service plan, again using the LCCE Mild Curriculum areas, competencies, and subcompetencies, is presented in Figure 8.12 to illustrate how they record transition planning activities.

Summary

The LCCE Mild/Moderate Curriculum Programs' approach provides educators with a method and the materials for implementing a transition component to the IEP that will meet students' functional skills needs as well as the requirements of federal legislation for an appropriate educational program and transition planning. The LCCE Mild/Moderate Curriculum assessment instruments presented in Chapter 7, the IEP form presented in Figure 8.10, and the LCCE Mild/Moderate instructional competency unit lesson plans provide educators with a comprehensive transition evaluation, planning, and instructional system.

"Since the end product of transition in special education is successful community adjustment as experienced by former special education students, adult adjustment may be viewed as a general measure of the effectiveness of special education programs."

(Weisenstein & Elrod, 1987, p. 39)

CHAPTER COMMENTARY

With the movement toward inclusive/integrated schools whereby students with special learning and/or behavior needs will be served to the maximum extent possible in general education classrooms, in their inclusive neighborhood schools, and in their community settings, community support becomes even more critical for successful transition endeavors. The CEC policy paper on inclusion (1994) notes that "there must be interagency agreements and collaboration with local governments and business to help prepare students to assume a constructive role in an inclusive community." Thus, systematic collaborative transition planning is essential for successful inclusive efforts and must include the support of the community.

The LCCE Curriculum (Mild/Moderate) transition model presented in Chapter 3 is the most comprehensive model to date. The model's three dimensions integrating 22 or 20 competencies, respectively; the three instructional settings (school, home, community); and four stages of career development, provide educators with a total scope and sequence approach from kindergarten through the postsecondary years. This functional approach provides an excellent framework for ensuring, first and foremost, that students with special learning and/or behavior needs and their families will benefit from a total approach to meeting all the instructional needs required for successful transition and adult adjustment.

TRANSITION PLANNING GUIDE SHEET
(Occupational Guidance and Preparation)

Annual Goals	Objectives/Competencies	Planning Options	Agency Support
		Prevocational Training	
17. Knowing and Exploring Occupational Possibilities	70. Identify Remunerative Aspects of Work 71. Locate Sources of Occupational and Training Information 72. Identify Personal Values Met Through Work 73. Identify Societal Values Met Through Work 74. Classify Jobs into Occupational Categories 75. Investigate Local Occupational and Training Opportunities	Classroom Programs Local School Programs Community-based Sites	JTPA Skills Center MRS MEGA
		Assessment	
18. Selecting and Planning Occupational Choices	76. Make Realistic Occupational Choices 77. Identify Requirements of Appropriate and Available Jobs 78. Identify Occupational Aptitudes 79. Identify Major Occupational Interests	Local Curriculum-Based Assessment MAISD Assessment	Goodwill MEGA
		Vocational Training	
19. Exhibiting Appropriate Work Habits and Behavior	80. Identify Major Occupational Needs 81. Follow Directions and Observe Regulations 82. Recognize Importance of Attendance 83. Recognize Importance of Supervision 84. Demonstrate Knowledge of Occupational Safety 85. Work with Others 86. Meet Demands for Quality Work 87. Work at a Satisfactory Rate	Regular Vocational Training Muskegon Consortium Newaygo Voc. Tech. Center Modified Vocational Training/Support Community-based sites/MAISD Community-based sites/LOCAL Individual Vocational Training (IVT) Work Study	MRS JTPA MEGA MOKA
21. Exhibiting Sufficient Physical/ Manual Skills	94. Demonstrate Stamina & Endurance 95. Demonstrate Satisfactory Balance and Coordination 96. Demonstrate Manual Dexterity 97. Demonstrate Sensory Discrimination		
		Employment	
20. Seeking, Securing, and Maintaining Employment	88. Search for a Job 89. Apply for a Job 90. Interview for a Job 91. Know How to Maintain Post-School Occupational Adjustment 92. Demonstrate Knowledge of Competitive Standards 93. Know How to Adjust to Changes in Employment	Competitive Competitive/Support Supported Employment Enclave Sheltered Volunteer	Michigan Rehab. Services (MRS) Competitive Competitive Support Supported Employment Goodwill Enclave Sheltered HGA JTPA

FIGURE 8.11 A Sample Guide Sheet for Transition Planning.

Note. From Muskegon, Michigan Area Intermediate School District.

INDIVIDUAL TRANSITION SERVICE PLAN (PAGE ____ OF ____)

NAME: ____________ DATE: ____________ SCHOLL: ____________ TRANSITION PLAN #: (CIRCLE ONE) (INITIAL) (2) (3) (4) (5)

(1) OUTCOMES

Check (√) "Transition Areas" that need to be addressed: (Attach additional pages if necessary)

( ) **DAILY LIVING SKILLS** OUTCOME: ____________	( ) **PERSONAL/SOCIAL SKILLS** OUTCOME: ____________
( ) **OCCUPATIONAL GUIDANCE AND/OR PREPARATION** OUTCOME: ____________	( ) **POST-SECONDARY EDUCATIONAL/TRAINING OPTIONS** OUTCOME: ____________

(2) GOALS/OBJECTIVES

(Attach additional pages if necessary)

ANNUAL GOALS	ANNUAL OBJECTIVES/COMPETENCIES	ACTIONS TO MEET GOALS	PERSON(S) RESPONSIBLE	EVALUATION PROCESS TIMELINE

(3) AGENCIES

(NEEDED ASSISTANCE/INVOLVEMENT)

AGENCY	PURPOSE	PERSON RESPONSIBLE/CONTACT	DATE CONTACT COMPLETED
( ) MRS ( ) CMH ( ) OTHER ________			

(4) SIGNATURES

STUDENT: DATE:	TEACHER/TRANSITION COORDINATOR: DATE:	OTHER: DATE:
PARENT: DATE:	AGENCY REPRESENTATIVE: DATE:	OTHER: DATE:

FIGURE 8.12 A Sample Form for Developing an individual Transition Service Plan.
Note. From Muskegon, Michigan Area Intermediate School District.

. . . .

ACTIVITIES

1. What transition areas would you include in the ITP component of your IEP? What differences would there be, if any, at the various grade levels?
2. Review the LCCE IEP form presented in Figure 8.10 and complete one of the following:

a. Write a statement defending the appropriateness of this form by your local education agency (LEA) for IEP/ITP planning.
b. Write a statement to explain changes you would need to make for your LEA.
c. Submit another format and defend its appropriateness for IEP/ITP planning.

CHAPTER 9

Functional Transition Materials and Resources

Iva Dean Cook, Robert J. Loyd,
Carol Opperman, and
Melody Thurman-Urbanic

PRELIMINARY QUESTIONS

1. What criteria should be considered when using functional materials/resources to teach the Life-Centered Career Education (LCCE)?
2. Mild/Moderate Curriculum Programs competencies/subcompetencies to students with special learning and/or behavior needs?
3. Examine a model and steps for matching functional materials to the student's personalized needs, and then discuss implications for its use.
4. How would you apply Cook's Task Analysis Model of Matching Materials/Resources to the Student's Personalized Needs functional materials model in Figure 9.1 to complete a student profile sheet in functional instruction planning for students with special learning and/or behavior needs in diverse settings?
5. Why is it important to adopt the Functional Materials/Resource Correlation Chart presented in Figure 9.2 for correlating materials to the LCCE Mild/Moderate Curriculum Programs?
6. If you were asked to share a brief, written description of your teacher-made functional materials with your colleagues, what would you include in your functional materials/resources guidelines?
7. What information about students with special learning and/or behavior needs would be helpful to you in selecting appropriate functional materials/resources to meet the personalized functional needs of individuals with special learning and/or behavior needs?
8. What sources would you access when searching for appropriate functional materials/resources related to the LCCE Mild/Moderate Curriculum Programs?
9. What steps would you take to facilitate lesson planning for all students with special learning and/or behavior needs, regardless of whether they are served in inclusive classes or segregated classes?
10. What are the educational implications for selecting functional materials/resources for students with various special learning and/or behavior needs?
11. How do the LCCE Mild/Moderate Curriculum objectives apply to each category of students with special learning and/or behavior needs?
12. How do the LCCE Mild/Moderate Curriculum Programs correlate to state standards/outcomes?

OVERVIEW

At one time, career education was defined as "the totality of experience through which one learns about and prepares to engage in work as part of her or his way of living" (Hoyt, 1975, p. 4). Currently, career education is viewed as a life experience program that teaches the skills to prepare students with special learning and/or behavior needs for a successful transition from school to postsecondary training, to the community, and to the working world. This concept of career education embraces transition so that both imply that many professionals, representing various agencies, are responsible for teaching transition/career education concepts and that these competencies should be integrated into the school's total curriculum. As stated by Luftig:

> A quick glance at the LCCE Curriculum reveals that all of the curriculum components are not directly related to school. That is, while many of the competencies deal directly with school-related subjects, other competencies are best taught under the auspices of other institutions and groups such as family or the community. Thus, a well-rounded career education curriculum should contain material found in the child's school, family, and community environment. (1987, p. 367)

The LCCE Mild/Moderate Curriculum provides the teacher with a clear idea of the functional skills needed to prepare the student with special learning and/or behavior needs for the many stages of transition. The LCCE Mild/Moderate Curriculum Programs CRS, Knowledge, and Performance Batteries

(Brolin, 1992a, 1992b) which are curriculum referenced, provide information to help teachers select the competencies (22 or 20)/subcompetencies (97 or 75) to teach the individual student with special learning and/or behavior needs. Knowledge of student characteristics, gleaned from other functional assessment data, can be used to help make transition process decisions. The teacher must analyze the data and create the instructional goals and objectives for writing the Individualized Education Plan and Individualized Transition Plan (IEP/ITP). The LCCE Mild/Moderate Curriculum competencies may be written as goals, and the subcompetencies as objectives. These goals and objectives lend themselves to a sequential selection and placement of transitional materials and resources in the instructional process, beginning in elementary school and extending into adulthood. Functional materials/resources needed to convey the curriculum goals and objectives to the student with special learning and/or behavior needs may be found in diverse environments.

The LCCE Mild/Moderate Curriculum instructional units, which are part of the LCCE Mild/Moderate Curriculum Programs, provide functional instruction. There are over 1,000 lesson plans in 21 competency units containing numerous functional materials and resources. Supplemental commercial functional materials/resources also can be added to enhance the lesson plans.

A transition instructional model is included in this chapter; it links the transition goals of a student with learning and/or behavior needs with the appropriate LCCE Mild/Moderate Curriculum transitional materials and resources. The steps for using this model also are described in this chapter.

TRANSITIONAL MATERIALS/RESOURCES SELECTION AND INSTRUCTION

Effective transition/career education instruction requires many of the "best practices" commonly iden-

tified in current special education textbooks (Mastropieri & Scruggs [2000], *The Inclusive Classroom: Strategies for Effective Instruction*; Mercer & Mercer [2001], *Teaching Students with Learning Problems*; & Lewis & Doorlag [2003], *Teaching Special Students in General Education Classroom*) on effective instruction of students with special learning and/or behavior needs. Most of these best practices are promoted and discussed in this text and include the following: (a) utilizing the "young adult projection" process; (b) promoting and implementing personalized planning; (c) teaching self-determination; (d) establishing reliable alliances with all support personnel; (e) establishing a learning community in all inclusion settings; (f) utilizing ecological analysis/behavior analysis assessment techniques; (g) implementing collaborative and/or team teaching service delivery approaches; (h) teaching learning strategies; (i) individualizing teaching based on preferred learning styles; (j) using technology instruction and assistance; (k) utilizing differentiated instruction; and (l) applying functional instructional techniques and transition materials/resources.

Selecting Transition Materials/Resources

The history and philosophy of special education philosophy is based on the application of differentiated instruction. This cannot be understated and is best applied by integrating real life/functional situations and materials into general academic content. Selection and application of transition materials/resources can be successfully implemented into both general education and community-based instruction environments.

Selecting the appropriate functional/transitional materials should always be based on the individualized goals of students with special learning and/or behavior needs, but most students can benefit from additional exposure to real-life application and functional instruction. When selecting transition materials/resources for students with special learning and/or behavior needs, educators should always consider the appropriateness of the materials. Making sure that the

CHAPTER OUTLOOK

Patricia Koppeis Burch is a special education teacher and transition coordinator at North St. Francois County R-I High School in Bonne Terre, Missouri. She is an LCCE Master Trainer for the Council for Exceptional Children and has been using the LCCE Curriculum Program for more than 15 years.

I have been a special education teacher at North St. Francois County R-1 School District in Bonne Terre, Missouri for 30 years. During this time, I have been committed to teaching and providing an education for my students that will ensure their success both now and in the future. Teaching the Life Centered Career Education (LCCE) curriculum has proven to be a very positive and rewarding experience not only for my students and their parents, but also for me.

I am often asked by other educators why I believe the LCCE curriculum is so valuable, and what is the secret to my students' successes. There are many answers to these questions, but first and foremost is that teaching the LCCE curriculum has enabled my students to graduate with essential functional skills in daily living, personal-social, and occupational areas. They are accessing the community through various agencies and businesses. These competencies and experiences combined enable students to reach their full potential as effective members of our community. LCCE students leave our school with skills, knowledge, and, most importantly, with positive self-esteem and respect for themselves and others.

The LCCE curriculum includes cooperation between the school, student, parents, and community. It provides a consistency and structure so that all areas of life are addressed. My students learn skills to become successful employees, citizens, and family members. It is a total person approach.

The vast amount of lesson plans provided with the LCCE curriculum guides as well as the competency units offer a logical scope and sequence for teaching the competencies and alleviate the burden of finding the appropriate materials and lesson plans for me as a teacher. In following the lesson plans provided, I feel confident that I am not leaving out significant lessons or concepts necessary for my students' success.

Through the LCCE lessons, parents, family members, and former graduates participate and provide information and shared experiences as team members and guest speakers within our classroom. This not only provides valuable and positive resources for my students, but it also elevates self-esteem for students and parents as well. My students and families feel a valuable sense of respect and accomplishment. They are proud of their accomplishments and can see a positive productive future for themselves.

The LCCE assessments help identify the students' strengths as well as their weaknesses. When writing a good transition plan, I believe it is imperative to build on the students' strengths and not just dwell on their weaknesses. My students are learning to live and function as contributing members of our community, not as failures. The LCCE curriculum has enabled me to refocus special education and included classes into positive, meaningful learning experiences. I no longer stress what the students can't do but build on what they can do well. Often I think about how difficult it is for parents to hear only the weaknesses of someone they love. This has to hurt. Special needs students try so hard to be successful but often fail to the point that sometimes they stop trying. If this happens, I believe it is because we, as educators, are not addressing their needs with positive functional curriculums like LCCE.

All of these factors are important, but one reason for success rises above all others. The students I work with are not just my students or "Individual Education, or Transition Plans." They are real, live people. They are my neighbors and friends. We live in the same community. We attend the same churches, shop in the same stores, and belong to the same organizations. They are citizens who help to make up our community. I want to help them to live and work to the best of their abilities. If I don't teach the critical skills provided through the LCCE curriculum to help them become productive and well-adjusted citizens, then I have failed. Not only will they

and their families suffer, but they may very well become dependent on tax-supported programs for the rest of their lives.

Because of the LCCE curriculum, transition goals for my students have become reality. I am pleased with all of my students, no matter what career field they pursue, because they are becoming productive citizens living as independently as possible within out community. I am proud of the LCCE Program and the benefits it brings my students.

I would like to sincerely thank the late Dr. Donn Brolin and Dr. Robert Loyd for their hard work, dedication, and determination in providing a curriculum that is truly making a difference in the lives of my special needs students and their families.

transition materials/resources are appropriate can be determined by answering the following questions:

- Are the transition materials/resources age appropriate for students with special learning and/or behavior needs?
- Do the selected transition materials/resources contain skills that are socially valid for students with special learning and/or behavior needs?
- Do the selected transition materials/resources contain skills that are community living valid for the students with special learning and/or behavior needs?
- Will the selected transition materials/resources meet the student with special learning and/or behavior needs' transition goals/objectives?
- Will the selected transition materials/resources meet the student with special learning and/or behavior needs' young adult projections?
- Can the selected transition materials/resources be used with general education students?
- Can the selected transition materials/resources be easily integrated into a general education content area/class?
- Can general educators use the selected transition materials/resources with the course's primary academic materials/resources?

- How much support/training must be given to the general education teacher in order to use the selected transition materials/resources?

Although this list of questions is not exhaustive by any means, it can guide educators when selecting transition materials/resources.

Transition Materials/Resources Instruction

Once transition materials/resources have been selected, students can receive this functional instruction utilizing a variety of service delivery options. Some educators have voiced the concern that functional instruction often ignores the basic skills/core competencies. In response to this criticism, most special educators believe that all students need functional instruction to be successful as adults no matter what career path is chosen by the student. Figure 9.1 clearly illustrates how Cronin and Patton (1993) believe transitional materials/resources instruction topics are interrelated to basic skills.

Cronin and Patton (1993) have identified a continuum of three option types for delivering transition materials/resources instruction. The first

	Employment/ Education	Home and Family	Leisure Pursuits	Community Involvement	Emotional/ Physical Health	Personal Responsibility/ Relationships
Reading	Reading classified ads for jobs	Interpreting bills	Locating and understanding movie information in newspaper	Following directions on tax forms	Comprehending directions on medication	Reading letters from friends
Writing	Writing a letter of application for a job	Writing checks	Writing for information on a city to visit	Filling in a voter registration form	Filling in your medical history on forms	Sending thank-you notes
Listening	Understanding oral directions of a procedure change	Comprehending oral directions about making dinner	Listening for forecast to plan outdoor activity	Understanding campaign ads	Attending lectures for stress	Taking turns in a conversation
Speaking	Asking your boss for a raise	Discussing morning routines with family	Inquiring about tickets for a concert	Stating your opinion at the school board meeting	Describing symptoms to a doctor	Giving feedback to a friend about the purchase of a compact disk
Math Applications	Understanding difference between net and gross pay	Computing the cost of doing laundry in a laundromat versus at home	Calculating the cost of a dinner out versus eating at home	Obtaining information for a building permit	Using a thermometer	Planning the costs of a date
Problem-Solving	Settling a dispute with a co-worker	Deciding how much to budget for rent	Role-playing appropriate behaviors for various places	Knowing what to do if your are the victim of fraud	Selecting a doctor	Deciding how to ask someone for a date
Survival Skills	Using a prepared career planning packet	Listing emergency phone numbers	Using a shopping center directory	Marking a calendar for important dates (e.g., recycling, garbage collection)	Using a system to remember to take vitamins	Developing a system to remember birthdays
Personal/ Social	Applying appropriate interview skills	Helping a child with homework	Knowing the rules of a neighborhood pool	Locating self-improvement classes	Getting a yearly physical exam	Discussing how to negotiate a price at a flea market

FIGURE 9.1   Secondary Matrix: Relationship of Basic Skills/Social Skills to Adult Domains

Note: From *Life Skills Instruction for All Students with Special Needs: A Practical Guide for Integrating Real-Life Content into the Curriculum* (p. 33) by M. E. Cronin and J. R. Patton, 1993, Austin, TX: Pro-Ed. Reprinted by permission.

and most popular inclusion approach involves developing a separate course based on the selected transition materials/resources. All students will be exposed to the transition materials/resources instruction and, if needed, individualized sessions will be provided to students who could benefit from additional functional instructional practice. Examples of this approach would be designing courses such as "Using Math Everyday," "Writing In The Adult World," "Health & My Safety," and "Reading For Community Living and Working." A second method for providing included students with special learning and/or behavior needs access to transition materials/resources is infusion into existing general education course content. An example of how this approach would be implemented is developing and teaching integrated thematic units around the topics/skills listed in Figure 9.1. The final option is to provide personalized community-based instruction. The students with special learning and/or behavior needs transitional goals would drive the selection of the appropriate transition materials/resources.

The students with special learning and/or behavior needs and their transition team members should decide which approach is more appropriate for each student. Through a collaborative effort, a personalized transition program can be developed and implemented for each student with special learning and/or behavior needs. The next section describes a functional approach for matching transition materials/resources to the characteristics and learning style of the student with special learning and/or behavior needs.

COOK'S TASK ANALYSIS MODEL OF MATCHING TRANSITION MATERIALS/ RESOURCES TO A STUDENT'S PERSONALIZED NEEDS

As demonstrated in Figure 9.2, Cook (1974) identified the major steps to consider when matching functional materials/resources to the personalized needs of students with special learning and/or behavior needs. This section deals with how to begin locating and obtaining functional materials/resources.

Locating and Obtaining Materials

The first step of Cook's Task Analysis Model of Matching Materials/Resources to Student Personalized Needs is to locate and then to obtain functional materials/resources that correlate to the student with special learning and/or behavior needs' IEP/ITP goals and objectives. Districts using the LCCE Mild/Moderate Curriculum approach will correlate the student with special learning and/or behavior needs' ITP goals and objectives with the LCCE Mild/Moderate Curriculum competencies and subcompetencies. Functional curricula like the LCCE Mild/Moderate Curriculum Program or others discussed in Chapter 5 can be sources to locate and obtain functional materials/resources. These functional curricula may be secured from the school resource center, community resource centers, and/or from state Instructional Materials Centers (IMCs).

Until the early 1960s, there was a scarcity of appropriate functional materials for students with special learning and/or behavior needs. Those available were developed for teaching basic skills and were not relevant to the functional needs and characteristics of all learners with special learning and/or behavior needs.

As a result of President John F. Kennedy's concern for the education/training of persons with mental retardation, a committee was appointed to study the concerns about a lack of instructional programs, instructional techniques, and available and appropriate functional materials/resources for this population. One outgrowth of this committee's efforts was the establishment of a national IMC identifying the materials/resources available to learners. Although this center did not intentionally focus on identifying materials/resources for learners who did not have special learning and/or behavior needs, few materials/resources were identified for students specifically targeted by President Kennedy. The success of this center resulted in these centers being established at regional, state, and local levels throughout the country. For example, in Georgia, the state educational agency (SEA) set up a regional IMC system that is referred to as the Georgia Learning Resource Services (GLRS).

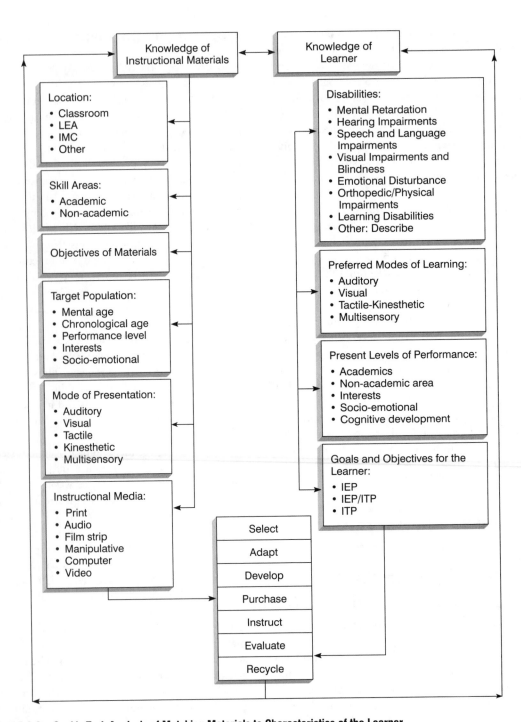

FIGURE 9.2 Cook's Task Analysis of Matching Materials to Characteristics of the Learner.

Note: From *Materials Handbook* (p. 8) by I. D. Cook, 1974, Institute, WV: West Virginia College of Graduate Studies. Copyright 1974 by West Virginia College of Graduate Studies. Reprinted by permission.

Over the last 30 years, instructional materials/resources have proliferated, and school systems have increased funding for purchasing instructional materials/resources for the their own resource centers and/or for teachers in the general education content areas. Thus, school district personnel who work with students with special learning and/or behavior needs are faced with the difficulty of accessing functional materials/resources from this array of sometimes inappropriate collections.

In reviewing all materials/resources, the model in Figure 9.2 suggests that several factors be analyzed to determine appropriate functional materials/resources:

1. Skill areas addressed
2. Objectives of the materials/resources
3. Target population
4. Mode of presentation
5. Instructional medium/technology

Skill Areas

An in-depth analysis is conducted to determine which skill areas are addressed in the instructional materials/resources. This analysis also evaluates whether the materials/resources will address academic or functional skill needs of students with special learning and/or behavior needs. The competency-based approach of the LCCE Mild/Moderate Curriculum Programs is not intended to de-emphasize the importance of basic academics and nonacademic instruction but is meant to be infused into other content/skill areas. The question to be answered is, *For which skill areas are the materials/resources designed?* For example, are the materials/resources intended to teach mathematical or functional mathematical concepts?

Objectives of the Materials

The model's next step is to determine what objectives/skills are addressed in the materials/resources and if they correlate with the competencies/subcom-

petencies of the LCCE Mild/Moderate Curriculum Programs or other functional curricula. If the skill area is math, can the materials/resources be used to teach some or all of the subcompetencies under competency 1, managing personal finances (mild) or competency 1, managing money (moderate)?

Target Population

A major consideration in selecting functional materials/resources is to determine the target population for whom the functional materials/resources would be suited. Attention should be directed to whether the materials are age appropriate and/or appropriate for the developmental levels of the students with special learning and/or behavior needs for whom they are being reviewed.

Schloss et al. (1990) cited two types of problems with functional materials/resources available to secondary teachers and students with special learning and/or behavior needs. First, instructional materials/resources may have been intended for elementary students with special learning and/or behavior needs. Second, some materials/resources may have originally been designed for general education secondary students (p. 14). As stated by Langone, "teachers should review many possible approaches and programs, deciding which individual programs or combination of them is the best match with each student's needs" (1990, p. 233).

Mode of Presentation

Central to learning and instruction is the idea that functional materials/resources must be based on the learning styles of students. "Because of their strengths and weaknesses in auditory, visual, and kinesthetic modalities, different students may require programs that meet specific learning styles" (Langone, 1990, p. 233). G. M. Clark and Kolstoe expanded this concept by citing the need to "consider logical and analogical styles as related to left- or right-brain functions" (1990, p. 199).

Instructional Media/Technology

As noted, for some students with special learning and/or behavior needs, the modality emphasized is important. This raises some important questions about the appropriateness of selecting media and technology utilized by the functional materials/resources. Is the material primarily print? Is it primarily auditory? Is the print supported by audiotapes, or are there other stimulus-response combinations (i.e., videotape, videodisc, computer-based combinations)?

A functional materials/resource correlation chart is presented in Figure 9.3 to correlate functional materials/resources once reviewed to the competencies and subcompetencies of the LCCE Mild/Moderate Curriculum (Cook, 1993, p. 207). The first column is used to identify the subject content area in which the LCCE Mild/Moderate Curriculum competencies and subcompetencies are to be infused. In the second column, the LCCE Mild/Moderate Curriculum competencies/subcompetencies are listed that are correlated to the functional materials/resources reviewed. The third column identifies the commercial functional materials/resources. The level in the educational system is reported in the third column. Finally, the last column records the modes of presentation.

Once a general collection of functional materials/resources has been identified and recorded, the second major step in instructional decision making is a thorough assessment of the learner characteristics.

KNOWLEDGE OF THE LEARNER

Knowledge of a student with a special learning and/or behavior needs' preferences and interests, of their learning styles, of their performance levels, and of their IEP/ITP goals and objectives all will help provide a basis for making decisions regarding personalized functional instruction and materials/resources. In this section, we will integrate the four steps comprising this component as we present several examples of students with different special learning and/or behavior needs.

Within the term *individuals with disabilities,* Public Law 101-476 (IDEA 1997) includes those with mental retardation, hearing impairments including deafness, speech and language impairments, visual impairments including blindness, serious emotional disturbance, orthopedic impairments, autism, traumatic brain injury, and other health impairments, or specific learning disabilities. The educational/functional needs of individuals with special learning and/or behavior needs may be met through many placement options including general and special education classrooms. In 1993, the Council for Exceptional Children (CEC) released an inclusion policy, which broadened the placement options and states:

> CEC believes the concept of inclusion is a meaningful goal to be pursued in our schools and communities. In addition, CEC believes children, youth, and young adults with disabilities should be served whenever possible in general education classrooms in inclusive neighborhood schools and community settings. Such settings should be strengthened and supported by an infusion of specially trained personnel and other appropriate supportive practices according to the individual needs of the child.

The concepts espoused in the policy have implications for making decisions regarding functional curriculum and materials/resources as well as staffing patterns. The nature of personnel preparation programs limits the effectiveness of cooperative instructional planning between general and special educators. The policy states that students with disabilities should be served whenever possible in general education classrooms and in neighborhood schools and community settings, and should be supported by an infusion of specially trained personnel. This implies that, in addition to placements in special education, separate classes, special schools, out-of-school environments, and in general education part-time, all individuals with disabilities have the option of full inclusion in general education classrooms. Such policy changes require that general educators and special educators be prepared to work together effectively in

			Levels			
Subject	**LCCE Competency/ Subcompetency**	**Commercial Materials**	**K–4**	**5–8**	**9–12**	**Mode of Presentation**

LCCE DOMAIN: _____

FIGURE 9.3   Functional Materials/Resource Correlation Chart.

Note: From Task Analysis of Matching Materials to Characteristics of the Learner by I. D. Cook in *Life Centered Career Education: Professional Development Activity Book* (p. 267) by D. E. Brolin, 1993, Arlington, VA: The Council for Exceptional Children. Copyright 1993 by The Council for Exceptional Children. Reprinted by permission.

making decisions regarding the use of appropriate curriculum, materials/resources, and instructional delivery in the least restrictive environment (LRE).

Preparing simple learning characteristics profiles for each student with special learning and/or behavior needs early in the school year and keeping up-to-date LCCE Mild/Moderate Curriculum materials/resources correlation charts will facilitate more appropriate instructional/functional programming regardless of whether they're served in inclusive schools or special classes. Curriculum and instructional tools, such as textbooks, media, materials, and technology, must all be carefully selected to assist those with special learning and/or behavior needs to learn to their maximum ability and make the transition from school to postsecondary training, to community living, and to the world of work.

Cook (1993) provides a series of profile sheets for developing learner characteristics profiles. These formats, which are illustrated in Figures 9.4 and 9.5, will guide the selection and adaptation of materials/resources to teach the diversity of students with special learning and/or behavior needs of all ages in a variety of environments. As the variation in students' abilities and special learning and/or behavior needs are reviewed, implications for functional materials/resources decisions will likely emerge.

The following sections contain case studies of students with special learning and/or behavior needs illustrating the principles and implications of making decisions regarding the selection of material and resources described earlier in this chapter and in the preceding chapters.

Mental Retardation

Students who have mental impairments are those who evidence significantly subaverage general intellectual functions resulting in or associated with impairments in adaptive behavior and manifested during the developmental periods. The term *mildly impaired* refers to those students who require specially designed instruction and basic academic and practical skills to develop adequate social, personal, and voca-

tional competence sufficient for self-maintenance. The term *moderately mentally impaired* refers to those students who require special instruction in basic communication, sensory motor, self-help and independent living skills, and vocational training to function in employment/supportive employment and community living/supervised community living. The term *severely mentally impaired* refers to those students who require systematic instruction in self-help skills and routines to function in society with assistance in all areas, including the possibility of functioning in specially designed work settings. Problems among these students are medical problems and dysfunctional behaviors. The term *profoundly mentally retarded* refers to those students who have limited capabilities in all areas of development and who are totally dependent on others.

Amos
......
Amos, a 12-year-old boy, is very quiet and insecure. He constantly needs to have directions repeated. Amos is easily distracted and darts from one activity to another. His mother was 17 when he was born. During Amos' birth, oxygen was cut off for a period of time due to the umbilical cord being wrapped around his neck, resulting in some brain damage. He has two siblings, an older brother and a younger sister. Tests of cognitive ability demonstrate that both siblings have normal intelligence. Adam has good health, other than the usual childhood illnesses, and there is nothing unusual in his health history.

Amos has a low socioeconomic background. He lives in a rural area, and his family receives Aid to Dependent Children from Human Services. In spite of this background, he is generally clean and dressed in clean clothes.

Amos is classified as mildly mentally impaired. He is included in general physical education, health, music, art, homeroom, recess, and lunch. Amos goes to a resource room for reading, language arts, mathematics, science, and social studies. In the classroom, he learns best when activities utilize visual-motor functioning. He has accept-

Student's Name: _____		Date: _____	
*Learning Characteristics	***Implications for for Materials/Resources**	****LCCE Competencies**	***Materials**
e.g., memory deficit	Materials should provide for short incremental steps and overlearning		

*   To be completed by special education teacher

** To be completed by regular education/special education teacher

FIGURE 9.4   Student Profile Sheet (for inclusion student).

Note: From Task Analysis of Matching Materials to Characteristics of the Learner by I. D. Cook in *Life Centered Career Education: Professional Development Activity Book* (p. 271) by D. E. Brolin, 1993, Arlington, VA: The Council for Exceptional Children. Copyright 1993 by The Council for Exceptional Children. Reprinted by permission.

Student's Name: _____		Date: _____	
*Learning Characteristics	***Implications for for Materials/Resources**	***LCCE Competencies**	***Materials**
e.g., memory deficit	Materials should provide for short incremental steps and overlearning		

* To be completed by special education teacher

FIGURE 9.5   Student Profile Sheet (Self-Contained Classroom Placement).
Note: From Task Analysis of Matching Materials to Characteristics of the Learner by I. D. Cook in *Life Centered Career Education: Professional Development Activity Book* (p. 273) by D. E. Brolin, 1993, Arlington, VA: The Council for Exceptional Children. Copyright 1993 by The Council for Exceptional Children. Reprinted by permission.

able handwriting, and his completed work is usually neat. His weaknesses include short-term memory ability, reading skills, and an extreme lack of confidence. Amos was retained in first grade. He has continually received speech therapy.

Educational Implications

The main goal of school personnel who teach students who are mentally impaired is to help them to achieve the functional behaviors necessary to assume adult roles and responsibilities when they transition from the school setting into the community and to the world of work. Programs for the mildly mentally impaired generally include academic, communication, functional academic, personal-social, self-determination/advocacy, and community living skills. Programs for the moderately mentally impaired include functional academic, basic communication, sensory motor, community use, self-determination/advocacy, and vocational skills. For students who are severely mentally impaired, programs generally include self-help, leisure, behavior management plans, communication/augmentative communication skills, social and vocational skills, daily routine, and personal care training. Programs for profoundly mentally impaired students include basic development in self-help, communication/augmentative, sensory motor training, and social responsiveness.

The student who is mentally impaired faces more problems in the area of adaptive behavior than in the area of low intellectual functioning. This will require the individual and other personal support providers to identify the level of support necessary to function appropriately in all ecological environments.

LCCE Mild/Moderate Curriculum Applications

The LCCE Mild/Moderate Curriculum provides ample opportunities to develop adaptive behavior. The competencies/subcompetencies contained in the three domains (daily living, personal-social, occupational guidance and preparation) are the thrust of all programs for students with mental impairments. These competencies and subcompetencies may be in-

fused into the general education curriculum. First-hand observation shows us that many adults who are mentally impaired struggle with daily functioning in these three domains. If the personalized needs of students with mental impairment are identified early and the appropriate functional instruction utilizing appropriate functional materials/resources is provided, all stakeholders (student, parents, teachers, agency personnel, etc.) can better prepare them for making the successful transition from school to work and community living. Whether the impairment is mild or severe, the LCCE Mild/Moderate Curriculum competencies and subcompetencies address the needs of students on their level. Again, as with most other exceptionalities, the emphasis is on providing hands-on, real-life learning activities and functional experiences, rather than the academic approach that has so dismally failed these students in the past.

Implications for Functional Materials and Resources

Many studies (Denny, 1966; Ellis, 1970; Fisher & Zeaman, 1973; Spitz, 1973; Zeaman & House, 1963; Zigler, 1966) have delineated specific characteristics of individuals with mental retardation and teaching implications. Some major conclusions from these studies were that persons with mental retardation have a deficit in short-term memory due to inadequate rehearsal strategies, have a deficit in input organization, have difficulty in selecting and attending to relevant dimensions, and are poor in incidental learning. Several teaching implications are provided (Mercer & Snell, 1977):

- Verbal or imagery rehearsal activities should be encouraged.
- Material should be grouped at input (e.g., redundancy and spacing).
- The number of irrelevant concepts should be reduced.

Individuals who have intellectual deficiencies have difficulty handling abstract concepts. Such concepts must either be avoided or presented in a manipulative, hands-on way (Luftig, 1987). Learning must be sequential and provide for overlearning. Because the mental age of individuals with mental impairments is below their chronological age, instructional strategies, materials, and resources must be interesting and have low vocabulary content. Concepts taught must be relevant and also age appropriate. When needed, print material should be accompanied by audiovisual or technological supports. For students who have difficulty completing tasks, small chunks of learning and distributed practice rather than mass practice should be provided.

Because of the limitations of students with mild mental impairments, concepts should be introduced in a number of settings, using a variety of materials/resources. The materials should be kept within the interest and performance range of the student. Therefore, the teacher may choose a basic text and still provide the student with supplementary books, teacher-prepared materials, videos, audiotapes, and computer-based programs. Transition guest speakers and community learning experiences also are a necessity to supplementing school activities. Do not have the students repeat activities to the point of boredom. Refer, instead, to the wealth of suggested ancillary materials/resources.

Hearing Impairments

Students who are deaf or hearing impaired/hard of hearing are those with auditory acuity delays that inhibit the development of speech and/or language skills and adversely affect developmental and educational performance. The deaf student is one with a profound or total loss of hearing sensitivity to the extent that processing linguistic information (with or without amplification) is impaired and requires specially designed instruction. The student with a hearing impairment is one whose sense of hearing is functional but whose hearing loss, whether permanent or fluctuating, causes a speech and/or language deficit to the extent that specifically designed instruction is required.

Stephanie
· · · · · · · · · ·
Stephanie is a 12-year-old girl. She has a hearing loss of 72 dB in her right and 80 dB in her left ear, which puts her within the deaf range. She is four grades behind her peers in general academic subjects, although she is of average intelligence. She is socially immature because of limited communication ability. She is currently placed in a self-contained classroom.

Educational Implications

As with other students with special learning and/or behavior needs, those with hearing impairments also require the same functional curriculum as their peers. The main goal of teachers of students with hearing impairments is to teach language and the means to communicate. The only adaptations a teacher needs to make for students with hearing impairments are in delivery and presentation. Teachers must be knowledgeable of signing, of assistive technology, of needed speech and pathology services, and of strategies for effectively communicating with students with hearing impairments. For instance, students should be seated in direct view of the teacher, and the teacher should face students with hearing impairments to allow for lip reading. Audiovisual presentations should always be preceded by a written outline or notes specific to the audiovisual materials. A functional curriculum addresses a key problem for students with hearing impairments—motivation.

LCCE Applications

The LCCE Mild/Moderate Curriculum Programs provide motivational considerations to the student with a hearing impairment by bypassing limited reading ability and involving the student in hands-on, life-centered learning activities. As with many other students with special learning and/or behavior needs, students with hearing impairments also need hands-on and functional activities, or they may become bored or lose motivation. The LCCE Mild/Moderate Curriculum Program competency instructional units provide functional, real-life learning activities that are not impeded by low reading ability in some students who are deaf or have hearing impairments.

Materials and Resources Implications

"The most common adaptations for students with hearing impairments are amplification devices, including auditory training units and hearing aids" (Bigge, 1988, p. 117). An augmentation, such as manual signing by interpreters, also may be provided for many students, but the pictorial format is another option. This approach requires that teachers adapt materials so that concepts are conveyed through signs, graphics, or other means of visual form.

Post-school opportunities are greater than ever for individuals who are deaf or have hearing impairments. Thus, it is critical that the public school programs teach the content outlined in the LCCE Mild/Moderate Curriculum Programs. The focus here is to select materials/resources appropriate for language levels. It is important to develop or adapt materials/resources to supplement or replace commercially available materials/resources. Examples of teacher-made materials include pictures, diagrams, and drawings. Extraordinary advances in technology applications for individuals who are deaf or have hearing impairments are increasing with a primary focus on both communication and educational difficulties caused by this sensory deficit.

Think It Through (Nugent & Stone, 1981), one example of a level-III videodisc-based program, was developed by staff of the Media Development Project for the Hearing Impaired (MDPHI). These programs help individuals with hearing impairments develop independent thinking skills. Students are presented with problematic situations by the videodisc and must define the problem and choose a solution (p. 98). This program addresses Competency 15 in the social skills domain and is one example of the emerging technology designed to assist educators in providing students who are deaf or with hearing impairments with the same opportunities for functional skills development as their peers.

"Many of the problems facing deaf adults in our society are job related. Limited English skills, poor educational and vocational training, and employer prejudice make finding appropriate jobs very difficult. The underemployment and low-level employment of deaf adults give them a financial handicap in addition to their physical disability."

(Kirk & Gallagher, 1989, p. 342)

Speech and Language Impairments

Students with communication disorders are those who evidence language, articulation, fluency, or voice disorders that adversely affect educational performance, including communication skills and social and emotional development within the school environment. Students with language disorders may exhibit deviant or delayed development or loss following development. Disorders may include difficulties with the form of language (semantics) or the function of language (pragmatics). Students with articulation disorders may exhibit the substitution of one phoneme (class of speech sounds) for another, distortion of phonemes or addition of phonemes, errors of syllable structure, or the presence of phonological process disorder. Students with fluency disorders may exhibit disruptions in the normal flow of speech that occur frequently or are markedly noticeable and are characterized by behaviors such as repetitions or prolongation of sounds or symbols, blocks, hesitations, revisions, incomplete phrases, and avoidance behaviors or ancillary movements indicative of stress or struggle; their voice is characterized by inappropriate voice or vocal quality, pitch, or loudness resulting from pathological conditions, psychogenic factors, or inappropriate use of the vocal mechanism.

Travis

Travis is a 14-year-old boy who has a moderate articulation-phonology disorder as well as a language deficit. He performs well below his grade level in subjects where language mediation is required. When he speaks, it is obvious that he has a speech disorder. This sets him apart from his peers at an age when peer acceptance is important.

Educational Implications

All too often, language disorders are given less attention than other categories of impairment. However, it is imperative that educators recognize these deficiencies as early as possible in the student with special learning and/or behavior needs' education. Early intervention of difficulties with speech and language will better facilitate the student's success and acceptance, not only by peers but also by the community. A large part of any transition/career education curriculum program consists of going into the community and meeting potential employers. Individuals who have communication problems are generally deemed less intelligent or less capable than peers without communication problems. Therefore, a program of activities that address deficiencies in language, articulation, and fluency or voice disorders should be implemented as early as possible. As with all populations with special learning and/or behavior needs, children who have difficulties with communication suffer from personal-social adjustment problems. Early screening and regular therapy by speech/language pathologists for these students will help them deal more effectively with social and personal-social adjustment.

LCCE Applications

The LCCE Mild/Moderate Curriculum Programs also is appropriate for students with communication disorders. The mild competency of communicating with others, which is under personal-social skills, addresses knowing subtleties of communication (subcompetency 69—mild) and demonstrating listening and responding skills (subcompetency 53—moderate), which is a vital skill for students who have speech and language deficits. Understanding the subtleties of communication and demonstrating listening and responding skills are recognized as extremely critical functional skills for adult living and working. Competency 11—mild—acquiring self-confidence—and competency 9—moderate—acquiring self-identity also address the functional needs of students with communication disorders. For instance, the following LCCE Mild Curriculum subcompetencies: 46—expressing feelings of self-worth; 47—describing others' perception of self; 48—accepting and giving praise; 49—accepting and giving criticism; and 50—expressing confidence

in one's self are all skills necessary for students with special learning and/or behavior needs to function in all adult career roles. Meanwhile, the following LCCE Moderate Curriculum subcompetencies: 33—demonstrating knowledge of personal interests and abilities; 34—demonstrating appropriate responses to emotions; 35—displaying self-confidence and self-worth; and 36—giving and accepting praise are all skills necessary for students with special learning and/or behavior needs to function successfully in all adult career roles.

This domain, as mentioned previously, is in many professionals' opinion the most important for all students with special learning and/or behavior needs.

Implications for Functional Materials and Resources

The ability to communicate is basic to learning and critical for achieving successful adult outcomes. Many students with special learning and/or behavior needs have communication deficits that necessitate intensive speech and/or language therapy. This also requires the selection of appropriate academic and functional academic materials/resources. "The preliminary challenge for the special education teacher, before considering modifications, is to identify student response methods or access activities" (Bigge, 1988, p. 67).

"Children with primary speech disorders typically respond to the regular education program with some additional help for their special communication needs."
(Kirk & Gallagher, 1989, p. 284)

Visual Impairments and Blindness

Students who are blind and partially sighted students are defined as those with such a visual limitation that even with the use of corrective lenses or magnification devices, the child requires modifications to obtain information visually or auditorily normally gained by reading printed material.

Alexandria

Alexandria is a 16-year-old girl who, as the result of a medical problem, lost her sight at the age of one. She is very alert and intelligent. Alexandria is one of seven children and attended a school for the blind until age 12, after which she was enrolled into general public education. During the last 4 years, she has been provided the support of an itinerant teacher as well as an orientation and mobility training specialist. Alexandria aspires to become a writer.

Educational Implications

The acquisition of knowledge and skills of students with visual impairment, probably more than any other population, depends on the ability of the student and her team to assess and utilize assistive technology when accessing academic and functional academic materials/resources in a meaningful way. Students with visual impairments need the same curriculum/functional curricula as their sighted peers. The major adaptation requires conveying curricular concepts in other mediums to students with visual impairments. Written information presented on a board, screen, or other written material is an example of when modifications may be required. The teacher must ensure that all written material is presented either orally or by the use of the most appropriately decided-upon assistive technology.

LCCE Applications

Because daily living skills acquisition is a major consideration of training students with visual impairments, the LCCE Mild/Moderate Curriculum Programs fits in quite appropriately to the functional training and educational needs of students with visual impairments. Also, because students with visual impairments, as it has been pointed out earlier with other students with special learning and/or behavior needs, may have significant problems with personal-social adjustment, the domain of personal-social skills addresses their needs quite adequately. The domain of occupational guidance and preparation offers a framework to assist students with visual impairments with the most

challenging career role of finding and maintaining employment. The following LCCE Mild Competencies contained in the occupational domains offer the functional skills to obtain this critical adult outcome:

17 Knowing and exploring occupational possibilities
18 Selecting and planning occupational choices
19 Exhibiting appropriate work habits and behaviors
20 Seeking, securing, and maintaining employment
21 Exhibiting sufficient physical-manual skills

No matter what functional program is used, it is critical for students with visual impairments to have a functional curriculum infused into their personalized program. These functional materials/resources can be presented orally, transcribed into Braille, or accessed through the use of assistive technology.

Implications for Functional Materials and Resources

Individuals with visual impairments can participate fully in the general education or a functional curriculum, when the individual and her team make the appropriate personalized accommodations. Examples of presentation alternatives include Braille, computer-based programs with voice output, electronic or auditory readers, and transcribers.

Current copiers enable teachers to enlarge printed material easily for students who can benefit with or without magnification. Computers also have the capability for increasing the font size of material presented in written format. Information, such introducing new vocabulary, can be largely projected, by using an overhead projector or slide show medium rather than only relying on regular enlarged printed text.

Braille is the primary tactile system for reading used by persons who are blind. Hard-copy Braille provides a permanent record, while paperless Braille allows immediate feedback for editing purposes. Many computer programs translate and print the written word into Braille.

Several other technological advancements have been developed for accessing print. A popular option is the Optacon, which "translates visual text into a raised, vibrating, tactile print that is not Braille but a tactile counterpart of visible symbols" (Lindsey, 1993, p. 186). Anna L. Hunt, in an interview response to a question about the developments in technology, stated:

> Other means of meeting communication needs of learners with visual impairments are auditory aids, such as recorded books, cassette tape recorders for taking notes and recording assignments, and the Language Master Special Edition. The Language Master, which is a speaking device, contains spellcheck, dictionary, thesaurus, grammar guide and word games. The word games are an activity related to the LCCE competency #8—Engaging in Leisure Time. The Kurzweil Reading Machine, from Kurzweil Computer Products, orally reads, in synthesized speech, any available printed material. (A. L. Hunt in an interview with I. D. Cook, October 1993)

The Tactile Graphics Display, an electronic, low-cost, assistive aid, produces textured lines and shapes that are important to learning history, geography, mathematics, and map study. The ability to read maps facilitates both communication and mobility (LCCE Mild Curriculum competencies 9 and 16 and LCCE Moderate Curriculum competencies 8 and 14). Speech synthesizers allow individuals with visual impairments to have access to much of the available computer software that translates print into speech.

Four commonly needed functional skill areas for visually impaired students are typing, listening, daily living, and orientation and travel skills. The IEP/ITP should address these personalized transition needs for persons with visual impairments. The inclusion of a functional curriculum that addresses daily living skills, personal-social skills, and occupational guidance and preparation, should be a point of discussion early in a student with visual impairments' educational/transitional program.

"All too frequently, even in recent years, otherwise capable, intelligent people with impaired vision have assumed dependent lives, remaining unemployed or returning to their parents' homes following graduation from high school or college because they have received no training in specific employment skills."

(N. G. Haring, 1982, p. 286)

Emotional/Behavior Disturbance

A student identified with an emotional/behavior disorder (EBD) is one whose condition adversely affects his educational performance and is manifested by one or more of the following characteristics over a long period of time and to a marked degree:

- An inability to learn that cannot be explained by intellectual, sensory, or health factors
- An inability to build or maintain satisfactory interpersonal relationships with peers and teachers
- Inappropriate types of behavior or feelings under normal circumstances
- A general pervasive mood of unhappiness, depression, or an emotional problem manifested by withdrawal
- A tendency to develop physical symptoms or fears associated with personal or school problems
- Or a schizophrenic condition

Emotional/behavior disorders do not include students who are socially maladjusted unless it is determined that they also meet the preceding definition.

Stephen

Stephen is a 16-year-old boy who has difficulty building and maintaining satisfactory relationships with his peers and teachers. In most of his general education classes, he is inattentive and fails to complete class assignments, which has resulted in a lack of academic progress. Stephen functions at the eighth grade level in both reading and mathematics. Sometimes Stephen appears to be depressed and unhappy. His behavior in class and in nonacademic settings is often inappropriate and immature.

Educational Implications

Special/general educators will need to provide a structured program assistance and guidance in helping students with EBD to develop and exhibit acceptable behaviors. These functional behavioral programs also should focus on helping students with EBD to develop positive interpersonal relationships as well as to continue effective learning in classroom settings. Effective teacher strategies for assisting students with EBD to attain their goals are the use of: applied behavior management programs, affective education to address the emotional and social needs of the child, and transition/career education to heighten that student's career roles development. The overall goal is to provide an environment that will help the student regulate their own behavior and will enhance the student's feeling of self-worth so that appropriate learning can occur.

LCCE Applications

The LCCE Mild/Moderate Curriculum competencies and subcompetencies under personal-social skills address the needs of students with behavior disorders very effectively. Many other prosocial skills have been developed to also help students with EBD to achieve more success in and out of school, as well as to help prepare them for adult living and working successfully.

The LCCE Mild/Moderate Curriculum succinctly addresses the critically important area of personal-social functioning for students with EBD. Unlike the general academic curriculum, which sometimes falls short motivating students with EBD, the LCCE Mild/Moderate Curriculum does hold the attention of students with special learning and/or behavior, because many state, "that LCCE is real-life, it is situational, and it elicits hands-on participation." This also is true of other functional type programs that are available for meeting the personalized needs of students with EBD.

Implications for Functional Materials and Resources

To the casual classroom observer, students with EBD may appear to be working with the same or similar materials/resources as other students in the classroom. This is usually true, but on closer inspection what is revealed that these materials/resources have been personalized or modified to consider the learning and/or social-emotional characteristics of these children (Meyen, 1990).

Wood (1986) presents selection principles that teachers should use when selecting appropriate materials/resources for students with EBD. These include: 1) selecting materials/resources that have qualities for catching and holding students' attention, 2) selecting materials/resources that address several objectives simultaneously, 3) selecting materials/resources that elicit active participation, 4) selecting materials/resources that are adaptable to the developmental levels of individual students, and 5) selecting materials/resources that provide for a successful outcome.

An educational/functional priority for most students with EBD is teaching them how to make successful personal-social adjustments so that personal interactions will not interfere with school or community functioning. They often exhibit a short attention span, a lack of motivation, a low frustration level, a poor self-concept, and are often easily distracted. Materials/resources selected must be relevant and interesting and at the appropriate age and instructional level. These materials/resources should be highly structured and elicit a great amount of student participation.

....

"One way for the school to increase the probability that students will misbehave or be truant is to offer instruction for which pupils have no real or imagined use. Not only will such 'education' fail to engage the attention of pupils, it will also hinder their social adaptation by wasting their time and substituting trivial information for knowledge that would allow them to pursue rewarding activities."

(Kaufman, 1985, pp. 159-160)

....

....

"Appropriate curriculum content can be a major vehicle for working with youths who have behavior disorders. Proper placement and appropriate curriculum materials can help eliminate many incipient behavior problems.

*The number of responses in a child's behavioral reper-
toire can be widened considerably through the medium
of curriculum."*

(Graubard, 1973, p. 271)

Orthopedic/Physical Impairments

Students with orthopedic/physical impairments have
physical disabilities, which may be congenital or
caused by accident or disease, resulting in permanent,
temporary, or intermittent medical disabilities. These
disabilities require modification of curriculum, instructional strategies, and/or related services. The
type, extent, and/or duration of services are determined by the nature of the individual's disability. The
term *physical disabilities* includes orthopedically impaired, which consists of the following:

- Disabilities caused by congenital anomaly (e.g.,
  spina bifida, congenital amputation, and os-
  teogenesis imperfecta)
- Disabilities from other causes (amputation,
  cerebral palsy, dystrophies and atrophies, and
  conditions that cause contractors)
- Other health impairments causing limited
  strength, vitality, or alertness as a result of
  chronic or acute health problems such as heart
  condition, rheumatic fever, asthma, sickle cell
  anemia, hemophilia, epilepsy, cystic fibrosis,
  cancer, or diabetes

Bea
. . . . .

Bea is a 6-year-old girl with a mental age of 3–11
and a chronological age of 6–3. Bea was born without use of her right arm and leg. No effective corrective measures were found until she was age 5,
when her leg and hip were operated on at a
Shriner's Hospital. After numerous trips to the hospital and three admissions, one of several months'
duration, Bea can now walk but with some difficulty. She is due for a follow-up this month. Her
right arm is presently immobilized by a cast, and
she has almost no control of her right hand.

Bea's mother says that her daughter had several seizures soon after her birth and was given
sleeping medications until the age of 2 weeks.
She has not taken antiseizure medication or experienced any seizures after those early incidents.

Bea's overall health is described as good. She
has about one cold per winter and sometimes
suffers from earaches with the colds. She sleeps
well but has a poor appetite. Bea did not learn to
walk until after surgery at age 5. Her mother says
that discipline is not a problem, because Bea is "a
really good kid." She notes that Bea does not
want to share toys and has a bad temper at times.
She was vague about methods of discipline used
but did mention the withholding of privileges.

The Stanford-Binet test revealed Bea's
strength on those items requiring purely visual
performance. She clearly had difficulty on items
requiring fine motor performance, and failed the
picture vocabulary item test at age IV level, although she passed it at age III level. The present
testing shows her functioning at a mental age of
3 years 11 months, with a consequent IQ in the
range of mild intellectual disabilities.

Raw score on the Vineland Social Maturity
Scale was 2, which yields an age equivalent of
3–0. Her human figure drawings consist solely of
faces with distinct eyes, noses, and mouths.

Cognitive factors observed include Bea's academic potential as measured by Stanford-Binet,
which is presently in the lowest 1% of all children
her age. It is not known, however, whether this is
the result of cognitive deficits or developmental
delays coincident to her physical disabilities. In
either case, she will be at a severe disadvantage if
placed with her general education age peers. Bea's
vision and hearing are apparently average, but it
is expected that they will be checked in a routine
screening during the first month of school.

Bea seems to be a happy, cheerful child, although she seems accustomed to having her own
way. There seems to be no reason why she cannot
socialize with her peers—provided that she is not
put into a position where her physical disabilities
will show to her disadvantage. Teachers should

cooperate with her parents on enforcing a firm but gentle discipline—stressing her competence to do things for herself and to persist at challenging activities.

Educational Implications

Because of the uniqueness of each student with physical impairments, the curriculum should consider a variety of instructional strategies, procedures, environmental arrangements, equipment, materials/resources, learning activities, skill sequences, and/or criteria for achieving successful educational performance. Some areas of consideration are the student's physical, psychological, and emotional adjustment to their physical disability. Other concerns to be considered when designing and implementing programming include: physical/occupational therapy, medical care and treatment, use of prosthetic or orthotic devices, eating, dressing, toileting, physical mobility, personal hygiene, communication skills, and use of assistive devices. The special educator's concern is not the origin of the disability but rather how the disability affects a child's learning and/or behavior. Unless the type and degree of severity of a disability interfere with or impede learning in a general education classroom, there is no need to specify special instruction or strategies for students with physical impairments.

LCCE Applications

The LCCE Mild/Moderate Curriculum and its three domains address the basic needs of students who are physically impaired. In Chapter 4, other functional curricula programs are discussed and also address the functional needs of students with physical impairments.

Implications for Functional Materials and Resources

Clark and Kolstoe stated "we have no substantial indication that persons with impaired physique or health differ as a group from other disabled or nondisabled group in their general or overall adjust-

ment" (1990, p. 68). Unless a disability interferes with a student's ability to work in a general education classroom, she is not identified as having a disability and served elsewhere.

As stated by Reynolds and Birch (1982), part of the school administrator's and teacher's daily work includes organizing educational programs in terms of the pupils' educational needs by matching instructional designs to cognitive rates, learning styles, and their present and projected educational achievements and making technology the servant of pupils and teachers.

One way that individuals with physical impairments may be helped, if they have difficulty engaging in appropriate motor activity, is through the use of computer technology:

> Three important factors must be considered when designing programming using computer technology: method of access to be used, chronological age of the individual, and educational or life functioning area(s) to be enhanced. (Lindsey, 1993, pp. 172–173)

Computers may be used for educational purposes, at home for leisure games and budgeting, and in the community (e.g., at work, at the bank) (Lindsey, 1993). Computer games allow persons with physical impairments to engage independently in recreation leisure skills. With the advent and use of the many assistive or adaptive devices, students with physical impairments can participate (fully or partially) in many ecological environments during the school years or as adults.

When it's necessary to adapt or develop materials for a person with a physical disability, the materials should approximate, as closely as possible, those used by students without physical impairments.

"...children and youth with physical impairments tend to experience problems related to environmental control, mobility, energy level, and access that make early and consistent career and occupational guidance, encouragement, and training especially necessary."

(Reynolds & Birch, 1982, p. 298)

Learning Disabilities

Learning disabilities (LD) is a disorder in one or more of the basic psychological processes involved in understanding or in using language, spoken or written, which may manifest itself in an imperfect ability to listen, think, speak, read, write, spell, or to do mathematical calculations. The term does not include a learning problem that is primarily the result of a visual or motor handicap, mental retardation, emotional disturbance, or environmental or cultural differences, or economic disadvantage.

Sebastian

Sebastian is an eighth grader with a learning disability. His tested intelligence is above average, and he learns most things easily and quickly. Sebastian communicates orally well but has difficulty with basic reading, handwriting, spelling, and written expression skills. Sebastian reads at the fifth-grade level with adequate word recognition and comprehension. He performs at the fourth-grade level in spelling and mathematics.

Educational Implications

The major goal of a program that addresses learning disabilities is to enable the student to achieve personalized goals in an integrated, sequential, and developmental manner. Strategies that work effectively for students with learning disabilities generally focus on four major curricular components:

1. Academic instruction
2. Social/emotional skills
3. Organized study skills
4. Transition/career education

Special educators need to be especially organized in working with these students. A successful teacher generally tries the simplest presentation of a flexible approach with students who have LD. Teachers should ask or assess the student with LD's preferred learning style (i.e., visual, auditory, tactile, or kinesthetic). Finally, early intervention is one of the best strategies in assisting students with LD to begin to cope with and effectively manage their learning difficulties.

Students with learning disabilities make up the largest group of students (50%) identified as needing special education. Many lack interpersonal skills (work habits and attitudes, social communication skills), job-related academic skills, and specific vocational skills to learn more than entry-level personal service jobs. This places them in a particularly difficult position: They have high-to-normal intellectual functioning, yet because of those areas in which they lack skill, they are often perceived unable to learn. Students with LD, when provided with the appropriate learning supports, could be as successful as any student who does not have an LD. Currently, many students with LD are achieving so much success in high school that they now represent the largest nontraditional group of students enrolling in postsecondary education. Once the personalized program is designed and appropriate learning strategies are used, there are no limits for many individuals with LD success in adult living and working

LCCE Applications

The practicality of the LCCE Mild Curriculum approach is appreciated by students with LD because they see its real-life skill application and it provides them with enough physical activity and movement to satisfy their physical needs. Other functional curricula discussed in Chapter 5 also are considered appropriate for use with students with special learning and/or behavior needs. Most students with special learning and/or behavior needs who have achieved the skills in these functional curricula programs skills usually can excel in areas of community living and working.

Students with LD generally have lived with a lot of failure in academic areas. Therefore, the LCCE Mild Curriculum and other functional curricula provide a better alternative in helping these students with LD in meeting their personal-social needs. The transition/functional approach is a better alternative than merely adhering to an academic curriculum.

Mercer (1983) emphasized the need to provide career and vocational options for students with LD and to make the necessary adaptations to accommodate their needs.

Implications for Functional Materials and Resources

As with other exceptional students, the diverse learning needs of those with learning disabilities imply that materials/resources need to be modified to meet individual needs. Polloway et al. (1989) provided several recommendations that briefly summarize the implications of learning research regarding students with LD. First, concrete, meaningful content should be emphasized in initial instruction. "Concrete concepts depend on direct observation (hence the term concrete) and often involve objects, but observable actions and events are also included" (Carpignano & Bigge, 1983, p. 223).

The second recommendation of Polloway et al. (1989) is to "ensure mastery of new material through overlearning and/or repetition." Gearheart also suggests that "repetition of items maintains information in a person's consciousness, whereas stimulus enrichment and elaboration are needed for deeper encoding" (1985, p. 122). To prevent boredom, a variety of materials/resources must be used when it is necessary to repeat concepts.

Third, Polloway et al. (1989) recommend that learners with LD be provided with methods of verbal mediation and strategies for learning, recalling, and problem solving. Understanding and learning what is needed to get around the community (LCCE Mild competency 9 and LCCE Moderate competency 8) and applying these concepts independent of others provide an example of problem-solving.

Fourth, Polloway et al. (1989) noted the need to increase attending skills. Several methods for increasing attention were discussed. "Using novel and varied stimuli properties in instructional materials/resources and increasing motivation through reinforcement are two other logical and effective ways to increase attention and thus capitalize on students' learning abilities" (p. 28).

Fifth, ensuring success in learning and/or in personal-social development was recommended. One way to ensure success is to select, modify, and/or adapt materials and resources to the student's ability. The student profile sheets, Figures 9.4 and 9.5, are formats used to indicate the student characteristics and major competencies and serve as a major approach to planning for successful task completion for the student.

Further recommendations by Polloway et al. (1989) were to provide incentives, to sequence instructions from easy to difficult, and to use a variety of academic and functional academic methods and materials/resources.

"Certainly the types of employment possibilities available to individuals with mild mental handicaps, learning disabilities, and behavior disorders in a highly technological society should be directly related to the quality of programs designed to instruct them. As professionals become effective at providing meaningful instruction and long-term services, the status of jobs available to these individuals should rise."

(Langone, 1990, pp. 374–375)

LEARNER-MATERIALS/ RESOURCES MATCH

Finally, the learner-material resources/match is made. Materials/resources may be selected, adapted, or when necessary, new ones may be developed or purchased if needed to convey the curriculum to the student. The process follows:

1. Review the LCCE materials correlation chart. Are there materials listed that correlate with the objectives on the student's IEP/ITP?
2. Are the materials appropriate as they are, or do they need to be adapted for use with the student based on specific learning characteristics?
3. Is there a need to develop or secure other functional materials?

The learning task stays the same. The LCCE Mild/Moderate Curriculum is appropriate for all students in regular and special education. However, if a student has difficulty acquiring skills and information through the available materials and resources, the first type of modification to try is adaptation of instructional materials and activities. Characteristics associated with different exceptionalities may necessitate minor and sometimes major modifications of available materials. The student profile formats presented in Figures 9.3 and 9.4 may be used to guide the adaptation/modification of materials.

Materials Development

A final option in the learner-material matching process is to develop materials. As teachers face the problem of individualizing instruction in the philosophy of mainstreaming or full inclusion, teacher-constructed materials are more important than ever.

Too often, suitable materials are not available; the steps in commercial materials may be too great for a student to understand and master and intermediate levels may need to be inserted. When it is necessary to substitute for or supplement commercially available materials, the skills to be taught, developmental levels of students, and cost should be the focus of materials development. Some possible formats include learning centers, learning packets, games, simulations, projects (art, etc.), media, charts, posters, bulletin boards, and more. A format for describing teacher-made materials is presented in Figure 9.6 (Cook, 1993).

Producer:

Title:

Focus Area:

Mode of Learning:

Description:

Objectives:

Content:

Procedure for Use:

Cost:

Equipment Needs:

Comments:

FIGURE 9.6   Outline for Describing Teacher-Developed Materials.
Note: From Outline for Describing Teacher Developed Materials by I. D. Cook in *Life Centered Career Education: Professional Development Activity Book* (p. 279) by D. E. Brolin, 1993, Arlington, VA: The Council for Exceptional Children. Copyright 1993 by The Council for Exceptional Children. Reprinted by permission.

Summary

The goal of this model is to reduce barriers and make the LCCE Mild/Moderate Curriculum or other functional curricula accessible to all students with special learning and/or behavior needs regardless of their ages. For this to occur, teachers must be knowledgeable of available materials/resources and learning characteristics. After materials/resources have been correlated to the LCCE Mild/Moderate Curriculum competencies, the second step in instructional decision making is a thorough assessment of the learner characteristics, which is then used for personalized IEP/ITP development. Having knowledge of specific disabilities, students' learning styles, performance levels, and goals and objectives for the learner (IEP/ITP) will provide a basis for making decisions regarding methods and materials for instructing learners with special learning and/or behavior needs.

STATE STANDARDS CORRELATION WITH LCCE MILD/MODERATE CURRICULUM PROGRAMS

As mentioned earlier in this chapter, concerns have been expressed about the difficulty of matching the functional skills with the state basic skills/standards. Several states (North Dakota, South Carolina, Florida, Alabama, Mississippi, etc.) have successfully correlated the LCCE Mild/Moderate Curriculum competencies with their state standards. Figure 9.7 illustrates how South Carolina has developed a matrix, which identifies how the LCCE competencies match to the state standards. Examples of reading/English/language arts and math standards correlated to the LCCE Mild Curriculum are illustrated in Figure 9.7.

State department personnel have found that LCCE corresponds easily to state standards, thus allowing the ability to meet graduation standards or develop IEP goals and objectives.

CHAPTER COMMENTARY

It is obvious that the market is full of transition materials/resources that address concepts covered in the LCCE Mild/Moderate Curriculum programs. The problem is not a lack of materials; it is ensuring that the materials succeed in facilitating learning. As we customize instruction for individual students, it may be necessary to use the options discussed in this chapter: selection, adaptation, and development of materials. After instruction, if a student doesn't reach a criterion or demonstrate attainment of the LCCE Mild/Moderate Curriculum competencies/subcompetencies, recycling of the stages as outlined in the model in Figure 9.2 should occur. A sampling of instructional materials, correlated to the competencies and subcompetencies of the LCCE Mild/Moderate Curriculum, is presented in Appendix F. This list is limited, and the materials included should not be regarded as an endorsement to their quality; further, it is not an exhaustive list. Many of the subcompetencies may be cross-referenced on the materials correlation list. For instance, materials listed under one competency also may be found under another if the materials are appropriate to both.

The materials in the list range from kindergarten to adulthood and address all competencies of the LCCE Mild/Moderate Curriculum. A variety of modalities are addressed. The title, author, publisher, content description, reading, and/or interest levels are also included. A listing of publishers follows the materials list. In addition to these materials listed, the LCCE Mild/Moderate Curriculum also provides instructional units/lesson plans, which include easily accessible, noncommercial materials and functional activities.

ACTIVITIES

1. For each individual student described in this chapter, summarize, in a short narrative, the provisions you would make to ensure that appropriate materials and resources are available to assist

Area Of Study	Curriculum Standard Objective	LCCE Behavioral Objective	K	1	2	3	4	5	6	7	8	9	10	11	12
Reading/ Literature	Identify common signs and logos.	9.38.1	X												
		9.38.3													
	Use number words.	1.6.3	X												
	Read a variety of texts, such as stories, poems, directories, newspapers, charts, and diagrams.	17.74.1		X	X	X									
		17.75.1								X					
		17.75.2													
	Read technical and career-related materials.	17.71.1								X	X				
		17.71.2													
		17.71.4													
		17.74.1													
		17.74.3													
		17.74.6													
		17.75.1													
		17.75.2													
		17.75.4													
		18.76.2													
	Read a variety of formats, such as stories, poems, plays, reports, and other technical writing across the curriculum.	18.76.2									X				
	Read and follow instructions to perform tasks.	19.81.2										X			X
	Complete an application for employment/ college admission.	20.89.1										X	X	X	
		20.89.2											X	X	
		20.89.3													
	Identify essential information needed to operate equipment.	2.8.2											X		
Measurement	Tell time.	19.82.1	X	X	X	X	X								
	Identify/choose appropriate instruments used to measure length/weight/time/ volume/temperature	3.14.1	X	X	X	X	X	X	X						
		5.23.2					X	X							
		6.27.2							X			X	X	X	X

Use standard/nonstandard units to measure length/weight/volume/temperature.

Code	
8.34.2	
8.37.5	
19.82.1	
5.23.3	X
5.23.5	X
6.27.2	X

Name/count coins.

Code	
1.1.1	X
1.1.2	X

Compare/make change for coins/dollars.

Code	
1.1.1	X
1.1.2	X
1.2.2	
1.2.6	

Read temperatures and determine temperature changes from Celsius and Fahrenheit temperatures.

Code	
3.14.1	X
5.22.1	
5.22.2	
5.23.1	
5.23.3	
8.33.2	

Estimate/calculate/justify amount of money needed to make purchases.

Code	
1.1.1	X
1.1.2	X
1.2.1	
1.2.2	
1.2.3	
1.2.4	
1.2.5	
1.3.1	
5.20.1	
6.27.4	
8.34.2	
8.37.5	

FIGURE 9.7 LCCE Correlation to South Carolina Reading/English Language Arts Curriculum Standards

these students in learning the concepts outlined in the LCCE Mild/Moderate Curriculum.

Amos
    Provisions:
Stephanie
    Provisions:
Travis
    Provisions:
Alexandria
    Provisions:
Stephen
    Provisions:

Sebastian
    Provisions:

2. In the following matrix (Figure 9.8), sketch out for one semester, in any subject matter you teach, the career education content you want to infuse and what you would recommend to be taught in separate programming. Address each of the components across the top of the matrix. Include the activities and materials to be used for teaching the unit. The materials may be selected from the list contained in Appendix F and/or other sources.

Subject ╲ Component	Daily Living	Personal Social	Occupational
Reading			
Language Arts			
Math			
Social Studies			
Other			

FIGURE 9.8   Cirriculum Matrix
Note: From *Curriculum Methods and Materials for the Handicapped in Career/Vocational Education, Part4, Developing Learning Activities* by I. D. Cook, 1979, Institute, WV: West Virginia Graduate College. Copyright 1979 by West Virginia Graduate College. Reprinted by permission.

CHAPTER 10

Self-Determination

**Robert J. Loyd and
Michael Wehmeyer**

PRELIMINARY QUESTIONS

1. Define self-determination and explain its importance and relationship to the LCCE Mild/Moderate Curriculum personal-social skills areas.
2. Identify Field and Hoffman's conceptual model for developing and providing self-determination instruction to students with special learning and behavior needs.
3. Identify Wehmeyer's conceptual model for developing and providing self-determination instruction to students with special learning and behavior needs.
4. Explain how the LCCE Mild/Moderate Curriculum can be used to provide self-determination instruction to your students with special learning and behavior needs.
5. Discuss the importance of personalized transition decision making with students with special learning and/or behavior needs.
6. Identify and discuss the importance of utilizing the "young adult projection" process.

OVERVIEW

During the late 1980s, federal funds became abundant for the development of transition model demonstration and personnel preparation projects. The U.S. Department of Education's Office of Special Education and Rehabilitation Services (OSERS) provided funding for special projects for the purpose of developing innovative transition models, materials, and personnel preparation methods. Considerable fundamental transition research resulted from this critical federal initiative and was used as a basis for the inclusion of the transition mandates which included both the Individuals with Disabilities Education Acts of 1990 and its amendments in 1997.

One of the most significant results of the transition research was the need to establish and implement self-determination models, materials, and methods for students with special learning and/or behavior needs. Wehmeyer (2001) noted that most special education

teachers were still making critical transition choices for students with special learning and/or behavior needs. Even with the abundance of transition models developed in the 1980s and 1990s, most placed little influence on the importance of personalized decision making and self-determination. Wehmeyer and others (Agran, Snow, & Swaner, 1999; Field, 1996) working in the area of transition believe that self-determination is an extremely important and often overlooked part of students with special learning and/or behavior needs' transition programming.

We, too, believe that self-determination is an extremely important component of transition/career education and have devoted a chapter to discussing its role in transition programming. Since the earliest edition in 1978, the Life-Centered Career Education (LCCE) Mild/Moderate Curriculum program has always addressed the importance of students with special learning and behavior needs acquiring and exhibiting self-determination skills.

The following section discusses the topic of self-determination and some recent work and concepts by leaders in the field. This section also explains how several LCCE Mild/Moderate Curriculum personal-social competencies have been incorporated into a self-determination curriculum developed by the Arc.

SELF-DETERMINATION

The concept of *self-determination* has been gaining considerable recognition recently as an important instructional need for people with special learning and/or behavior needs. In this section, the basic concept is further discussed as it relates to the needs of students with special learning and/or behavior needs.

Basic Concepts

An individual's ability and subsequent efforts to make transition decisions and goals are crucial to transition/career education. The student with special learning and/or behavior needs' self-concept is an extremely important factor to successful learning and functioning. Self-concept or image is a

CHAPTER OUTLOOK

Dr. Michael Wehmeyer is an Associate Professor in the Department of Special Education and Director of Kansas University Center on Developmental Disabilities at the University of Kansas.

One of the fundamental tenets of career education and transition services is that such supports should prepare students with disabilities for success as adults. This text has many strategies that will enable educators and others to do so for students with disabilities. Perhaps none, however, are more important than promoting and enhancing the self-determination of children and youth with disabilities.

What is self-determination? Although there are several ways to define the construct, fundamentally promoting self-determination involves preparing young people to make things happen in their lives. Self-determined people are causal agents in their lives; they make or cause things to happen to them. More precisely, people who are self-determined set goals based on personal preferences, interests, and abilities; solve problems that pose barriers to achieving these goals; make decisions that impact the quality of their lives; advocate for themselves and others; and self-manage or self-regulate their actions to achieve goals.

Why is this important? For one thing, our society essentially defines adulthood by the degree to which we assume responsibility for and the control we have over our lives. If students are unable to assume greater responsibility for making decisions, setting goals, solving problems, and so forth, or if they are denied the opportunity to do so, they will not be able to assume the role of an adult. Living as an adult in the community requires people to solve large and small problems on a day-to-day basis. Students who are not prepared to do so will not function independently, even if they have prerequisite vocational, social, or other skills. Second, experiencing control over one's life is something that is valued by all people. We define ourselves, and others define us, by the degree to which we are autonomous and self-determining. There is also research to suggest that students who are more self-determined are better able to achieve educationally relevant goals.

Promoting self-determination became a focus of transition services for adolescents with disabilities in part due to the student involvement language in the IDEA transition mandates. Students with disabilities are required by law to be invited to attend their IEP meeting if transition is to be discussed. This requirement resulted in considerable interest in the field in promoting student involvement in transition planning, based on the common-sense assumption that if students are actively involved in setting goals for their future, they will be more likely to take ownership over and work toward those goals. There are now a number of methods, materials, and strategies to promote self-determination and student involvement available to educators.

Students who are not taught to set goals, solve problems, make decisions, self-advocate, and self-direct their learning will, in the end, lack the basic skills and knowledge they will need to succeed as adults. Only by focusing on this area can we, as educators, fulfill our mission to promote positive adult outcomes for students with disabilities.

learned phenomenon and can change based on new learning and personal-social experiences. One's self-concept influences what one will learn from experience and how one will ultimately act when making decisions critical for transition programming. The self-concept is also influenced by significant others such as parents, family members, teachers, peers, and those who deliberately help to foster a change in a person's self-concept. Thus, the educational program, and specifically a functional curriculum, can provide an important influence on each student with special learning and/or behavior needs' self-concept development. This recent attention on the need for a more substantial self-determination focus in our educational/transitional programs relates directly to addressing the positive self-concept needs of the many students with special learning and/or behavior needs. In the next two sections, two basic conceptual self-determination models are presented, specifically as they relate to the personal-social curriculum domains skills of the LCCE Mild/Moderate Curriculum competencies and subcompetencies.

"Clearly, our state's youth in transition need to increasingly discover the right to self-determination, for it is through this self-empowerment that their level of human decency, pride, and sense of self-worth will be heightened and their quality of life enhanced."

(Browning, 1994)

FIELD AND HOFFMAN SELF-DETERMINATION MODEL

Self-determination is rapidly gaining attention and acceptance as an important instructional focus that general and special educators need to emphasize much more if students with special learning and/or behavior needs are to successfully make the transition from school to adulthood (Field & Hoffman, 1994). Field and Hoffman describe the concept

> as the ability to define and achieve goals based on a foundation of knowing and valuing oneself. It is promoted, or discouraged, by both internal factors (e.g., values, knowledge, and skills) and external factors (e.g., opportunities for choice-making, attitudes of others, etc.). (p. 162)

They have developed a self-determination model focusing on the internal factors that are to be used as a guide for developing strategies and materials that promote the knowledge, skills, and values leading to a person's ability to perform self-determination. Their model contains six major components: ecological environments in which the five other components occur; know yourself, value yourself, plan, act, and experience outcomes and learn. The model is illustrated in Figure 10.1.

Environment

The model is based on the ability to apply self-determination in all of the ecological environments in which a person with special learning and/or behavior needs performs his career roles. These critical ecological environments in which all persons with special learning and/or behavior needs should exhibit self-determination include the following: the school, the home, the workplace, and the community. On a daily basis, all individuals need to be able to set goals and make decisions, as well as to achieve their goals in all of the ecological environments. These skills are learned by many people, but many of our students with special learning and/or behavior needs are leaving our education system without having this extremely important ability. Additionally, our education system is beginning to endorse the idea that goal setting and self-determination need to be a personalized process with support provided to the student with special learning and/or behavior needs as needed. It has not been too many years ago that special educators and family members of students with special learning and/or behavior needs did not encourage student participation in setting transition goals and making their own decisions about career roles. Most educators working in the area of self-determination concur that it needs to be included in the student with special learning and/or behavior needs' transition planning and include the student's participation.

Know Yourself

The second component, know yourself, is an important ability in setting personalized goals. This internal

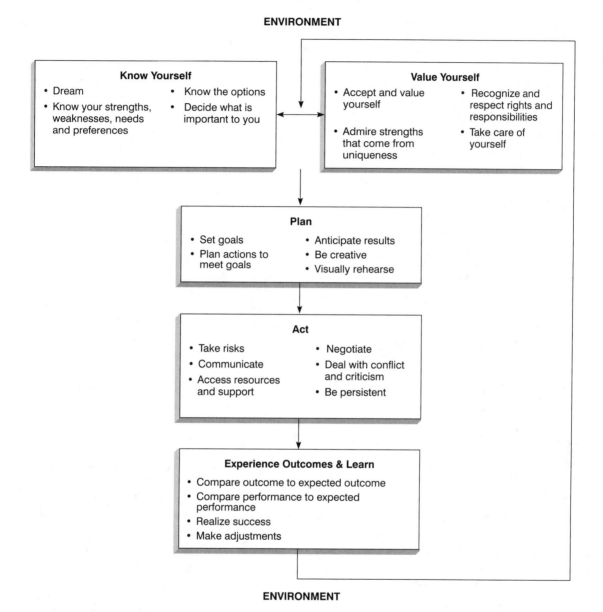

ENVIRONMENT

Know Yourself
- Dream
- Know your strengths, weaknesses, needs and preferences
- Know the options
- Decide what is important to you

Value Yourself
- Accept and value yourself
- Admire strengths that come from uniqueness
- Recognize and respect rights and responsibilities
- Take care of yourself

Plan
- Set goals
- Plan actions to meet goals
- Anticipate results
- Be creative
- Visually rehearse

Act
- Take risks
- Communicate
- Access resources and support
- Negotiate
- Deal with conflict and criticism
- Be persistent

Experience Outcomes & Learn
- Compare outcome to expected outcome
- Compare performance to expected performance
- Realize success
- Make adjustments

ENVIRONMENT

FIGURE 10.1 Model for Self-Determination.
Note. From "Development of a Model for Self-Determination" by S. Field and A. Hoffman, 1994, *Career Development for Exceptional Individuals, 17*(2), p. 165. Copyright 1994 by the Division on Career Development and Transition, The Council for Exceptional Children. Reprinted by permission.

factor includes the following skills: being able to dream and visualize your life; knowledge of your strengths, weaknesses, interests, and preferences; knowledge of your options; and deciding what is im-portant in your current and future ecological roles. In elementary school, teachers can help students with special learning and/or behavior needs gain an aware-ness of these skills in classroom discussions. Family members should also be encouraged to discuss these skills in all ecological environments with their family member with special learning and/or behavior needs. Many schools are now teaching students with special learning and/or behavior needs to direct or have more involvement in the IEP/ITP process. The "young adult projection" is an example of how these skills can be facilitated in the IEP/ITP meeting. Young adult projections permit the student with special learning and/or behavior needs to dream and visualize what they want as their quality of life as young adults in the adult functioning areas of postsecondary education, working, and community living. This process should occur with the support of the IEP/ITP team at each year's IEP/ITP meeting. Students can prepare for the young adult projection discussion by developing a pictorial map, drawing, or creating a collage of their future career roles and quality of life. Secondary students with special learning and behavior needs' functional transitional evaluation results can be shared in helping to create appropriate personalized transition plans.

The following LCCE Mild Curriculum competencies (1st number)/subcompetencies (2nd number) are related to this second component of Field and Hoffman's self-determination model.

10.42 Identify Physical and Psychological Needs

The skills involved in identifying needs enter into the physical, psychological, and social domains. There are some minimal needs for physical existence, but it is much harder to describe basic requirements in the social and psychological realms. How do we measure quantities of security, self-worth, esteem, and love? One way to determine the answer to that question is for students to identify their needs, talk about them, draw them, collect examples of them, and examine the ways in which other persons attempt to meet their needs. Varied classroom activities concerning the necessities of life will lead students with special learning and/or behavior needs to a realization about those things that they regard as essential to their lives.

10.45 Demonstrate Knowledge of Physical Self

Understanding the physical self contains functional objectives that are specific to the sexual role of the individual. The activities should enable students with special learning and/or behavior needs to develop an awareness of the similarities and differences in the anatomy and functioning of the male and female. This subject material has received increased attention among researchers, parents, consumer groups, and publishing firms primarily because of the long absence of discussion on the sexual role of individuals who are mentally retarded or physically disabled. Teachers should be aware that, if they encourage classroom or small-group discussion and questions, they must be prepared to provide information. Objectives involve identifying general systems of the body, listing and describing physical characteristics, and identifying major parts of the body.

11.50 Develop Confidence in Oneself

Students with special learning and/or behavior needs should be aware of their innate dignity. At times, they may have to assert their rights to protect that dignity. These actions are founded on a trust in their ability to accomplish functional objectives. Trust begins with the first completed task in infancy and is subsequently nurtured by the individual's efforts to accomplish more difficult functional objectives. Often, the act of attempting a task strengthens one's trust in oneself. After developing faith in oneself, the individual can begin to form objectives and seek the means, appropriate to his ability, of accomplishing his goals.

Students with special learning and/or behavior needs should be familiar with those personality factors that generally allow them to participate in a group situation that results in a positive attitude of others. What are some of these positive traits? Cooperation, cheerfulness, and dependability form a solid foundation and are also considered necessary in employment situations. There are other traits, but each individual with special learning and/or behavior needs must discover them. This is where experience and observation of others are important factors in helping individuals to change. The ability to look at oneself with a critical eye is not reserved for those with advanced degrees; it comes from practice, with encouragement, at home and in the classroom. Teachers can help students with special learning and/or behavior needs build their observational skills by assigning projects in which students with special learning and/or behavior needs interview or consider someone of their choice and list outstanding characteristics. Once the characteristics are defined, teachers can translate them into behaviors students with special learning and/or behavior needs should attempt. Together, students with special learning and/or behavior needs and teachers should work on a plan of practicing and reporting the behaviors. For students who experience problems in performing acceptable behaviors, the teacher may structure a system in which there is a conscious effort to modify the behavior toward prearranged objectives. Another functional objective should be identifying character traits that inhibit acceptance.

18.76 Make Realistic Occupational Choices

Experiences from the previous subcompetency will help students with special learning and/or behavior needs discover many jobs that really do not meet their occupational needs, interests, or aptitudes. For those jobs that do, a second level of decisions needs to be made relative to jobs of highest preference. The demand for the occupation, required education and training, and other factors are significant at this level. Students with special learning and/or behavior needs should learn the career ladder that the occupation offers and occupations for which they might qualify. These tentative personalized occupational choices should be based on an analysis of the whole person and should be systematically determined primarily by the students with special learning and/or behavior needs and their parents, employers, and school personnel. Professional guidance and counseling are important for this subcompetency. Another functional objective that should be attempted is for the individual to be able to identify specific work sites where the job of choice is available and to try out the job.

18.77 Identify Requirements of Appropriate and Available Jobs

With knowledge of sources of occupational information (subcompetency 17.2) and their major occupational needs, interests, and aptitudes, students should be ready to review the specific requirements and characteristics of appropriate and available jobs. Publications such as the *Dictionary of Occupational Titles* should be useful for individual and group sessions. The *Dictionary*, published by the Department of Labor, is a compendium of over 20,000 occupations representing the majority of jobs in the country. These activities can begin seriously during the 10th grade and can become a stimulus for independent job searching and decision making. Vocational assessment adds an important dimension to realistic decision making and planning, as do community resource personnel, who can give an in-depth personal analysis of the job's characteristics. A wide range of commercial games, materials, and packages are available for students. Another objective that should be attempted is to help students identify alternative, related occupations for which they are best qualified.

18.78 Identify Occupational Aptitudes

Use of extensive vocational assessment techniques can help students with special learning and/or behavior needs understand their vocational potentials and specific aptitudes. Before formalized vocational assessment, students with special learning and/or behavior needs will have had some indication of job areas that they are able to learn and perform successfully. Aptitudes or abilities in the following areas should be ascertained: verbal, numerical, spatial, form perception, clerical, motor coordination, finger dexterity, manual dexterity, and mechanical. The General Aptitude Test Battery (GATB) of the U.S. Employment Service is one instrument for identifying the strengths and weaknesses of some students with special learning and/or behavior needs. For others, work sample batteries can be particularly beneficial and provide a better indication of aptitudes than standardized test batteries such as the GATB, which some claim to be discriminating toward minorities relative to its cutoff scores. A substantial number of vocational assessment systems are new on the market and will be discussed in greater detail in the occupational guidance techniques section. Another objective associated with this subcompetency should be to help the student with special learning and/or behavior needs identify ways of developing needed aptitudes for occupational interests.

18.79 Identify Major Occupational Interests

By 9th or 10th grade, most students should have a basic idea of occupational areas that would interest them. These decisions are related more to what they think they would like to do, for example, "help people by working in a hospital as an aide or orderly," regardless of whether the job meets all or most occupational needs and aptitudes. If the jobs that the student with special learning and/or behavior needs identifies are not within her capability or need structure, she can explore related but more appropriate ones later. What is important is that each individual with special learning and/or behavior needs is beginning to focus on specific occupational areas or jobs based on her knowledge of occupations and self. In some situations interest inventories can be valuable, but for the most part, interests evolve from experiences and explorations in the workplace. Although occupational interests are unique to each individual, students with special learning and/or behavior needs can learn how others arrived at such decisions by engaging in group interactions. For students who are poor readers or nonreaders, pictorial interest inventories are available. Other objectives that relate to this subcompetency are to help students with special learning and/or behavior needs identify occupations that permit the pursuit of personal interests and the occupational needs that can be met from these jobs.

18.80 Identify Major Occupational Needs

As students with special learning and/or behavior needs acquire the personal-social skills of self-awareness, self-confidence, socially responsible behavior, interpersonal skills, independence, and problem-solving,

they should be ready to identify those major occupational needs that are presently part of their work personality. They should be able to determine whether needs such as high pay, independence, achievement, praise, responsibility, authority, use of talents and abilities, advancement, security, social service, variety, and social status are of major importance in their future work life. Group discussions on the topic, supplemented with presentations given by persons working in various occupations, should be provided so that students with special learning and/or behavior needs can make these decisions and other choices related to an appropriate work environment (e.g., outdoor vs. indoor work, sedentary vs. active, urban vs. rural settings). These discussions can serve as a basis for lively and soul-searching inquiry. Teachers also can attempt to have students with special learning and/or behavior needs identify the occupational needs that persons in occupations they are interested in tend to have.

The following LCCE Moderate Curriculum competencies (1st number)/subcompetencies (2nd number) are related to this second component of Field and Hoffman's self-determination model.

9.33 Demonstrate Knowledge of Personal Interests

Individuals with special learning and/or behavior needs discover their abilities through their interests. How can a child try or attempt to accomplish anything if his interest cannot be aroused? Aren't childhood hobbies a means of building confidence through interest? If individuals with special learning and/or behavior needs are to achieve independence through competent behavior, they must have numerous experiences with those things they like to do, can do, and would attempt to do if given adequate support. With support, trial and error can help the individual with special learning and/or behavior needs build an awareness of physical and spiritual capabilities. This is especially important for able-bodied people who, through accident, injury, or operation, enter the category of disabled. For these individuals, the rehabilitative process involves supportive efforts that help them identify interests that correspond to their altered abilities. Teachers should plan activities that require students with special learning and/or behavior needs to identify interests and abilities that are common to most people. They should engage their students with special learning and/or behavior needs in activities that will help them identify their own interests and abilities, set future goals, and devise strategies for implementing and reaching these goals.

9.34 Demonstrate Appropriate Responses to Emotions

Teachers can begin classroom activities that deal with emotions by creating a nonjudgmental climate in which students (whether children or adults) feel free to talk about feelings. Primary-grade students should identify such emotions as happiness, sadness, and anger and should have had exposure to these emotions long before entering school. Older children with special learning and/or behavior needs should begin to work with the problem of recognizing the various ways in which emotions can be expressed. Students with special learning and/or behavior needs should be involved in role-playing situations or should report observations that emphasize various indices of emotions, for example, body language, facial expressions, and tone of voice. A second major functional objective should be for teachers to develop students with special learning and/or behavior needs' ability to distinguish the consequences of the emotion for others, but particularly, for the self. For example, an expression of anger by an employer may have different consequences than a similar demonstration by an employee. The employer is allowed to let off steam, but the employee may lose his job. Finally, teachers should identify a means through which students with special learning and/or behavior needs can release emotions constructively. An appropriate expression of emotion is unique to each individual. Teachers and parents should exert a great deal of time and effort in establishing a foundation of trust that will encourage students to explore feelings and

find adequate ways of expressing them. Another functional objective should be identifying ways in which emotions affect behavior.

9.35 Display Self-Confidence and Self-Worth

Individuals begin to feel worthy when they experience expressions of value from parents, teachers, and friends. These declarations of worth may be difficult for the person with special learning and/or behavior needs to formulate. In our society, an individual's perceived worth is based on comparison to other people. Comparative statements are common in a culture that rewards individuals who demonstrate the drive to excel. The problem is that "doing better" is often determined in comparison to someone else. Individuals with special learning and/or behavior needs can find themselves at a serious disadvantage if their abilities are always placed in some type of "better than the other person" derby. If the individual with special learning and/or behavior needs loses the race, he might perceive himself as being inferior to others, which in turn may cause him to lose his sense of self-worth. The parent's and teacher's ability to work with the assets an individual with special learning and/or behavior needs has at his disposal is the key to this potential dilemma. They must move away from "you versus them" situations to "I can do" experiences. By emphasizing the "I can," the parent and teacher opinions change, with a corresponding influence on the attitudes and values of the individual. "I can" is a positive statement of value and worth in this society. How many times have we heard stories about individuals who were told they would never walk, run, or dance only to accomplish that very thing and more? The emergence and success of such events as the Special Olympics and Wheelchair Games illustrate that individuals with disabilities have a strong desire to demonstrate their worth through physical accomplishments regardless of how long it may take them to run a certain distance. Teachers and parents should provide opportunities in which students with special learning and/or behavior needs express how they feel about themselves in relationship to their accomplishments, successes, and failures. What experiences cause students to feel good, worthy, or pleased with their accomplishments? What experiences frustrate them? These expressions provide professionals with an opportunity to plan subsequent activities that will increase the quality and quantity of success experiences. Another functional objective should be identifying ways in which other people affect an individual's feelings of worth.

10.38 Identify Current and Future Personal Roles

Several roles are identified across competency areas. Some of these roles are employee, citizen, parent, relative, and friend. Students with special learning and/or behavior needs should be able to describe and demonstrate responsible behavior to individuals (employer, parent, child) as well as groups (union, passengers, clubs) identified with a specific role. This LCCE Mild Curriculum subcompetency requires students with special learning and/or behavior needs to be actively involved in each role so they can realize its full meaning. For example, a student with special learning and/or behavior needs may be a member of a family by birth, but not in practice. Parents should involve their children in as many family activities and decisions as possible, especially if the student with special learning and/or behavior needs has chosen a future role as parent and spouse. Teachers should place students with special learning and/or behavior needs in situations that provide understanding of the expectations of others for a particular role. For example, community personnel such as police officers, fire fighters, and employers should discuss their expectations of student behaviors and responsibilities in the roles of citizen and employee. Another functional objective should be identifying all possible future roles. The growth of self-esteem is woven into the personal-social competencies.

16.58 Demonstrate Knowledge of Occupational Interests

By 9th or 10th grade, most students should have a basic idea of occupational areas that would interest them. These decisions are related more to what they think they would like to do, for example, "help people by working in a hospital as an aide or orderly," regardless of whether the job meets all or most occupational needs and aptitudes. If the jobs that the student with special learning and/or behavior needs identifies are not within her capability or need structure, she can explore related but more appropriate ones later. What is important is that each individual with special learning and/or behavior needs is beginning to focus on specific occupational areas or jobs based on her knowledge of occupations and self. In some situations, interest inventories can be valuable, but for the most part, interests evolve from experiences and explorations in the workplace. Although occupational interests are unique to each individual, students with special learning and/or behavior needs can learn how others arrived at such decisions by engaging in group interactions. For students who are poor readers or nonreaders, pictorial interest inventories are available. Other objectives that relate to this subcompetency are to help students with special learning and/or behavior needs to identify occupations that permit the pursuit of personal interests and the occupational needs that can be met from these jobs.

16.59 Demonstrate Knowledge of Occupational Strengths and Weaknesses

Use of extensive vocational assessment techniques can help students with special learning and/or behavior needs understand their vocational potentials and specific aptitudes. Before formalized vocational assessment, students with special learning and/or behavior needs will have had some indication of job areas that they are able to learn and perform successfully. Aptitudes or abilities in the following areas should be ascertained: verbal, numerical, spatial, form perception, clerical, motor coordination, finger dexterity, manual dexterity, and mechanical. The General Aptitude Test Battery (GATB) of the U.S. Employment Service is one instrument for identifying the strengths and weaknesses of some students with special learning and/or behavior needs. For others, work sample batteries can be particularly beneficial and provide a better indication of aptitudes than standardized test batteries such as the GATB, which some claim to be discriminating toward minorities relative to its cutoff scores. A substantial number of vocational assessment systems are new on the market and will be discussed in greater detail in the occupational guidance techniques section. Another objective associated with this subcompetency should be to help the student with special learning and/or behavior needs identify ways of developing needed aptitudes for occupational interests.

16.60 Identify Possible and Available Matching Interests and Strengths

Students should learn very early that many personal needs and values can be met by work and that work can become a personally meaningful part of their lives. At the same time, they must also learn that some personal needs and values may have to be gratified through leisure activities and other pursuits. One of the teacher's major goals should be to help students with special learning and/or behavior needs identify and choose a personally meaningful set of work values that fosters their desire to become productive members of society. Values such as a sense of fulfillment, self-sufficiency, personal worth, positive self-concept, success, self-support, acceptance by others, satisfying social relationships, independence, and monetary gratification are examples of needs that students can meet through working. Community-based experiences and classroom visits can give elementary students with special learning and/or behavior needs an opportunity to interact with various types of employed people and can expose them to ways in which these workers meet personal needs and develop values. Students with special learning and/or behavior needs can begin to identify the kind of personal values they presently possess and can visualize how to meet their needs through work.

Group discussions can give students with special learning and/or behavior needs an opportunity to hear how others arrive at their decisions. Parents can discuss the positive aspects of their jobs as well as ways in which they would like to change their jobs (e.g., more responsibility, variety, and physical activity). They should explain how they meet these missing values and needs in their nonoccupational time. Secondary-level students with special learning and/or

behavior needs who are on job sites and former students who are employed can also discuss many features of their jobs. Adult learners can identify what personal values they met and didn't meet while working at various jobs. Other functional objectives related to this subcompetency are helping students with special learning and/or behavior needs recognize the importance of work for economic functioning and building self-esteem.

As students with special learning and/or behavior needs acquire the personal-social skills of self-awareness, self-confidence, socially responsible behavior, interpersonal skills, independence, and problem-solving, they should be ready to identify those major occupational needs that are presently part of their work personality. They should be able to determine whether needs such as high pay, independence, achievement, praise, responsibility, authority, use of talents and abilities, advancement, security, social service, variety, and social status are of major importance in their future work life. Group discussions on the topic, supplemented with presentations given by persons working in various occupations, should be provided so that students with special learning and/or behavior needs can make these decisions and other choices related to an appropriate work environment (e.g., outdoor vs. indoor work, sedentary vs. active, urban vs. rural settings). These discussions can serve as a basis for lively and soul-searching inquiry. Teachers can also attempt to have students with special learning and/or behavior needs identify the occupational needs that persons in occupations they are interested in tend to have.

16.61 Plan and Make Realistic Occupational Training and Job Placement Decisions

Experiences from the previous subcompetency will help students with special learning and/or behavior needs discover many jobs that really do not meet their occupational needs, interests, or aptitudes. For those jobs that do, a second level of decisions needs to be made relative to jobs of highest preference. The demand for the occupation, required education and training, and other factors are significant at this level. Students with special learning and/or behavior needs should learn the career ladder that the occupation offers and occupations for which they might qualify. These tentative personalized occupational choices should be based on an analysis of the whole person and should be systematically determined primarily by the students with special learning and/or behavior needs and their parents, employers, and school personnel. Professional guidance and counseling are important for this subcompetency. Another functional objective that should be attempted is for the individual to be able to identify specific work sites where the job of choice is available and to try out the job.

Value Yourself

The third component, value yourself, is an important ability in setting personalized goals. This internal factor includes the following skills: being able to value and accept self; admire your strengths that are from your uniqueness; recognize and respect rights and responsibilities; and take care of yourself. In elementary school, teachers can help students with special learning and/or behavior needs gain an awareness of these skills in classroom discussions. Family members should also be encouraged to discuss these skills in all ecological environments with their family member with special learning and/or behavior needs. Many schools are now teaching students with special learning and/or behavior needs to direct or have more involvement in the IEP/ITP process.

The following LCCE Mild Curriculum competencies/subcompetencies are related to this third component of Field and Hoffman's self-determination model.

3.12 Demonstrate Knowledge of Physical Fitness, Nutrition, and Weight

Development of the Special Olympics was motivated by the fact that individuals with mental retardation had received little or no instruction in physical education or recreation in public schools and institutions. The Special Olympics help underscore that all individuals possess physical competence. Proper care and development of the body are vital to meet the physical demands of everyday life. Students with special learning and/or behavior needs should demonstrate knowledge of major body parts and perform exercises or activities that benefit development. As students with special learning and/or behavior needs develop a fundamental knowledge of basic food groups, nutrition, and weight control, teachers should enlist the cooperation of physical education, recreation, and home economics professionals. Students with special learning and/or behavior needs can maintain their own health charts by recording maturation, eating habits, or games and exercises. Other functional objectives include performing activities that maintain appropriate physical fitness and demonstrating eating practices that contribute to proper nutrition.

3.13 Exhibit Proper Grooming and Hygiene

Students with special learning and/or behavior needs should demonstrate the ability to brush their teeth; wash their hands and face; use handkerchiefs, towels, and napkins; and maintain a clean appearance. Teachers from intermediate grades through adult education should continue to help students with special learning and/or behavior needs develop these abilities and expand their awareness of personal hygiene and grooming habits that are appropriate for males and females. This is one of the most vital LCCE Mild Curriculum subcompetencies because acceptance of an individual by peers, adults, and employers is usually based on personal appearance. Another functional objective should include demonstrating the use of appropriate health and grooming aids.

3.15 Demonstrate Knowledge of Common Illness Prevention and Treatment

Demonstrating knowledge of illness prevention and treatment methods is one of the most complex LCCE Mild Curriculum subcompetencies. This area includes information about illnesses and basic symptoms, hazards to health that occur in the home, basic first-aid techniques, and obtaining assistance for various medical problems. The lessons on illness will be significant to individuals who must guard against dangers in the environment that can complicate a primary disability, for example, respiratory infections for the physically disabled, or an inflamed eyelid for the deaf. Students with special learning and/or behavior needs in the primary grades should begin learning basic health measures that will prevent illnesses or injury. The students with special learning and/or behavior needs' experiences will provide ample subject matter, and the instructor should provide numerous practice sessions requiring students to contact emergency facilities in the event of illness or injury. The range of subject matter increases as instruction includes first aid, safety considerations, health facilities, and professionals. Local public health facilities or agents can provide demonstrations and audiovisual aids to assist instruction in these competencies.

3.16 Practice Personal Safety

Functional objectives for the subcompetency of practicing personal safety focus on home security, personal assault, and self-defense techniques. This functional skill area has become extremely important with the rising violence and crime in our society. The involvement of parents, law enforcement officials, self-defense specialists, and community services such as gas and electric companies can help students with special learning and/or behavior needs learn safety precautions and potential hazards. Role-play activities will enhance this instruction, which should begin at the elementary level.

7.29 Demonstrate Knowledge of Civil Rights and Responsibilities

Subcompetency 7.29 includes knowledge of the individual's rights when being questioned by officers of the law and knowledge of sources of legal assistance that can be used to help individuals answer the questions. Teachers cannot help students with special learning and/or behavior needs develop this combination of skills very easily. Students with spe-

cial learning and/or behavior needs should role play situations in which they are confronted by officers. Law enforcement officials or members of legal aid associations may also give classroom presentations that concern violations and citizen responses during interrogation. Students should register for selective service classification at age 18. In some instances, the military may be a possible occupational choice. Another functional objective should be identifying information required for registration with the selective service.

7.32 Demonstrate Knowledge of Citizen Rights and Responsibilities

The reasons for voting should be emphasized throughout the elementary years. Many secondary students who have the opportunity to register and vote will enroll in training programs. This situation provides teachers with a chance to use practical lesson plans based on student experiences with the process of registering and voting. Other functional objectives should be identifying the dates, issues, and offices to be decided in coming elections and soliciting sources of information to speak to the class.

11.46 Express Feelings of Self-Worth

Individuals begin to feel worthy when they experience expressions of value from parents, teachers, and friends. These declarations of worth may be difficult for the person with special learning and/or behavior needs to formulate. In our society, an individual's perceived worth is based on comparison to other people. Comparative statements are common in a culture that rewards individuals who demonstrate the drive to excel. The problem is that "doing better" is often determined in comparison to someone else. Individuals with special learning and/or behavior needs can find themselves at a serious disadvantage if their abilities are always placed in some type of "better than the other person" derby. If the individual with special learning and/or behavior needs loses the race, he might perceive himself as being inferior to others, which in turn may cause him to lose his sense of self-worth. The parent's and teacher's ability to work with the assets an individual with special learning and/or behavior needs has at his disposal is the key to this potential dilemma. They must move away from "you versus them" situations to "I can do" experiences. By emphasizing the "I can," the parent and teacher opinions change, with a corresponding influence on the attitudes and values of the individual. "I can" is a positive statement of value and worth in this society. How many times have we heard stories about individuals who were told they would never walk, run, or dance only to accomplish that very thing and more? The emergence and success of such events as the Special Olympics and Wheelchair Games illustrate that individuals with disabilities have a strong desire to demonstrate their worth through physical accomplishments regardless of how long it may take them to run a certain distance. Teachers and parents should provide opportunities in which students with special learning and/or behavior needs express how they feel about themselves in relationship to their accomplishments, successes, and failures. What experiences cause students to feel good, worthy, or pleased with their accomplishments? What experiences frustrate them? These expressions provide professionals with an opportunity to plan subsequent activities that will increase the quality and quantity of success experiences. Another functional objective should be identifying ways in which other people affect an individual's feelings of worth.

11.47 Describe Others' Perception of Self

Students with special learning and/or behavior needs should be able to describe overt expressions and subtle hints made by other people. Because most people are more sensitive to communications relative to themselves, they are more apt to interject their own interpretations onto the behavior of another person. The individual with a health or physical impairment encounters a particularly puzzling situation when she wonders whether a person is reacting to her personality or to the particular disability. If someone does not invite her to another party, was it because

she did not conduct herself properly, or was it due to her prosthesis? She may never get the answer, and repeated instances of these nebulous situations damage the individual's self-confidence. What others think of us influences our attitudes toward the self. These attitudes are used as a basis for further judgments. Parents and teachers cannot control the attitudes of other people—in some cases, their own attitudes may be enough of a challenge. But they can instruct the student with special learning and/or behavior needs to observe another person's overt and subtle responses that reflect either positive or negative attitudes. Many of the lessons on communication (refer to competency 16) should include such reactions that convey attitudes of pity, disgust, condescension, and the like. The lessons should, however, emphasize positive reactions that reflect the individual's self-respect. She must guard against reactions that would be interpreted by other members of society as justification for their folly. Another functional objective should be constructing personal views of others toward her.

12.54 Know Character Traits

Students with special learning and/or behavior needs should be familiar with those personality factors that generally allow them to participate in a group situation that results in a positive attitude of others. What are some of these positive traits? Cooperation, cheerfulness, and dependability form a solid foundation and are also considered necessary in employment situations. There are other traits, but each individual with special learning and/or behavior needs must discover them. This is where experience and observation of others are important factors in helping individuals to change. The ability to look at oneself with a critical eye is not reserved for those with advanced degrees; it comes from practice, with encouragement, at home and in the classroom. Teachers can help students with special learning and/or behavior needs build their observational skills by assigning projects in which students with special learning and/or behavior needs interview or consider someone of their choice and list outstanding characteristics. Once the characteristics are defined, teachers can translate them into behaviors students with special learning and/or behavior needs should attempt. Together, students with special learning and/or behavior needs and teachers should work on a plan of practicing and reporting the behaviors. For students who experience problems in performing acceptable behaviors, the teacher may structure a system in which there is a conscious effort to modify the behavior toward prearranged objectives. Another functional objective should be identifying character traits that inhibit acceptance.

12.55 Recognize Personal Roles

Several roles are identified across competency areas. Some of these roles are employee, citizen, parent, relative, and friend. Students with special learning and/or behavior needs should be able to describe and demonstrate responsible behavior to individuals (employer, parent, child) as well as groups (union, passengers, clubs) identified with a specific role. This LCCE Mild Curriculum subcompetency requires students with special learning and/or behavior needs to be actively involved in each role so they can realize its full meaning. For example, a student with special learning and/or behavior needs may be a member of a family by birth, but not in practice. Parents should involve their children in as many family activities and decisions as possible, especially if the student with special learning and/or behavior needs has chosen a future role as parent and spouse. Teachers should place students with special learning and/or behavior needs in situations that provide understanding of the expectations of others for a particular role. For example, community personnel such as police officers, fire fighters, and employers should discuss their expectations of student behaviors and responsibilities in the roles of citizen and employee. Another functional objective should be identifying all possible future roles.

The following LCCE Moderate Curriculum competencies/subcompetencies are related to this third component of Field and Hoffman's self-determination model.

3.12 Maintain Physical Fitness

Development of the Special Olympics was motivated by the fact that individuals with mental retardation had received little or no instruction in physical education or recreation in public schools and institutions. The Special Olympics help to underscore that all individuals possess physical competence. Proper care and development of the body are vital to meet the physical demands of everyday life. Students with special learning and/or behavior needs should demonstrate knowledge of major body parts and perform exercises or activities that benefit development. As students with special learning and/or behavior needs develop fundamental knowledge of basic food groups, nutrition, and weight control, teachers should enlist cooperation of physical education, recreation, and home economics professionals. Students with special learning and/or behavior needs can maintain their own health charts by recording maturation, eating habits, or games and exercises. Another functional objective is performing activities that maintain appropriate physical fitness daily.

3.13 Recognize and Seek Help for Illness

Demonstrating knowledge of illness prevention and treatment methods is one of the most complex subcompetencies. This area includes information about illnesses and basic symptoms, hazards to health that occur in the home, basic first-aid techniques, and obtaining assistance for various medical problems. The lessons on illness will be significant to individuals who must guard against dangers in the environment that can complicate a primary disability, for example, respiratory infections for the physically disabled, or an inflamed eyelid for individuals who are deaf. Students with special learning and/or behavior needs in the primary grades should begin learning basic health measures that will prevent illnesses or injury. The students with special learning and/or behavior needs' experiences will provide ample subject matter, and the instructor should provide numerous practice sessions requiring students to contact emergency facilities in the event of illness or injury. The range of subject matter increases as instruction includes first aid, safety considerations, health facilities, and professionals. Local public health facilities or agents can provide demonstrations and audiovisual aids to assist instruction in these competencies.

3.14 Practice Basic First Aid

All adults with special learning and/or behavior needs will need to know how to perform basic first aid procedures. Examples include cleaning cuts and abrasions and applying appropriate dressings. Elementary students should discuss emergency situations and how to contact emergency assistance. Secondary-level students should demonstrate how to follow emergency procedures. Another functional objective is seeking emergency assistance when needed.

3.15 Practice Personal Safety

Functional objectives for the subcompetency of practicing personal safety focus on home security, personal assault, and self-defense techniques. This functional skill area has become extremely important with the rising violence and crime in our society. The involvement of parents, law enforcement officials, self-defense specialists, and community services such as gas and electric companies can help students with special learning and/or behavior needs learn safety precautions and potential hazards. Role-play activities will enhance this instruction, which should begin at the elementary level. Another functional objective is understanding and practicing precautions when dealing with strangers.

9.35 Display Self-Confidence and Self-Worth

See pages 259–260 for a description of this competency/subcompetency.

10.39 Demonstrate Respect for Others' Rights and Property

Developing respect for the rights and properties of others involves one of the fundamental concerns on which this country was founded. It is a continuous subject of interest in television, radio, and newspaper reports and, therefore, offers ample opportunity for teachers and parents to pinpoint the reasons for respecting the rights of others and their possessions. Parents are the initial vital link in this competency. They are the ones who have to teach children to differentiate between what belongs to them and what belongs to someone else. Teachers reinforce these basic lessons as instances of ownership that will, no doubt, occur in the classroom. Respecting the rights of others becomes more complicated as individuals grow older and begin to exert their own opinions and power in taking command of possessions. This requires teachers to initiate lessons and draw on the student's experiences that emphasize the relationships of laws, ownership, and the protection of the community.

10.40 Demonstrate Respect for Authority

All adults are confronted with authority figures often. Students with special learning and/or behavior needs should know the role of the authority figure and demonstrate the appropriate respect. Another functional objective is to know the consequences of not respecting authority figures.

Plan

The fourth component, plan, is an important ability in setting personalized goals. This internal factor includes the following skills: set goals, plan actions to meet goals, anticipate results, be creative, and visually rehearse. In elementary school, teachers can help students with special learning and/or behavior needs to gain an awareness of these skills in classroom discussions. Family members also should be encouraged to discuss these skills in all ecological environments with their family member with special learning and/or behavior needs. Many schools are now teaching students with special learning and/or behavior needs to direct or have more involvement in the IEP/ITP process. The "young adult projection" is an example of how these skills can be facilitated in the IEP/ITP meeting. Young adult projections permit the students with special learning and/or behavior needs to dream and visualize what they want as their quality of life as young adults in the adult functioning areas of post-secondary education, working, and community living. This process should occur with the support of the IEP/ITP team at each year's IEP/ITP meeting. Students can prepare for the young adult projection discussion by developing a pictorial map, drawing, or creating a collage of their future career roles and quality of life. Secondary students with special learning and behavior needs' functional transitional evaluation results can be shared in helping to create appropriate personalized transition plans.

The following LCCE Mild Curriculum competencies/subcompetencies are related to this fourth component of Field and Hoffman's self-determination model.

15.63 Anticipate Consequences

Anticipating the consequences of a decision is the most difficult component to examine in the problem-solving process and the most neglected component of the process. How can students with special learning and/or behavior needs examine what is only anticipated? At this point, observation and inquiry will be of greatest assistance to students with special learning and/or behavior needs. Although students with special learning and/or behavior needs may have had little, if any, experience with potential consequences of a course of action, they may ask others how they handled a similar problem and what the consequences were. Everyone makes everyday decisions, and the consequences can be used as guides for those who are first examining similar problems and alternatives.

15.64 Develop and Evaluate Alternatives

At first glance, a problem may appear to have only one or two possible solutions. Students with special learning and/or behavior needs obviously limit the range of alternatives if they accept the visible solutions. Exercises related to differentiation of bipolar concepts expose students with special learning and/or behavior needs to the possibility that other solutions or positions can be used to solve problems, and that they must search for alternatives. The deep attraction of fictional mysteries, whether Sherlock Holmes or Nancy Drew, is that the characters refuse to accept answers that are easily available and seek other solutions to the puzzle. This principle should be applied to human relationships. Students with special learning and/or behavior needs should demonstrate the ability to seek information and examine alternatives involved in individual and group relationships.

The following LCCE Mild Curriculum lesson plan addresses subcompetency 15.64 relative to developing alternatives for personal goal planning. The lesson plan is a career preparation level of instruction and spans all career roles. Family involvement in the lesson is encouraged. The worksheets are not included for the illustration.

Lesson Plan 6

LCCE Objective 15.64.2   List possible alternatives with respect to a personal goal.

Lesson Objective: Student will develop alternatives to personal goals in different areas of life.

Instructional Resources: Worksheets **Personal Goal Alternatives**, **Goals Flowchart**, Home Worksheet **Personal Goals at Home**, Worksheet **Your Goal Flowchart**.

Lesson Introduction: How many of you would start off on a trip without knowing what your goal is—where you're headed? It's the same in your personal life. With a goal you know where you're headed. But you may find that you can't reach your goal. Maybe you need more time—or maybe it's no longer important to you. Sometimes you need to develop a "Plan B" alternative goal.

School Activity:

Task:
1. Suggest these six areas in which people may have personal goals:
   - money (financial)
   - people (social)
   - body (physical)
   - school (educational)
   - worship (spiritual)
   - job (vocational)
2. Clarify concept of "Plan B" alternatives—a backup plan, in case the original plan is not attainable.
   - What might make a plan unattainable? Examples include: not enough time; goal might not be appropriate to the individual; circumstances change.
   - Distribute and complete Worksheet **Personal Goal Alternatives** together as a class exercise.
3. Divide the class into small groups of three to four students and distribute Worksheet **Goals Flowchart**.
   - Students complete the worksheet including "Plan B" alternatives for both Barry and Alice.
   - "Plan B" alternatives can include any other choices within the designated career roles.
   - Emphasize that it's okay to change goals; this does not imply failure, only growth.
   - Discuss the worksheet with class, reviewing each group's "Plan B" alternatives for Barry and Alice.
4. Distribute and explain Home Worksheet **Personal Goals at Home**.

Home/School Activity:

Task:
1. Each student asks a parent or another adult to assist him or her in completing **Personal Goals at Home**, identifying "Plan B" alternatives.
2. Lead a class discussion of each student's goals and alternatives as they are listed on the home worksheet.
   - Emphasize that some decisions provide more options or flexibility than others. They could lead in two or more ways—for example, deciding to graduate from high school could allow you to get a good job or go to college. Dropping out would limit your possible options. Relate to students' personal goals.
   - Explain the fact that not to make a choice is really to decide—for example, if you don't decide to have anything for lunch, you really are deciding to eat nothing. Relate to students' choices.
3. Illustrate goal attainment with flowchart. Distribute Worksheet **Your Goal Flowchart** and explain example.
   - Students create their own goal flowchart, identifying a personal goal and "Plan B" alternatives in any career role.
   - Students who finish quickly may help those who have difficulty with this.

Lesson Plan Evaluation:

Activity: Students complete Worksheet **Your Goal Flowchart**.
Criteria: Student will complete worksheet with six out of eight appropriate steps.
Career Role: Family Member/Homemaker, Employee, Citizen/Volunteer, Avocational
Career Stage: Preparation

Note. From *Life Centered Career Education Competency Units for Personal-Social Skills* (pp. 1015-1016) by D. E. Brolin, 1992, Arlington: VA: The Council for Exceptional Children. Copyright 1992 by The Council for Exceptional Children. Reprinted by permission.

15.65 Recognize the Nature of a Problem

Bipolar concepts include such examples as good and evil, positive and negative, pro and con. These terms are often used in reference to issues and relationships. However, more often than not, problems and relationships do not fall into such a neat dichotomy. There may be several solutions to a problem or positions on an issue. The favored solutions are of greatest advantage to the individual and her set of values. Students with special learning and/or behavior needs should demonstrate the ability to identify the extreme positions within a problem area, search for many solutions, and place each alternative on a progression. In using a methodology that includes this ordering of possible solutions, alternatives, or approaches, students can identify several ingredients that are intrinsic to the problem. Another functional objective should be examining various positions relative to a group's interpretation of ideas, feelings, and behaviors.

15.66 Develop Goal-Seeking Behavior

Behavior leading to the accomplishment of a goal is one of the most powerful ingredients to the success of people with special learning and/or behavior needs. Indeed, the successful individual who obtains a goal despite an inconvenience is often used as a role model for others who have disabilities. To replicate those successes, students with special learning and/or behavior needs should be able to identify goals and execute the appropriate behavior that will help them reach defined functional objectives. Teachers should discriminate between short- and long-term, realistic and unrealistic goals. Students with special learning and/or behavior needs should practice the organization of goals, outline behaviors they will need to reach those goals, practice the behaviors, and evaluate the results. Other functional objectives should include identifying potential barriers to goals and identifying resources that can help students to achieve their goals.

The following LCCE Moderate Curriculum competency/subcompetency is related to this

fourth component of Field and Hoffman's self-determination model.

12.46 Set and Reach Personal Goals

Behavior leading to the accomplishment of a goal is one of the most powerful ingredients to the success of people with special learning and/or behavior needs. Indeed, the successful individual who obtains a goal despite an inconvenience is often used as a role model for others who have disabilities. To replicate those successes, students with special learning and/or behavior needs should be able to identify goals and execute the appropriate behavior that will help them reach defined functional objectives. Teachers should discriminate between short- and long-term, realistic and unrealistic goals. Students with special learning and/or behavior needs should practice the organization of goals, outline behaviors they will need to reach those goals, practice the behaviors, and evaluate the results. Other functional objectives should include identifying potential barriers to goals and identifying resources that can help students to achieve their goals.

Act

The fifth component, act, is an important ability in meeting personalized goals. This internal factor includes the following skills: take risks; communicate; access resources and support, negotiate, and deal with conflict and criticism; and be persistent. In elementary school, teachers can help students with special learning and/or behavior needs gain an awareness of these skills in classroom discussions. Family members should also be encouraged to discuss these skills in all ecological environments with their family member with special learning and/or behavior needs. Many schools are now teaching students with special learning and/or behavior needs to direct or have more involvement in the IEP/ITP process. The "young adult projection" is an example of how these skills can be facilitated in the IEP/ITP meeting. Young adult projections permit the student with special learning and/or behavior needs to set and meet goals as to what they want as their quality of life as young adults in the adult functioning areas of postsecondary education, working, and community living. This process should occur with the support of the IEP/ITP team at each year's IEP/ITP meeting. Students can prepare for the young adult projection discussion by developing a pictorial map, drawing, or creating a collage of their future career roles and quality of life. Secondary students with special learning and/or behavior needs' functional transitional evaluation results can be shared in helping create appropriate personalized transition plans.

The following LCCE Mild Curriculum competencies/subcompetencies are related to this fifth component of Field and Hoffman's self-determination model.

15.62 Locate and Utilize Sources of Assistance

Throughout the discussions on the LCCE Mild Curriculum subcompetencies, teachers and parents have been reminded that students with special learning and/or behavior needs should identify the resources in their communities that can provide assistance in personal and family decision making. These resources should be experts in their given subject content area, have experience in advising members of the community, and should be able to subdivide the decision-making process for their given subject content area into sequential parts. Students with special learning and/or behavior needs should learn under what circumstances resources should be used and what potential outcomes will result.

15.63 Anticipatie Consequences

See page 267 for a description of this competency/subcompetency.

15.64 Develop and Evaluate Alternatives

See page 267 for a description of this competency/subcompetency.

15.65 Recognize the Nature of a Problem

See page 269 for a description of this competency/subcompetency.

16.68 Communicate with Understanding

In a society that places value on verbal skills (singing, acting, political oratory, salesmanship), the individual who has speech disabilities or problems speaking fluently is at a disadvantage. Individuals with speech problems experience many frustrations in their everyday dealings with other members of society. Even competent persons have occasional bad days when they mispronounce the boss's name, flounder among sentences in an interview, or are tongue-tied when meeting a prospective date. Teachers, parents, counselors, and therapists have a formidable task in preparing students to demonstrate proficiency in basic language skills, skill in regulating the loudness of voice according to the social setting, ability to participate in conversation, and verbal expression of emotion, information, and inquiry.

16.69 Know Subtleties of Communication

Teachers should explore the area of what is meant in communication in contrast to what is said, signed, or written. In other words, we live in a world of intention. Students with special learning and/or behavior needs should realize that sometimes people disguise their messages to protect themselves. They may say or imply things so they cannot be held accountable. Schoolchildren soon learn that they can only be held accountable for what they say (or do). They realize that communication can occur through many channels and can operate at both the overt and covert levels. Commercials can be, perhaps, the biggest and most accessible source of lessons. Numerous advertisements on radio and television and in print use nonverbal components—the subtleties—of communication to convey messages other than what is stated or pictured. Students with special learning and/or behavior needs should be able to distinguish between the verbal and nonverbal messages so that they can improve their communication skills. They should be aware of those instances when they are producing dual messages (i.e., one level of acknowledged symbols and another one of intended meaning). Another functional objective should be practicing verbal and nonverbal forms of communication that are congruent with an individual's feelings.

The following LCCE Moderate Curriculum competencies/subcompetencies are related to this fifth component of Field and Hoffman's self-determination model.

12.48 Demonstrate Self-Determinaton

Students with special learning and/or behavior needs should be familiar with those personality factors that generally allow them to participate in individual and group situations enabling them to request their wants and needs. What are some of these positive traits? Confidence, knowledge of interests, and communication skills form a solid foundation for engaging in self-determination, which is also considered necessary in employment situations. There are other traits, but each individual with special learning and/or behavior needs must discover them. This is where experience and observation of others are important factors in helping individuals to change. The ability to look at oneself with a critical eye is not reserved for those with advanced degrees; it comes from practice, with encouragement, at home and in the classroom. Teachers can help students with special learning and/or behavior needs build their observational skills by assigning projects in which the students make lists of their basic wants, desires, and needs to help in making personalized decisions. Together, students with special learning and/or behavior needs and teachers should practice self-determination. For students who experience problems in performing this acceptable behavior, the teacher may structure a system in which there is a conscious effort to modify the behavior toward prearranged objectives.

13.49 Identify Problems/Conflicts

Bipolar concepts include such examples as good and evil, positive and negative, pro and con. These terms are often used in reference to issues and relationships. However, more often than not, problems and rela-

tionships do not fall into such a neat dichotomy. There may be several solutions to a problem or positions on an issue. The favored solutions are of greatest advantage to the individual and her set of values. Students with special learning and/or behavior needs should demonstrate the ability to identify the extreme positions within a problem area, search for many solutions, and place each alternative on a progression. In using a methodology that includes this ordering of possible solutions, alternatives, or approaches, students can identify several ingredients that are intrinsic to the problem. Another functional objective should be examining various positions relative to a group's interpretation of ideas, feelings, and behaviors.

13.50 Use Appropriate Resources to Assist in Problem Solving

Throughout the discussions on the LCCE Moderate Curriculum subcompetencies, teachers and parents have been reminded that students with special learning and/or behavior needs should identify the resources in their communities that can provide assistance in personal and family decision making. These resources should be experts in their given subject content area, have experience in advising members of the community, and should be able to subdivide the decision-making process for their given subject content area into sequential parts. Students with special learning and/or behavior needs should learn under what circumstances resources should be used and what potential outcomes will result.

13.51 Develop and Select Best Solution to Problems/Conflicts

At first glance, a problem may appear to have only one or two possible solutions. Students with special learning and/or behavior needs obviously limit the range of alternatives if they accept the visible solutions. Exercises related to differentiation of bipolar concepts expose students with special learning and/or behavior needs to the possibility that other solutions or positions can be used to solve problems, and that they must search for alternatives. The deep attraction of fictional mysteries, whether Sherlock Holmes or Nancy Drew, is that the characters refuse to accept answers that are easily available and seek other solutions to the puzzle. This principle should be applied to human relationships. Students with special learning and/or behavior needs should demonstrate ability to seek information and examine alternatives involved in individual and group relationships.

13.52 Demonstrate Decision Making

Anticipating the consequences is a critical activity in making decisions and is sometimes the most neglected component of the process. How can students with special learning and/or behavior needs examine what is only anticipated? At this point, observation and inquiry will be of the greatest assistance to students with special learning and/or behavior needs. Although students with special learning and/or behavior needs may have had little, if any, experience with potential consequences of a course of action, they may ask others how they handled a similar problem and what the consequences were. Everyone makes everyday decisions, and the consequences can be used as guides for those who are first examining similar problems and alternatives.

14.53 Demonstrate Listening and Responding Skills

Communication depends on the correct interchange of ideas or objects between people. Computers can be programmed to exchange information, but people depend on the meaning and implications of the message. They accomplish this by attending to the source of the message as well as to other nonverbal clues that may accompany it. The teacher should develop several abilities so students can complete this competency. Students with special learning and/or behavior needs should be able to attend to the message by using all available senses; develop adequate means of response, such as speaking, signing, communication board, or typing; determine the appropriate meaning of the message (verbal or nonverbal); and determine the correct manner of response. Another objective should be identifying negative aspects of listening and responding inappropriately.

14.54 Demonstrate Effective Communication

In a society that places value on verbal skills (singing, acting, political oratory, salesmanship), the individual who has speech disabilities or problems speaking fluently is at a disadvantage. Individuals with speech problems experience many frustrations in their everyday dealings with other members of society. Even competent persons have occasional bad days when they mispronounce the boss's name, flounder among sentences in an interview, or are tongue-tied when meeting a prospective date. Teachers, parents, counselors, and therapists have a formidable task in preparing students to demonstrate proficiency in basic language skills, skill in regulating the loudness of voice according to the social setting, ability to participate in conversation, and verbal expression of emotion, information, and inquiry.

Teachers should explore the area of what is meant in communication in contrast to what is said, signed, or written. In other words, we live in a world of intention. Students with special learning and/or behavior needs should realize that sometimes people disguise their messages to protect themselves. They may say or imply things so they cannot be held accountable. Schoolchildren soon learn that they can only be held accountable for what they say (or do). They realize that communication can occur through many channels and can operate at both the overt and covert levels. Commercials can be, perhaps, the biggest and most accessible source of lessons. Numerous advertisements on radio and television and in print use nonverbal components—the subtleties—of communication to convey messages other than what is stated or pictured. Students with special learning and/or behavior needs should be able to distinguish between the verbal and nonverbal messages so that they can improve their communication skills. They should be aware of those instances when they are producing dual messages (i.e., one level of acknowledged symbols and another one of intended meaning). Another functional objective should be practicing verbal and nonverbal forms of communication that are congruent with an individual's feelings.

Experience Outcomes and Learn

The final component, experience outcomes and learn, is an important ability in meeting personalized goals, not meeting personalized goals, and revising personalized goals. This internal factor includes the following skills: compare outcome to expected performance, realize success, and make adjustments. In elementary school, teachers can help students with special learning and/or behavior needs gain an awareness of these skills in classroom discussions. Family members should also be encouraged to discuss these skills in all ecological environments with their family member with special learning and/or behavior needs. Many schools are now teaching students with special learning and/or behavior needs to direct or have more involvement in the IEP/ITP process. The "young adult projection" is an example of how these skills can be facilitated in the IEP/ITP meeting. Young adult projections permit the students with special learning and/or behavior needs to set goals, meet goals, not meet some goals, and revise goals as to what they want as their quality of life as young adults in the adult functioning areas of postsecondary education, working, and community living. This process should occur with the support of the IEP/ITP team at each year's IEP/ITP meeting. Students can prepare for the young adult projection discussion by developing a pictorial map, drawing, or creating a collage of their future career roles and quality of life. Secondary students with special learning and behavior needs' functional transitional evaluation results can be shared in helping to create appropriate personalized transition plans.

The following LCCE Mild Curriculum competencies/subcompetencies are related to this final component of Field and Hoffman's self-determination model.

15.64 Develop and Evaluate Alternatives

See page 267 for a description of this competency/subcompetency.

20.93 Know How to Adjust to Changes in Employment

Most people change jobs about four or five times during their working career. Some people lose their jobs for various employment and nonemployment reasons. Others are promoted or find better positions. Students with special learning and/or behavior needs need to learn the factors that determine successful and unsuccessful job adjustment and how to deal with them. Another important objective of this unit of study is to know how to recognize and apply for promotional opportunities. The following career preparation lesson plan is designed to help students with special learning and/or behavior needs know how to appropriately resign from a job.

Lesson Plan 5

LCCE Objective 20.93.4 Identify factors that lead to termination of employment.

Lesson Objective: Student will demonstrate the procedures to follow when leaving a job.

Instructional Resources: Worksheet **Quitting a Job**, Home Worksheet **Letter of Resignation**, Fact Sheet **Writing an Appropriate Letter**.

Lesson Introduction: Something happens on the job that upsets you. You say to yourself, "That's it. I quit." Have you just given yourself a bigger problem? Today, we will talk about what is involved in leaving a job.

School Activity: **Time: 2 sessions**
1. Students discuss reasons for quitting a job, for example:
   - found a better job (economic reasons)
   - family/spouse relocation

- career interest changes
- same work all the time
- poor working conditions
- disagreeable supervisor

2. Small groups develop acceptable procedures (guidelines) to follow when quitting a job. Have the groups list their guidelines on the board.
3. Students review the rules on Worksheet **Quitting a Job** and answer the questions. Have them discuss responses when finished.
4. Students study Fact Sheet **Writing an Appropriate Letter** and identify the parts of a letter of resignation.
5. Explain the home activity to the students. Have them take Home Worksheet **Writing a Letter of Resignation** with them.

Home/School Activity: **Time: 2 sessions**

Task:
1. Students complete the worksheet at home. Have them select an employer and job for the letter.
2. Students ask a parent and/or friends about procedures they followed when resigning from a job.
3. Students discuss in pairs their letters of resignation. Students discuss in class what their parents and/or friends said about leaving a job.

Lesson Plan Evaluation:
Activity: Students will complete Worksheet **Quitting a Job** and Home Worksheet **Letter of Resignation**.
Criteria: Students will complete Worksheet **Quitting a Job** with 80% accuracy and write a letter of resignation.
Career Role: Employee
Career Stage: Preparation

Note. From *Life Centered Career Education Competency Units for Occupational Guidance and Preparation* (Vol. 2, pp. 580–581) by R. T. Roessler and D. E. Brolin, 1992, Arlington, VA: The Council for Exceptional Children. Copyright 1992 by The Council for Exceptional Children. Reprinted by permission.

The following LCCE Moderate Curriculum competencies/subcompetencies are related to this final component of Field and Hoffman's self-determination model.

13.49 Identify Problems/Conflicts

See page 271 for a description of this competency/subcompetency.

13.50 Use Appropriate Resources to Assist in Problem Solving

See page 271 for a description of this competency/subcompetency.

13.51 Develop and Select Best Solution to Problems/Conflicts

See page 271 for a description of this competency/subcompetency.

13.52 Demonstrate Decision Making

See page 272 for a description of this competency/subcompetency.

17.65 Make Adjustments to Change in Employment Status

Most people change jobs about four or five times during their working career. Some people lose their jobs for various employment and nonemployment reasons. Others are promoted or find better positions. Students with special learning and/or behavior needs need to learn the factors that determine successful and unsuccessful job adjustment and how to deal with them. Another important objective of this unit of study is to know how to recognize and apply for promotional opportunities.

Summary

This was brief overview of this excellent self-determination model. People interested in gaining further information should contact the authors at the College of Education, Wayne State University, Detroit, Michigan.

We hope that the reader realizes that many excellent materials and methods have been developed to help implement this model. Although the LCCE

Mild/Moderate Curriculum program strongly integrates the concept of self-determination in all competencies and subcompetencies, the preceding are some of the most obvious subcompetencies where self-determination is evident. Currently, many instructional materials and models are available for additional information on teaching students with special learning and/or behavior needs self-determination skills.

The next section will discuss an additional self-determination approach as developed by Michael Wehmeyer.

WEHMEYER'S SELF-DETERMINATION MODEL

Another excellent conceptualization of a self-determination model (see Figure 10.2) was devel-

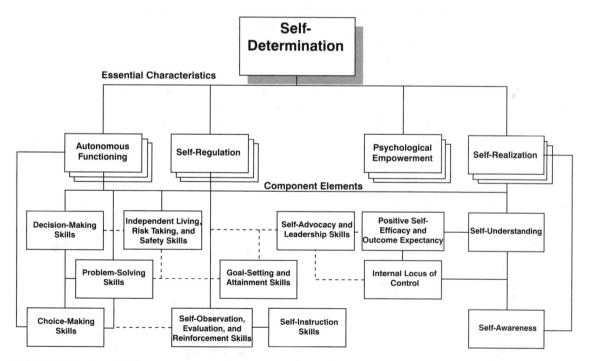

FIGURE 10.2   Essential Characteristics of Self-Determination and Their Component Elements. (———— = direct relationship; - - - = indirect relationship.)
Note. From Wehmeyer, M. L., Agran, M., & Hughes, C. (1998), *Teaching self-determination to students with disabilities: Basic skills for successful transition* (p. 8). Baltimore: Paul H. Brookes Publishing Co.; reprinted by permission.

oped by Wehmeyer (2001). He conceptualizes self-determination as:

> actions that identified by four essential characteristics: 1.) the person acted autonomously, 2.) the behavior(s) are self-regulated, 3.) the person initiated and responded to the event(s), and 4.) the person acted in a self-realizing manner. Self-determination emerges across the lifespan as children and adults learn skills, attitudes, and abilities necessary to act as the primary causal agent in one's life and to make choices and decisions regarding one's quality of life, free from undue external influence or interference. (p. 7)

Persons who are self-determined control their own lives and make their own decisions without the undue influence of others.

He notes that to be self-determined, students with special learning and/or behavior needs must believe they can control their outcomes, be effective people, know their strengths and needs, and build a positive self-concept and self-esteem. If this happens, they can become adults who can assume their own responsibility for choices and decisions, find their own jobs, and advocate for themselves.

According to Wehmeyer (1992), educational programs need to institute appropriate functional curricula, environments that encourage student choice and preferences, interactions with peers without disabilities, access to role models, experiences with success, and control in decision making. He notes that the limited research available on the subject has found that, in most instances, students with special learning and/or behavior needs are given too little opportunity to express preferences and make choices or take responsibility for their actions in the classroom. In addition, appropriate involvement of the student with special learning and/or behavior needs' family and community is critical. These components are similar to those that have been noted in this book as important for providing a comprehensive career education, functional skills effort.

> *"Self-determination leads to enhanced motivation and performance. Also, others note that a substantial number of experiments show that the opportunity to make direct decisions and therefore exercise control has been associated with an increased perception of psychological and emotional well-being."*
>
> (Browning, 1994, p. 94)

Students with special learning needs must learn the behaviors and skills needed to work and live independently in their communities. Thus, a curriculum must embody self-directed decision-making skills that include three important cognitive-behavioral decision-making skills: goal setting, social problem solving, and requesting assistance (Browning, 1994). According to Browning, our transitional programs fall short of instilling in their students enabling self-directing skills with which to choose, decide, and express interests and preferences regarding their own destiny. Such skills are sorely needed to enhance their ability to plan, manage, and direct their own lives and thus exert greater control over their own future (1994, p. 102).

The importance of giving more attention to the self-determination instructional needs of students should be more apparent by now. This area of need falls clearly within the personal-social curriculum area. An example of one curricular effort using LCCE Mild/Moderate Curriculum components to meet this need is described next.

Readers interested in learning more about Wehmeyer's self-determination model are referred to *Teaching Self-Determination to Students with Disabilities: Basic Skills for Successful Transition* by M. L. Wehmeyer, M. Agran, and C. Hughes (Baltimore, MD: Paul H. Brookes Publishing Company, 2001).

Wehmeyer's Self-Determination Model and the LCCE Mild/Moderate Curriculum

Drs. Sharon Davis and Michael Wehmeyer of the Arc (formerly, Association for Retarded Citizens, National

Headquarters) have developed a comprehensive self-determination curriculum based on several competencies and lesson plans from the personal-social curriculum area of the LCCE Mild Curriculum. Based on federal funding for the period 1990 to 1993, the Arc conducted an extensive literature review and discussions with and surveys of adults with mild cognitive disabilities to discern how well these individuals were able to make choices and decisions relative to their quality of life. The results were as expected; these individuals were quite limited in their ability to make such choices and decisions (Wehmeyer, 1992).

Based on the results of their study, the Arc staff reviewed various curricula that held promise for teaching self-determination skills to students with special learning and/or behavior needs. They then devised a core curriculum that would result in a framework for promoting self-determination. This core curriculum consists of four major domains:

1. Self-awareness
2. Self-confidence
3. Choice and autonomy
4. Goal attainment

For each domain area, a list of attitudes and abilities related to this outcome (self-determination) was identified. Project staff then selected the LCCE Mild/Moderate Curriculum as being most applicable to their framework and identified 4 LCCE competencies and 17 subcompetencies that matched the structure of the model. Table 10.1 presents the structure of the resulting model.

The approximately 350 LCCE lesson plans composing the 17 subcompetency areas were field tested by project staff with over 500 students (ages 14 to 20) labeled as having mental retardation or learning disabilities. The lesson plans were organized sequentially, beginning with instruction in the self-awareness area

TABLE 10.1   LCCE Competency and Subcompetency Areas Used to Promote Self-Determination

Model Domain	LCCE Competency	LCCE Subcompetency
Self-awareness	10. Achieving self-awareness	42. Identify physical and psychological needs
		43. Identify interests and abilities
		44. Identify emotions
		45. Demonstrate knowledge of physical self
		61. Awareness of how behavior affects others
Self-confidence	11. Acquiring self-confidence	46. Express feelings of self-worth
		47. Describe others' perception of self
		48. Accept and give praise
		49. Accept and give criticism
		50. Develop confidence in oneself
Choice and decision making	15. Making adequate decisions	62. Locate and use sources of assistance
		63. Anticipate consequences
		64. Develop and evaluate alternatives
Goal attainment	14. Achieving independence	59. Strive toward self-actualization
		60. Demonstrate self-organization
		65. Recognize nature of a problem
		66. Develop goal-seeking behavior

(competency 10), then moving to self-confidence instruction (competency 11), and then to the choice and decision making and goal setting later (competencies 14 and 15). The Arc staff found the LCCE materials to be a comprehensive treatment of self-determination and recommended students begin instruction by at least ages 12 to 14 in regular classrooms with same-age peers without disabilities whenever possible.

The self-determination curriculum is now available from the CEC as part of its total LCCE Mild/Moderate Curriculum package, including the Self-Determination Scale, described in Chapter 7.

CHAPTER COMMENTARY

It is widely recognized that possessing adequate self-determination skills is extremely important for all students in American schools, including those with special learning and/or behavior needs. Yet, Wehmeyer (2001) has indicated that very few students with special learning and/or behavior needs' IEP/ITPs examined included goals to promote self-determination.

With the lack of employment and community living success of adults with special learning and/or behavior needs, there is an immediate need to restructure curricula to provide more and better self-determination skills. Despite this obvious need, many teacher training institutions are not instructing our future teachers to infuse self-determination into all content area instruction.

Teaching the competencies in the LCCE Mild/Moderate Curriculum personal-social skills domain and self-determination skills will likely increase the probability that students with special learning and/or behavior needs will function more adequately in interpersonal relationships and problem-solving situations. These skills are needed for home, community, recreational, and employment settings. People who have a successful quality of life and satisfactory adult adjustment can acquire the LCCE Mild/Moderate Curriculum competencies outlined in this chapter related to self-determination instruction. An individual's opinion of his ability and his subsequent efforts to obtain goals are crucial to suc-

cessful career development. Educators must provide the opportunity for students to learn and demonstrate all of the important prosocial skills, including those that build the important skills relating to self-determination, that will be needed for adult functioning. More career-oriented prosocial skills instruction is critically needed in most schools. Educators cannot do this by themselves; they must involve not only the entire school community but family and community resources. As general and special education services are integrated into a more unified educational system, the opportunity becomes even greater for students with special learning and/or behavior needs to be better integrated and embraced into the entire school program by other students and teachers. Integrated self-determination skills instruction, such as that being promoted in this chapter, can help enhance this process.

ACTIVITIES

1. Review the LCCE Mild/Moderate Curriculum competencies and subcompetencies identified in the Field & Hoffman Self-Determination model and then determine what general education and special education courses would be most appropriate for teaching self-determination to your particular students. Then identify those LCCE Mild/Moderate Curriculum subcompetencies/skills in which you would attempt to involve family members in teaching self-determination skills at home. Finally, identify the LCCE Mild/Moderate Curriculum subcompetencies for which you would teach self-determination in community-based instruction and what community resources you would use to help you teach the LCCE Mild/Moderate Curriculum subcompetencies.

2. Review the LCCE Mild/Moderate Curriculum competencies and subcompetencies identified in the Wehmeyer Self-Determination model and then determine what general education and special education courses would be most appropriate for teaching self-determination to your particular

students. Then, identify those LCCE Mild/Moderate Curriculum subcompetencies/skills in which you would attempt to involve family members in teaching self-determination skills at home. Finally, identify the LCCE Mild/Moderate Curriculum subcompetencies for which you would teach self-determination in community-based instruction and what community resources you would use to help you teach the LCCE Mild/Moderate Curriculum subcompetencies.

3. Develop a self-determination instructional lesson and materials around one of the LCCE Mild Curriculum subcompetencies, and address one of the career stages, instructional settings, and career roles, as well as the concept of self-determination.

4. Develop a self-determination instructional lesson and materials around one of the LCCE Moderate Curriculum subcompetencies, and address one of the career stages, instructional settings, and career roles, as well as the concept of self-determination.

PART 4

TRANSITION INSTRUCTIONAL DELIVERY

CHAPTER 11

Daily Living Skills

PRELIMINARY QUESTIONS

1. Develop a list of all the daily living skills you believe students with special learning and/or behavior needs should learn before they leave the school system.

2. What general education content areas and special class subjects would be appropriate for teaching these functional skills?

3. List what you consider to be particularly important instructional strategies to use in teaching these functional skills.

4. How would you involve families in the instructional effort needed for their children with special learning and/or behavior needs to learn these functional skills?

5. How would you convince reluctant parents to become involved in this functional area?

6. Why would community-based instruction be an important component of your instructional/transitional program?

7. Which of the daily living skills that you have identified would need to be taught in your transition program's community-based component?

8. How would you capitalize on the interests and aptitudes some of your students with special learning and/or behavior needs would have in certain daily living skills areas for vocational planning and placement?

9. What would be some convincing and compelling reasons you could use to get general educators to teach daily living skills in their content areas?

10. Who should assume the major responsibility in ensuring that the students with special learning and/or behavior needs are being taught sufficient daily living skills at the various levels?

OVERVIEW

Only 40% of former students who have had special learning and/or behavior needs can perform such basic daily living and functional mental skills as looking up telephone numbers, using the telephone, counting change, telling time, and reading common signs. This was the finding of SRI International from their National Longitudinal Transition Study of individuals who were followed for a 5-year period in the late 1980s (U.S. Department of Education, Office of Special Education Programs, 1992). This national study concluded that daily living skills are an extremely critical instructional need for students with special learning and/or behavior needs and that schools need to give considerably more attention to this area of the curriculum if these individuals are to attain the level of competence needed for independent community living.

Although considerable recognition of the importance of teaching daily living skills has been professed by many writers in the field (e.g., Sitlington, Clark, & Kolstoe, 2000; Cronin & Patton, 1993; Mercer & Mercer, 1993), these skills usually are not taught enough; consequently, there is considerable need to increase instructional efforts in this area. The evidence clearly reveals that most students with special learning and/or behavior needs do not learn these skills incidentally; rather, direct instruction must be provided so they acquire them at a satisfactory level of competence.

This chapter first presents an introductory discussion of some considerations and techniques for teaching daily living skills. The next section describes each of the nine daily living skills competencies and 41 subcompetencies contained within the Life Centered Career Education (LCCE) Mild Curriculum. Instructional objectives and activities are suggested. Several activity tips and sample lesson plans are interspersed to illustrate how career education concepts and materials can be infused into various subjects. Next, this section describes each of the eight daily living skills competencies and 32 subcompetencies contained within the Life Centered Career Education (LCCE) Moderate Curriculum. Instructional objectives and activities are suggested. Several activity tips and sample lesson plans are interspersed to illustrate how career education concepts and materials can be infused into various subjects.

In the next section, teachers who have implemented the LCCE Mild Curriculum approach into their classes at the elementary and high school levels provide their explanations of how they are doing it. Next, the implications of daily living skill instruction for occupational preparation are explained. An exam-ple of how LCCE infusion into a leisure-science cur-riculum also is presented. The chapter concludes, like previous chapters, with some final comments and suggested activities for the readers.

CHAPTER OUTLOOK

Carol Ellington-Pinske is a former middle school teacher at Hillsborough School in Plant City, Florida.

Transition/career education is an area of concern to all persons involved with children, adolescents, and adults with special learning and/or behavior needs today in our work-related society. The main prob-lem I address here is beginning transition/career education early enough in a student's life, through the cooperative efforts of particularly the students and her parents, teachers, and the community.

Elements of transition/career education, such as daily living skills, self-awareness, attitudes toward work, decision-making skills, and employability skills, must be dealt with early in each student with special learning and/or behavior needs' life. This training will provide a valuable beginning that will shape each student with special learning and be-havior needs' attitudes and behavior toward the working world and community living.

The school has an obligation to continue the transition/career education process that should begin at home. Daily living skills fit nicely into this plan, when guidance and counseling runs concurrently with functional academic instruction and survival skill development. Young students can begin preparation, not only for work but also for day-to-day survival skills.

Parents, teachers, guidance counselors, occupa-tional specialists, work experience teachers, the business community, and the students all play a vital role in formulating and carrying out this as-pect of transition/career education.

Teachers can use the classroom as a learning facility that can help students learn daily living skills. For instance, in teaching employability skills, the teacher becomes the employer and the student becomes the employee. Grades and, in some instances, token money may become the wages. A classroom store can be set up where stu-dents can purchase school supplies with token money they have earned from working in the classroom. The idea of incorporating a money system leads the way to setting up a classroom banking system, savings accounts, and loans. In this way, the students learn not only the expected curriculum, but also survival skills such as bud-geting money.

Hardly a subject within the school curriculum does not have some relationship to daily living skills. Math (e.g., time, money, measurement), English (e.g., reading), language arts (e.g., writing skills), and social studies (e.g., map skills) include teaching career concepts.

The special education teacher should assume the leadership role in helping other professionals apply the best of their knowledge and skills on be-half of the students with special learning and/or behavior needs. Without the leadership of the spe-cial educator, little will be accomplished; it is the special educator who knows the students best and must acquaint other general education personnel with each student's strengths, interests, and preferences, along with her limitations and its potential effect on future accomplishments.

Transition/career education brings meaning to the learning and practice of basic academic skills by demonstrating to students the multitude of ways in which these skills are applied in daily community living. It answers the frequently asked questions, "What am I learning this for? Is this going to help when I leave school?"

Methods of daily living skills instruction vary widely, but the basic principle is to show students how their learning relates to community living and to work, along with teaching them employability skills such as good work habits, decision-making capabilities, and basic economic education. If you are a general education or special education teacher who wants to increase the relevancy of the education you are providing, stimulate students' interest, increase the use of community resources, and create an awareness of the community living and working, infuse daily living skills into your curriculum.

TEACHING LCCE MILD CURRICULUM DAILY LIVING SKILLS

Daily living skills, sometimes referred to as *independent* or *survival living skills,* are those required to function independently or within a family environment. Some examples of daily living skills are budgeting, banking, personal care, cleaning, purchasing necessities, cooking, driving a car, planning and preparing balanced meals, practicing first aid, using public transportation, and engaging in meaningful leisure-time activities. These skills are those needed to become responsible adults within the home, school, community, and the job. Responsibility for teaching these skills rests jointly with special and regular educators, parents, and peers (West et al., 1992).

Throughout this book, the importance of family and community involvement and partnerships has been stressed. Successful transition/career education in this functional curriculum area is extremely dependent on the involvement of these resources. In the case of family members willing to participate in helping to meet the functional needs of their child with special learning and/or behavior needs, much of the teacher's focus in this functional curriculum area can be reinforced and further expanded in the home setting. In addition, community resources such as grocery stores, clothing stores, banks, recreational centers, transportation companies, governmental agencies, and many others can provide valuable assistance. Suggestions for the involvement of these resources has been addressed in previous chapters and so is not repeated here. Rather, attention is directed primarily to the teacher's role in this functional curriculum area.

Daily living skills are necessary for successful independent living and working in modern society. Acquisition of these skills also can lead to vocational possibilities for students with special learning and/or behavior needs, depending on their particular abilities, interests, and personalized needs. These functional skills must be systematically infused into daily lessons rather than taught haphazardly or overlooked entirely. Teachers will need to consider the personalized functional needs of the individual with special learning and/or behavior needs before they plan functional objectives and methods and evaluate the progress of the student with special learning and/or behavior needs. These functional efforts will help teachers and most importantly learners with special learning and/or behavior needs to notice improvements in such daily living skills functions as maintaining personal appearance, managing finances, and getting around in the community.

Daily living skills can and should be taught in various general education content areas, community-based activities, and in home assignments. In addition to the many obvious benefits for teaching these functional skills substantially to students with special learning and/or behavior needs, this functional focus "can provide exciting and realistic activities for reaching academic, general cognitive, and language and communication, as well as social skills" (Langone, 1990).

Daily living skills can be infused into a wide range of basic academic content areas, for example, reading, English, math, government, social studies, science, and such courses as home economics, physical education, and health. Through a process such as curriculum mapping (i.e., determining what subjects and levels to teach each of the agreed-on life skills), a transition committee and/or other general educators in the school identify how these functional skills can be infused into the school's curriculum.

Some of the instructional approaches or strategies that are particularly important to provide students in this functional curriculum area follow:

- Numerous hands-on experiences with real materials such as tools and appliances
- School resources such as the cafeteria, nurse, clerical, transportation, and housekeeping services to reinforce the importance of these skills for not only personal functioning but also for employment
- Community-based experiences such as tours, job shadowing, mentoring, and instructional opportunities
- Volunteers such as parents and community members to provide classroom demonstrations and activities for students in these skill areas
- Games, simulations of community resources, role-playing, computers, and videotapes to provide interesting and challenging activities and demonstrations for skills development
- Peer tutors who have particular expertise and enthusiasm for tutoring the students in areas of special need
- The cooperative learning approach

The cooperative learning approach has gained considerable attention and use by many educators over the past three decades and is an excellent technique to integrate students with special learning and/or behavior needs in with general class students. Cooperative learning is a mainstream alternative to ability grouping, remediation, or special education pull-out programs. It provides both special education and at-risk students with the opportunity to develop significant relationships with other students in class. The teacher must carefully structure the learning situation so all students have an important contribution to the successful completion of the task. Group members can help each other learn various material, but everyone has her own responsibility for achieving the goal. For students with special learning and/or behavior needs, a cooperative rather than a competitive or individual approach is particularly appropriate. Teaching daily living skills lends itself very well to a cooperative learning endeavor.

Team teaching is another effective approach for providing students with special learning needs access to regular classes. LCCE Mild/Moderate Curriculum instruction is being provided in many schools, with a special education teacher teaming with a regular class teacher to teach many of the daily living skills. One example is the teaming with home economics teachers for the functional skill areas of cooking, clothing, home management, and personal care. One cannot help but be impressed, when witnessing such a collaborative atmosphere, by the effectiveness of the instructional effort that usually results from carefully designed team teaching efforts that have a specified and important outcome for the students.

Community-based instruction (CBI) is an extremely common functional approach in many school districts throughout the country. This transitional approach generally involves individualized or small group experiences that occur routinely or more than once as contrasted to field trips. CBI provides students with special learning and/or behavior needs an opportunity to draw on their skills and use functional problem-solving strategies with guidance as needed from the teacher. As noted by J. Beck et al., "the general education curriculum divides information into content areas, but in the real world, students must combine skills and knowledge, and use them in functional ways" (1994, p. 45). Thus, a community-based component is very important to instructional success with students, especially those with special learning and/or behavior needs. In the section on the LCCE Mild and Moderate competencies, suggestions for incorporating CBI are presented.

Peer tutoring, which has been used for years, has gained greater recognition as an effective technique for engaging all students with special learning and/or behavior needs in the learning of daily living and other functional skills. Basically, it is an interchange between two students in which the tutor helps the tutee learn content material. Tutors may be of the same age or older than the tutee. Tutoring can take place within the classroom with all students participating, or it can occur outside the classroom or with only one or a few students off to the side of the classroom. The tutor can be the expert, or there can be reverse-role tutoring where the student who is having difficulty serves as tutor to the more able tutee. Teachers who use this approach are generally quite positive about it. To be successful, however, it is important to provide positive feedback to the students, supervise the students adequately, train the tutors, and make regular use of the technique to keep the students familiar with the system (Warger, 1991).

A wide variety of functional strategies and approaches can be used in teaching daily living skills. In this section, only some have been discussed. Good teachers will be creative, flexible, and collaborative in designing functional experiences and effective strategies to meet the needs of their students with special learning and/or behavior needs.

LCCE MILD CURRICULUM COMPETENCIES

The Division on Career Development and Transition's (DCDT) publication *Integrating Transition Planning Into the IEP Process* identifies the LCCE Mild Curriculum as "a good example of a comprehensive functional curriculum" (West et al., 1992, p. 24) because it includes life skills in the three major environments or domains of adjustment identified by Halpern for the post-school years: personal-social networks, daily living, and employment (1985, p. 24).

In addition to general life skills development, the daily living skills curriculum area of LCCE Mild Curriculum focuses on three of the four major career roles composing the concept of career development advocated in this book: the work of a family member, citizen/volunteer, and productive avocational activities such as hobbies and other leisure pursuits. Daily living skills instruction also promotes, to a somewhat lesser extent, occupational development and future employment possibilities. This area is addressed later in the chapter.

In this section, the nine LCCE Mild Curriculum daily living skills competencies and their 41 subcompetencies are presented. The competencies and subcompetencies are illustrated in Figure 11.1. As each of these is presented in the following discussion, several activity tips and sample lesson plans—including those taken from the more extensively written LCCE competency unit curriculum materials published by the Council for Exceptional Children (CEC) (Brolin, 1992b)—are interspersed to illustrate how instructional activities could be organized within such a framework.

1.0 Managing Personal Finances

The ability to regulate finances is a crucial determinant of adult success for everyone. Therefore, teachers must provide numerous activities that prepare students with special learning and/or behavior needs for their roles as spenders, savers, and managers of their money. This should include the following LCCE Mild Curriculum subcompetencies:

1.1 Count Money and Make Correct Change

The beginning skill for this LCCE Mild Curriculum subcompetency is the successful identification of several forms of currency. Students with visual impairments may accomplish this functional skill by becoming familiar with the size of metal coins and by folding paper money of various denominations at different corners. Arithmetic exercises or play stores can be used to teach primary-grade students how to count and manipulate coins and bills.

Curriculum Area	Competency	Subcompetency: The student will be able to:	
	1. Managing Personal Finances	1. Count money & make correct change	2. Make responsible expenditures
	2. Selecting & Managing a Household	7. Maintain home exterior/interior	8. Use basic appliances and tools
	3. Caring for Personal Needs	12. Demonstrate knowledge of physical fitness, nutrition & weight	13. Exhibit proper grooming & hygiene
	4. Raising Children & Meeting Marriage Responsibilities	17. Demonstrate physical care for raising children	18. Know psychological aspects of raising children
DAILY LIVING SKILLS	5. Buying, Preparing & Consuming Food	20. Purchase food	21. Clean food preparation areas
	6. Buying & Caring for Clothing	26. Wash/clean clothing	27. Purchase clothing
	7. Exhibiting Responsible Citizenship	29. Demonstrate knowledge of civil rights & responsibilities	30. Know nature of local, state & federal governments
	8. Utilizing Recreational Facilities & Engaging in Leisure	33. Demonstrate knowledge of available community resources	34. Choose & plan activities
	9. Getting Around the Community	38. Demonstrate knowledge of traffic rules & safety	39. Demonstrate knowledge & use of various means of transportation

FIGURE 11.1   Life Centered Career Education Competencies: Daily Living Skills Curriculum.
Note: From *Life Centered Career Education: A Competency-Based Approach* (5th ed., pp. 12–13) by D. E. Brolin, 1997, Arlington, VA: The Council for Exceptional Children. Copyright 1997 by The Council for Exceptional Children. Reprinted by permission.

Numerous teaching aids and commercial workbooks are available to help teachers initiate activities that would require students to make correct change and use money in various situations. Parents can provide students with money to buy lunch or spend on field trips. Other functional objectives related to this LCCE Mild Curriculum subcompetency should include demonstrating the ability to make change and identifying uses of money in society.

1.2 Make Reasonable Expenditures

The ability to select goods and services is valuable in a society that experiences inflation, economic stagnation, and prosperity. This LCCE Mild Curriculum subcompetency focuses on the student with special learning and/or behavior needs as a consumer who can use tags and labels to evaluate merchandise, who considers the advantages and disadvantages of discount stores, and who develops strategies for buying during bargain sales. These functional skills are especially helpful to those with low incomes. Teachers can acquire commercial

materials that include specific exercises in consumer education. However, in general, the instructor should conduct classroom activities that require students with special learning and/or behavior needs to compare products sold at different stores or markets, itemize their family's purchases during a given period of time, or construct a shopping list and record prices of items at a given store. These assignments can begin at the primary level, and experience has taught us that students with special learning and/or behavior needs use these skills repeatedly through the adult years. These practices also sharpen the students with special learning and/or behavior needs' ability to make decisions regarding which products and services to use.

A final consideration for all consumers is an awareness of common advertising gimmicks and traps. Local consumer protection agencies and groups can provide the class with materials and demonstrations that will further supplement this part of the curriculum. Other functional objectives should include distinguishing essential items from luxuries and engaging in comparative shopping.

3. Keep basic financial records	4. Calculate & pay taxes	5. Use credit responsibly	6. Use banking services
9. Select adequate housing	10. Set up household	11. Maintain home grounds	
14. Dress appropriately	15. Demonstrate knowledge of common illness, prevention & treatment	16. Practice personal safety	
19. Demonstrate marriage responsibilities			
22. Store food	23. Prepare meals	24. Demonstrate appropriate eating habits	25. Plan/eat balanced meals
28. Iron, mend & store clothing			
31. Demonstrate knowledge of the law & ability to follow the law	32. Demonstrate knowledge of citizen rights & responsibilities		
35. Demonstrate knowledge of the value of recreation	36. Engage in group & individual activities	37. Plan vacation time	
40. Find way around the community	41. Drive a car		

• • • • • • • • **Activity Tip** • • • • • • • •

Students with special learning and/or behavior needs can keep a record and calculate their parents' expenditures for a week or their own expenses for a longer period. The student with special learning and/or behavior needs should place budget headings on the left-hand side of a ruled sheet of paper. The days of the week or months of the year are placed at the top of the page. Dollar amounts are entered for the following budget headings: rent, utilities, food, transportation, clothing, medical expenses, insurance, taxes, entertainment, savings, others. Advanced students can calculate the percentage of expenditures per budget heading.

• •

1.3 Keep Basic Financial Records

Successful adults can maintain a minimum number of records. However, they must be able to identify those receipts, bank statements, or contracts that should be preserved to plan a budget, meet bills, and file tax returns. The goal of these functional activities is to help the student with special learning and/or be-

havior needs develop a personal system of record keeping and filing. Children are introduced to logical systems when they develop hobbies that involve organizing events or materials, such as collecting stamps, pictures, or bubble gum cards. Several commercial publishers provide instructional materials explaining banking procedures and how to maintain records and calculate taxes. The crucial concern for the teacher is whether the student with special learning and/or behavior needs has practiced and uses a record-keeping system. Once students with special learning and/or behavior needs incorporate a system into their daily activities, they have acquired the necessary functional skills for the development of this LCCE Mild Curriculum subcompetency. Other functional objectives should include constructing a personal budget for a given length of time and recording income and expenses and balance over time.

1.4 Calculate and Pay Taxes

Students with special learning and/or behavior needs will not need to calculate and pay taxes in authentic situations until they have earned incomes subject to local, state, and federal taxes. However, the instructor should prepare the student with special learning and/or behavior needs by conducting classroom activities examining the several kinds of taxes (sales, luxury, gas) that affect the student's earnings and savings. These activities can help students with special learning and/or behavior needs identify which items are taxed, how much tax they should pay, and how taxes are collected and used. Secondary school programs should include exercises that will familiarize students with special learning and/or behavior needs with income tax forms, procedures for filing returns, and agencies that provide tax assistance. Other functional objectives should include demonstrating the ability to complete a tax form.

1.5 Use Credit Responsibly

This LCCE Mild Curriculum subcompetency covers loans and credit cards. Initial familiarity with banks, savings accounts, checking accounts, Automatic Transfer Machines (ATM), deposits, and the like can begin in the elementary grades. Teachers can establish classroom banks and accounts in conjunction with exercises on the use of money. Shopping trips, as discussed in LCCE Mild Curriculum subcompetency 1.2, can be financed by checking, savings, or charge accounts maintained through the classroom deposits. All of these exercises depend on an actual acquaintance with the community's financial establishments. Although teachers have an opportunity to visit banks, savings and loan facilities, and credit unions, the family has access to these establishments over a longer period of time. Teachers should encourage parents to

explain how to use these facilities when they take their children with special learning and/or behavior needs with them to make deposits or withdrawals at their bank. Teachers can supplement these activities by asking representatives from these establishments to show the class how to use these services. Other functional objectives should include proper credit card use, which could present major problems to students with special learning and/or behavior needs if not used wisely within their budget.

1.6 Use Banking Services

Students with special learning and/or behavior needs must learn how to manage checking and savings accounts so they can pay their bills and manage other financial manners. Thus, it is important for students with special learning and/or behavior needs to learn —to the extent possible—instructional objectives that focus on writing checks, making deposits, recording transactions, using the ATM, making deposits and withdrawals, and recording savings transactions. The following lesson plan is an example of how one of the objectives comprising this LCCE Mild Curriculum subcompetency area can be taught to an elementary or middle school class at the career awareness level. The instructional resources included in the lesson plan (i.e., checks, fact sheet about checks and checking accounts, bank statement, and work sheet) are not included in the sample. The lesson plan was taken from the daily living skills competency unit manual published by the CEC (Brolin, 1992c).

Lesson Plan 1   **1.6.1A:1**

LCCE Objective 1.6.1   Open a checking account

Lesson Objective: Student will learn what a checking account is and will be able to identify basic vocabulary associated with opening a checking account

Instructional Resources: Fact Sheet **Checks and Checking Accounts**, Worksheet **Checks and Checking Accounts**, Sample Sheet **Checks, Bank Statement**.

Lesson Introduction: How many of you have received and cashed a check? Today you will learn about checks and checking accounts. You will learn what a check is, why we use checks, and what a checking account is.

School Activity: **Time: 1 session**

Task:
1. **Advance Preparation:** Use Sample Sheet **Checks** to write a check for each student. (Checks also are used in Lesson Plans 8, 9, and 10.)
2. Distribute checks to students. Ask students why they might not be able to cash their checks. Be sure to include ideas such as the check writer has not opened a checking account and does not have a balance.
3. Distribute Fact Sheet **Checks and Checking Accounts**. Use the students' checks to facilitate the fact sheet discussion.
4. Distribute and discuss Sample Sheet **Bank Statement**. Use the students checks and the fact sheet to facilitate discussion.
5. Distribute and explain Worksheet **Checks and Checking Accounts**. Students should work with a partner and discuss responses with the class after completing the task.
6. Have students identify times when they may write checks or use a checking account as a family member/homemaker, citizen/volunteer, employee or for avocational activities.

Lesson Plan Evaluation:
Activity: Students will complete Worksheet **Checks and Checking Accounts**.
Criteria: Student will complete the worksheet with 80% accuracy.
Career Role: Family Member/Homemaker, Employee, Citizen/Volunteer, Avocational
Career Stage: Awareness

Note: From *Life Centered Career Education: Competency Units for Daily Living Sklls* (Vol. 1., p. 203) by D. E. Brolin, 1992, Arlington, VA: The Council for Exceptional Children. Reprinted by permission.

2.0 Select and Manage Household

A major portion of the average person's salary is spent on housing. In certain parts of the country, the monthly rent for an apartment or house may exceed the costs for food. Housing costs that exceed the average worker's salary place increased stress on his ability to maintain independence. The young person may have to reside with the family for a longer period of time or seek peers who will share costs as a roommate. These situations require individuals with special learning and/or behavior needs to be alert for ways to minimize expenses for maintaining a home. This competency includes the following LCCE Mild Curriculum subcompetencies:

2.7 Maintain Home Exterior/Interior

Although the majority of young adults will live in apartments, they should understand and practice

● ● ● ● ● ● ● ● **Activity Tip** ● ● ● ● ● ● ● ●
Students with special learning and/or behavior needs and parents should cooperate in constructing a large diagram of their house or apartment. Symbols that represent various tools required for maintaining and cleaning the dwelling and that the student with special learning and/or behavior needs can use successfully should be entered at the bottom of the diagram. Students with special learning and/or behavior needs can create their own symbols for such functions as sweeping and dusting. A chart can be added indicating the functions and the days of the week. This chart can help parents and teachers keep track of the progress of the student with special learning and/or behavior needs. Both the diagram and chart can be expanded to fit the student with special learning and/or behavior needs' abilities.

skills that contribute to the preservation of both the exterior and interior of the dwelling. Students with special learning and/or behavior needs should learn the common tools, products, and equipment used both inside and outside for home maintenance work. Students with special learning and/or behavior needs should review owner's manuals, observe demonstrations, learn safety procedures, and then learn to use the various materials required for satisfactory interior and exterior home maintenance.

2.8 Use Basic Appliances and Tools

Appliances can be used to clean or repair the home. The latter include such tools as a hammer, saw, screwdriver, or wrench. The teacher's goal is to develop students with special learning and/or behavior needs' competence with appliances and tools that would be used in the home to maintain cleanliness and ensure that doors, windows, and locks are in working order. This means that students with special learning and/or behavior needs would be able to make basic home repairs and improvements such as replacing screens or light bulbs, tightening screws or bolts, and painting doors or walls. The special education teacher should plan these activities with the assistance of home economics and trade and industrial technology teachers. Other objectives should include using safety procedures in working with tools and appliances. A sample lesson plan written by a teacher using her own format for teaching this LCCE Mild Curriculum subcompetency is presented next.

Sample Lesson Plan

Author: Lynn S. Miller

Level: Elementary

Period: Language arts

Situation: Students with multiple disabilities

Time Span: One week

Objective: Subcompetency 2.2: Students will identify and demonstrate the use of basic appliances and tools found in the home.

Activity Title: *Field Trip to an Appliance Store*

Goal of Activity: Students will participate in a field trip to a local appliance store and will identify a variety of home appliances and tools.

Activity: Students will take a field trip to an appliance store in the community. While touring the store, each student will compile a list of as many appliances and tools as possible. Students may need assistance from the teacher to develop a list. The students should ask a store employee for any catalogs or advertising material concerning home appliances and tools that are available. Students also should collect a business card that they can put into their field trip file.

Activity Title: *My Home Appliances and Tools Notebook*

Goal of Activity: Students will compile a booklet picturing basic home appliances and tools.

Activity: Students will look for pictures of a variety of home appliances and tools found in magazines, newspapers, catalogs, and brochures that they have received from an appliance store. After pasting their pictures onto a piece of construction paper, students will label each tool and appliance. These pages will be placed in a booklet form and titled *My Home Appliances and Tools Notebook*. The students also will discuss the function of each appliance and tool.

Activity Title: *Are You Using Your Appliances and Tools Correctly?*

Goal of Activity: Students will become familiar with safety procedures involved in using various home appliances and tools.

Activity: The teacher will bring several home appliances and tools to the classroom and will discuss and demonstrate procedures for using these items safely. While showing students how to use each device, the teacher should explain what the appliance or tool is used for. Before each student has the opportunity to operate the appliance or tool, the student should be aware of the safety procedures involved in operating the device. A photograph will be taken as the student demonstration is taking place. Students will construct a bulletin board using these photos. They will label each appliance and tool and make a list of safety procedures that will accompany each photo.

Evaluation: After discussing their field trip to the appliance store, students will illustrate and write a sentence or a short story about their experience. Students also will share *My Home Appliances and Tools Notebook* with their parents and should list the appliances and tools found in their homes. Finally students will discuss the function and safety procedures of a variety of home appliances and tools.

Related Subcompetencies:

3.16	Practice personal safety
12.53	Demonstrate proper behavior in public places
16.68	Communicate with understanding

2.9 Select Adequate Housing

Awareness of a family's needs for living space and facilities begins in the primary grades. Students with special learning and/or behavior needs can draw their homes or apartments, collect pictures of various rooms, and identify family functions in each part of the dwelling. This general inquiry leads to expanded knowledge of various types of housing available in the community. The teacher should stress the advantages and disadvantages of each dwelling. This includes discussions about space, costs, utilities, and location. Students with special learning and/or behavior needs in the intermediate grades can gather information by interviewing realty agents, family members, and newspaper advertisers. Secondary students with special learning and/or behavior needs should continue with specific exercises related to renting a home or apartment, deposits, leases, tenant rights and responsibilities, and community agencies that can assist the individual with more complicated decisions involving the purchase of property. Another functional objective should be identifying important considerations in renting an apartment or buying a house.

2.10 Set Up Household

Setting up a household requires students with special learning and/or behavior needs to learn how to obtain utility services, basic household items, and furniture and appliances. Parent and community-based experiences are critical activities to include in these lessons. For example, parents can discuss with their child with special learning and/or behavior needs the utilities used in the home, show records of bills and installation agreements, and take them to visit stores that sell basic household items, furniture, and major appliances. The use of telephone directories and newspapers also is important in gaining an adequate understanding of the use of services and the purchase of basic household items.

2.11 Maintain Home Grounds

The LCCE Mild Curriculum subcompetency called maintain home grounds is an extension of 2.7 and requires the student with special learning and/or behavior needs to perform home maintenance and repairs such as grass cutting, painting, bush trimming, and the like. Parents and persons employed in this type of business are to be involved in the students' career development.

3.0 Caring for Personal Needs

Adequate hygiene, physical condition, and health care are of special importance to those individuals who are susceptible to injury, illness, or irritation associated with their impairment. Relatives will probably try to help these individuals learn how to take care of personal needs, but the teacher's objectivity can help to balance the emotional involvement of relatives who identify with the individual with special learning and/or behavior needs. This competency includes the following LCCE Mild Curriculum subcompetencies:

3.12 Demonstrate Knowledge of Physical Fitness, Nutrition, and Weight

Development of the Special Olympics was motivated by the fact that individuals with mental retardation had received little or no instruction in physical education or recreation in public schools and institutions. The Special Olympics help to underscore that all individuals possess physical competence. Proper care and development of the body are vital to meet the physical demands of everyday life. Students with special learning and/or behavior needs should demonstrate knowledge of the major body parts and perform exercises or activities that benefit development. As students with special learning and/or behavior needs develop fundamental knowledge of basic food groups, nutrition, and weight control, teachers should enlist cooperation of physical education, recreation, and home economics professionals. Students with special learning and/or behavior needs can maintain their own health charts by recording maturation, eating habits, or games and exercises. Other functional objectives include performing activities that maintain appropriate physical fitness and demonstrating eating practices that contribute to proper nutrition.

3.13 Exhibit Proper Grooming and Hygiene

Students with special learning and/or behavior needs should demonstrate the ability to brush their teeth,

wash their hands and face, use handkerchiefs, towels, and napkins, and maintain a clean appearance. Teachers from intermediate grades through adult education should continue to help students with special learning and/or behavior needs develop these abilities and expand their awareness of personal hygiene and grooming habits that are appropriate for males and females. This is one of the most vital LCCE Mild Curriculum subcompetencies because acceptance of an individual by peers, adults, and employers is usually based on personal appearance. Another functional objective should include demonstrating the use of appropriate health and grooming aids.

• • • • • • • • **Activity Tip** • • • • • • • •

Each student with special learning and/or behavior needs should construct a grooming card that he or she can carry in a wallet or purse. The grooming card is similar to an identification card but contains reminders of grooming appropriate to the student's concern (i.e., hair style, make-up, and clean glasses). Teachers, counselors, and parents periodically check the grooming card for proper identification!

3.14 Dress Appropriately

Social standards concerning acceptable attire for both men and women have become less rigorous. The broad range of acceptable attire presents a new burden to teachers who must instruct students on the types of clothing that are appropriate for different weather conditions, social settings, and work situations. Elementary school students with special learning and/or behavior needs could construct bulletin boards containing displays that illustrate the major forms of dress. When planning activities related to this skill, teachers should focus on the relationship between health and appropriate attire. Teachers also can use role-playing techniques to help adolescents with special learning and/or behavior needs become more aware of the social ramifications involved in dressing to meet the occasion. Students with special learning and/or behavior needs can use the feedback provided by role playing to evaluate the appropriateness of their attire. Another functional objective should include demonstrating competence in selecting appropriate leisure and work attire.

3.15 Demonstrate Knowledge of Common Illness Prevention and Treatment

Demonstrating knowledge of illness prevention and treatment methods is one of the most complex LCCE Mild Curriculum subcompetencies. This area includes information about illnesses and basic symptoms, hazards to health that occur in the home, basic first-aid techniques, and obtaining assistance for various medical problems. The lessons on illness will be significant to individuals who must guard against dangers in the environment that can complicate a primary disability, for example, respiratory infections for the physically disabled, or an inflamed eyelid for individuals who are deaf. Students with special learning and/or behavior needs in the primary grades should begin learning basic health measures that will prevent illnesses or injury. The students with special learning and/or behavior needs' experiences will provide ample subject matter, and the instructor should provide numerous practice sessions requiring students to contact emergency facilities in the event of illness or injury. The range of subject matter increases as instruction includes first aid, safety considerations, health facilities, and professionals. Local public health facilities or agents can provide demonstrations and audiovisual aids to assist instruction in these competencies.

Sample Lesson Plan

Author: Lynda Glascoe

Level: Junior high school

Situation: Resource specialist program

Period: Four (home activity included)

Time Span: One week

Objective: Subcompetency 3.15: The student will differentiate between healthful and unhealthful products advertised in magazines and on television. These activities should be used after basic instruction on nutrition and chemical abuse.

Activity Title: *Do Magazines Advertise Healthful Products?*

Goal of Activity: Students rate products advertised in magazines according to their appropriateness to good health.

Activity: The teacher leads a discussion on how advertising affects eating habits and how this could influence health. Provide different types of magazines (women's, teens', and sports). The student cuts out advertisements of products that can be eaten or are related to health (e.g. food, drinks, medicine, and cigarettes). The student glues each advertisement on a separate piece of paper and answers the following questions about each product (this can be done in questionnaire form or written in a paragraph).

1. Is this product good for you?
    Yes   No   Don't know
2. Do you like it?
    Yes   No   Don't know

3. Would you use it?
   Yes, a lot
   Yes, sometimes
   Yes, but only when an adult says it's okay
   No

Activity Title: *Does Television Advertise Healthful Products?*

Goal of Activity: Students rate the appropriateness of products advertised on television to good health.

Activity: Students will watch television during *normal* viewing hours and will record the time and the program they watched. Since this activity will probably be conducted almost entirely at home (unless a television is available for classroom use), parent involvement is important. Teachers should contact parents to explain the objectives of this activity and encourage their assistance. After students have listed all commercials that advertise products to eat or drink (including medicines), students will answer the questions given in the previous activity. These activities will be included in a folder with the previous cutouts.

Evaluation: Students will list five healthful and five unhealthful products that are frequently advertised in magazines or on television. Given five advertisements, the student will state reasons why the product is healthful or unhealthful.

| **Related Subcompetencies**: | 15.64 | Look at alternatives |
| | 15.63 | Anticipate consequence |

3.16 Practice Personal Safety

Functional objectives for the subcompetency of practicing personal safety focus on home security, personal assault, and self-defense techniques. This functional skill area has become extremely important with the rising violence and crime in our society. The involvement of parents, law enforcement officials, self-defense specialists, and community services such as gas and electric companies can help students with special learning and/or behavior needs learn safety precautions and potential hazards. Role-play activities will enhance this instruction, which should begin at the elementary level.

4.0 Raising Children—Family Living

Learning to raise a family begins with the individual's experiences as a family member. Teachers should help students with special learning and/or behavior needs observe child-rearing practices of their families, relatives, or neighbors. Many of the functional skills required in mastering the subcompetencies will be based on students with special learning and/or behavior needs' observations and reporting skills. Students with special learning and/or behavior needs' observations can help teachers prepare lessons on successful child-parent interactions. Experience is the best teacher, but when room for experimentation is limited, observation of others' experiences also avoids needless trial and error. Teachers in secondary and adult programs also can provide students with special learning and/or behavior needs with ample opportunity to ask questions about raising children and can provide them with enough sources of information so that students with special learning and/or behavior needs may obtain in-depth answers. This competency includes the following LCCE Mild Curriculum subcompetencies:

4.17 Demonstrate Physical Care for Raising Children

Children have various needs at successive developmental stages. Infant care and feeding, inoculation for diseases, appropriate diet, clothing, exercise, and protection are important throughout all stages of development. The intensity of these needs may vary depending on all particular personalized needs for the individual with special learning and/or behavior needs. Students with special learning and/or behavior needs can use their own life experiences with each topic area to develop appropriate methods of working with their future children. This is one way the teacher can emphasize child-rearing procedures when, in actuality, the main topic of consideration is projected to some time in the future. Other functional objectives should include demonstrating proper care of a child and demonstrating basic protection measures for a child.

• • • • • • • • **Activity Tip** • • • • • • • •

Each student with special learning and/or behavior needs is given an egg and a shoebox. The egg represents a new baby, and each shoe box is a bed or home. The student with special learning and/or behavior needs is to provide and care for the "child." The student with special learning and/or behavior needs must plan a schedule that includes bathing, feeding, changing, and so on. Classroom discussions can include the difficulties and fun aspects of the assignment.

4.18 Know Psychological Aspects of Raising Children

In preparing the student to meet the psychological responsibilities of marriage and child rearing, the teacher must develop the student with special learning and/or behavior needs' awareness of some basic emotional needs. Discussions of love, support, and acceptance probe the structure of the student with special learning and/or behavior needs sense of self and identify the conceptions and attitudes that are basic to the individual with special learning and/or behavior needs' behavior. These encounters may include identification of the student's needs as a child or at various stages of development, reflections on behaviors that meet these needs, and the parent's role in providing for this aspect of the child. In understanding their emotional needs as children, students with special learning and/or behavior

needs can approach the problem of building a psychological environment that fosters personal growth. Other functional objectives should include identifying potential family problems and identifying community agencies that provide assistance with family problems.

• • • • • • • • **Activity Tip** • • • • • • • •

The teacher or counselor arranges the class into a "family circle." All students with special learning and/or behavior needs are members of the same family. Each session focuses on an incident or problem that confronts a family (i.e., planning a vacation or sending a child to summer camp). Teachers should select problem areas that have particular importance to the class. The students with special learning and/or behavior needs can question the professional for more details but must present alternative solutions, writing, and other creative endeavors that reflect individual and group solutions.

4.19 Demonstrate Marriage Responsibilities

The focus of the teacher's lessons should be on the personal adjustments that each partner must make during marriage. Students with special learning and/or behavior needs can certainly observe the give and take in decision-making processes that occur in their families: They may also have some experience adjusting to brothers and sisters, playmates, club members, or peers. Of course, these situations hedge around the actual experiences accompanying marriage. Nevertheless, these experiences test students with special learning and/or behavior needs' abilities to plan cooperatively with others, express their opinions, and develop other basic skills that contribute to a successful marriage. The teacher may discuss various aspects of marriage that require careful decision making. Mutual concern and respect, shared responsibilities in the home, earning a living, managing the household, visiting relatives, and planning a family are just a few issues for discussion. Other functional objectives should include identifying personal and joint adjustments in life-style necessary in marriage.

5.0 Buying and Preparing Food

Competency 5 relates to the purchase, preparation, and consumption of food. It also involves an area of life that functions as a reward; thus, food is used frequently as a reinforcer for student performance in the classroom. The role of food as both a necessary substance for life and reward for behavior places an additional responsibility on teachers who must develop student abilities in distinguishing between the two. The following LCCE Mild Curriculum subcompetencies are by no means the last word in planning, purchasing, and preparing food, so teachers should expand this area to meet the particular needs and abilities of their students. This competency includes the following LCCE Mild Curriculum subcompetencies:

5.20 Purchase Food

Purchasing food is related to the LCCE Mild Curriculum subcompetency on making responsible expenditures (1.2) and provides ample opportunity for teachers to train students with special learning and/or behavior needs in the use of measuring units of food and calculating costs. Unfortunately, students with special learning and/or behavior needs are often immersed in a world of advertisements for foods. Buying goodies can become the subject matter for daily assignments in purchasing meals at the school cafeteria, calculating the cost of a bag lunch, or projecting future expenses for after school snacks. In later years, with the recommended assistance of home economics instructors or representatives from community consumer organizations, students should be exposed to lessons that will help them recognize differences in the quality of foods, various types and cuts of meat and fish, and the advantages of sales and specials. Other functional objectives should include identifying community sources of information about food prices and constructing a shopping list within a budget.

• • • • • • • • **Activity Tip** • • • • • • • • •

The teacher provides the class with a list of basic food items. Students with special learning and/or behavior needs price each item at their local store or supermarket. These prices form the basis for activities requiring students with special learning and/or behavior needs to compare prices of food items, compute costs for a given number of items, and select items based on a fixed amount of money. The complexity of the activity can be adjusted to the ability of the individual student.

5.21 Clean Food Preparation Areas

Teachers should stress that the cleaning process is just as important as preparation of food. After all, food disappears, but dirty dishes remain for the next meal. This LCCE Mild Curriculum subcompetency includes skills involved in the use of various cleaning measures and materials, disposal and removal of waste products, and storage of utensils. Cleaning up is also an appropriate area for lessons emphasizing safety factors and measures involved in the entire preparation and clean-up process.

The lesson plan presented next is an example of how two of the LCCE objectives that are contained in this LCCE Mild Curriculum subcompetency area can be taught in conjunction with a community-based field experience. Note that this is a career exploration lesson plan and that it addresses two of the career roles composing the LCCE model: family member/homemaker and employee.

Lesson Plan 3   **5.21.1E:3**
                                                                                      5.21.2E:3

LCCE Objective 5.21.1 Identify importance of personal hygiene in food preparation areas.

LCCE Objective 5.21.2 List reasons for cleaning work area and materials after food preparation.

Lesson Objective: Student will learn the importance of cleanliness practices when working with food.

Instructional Resources: Field trip to fast-food restaurant.

Lesson Introduction: Recent studies in the health field have found that disease is spread more quickly by touching than by any other way. Consider a person who has a slight cold and coughs into his hand. If he then makes a sandwich for someone and shakes hands with someone else, those two people are exposed to the cold. The cold germ is passed on to other people through touch. No wonder hospitals are placing such importance on simple hand washing carefully and often as a way to stop the spread of disease.

Community/School Activity: **Time**: 2 sessions

Task:

1. Take a field trip to a fast-food restaurant. Ask the manager to explain clean work area procedures to the students and the importance of personal hygiene, emphasizing washing hands properly. Direct the students to each notice two cleanliness practices they think are important to report to the class the next day.

2. In the second session, have students discuss their experiences on the field trip and report the two practices they observed.

3. Have students break into small groups.

   • Each student is asked to think of one example of when or where it is important to wash hands afterwards or before.

   • See which group can come up with more examples. Have them share their lists.

   • Also have them discuss why washing hands is important as a family member and as an employee.

Lesson Plan Evaluation:

Activity: Students will participate in the field trip.

Criteria: Student will report to the class two cleanliness practices observed on the field trip.

Career Role: Family Member/Homemaker, Employee

Career Stage: Exploration

Note: From *Life Centered Career Education, Competency Units for Daily Living Skills* (Vol. 2, p. 745) by D. E. Brolin, 1992, Arlington, VA: The Council for Exceptional Children. Copyright 1992 by The Council for Exceptional Children. Reprinted by permission.

Developing food preparation skills is necessary to perform all four career roles (employee, family member, citizen, and participant) in recreational and leisure activities.

5.22 Store Food

Proper food storage is useful in the overall management of financial resources and family health. This process requires that students learn how to store food and identify when food is spoiled. Teachers can use numerous instructional aids available from consumer organizations or companies that manufacture storage devices. Another functional objective should be demonstrating techniques for storing food.

5.23 Prepare Meals

To prepare an entire meal, the student with special learning and/or behavior needs will need to know how to use utensils, follow directions, identify various forms of measures, clean, cut, and prepare food, and use devices for cooking and baking. Every school curriculum should train the student with special learning and/or behavior needs in the skills involved in managing the preparation of a meal, either by direct manipulation or instruction. Teachers can certainly include parents in the instruction of buying and preparing food. Other functional objectives should include preparing a meal according to directions and demonstrating kitchen safety measures.

5.24 Demonstrate Appropriate Eating Habits

Society has developed standards of behavior pertaining to eating in the company of other individuals, whether in family or public situations. These standards of etiquette are bent only slightly for some students with special learning and/or behavior needs. Individuals who are blind must eat peas with the same skill as their companions who can watch peas rolling around on the dinner plate. An inability to conform to these standards even with some slight modification to accommodate the disability places these individuals in situations that elicit disapproval and rejection by other members of society. Therefore, the student with special learning and/or behavior needs should be made aware of the standards and should demonstrate the ability to use necessary eating utensils and the accessories available to people with physical limitations. These skills should be taught in the primary grades, reinforced in the home, and practiced in specifically designed field trips in the community. Another functional objective should be demonstrating abilities in restaurants or other public eating places.

5.25 Plan and Eat Balanced Meals

It is quite a step from eating properly to planning appropriate foods for breakfast, lunch, and dinner. Planning does not need to include actual preparation of a meal. Even if students with special learning and/or behavior needs cannot or do not choose to prepare foods, they should know the nutritional value and relationships between food, health, and growth so that they can choose meals that provide the greatest benefits. Many individuals eat "junk foods" that are high in sugar content but low in protein. This is the type of situation that the individual with special learning and/or behavior needs must avoid. Second, adequate meals are important for those individuals with special learning and/or behavior needs who receive supplementary ingredients to their diets, such as calcium for bone development, medications of various sorts, and injections. These supplements balance and interact with other nutrients. If a student with special learning and/or behavior needs is careless about her diet, her mental and physical performance will be lowered and her health endangered. Teachers should note that this LCCE Mild Curriculum subcompetency is also related to the one on physical fitness, nutrition, and weight (3.12). Other functional objectives should include developing a list of foods that are beneficial to health and planning meals within a specified budget.

6.0 Buying and Caring for Clothes

The old expression that "clothes make the man" has undergone some alterations, but it still signifies a cultural standard that serves as a powerful tool in the classroom. Whether blue jeans or formal dress, running/cross-training/walking/exercise shoes or high heels, fashions, styles, and the latest "in thing" interest students with special learning and/or behavior needs from elementary through adult education classes, because clothes are related to identity and social acceptance. Proper choice or modification of clothing can improve the appearance of individuals with special learning and/or behavior needs and minimize physical deficiencies. This competency includes the following LCCE Mild Curriculum subcompetencies:

6.26 Wash/Clean Clothing

The principal objective in LCCE Mild Curriculum subcompetency 6.26 is to teach students with special learning and/or behavior needs how to care for clothing. This skill will enhance the students with special learning and/or behavior needs' appearance and use of appliances. Primary-grade students with special learning and/or behavior needs can become familiar with the effects of various laundry detergents and water temperatures by washing dust cloths, handkerchiefs, and towels. When students with special learning and/or behavior needs begin to wash their clothes, they will need instruction about the various laundry products and about operating washing machines and dryers. These steps require cooperation from parents, who are in a better position to evaluate these functional skills.

6.27 Purchase Clothing

Some students with special learning and/or behavior needs will have experience with or influence over the purchase of clothing and food products before they have learned other basics of consumer buying (i.e., shelter, health, transportation, and leisure). The observant teacher will recall the numerous children who accompany their parents on shopping ventures in the supermarket and clothing stores. These same teachers may face a bitter battle in attempting to counteract students' impulse buying habits. If successful, the teacher will have impressed the student with special learning and/or behavior needs with such considerations as how to select appropriate clothing for different occasions, balance clothing needs with available funds, identify well-made versus poorly made garments, and coordinate purchases relative to the student's needs and finances. Other functional objectives

should include recording one's measurements, identifying clothing for a basic wardrobe, and planning a wardrobe based on a specific budget.

6.28 Iron and Store Clothing

Home economics teachers can help students with special learning and/or behavior needs acquire skills involved in preparing and ironing various types of clothing. Teachers should provide instruction about the why, when, how, and where of storing seasonal clothing. Once again, every attempt should be made to coordinate classroom and home instruction. Skills for this subcompetency include matching thread color and learning the mechanics of preliminary planning and basting, simple hand sewing, machine sewing, and appropriate stitches for different types of tears.

· · · · · · · · **Activity Tip** · · · · · · · ·
Each student with special learning and/or behavior needs should have access to a clothing repair kit either at school or home. The classroom or home economics teacher should assign specific repairs to be completed at home or the student with special learning and behavior needs may bring items from home to repair sessions at school. Teachers and parents can monitor materials for the kit, its location, and use according to the abilities and attitude of the student with special learning and behavior needs.

7.0 Exhibiting Responsible Citizenship

Over the past decade, the community participation of people with special learning and behavior needs has steadily increased. This participation has been encouraged by the success of other groups of individuals who have demonstrated and lobbied for legislation to ensure equality in housing, education, and employment. Once significant laws have been passed at the local, state, and federal levels, these citizens must be prepared to continue their roles as advocates to translate legislation and regulations into daily social practice.

7.29 Demonstrate Knowledge of Civil Rights and Responsibilities

Subcompetency 7.29 includes knowledge of the individuals' rights when being questioned by officers of the law and knowledge of sources of legal assistance that can be used to help individuals answer the questions. Teachers cannot help students with special learning and behavior needs develop this combination of skills very easily. Students with special learning and behavior needs should role play situations in which they are confronted by officers. Law enforcement officials or members of legal aid associations may also give classroom presentations that concern violations and citizen responses during interrogation. Students should register for selective service classification at age 18. In some instances, the military may be a possible occupational choice. Another functional objective should be identifying information required for registration with the selective service.

7.30 Know Nature of Local, State, and Federal Governments

The teacher should help each student understand fundamental reasons for the existence of laws, government, and the various roles and duties of government officials. Instead of emphasizing the consequences of violating a law, the teachers should explain how officials and citizens within the community effect changes in the law and how already existing laws benefit them. The teacher may approach the larger federal structure from the same vantage point as in the previous LCCE Mild Curriculum subcompetency. Local and federal structures contain three major administrative, legislative, and judicial areas, as well as a set of statutes, regulations, and agencies. The student with special learning and behavior needs should be aware of the instances in which federal law takes precedence over local and state laws. Another functional objective should be identifying appropri-ate elements of the Constitution and Declaration of Independence.

7.31 Demonstrate Knowledge of the Law and the Ability to Follow the Law

Citizenship rights and responsibilities are a major element in the entire competency. LCCE Mild Curriculum subcompetency 7.31 involves identification of laws enacted to assist citizens, including those with special learning and behavior needs. But each right contains a responsibility of citizenship, and students with special learning and behavior needs should be aware of obligations that include obeying laws, paying taxes, and being informed on problems and issues within the society. Another functional objective should focus on an adequate understanding of the basic court system and its procedures.

7.32 Demonstrate Knowledge of Citizen Rights and Responsibilities

The reasons for voting should be emphasized throughout the elementary years. Many secondary students who have the opportunity to register and vote will enroll in training programs. This situation provides teachers with a chance to use practical lesson plans based on student experiences with the process of registering and voting. Other functional objectives should be identifying the dates, issues, and offices to be decided in coming elections, and soliciting sources of information to speak to the class.

· · · · · · · · **Activity Tip** · · · · · · · · ·

Students should collect an "Advocacy Notebook" of pictures, articles, and information pertaining to the rights of individuals with special learning and behavior needs. The material should reflect the expanding role of individuals in civic and social functions. It can be gathered from newspapers, magazines, or brochures collected on field trips or distributed by classroom speakers. Teachers should enlist the cooperation of individuals who have been active in community affairs.

· ·

8.0 Utilizing Recreation and Leisure

A steady decrease in the number of hours in the average work week has resulted in an increase in the amount of time, energy, and attention that workers can devote to recreation and leisure. Various professional and parent organizations have placed great emphasis on physical education, leisure, recreation, and art. Expanded programs, special events, and conferences will contribute to the development of physical abilities, as well as public acceptance of the individual's participation in society. The activities involved in this competency prepare them for yet another area of integration and, therefore, must be considered a distinct and valuable part of the overall curriculum. The career cluster of hospitality and recreation occupations also provides opportunities for future employment if the individual with special learning and behavior needs demonstrates particular interest and skill in these competencies. This competency includes the following LCCE Mild Curriculum subcompetencies:

8.33 Demonstrate Knowledge of Available Community Resources

Teachers can begin to teach elementary school students about functions, events, and facilities available in community agencies, schools, or churches. The next step includes cooperative efforts between teachers, parents, and recreation leaders to encourage and include the students with special learning and behavior needs as participants, as well as observers. Based on this encouragement, students with special learning and behavior needs can develop an awareness of the range of recreational activities in which they can participate, as well as the resources and facilities accessible to them in the community. An important functional objective is to strongly promote participation in recreational activities outside the home as soon as possible.

8.34 Choose and Plan Activities

Many LCCE Mild Curriculum subcompetencies related to the use of recreation and leisure require actual field experiences. These experiences enable the student with special learning and behavior needs to plan leisure activities. Planning should include factors such as cost, location, travel, physical requirements, use of equipment, and number of participants. The planning and decision making will incorporate the students' experience with prior activities and test their self-awareness (refer to competency 10 in Chapter 12). An important functional objective is to have each student with special learning and behavior needs develop an individual plan of leisure activities.

8.35 Demonstrate Knowledge of the Value of Recreation

Understanding recreational values is closely linked to development of self-awareness. It includes students with special learning and behavior needs' understanding of the role of recreation in the overall development of life and can function as a balance to everyday pressures that they may confront in striving toward independence. But students with special learning and behavior needs only can internalize this understanding by using leisure time effectively and by becoming involved in activities, clubs, or hobbies. This requires a coordinated effort among parents, teachers, and recreational personnel.

• • • • • • • • • **Activity Tip** • • • • • • • •
Teachers, recreation and physical education personnel, parents, and students with special learning and behavior needs should contribute to the construction of a leisure grid. This grid lists the skills required of students with special learning and behavior needs as (1) participants, (2) observers, and (3) employees in each leisure area. Each sport, activity, or hobby provides students with special learning and behavior needs with opportunities to record their observations about recreation and employment possibilities. The grid can be supplemented by pictures, newspaper or magazine articles, and student essays.
• •

8.36 Engage in Group and Individual Activities

Adequate participation in group activities depends, in part, on the individuals with special learning and behavior needs' physical fitness and ability to interact with other members of the group. Therefore, the teacher should design or adapt games and group activities that contribute to both goals. The students with special learning and behavior needs' physical characteristics are a consideration, but we have enough examples—from blind skiers to basketball players in wheelchairs—to know that physical constraints do not always prevent an individual with special learning and behavior needs from engaging in particular activities. Other functional objectives should include demonstrating the proper care of equipment used in an activity, learning safety rules, and sportsmanship.

8.37 Plan Vacation Time

Adults initiate vacations, but children can be included in some of the planning. Children can wrestle with such major questions as, "When should the family take a vacation? Where should we go? Why should we go there? What will we do when we get there? How much will it cost? Do we have enough money for a vacation?" Throughout the questioning process, teachers and parents should present several considerations so children with special learning and behavior needs can understand that the final plan is composed of several decisions involving family needs and resources. Other functional objectives should include identifying available sources of information that assist in planning and constructing a vacation plan.

9.0 Getting Around the Community (Mobility)

In a society that encourages mobility and places importance on such things as cars, campers, ski trips, and coast-to-coast air flights, it is no wonder that teenagers and adults value their ability to move at will. This ability is even more important for those who struggle to commute between home and places of employment, recreation, or health services. Diligent training can prepare individuals who have visual, physical, and mental disabilities to move freely within the community. These individuals with special learning and/or behavior needs should receive training on how to use guide dogs or canes, drive cars, use wheelchairs or carts, and use other forms of transportation. The following LCCE Mild Curriculum subcompetencies are based on the assumption that individuals can move within the community with or without the assistance of devices such as artificial limbs, mechanical devices, or sonic sensory aids. This competency includes the following LCCE Mild Curriculum subcompetencies:

9.38 Demonstrate Knowledge of Traffic Rules and Safety

The basics of traffic rules, signs, symbols, and sounds should be taught in the elementary grades. Their importance is based on safety for all members of the community. Teachers should use posters, field trips, and numerous audiovisual aids to emphasize the responsibilities of both pedestrians and motorists.

9.39 Demonstrate Knowledge and Use of Various Means of Transportation

Students should be acquainted with the specific forms of transportation available within the community. Teachers should construct lessons that emphasize advantages and disadvantages, costs, schedules, availability, and convenience of various forms of transportation. The lessons should include information on how students can use aids such as tickets or tokens, route maps, and illustrations provided by various carriers. A second important area of instruction would include the students with special learning and/or behavior needs' ability to interpret maps and locate addresses within the community. Finally, students with special learning and/or behavior needs use appropriate forms of transportation to reach school, work, or recreational destinations.

• • • • • • • • Activity Tip • • • • • • • •

The treasure hunt game can be used to test students with special learning and/or behavior needs' mobility skills. Parents, friends, and other teachers can assist on hunts that expand from the classroom or home, to the neighborhood, and to the larger community. The hunt should emphasize all aids that students with special learning and/or behavior needs may use to reach their final destinations and should help them understand the roles of various community workers who can provide assistance.

9.40 Find Way Around the Community

LCCE Mild Curriculum subcompetency 9.40 focuses on teaching students with special learning and/or behavior needs how to find specific addresses so they can locate not only friends but places of business and recreation or leisure. Students with special learning and/or behavior needs will learn how to use city and state maps with the help of family members who should expose them to actual community-based experiences. Another functional objective is to help students become knowledgeable of community resources and to become familiar with everyday symbols and signs encountered in community mobility.

9.41 Drive a Car

One of the major goals of most high school students is to sit behind the wheel of a car. Teachers can use this to help students with special learning and/or behavior needs develop several other LCCE Mild Curriculum subcompetencies, as well as functional academic skills. The teacher should work with other instructors to coordinate driver's education lessons. This is especially important if driver educators are responsible for instruction in the driver's manual, state examination, and behind-the-wheel training. Classroom teachers also could be of assistance in teaching aspects of the manual. Teachers can construct layouts of highways and streets (from posterboard or plywood) that contain numerous traffic signals and signs. Other functional objectives should include identifying appropriate procedures for a driver after being involved in an auto accident and demonstrating ability to make minor repairs on a vehicle.

The final lesson plan presented for daily living skills instruction relates to this final LCCE Mild Curriculum subcompetency. The lesson plan is a career preparation level of instruction and involves learning road signs, reviewing state driver's manuals, and taking a relevant vehicle safety sign test. The lesson plan spans all career roles as noted at the bottom of the sheet. The lesson may need to be taught over more than the one session indicated. More detailed and specific instructional objectives and lesson plan activities can be obtained by obtaining the LCCE competency unit manuals (Brolin, 1992a to 1992d; Roessler & Brolin, 1992), which are described in Appendix E.

Lesson Plan 11   9.38.3P:11

LCCE Objective 9.38.3 Identify vehicle safety signs of the driver's education sign test.

Lesson Objective: Student will successfully identify vehicle safety signs from a practice driver's test.

Instructional Resources: Fact Sheet **Road Signs**, colored pencils or markers, state driver's manuals, Worksheet **Vehicle Safety Sign Test**.

Lesson Introduction: Today we are going to take a practice test that is very nearly like the vehicle safety sign test which you must pass to get a driver's license. When you have finished, we will evaluate how well you did.

School Activity: **Time: 1 session**

Task:

1. Distribute copies of Fact Sheet **Road Signs** and colored pencils or markers.
   - Have students color the signs to make them more realistic.
   - Students may refer to the fact sheet and to driver's manuals as needed.
2. Divide class into pairs, and have students drill each other on identification and meanings of signs.
3. When students are satisfied that they know the signs and meanings, distribute and administer Worksheet **Vehicle Safety Sign Test**.
   - Students are to refer to the Fact Sheet **Road Signs** while completing the test.
   - It is suggested that the class be allowed the same amount of time to complete the test as is permitted in your state for the actual test.
4. When students are finished, read correct responses to items, and allow students to correct their own tests. Discuss any incorrect answers.

Lesson Plan Evaluation:

Activity: Students will complete Worksheet **Vehicle Safety Sign Test**.

Criteria: Student will complete the test with 12 of 15 accurate responses.

Career Role: Family Member/Homemaker, Employee, Citizen/Volunteer, Avocational

Career Stage: Preparation

Note: From *Life Centered Career Education: Competency Units for Daily Living Skills* (Vol. 3, p. 1430) by D. E. Brolin, 1992, Arlington, VA: The Council for Exceptional Children. Copyright 1992 by The Council for Exceptional Children. Reprinted by permission.

Developing appropriate communication skills is critical for functioning in current and future ecological environments.

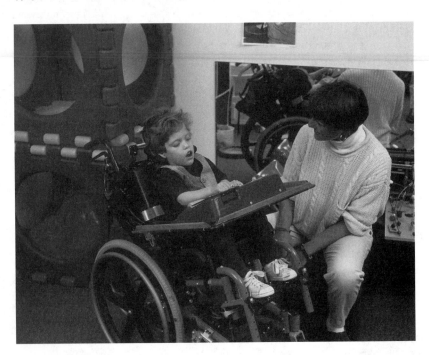

TEACHING LCCE MODERATE CURRICULUM DAILY LIVING SKILLS

Daily living skills, sometimes referred to as *independent or survival living skills,* are those required to function independently, semi-independently, or within a family environment. Some examples of daily living skills are counting money, using vending machines, performing banking skills, dressing appropriately, maintaining physical fitness, practicing personal safety, preparing meals, practicing basic first aid, accessing available transportation, and selecting and participating in group travel. These skills are those needed to become responsible adults within the home, school, community, and the job. Responsibility for teaching these skills rests jointly with special and regular educators, parents, and peers (West et al., 1992).

Most LCCE Mild Curriculum lesson plans from Life Centered Career Education: Competency Units for Daily Living Skills *by D. E. Brolin (Arlington, VA: The Council for Exceptional Children, 1992) can be modified for use with the LCCE Moderate Curriculum competencies and subcompetencies*

Throughout this book, the importance of family and community involvement and reliable alliances has been stressed. Successful transition/career education in this functional curriculum area is extremely dependent on the involvement of these resources. In the case of family members willing to participate in helping to meet the functional needs of their child with special learning and/or behavior needs, much of the teacher's focus in this functional curriculum area can be reinforced and further expanded in the home setting. In addition, community resources such as grocery stores, clothing stores, banks, recreational centers, transportation companies, governmental agencies, and many others can provide valuable assistance. Suggestions for the involvement of these resources has been addressed in previous chapters and so is not repeated here. Rather, attention is directed primarily to the teacher's role in this functional curriculum area.

Daily living skills are necessary for successful independent living and working in modern society. Acquisition of these functional skills also can lead to vocational possibilities for students with special learning and/or behavior needs, depending on their particular abilities, interests, and personalized needs. These functional skills must be systematically infused into daily lessons rather than taught haphazardly or overlooked entirely. Teachers will need to consider the personalized functional needs of the individual with special learning and/or behavior needs before they plan functional objectives and methods and evaluate the progress of the student with special learning and/or behavior needs. These functional efforts will help teachers and most importantly learners with special learning and/or behavior needs to notice improvements in such daily living skills functions as maintaining personal appearance, managing finances, and getting around in the community.

Daily living skills can and should be taught in various general education content areas, community-based activities, and in home assignments. In addition to the many obvious benefits for teaching these functional skills substantially to students with special learning and/or behavior needs, this functional focus "can provide exciting and realistic activities for reaching academic, general cognitive, and language and communication, as well as social skills" (Langone, 1990).

Daily living skills can be infused into a wide range of basic academic content areas, for example, reading, English, math, government, social studies, science, and such courses as home economics, physical education, and health. Through a process such as curriculum mapping (i.e., determining what subjects and levels to teach each of the agreed-on life skills), a transition committee and/or other general educators in the school identify how these functional skills can be infused into the school's curriculum.

Some of the instructional approaches or strategies that are particularly important to provide students with moderate learning and/or behavior needs in this functional curriculum area follow:

Curriculum Area	Competency	Subcompetency: The student will be able to:	
DAILY LIVING SKILLS	1. Managing Money	1. Count money	2. Make purchases
	2. Selecting & Maintaining Living Environments	6. Select appropriate community living environment	7. Maintain living environment
	3. Caring for Personal Health	10. Perform appropriate grooming and hygiene	11. Dress appropriately
	4. Developing and Maintaining Appropriate Intimate Relationships	16. Demonstrate knowledge of basic human sexuality	17. Demonstrate knowledge of appropriate dating behavior
	5. Eating at Home and in the Community	18. Plan balanced meals	19. Purchase food
	6. Cleaning and Purchasing Clothing	24. Wash/dry clothes	25. Buy clothes
	7. Participate in Leisure/Recreational Activities	26. Identify available community leisure/recreational activities	27. Select and plan leisure/recreational activities
	8. Getting Around in the Community	30. Follow traffic rules and safety procedures	31. Develop and follow community access routes

FIGURE 11.2   Life Centered Career Education—Moderate Curriculum (LCCE-M): Daily Living Skills Competencies
Note: From *Life Centered Career Education: Modified Curriculum for Individuals with Moderate Disabilities* by R. J. Loyd and D. E. Brolin, 1997, Arlington, VA: The Council for Exceptional Children. Copyright 1997 by the Council for Exceptional Children. Reprinted with permission.

- Numerous hands-on experiences with real materials such as tools and appliances
- School resources such as the cafeteria, nurse, clerical, transportation, and housekeeping services to reinforce the importance of these skills for not only personal functioning but also for employment
- Community-based experiences such as tours, job shadowing, mentoring, and instructional opportunities
- Volunteers such as parents and community members to provide classroom demonstrations and activities for students in these skill areas
- Games, simulations of community resources, role-playing, computers, and videotapes to provide interesting and challenging activities and demonstrations for skills development
- Peer tutors who have particular expertise and enthusiasm for tutoring the students in areas of special need
- The cooperative learning approach

All of these important functional instructional strategies were addressed earlier during the discussion of the LCCE Mild Curriculum competencies and subcompetencies.

Other critical instructional strategies for students with moderate learning and/or behavior needs include: using age-appropriate transition materials/resources; providing adequate support and assistance; instruction in utilizing natural supports; facilitating school/community integration success; instruction in multiple ecological environments; and instruction in seeking assistance when needed.

LCCE MODERATE CURRICULUM COMPETENCIES

In addition to general life skills development, the daily living skills curriculum area of LCCE Moderate Curriculum focuses on three of the four major career roles composing the concept of career development advocated in this book: the work of a family member, citizen/volunteer, and productive avocational activities such as hobbies and other

3. Use vending machine	4. Budget money	5. Perform banking skills		
8. Use basic appliances and tools	9. Set up personal living space			
12. Maintain physical fitness	13. Recognize and seek help for illness	14. Practice basic first aid	15. Practice personal safety	
20. Prepare meals	21. Demonstrate appropriate eating habits	22. Demonstrate meal clean-up and food storage	23. Demonstrate appropriate restaurant dining	
28. Participate in individual and group leisure/recreational activities	29. Select and participate in group travel			
32. Access available transportation				

leisure pursuits. Daily living skills instruction also promotes, to a somewhat lesser extent, occupational development and future employment possibilities. This area is addressed later in the chapter.

In this section, the LCCE Moderate Curriculum 8 daily living skills competencies and their 32 subcompetencies are presented. The competencies and subcompetencies are illustrated in Figure 11.2. As each of these is presented in the following discussion, several activity tips are provided. LCCE competency unit curriculum manuals (Loyd & Brolin, in press), similar to the ones already developed for the LCCE Mild Curriculum Program, will be published by the Council for Exceptional Children (CEC).

1.0 Managing Money

The ability to manage money is a crucial determinant of adult success for everyone. Therefore, teachers and reliable alliances must provide numerous activities that prepare students with moderate special learning and/or behavior needs for their roles as spenders, savers, and managers of their money with or without support. Although these skills may be limited in scope and sequence to activities included in the LCCE Mild Curricu-

lum, many of the lower level money skills need to be included in students with moderate disabilities' personalized programs. Many will become actively involved in the community, thus needing to understand the concept of making money, saving money, and spending money. This should include the following subcompetencies:

1.1 Count Money

Counting money can be successfully taught to students with moderate disabilities. Some students may be able to count out money for some level of purchasing items. As with all students, money identification is the beginning skill for this subcompetency. Teachers and families should encourage handling money at every opportunity. Teachers can use token economies and checking/savings programs to practice counting coins and bills. Family members can put money out on a table from pockets and wallets and let the individual count out their allowance.

As it has been noted with the LCCE Mild Curriculum, simple teaching aids and commercial workbooks are available to help teachers initiate activities that would require students to count coins and bills up to twenty dollar bills.

1.2 Make Purchases

Being able to purchase items is an important skill to be performed either fully or partially with support by all individuals with more moderate disabilities. Teachers can set up a classroom store to have students with more moderate disabilities practice the skill of purchasing items. Community-based experiences, even at the elementary school level, provide opportunities for students to purchase lunch from a restaurant or items from a retail store. School snack/supply shops also provide opportunities for students to practice making purchases. Selecting the item that is the best priced is another activity needing to be reinforced in school or in the community.

Families can enable the individual to purchase items when it is convenient and can provide practice counting money and receiving the correct change. Families can discuss how to select discounted items and how coupons can reduce the price. Students need to be aware of any store providing discount cards and how to select the store's discounted products or own brand as a savings on the overall total bill.

A final consideration for all consumers is recognizing from whom to request help and then requesting assistance when needed.

• • • • • • • • Activity Tip • • • • • • • •

Students with moderate special learning and/or behavior needs can help with the family's grocery shopping. The grocery list can be divided into two separate lists: the longer list can be a family project to purchase and a shorter list designed for the individual with moderate special learning and/or behavior needs to select and purchase. Pictorial lists can support both in selection and purchasing the best buy. The individual should check out and purchase his or her items ahead of the family purchasing the remaining items.

1.3 Use Vending Machines

Almost on a daily basis, adults use vending machines to make purchases of food or product items. Previously, most vending machines operated similarly, but now many vary in operating procedures and payment options. Students with moderate special learning and/or behavior needs should be exposed to as many different types of machines as possible to help learn the basic operation of vending machines. The use of the next quarter technique is a good strategy for use in making purchases from vending machines. Students with moderate special learning and/or behavior needs should keep a good reserve of quarters at their disposal when out in the community. Students with moderate special learning and/or behavior needs also should learn how to operate vending machines that accept dollar bills. Another functional activity should be to always check the coin return after purchasing and receiving vending items.

A final consideration for all consumers is recognizing from whom to request help and then requesting assistance when needed.

1.4 Budget Money

Students with moderate special learning and/or behavior needs will need to learn the rudimentary elements of budgeting earned incomes. Teachers can set up practice sessions of budget situations for students with moderate special learning and/or behavior needs in the classroom. Family members can develop and review family budgeting practices for their lifestyles. If students with moderate special learning and/or behavior needs are paid monthly, it is important to discuss with a support person how to itemize weekly so as to budget for the month. Nonreaders should use a pictorial representation of the budget—daily, weekly, and monthly. This should include a discussion of income received versus expenses spent.

A final consideration for all consumers is recognizing from whom to request help and then requesting assistance when needed.

1.5 Perform Banking Skills

Presently, the majority of consumers use a checking account. This practice provides the person the benefit of not having to use cash to pay for typical daily, weekly, and/or monthly budgeted items. Thus, it is important for students with moderate special learning and/or behavior needs to learn—to the extent possible—instructional objectives that focus on banking transactions with or without support. This subcompetency covers a wide spectrum of skills for performing personalized banking skills. It also can include opening and maintaining a checking and savings account with or without the support of reliable alliances. Teachers should schedule community-based teaching experiences in banking facilities. Currently, the debit card or ATM (Automatic Transfer Machine) card is a convenient form of paying for purchases, but requires the same recording process as writing checks. Teachers can establish classroom banks and accounts in conjunction with exercises on the use of money. Teachers should encourage family members to explain how to use these facilities when they take their children with special learning and/or behavior needs with them to make deposits or withdrawals at their bank. Families can play an important role in helping to teach how to use their personal banking activities. Teachers can supplement these activities by asking representatives from these establishments to show the class how to use these services. Other functional objectives should include being able to request assistance from the appropriate banking official when needed.

2.0 Selecting and Maintaining Living Environments

An important normalized goal for most adults is community living. For some individuals with moderate special learning and/or behavior needs, this may require some form of a supported living option. Housing expenses generally are a major portion of a person's monthly budget. In some urban areas of the country, these expenses are high and generally require living in apartment complexes of all sizes, both externally and the interior. Although there is a trend for a young adult to reside with the family for longer periods of time, an activity that still is critical for students with moderate special learning and/or behavior needs is to participate in selecting and maintaining community living. This competency includes the following subcompetencies:

2.6 Select Appropriate Community Living Environment

Although many young adults with moderate special learning and/or behavior needs will initially live in group homes or supported apartments, they should understand and practice skills that are necessary for selecting the appropriate living environment. Teachers should discuss the following community living options: supported living, semi-independent, group homes, living with a reliance alliance roomate, and living alone with an emergency support service. The teacher needs to stress the advantages and disadvantages of each community living option. This includes discussions about space, costs, utilities, and location. Secondary students with moderate special learning and/or behavior needs should continue with specific exercises related to renting a home or apartment, deposits, leases, tenant rights and responsibilities, and community agencies providing community living support services. Families and other reliable alliances need to reinforce and discuss these community living options in their own communities. Another functional objective should be to identify who to contact and request assistance from when utilities are connected.

2.7 Maintaining Living Environment

Many teachers provide students with moderate special learning and/or behavior needs with practice maintaining their living environment. Although many community living options include exterior care of the living unit in the housing cost, interior preservation of the dwelling is the tenant's responsibility. Students with moderate special learning and/or behavior needs should learn the common tools, products, and equipment used for inside home maintenance work. This includes identifying routine cleaning tasks and safety factors required for maintaining the total living environment. Families can assist students in learning these cleaning tasks while living at home. Also, families can make sure that daily and weekly tasks are identified and performed in the home. Other functional objectives include knowing who to ask for support and assistance when needed.

Students with moderate special learning and/or behavior needs and families cooperate in constructing pictorial posters in each room displaying dates for and products, tools, and equipment necessary for cleaning each area of the home interior. A success chart can be added, indicating the performance of each function. The student and families can evaluate the performance and discuss needs to improve areas not adequately cleaned. This can be paired with an allowance or checking/savings program.

2.8 Use Basic Appliances and Tools

Concurrent to maintaining the living enironment is learning to safely use appliances to clean or make simple repairs to the living environment. The latter include such tools as a hammer, saw, screwdriver, or wrench. Teachers need to develop the skills that the student with moderate special learning and/or behavior will need to competently use appliances and tools in order to maintain cleanliness and ensure that doors, windows, and locks are in working order. This means that students with moderate special learning and/or behavior needs should be able to make some basic home repairs and improvements such as replacing light bulbs, tightening screws or bolts, and painting doors or walls with or without support. Teachers should plan these activities with the assistance of home economics, trade, and industrial technology teachers. Families can assist in helping teach the safe use of tools and appliances and make some minor home repairs. Other objectives should include knowing who to contact for support or assistance in using appliances and tools.

2.9 Set Up Personal Living Space

One of the most exciting events of moving into a community living environment is setting up a household. Some apartment complexes come furnished but without cooking and pantry supplies. The community living option requires students to learn how to obtain basic household items, furniture, and appliances. Teachers can have students develop posters that illustrate basic personal living space needs. As the student gets older, family members can help in selecting or give students basic second-hand items that can be used in their personal living space.

A final consideration for all students is recognizing from whom to request help and then requesting assistance when needed in helping setting up personal living space.

3.0 Caring for Personal Health

Personal health care is an important skill for ensuring that people maintain a good quality of life. Persons with moderate special learning and/or behavior needs who are integrated into community living and working must practice adequate personal hygiene, maintenance of physical fitness, and health care with or without support. Reliable alliances will assist these individuals in learning how to take care of these personal needs. Teachers need to work annually with the student and his/her reliable alliances to determine and instruct them in the most critical personal health skills needed in their current ecological environments. This competency includes the following subcompetencies:

3.10 Perform Appropriate Grooming and Hygiene

Students with moderate special learning and/or behavior needs should demonstrate the following skills to maintain appropriate grooming and personal hygiene: brushing their teeth; showering; washing their hands and face; using handkerchiefs/tissues, towels, and napkins; and dressing in appropriate clothing. Starting as early as preschool, families and teachers should determine and help students with moderate special learning and/or behavior needs develop these abilities and expand their awareness of personal hygiene and grooming habits that are appropriate for each age level that is normalized with or without support. This is one of the most vital subcompetencies because acceptance of an individual by peers, adults, and employers is usually based on personal appearance and personal hygiene practices. Another functional objective should include identifying the appropriate hygiene and grooming products.

A final consideration for all students is recognizing from whom to request help and then requesting assistance when needed in performing appropriate grooming and personal hygiene, as well as knowing who to ask when purchasing items.

•••••••• **Activity Tip** ••••••••
Each student with moderate special learning and/or behavior needs to construct a pictorial grooming card that he can carry in a wallet or purse. The pictorial grooming card is similar to an identification card but contains pictorial reminders of personal hygiene and grooming appropriate to the student's needs with or without support. Teachers, families, and other reliable people should check the grooming card daily for proper performance; they can also ask the student about the status of their supply of products used.

3.11 Dress Appropriately

Although dress requirements for most community settings have lessened, there are still standards that need to be followed. For many social settings (i.e., parties, weddings, theaters, etc.), coats and ties for men and dresses for women are no longer required attire. Other activities, such as attending funerals, religious services, and interviews still require more formal attire. Even though dressing down is more acceptable, students with moderate special learning and/or behavior needs must know the correct dress for the community activity. In reality, it is probably more difficult today than in the past to know the appropriate dress for the various community activities. This broad range of acceptable attire presents a new burden to teachers who must instruct students on types of clothing that are appropriate for different weather conditions, social settings, and work situations. Teachers in elementary school can keep boxes of oversized but shortened clothing so that students with moderate special learning and/or

behavior needs can practice selecting the appropriate dress for different situations. Videotapes can present a scenario in which the student then selects the appropriate clothing from the appropriate box of clothing. Teachers also can use role-playing techniques for helping adolescents with moderate special learning and/or behavior needs to become more aware of the social and health ramifications involved in dressing to meet the occasion.

A final consideration for all students is recognizing from whom to request help and then requesting assistance when selecting the appropriate dress for different situations in the community.

3.12 Maintain Physical Fitness

In the latest reauthorizations of the Individuals with Disabilities Education Act (IDEA), greater emphasis is placed on integrating students with moderate special learning and/or behavior needs in general education classes. This includes the content of physical education. Currently, there is a trend in many states to eliminate or reduce the daily physical education classes due to raising academic content standards. Prior to IDEA's mandates, many students with moderate special learning and/or behavior needs received little or no instruction in physical education or adapted physical education in public schools. As a result, many schools have initiated Special Olympics programs in an attempt to provide a means for these students to maintain physical fitness. The Special Olympics help to underscore that all individuals possess physical competence. Proper care and development of the body are vital to meet the physical demands of everyday life. Students with moderate special learning and/or behavior needs should demonstrate knowledge of the major body parts and perform exercises or activities that benefit health and fitness development. Teachers should enlist the cooperation of physical education or adapted physical education teachers and provide structured activities to help students with moderate special learning and/or behavior needs to develop fundamental knowledge of the basic food groups, nutrition, physical fitness, and weight control. Family members can help by having their child with moderate special learning and/or behavior needs develop and maintain their own health charts by recording weight (as compared to correct BMI) and physical fitness program participation.

A final consideration for all students is recognizing from whom to request help and then requesting assistance when needing support in developing and maintaining physical health and fitness.

3.13 Recognize and Seek Help for Illness

Most students will experience minor illnesses annually. This may include colds, flu, or allergy symptoms. Teachers and families must help students with moderate special learning and/or behavior needs to learn some basic first-aid techniques and know when to obtain assistance for various medical problems. Teachers should help students with moderate special learning and/or behavior needs in the primary grades to learn basic health measures that will prevent illnesses or injury. Community visits to local public health facilities or agents can provide demonstrations and audiovisual aids to assist instruction in these competencies. School nurses or hospital medical staff can discuss in class the appropriate measures for recognizing and seeking help for illnesses.

A final consideration for all students is recognizing who to request help from and then requesting assistance when needing help for illness.

3.14 Practice Basic First Aid

With or without support, all adults with moderate special learning and/or behavior needs will need to know how to perform basic first aid procedures. Examples include the appropriate intitial treatment for cuts, abrasions, and burns and then applying appropriate dressings. Families should discuss and demonstrate appropriate procedures and supplies to be used in practicing first aid for minor injuries occurring at home. Teachers and/or nurses can discuss the proper care for minor injuries in the community and how to contact emergency assistance when more serious injuries occur. Secondary level students should demonstrate how to follow emergency procedures.

A final consideration for all students is recognizing from whom to request help and then requesting assistance when needing help for emergency situations.

3.15 Practice Personal Safety

This subcompetency emphasizes the importance of students with moderate special learning and/or behavior practicing personal safety in the home, community, and work. Other functional objectives focus on knowing appropriate self-defense techniques and practices to take when being personally assaulted. This functional skill area has become extremely important with the rising violence and crime in our society. Teachers must address in elementary school the importance of knowing how to keep the living environment safe from hazards and how to practice safety issues in the community and at work. The involvement of families, law enforcement officials, and self-defense specialists can discuss and teach ways to practice safe living and working. Visits to community utility services such as gas and electric companies can help students with moderate special learning and/or behavior needs learn safety precautions and potential hazards in the living environment. Teachers should use role-playing activities to enhance this instruction. Another functional objective is understanding and practicing precautions when dealing with strangers.

A final consideration for all students is recognizing from whom to request help and then requesting assistance when needing help for emergency situations.

4.0 Developing and Maintaining Appropriate Intimate Relationships

For most adults with moderate special learning and/or behavior needs developing and maintaining appropriate intimate relationships is an important and normal activity. Teachers should help elementary students with moderate special learning and/or behavior needs to know what are appropriate levels of intimacy with various family members and friends, and when dating. Students with moderate special learning and/or behavior needs should role play these various interactions with the appropriate level of intimacy. Family members, church officials, and teachers in secondary and adult programs also can provide students with special learning and/or behavior needs with ample opportunity to ask questions about relationships and appropriate intimacy. This competency includes the following subcompetencies:

4.16 Demonstrate Knowledge of Basic Human Sexuality

Demonstrating a basic knowledge and understanding of human sexuality is an important functional skill for students with moderate special learning and/or behavior needs. Family discussions on a regular basis regarding maleness and femaleness are important in helping students with moderate special learning and/or behavior needs understand the differences between the genders. Family members or church officials should discuss the process that married couples engage in for having a family. These experiences must include serious discussions and questions addressing the responsibility of marriage and parenting. A basic understanding of the male or female physical self contains functional objectives that are specific to the sexual role of the individual. Awareness activities should be provided to help students with moderate special learning and/or behavior needs know the similarities and differences in the anatomy and functioning of the male and female. Although some educational institutions have excluded this subject material from the curriculum, families and other professionals should provide human sexuality education. Students with moderate special learning and/or behavior needs must make informed decisions to protect and participate in appropriate human sexuality experiences.

A final consideration for all students is recognizing from whom to request help and then requesting knowledge about basic human sexuality needs or concerns.

4.17 Demonstrate Knowledge of Appropriate Dating Behavior

Dating is a normalized activity for all young adults and needs to be included in the education of students with moderate special learning and/or behavior needs. Some areas of the country feel that home or the religious community are responsible for providing this information. No matter what the philosophy, it is critical that students with moderate special learning and/or behavior needs should understand the process of dating, various customs relative to the

relationship of individuals in the dating situation, and the responsibilities of each role. Family members or teachers can address such critical questions as, "When do I start dating? Should I date this type of person? How do I act on a date? Where do I go on a date?" These few questions provide enough fuel for years of home or classroom discussions, heart-to-heart talks, and personal growth. Other functional objectives should include identifying activities in the community that are appropriate for dating relationships and identifying ways to demonstrate that one is pleased on a date.

Families can nurture the skills for developing close relationships. Children learn about personal relations and respect by observing their parents and by interacting with brothers, sisters, or relatives. Before the primary grades, students with moderate special learning and/or behavior needs may have already developed relationships of varying intensities with family members, neighbors, playmates, and specialists. Students with moderate special learning and/or behavior needs should formulate answers to such questions as "What are the characteristics of a close relationship? In what manner do people respond to one another in a close relationship? What is its function?" By trying to find answers to questions such as these, students develop an awareness of those individual needs that lead to the development of close relationships. Another functional objective should be identifying persons with whom the student with special learning and/or behavior needs could establish a close relationship.

A final consideration for all students is recognizing from whom to request help and then requesting knowledge about dating behavior and concerns.

5.0 Eating at Home and in the Community

Along with eating at home, individuals are choosing to eat more meals in the community. This competency relates to process of purchasing, preparing, and consuming food at home and in the community. The role of food as both a necessary substance for life and reward for behavior places an additional

Teachers can set up role playing situations where each student with moderate special learning and/or behavior needs can practice asking another student for a date. The student asking should address all the specifics of the date (i.e., activity, time, transportation, etc.). Students also should practice how to accept rejection from a person. Group dating activities should be discussed and practiced. Classroom discussions can include the difficulties and fun aspects of dating. Adolescents with chaperones can engage in double-dating activities.

responsibility on teachers and families who must develop student abilities in distinguishing between the two for health purposes. The following subcompetencies are by no means the last word in planning, purchasing, and preparing food, so teachers should expand this area to meet the particular needs and abilities of their students. This competency includes the following subcompetencies.

5.18 Plan Balanced Meals

Getting to the step of enjoying eating properly requires careful planning of appropriate foods for breakfast, lunch, and dinner. Planning needs to be the first step involved the actual preparation of a meal. Even if students with moderate special learning and/or behavior needs cannot or do not choose to prepare foods, they need to know the nutritional value and relationships between food, health, and growth to choose meals that provide the greatest nutritional benefits. Many Americans are choosing to eat more "fast foods" that are high in sugar and carbohydrate content but low in protein. This is the type of situation that the individual with moderate special learning and/or behavior needs must be taught to avoid. If a student with moderate special learning and/or behavior needs is careless about her diet, her mental and physical performance will be lowered and her health could be endangered. Families and teachers should note that this subcompe-

tency also is related to the one on maintaining physical fitness and proper weight control (3.12). Other functional objectives should include planning a list of foods that are beneficial to health and planning meals following the food pyramid and within a specified budget.

A final consideration for all students is recognizing from whom to request help and then requesting knowledge about planning appropriate meals.

5.19 Purchase Food

With or without support purchasing food is related to the subcompetency on making responsible purchasing (1.2) and provides ample opportunity for families and teachers to train students with moderate special learning and/or behavior needs in the use of selecting appropriate quantities of food and calculating costs. Unfortunately, students with moderate special learning and/or behavior needs are often immersed in a world of advertisements for fast or junk foods. Buying junk food can become the subject matter for daily assignments in purchasing meals at the school cafeteria, calculating the cost of a bag lunch, or projecting future expenses for after school snacks. In later years, with the recommended assistance of home economics instructors or representatives from community consumer organizations, students should be exposed to lessons that will help them recognize differences in the quality of foods, various types and cuts of meat and fish, and the advantages of sales and specials. Other functional objectives should include identifying community sources of information about food prices, sales, and coupons, and constructing a shopping list within a budget.

5.20 Prepare Meals

Families and teachers should stress that selecting appropriate foods in the food pyramid is just as important as the preparation of food. This subcompetency also includes skills involved in the use of various kitchen tools and appliances. When preparing an entire balanced meal, the student with moderate special learning and/or behavior needs will need to know how to use cooking utensils; follow simple recipe

In preparation for a community visit to a grocery story, the teacher should provide the class with a pictorial list of basic food items from the food pyramid. Students with moderate special learning and/or behavior needs print prices on their pictorial list for each item from the local grocery store or supermarket. Students then compare these same items when shopping with family members. The complexity of the activity can be adjusted to the ability of the individual student.

(pictorial) directions; identify various forms of measures; clean, cut, and prepare food; and use devices for cooking and baking. Family members, as well as every school curriculum, should teach students with moderate special learning and/or behavior needs the skills involved in managing the preparation of a meal, either by direct manipulation or instruction. Other functional objectives should include preparing a meal according to directions and demonstrating kitchen safety measures.

A final consideration for all students is recognizing from whom to request help and then requesting knowledge about preparing meals.

5.21 Demonstrate Appropriate Eating Habits

Most adults know the standards of behavior pertaining to preparing for and eating in the company of other individuals. Individuals with moderate special learning and/or behavior needs should learn to set the table, serve, and eat food appropriately. Therefore, the student with moderate special learning and/or behavior needs should be made aware of the standards and should demonstrate the ability to use necessary eating utensils. These skills should be taught in the primary grades, reinforced at home, and practiced in specifically designed community visits to restaurants.

A final consideration for all students is recognizing from whom to request help and then requesting knowledge about appropriate eating habits.

5.22 Demonstrate Meal Clean-Up and Food Storage

After having a meal, it is just as important to perform appropriate cleaning measures and materials, disposal and removal of waste products, and storage of utensils. Cleaning up also is an appropriate area for lessons emphasizing safety factors and measures involved in the entire preparation and clean-up process. Proper food storage is useful in the overall management of financial resources and family health. Many people have become ill after eating leftover or spoiled food due to the improper storage of food. This process requires that students learn how to store food and identify when food is spoiled. Families can demonstrate food storage and the identification of spoiled food. Teachers can use numerous instructional aids available from consumer organizations or companies that manufacture storage devices. Another functional objective should be demonstrating techniques for storing food.

A final consideration for all students is recognizing from whom to request help and then requesting knowledge about meal clean-up and food storage.

5.23 Demonstrate Appropriate Restaurant Dining

Adults have to learn the standards of behavior pertaining to eating in public situations. An inability to conform to these standards even with some slight modification to accommodate the disability places these individuals in situations that elicit disapproval and rejection by other members of society. Therefore, the student with moderate special learning and/or behavior needs should be made aware of the standards and should demonstrate the ability to select foods and use necessary eating utensils. Family members should teach these skills at home and they should be reinforced in the primary grades. These skills should be practiced in specifically designed community trips to various types of restaurants.

A final consideration for all students is recognizing from whom to request help and then requesting knowledge about eating in public restaurants.

6.0 Cleaning and Purchasing Clothing

Cultural standards still require that certain clothes are stylish and that they are kept neat and clean. Whether blue jeans or formal dress, running/cross-training/walking/exercise shoes or high heels, fashions, styles, and the latest "in thing" interest students with moderate special learning and/or behavior needs from elementary through adult education classes, because clothes that are clean are related to social acceptance. Proper choice or modification of clothing can improve the appearance of individuals with moderate special learning and/or behavior needs and minimize physical deficiencies. This competency includes the following subcompetencies:

6.24 Wash/Dry Clothes

Cleaning clothing is the principal objective in subcompetency 6.24. This skill will enhance the students with moderate special learning and/or behavior needs' appearance and use of critical appliances with or without support. Family members can start early by having the child help by learning to sort clothes. Teachers can help primary-grade students with moderate special learning and/or behavior needs become familiar with the effects of various laundry detergents and water temperatures by washing dust cloths, handkerchiefs, and towels. When students with moderate special learning and/or behavior needs at home begin learning to wash their clothes, they will need instruction about the various laundry products and about operating washing machines and dryers. This also may require that they learn to use these appliances in commercial laundromats. Some schools have classrooms equipped with washing machines and dryers for teaching these basic procedures.

A final consideration for all students is recognizing from whom to request help and then requesting knowledge about washing and drying clothes.

6.25 Buy Clothing

Sometimes, families provide students with moderate special learning and/or behavior needs with early experiences or influence over the purchase of clothing and food products before they have learned other basics of consumer buying (i.e., health, transportation, and leisure). Teachers can help teach students how to counteract impulse buying habits with or without support. If successful, the teacher will have impressed upon the student with moderate special learning and/or behavior needs such considerations as how to select appropriate clothing for different occasions, balance clothing needs with available funds, identify well-made versus poorly made garments, and coordinate purchases relative to the student's needs and finances. Other functional objectives should include recording one's measurements, identifying clothing for a basic wardrobe, and planning a wardrobe based on a specific budget with or without support. Home economics teachers can help students with moderate special learning and/or behavior needs acquire skills involved in preparing and ironing various types of clothing. Teachers should provide instruction about the why, when, how, and where of storing seasonal clothing. Once again, every attempt should be made to coordinate classroom and home instruction. Skills for this subcompetency also include matching thread color and learning the mechanics of simple hand sewing and appropriate stitches for different types of tears with or without support.

A final consideration for all students is recognizing from whom to request help and then requesting knowledge about purchasing and making simple repairs to clothing.

• • • • • • • •   **Activity Tip**   • • • • • • • •

Families and teachers should provide the necessary practice for repairing torn clothing and provide sewing kits. The classroom or home economics teacher should assign specific repairs to be completed at home or the student with moderate special learning and/or behavior needs may bring items from home to repair sessions at school. Teachers and parents can monitor materials for the kit, its location, and use according to the abilities and aptitude of the student with moderate special learning and/or behavior needs.

• •

7.0 Participate in Leisure Recreational Activities

Fortunately, we have seen over the past two decades a tremendous increase in community recreational participation (either full or partially) of people with moderate special learning and/or behavior needs. This participation has been encouraged by the success of other groups of individuals who have demonstrated and lobbied for legislation to ensure equality in housing, education, and employment. Once significant laws have been passed at the local, state, and federal levels, these citizens must be prepared to continue their roles as advocates to translate legislation and regulations into daily social practice. A steady decrease in the number of hours in the average workweek has resulted in an increase in the amount of time, energy, and attention that workers can devote to recreation and leisure. Various professional and parent advocacy organizations have placed great emphasis on physical education, leisure, recreation, and the arts. Expanded programs, special events, and conferences will contribute to the development of physical abilities, as well as public acceptance of the individual's participation in normalized community activities. The activities involved in this competency prepare them for yet another area of integration and, therefore, must be considered a distinct and valuable part of the overall curriculum and their quality of life. The career cluster of hospitality and recreation occupations also provides opportunities for future employment if the individual with moderate special learning and/or behavior needs demonstrates particular interest and skill in these competencies. This competency includes the following subcompetencies:

7.26 Identify Available Community Leisure/Recreational Activities

Families can play a vital role in the identification and participation of their child with moderate special learning and/or behavior needs in community recreational and leisure opportunities. Teachers can begin to teach elementary school students about functions, events, and facilities available in community agencies, schools, or churches. The next step includes cooperative efforts among teachers, parents, and recreation leaders to encourage and include the students with moderate special learning and/or behavior needs as participants, as well as observers. Based on this encouragement, students with moderate special learning and/or behavior needs can develop an awareness of the range of recreational activities in which they can participate, as well as the resources and facilities accessible to them in the community. An important functional objective is to strongly promote participation in recreational activities outside the home as soon as possible.

A final consideration for all students is recognizing from whom to request help and then requesting knowledge about participating in community recreational and leisure activities with or without support.

7.27 Select and Plan Leisure/ Recreational Activities

Many activities related to participating in recreation and leisure requires utilizing actual community facilities. Families can help the student with moderate special learning and/or behavior needs know which activities require or do not require accessing community facilities. These experiences enable the student with moderate special learning and/or behavior needs to plan leisure activities. Planning should include factors such as cost, location, travel, physical requirements, use of equipment, and number of participants. The planning and decision making will incorporate the students' experience with prior activities and test their self-awareness (refer to competency 10 in Chapter 12). An important functional objective is to have each student with moderate special learning and/or behavior needs develop an individual plan of leisure activities.

A final consideration for all students is recognizing from whom to request help and then requesting knowledge about selecting and planning leisure/recreational experiences with or without support.

7.28 Participate in Individual and Group Leisure/Recreational Activities

Today, many opportunities are available for either participating in a variety of individual or group leisure/recreational activities. Understanding recreational values is closely linked to development of self-awareness. It includes students with moderate special learning and/or behavior needs' understanding the role of recreation in the overall development of life and can function as a balance to everyday pressures that they may confront in striving toward independence. But, students with moderate special learning and/or behavior needs can only internalize this understanding by learning about making choices, using leisure time effectively, and by becoming involved in individual activities, clubs, or hobbies. This requires coordinated effort between parents, teachers, and recreational personnel.

Adequate participation in group activities depends, in part, on the individual with moderate special learning and/or behavior needs' physical fitness and ability to interact with other members of the group. Therefore, the teacher and adapted physical education teacher should design or adapt games and group activities that contribute to both goals. The student with moderate special learning and/or behavior needs' physical characteristics are a consideration, but we have enough examples—from blind skiers to basketball players in wheelchairs—to know that physical constraints do not always prevent an individual with special learning and/or behavior needs from engaging in particular activities. Other functional objectives should include demonstrating the proper care of equipment used in an activity, learning safety rules, and sportsmanship.

A final consideration for all students is recognizing from whom to request help and then requesting knowledge about participating in individual and/or group recreational activities.

7.29 Select and Participate in Group Travel

Parents and other adults usually are the ones to initiate group vacations, but students with moderate special learning and/or behavior needs can be included in the planning. Children can wrestle with such major questions as, "When should the family take a vacation? Where should we go? Why should we go there? What will we do when we get there? How much will it cost? Do we have enough money for a vacation?" Throughout the questioning process, teachers and family members should present several considerations so children with moderate special learning and/or behavior needs can understand that the final plan is comprised of several decisions involving family needs and resources. Other functional objectives should include identifying available sources of information that assist in planning and constructing a group vacation plan.

A final consideration for all students is recognizing from whom to request help and then requesting knowledge about selecting and participating in group vacations.

• • • • • • • • **Activity Tip** • • • • • • • •

Students should collect an "Advocacy Notebook" of pictures, articles, and information pertaining to the group travel events. The material should reflect the expanding role of individuals in various travel adventures. It can be gathered from newspapers, magazines, or brochures collected on field trips or distributed by classroom speakers. Teachers should enlist the cooperation of individuals who have are involved with travel agencies and/or planning.

8.0 Getting Around in the Community

We are a mobile society and engage in learning to use transportation means, such as public transportation, trains, and coast-to-coast air flights. This ability is even more important for those who struggle to commute among home and places of employment, recreation, or health services. Diligent training can prepare individuals who have visual, physical, and mental disabilities to move freely within the community. These individuals with moderate special learning and/or behavior needs should receive training on how to use multiple forms of transportation. The following subcompetencies are based on the assumption that individuals can move within the community with or without support. This competency includes the following subcompetencies:

8.30 Follow Traffic Rules and Safety Procedures

Families should begin teaching their children safe travel procedures at a very early age. The basics of traffic rules, signs, symbols, and sounds also should be taught in the elementary grades. Their importance is based on safety for all members of the community. Teachers should use posters, community experiences, and numerous audiovisual aids to emphasize the responsibilities of both pedestrians and motorists.

A final consideration for all students is recognizing from whom to request help and then requesting knowledge about traveling about the community safely.

8.31 Develop and Follow Community Access Routes

Families should teach their child with moderate special learning and/or learning needs familiar routes to routine community resources. Subcompetency 8.31 focuses on teaching students with moderate special learning and/or behavior needs how to find specific addresses so they can locate not only friends but also places of business and recreation or leisure. Students with moderate special learning and/or behavior needs will learn how to use simple city and state maps with the help of family members who should expose them to actual community-based experiences. Another functional objective is to help students become knowledgeable of community resources and to become familiar with everyday symbols and signs encountered in community mobility.

A final consideration for all students is recognizing from whom to request help and then requesting knowledge about moving about the community safely.

8.32 Access Available Transportation

Students with moderate special learning and/or behavior needs should be acquainted with the specific forms of private and/or public transportation available within the community. Teachers should construct lessons that emphasize the advantages and disadvantages, costs, schedules, availability, and convenience of various forms of transportation. The lessons should include information on how students can use aids such as tickets or tokens, route maps, and illustrations provided by various carriers. A second important area of instruction would include the student with moderate special learning and/or behavior needs' ability to decide which is the best available transportation within their community. Finally, students with special learning and/or behavior needs use appropriate forms of transportation to reach school, work, or recreational destinations.

A final consideration for all students is recognizing from whom to request help and then requesting knowledge about available community transportation.

• • • • • • • • **Activity Tip** • • • • • • • •

The treasure hunt game can be used to test students with moderate special learning and/or behavior needs' mobility skills. Parents, friends, and other teachers can assist on hunts that expand from the classroom or home, to the neighborhood, and to the larger community. The hunt should emphasize all transportation and travel aids that students with special learning and/or behavior needs may use to reach their final destinations and should help them understand the roles of various community workers who can provide assistance.

EXAMPLES OF LCCE MILD/MODERATE CURRICULUM INFUSION

Elementary Level

One example of the use of the LCCE Mild Curriculum approach at the elementary level has been reported by J. Beck et al. (1994), who developed and implemented a life skills program oriented to adult outcomes for children with special learning and/or behavior needs in inclusive settings beginning at age 5. These educators note that an examination of the functional skills outlined by Brolin reveals a number of areas that also are taught in the elementary general education curriculum for students without disabilities; examples are time, money, seasons (appropriate clothing), and health (body care). When general education and special education teachers collaborate to plan age-appropriate lessons, these functional skills can be incorporated into lessons and units (J. Beck et al., 1994, p. 47). The authors note that the objectives they incorporated into their students' Individualized Education Plans (IEPs) were based on the LCCE Mild Curriculum competencies/subcompetencies for both the classroom and CBI.

An elementary teacher in Grand Rapids, Michigan, Diane Wisniewski, provides the following account of her use of the LCCE curriculum at Thornapple Elementary School:

I teach in a categorical learning disabled classroom. My students are third and fourth graders who range in ability from first- to fourth-grade level. I service children with learning disabilities, emotional impairments, and speech and language impairments. I have found that all of my students have benefited from the use of the LCCE tasks and objectives. Some examples of objectives that I have incorporated in my room follow:

Competency 1. Managing personal finances: Subcompetency 1. Count money and make correct change. At class centers in my room, the students start by identifying different coins and bills by name and value. Then, as they progress, I give them work sheets saying "Show me $34.16," "Show me 46 cents or $.46 or 46¢." The students then count out the different amounts. When they are finished, they are checked by a peer or staff. This also promotes cooperative learning.

We take this one step further, opening a school store, where the students run it exclusively. They make posters for advertising, they set up the shop, name the shop, fill the jars with the sale items, count out the items for a sale, and calculate the costs to the buyers. Additionally, they make change with staff assistance and cooperatively count out the profit. This

objective addresses many areas across the regular curriculum and LCCE objectives.

In this store operation, we incorporate all of our special needs students in our building. We are working for a group outing and also to put some of the profit back into the community. This entire project also relates to other LCCE competencies and subcompetencies, mainly, competency 5, subcompetencies 20 and 21, and competency 19, and subcompetencies 81 and 85.

Competency 9. Getting Around the Community: Subcompetency 38. Demonstrate knowledge of traffic rules and safety. In this lesson, I incorporate a social studies lesson, which is called "communities." In each lesson, I displayed one or two new directional signs from our community. We have open discussions on each, talk about their importance, where we would see and use these, and then draw and display them. At the end of each unit, the students sketch their community and incorporate the signs in the appropriate places. This activity can be used across the curriculum as well as reinforced on outings in the community.

Wisniewski and her colleagues have conducted curriculum mapping to categorize the LCCE Mild Curriculum skills (competencies and subcompetencies) so they can be incorporated into a K–12 scope and sequence. They have broken down the skills into even smaller units to meet the needs of all of their students with special learning and/or behavior needs.

Secondary Level

Pat Burch, Special Education Teacher/Transition Coordinator from North St. Francois County R-1 Public Schools in Bonne Terre-Desloge, Missouri, has used the LCCE Mild Curriculum with her students for many years. She provides this example of how she teaches one of the daily living skills competencies to her students.

I would like to share a few unique approaches and teaching strategies that we have implemented while teaching daily living skills competency 4, raising children and meeting marriage responsibilities. This area is a most valuable life skill and should not be regarded as something our students with special learning and/or behavior needs will acquire on their own. Many of our students with special learning and/or behavior needs develop relationships, marry, and raise a family after graduation. A successful marriage and the knowledge, skills, and ability necessary to make this commitment are critical for them to be happy and well adjusted. It is important to teach our students with special learning and/or behavior needs to show love, concern, understanding, support, and to share responsibilities in a marriage.

The demands of raising a family and working in today's society can be extremely stressful, especially for students with special learning and/or behavior needs. Learning to cope with these stresses in a positive way is provided through unit 4 LCCE lesson plans. Along with independence comes responsibility. For our students to develop successful relationships and raise their children in safe, loving, satisfying homes it is critical. The children of our students also deserve the opportunity to grow and mature in safe, happy homes. Teaching LCCE competency 4, raising children and meeting marriage responsibilities, helps to ensure that this happens.

The following strategies and activities that we have successfully implemented in teaching LCCE unit 4 have helped to bring the unit alive and have made teaching the various subcompetencies an enjoyable, positive learning experience for students with special learning and/or behavior needs, parents, and their teachers.

The LCCE Mild Curriculum approach stresses community and agency involvement. In teaching unit 4, as well as other units, I believe experiences with and obtaining assistance from various agencies are critical. We have established a working relationship with our County Health Department. Their staff has graciously provided us with informative pamphlets, materials, videos, samples, and packets pertaining to a number of LCCE Mild Curriculum lessons dealing with stress, prenatal care, immunizations, safety, child care, diseases, and so on. We have also opened our classroom doors to various health department personnel, who have shared valuable knowledge and expertise with our students with special learning and/or behavior needs, thus enhancing our LCCE Mild Curriculum program.

Our students with special learning and/or behavior needs, as well as other community members, have the opportunity to receive valuable help and assistance through this agency for numerous services, such as child care, nutrition, and immunizations. Unfortunately, many of our students with special learning and/or behavior needs in the past did not follow through and seek this assistance, although it was stressed within the classroom. I believe the primary barrier to students with special learning and/or behavior needs' acquiring needed services was a fear of the unknown. Students with special learning and/or behavior needs were not sure where specific agencies were located or what to expect from personnel once they were contacted. We have helped alleviate this barrier, not only by having the agency visit our classroom, but by also expanding the classroom into the community to include visits to the agency. We have found that, once given the opportunity to experience an actual visit to the agency in a controlled setting, our students with special learning and/or behavior needs' fears are relieved. They now not only know and understand where the County Health Department is located but also have become familiar with personnel and services provided.

The County Health Department becomes a valuable source of assistance to our students with special learning and/or behavior needs in raising children and meeting marriage responsibilities.

Parents, family members, and former graduates of our program also provide information and shared experiences as guest speakers within our classroom. This not only provides and brings meaningful life experiences into the classroom, but it elevates the self-esteem of our students with special learning and behavior needs, their parents, and former students. They feel a valuable sense of respect and accomplishment. Our students with special learning and/or behavior needs are proud of their accomplishments, and they can see hope for a positive, productive future for themselves.

We always strive to make our LCCE lessons as realistic as possible. Our students with special learning and/or behavior needs definitely relate to and learn more from real materials and people than just reading about or discussing written information in the classroom. We obtain and use real materials when possible, whether comparing one baby formula to another, the proper way to feed a baby, or taking a budget-making field trip to the baby department of a local store to choose necessary and appropriate clothing and items for an infant. Former students have also visited our classrooms with their own new infants, allowing us to experience these lessons with a real baby. All of these opportunities provide meaningful experiences in a controlled setting (Burch, 1994, personal communication).

Burch's strong support for the LCCE curriculum has been contagious in her school district, which is moving toward implementing the approach in a K–12 scope and sequence. In addition, Burch has been called on to give hundreds of presentations on her work and has become the primary trainer employed by the CEC to conduct LCCE Training Academies throughout the country.

OCCUPATIONAL POSSIBILITIES

Teaching daily living skills not only enhances students' abilities to function independently in their home and community, but results in students with special learning and/or behavior needs' developing occupational interests and abilities. In Table 11.1, the nine LCCE daily living skills competencies and

their subcompetencies are listed with examples of occupational possibilities that relate to each competency. These are just a few examples of the large number of potential jobs that students with special learning and/or behavior needs who become interested and competent in one or more of these areas may qualify for, with further training, in later life.

One additional effort to illustrate the application of the LCCE Mild Curriculum approach to career development has been reported by Elrod and Gilliland (1991–1992). They note that transition/career education concepts can be infused into a blended leisure-science curriculum using a functional application so that students with mild disabilities and disadvantaged environments can gain an expanded view of career options. Elrod and Gilliland have developed instructional units using the subcompetencies of competency 8, and utilizing recreation and leisure, to demonstrate a neoprogressive curricular example of what they call "eclectic functionalism," that is, where "traditional subject areas are blended and taught in non-traditional ways, emphasizing experiential learning where possible" (1991–1992, p. 21). Interested readers should refer to their article in the *National Forum of Special Education Journal* for specific information on their work.

Learning to manage money is a critical functional skill.

TABLE 11.1   The Daily Living Skills with Occupational Possibilities

Competencies and Subcompetencies	Occupational Possibilities
1. Managing personal finances	
Manage money	Clerk
Keeping financial records	Ticket seller
Banking and credit	Checker at supermarket
Buying wisely	Bookkeeper
Taxes	
Keep bills paid	
2. Selecting and managing a household	
Care for a home	Maintenance worker
Repair appliances	Plumber's assistant
Repair broken furniture	Electrician's assistant
Repair electrical items and plumbing	Groundskeeper
Renting or buying	Painter
Maintenance of lawn and grounds	Bricklayer's assistant
3. Caring for personal needs	
Grooming and hygiene methods	Cosmetologist
Sex education	Nurse's aid
Physical fitness	Dental assistant
	Personal care attendant
4. Raising children and meeting marriage responsibilities	
Setting goals	Day-care attendant
Making decisions	Nursery attendant
Choosing lifestyles	
Managing available resources	
Expanding and controlling family size	
Providing for the needs of children and adults	
Ensuring the safety and health of all family members	
5. Buying, preparing, and consuming food	
Planning meals	Waiter/waitress
Purchasing, caring for, and storing food	Food preparation
Preparing proper meals	Bus girl/boy
Work safety in the kitchen	Restaurant custodian
Proper use and care of kitchen equipment, e.g., stove, blender, knives, etc.	

continues

TABLE 11.1   Continued.

Competencies and Subcompetencies	Occupational Possibilities
6. Buying and caring for clothing Purchase appropriate clothing Clean, press, and repair clothing Construct garments Construct drapes, wall hangings, etc.	Clothing alterations Laundry facility attendant Dry cleaner Clothing sales Interior design worker Textiles factory worker
7. Exhibiting responsible citizenship Know about laws of this country Know about one's rights Know how to register and vote Know about local laws Know about other pertinent citizenship matters	Nightwatchman Security guard Dispatcher County/city clerical worker
8. Using recreational facilities and leisure Know and engage in leisure activities Know and use leisure resources Engage in avocational interests/hobbies	Park attendant Pool attendant City facility upkeep Sports equipment repair
9. Getting around the community (mobility) Use of intercity and intracity travel resources Drive a car Obey traffic laws Know agencies that can increase mobility In general, know how to get around efficiently	Taxi driver Bus driver Forklift operator Tractor operator

Note: From *Life Centered Career Education: Professional Development Activity Book* (pp. 161–163) by D. E. Brolin, 1993, Arlington, VA: The Council for Exceptional Children. Copyright 1993 by The Council for Exceptional Children. Reprinted by permission.

CHAPTER COMMENTARY

All of the LCCE Mild/Moderate Curriculum competencies presented in this chapter are important for individuals with special learning and/or behavior needs to learn so they can function successfully as adults. The great challenge of teaching daily living skills is to translate educational goals into manageable components of instruction for individual students, given the circumstances that teachers encounter during the "average" day. It is important to consider the teacher's circumstances as well as the unique learning styles of the students in the class. The increased emphasis on inclusion places even greater demands on all educators to handle the complexities of meeting all of the personalized needs of students with special learning and/or behavior needs.

Teachers should identify areas of the LCCE Mild/Moderate Curriculum that already contain lessons relative to the daily living skills competencies. Ideally, lesson plans should be developed for each LCCE Curriculum Mild/Moderate subcompetency to meet the multiple learning characteristics of the students with special learning and/or behavior needs. Because such a task would take years to accomplish, an extensive set of LCCE lesson plans is available for this curriculum area, as well the personal-social and occupational area (Brolin, 1992b).

Daily living skills should be the easiest group of competencies to integrate and teach to students with special learning and/or behavior needs, with the assistance of family and community resource persons. Although much of this area is already being taught, in many cases, it is not done extensively enough. This chapter is intended to provide enough information and examples to help educators and parents provide a comprehensive approach to this important functional curriculum area.

. . . .

ACTIVITIES

1. Review the LCCE Mild Curriculum daily living skills matrix in Figure 11.1, and the LCCE Moderate Curriculum daily living skills in Figure 11.2, and then determine what general education and special education courses would be most appropriate for teaching each of the subcompetencies to your students with special learning and/or behavior needs. Then, identify those subcompetencies/skills in which you would attempt to involve the parents. Finally, identify the subcompetencies for which you would include CBI and what community resources you would use to help you teach the subcompetencies.

2. Develop an instructional objective around one of the subcompetencies, and then write a lesson plan for your students, using the LCCE lesson plan format, addressing one of the career stages, instructional settings, and career roles. An LCCE lesson plan outline is provided in Appendix G. The three lesson plans presented in this chapter also can be used for reference purposes. Note the code number in the upper right-hand corner of the lesson plans appearing in the chapter. This coding system is a method to identify exactly what LCCE competency, subcompetency, objective, career education stage, and lesson plan number is to be taught. For example, for competency 1, managing personal finances, the first lesson plan in the daily living skills domain is 1.1.1A:1, where 1 = competency number, 1 = subcompetency number, 1 = objective (identify coins and bills less than or equal to $100 in value), A = career awareness stage or level, and 1 = lesson plan 1. You may want to use this coding system in writing your lesson plan.

CHAPTER 12

Personal-Social Skills

PRELIMINARY QUESTIONS

1. Why should Life Centered Career Education (LCCE) Mild/Moderate Curriculum personal-social skills be emphasized in the curriculum/transition program of every school?

2. What are the important personal-social skills that should be taught in the schools?

3. Identify as many instructional strategies as possible that are useful for teaching personal-social skills.

4. What are the major ecological environments in which personal-social skills should be taught?

5. What are the seven/six Life Centered Career Education (LCCE) Mild/Moderate Curriculum competencies that comprise the personal-social curriculum area?

6. Give an example of an activity tip that would be useful in teaching the LCCE Mild Curriculum subcompetency "identifying emotions."

7. Give an example of an activity tip that would be useful in teaching the LCCE Moderate Curriculum subcompetency "demonstrate appropriate responses to emotions."

8. Explain how you would use the community to provide appropriate functional instruction and experiences in an LCCE Mild/Moderate Curriculum subcompetency area.

OVERVIEW

Violence and crime have become increasingly critical problems in American schools. Numerous students bring weapons to school, thousands of violent crimes occur in and around school, many teachers and students fear for their lives every day, and the incidence of criminal behavior continues to rise dramatically in young people, who now account for over 40% of reported crimes despite representing only 20% of the population (Walker & Sylvester, 1991). Other problems related to prosocial skill deficits include racial and ethnic discrimination, gang wars, school dropouts, post-high school unemployment, teenage pregnancy, teenage suicide, drug and alcohol abuse, and general socially maladapted behaviors (Iannacone, Wienke, & Cosden, 1992).

Almost all State Boards of Education have developed lists of outcomes or specific competencies they expect their students to achieve. They have identified personal-social adjustment as one of the most critical areas to provide their students (National Center on Educational Outcomes, 1993). Only academic and functional literacy was rated higher. However, this functional curriculum area is probably the most neglected and perhaps the most difficult for educators to address; consequently, in most schools students do not receive an organized, systematic, comprehensive, and continuous instructional program of personal-social skills development. Thus, prosocial skills instruction is typically not considered an important component of the school's curriculum. Compounding this problem is that few teacher preparation programs include prosocial instructional strategies training to the future teachers who will be teaching students with special learning and/or behavior needs.

Who will or should teach students with special learning and/or behavior needs appropriate personal-social behaviors and skills? Many critics believe that schools should not assume a social work function, that their responsibility is to teach academic basic skills. This is not difficult to understand because SEAs and LEAs are feeling the pressure from the national reform initiatives that call for increasingly higher standards for graduation. However, because academic, interpersonal, and occupational success depend so much on prosocial competence, and because many families are themselves unable or unwilling to provide this guidance and instruction, schools must give more emphasis to incorporating this functional curriculum area into their programs.

This chapter focuses on the seven LCCE Mild Curriculum personal-social skills competencies and the six LCCE Moderate Curriculum personal-social skills competencies. The first section presents a discussion of suggested techniques and strategies for teaching the personal-social skills. This section refers to the extensive work by Joni Alberg and her colleagues at the Research Triangle Institute in North Carolina.

Some of the many prosocial skills curricula in use are also identified in this section. The next section provides a detailed description of each of the seven LCCE Mild Curriculum competencies and their 28 subcompetencies with suggested instructional objectives and activities, activity tips, and several sample lesson plans to illustrate the infusion of transition/career education concepts and materials. Then, in the final section, a detailed description of each of the six LCCE Moderate Curriculum competencies and their 21 subcompetencies with suggested instructional objectives and activities, activity tips, and several sample lesson plans to illustrate the infusion of career education concepts and materials is provided.

TEACHING LCCE MILD CURRICULUM PERSONAL-SOCIAL SKILLS

As in the case of the daily living skills, personal-social skills instruction can and should be taught in a variety of content areas, community-based activities, and home settings. It is astonishing that personal-social skills instruction receives such limited attention in our schools. With the wide recognition of its importance and the large number of commercial and teacher-made materials developed to implement it, one would expect a greater effort to teach these skills.

CHAPTER OUTLOOK

Dr. Sharon Field is an Associate Professor (Research), Wayne State University, Detroit, Michigan, and a former President of the Division on Career Development and Transition (DCDT).

The concepts of self-determination and quality of life have recently taken on increased importance in the disability-related fields, including special education. The focus on self-determination is occurring as persons with disabilities, their families, educators, and service providers are questioning the passive stereotypes and roles often assigned to individuals with disabilities. These stereotypes are in direct conflict with typical expectations of adults. According to Ward, "self-determination, which includes self-actualization, assertiveness, creativity, pride and self-advocacy, must be part of the career development process that begins in early childhood and continues throughout adult life" (1992, p. 389).

In addition to the emphasis on self-determination, there is an increasing focus in special education on preparation that is rooted in a quality of life focus. The quality of life orientation requires that we consider the wide range of variables that contribute to the student's quality of life rather than taking a more narrow view that focuses only on more traditional outcomes, such as academics and work preparation.

Personal-social skills, as defined by LCCE, have a great influence on one's ability to be self-determined and on the quality of life one experiences. Personal-social skills development therefore is valuable in and of itself. However, the degree to which these skills are mastered also affects the development of academics and employment skills. Generalization research supports the importance of teaching critical skills in all environments in which we expect students to be able to use the skills. The importance of personal-social skills and the need to promote generalization make it imperative that personal-social skills be taught and reinforced in the home and the school. These skills are far too important to be delegated to an isolated setting, and they are integral to preparing students for satisfying and successful lives.

Reasons for this problem can only be left to conjecture: for example, they are too difficult to teach, there is too little time with other requirements to meet, they are not deemed that important, or teachers feel others should do it. Yet, as noted previously, the evidence is clear that a large proportion of students with special learning and/or behavior needs are not being equipped with appropriate personal-social skills and behaviors.

Teachers use numerous techniques to teach personal-social skills. Many of the strategies and approaches identified in Chapter 11 for daily living skills (e.g., community-based experiences, volunteers, games, role playing, videotapes, and cooperative learning) are also appropriate for personal-social skills. Other techniques relevant to this functional curriculum area include the following:

- Various small-group activities incorporated into the lesson plans
- Positive reinforcement for certain activities
- Brainstorming and consensus-forming activities
- Organizing debates or panels of students with special learning and/or behavior needs and/or guests to discuss topics and appropriate behaviors given various scenarios
- Bibliotherapy to expose the students with special learning and/or behavior needs to works of literature in which characters with limitations successfully confront life's challenges
- Individualized learning centers in which students work at specific tasks at their own pace
- Regular classroom discussions covering topics within this area
- Coaching and modeling
- Life space interviews to help students discover the crisis and come up with solutions to address future incidents with self-reinforcement
- Turtle technique to retreat, relax, and regroup before striking out

According to Iannacone et al. (1992), teachers generally prefer integrating social skills instruction into other academic content areas to addressing it in a discrete content area. Many good teachers will use prosocial teachable moments at every opportunity to address prosocial skills individually or with all class members.

Values clarification is a process that focuses on the student's particular mode of reaching decisions and the special importance of his actions and goals. One of the strengths of this approach is that it does not advocate a special set of values that supersedes those of the student with special learning and/or behavior needs. The approach concentrates on the process so that the student with special learning and/or behavior needs becomes aware of the value, its relationship to other values, and fundamental aspects of change that the student could use if he decided to modify his beliefs.

A strength of values clarification rests on the numerous activities that have been suggested by advocates. Activities are applicable to classes for adolescent and adult groups and have been used with elementary-grade students. It is recommended that teachers and counselors review the activities carefully if they attempt to engage certain individuals with special learning and/or behavior needs, because mental ability and emotional factors are variables in the anticipated results.

• • • • • • • • **Activity Tip** • • • • • • • •

The following game can help students clarify values related to employment and personal goals: A former student has a comfortable job at Company A. She learns about an attractive job opening at a new Company B. The position at Company B pays more and provides training that the company will finance. But, if she decided to accept the position at Company B, she would have to travel a greater distance to work. The former student could cut the travel time by moving from her current dwelling, but her boyfriend would then be farther away. Her relatives encourage her to explore the possible job. Some of her pals at Company A tell her to forget it, because Company B may fold, and besides, they need her for their sports team. What should she do?

• •

Alberg, Petry, and Eller (1994) reviewed the literature and identified the strategies listed in Table 12.1

TABLE 12.1   Instructional Strategies for Teaching Social Skills

Instructional Strategy	Description
Modeling	Exposing target student(s) to live or film/tape models who perform the desired skill. Stories and books can also be used.
Practice/rehearsal	Practicing a specific skill or sequence of behavior in a structured setting; this is similar to role playing the desired response.
Role playing/taking	Assuming various roles in interpersonal situations.
Incidental teaching	Making use of "teachable moments" to provide instruction as opportunities arise in natural contexts throughout the day.
Positive reinforcement	Rewarding the use of socially appropriate behaviors (e.g., approval, special privileges, tokens or points that can be exchanged for rewards). Reinforcement should occur frequently when the student is first learning a skill.
Prompting	Giving a student cues that help evoke the desired behavior.
Coaching	Prompting a student to use a skill by (1) giving clear instructions for what to do, (2) allowing the student to practice the skill, and (3) providing feedback on the correct aspects of the response.

Note: From *The Social Skills Planning Guide* (pp. 2-13) by J. Alberg, C. Petry, & S. Eller, 1994, Longmont, CO: Sopris West. Reprinted by permission.

as well-demonstrated strategies for teaching prosocial skills. As the authors note, these strategies can be used alone or in combination and should be adapted to meet your learning style, those of your students with special learning and/or behavior needs, and their developmental age. Because the goal of this instruction, and all functional skill instruction, is for the students with special learning and/or behavior needs to apply what they learn in the many settings of the real world, it is important not only to integrate the instruction throughout the curriculum, but also to provide many community-based experiences so generalization and maintenance will occur.

Carter and Sugai (1989) have also studied the prosocial skills curriculum area relative to training techniques and available curricula. They note that "selection of a given strategy or curriculum rests on

the teacher's ability to assess the individual's learning difficulties, identify and implement the most viable strategy, and measure its effects on the student's performance" (Carter & Sugai, 1989, p. 36). They note that teachers have many strategies at their disposal that can be used individually or in combination. In Table 12.2, Carter and Sugai provide a list of instructional strategies for teaching prosocial skills and identify some of the advantages and disadvantages of each strategy. This information should be helpful to teachers contemplating a prosocial skills curricular effort.

How can educators find the time and space to integrate sufficient prosocial skills instruction into their curriculum? Alberg and her colleagues (1993) interviewed many educational practitioners who, although they stated finding time to teach social skills was very difficult, found the time because of their strong belief

TABLE 12.2   Descriptions, Advantages, and Disadvantages of Instructional Tactics for Teaching Social Skills

Instructional Strategy	Description	Advantages	Disadvantages
Modeling	Exposing target student to display of prosocial behavior.	Easy to implement.	Not sufficient if used alone.
Strategic placement	Placing target student in situations with other students who display prosocial behaviors.	Employs peers as change agents. Facilitates generalization. Is cost effective.	Research data inconclusive when used alone.
Instruction	Telling students how and why they should behave a certain way, and/or giving rules for behavior.	Overemphasizes norms/expectations.	Not sufficient if used alone.
Correspondence training	Students are positively reinforced for accurate reports regarding their behavior.	Facilitates maintenance and generalization of training. Is cost effective.	Very little documentation of effectiveness.
Rehearsal and practice	Structured practice of specific prosocial behavior.	Enhances skill acquisition.	Not sufficient to change behavior if used alone.
Positive reinforcement or shaping	Prosocial behaviors or approximations are followed by a reward or favorable event.	Strong research support for effectiveness.	Maintenance after treatment termination is not predictable.
Prompting and coaching	Providing students with additional stimuli/prompts which elicit the prosocial behavior.	Particularly effective after acquisition to enhance transfer to natural settings.	Maintenance after treatment termination is not predictable.
Positive practice	A consequence strategy in that student repeatedly practices correct behavior.	May produce immediate increases in prosocial behavior.	Long-term effectiveness not documented. Less restrictive approaches should be used first.
Multimethod training packages	Multicomponent instructional package which incorporates several behavioral techniques.	Greater treatment strength and durability. Applicable to a wide range of children and settings.	

Note: From "Social Skills Curriculum Analysis" by J. Carter & G. Sugai, 1989, *Teaching Exceptional Children, 22*(1), p. 38. Copyright 1989 by The Council for Exceptional Children. Reprinted by permission.

in its importance for the students' total education. In their visits to many programs, Alberg et al. noted that many teachers were integrating the instruction into existing curricula and into other aspects of the school day. They also found that the involvement of a variety of school personnel greatly enhances the generalization and maintenance of the skills learned to different settings and events. Readers interested in a more in-depth presentation of prosocial skills instruction and program selection are encouraged to obtain the publication *The Social Skills Planning Guide* (1994) by Alberg et al., published by Sopris West, Inc., Longmont, CO.

Numerous prosocial skills curricula and programs have been developed and are commercially available for educators. Alberg and associates (1993) conducted an extensive review of available prosocial skills programs and selected eight for field study of their use by educators. The authors selected two curricula each for preschool, elementary, middle/junior high, and high school/adult levels:

Preschool	*My Friends and Me* (Davis, 1988) American Guidance Service
	Play Time/Social Time (Vanderbilt/Minnesota Social Interaction Project,1993) Communication Skills Builders
Elementary	*Skillstreaming the Elementary School Child* (McGinnis, Goldstein, Sprafkin, & Gershaw, 1984) Research Press
	TRIBES: A Process for Social Development and Cooperative Learning (Gibbs, 1987) Center Source Publications
Middle/Junior	*The Walker Social Skills Curriculum* (Walker, Todis, Holmes, & High Horton, 1988) Pro-Ed
	The Prepare Curriculum (Goldstein, 1988) Research Press
Senior High/ Postsecondary	*Learning to Get Along: Social Effectiveness Training for People with Developmental Disabilities* (Jackson, Jackson, Bennett,

Bynum, & Faryna, 1991) Research Press
Life Centered Career Education Mild Curriculum (Brolin, 1992a, 1992b, 1993a, 1997) The Council for Exceptional Children
Life Centered Career Education Moderate Curriculum (Loyd, 1997) The Council for Exceptional Children

Further information on these and other social skills curriculums can be obtained by securing the publication noted earlier, *The Social Skills Planning Guide* (Alberg et. al., 1994). Students with special learning and/or behavior needs should be able to learn adequate prosocial skills so they can function adequately in the four major career roles.

Elksnin and Elksnin (1991) reviewed nine commercial social skills programs designed for adolescent populations:

1. *ACCESS* by Walker, Todis, Holmes, and Horton (1988, Pro-Ed)
2. *ASSET* by Hazel, Schumacher, Sherman, and Sheldon-Wildgen (1981, Research Press)
3. *Getting Along with Others* by Jackson, Jackson, and Monroe (1983, Research Press)
4. *The Prepare Curriculum* by Goldstein (1988, Research Press)
5. *Skillstreaming the Adolescent* by Goldstein, Sprafkin, Gershaw, and Klein (1980, Research Press)
6. *Skillstreaming the Elementary* by Goldstein, Sprafkin, Gershaw, and Klein (1980, Research Press)
7. *Social Skills for Daily Living* by Schumacher, Haze, and Pederson (1988, American Guidance Service)
8. *Social Skills in the Classroom* by Stephens (1978, Cedars Press)
9. *Waksman Social Skills Curriculum* by Waksman and Messmer (1985, AIEP Education)

Elksnin and Elksnin studied these programs to determine whether their content contained instruction in the 20 interpersonal skills areas identified by Greenan

(1986) as important generalizable skills necessary for success in vocational training programs and jobs. Elksnin and Elksnin found that only 15% to 70% of these generalizable interpersonal skills were contained in the various programs. The authors called for more job-related social skills instruction to be instituted for students with special learning and/or behavior needs in *Skillstreaming the Adolescent* by Goldstein, Sprafkin, Gershaw, and Klein (1980, Research Press). This recommendation is very important for educators. In providing prosocial skills training to their students, according to *Skillstreaming the Adolescent* by Goldstein, Sprafkin, Gershaw, and Klein (1980, Research Press), educators must keep in mind the ultimate purpose of the effort; that is, to teach students with special learning and/or behavior needs how to function in the various career roles—family member, citizen, employee, and as a contributing and acceptable participant in prosocial and recreational activities.

So many prosocial skills curricula are on the market that deciding what to use is often overwhelming to educators. Carter and Sugai (1989) have developed a Social Skills Analysis Checklist, which seems to hold promise for educators seeking some guidance on this matter. They propose several "yes" or "no" questions for the potential user to ask that relate to the instructional strategies presented in Table 12.2.

> Does the curriculum use: 1) modeling, 2) strategic placement, 3) instruction, 4) correspondence training, 5) rehearsal/practice, 6) prompting/coaching, 7) positive reinforcement shaping or 8) positive practice? Then, six programming questions are posed: 1) are assessment procedures/instruments included, 2) is the curriculum adaptable to individual needs, 3) can the curriculum be used with small groups, 4) can personnel implement the curriculum without specialized training beyond that described in the curriculum, 5) is the cost of implementation reasonable and manageable and 6) are strategies included that will promote maintenance and generalization of skills. (p. 38)

Based on the answers to these questions, the educator should be able to make a more informed decision.

If students with special learning and/or behavior needs can better understand that the purpose of the education program is to help them acquire the proper behaviors and skills they will need to become successfully and happily employed, to attain satisfactory friendships and acceptance by others, and to become an independent and productive member of the community, a greater reduction in the socially maladaptive behaviors of many students should result in schools that embrace this functional, life-centered, student-focused approach.

"Career education at the elementary level consists primarily of an evolvement of social skills necessary in job, family, and societal adjustment; an understanding of oneself; a development of basic communication skills; an introduction to the general idea of the world of work; and an exploration of a variety of meaningful careers."

(Gillet, 1980)

LCCE MILD CURRICULUM COMPETENCIES

As mentioned, the LCCE Curriculum personal-social skills curriculum area involves those abilities that are necessary for personal achievement and satisfactory interpersonal relationships. While the LCCE Curriculum daily living skills form the structure of the individual's abilities, the LCCE Curriculum personal-social skills are the muscle and blood that propel the individual toward fulfillment. One's sense of achievement and fulfillment determines quality of life. The individual with special learning and/or behavior needs' ideas about his present status, potentials, and interactions with other people should also be considered. Today, the term *self-determination* is the common reference for this concept and is presented in Chapter 10.

An individual's potential for successful, independent living cannot be judged merely on the basis of academic performance or competency assessments.

Curriculum Area	Competency	Subcompetency: The student will be able to:	
PERSONAL-SOCIAL SKILLS	10. Achieving Self-Awareness	42. Identify physical & psychological needs	43. Identify interests & abilities
	11. Acquiring Self-Confidence	46. Express feelings of self-worth	47. Describe others' perception of self
	12. Achieving Socially Responsible Behavior—Community	51. Develop respect for the rights & properties of others	52. Recognize authority & follow instructions
	13. Maintaining Good Interpersonal Skills	56. Demonstrate listening & responding skills	57. Establish & maintain close relationships
	14. Achieving Independence	59. Strive toward self-actualization	60. Demonstrate self-organization
	15. Making Adequate Decisions	62. Locate & utilize sources of assistance	63. Anticipate consequences
	16. Communicating with Others	67. Recognize & respond	68. Communicate with understanding

FIGURE 12.1   Life Centered Career Education Competencies: Personal-social Curriculum
Note: From *Life Centered Career Education: A Competency-Based Approach* (5th ed., pp. 12–13) by D. E. Brolin, 1997, Arlington, VA: The Council for Exceptional Children. Copyright 1997 by The Council for Exceptional Children. Reprinted by permission.

In this section, the seven LCCE Mild Curriculum personal-social skills competencies and their 28 subcompetencies appearing in Figure 12.1 are presented. Instructional objectives and activities for each are suggested. Several activity tips and some sample lesson plans from the three LCCE Mild Curriculum personal-social skills competency unit curriculum manuals (Brolin, 1997), published by the Council for Exceptional Children (CEC), are interspersed throughout the section to illustrate teaching ideas.

10.0 Achieving Self-Awareness

Individuals with special learning and/or behavior needs are part of the new sense of freedom in America. They have been the subjects of an increased number of television documentaries, magazine articles, and newspaper reports. Legislation now guarantees these individuals with special learning and/or behavior needs equal rights to transportation, education, housing, and employment. Individuals with special learning and/or behavior needs are entering the mainstream of society now more than ever before. Being able to know oneself (self-awareness) therefore has much to do with becoming a contributing and productive member of society. Critical LCCE Mild Cur-

riculum subcompetencies that make up this important competency area are discussed next.

10.42 Identify Physical and Psychological Needs

The skills involved in identifying needs enter into the physical, psychological, and social domains. There are some minimal needs for physical existence, but it is much harder to describe basic requirements in the social and psychological realms. How do we measure quantities of security, self-worth, esteem, and love? One way to determine the answer to that question is for students to identify their needs, talk about them, draw them, collect examples of them, and examine the ways in which other people attempt to meet their needs. Varied classroom activities concerning the necessities of life will lead students with special learning and/or behavior needs to a realization about those things that they regard as essential to their lives.

10.43 Identify Interests and Abilities

Individuals with special learning and/or behavior needs discover their abilities through their interests.

44. Identify emotions	45. Demonstrate knowledge of physical self	
48. Accept and give praise	49. Accept & give criticism	50. Develop confidence in oneself
53. Demonstrate appropriate behavior in public places	54. Know important character traits	55. Recognize personal roles
58. Make & maintain friendships		
61. Demonstrate awareness of how one's behavior affects others		
64. Develop & evaluate alternatives	65. Recognize nature of a problem	66. Develop goal-seeking behavior
69. Know subtleties of communication		

• • • • • • • • **Activity Tip** • • • • • • • •

The want ads of the local newspaper can provide a rich resource of ideas that can help students identify personal needs. People advertise so they can gain employment, sell home furniture, or join a car pool. Students with special learning and/or behavior needs can cut, paste, and place ads in various categories of interest.
• •

How can a child try or attempt to accomplish anything if his interest cannot be aroused? Aren't childhood hobbies a means of building confidence through interest? If individuals with special learning and/or behavior needs are to achieve independence through competent behavior, they must have numerous experiences with those things they like to do, can do, and would attempt to do if given adequate support. With support, trial and error can help the individual with special learning and/or behavior needs build an awareness of physical and spiritual capabilities. This is especially important for able-bodied persons who through accident, injury, or operation enter the category of disabled. For these individuals, the rehabilitative process involves supportive efforts that help them identify interests that correspond to their altered abilities. Teachers should plan activities that require students with special learning and/or behavior needs to identify interests and abilities that are com-

mon to most people. They should engage their students with special learning and/or behavior needs in activities that will help them identify their own interests and abilities, set future goals, and devise strategies for implementing and reaching these goals.

10.44 Identify Emotions

Teachers can begin classroom activities that deal with emotions by creating a nonjudgmental climate in which students (whether children or adults) feel free to talk about feelings. Primary-grade students should identify such emotions as happiness, sadness, and anger and should have had exposure to these emotions long before entering school. Older children with special learning and/or behavior needs should begin to work with the problem of recognizing the various ways in which emotions can be expressed. Students with special learning and/or behavior needs should be involved in role-playing situations or should report observations that emphasize various indices of emotions, for example, body language, facial expressions, and tone of voice. A second major functional objective should be for teachers to develop students with special learning and/or behavior needs' abilities to distinguish the consequences of the emotion for others, but particularly for the self. For example, an expression of anger by an employer may have different consequences a similar demonstration by an employee. The employer is allowed to let off steam, but the employee may lose his job. Finally, teachers should identify means through which students with special learning and/or behavior needs can release emotions constructively. An appropriate expression of emotion is unique to each individual. Teachers and parents should exert a great deal of time and effort in establishing a foundation of trust that will encourage students to explore feelings and find adequate ways of expressing them. Another functional objective should be identifying ways in which emotions affect behavior.

The following lesson plan is an example of how one of the functional objectives of this LCCE Mild

• • • • • • • • **Activity Tip** • • • • • • • •
The Emotions Bulletin Board is a sure hit. Students can photograph each other in "typical" expressions, cut photos from newspapers and magazines, superimpose one photo on another, and add their own zany captions and quotes.
• •

Curriculum subcompetency area can be taught to an elementary or middle school class of students at the career awareness level. The worksheet is not included. The lesson plan was taken from the Personal-Social Skills competency unit manual published by the CEC (Brolin, 1992d).

Lesson Plan 17   10.44.4A:17

LCCE Objective 10.44.4   Differentiate particular emotions in self and others.

Lesson Objective: Student will become aware of how particular emotions appear in self and others.

Instructional Resources: Worksheet **Identifying Emotions**, panel (three or four actors or dramatic readers from community drama troupe, performing arts company, or school drama class).

Lesson Introduction: Today we have several guests with us from _____. Their names are _____. They are going to show us what emotions *look* like when actors are on stage. They have agreed to play characters that are going through various feelings and emotions. Watch for the emotions they show us and we'll discuss them later.

School Activity: **Time: 1 session**

Task:
1. Define the following terms:
   • "verbal cues"—what an actor *says* to indicate emotions
   • "nonverbal cues"—what an actor *does* to indicate emotions
2. Instruct the class to watch for emotions demonstrated by the actors. Possibilities include: anger, sadness, fear, joy, happiness, surprise.
3. The actors perform short role-plays, demonstrating a variety of human emotions. Their demonstrations convey situations in various career roles, including examples from home, work, and community life and from leisure activities as well.
4. Four role-plays (or dramatic readings) will be performed. Use the first two as examples. After each of them, record class input on the board:
   • The students look for a variety of emotions in the person who is acting (or reading) *and* in the people who are observing (students).
   • The class members classify cues of various emotions as verbal or nonverbal.
   • The students identify the career roles the actors portray, and relate the emotions to those career roles.

5. Distribute and explain Worksheet **Identifying Emotions**
   - After the third role-play, the students work individually to record on their worksheet the emotions they observe, including verbal and nonverbal cues of each emotion.
   - The fourth role-play is handled in the same fashion.
6. The students share their worksheet responses with the class, and panel members affirm their responses whenever possible.

Lesson Plan Evaluation:

Activity:	Students will complete Worksheet **Identifying Emotions**.
Criteria:	Student will record at least six emotions observed, identifying the cues as verbal or nonverbal.
Career Role:	Family Member/Homemaker, Employee, Citizen/Volunteer, and Avocational
Career Stage:	Awareness

Note: From *Life Centered Career Education Competency Units for Personal-Social Skills* (Vol. 1, pp. 134–135) by D. E. Brolin, 1992, Arlington, VA: The Council for Exceptional Children. Copyright 1992 by The Council for Exceptional Children. Reprinted by permission.

Vocational rehabilitation counselors can help students build their self-confidence in preparation for their job-seeking activities.

10.45 Demonstrate Knowledge of Physical Self

Understanding the physical self contains functional objectives that are specific to the sexual role of the individual. The activities should enable students with special learning and/or behavior needs to develop an awareness of the similarities and differences in the anatomy and functioning of the male and female. This subject material has received increased attention among researchers, parents, consumer groups, and publishing firms primarily because of the long absence of discussion on the sexual role of individuals who are mentally retarded or physically disabled. Teachers should be aware that if they encourage classroom or small-group discussion and questions, they must be prepared to provide information. Objectives involve identifying general systems of the body, listing and describing physical characteristics, and identifying major parts of the body.

11.0 Acquiring Self-Confidence

Individuals with special learning and/or behavior needs have been confronted for centuries with stories, fairy tales, works of art, and popular expressions depicting them as incapable. In some instances, they were not even regarded as human beings but as the embodiment of evil spirits. These ideas and stereotypes linger to this day, and most individuals with special learning and/or behavior needs have had experience with abuse or pity by peers or elders. Despite these opinions and attitudes, the students with special learning and/or behavior needs must build self-concepts as capable human beings so that they can reach personal objectives and attain dreams. Subcompetencies and some of their respective functional objectives are described next.

11.46 Express Feelings of Self-Worth

Individuals begin to feel worthy when they experience expressions of value from parents, teachers, and friends. These declarations of worth may be difficult for the person with special learning and/or behavior needs to formulate. In our society, an individual's perceived worth is based on comparison to other people. Comparative statements are common in a culture that rewards individuals who demonstrate the drive to excel. The problem is that "doing better" is often determined in comparison to someone else. Individuals with special learning and/or behavior needs can find themselves at a serious disadvantage if their abilities are always placed in some type of "better than the other person" derby. If the individual with special learning and/or behavior needs loses the race, he might perceive himself as being inferior to others, which in turn may cause him to lose his sense of self-worth. The parent's and teacher's abilities to work with the assets an individual with special learning and/or behavior needs has at his disposal is the key to this potential dilemma. They must move away from "you versus them" situations to "I can do" experiences. By emphasizing the "I can," the parent and teacher opinions change, with a corresponding influence on the attitudes and values of the individual. "I can" is a positive statement of value and worth in this society. How many times have we heard stories about individuals who were told they would never walk, run, or dance only to accomplish that very thing and more? The emergence and success of such events as the Special Olympics and Wheelchair Games illustrates that individuals with disabilities have a strong desire to demonstrate their worth through physical accomplishments regardless of how long it may take them to run a certain distance. Teachers and parents should provide opportunities in which students with special learning and/or behavior needs express how they feel about themselves in relationship to their accomplishments, successes, and failures. What experiences cause students to feel good, worthy, or pleased with their accomplishments? What experiences frustrate them? These expressions provide professionals with an opportunity to plan subsequent activities that will increase the quality and quantity of success experiences. Another functional objective should be identifying ways in which other people affect an individual's feelings of worth.

11.47 Describe Others' Perception of Self

Students with special learning and/or behavior needs should be able to describe overt expressions and subtle hints made by other people. Because most people are more sensitive to communications relative to themselves, they are more apt to interject their own interpretations onto the behavior of another person. The individual with a health or physical impairment encounters a particularly puzzling situation when she wonders whether a person is reacting to her personality or to the particular disability. If someone does not invite her to another party, was it because she did not

conduct herself properly, or was it due to her prosthesis? She may never get the answer, and repeated instances of these nebulous situations damage the individual's self-confidence. What others think of us influences our attitudes toward the self. These attitudes are used as a basis for further judgments. Parents and teachers cannot control the attitudes of other people—in some cases, their own attitudes may be enough of a challenge. But they can instruct the student with special learning or behavior needs to observe another person's overt and subtle responses that reflect either positive or negative attitudes. Many of the lessons on communication (refer to competency 16) should include such reactions that convey attitudes of pity, disgust, condescension, and the like. The lessons should, however, emphasize positive reactions that reflect the individual's self-respect. She must guard against reactions that would be interpreted by other members of society as justification for their folly. Another functional objective should be constructing personal views of others toward her.

• • • • • • • • **Activity Tip** • • • • • • • •
An effective exercise requires all students to say positive things about an individual. The class may be seated in a circle or at their desks, but the student under discussion should be facing the class. Each student has 15 to 20 seconds, during which time other students say such things as, "He helped our team win the game. He came to school on time every day of the week. He knew the right answer to the weekly quiz." This activity helps build class unity as well as individual confidence.
• •

11.48 Accept and Give Praise

Individuals with disabilities need legitimate experiences in which others confirm and show respect for their behavior. Legitimate experiences include those daily activities in home, school, or other environments that involve students as contributing members. Students with special learning and/or behavior needs may receive respect and validation for their contributions from family, peers, teachers, or others. Students

Making adequate decisions is critical for successful adult functioning.

with special learning and/or behavior needs not only should receive recognition for their accomplishments but also should be supported for behaviors that will eventually result in accomplishment. Otherwise students with special learning and/or behavior needs are only rewarded for one achievement, and this may be disproportionate to their total effort at home, in school, or on a team. It is easier to know how to accept praise after having experienced various forms of reward. Other functional objectives should include listing effects of praise on the self and others and demonstrating ability to offer praise to others.

Sample Lesson Plan

Author: Lynda Glascoe

Level: High school through community college

Situation: Resource setting or group meetings
Time Span: One class period

Objective: The student will be able to act out appropriate responses after he has received praise or criticism.

Activity: This is a role-playing activity that can simulate actual employment situations. Each situation is described on 3-by-5-inch cards. Each card should contain enough detail to allow the student to understand the situation yet still encourage him to use his creativity. Second, two or more students are chosen for each activity. After the students have read the situation and chosen their roles, they will decide what they will do and say during the play. Third, the class discusses the situation, responses, and possible alternatives.

Examples: (1) your best friend quit his job and you are hired to take his place. After one week, your boss praises your work and begins to tell you about your friend's problems on the job. (2) You don't feel like working today and your boss notices it. He says "Unless you shape up, you won't have this job much longer." (3) You worked late last night on the job and your supervisor tells you "Pretty good. But, you could have done better."

Evaluation: Students will be able to identify appropriate responses to each situation.

Related Subcompetencies: 11.48   Accepting praise
                                 11.49   Accepting criticism
                                 19.81   Accepting supervision

11.49 Accept and Give Criticism

Criticism can have a positive effect when it refers to astute judgments relative to standards. However, it is more often taken in the negative vein of fault finding. Unfortunately, criticism causes individuals with special learning and/or behavior needs to feel less than adequate about themselves. This is one reason why students with special learning and/or behavior needs in secondary or college classes hate to receive a critical analysis of their assignments. Fearing a potentially harsh review, they produce less than they can. In a sense, they are already protecting themselves from devaluation. Is it any wonder, then, that when teachers begin to criticize, students with special learning and/or behavior needs become disinterested? Teachers have the arduous task of first convincing students with special learning and/or behavior needs to be open to criticism, and second, helping them recognize situations in which critical statements are of little value in changing or improving on a mistake. The teacher can accomplish these goals by providing respect for students with special learning and/or behavior needs while their work is being analyzed. Respect with criticism builds self-confidence. An attitude of respect says to the student with a special learning and/or behavior need, "You are someone." The critical element conveys the message, "You are someone who can improve on this mistake." The improvement reinforces the previous steps in the process. Another functional objective should be identifying positive and negative effects of criticism on self and others.

11.50 Develop Confidence in Oneself

Students with special learning and/or behavior needs should be aware of their innate dignity. At times, they may have to assert their rights to protect that dignity. These actions are founded on a trust in their ability to accomplish functional objectives. Trust begins with the first completed task in infancy and is subsequently nurtured by the individual's efforts to accomplish more difficult functional objectives. Often, the act of attempting a task strengthens one's trust in oneself. After developing faith in oneself, the individual can begin to form objectives and seek the means, appropriate to his ability, of accomplishing his goals.

For example, the movie *A Matter of Inconvenience* (Stanfield House, 1974) is based on individuals who, without sight or a leg, attempt to ski. The war veterans without a limb use one ski and two poles fashioned with small runners at the ends. The three skis function as supports to balance the transfer of weight at each turn. Experienced skiers who provide instructions on turning, plowing, and breaking follow the women who are blind. These individuals experience skiing and enjoy themselves. Their accomplishments are judged by themselves and not in comparison to Olympic competitors. The experience is of value because it accomplishes an objective through a means that is appropriate to the individual with the special learning and/or behavior needs. We are sure that these individuals' self-confidence is extended and that they will attempt other tasks because their trust in their abilities has been reinforced. They are, in a sense, developing

• • • • • • • • **Activity Tip** • • • • • • • •

The teacher leads the class in a role-playing activity in which the classroom is the "work setting;" half of the class are "employees," and the other half of the class are "employers." For one day, the "employers" note characteristics such as promptness, response to instructions, attitude, proper attire, and quality of work. The "employers" share their reviews at the end of the day only to become "employees" on the next day.

• •

faith in themselves. Another functional objective should be evaluating the self in a variety of activities.

12.0 Achieving Socially Responsible Behavior

Society is held together by laws and understandings relative to the conduct of individuals with special learning and/or behavior needs toward each other. These laws have been gradually increased to extend protection to people with disabilities. However, acceptance of the individual depends more on the ability to demonstrate responsible behavior in various kinds of social situations. Critical LCCE Mild Curriculum subcompetencies that make up this important competency area are discussed next.

12.51 Develop Respect for the Rights and Properties of Others

Developing respect for the rights and properties of others involves one of the fundamental concerns on which the country was founded. It is a continuous subject of interest in television, radio, and newspaper reports and, therefore, offers ample opportunity for teachers and parents to pinpoint the reasons for respecting the rights of others and their possessions. Parents are the initial vital link in this competency. They are the ones who have to teach children to differentiate between what belongs to them and what belongs to someone else. Teachers reinforce these basic lessons as instances of ownership that will, no doubt, occur in the classroom. Respecting the rights of others becomes more complicated as individuals grow older and begin to exert their own opinions and power in taking command of possessions. This requires teachers to initiate lessons and draw on the student's experiences that emphasize the relationships of laws, ownership, and the protection of the community.

12.52 Recognize Authority and Follow Instructions

Just about everything students with special learning and/or behavior needs do in school is preceded by

• • • • • • • • **Activity Tip** • • • • • • • •

"Who Owns This?" is an activity that focuses on situations and decisions related to ownership of property. School situations, newspaper articles, and student experiences provide the teacher with material for discussions and students' essays. The teacher constructs the situation and possible questions to consider. For example, a boy brings a pair of goggles to a swimming pool. He lays them on a deck chair and goes for a drink. He returns to put them on, and another swimmer says that the goggles are his. There is one pair of goggles and two swimmers. What should the boys do?

• •

directions. The routine and even monotony of the school situation makes it difficult for teachers to impress on students with special learning and/or behavior needs that things are different in the employment world. If students with special learning and/or behavior needs don't pay attention or forget an instruction, they may have to do the assignment again, visit the principal, or lose points. The results become commonplace if they are experienced often enough. But if these lapses occur in an employment situation, students with special learning and/or behavior needs must face the consequences (i.e., "You're fired!"). An equally difficult task is for teachers to determine whether students with special learning and/or behavior needs can accomplish an objective or whether they lack the skills to follow directions. Teachers often infer that students with special learning and/or behavior needs cannot follow instructions because the assignment has not been completed.

For example, a student with special learning and/or behavior needs is instructed to clean a room in the home economics model house. He is to dust, sweep, and operate a vacuum cleaner. If he did not receive prior instructions on how to operate a vacuum cleaner, he may be unable to fulfill the assignment. One possible teacher response is "Didn't you hear what I said?" This is one reason why students with special learning and/or behavior needs must be encouraged to ask questions or identify those things they do not know how to do before attempting a task. Employers have often said that employees with mental retardation are easier to work with because they will tell the employer about those things they don't understand. This is not always the case; some employees may not have the confidence or self-advocacy skills, and just sit idly waiting for more information, affirmation, or criticism for nonperformance. Another person may try to fake his way through the job.

12.53 Demonstrate Appropriate Behavior in Public Places

Students with special learning and/or behavior needs should be able to identify behaviors that are appropriate and expected in such places as restaurants, transportation facilities, churches, recreational settings, and public meetings. Students with special learning and/or behavior needs acquire this behavior by imitating other members of the family or peer group. If it is necessary for the teacher to modify these behaviors, most importantly, the student with special learning and/or behavior needs, her teacher, and her family should all agree on common objectives.

There are common denominators to acceptable behavior across all public and ecological environments. Teachers should examine these similarities in classroom role-playing encounters, where students with special learning and/or behavior needs report on experiences with family or friends, field trips, or critical reviews of televised events. Like a seasoned athlete before the "big game," the student needs practice that should be supervised by teachers or parents. Another functional objective should be identifying reasons for appropriate behavior in public places.

Sample Lesson Plan 12.53

Author: Paul Perencevic

Level: High school   **Situation:** Self-contained class composed of students with behavior disorders

Time Span: Over one semester

Objective: The student will be able to demonstrate proper behavior in public places and learn to follow instructions.

Activity: This is a field trip activity in which members of the class visit a local mall. Teachers should identify target behaviors for the class as well as for individual students. They should give students instructions for following certain procedures, selecting items, standing in line, and responding to questions or comments by sales personnel.

Examples: (1) Students are told to stand in line with the selected items and wait their turns at the cash register; (2) students are provided with written instructions on how to purchase certain items. They follow the instructions from entrance to exit of the mall.

Evaluation: Teachers or aides should observe the target behaviors that they identified before the activity. The teacher can make immediate evaluations and should reinforce acceptable behavior while the students are in a community setting.

Related Activities: Prior practice of the expected behaviors can be accomplished through role-playing exercises in the classroom

12.54 Know Character Traits

Students with special learning and/or behavior needs should be familiar with those personality factors that generally allow them to participate in a group situation that results in a positive attitude of others. What are some of these positive traits? Co-operation, cheerfulness, and dependability form a solid foundation and are also considered necessary in employment situations. There are other traits, but each individual with special learning and/or behavior needs must discover them. This is where experience and observation of others are important factors in helping individuals to change. The ability to look at oneself with a critical eye is not reserved for those with advanced degrees; it comes from practice, with encouragement, at home and in the classroom. Teachers can help students with special learning and/or behavior needs build their observational skills by assigning projects in which students with special learning and/or behavior needs interview or consider someone of their choice and list outstanding characteristics. Once the characteristics are defined, teachers can translate them into behaviors students with special learning and/or behavior needs should attempt. Together, students with special learning and/or behavior needs and teachers should work on a plan of practicing and reporting the behaviors. For students who experience problems in performing acceptable behaviors, the teacher may structure a system in which there is a conscious effort to modify the behavior toward prearranged objectives. Another functional objective should be identifying character traits that inhibit acceptance.

12.55 Recognize Personal Roles

Several roles are identified across competency areas. Some of these roles are employee, citizen, parent, relative, and friend. Students with special learning and/or behavior needs should be able to describe and demonstrate responsible behavior to individuals (employer, parent, child) as well as groups (union, passengers, clubs) identified with a specific role. This LCCE Mild Curriculum sub-competency requires students with special learning and/or behavior needs to be actively involved in each role so they can realize its full meaning. For example, a student with special learning and/or behavior needs may be a member of a family by birth but not in practice. Parents should involve their children in as many family activities and decisions as possible, especially if the student with special learning and/or behavior needs has chosen a future role as parent and spouse. Teachers should place students with special learning and/or behavior needs in situations that provide understanding of the expectations of others for a particular role. For example, community personnel such as police officers, fire fighters, and employers should discuss their expectations of student behaviors and responsibilities in the roles of citizen and employee. Another functional objective should be identifying all possible future roles.

It is no accident that the seven personal-social competencies appear in the middle of the 22 competencies. Acquisition of these functional skills is essential to the fulfillment of individuals with special learning and/or behavior needs; moreover, once these individuals with special learning and/or behavior needs have command over personal-social skills, it is easier for them to learn and incorporate the daily living and occupational competencies in their lives.

The growth of self-esteem is woven into the personal-social competencies. Self-understanding (i.e., abilities, interests, needs, wants) and learning to interact constructively, appropriately, and responsibly lead to heightened positive attitudes about self-worth.

We must provide an environment in which self-esteem can be nurtured with the systematic infusion of the personal-social skills into a structured, continuous program. Isolated lessons and transition/career education classes are fragmented efforts that yield fragmented results. This chapter provides educators with a focal point for weaving the competencies into a program that will raise the esteem of students with special learning and/or behavior needs.

13.0 Maintaining Good Interpersonal Skills

Competency 13 explores the functional skills needed to establish and maintain successful forms of interpersonal relationships. It does not include all skills or offer a cookbook approach to an area that has received enough attention in books, magazines, and newspapers to fill a lifetime. It is a skill that interacts with the individual with special learning and/or behavior needs' feelings of confidence and independence and is a key to successful career functioning. Practice is the most crucial element of these competencies for teachers, parents, and students. Students with special learning and/or behavior needs should have the opportunity to role play expected behaviors and responses for such everyday events as listening to another person, asking questions, providing information, telling a story, and expressing emotions. LCCE Mild Curriculum subcompetencies and the sense of these functional objectives' relation to this competency follow.

13.56 Demonstrate Listening and Responding Skills

Communication depends on the correct interchange of ideas or objects between people. Computers can be programmed to exchange information, but people depend on the meaning and implications of the message. They accomplish this by attending to the source of the message as well as to other nonverbal clues that may accompany it (refer to competency 16). The teacher should develop several abilities so students can complete this competency. Students with special learning and/or behavior needs should be able to attend to the message by using all available senses; develop adequate means of response, such as speaking, signing, using a communication board, or typing; determine the appropriate meaning of the message (verbal or nonverbal); and determine the correct manner of response. Another objective should be identifying negative aspects of listening and responding inappropriately.

13.57 Establish and Maintain Close Relationships

Students with special learning and/or behavior needs should understand the process of dating, various customs relative to the relationship of individuals in the dating situation, and the responsibilities of each role. Parents and teachers face many difficult questions when they counsel young people. "When do I start dating? Should I date this type of person? How do I act on a date? Where do I go on a date?" These few questions provide enough fuel for years of classroom discussions, heart-to-heart talks, and personal growth. Other functional objectives should include identifying activities in the community that are appropriate for dating relationships and identifying ways to demonstrate that one is pleased on a date.

Families can nurture the skills for developing close relationships. Children learn about personal relations and respect by observing their parents and by interacting with brothers, sisters, or relatives. Before the primary grades, students with special learning and/or behavior needs may have already developed relationships of varying intensities with family members, neighbors, playmates, and therapists. The teacher can begin with exercises that help students with special learning and/or behavior needs identify the different types of relationships that already exist or can be observed in the family's community. Students with special learning and/or behavior needs should formulate answers to such questions as "What are the characteristics of a close relationship? In what manner do people respond to one another in a close relationship? What is its function?" By trying to find answers to questions like these, students develop an awareness of those individual needs that leads to the development of close relationships. Another functional objective should be identifying people with whom the student with special learning and/or behavior needs could establish a close relationship.

The following lesson plan combines two LCCE Mild Curriculum objectives for this subcompetency area. The worksheet is not illustrated. This is a career exploration lesson plan that has application for all four-career roles.

Lesson Plan 11   13.57.4E:11
                                                      13.57.5E:11

LCCE Objective 13.57.4 Identify characteristics of close relationships.

LCCE Objective 13.57.5 List different types of close relationships.

Lesson Objective: Student will explore the nature of different types of close relationships.

Instructional Resources: Worksheet **Who Am I Close To?**

Lesson Introduction: Close relationships are not always the same. You may feel close to different people now than you did last year. We are always meeting new people and, unfortunately, sometimes we lose track of people we were close to before. Today we will talk more about close relationships, and look more closely at some of the people you are close to now.

School Activity: **Time: 1 session**

Task:
1. Point out that close relationships are not always the same. The people we are close to now may not be the same people we were close to last year. Ask students to think about why this happens.
2. Distribute and explain Worksheet **Who Am I Close To?** for students to complete individually.
3. Lead class discussion of worksheet responses.
   - Ask students to share those characteristics they value the most in close relationships.
   - How have students' close relationships changed over the last year? (more of them, fewer of them, relationships with different people?)
4. Students take turns telling the class about one close relationship they have.
   - What characteristics does the person have with whom they share the relationship?
   - How long have they shared this relationship?
   - Does the student have good communication with the person?
5. Lead a class discussion about the students' relationship choices and why they feel close to those people.

Lesson Plan Evaluation:
Activity: Students will explore the nature of one close relationship they have.
Criteria: Student will answer the three questions in Task 4 about his or her relationship.
Career Role: Family Member/Homemaker, Employee, Citizen/Volunteer, and Avocational
Career Stage: Exploration

Note: From *Life Centered Career Education Competency Units for Personal-Social Skills* (Vol. 2, p. 680) by D. E. Brolin, 1992, Arlington, VA: The Council for Exceptional Children. Copyright 1992 by The Council for Exceptional Children. Reprinted by permission.

13.58 Make and Maintain Friendships

"Dear Abby" columns in newspapers and magazines are filled with the laments of people without friends. "What is a friend? What do students with special learning and/or behavior needs want in a friendship? What can they offer as a friend to someone else? How can they meet people who may become friends? What happens when a friend leaves?

Do friends change as one becomes older?" These are just a few of the topic questions that can be used in individual and group activities throughout the year. Students with special learning and/or behavior needs can identify what they want in a friendship, various ways of meeting people and sharing interests, and responsibilities involved in being a friend. Teachers should help students with special learning and/or behavior needs form personal solutions to problems, because in the final analysis, the formula for "how to make friends and keep them" is unique to each person. Another functional objective should be identifying activities that can be shared with friends.

• • • • • • • • **Activity Tip** • • • • • • • •

The teacher should use a coming event in students' lives to help them practice interpersonal skills. For example, a class member has been invited to a party given by a relative. All students can rehearse appropriate questions and responses by taking on the various roles of participants at the party. These rehearsals are applicable from elementary school through the adult years and can be applied to a variety of social situations.

14.0 Achieving Independence

There is no magic in the term *independence,* and yet it looms as an ever-present goal in the lives of almost everyone. Our lives involve a mixture of relationships, from dependence, through independence, to interdependence. Writers have debated whether an individual can ever be truly independent. Writers, who already have a measure of freedom, can debate concepts; persons with disabilities, who only recently have been acknowledged as first-class citizens, would just like to experience the feeling.

Independent persons can assume responsibility for their jobs and other daily affairs in a competent manner. Critical LCCE Mild Curriculum subcompetencies that make up this important competency area are discussed next.

14.59 Strive Toward Self-Actualization

Self-actualization is the point at which an individual is producing as near to her potential as possible, is aware of these accomplishments, and feels a sense of fulfillment in them. The emphasis is on current talents and abilities and the individual's feeling that she is doing her best. This LCCE Mild Curriculum subcompetency may remind parents, counselors, teachers, and therapists of the part that self-actualization plays in their own lives. Teachers can create an atmosphere that is conducive to self-actualization by emphasizing students with special learning and/or behavior needs' positive qualities and by teaching them that what they can do is more important than what they cannot do. Self-actualization is not a final end-all goal, but a realization that results from many incidents that cause individuals to achieve and feel satisfaction.

During the first 20 years of life, children and adolescents become aware of physical changes in their bodies and become too concerned about whether they measure up to standards. The psychological aspects of physical change are realized in later years, but their beginnings are established during those days when children have so little time for them. It is the responsibility of parents and professionals to plant those seeds of discovery. Other functional objectives should include identifying elements necessary for a satisfactory day and identifying important characteristics of personal growth.

14.60 Demonstrate Self-Organization

Numerous proverbs and sayings in our culture convey the idea that larger goals are accomplished by taking one step at a time. Self-organization is the process of arranging these steps into a pattern. The importance of self-organization is found in the fact that a task such as getting dressed in the morning has to be repeated daily and is subject to a pattern of behavior that facilitates its accomplishment. Among other things, children's puzzles convey the idea that an organization—a pattern—is involved in solving the problem. After children learn to piece the puzzle together, they may use the same steps to complete the task again—because the method was efficient or just because they enjoy solving the problem in that particular way. Once students have developed the fundamental ability of creating and replicating patterns of behavior to solve problems, teachers can present an overview of a problem and ask the students to choose the best course of action. In other words, students learn to make current decisions. Completing mazes and the yearly income tax forms are examples of such a whole-part-whole approach. Commuting, dating, and shopping are other subjects for further review, analysis, and organization. Another functional objective should be demonstrating ability to organize daily activities.

• • • • • • • • **Activity Tip** • • • • • • • •

Teachers and parents can cooperate effectively on the familiar "Things to Do" lists that students make for weekly projects or tasks. The lists provide students with an opportunity to identify goals and can serve as reminders of resources for accomplishing the functional objectives. They can also be used as sources for classroom discussions related to daily events and accomplishments. Some students may organize such a list for each subject in the curriculum.

• •

14.61 Demonstrate Awareness of How One's Behavior Affects Others

The goal of personal independence involves students with special learning and/or behavior needs' awareness of those behaviors that promote acceptance or rejection within society. This anticipation influences interaction within a family, social, or employment setting. Teachers and parents want students with special learning and/or behavior needs to understand and to foresee the effect of their conduct on others. Teachers at the primary level can begin with simple exercises in which students identify the way one person's behavior produces another's response. This is not a difficult task because the basic "cat and mouse" cartoons on television and in the comics depict these cause-and-effect relationships. The attraction of these stories is con-

tained in the viewer's anticipation. Children know what is going to happen, and it does. The teacher can apply this principle to lessons in the classroom. Given a specific behavior, what will be the response? Of course, the subtleties of behavior and communication become more complicated at successive levels of development, but understanding consequences should be emphasized throughout education. Another functional objective should be identifying several aspects of behavior (i.e., appearance, manner, and speech) and their effect on others.

15.0 Making Adequate Decisions

The process of making adequate decisions and problem solving is intrinsic to education. Reading, writing, calculating, and other basic skills prepare students to make appropriate decisions. Problem solving is usually identified with the previous curriculum areas and the sciences. But several facets of methodology can be applied to the broad area of personal-social skills to help students examine and improve their relationships with other individuals. Critical LCCE Mild Curriculum subcompetencies that make up this important competency area are discussed next.

15.62 Locate and Utilize Sources of Assistance

Throughout the discussions on the LCCE Mild Curriculum subcompetencies, teachers and parents have been reminded that students with special learning and/or behavior needs should identify the resources in their communities that can provide assistance in personal and family decision making. These resources should be experts in their given subject content area, have experience in advising members of the community, and should be able to subdivide the decision-making process for their given subject content area into sequential parts. Students with special learning and/or behavior needs should learn under what circumstances resources should be used and what potential outcomes will result.

15.63 Anticipate Consequences

Anticipating the consequences of a decision is the most difficult component to examine in the problem-solving process and the most neglected component of the process. How can students with special learning and/or behavior needs examine what is only anticipated? At this point, observation and inquiry will be of greatest assistance to students with special learning and/or behavior needs. Although students with special learning and/or behavior needs may have had little, if any, experience with potential consequences of a course of action, they may ask others how they handled a similar problem and what the consequences were. Everyone makes everyday decisions, and the consequences can be used as guides for those who are first examining similar problems and alternatives.

15.64 Develop and Evaluate Alternatives

At first glance, a problem may appear to have only one or two possible solutions. Students with special learning and/or behavior needs obviously limit the range of alternatives if they accept only the visible solutions. Exercises related to differentiation of bipolar concepts expose students with special learning and/or behavior needs to the possibility that other solutions or positions can be used to solve problems, and that they must search for alternatives. The deep attraction of fictional mysteries, whether Sherlock Holmes or Nancy Drew, is that the characters refuse to accept answers that are easily available and seek other solutions to the puzzle. This principle should be applied to human relationships. Students with special learning and/or behavior needs should demonstrate the ability to seek information and examine alternatives involved in individual and group relationships.

See Chapter 10, pages 267–268, for a lesson plan that addresses subcompetency 15.64 relative to developing alternatives for personal goal planning.

15.65 Recognize the Nature of a Problem

Bipolar concepts include such examples as good and evil, positive and negative, pro and con. These terms are often used in reference to issues and relationships. However, more often than not, problems and relationships do not fall into such a neat dichotomy. There may be several solutions to a problem or positions on an issue. The favored solutions are of greatest advantage to the individual and her set of values. Students with special learning and/or behavior needs should demonstrate the ability to identify the extreme positions within a problem area, search for many solutions, and place each alternative on a progression. In using a methodology that includes this ordering of possible solutions, alternatives, or approaches, students can identify several ingredients that are intrinsic to the problem. Another functional objective should be examining various positions relative to a group's interpretation of ideas, feelings, and behaviors.

15.66 Develop Goal-Seeking Behavior

Behavior leading to the accomplishment of a goal is one of the most powerful ingredients to the success of persons with special learning and/or behavior needs. Indeed, the successful individual who obtains a goal despite an inconvenience is often used as a role model for others who have disabilities. To replicate those successes, students with special learning and/or behavior needs should be able to identify goals and execute the appropriate behavior that will help them reach defined functional objectives. Teachers should discriminate between short- and long-term, realistic and unrealistic goals. Students with special learning and/or behavior needs should practice the organization of goals, outline behaviors they will need to reach those goals, practice the behaviors, and evaluate the results. Other functional objectives should include identifying potential barriers to goals and identifying resources that can help students achieve their goals.

16.0 Communicating Adequately with Others

Without adequate communication, individuals with special learning and/or behavior needs are isolated. No person, disabled or not, is an island. Individuals who cannot convey their thoughts and feelings to others

Goal of the Week activity sheets require students to identify successive steps to accomplish functional objectives. The functional objective should include activities outside the classroom such as fixing a bike, shopping for clothes, or attending a school event. The reports provide a weekly record of accomplishments that reinforce goal-seeking behaviors.

will have difficulty reaching fulfillment. In the final analysis, educators should focus on helping students with special learning and/or behavior needs develop communication skills. With these skills, students with special learning and/or behavior needs can gain protection, companionship, and understanding. Critical LCCE Mild Curriculum subcompetencies that make up this important competency area are discussed next.

16.67 Recognize and Respond to Emergency Situations

Darley and Latane (1968) developed The Decision Tree to describe people's reactions in emergency situations. For a person to assist another who is in need, the bystander must (1) recognize that something is happening; (2) interpret the occurrence as an emergency; (3) assume some personal responsibility in relationship to the situation or person; and (4) intervene. If any of these steps is not completed, the needed assistance will not be provided. This progression gives teachers a structure for planning training activities. Students with special learning and/or behavior needs first must be able to attend to instances within the environment that either are direct signs of an emergency (fire, earthquake) or that could be interpreted as a danger signal (screeching car brakes followed by a loud "thud," or an individual collapsing in a restaurant). Assuming that students with special learning and/or behavior needs do take personal responsibility for action (which is a test of their values), they should be able to provide the appropriate form of communication with participants ("Can I help you?" or "What do you need?") and emergency personnel ("I wish to report an accident" or "I observed the following things"). These functional skills can be practiced in conjunction with subcompetencies 3.4 and 4.4. Another functional objective should be preparing a list of emergency information to be carried by the student with special learning and/or behavior needs.

16.68 Communicate with Understanding

In a society that places value on verbal skills (singing, acting, political oratory, salesmanship), the individual who has speech disabilities or problems speaking fluently is at a disadvantage. Individuals with speech problems experience many frustrations in their everyday dealings with other members of society. Even competent persons have occasional bad days when they mispronounce the boss's name, flounder among sentences in an interview, or are tongue-tied when meeting a prospective date. Teachers, parents, counselors, and therapists have a formidable task in preparing students to demonstrate proficiency in basic language skills, skill in regulating the loudness of voice according to the social setting, ability to participate in conversation, and verbal expression of emotion, information, and inquiry.

Sample Lesson Plan

Author: Christine Hughes

Period: Second

Time Span: Six weeks

Activity Title: *Using the Telephone*

Situation: A resource room or special day class setting

Objective: Competency 16.2: Students will be able to communicate adequately with others and will use the telephone as a means of obtaining information.

Goal of Activity: Students will role play and practice various telephone skills using a classroom telephone learning center.

Activity: Upon written request, local telephone companies are usually willing to provide used, gutted telephones that are no longer in use. Obtain a set of phones and organize a telephone learning center in your classroom in which students can practice various telephone skills. On separate pieces of posterboard, creatively describe and illustrate situations for students to role play and practice. Include the following sample student responses or invent your own.

Situation 1	Call a friend to talk for a while.
What to Say:	"How did your day go today?"
	"What did you do last weekend?"
	"What do you plan to do this weekend?"
Situation 2	Call a friend to make plans to go somewhere.
What to Say:	"Where would you like to go this weekend?"
	"I would like to go to _____."
	"I agree. We should go to _____."
Situation 3	Place an emergency phone call to the police department, fire department, or family doctor.
What to Say:	"I want to report a prowler at _____." (Give address)
	"I want to report an accident at the corner of _____ and _____."
	"I want to report a fire at _____." (Give address)
Situation 4	Call a business establishment to determine job openings.
What to Say:	"Does your company have any job openings at this time?"
	"What positions are available?"
	"What is the application procedure?"
	"Could I schedule an interview at this time?"
Situation 5	Practice taking messages.
What to Say:	"May I ask who is calling, please?"
	"May I take a message?"
	"What is your phone number?"
Situation 6	Call to schedule an appointment with your doctor, dentist, etc.
What to Say:	"My name is _____, and I'd like to make an appointment with Dr._____ on _____ for _____."

Evaluation: Let students choose partners and act out the situation of the week. Students will take turns being the caller and receiver of the call. Inform parents of your classroom activities. Encourage them to allow students to make these types of calls at home.

Activity Title: *Dialing for Information*

Objective: Competency 16.4: The student will be able to communicate adequately with others and will use the telephone as a means of obtaining information.

Goal of Activity: Under teacher supervision, students will use school telephones to obtain simple information.

Activity: Let students use school telephones under your supervision to make simple phone calls. Listed below are some suggested calls to make.

1. Call to order a pizza for the class.
2. Call to find out bus routes and schedules for a class field trip.
3. Call to find out the business hours of a field trip destination.
4. Call to find out the business hours of a local bank or store.
5. Call to find out the cost of bowling for a class field trip.
6. Call to find out the admission price to the local zoo, museum, or amusement park.
7. Call to find out what movie is playing and the admission price at a local theater.

Help students write a script to use while calling. Allow them to practice several times before making the call. This could be done individually or as a group. Have the student making the call look the phone number up in the telephone directory. If the number is unlisted, have the student call directory assistance. Provide students with a checklist of skills to keep in mind while making the call. This checklist could include such items as speaks clearly, speaks with expression, requests correct information, and accurately records information received.

Evaluation: Allow a different student to place calls for you or the class whenever necessary. Use the checklist as a means of evaluation. Inform parents of your classroom activities. Encourage them to allow students to make these types of calls.

16.69 Know Subtleties of Communication

Teachers should explore the area of what is meant in communication in contrast to what is said, signed, or written. In other words, we live in a world of intention. Students with special learning and/or behavior needs should realize that sometimes people disguise their messages to protect themselves. They may say or imply things so they cannot be held accountable. Schoolchildren soon learn that they can only be held accountable for what they say (or do). They realize that communication can occur through many channels and can operate at both the overt and covert levels. Commercials can be, perhaps, the biggest and most accessible source of lessons. Numerous advertisements on radio and television and in print use nonverbal components—the subtleties—of communication to convey messages other than what is stated or pictured. Students with special learning and/or behavior needs should be able to distinguish between the verbal and nonverbal messages so that they can improve their communication skills. They should be aware of those instances when they are producing dual messages (i.e., one level of acknowledged symbols and another one of intended meaning). Another functional objective should be practicing verbal and nonverbal forms of communication that are congruent with an individual's feelings.

TEACHING LCCE MODERATE CURRICULUM PERSONAL-SOCIAL SKILLS

As in the case of the daily living skills, personal-social skills instruction can and should be taught in a variety of content areas, community-based activities, and home settings. It is astonishing that personal-social skills instruction receives such limited attention in our schools. With the wide recognition of its importance and the large number of commercial and teacher-made materials developed to implement it, one would expect a greater effort to teach these skills. Reasons for this problem can only be left to conjecture: for example, they are too difficult to teach, there is too little time with other requirements to meet, they are not deemed that important, or teachers feel others should do it. Yet, as noted previously, the evidence is clear that a large proportion of students with special learning and/or behavior needs are not being equipped with appropriate personal-social skills and behaviors.

Teachers use numerous techniques to teach personal-social skills. Many of the strategies and approaches identified in Chapter 11 for daily living skills (e.g., community-based experiences, volunteers, games, role playing, videotapes, and cooperative learning) are also appropriate for personal-social skills. Other techniques relevant to this functional curriculum area include the following:

- Various small-group activities incorporated into the lesson plans
- Positive reinforcement for certain activities
- Brainstorming and consensus-forming activities
- Organizing debates or panels of students with special learning and/or behavior needs and/or guests to discuss topics and appropriate behaviors given various scenarios
- Bibliotherapy to expose the students with special learning and/or behavior needs to works of literature in which characters with limitations successfully confront life's challenges
- Individualized learning centers in which students work at specific tasks at their own rate
- Regular classroom discussions covering topics within this area
- Coaching and modeling
- Life space interviews to help students discover the crisis and come up with solutions to address future incidents with self-reinforcement
- Turtle technique to retreat, relax, and regroup before striking out

According to Iannacone et al. (1992), teachers generally prefer integrating social skills instruction into other academic content areas to addressing it in a discrete content area. Many good teachers will use prosocial teachable moments at every opportunity to address prosocial skills individually or with all class members.

If students with special learning and/or behavior needs can better understand that the purpose of the educational program is to help them acquire the proper behaviors and skills they will need to become successfully and happily employed, attain satisfactory

friendships and acceptance by others, and become an independent and productive member of the community, a greater reduction in the socially maladaptive behaviors of many students should result in schools that embrace this functional, life-centered, student-focused approach.

LCCE MODERATE CURRICULUM COMPETENCIES

As it has been described earlier, the LCCE Mild and Moderate Curriculum personal-social skills involve the abilities that are critical for personal achievement and satisfactory interpersonal relationships. While the LCCE Mild and Moderate Curriculum's daily living skills and occupational skills form the structure of the individual's community living and working abilities, the LCCE personal-social skills are the life's blood that propel the individual toward self-fulfillment and an improved quality of life. The individual with moderate special learning and/or behavior needs' ideas about his present status, potentials, and interactions with other people should also be considered. Today, the term *self-determination* is the common reference for this concept and was presented in Chapter 10.

Given adequate support, opportunities, and instruction, individuals with moderate learning and/or behavior needs have the potential for successful independent/semi-independent living and working.

Most LCCE Mild Curriculum lesson plans from Life Centered Career Education: Competency Units for Personal-Social Skills *by D. E. Brolin (Arlington, VA: The Council for Exceptional Children, 1992) can be modified for use with the LCCE Moderate Curriculum competencies and subcompetencies.*

It is no accident that the six personal-social competencies appear in the middle of the 20 competencies. Acquisition of these functional skills is essential to the fulfillment of individuals with moderate special learning and/or behavior needs' community living and working needs; moreover, once these individuals have command over personal-social skills, it is easier for them to learn and incorporate the daily living and occupational competencies into their lives.

The growth of self-esteem is woven into the personal-social competencies. Self-understanding (i.e., abilities, interests, needs, wants) and learning to interact constructively, appropriately, and responsibly lead to heightened positive attitudes about self-worth.

We must provide activities in the school, home, and community environments in which self-esteem can be nurtured with the systematic infusion of the personal-social skills into a structured, continuous program. Isolated lessons and transition/career education classes are fragmented efforts that yield fragmented results. This chapter provides educators with a focal point for weaving the competencies into a program that will raise the esteem of students with moderate special learning and/or behavior needs.

Students with special learning and/or behavior needs should be able to describe overt expressions and subtle hints made by other people. Because most people are more sensitive to communications relative to themselves, they are more apt to interject their own interpretations onto the behavior of another person. The individual with a health or physical impairment encounters a particularly puzzling situation when she wonders whether a person is reacting to her personality or to the particular disability. If someone does not invite her to another party, was it because she did not conduct herself properly, or was it due to her prothesis? She may never get the answer, and repeated instances of these nebulous situations damage the individual's self-confidence. What others think of us influences our attitudes toward the self. These attitudes are used as a basis for further judgments. Parents and teachers cannot control the attitudes of other people—in some cases, their own attitudes may be enough of a challenge. But they can instruct the student with special learning or behavior needs to observe another person's overt and subtle responses that reflect either positive or negative attitudes. Many of the lessons on communication (refer to competency

14) should include such reactions that convey attitudes of pity, disgust, condescension, and the like. The lessons should, however, emphasize positive reactions that reflect the individual's self-respect. She must guard against reactions that would be interpreted by other members of society as justification for their folly. Another functional objective should be constructing personal views of others toward her.

In this section, the six LCCE Moderate Curriculum personal-social skills competencies and their 21 subcompetencies appearing in Figure 12.2 are presented. Instructional objectives and activities for each are suggested. As each of these is presented in the following discussion, several activity tips are provided. The Council will publish LCCE competency unit curriculum manuals (Loyd & Brolin, in press) similar to the ones already developed for the LCCE Mild Curriculum Program.

9.0 Achieving Self-Identity

Of all the competencies in the personal-social curriculum domain, demonstrating self-identity is paramount to the performance of all the other competencies in this domain. As a by-product of the freedoms gained from the civil rights laws, more pervasive minority groups comprise the small incidence population of individuals with moderate special learning and/or behavior needs who have gained a new sense of freedom and inclusion in American life activities. Before these laws, many of these individuals were institutionalized or not given the opportunities to participate (fully or partially) in community living and working. Legislation now guarantees that individuals with moderate special learning and/or behavior needs have equal rights to community transportation, education, housing, and employment. Individuals with moderate special learning and/or behavior needs are integrating into all aspects of society now more than ever before. Being able to know oneself (self-awareness) therefore has much to do with becoming a contributing and productive member of society. Critical LCCE Moderate Curriculum subcompetencies that make up this important competency area are discussed next.

Curriculum Area	Competency	Subcompetency: The student will be able to:	
PERSONAL-SOCIAL SKILLS	9. Acquiring Self-Identity	33. Demonstrate knowledge of personal interests and abilities	34. Demonstrate appropriate responses to emotions
	10. Exhibiting Socially Responsible Behavior	37. Demonstrate appropriate behavior	38. Identify current and future personal roles
	11. Developing and Maintaining Appropriate Social Relationships	44. Develop friendships	45. Maintain friendships
	12. Exhibiting Independent Behavior	46. Set and reach personal goals	47. Demonstrate self-organization
	13. Making Informed Decisions	49. Identify problems/conflicts	50. Use appropriate resources to assist in problem-solving
	14. Communicating with Others	53. Demonstrate listening and responding skills	54. Demonstrate effective communication

FIGURE 12.2 Life Centered Career Education—Moderate Curriculum (LCCE-M): Personal-Social Skills Competencies
Note: From *Life Centered Career Education: Modified Curriculum for Individuals with Moderate Disabilities* by R. J. Loyd and D. E. Brolin, 1997, Arlington, VA: The Council for Exceptional Children. Copyright 1997 by the Council for Exceptional Children. Reprinted with permission.

9.33 Demonstrate Knowledge of Personal Interests

Individuals with moderate special learning and/or behavior needs discover their abilities through gaining an understanding of their interests. Students with moderate special learning and/or behavior needs should be given many opportunities in elementary education to discover their own personal interests. We know that for learning to occur the child must be motivated to attempt and accomplish a task. Aren't childhood hobbies a means of building confidence through interest? If individuals with moderate special learning and/or behavior needs are to achieve full or partial independence through competent behavior, they must discover those things they like to do, can do, and would attempt to do if given adequate support. With support, trial and error can help the individual with special learning and/or behavior needs build an awareness of physical and spiritual capabilities. This is especially important for able-bodied persons who, through accident, injury, or operation, enter the category of disabled. For these individuals, the rehabilitative process involves supportive efforts that help them identify interests that correspond to their altered abilities. Teachers should plan activities that require students with moderate special learning and/or behavior needs to identify interests and abili-

ties that are common to most people. They should engage their students with moderate special learning and/or behavior needs in community-based activities that will help them identify their own interests and abilities, set future goals, and devise strategies for implementing and reaching these goals. During a community-based experience, many skills can be acquired or mastered while making sure that the student becomes aware of community activities of interest that are available to the students. Guest speakers and family members can discuss their own personal interests to the students. The key for the acquisition of this subcompetency is exposure to numerous community living and working areas that are of interest to most people.

A final consideration for all students is recognizing from whom to request help and then requesting knowledge about their own personal interests.

9.34 Demonstrate Appropriate Responses to Emotions

The classroom environment is critical in helping create an environment where teachers can model and teach appropriate responses to emotions. All people are confronted with emotional situations on a daily basis and must learn how to respond in an appropri-

35. Display self-confidence and self-worth	36. Demonstrate giving and accepting praise and criticism			
39. Demonstrate respect for others' rights and property	40. Demonstrate respect for authority	41. Demonstrate ability to follow directions/ instructions	42. Demonstrate appropriate citizen rights and responsibilities	43. Identify how personal behavior affects others
48. Demonstrate self-determination				
51. Develop and select best solution to problems/conflicts	52. Demonstrate decision-making			
55. Communicate in emergency situations				

• • • • • • • • **Activity Tip** • • • • • • • •

The department store advertisements included in the local newspaper provide a rich resource of ideas that can help students identify personal needs. Advertisements provide a wealth of areas to be discussed such as areas of community living and working interests. Families can use the Sunday newspaper also to reinforce family interests and stress the importance of discovering personal interests. Students with moderate special learning and/or behavior needs can cut, paste, and place ads in various categories of interest on a poster board to discuss with their classmates.

• •

ate way. Inappropriate emotional responses can result in hurt feelings, losing friends, or outbursts that may result in the loss of a job. Teachers need to help elementary students identify emotions such as happiness, sadness, and anger. Families should also help preschoolers learn about emotions long before entering school. Older children with moderate special learning and/or behavior needs should begin to work with the problem of recognizing the various ways in which emotions can be expressed. Students with moderate special learning and/or behavior needs should be involved in role-playing situations or should report observations that emphasize various indices of emotions, for example, body language, facial expressions, and tone of voice. A second major functional objective should be for teachers to develop stu-

dents with moderate special learning and/or behavior needs' ability to distinguish the consequences of the emotion for others, but particularly, for the self. For example, an expression of anger by an employer may have different consequences than a similar demonstration by an employee. The employer is allowed to let off steam, but the employee may lose his job. Finally, teachers should identify means through which students with moderate special learning and/or behavior needs can release emotions constructively. Many commercial videotapes are available to demonstrate expression of both appropriate and inappropriate emotions and give examples of how to respond to emotional situations. An appropriate expression of emotion is unique to each individual. Teachers and parents should exert a great deal of time and effort to establish a foundation of trust that will encourage students to explore feelings and find adequate ways of expressing them. Another functional objective should be identifying ways in which emotions affect behavior.

A final consideration for all students is recognizing from whom to request help and then requesting knowledge about how to manage emotions when unaware of appropriate responses to emotions.

9.35 Display Self-Confidence and Self-Worth

Preschool students can learn to feel worthy when they experience expressions of value from family members and when involved in community activities with family and friends. These declarations of worth may be difficult for the person with moderate special learning and/or behavior needs to formulate. Society judges an individual's perceived worth by comparing him to other people. Comparative statements are common in a culture that rewards individuals who demonstrate the drive to excel. The problem is that "doing better" is often determined in comparison to someone else. Individuals with moderate special learning and/or behavior needs can find themselves at a serious disadvantage if their abilities are always placed in some type of "better than the other person" derby. If the individual with moderate special learning and/or behavior needs loses the race, he might perceive himself as being inferior to others, which, in turn, may cause him to lose his sense of self-worth. Families and teachers must begin early to help the individual with moderate special learning and behavior needs to identify and to work with the assets that the individual has at her disposal. Families and teachers must stress the importance of moving to situations that present the individual with "I can do" experiences. By emphasizing the "I can," the family and teacher opinions change, with a corresponding influence on the attitudes and values of the individual. "I can" is a positive statement of value and worth in this society. How many times have we heard stories about individuals who were told they would never walk, run, or dance only to accomplish that very thing and more? The emergence and success of such events as the Special Olympics and Wheelchair Games illustrate that individuals with disabilities have a strong desire to demonstrate their worth through physical accomplishments regardless of how long it may take them to run a certain distance. Teachers and families should provide opportunities in which students with moderate special learning and/or behavior needs express how they feel about themselves in relationship to their interests, accomplishments, successes, and failures. The successful and unsuccessful teachable moments are excellent opportunities to practice the following questions. What experiences cause students to feel good, worthy, or pleased with their accomplishments? What experiences frustrate them? These expressions provide professionals and families with an opportunity to plan subsequent activities that will increase the quality and quantity of success experiences. Another functional objective should be identifying ways in which other people affect an individual's feelings of worth.

Students with moderate special learning and/or behavior needs should be aware of their innate dignity. At times, they may have to assert their rights to protect that dignity. These actions are founded on a trust in their ability to accomplish functional objectives. Trust begins with the first completed task in infancy and is subsequently nurtured by the individual's efforts to accomplish more difficult functional objectives. Often, the act of attempting a task strengthens one's trust in oneself. After developing faith in oneself, the individual can begin to form objectives and seek the means, appropriate to his ability, of accomplishing his goals.

For example, the movie *A Matter of Inconvenience* (Stanfield House, 1974) is based on individuals who, without sight or a leg, attempt to ski. The war veterans without a limb use one ski and two poles fashioned with small runners at the ends. The three skis function as supports to balance the transfer of weight at each turn. Experienced skiers who provide instructions on turning, plowing, and breaking follow the women who are blind. These individuals experience skiing and enjoy themselves. Their accomplishments are judged by themselves and not in comparison to Olympic competitors. The experience is of value because it accomplishes an objective through a means that is appropriate to the individual with the special learning and/or behavior needs. We are sure that these individuals' self-confidence is extended and that they will attempt other tasks because their trust in their abilities has been reinforced. They are, in a sense, developing faith in themselves.

Another functional objective should be evaluating the self in a variety of activities. A final consideration for all students is recognizing from whom to request help and then requesting knowledge about their own basic identities to understand their self-worth/confidence.

9.36 Demonstrate Giving and Accepting Praise and Criticism

Many adults have difficulty with these difficult social skills. Individuals with moderate disabilities

The Emotions Bulletin Board is a sure hit. Students can photograph each other in "typical" expressions, cut photos from newspapers and magazines, superimpose one photo on another, and add their own zany captions and quotes.

Posters expressing pictures of different "I can" situations can help in discussing current and future activities demonstrating self-worth. Role playing strengths is an activity to reinforce the "I can" importance of self.

need legitimate experiences in which others confirm and show respect for their behavior. Legitimate experiences include those daily activities in home, school, or community environments that involve students as contributing members. Students with moderate special learning and/or behavior needs may receive respect and validation for their contributions from family, peers, teachers, or others. Teachers have ample opportunities daily to provide to students or have one student provide another student with practice at providing praise and constructive criticism. Students with moderate special learning and/or behavior needs not only should receive recognition for their accomplishments, but also should be supported for behaviors that will eventually result in accomplishment. Otherwise students with moderate special learning and/or behavior needs are only rewarded for one achievement, and this may be disproportionate to their total effort at home, in school, or on a team. It is easier to know how to accept praise after having experienced various forms of reward. Other functional objectives should include listing effects of praise on the self and others and demonstrating ability to offer praise to others.

Criticism can have a positive effect when it refers to astute judgments and constructive support relative to improving standards. However, it is more often taken in the negative vein of fault finding. Unfortunately, criticism causes individuals with moderate special learning and/or behavior needs to feel less than adequate about themselves. This is one rea-

son why students with moderate special learning and/or behavior needs in secondary school hate to receive a critical analysis of their school work. Teachers, in an attempt to be constructive, often use intimidation or ridicule to address this important area of functioning. Once ingrained in the person, it often leads to fearing more potentially harsh reviews, resulting in poorer performances as opposed to demonstrating appropriate behaviors. In a sense, they are already protecting themselves from devaluation. Is it any wonder, then, that when teachers begin to criticize, students with moderate special learning and/or behavior needs become disinterested? Teachers have the arduous task of first convincing students with moderate special learning and/or behavior needs to be open to criticism, and second, helping them recognize situations in which critical statements are of little value in changing or improving on a mistake. But where is constructive criticism intended to help the person and not belittle or devalue the attempts? The teacher can accomplish these goals by providing respect for students with moderate special learning and/or behavior needs while their work is being analyzed.

When respect is paired with criticism, we generally see a sense of building self-confidence. An attitude of respect says to the student with a moderate special learning and/or behavior need, "You are someone." The critical element conveys the message, "You are someone who can improve on this mistake." The improvement reinforces the previous steps in the process. Another functional objective should be identifying positive and negative effects of criticism on self and others. Families have a great opportunity to express and convey these messages to the preschool child so that they help understand a teacher's intervention into changing behaviors. Families during the elementary school years need to conduct family discussions about accepting praise graciously and how to respond to either constructive criticism or criticism from others in the community.

A final consideration for all students is recognizing from whom to request help and then requesting knowledge about how to accept and give praise and criticism when not understanding how to appropriately respond.

10.0 Acquiring Socially Responsible Behavior

All individuals must learn appropriate behaviors beginning early in life and all the way through life to survive. Our society is governed by official and social laws and understandings relative to the conduct of individuals with moderate special learning and/or behavior needs toward each other. These laws have been greatly increased to extend protection to people with disabilities. Along with this protection comes more freedom that must be practiced appropriately. Nevertheless, acceptance of the individual depends more on her ability to demonstrate responsible behavior in various kinds of social situations. Critical LCCE Moderate Curriculum subcompetencies that make up this important competency area are discussed next.

10.37 Demonstrate Appropriate Behavior

Most students have acquired a large repertoire of acceptable behaviors by the time they start school. Some students who are developmentally delayed have not learned some of the school and community behaviors by the time they start school. All students with moderate special learning and/or behavior needs should learn as early as elementary school to identify behaviors that are appropriate and expected in such places as restaurants, transportation facilities, churches, recreational settings, and public meetings. Students with moderate special learning and/or behavior needs may or may not acquire this behavior by imitating other members of the family or peer group. If it is necessary for the teacher to modify these behaviors, most importantly, the student with moderate special learning and/or behavior needs, her teacher, and her family should all agree on common objectives of behaviors needing to be acquired.

There are common standards to acceptable behavior across all public and ecological environments. Teachers should examine these similarities in classroom role-playing encounters, where students with moderate special learning and/or behavior needs report on experiences with family or friends, community-based training, or critical reviews of televised events. Like a seasoned athlete before the "big game," the student needs practice that should be supervised by teachers or family members. Another functional objective should be identifying reasons for appropriate behavior in public places.

A final consideration for all students is recognizing from whom to request help and then requesting knowledge about understanding what the appropriate behaviors are to be exhibited.

10.38 Identify Current and Future Personal Roles

The LCCE Moderate Curriculum has recognized that across all competency areas the career roles of employee, citizen, parent, relative, and friend are critical to succeeding in community living and working. Students with moderate special learning and/or behavior needs should be able to describe and demonstrate responsible behavior to individuals (employer, parent, child) as well as groups (union, passengers, clubs) identified with a specific role. This LCCE Moderate Curriculum subcompetency requires students with moderate special learning and/or behavior needs to be actively involved in each role so they can realize its full meaning. Family members should involve their children in as many family activities and decisions as possible, especially if the student with moderate special learning and/or behavior needs has chosen their future roles as an employee, citizen, family member, and friend. Teachers should place students with moderate special learning and/or behavior needs in situations that provide understanding of the expectations of others for each particular career role. For example, community personnel such as police officers, fire fighters, and employers should discuss their expectations of student behaviors and responsibilities in the roles of citizen and employee. Family members should frequently discuss with the individual with moderate special learning and/or behavior needs potential current and future career roles. Another functional objective should be for the teacher to help the individual with moderate special learning and/or behavior needs to identify all possible future career roles.

A final consideration for all students is recognizing from whom to request help and then requesting knowledge about their personal roles.

• • • • • • • • **Activity Tip** • • • • • • • •

An effective exercise (circle discussion groups) requires all students to say positive things about individuals in their small group circle. The classmates may be seated in a circle or at their desks, but the student under discussion should be facing the class. Each student has 15 to 20 seconds, during which time other students say such things as, "He helped our team win the game. He came to school on time every day of the week. He knew the right answer to the weekly quiz." This activity helps build class unity, as well as individual confidence.

10.39 Demonstrate Respect for Others' Rights and Property

Preschool children who have siblings should learn the importance of respecting their siblings' rights and property. However, these skills are not always found in all students with moderate special learning and/or behavior needs. Developing respect for the rights and property of others involves one of the fundamental concerns on which the country was founded. It is a continuous subject of interest in television, radio, and newspaper reports and, therefore, offers ample opportunity for teachers and families to pinpoint the reasons for respecting the rights of others and their possessions. Parents are the initial vital link in this competency. They are the ones who have to teach children to differentiate between what belongs to them and what belongs to someone else or their siblings. Teachers reinforce these basic lessons as instances of ownership that will, no doubt, occur in the classroom. Respecting the rights of others becomes more complicated as individuals grow older and begin to exert their own opinions and power in taking command of possessions. This requires teachers to initiate lessons and draw on the students' experiences that emphasize the relationships of laws, ownership, and the protection of the community.

A final consideration for all students is recognizing from whom to request help and then requesting knowledge about exhibiting behaviors related to other individuals' rights and property.

• • • • • • • • **Activity Tip** • • • • • • • •

"Who Owns This?" is an activity that focuses on situations and decisions related to ownership of property. School situations, newspaper articles, and student experiences provide the teacher with material for discussions and students' essays. The teacher constructs the situation and possible questions to consider. For example, a boy brings a pair of goggles to a swimming pool. He lays them on a deck chair and goes for a drink. He returns to put them on, and another swimmer says that the goggles are his. There is one pair of goggles and two swimmers. What should the boys do?

10.40 Demonstrate Respect for Authority

On almost a daily basis, adults are confronted with authority figures. Students with moderate special learning and/or behavior needs should know the role of the authority figure and demonstrate the appropriate respect. Families need to begin with their preschool children, discussing the importance of and demonstrating the practice of respecting authority figures. Teachers need to include discussions of who the authority figures are that we should trust and respect. Another functional objective is to know the consequences of not respecting authority figures.

A final consideration for all students is recognizing from whom to request help and then requesting knowledge about behaviors related to respecting authorities.

10.41 Demonstrate Ability to Follow Directions/Instructions

One of the basic skills that needs to be learned and practiced for all students at the preschool level as well as when in school is following directions. Just about everything students with moderate special learning

The teacher leads the class in a role-playing activity in which the classroom is the "work setting;" half of the class are "employees," and the other half of the class are "employers." For one day, the "employers" note characteristics such as promptness, response to instructions, attitude, proper attire, and quality of work. The "employers" share their reviews at the end of the day only to become "employees" on the next day.
• •

and/or behavior needs do in school is preceded by directions. The routine and even monotony of the school situation makes it difficult for teachers to impress on students with moderate special learning and/or behavior needs that things are different in the employment world. If students with moderate special learning and/or behavior needs don't pay attention or forget an instruction, they may have to do the assignment again, visit the principal, or lose points. The results become commonplace if they are experienced often enough. But if these lapses occur in an employment situation, individuals with moderate special learning and/or behavior needs must face the consequences (i.e., "You're fired!"). An equally difficult task for teachers is to determine whether students with moderate special learning and/or behavior needs can accomplish an objective or whether they lack the skills to follow directions. Teachers often infer that students with moderate special learning and/or behavior needs cannot follow instructions because the assignment has not been completed. This is one reason that students with moderate special learning and/or behavior needs must be encouraged to ask for assistance or identify those things they do not know how to do before attempting a task. Employers have often said that employees with mental retardation are easier to work with because they will tell the employer about those things they don't understand. This is not always the case; some employees may not have the confidence or self-advocacy skills, and just sit idly waiting for more information, affirmation, or criticism for nonperformance. Another person may try to fake his way through the job.

A final consideration for all students is recognizing from whom to request help and then requesting knowledge when not understanding directions.

10.42 Demonstrate Appropriate Citizen Rights and Responsibilities

Subcompetency 10.42 includes knowledge of the individuals' rights when being questioned by officers of the law and knowledge of sources of legal assistance that can be used to help individuals answer the questions. Teachers cannot help students with moderate special learning and/or behavior needs develop this combination of skills very easily. Students with moderate special learning and/or behavior needs should role play situations in which they are confronted by police officers or other authority figures. Law enforcement officials or members of legal aid associations may also give classroom presentations that concern violations and citizen responses during interrogation.

A final consideration for all students is recognizing from whom to request help and then requesting knowledge about their rights and responsibilities as a citizen.

10.43 Identify How Personal Behavior Affects Others

The goal of personal independence involves students with special learning and/or behavior needs' awareness of those behaviors that promote acceptance or rejection within society. This anticipation influences interaction within a family, social, or employment setting. Teachers and parents want students with special learning and/or behavior needs to understand and to foresee the effect of their conduct on others. Teachers at the primary level can begin with simple exercises in which students identify the way one person's behavior produces another's response. This is not a difficult task because the basic "cat and mouse" cartoons on television and in the comics depict these cause-and-effect relationships. The attraction of these stories is contained in the viewer's anticipation. Children know what is going to happen, and it does. The teacher can apply this principle to lessons in the classroom. Given a specific behavior, what will be the response? Of course, the subtleties of behavior and communication become more complicated at successive levels of development, but understanding consequences should be emphasized throughout education. Another functional objective should be identifying several aspects of behavior (i.e., appearance, manner, and speech) and their effect on others.

11.0 Developing and Maintaining Appropriate Social Relationships

Competency 11 explores the functional skills needed to establish and maintain successful forms of interpersonal relationships. It does not include all skills or offer a cookbook approach to an area that has received enough attention in books, magazines, and newspapers to fill a lifetime. It is a skill that interacts with the individuals with moderate special learning and/or behavior needs' feelings of confidence and independence and is a key to successful career functioning. Practice is the most crucial element of these competencies for teachers, parents, and students. Students with moderate special learning and/or behavior needs should have the opportunity to role play expected behaviors and responses for such everyday events as listening to another person, asking questions, providing information, telling a story, and expressing emotions. LCCE Moderate Curriculum subcompetencies and the sense of these functional objectives' relation to this competency follow.

11.44 Develop Friendships

A difficult skill for many individuals is the ability to establish genuine friendships. Many adults do not understand or practice the true skills of being a friend. Family members are vital in helping preschool students learn about friendship. Still, many students begin their educational experience without knowing how to develop true friends. Thus, some children are isolated and lonely. "Dear Abby" columns in newspapers and magazines are filled with the laments of people without friends. "What is a friend? What do students with moderate special learning and/or behavior needs want in a friendship? What can they offer as a friend to someone else? How can they meet people who may become friends? What happens when a friend leaves? Do friends change as one becomes older?" These are just a few of the topic questions that can be used in individual and group activities throughout the year. Students with moderate special learning and/or behavior needs can identify what they want in a friendship, various ways of meeting people and sharing interests, and responsibilities involved in being a friend.

A final consideration for all students is recognizing from whom to request help and then requesting knowledge about developing friendships.

11.45 Maintain Friendships

Teachers should help students with moderate special learning and/or behavior needs form personal solutions to personal-social problems because, in the final analysis, the formula for "how to make friends and keep them" is unique to each person. Another functional objective should be identifying activities that can be shared with friends.

Students with a moderate special learning and/or behavior needs should understand the process of dating, various customs relative to the relationship of individuals in the dating situation, and the responsibilities of each role. Parents and teachers face many difficult questions when they counsel young people. "When do I start dating? Should I date this type of person? How do I act on a date? Where do I go on a date?" These few questions provide enough fuel for years of classroom discussions, heart-to-heart talks, and personal growth. Other functional objectives should include identifying activities in the community that are appropriate for dating relationships and identifying ways to demonstrate that one is pleased on a date.

Families can nurture the skills for developing close relationships. Children learn about personal relations and respect by observing their parents and by interacting with brothers, sisters, or relatives. Before the primary grades, students with moderate special learning and/or behavior needs may have already developed relationships of varying intensities with family members, neighbors, playmates, and therapists. The teacher can begin with exercises that help students with moderate special learning and/or behavior needs identify the different types of relationships that already exist or can be observed in the family's community. Students with moderate special learning and/or behavior needs should formulate answers to such questions as "What are the characteristics of a close relationship? In what manner do people respond to one another in a close relationship? What is its function?" By trying to find answers to questions like these, students develop an awareness of those individual needs that lead to the development of close relationships. Another functional objective should be identifying people with whom the student with special learning and/or behavior needs could establish a close relationship.

A final consideration for all students is recognizing from whom to request help and then requesting knowledge about maintaining friendships.

• • • • • • • • **Activity Tip** • • • • • • • •

Roleplaying is a good activity to practice the skills of friendships and dating. The teacher should use a coming event in students' lives to help them practice interpersonal skills. For example, a class member has been invited to a party given by a relative. All students can role play appropriate questions and responses by taking on the various roles of participants at the party. These roleplaying activities are applicable from elementary school through the adult years and can be applied to a variety of social situations.

12.0 Exhibiting Independent Behaviors

More than ever before, society is realizing that individuals with moderate special learning and/or behavior needs are capable of becoming independent with or without support. There is no magic in the term *independence,* yet it looms as an ever-present goal in the lives of almost everyone. Our lives involve a mixture of relationships, from dependence, through independence, to interdependence. Writers have debated whether an individual can ever be truly independent. Writers, who already have a measure of freedom, can debate concepts; persons with moderate disabilities, who only recently have been acknowledged as first-class citizens, want the opportunity to experience the feeling of being more independent.

Independent persons can assume responsibility for their jobs and other daily affairs in a competent manner. Critical LCCE Moderate Curriculum subcompetencies that make up this important competency area are discussed next.

12.46 Set and Reach Personal Goals

Behavior leading to the accomplishment of a goal is one of the most powerful ingredients to the success of people with moderate special learning and/or behavior needs, even though this has been an extremely difficult skill for some students with moderate special learning and/or behavior needs to master. Indeed, the successful individual who obtains a goal despite an inconvenience is often used as a role model for others who have disabilities. To replicate those successes, students with moderate special learning and/or behavior needs should be able to identify goals and execute the appropriate behavior that will help them reach defined functional objectives. Teachers should discriminate between short- and long-term, realistic and unrealistic goals. Family members and other reliable alliances must all participate with the student to ensure realistic goals are set and accomplished. Students with moderate special learning and/or behavior needs should practice the organization of goals, outline behaviors they will need to reach those goals, practice the behaviors, and evaluate the results. Other functional objectives should include identifying potential barriers to goals and identifying resources that can help students achieve their goals.

A final consideration for all students is recognizing from whom to request help and then requesting knowledge about setting and maintaining goals.

• • • • • • • • **Activity Tip** • • • • • • • •

Goal of the Week activity sheets requires students to identify successive steps to accomplish functional objectives. The functional objective should include activities outside the classroom such as fixing a bike, shopping for clothes, or attending a school event. The reports provide a weekly record of accomplishments that reinforce goal-seeking behaviors.

• •

12.47 Demonstrate Self-Organization

Every day, all people have to organize their lives to successfully accomplish the numerous requirements of community living and working. Numerous proverbs and sayings in our culture convey the idea that larger goals are accomplished by taking one step at a time. Self-organization is the process of arranging these steps into a pattern. The importance of self- organization is found in the fact that a task such as getting dressed in the morning has to be repeated daily and is subject to a pattern of behavior that facilitates its accomplishment. Among other things, children's puzzles convey the idea that an organization—a pattern—is involved in solving the problem. After children learn to piece the puzzle together, they may use the same steps to complete the task again—because the method was efficient or just because they enjoy solving the problem in that particular way. Once students have developed the fundamental ability of creating and replicating patterns of behavior to solve problems, teachers can present an overview of a problem and ask the students to choose the best course of action. In other words, students learn to make current decisions. Commuting, dating, and shopping are other subjects for further review, analysis, and organization. Another functional objective should be demonstrating the ability to organize daily activities.

A final consideration for all students is recognizing from whom to request help and then requesting knowledge about daily organization tasks.

12.48 Demonstrate Self-Determination

Learning to make decisions without being coerced is now being recognized as a skill that most individuals

with moderate special learning and/or behavior needs are capable of exhibiting. Students with moderate special learning and/or behavior needs should be familiar with those personality factors that generally allow them to participate in individual and group situations enabling them to request their own personal wants and needs. What are some of these positive traits? Confidence, knowledge of interests, and communication skills form a solid foundation for engaging in self-determination, which is considered necessary in employment situations. There are other traits, but each individual with special learning and/or behavior needs must discover them. This is where experience and observation of others are important factors in helping individuals to change. The ability to look at oneself with a critical eye is not reserved for those with advanced degrees; it comes from practice, with encouragement, at home and in the classroom. Teachers can help students with moderate special learning and/or behavior needs build their observational skills by assigning projects in which students with moderate special learning and/or behavior needs make lists of their basic wants, desires, and needs to help make personalized decisions. Together, students with moderate special learning and/or behavior needs and teachers should practice self-determination. For students who experience problems in performing this acceptable behavior, the teacher may structure a system in which there is a conscious effort to modify the behavior toward prearranged objectives.

A final consideration for all students is recognizing from whom to request help and then requesting knowledge about making personalized decisions about their wants and needs. Chapter 10 has more information regarding the importance of learning and practicing self-determination.

13.0 Making Informed Decisions

The process of making adequate decisions and problem solving is intrinsic to education. Reading, writing, calculating, and other basic skills prepare students to make appropriate decisions. Problem solving is usually identified with the previous curriculum areas and the sciences, but several facets of methodology can be applied to the broad area of personal-social skills to help students examine and improve their relationships with other individuals. Critical LCCE Moderate Curriculum subcompetencies that make up this important competency area are discussed next.

13.49 Identify Problems/Conflicts

Early awareness and resolution of problems and conflicts can help all adults live and work successfully in their ecological environments. Bipolar concepts include examples such as good and evil, positive and negative, pro and con. These terms are often used in reference to issues and relationships. However, more often than not, problems and relationships do not fall into such a neat dichotomy. There may be several solutions to a problem or positions on an issue. The favored solutions are of greatest advantage to the individual and her set of values. Students with moderate special learning and/or behavior needs should demonstrate the ability to identify issues within a problem area, search for appropriate solutions, seek the best solution, and then use it in resolving problems in life. In using a methodology that includes this ordering of possible solutions, alternatives, or approaches, students can identify several ingredients that are intrinsic to the problem. Another functional objective should be examining various positions relative to a group's interpretation of ideas, feelings, and behaviors.

A final consideration for all students is recognizing from whom to request help and then requesting knowledge about identifying problems and resolving them.

13.50 Use Appropriate Resources to Assist in Problem Solving

Throughout the discussions on the LCCE Moderate Curriculum subcompetencies, teachers and family members have been reminded that students with moderate special learning and/or behavior needs should identify the appropriate reliable alliances/resources in their communities who can provide assistance in making personal and family decisions. These alliances/resources should be experts in their given subject content area, have experience in advising members of the community, and should be able to subdivide the decision-making process for their given subject content area into sequential parts. Students with moderate special learning and/or behavior needs should learn under what circumstances resources should be used and what potential outcomes will result.

A final consideration for all students is recognizing from whom to request help and then requesting knowledge about how to solve problems.

13.51 Develop and Select Best Solution to Problems/Conflicts

At first glance, a problem may appear to have only one solution. Students with moderate special learning and/or behavior needs obviously limit the range of alternatives if they accept the visible solutions. Exercises related to differentiation of bipolar concepts expose students with moderate special learning and/or behavior needs to the possibility that other solutions or positions can be used to solve problems, and that they must search for alternatives. The deep attraction of fictional mysteries, whether Sherlock Holmes or Nancy Drew, is that the characters refuse to accept answers that are easily available and seek other solutions to the puzzle. This principle should be applied to human relationships. Students with moderate special learning and/or behavior needs should demonstrate the ability to seek information and examine alternatives involved in individual and group relationships.

A final consideration for all students is recognizing from whom to request help and then requesting knowledge about how to solve problems.

13.52 Demonstrate Decision Making

Anticipating consequences is a critical activity in making decisions and is sometimes the most neglected component of the process. How can students with moderate special learning and/or behavior needs examine what is only anticipated? At this point, observation and inquiry will be of greatest assistance to students with moderate special learning and/or behavior needs. Although students with moderate special learning and/or behavior needs may have had little, if any, experience with potential consequences of a course of action, they may ask others how they handled a similar problem and what the consequences were. Everyone makes everyday decisions, and the consequences can be used as guides for those who are first examining similar problems and alternatives.

A final consideration for all students is recognizing from whom to request help and then requesting knowledge about the decisions they are making.

• • • • • • • • **Activity Tip** • • • • • • • •

"Pictorial To Do Lists" that students make for weekly projects or tasks can be used with the support of teachers and family members. These pictorial lists provide students with an opportunity to identify goals and can serve as reminders of resources for accomplishing the functional objectives. They can also be used as sources for classroom discussions related to daily events and accomplishments. Some students may organize such a list for each subject in the curriculum.

• •

14.0 Communication with Others

Ineffective communication skills do much to handicap a person's success in community living and working. Without adequate communication, individuals with moderate special learning and/or behavior needs are isolated, misunderstood, and prevented from achieving the success many are capable of achieving. No person, disabled or not, is an island. Individuals who cannot convey their thoughts and feelings to others will have difficulty reaching fulfillment. In the final analysis, educators should focus on helping students with special learning and/or behavior needs develop communication skills. With these skills, students with moderate special learning and/or behavior needs can gain protection, companionship, and understanding. Critical LCCE Moderate Curriculum subcompetencies that make up this important competency area are discussed next.

14.53 Demonstrate Listening and Responding Skills

Communication depends on the correct interchange of understanding and sharing ideas or objects between people. Computers can be programmed to exchange information, but people depend on the meaning and implications of the message. They accomplish this by attending to the source of the message as well as to other nonverbal clues that may accompany it. The teacher should develop several abilities so students can complete this competency. Students with moderate special learning and/or behavior needs should be able to attend to the message by using all available senses; develop adequate means of response, such as speaking, signing, using a communication board, or typing; determine the appropriate meaning of the message (verbal or nonverbal); and determine the correct manner of response. Another objective should be identifying negative aspects of listening and responding inappropriately. Family members can also contribute to the acquisition of appropriate listening and understanding skills.

A final consideration for all students is recognizing from whom to request help and then requesting people to repeat or to restate what the student with moderate learning and/or behavior needs did not understand.

14.54 Demonstrate Effective Communication

In a society that places value on verbal skills (singing, acting, political oratory, salesmanship), the individual who has speech disabilities or problems speaking fluently is at a disadvantage. Individuals with speech problems experience many frustrations in their everyday dealings with other members of society. Even competent persons have occasional bad days when they mispronounce the boss's name, flounder among sentences in an interview, or are tongue-tied when meeting a prospective date. Teachers, parents, counselors, and therapists have a formidable task in preparing students to demonstrate proficiency in basic language skills, skill in regulating the loudness of voice according to the social setting, ability to participate in conversation, and verbal expression of emotion, information, and inquiry.

Teachers should explore the area of what is meant in communication in contrast to what is said, signed, or written. In other words, we live in a world of intention. Students with moderate special learning and/or behavior needs should realize that sometimes people disguise their messages to protect themselves. They may say or imply things so they cannot be held accountable. Schoolchildren soon learn that they can only be held accountable for what they say (or do). They realize that communication can occur through many channels and can operate at both the overt and covert levels. Commercials can be, perhaps, the biggest and most accessible source of lessons. Numerous advertisements on radio and television and in print use nonverbal components—the subtleties—of communication to convey messages other than what is stated or pictured. Students with moderate special learning and/or behavior needs should be able to distinguish between the verbal and nonverbal messages so that they can improve their communication skills. They should be aware of those instances when they are producing dual messages (i.e., one level of acknowledged symbols and another one of intended meaning). Another functional objective should be practicing verbal and nonverbal forms of communication that are congruent with an individual's feelings.

A final consideration for all students is recognizing from whom to request help and then requesting knowledge about how to improve their current and future communication activities.

14.55 Communicate in Emergency Situations

Darley and Latane (1968) developed The Decision Tree to describe people's reactions in emergency situations. For a person to assist another who is in need, the bystander must (1) recognize that something is happening; (2) interpret the occurrence as an emergency; (3) assume some personal responsibility in relationship to the situation or person; and (4) intervene. If any of these steps is not completed, the needed assistance will not be provided. This progression gives teachers a structure for planning training activities. Students with special learning and/or behavior needs must first be able to attend to instances within the environment that either are direct signs of an emergency (fire, earthquake) or could be interpreted as a danger signal (screeching car brakes followed by a loud "thud" or an individual collapsing in a restaurant). Assuming that students with moderate special learning and/or behavior needs do take personal responsibility for their actions (which is a test of their values), they should be able to provide the appropriate form of communication to participants ("Can I help you?" or "What do you need?") and emergency personnel ("I wish to report an accident" or "I observed the following things"). These functional skills can be practiced in conjunction with subcompetencies 3.4 and 4.4. Another functional objective should be preparing a list of emergency information to be carried by the student with special learning and/or behavior needs.

A final consideration for all students is recognizing from whom to request help and then requesting knowledge about what to do in emergency situations.

CHAPTER COMMENTARY

It is widely recognized that possessing adequate prosocial skills is extremely important for all students in American schools, including those with special learning and/or behavior needs. Yet, as Iannacone et al. note, "there is little evidence to suggest that comprehensive and continuous social skills curriculum and instruction have a definite presence" (1992, p. 111).

With drug abuse as the number one problem in our schools, the immediate need to restructure curricula to provide more and better prosocial skills training and to address transition/career development issues becomes more obvious and critical. Despite this obvious need, prosocial skills instruction is not considered a vital component of the school curriculum and we appear to have lost sight of one of the most fundamental goals of our educational system: to foster the development of human relationships and to help students to live and work cooperatively with others in their communities (National Education Association, 1938, 1952).

Teaching the competencies in the LCCE Mild/Moderate Curriculum personal-social skills domain will increase the probability that students with special learning and/or behavior needs will function more adequately in interpersonal relationships and problem-solving situations. These skills are needed for home, community, recreational, and employment settings. People who have a successful quality of life and satisfactory adult adjustment can acquire the seven LCCE Mild/Moderate Curriculum personal-social competencies: adequate self-awareness, self-confidence, socially responsible behavior, good interpersonal skills, independence, decision-making, and communication skills.

An individual's opinion of his ability and his subsequent efforts to obtain goals are crucial to successful career development. Educators must provide the opportunity for students to learn and demonstrate all of the important prosocial skills, including those that build the important skills relating to self-determination, that will be needed for adult functioning. More career-oriented prosocial skills instruction is critically needed in most schools. Educators cannot do this by themselves; they must involve not only the entire school community but also family and community resources. As general and special education services are integrated into a more unified educational system, the opportunity becomes even greater for students with special learning and/or behavior needs to be better integrated and embraced into the entire school program by other students and teachers. Integrated prosocial skills instruction, such as that being promoted in this chapter, can help enhance this process.

. . . .

ACTIVITIES

1. Review the personal-social skills matrix in Figure 12.1, and then determine what general education and special education courses would be most appropriate for teaching each of the LCCE Mild Curriculum subcompetencies for your particular students. Then, identify those LCCE Mild Curriculum subcompetencies/ skills in which you would attempt to involve the parents. Finally, identify the LCCE Mild Curriculum subcompetencies for which you would include community-based instruction and what community resources you would use to help you teach the LCCE Mild Curriculum subcompetencies.

2. Develop an instructional functional objective around one of the LCCE Mild Curriculum subcompetencies, then write a lesson plan for your students using the LCCE Mild Curriculum lesson plan format that addresses one of the career stages, instructional settings, and career roles, as well as the concept of self-determination. The LCCE Mild Curriculum lesson plan outline is contained in Appendix G.

3. Review the personal-social skills matrix in Figure 12.2, and then determine what general education and special education courses would be most appropriate for teaching each of the LCCE Moderate Curriculum subcompetencies for your particular students. Then, identify those LCCE Moderate Curriculum subcompetencies/skills in which you would attempt to involve the parents. Finally, identify the LCCE Moderate Curriculum subcompetencies for which you would include community-based instruction and what community resources you would use to help you teach the LCCE Moderate Curriculum subcompetencies.

4. Develop an instructional functional objective around one of the LCCE Moderate Curriculum subcompetencies, then write a lesson plan for your students using the LCCE Moderate Curriculum lesson plan format that addresses one of the career stages, instructional settings, and career roles, as well as the concept of self-determination. The LCCE Moderate Curriculum lesson plan outline is contained in Appendix H.

CHAPTER 13

Occupational Guidance and Preparation Skills

PRELIMINARY QUESTIONS

1. Identify what LCCE Mild/Moderate Curriculum occupational knowledge and skills you believe students with special behavior needs should acquire before leaving the secondary program.
2. Who should be involved in the LCCE Mild/Moderate Curriculum occupational guidance and preparation of these students with special behavior needs?
3. When should instruction in the LCCE Mild/Moderate Curriculum occupational skills area begin, and what should be the focus at the beginning stages?
4. What contributions can the school counselor make toward the career/transition development of students who have special behavior needs?
5. What occupational information systems are available to help students with behavior needs identify realistic occupational goals?
6. What community resources are available to provide additional training for students with special behavior needs who need postsecondary vocational training?
7. How can educators avoid violating the Fair Labor Standards Act (FLSA) relative to child labor and compensation requirements?
8. What are the various employability enhancement strategies materials available to assess and instruct students with special behavior needs in important LCCE Mild/Moderate Curriculum occupational areas and behaviors?
9. What responsibilities should educators at each of the levels assume in providing LCCE Mild/Moderate Curriculum occupational guidance and instruction to their students with special learning and/or behavior needs?
10. What percentage of students with special learning and/or behavior needs could be competitively employed if they were provided with sufficient guidance and training?

OVERVIEW

The workplace is changing dramatically in American society. Changes are occurring relative to the characteristics of the work force itself (age, sex, and ethnic composition), legislative mandates requiring adaptations in the work environments for persons with special learning and/or behavior needs, and in the nature of jobs available as a result of the high-tech explosion and movement into the Communication Information Age. Because three fourths of high school students will not complete college, considerable concern exists at all levels of government and industry to address the question of how this majority of individuals will be prepared for satisfying and well-paying employment.

The federal government is promoting The School-to-Work Opportunities Act to encourage schools to enrich and expand their existing school-to-work programs, including those of vocational education, youth apprenticeship, tech-prep education, cooperative education, career/functional academics, and school-to-apprenticeship programs. The bill helps states develop work-based learning so students can work in chosen fields their last 2 years of high school and school-based learning opportunities so they can explore career opportunities with counselors and receive instruction in a career major. Postsecondary education also will be available.

Where do students with special learning and/or behavior difficulties fit into the future plans? The answer still remains to be seen. But it should be obvious to professionals and parents that these students will need to learn as early as possible the basic academic, daily living, personal-social, prevocational, and occupational skills that will be required to qualify for and benefit from the new programmatic efforts.

This chapter begins with a section on occupational guidance and includes a description of the Missouri Comprehensive Guidance System, developed by Professor Norman C. Gysbers, which is being implemented in numerous school districts throughout the country and beyond. A section follows this on occupational preparation techniques. The next section focuses on the six occupational competencies in the

Life-Centered Career Education (LCCE) Mild Curriculum, which covers the major knowledge and skills students need to learn for occupational success. Each competency and subcompetency is described, sample lesson plans are presented, and a teacher using the LCCE approach and materials explains her use of

CHAPTER OUTLOOK

Dr. Richard T. Roessler is a professor emeritus of rehabilitation, Department of Rehabilitation, University of Arkansas-Fayetteville. He is the co-author of the LCCE Competency Units for Occupational Guidance and Preparation *(1992) published by The Council for Exceptional Children.*

Instructing students with disabilities in the occupational skills—that focus on choosing a job (guidance) and preparing for a job (preparation)—is an extremely important, but often overlooked, aspect of American education. Although occupational guidance and preparation are important for all students, they are particularly significant for young people who are coping with the impact of disabilities on their lives. They need the foundation provided by occupational skill training throughout their vocational lives. Think of how such instruction might have made a difference in these three scenarios:

A high school junior with developmental disabilities that affect both her cognitive and mobility functions has no work experience, has never discussed employment with a counselor or her parents, and has never heard of the Division of Vocational Rehabilitation.

A second-semester college senior with a hearing impairment is 1 month from graduation and has no idea what jobs are possible within his major field of study.

A young employee with multiple sclerosis is having difficulty remembering, standing during the workday, and lifting heavy order catalogs; but she is unfamiliar with Title I of the Americans with Disabilities Act and the concept of job accommodation.

With instruction in occupational skills during their K–12 years, each of these individuals would be much better prepared to solve the problems associated with disability, job acquisition, and job retention. Hence, the occupational skills curriculum described in this chapter is a curriculum for all seasons of one's career development. It helps young people with disabilities understand their abilities and interests and relate them to a wide range of occupational roles. It involves students in practical work experiences in the home, school, and community that broaden their knowledge of the types of jobs people hold to make a living and the skills needed to retain employment. It prepares students for the challenges of job seeking such as organizing a job search, completing job applications, and conducting a job interview. And, finally, it introduces students to the many employment resources in their communities such as the Division of Vocational Rehabilitation, employment counselors, and facilities that specialize in vocational training and placement.

Choosing a job is, of course, only the first step. Students must learn how to get and keep a job. The occupational skills curriculum addresses each of those three important steps—choose, get, and keep. In fact, Chapter 13 brings to mind a popular country song with a slightly amended title, "Take this job and keep it."

them. And the final section focuses on the six occupational competencies in the LCCE Moderate Curriculum. Each LCCE Moderate Curriculum competency and subcompetency is described and a sample lesson plan is presented.

OCCUPATIONAL GUIDANCE

In a survey taken by the National Alliance of Business (NAB) of 4,170 high school principals and 2,675 small businesses, 95% of the principals said they would be willing to alter their school's curriculum to include courses that relate to specific careers, 74% of the employers said they would be willing to spend time and money working with a school and part-time workers to have better-trained employees, and 86% of the principals said they would be willing to spend time and money working with a local business to help students prepare for careers (National Association for Industry-Education, 1993).

With greater recognition by school administrators that more career/transitional development components need to be instituted and a greater willingness to make changes that lead in this direction, the opportunity for improving the occupational guidance for students with special learning and/or behavior needs appears brighter than in the past. Many people have the capability to assist students in this area: school counselors, rehabilitation counselors, employment counselors, employers, teachers, family members, peers, and others are all critically important in helping self-determined students learn more about their job potentials and the possibilities related to their own unique set of interests and abilities.

What kind of occupational guidance services can be instituted? Occupational guidance does not need to be only a professional counseling endeavor; rather, it also should consist of a variety of classroom and community-based experiences. The remainder of this section presents some of the important services or techniques that can be employed for students with special learning and/or behavior needs. It also provides one example of a comprehensive guidance program that is being implemented in many states to meet the needs of all students in a school system: the Missouri Comprehensive Guidance Program.

Counseling

Ironically, most of the counseling and advice that students receive, including those with special learning and/or behavior needs, is not from persons trained to conduct professional counseling. Rather, it comes mainly from family members, friends, peers, and some teachers. Professional counselors complain of heavy caseloads and too many noncounseling responsibilities to be able to do what they have been trained and hired to do. Thus, the counseling many students receive is not always based on what professionals believe to constitute a more scientific and knowledgeable helping relationship. Yet, if the three fourths or more of students with disabilities and other special behavior needs are to reach their employment potential and become competitively employed, school counselors and others who are well-trained in occupational guidance must become more engaged in the guidance and counseling of these individuals.

Decision-making skills are the cornerstone of transition/career education. If individuals can be provided with appropriate educational experiences, they should be able to make more effective decisions. Counseling may help individuals learn how to take risks, solve problems, select from alternatives, and explore their potentials in relationship to the occupational possibilities available in the real world. Counseling should be the responsibility of a variety of helping professionals who should use the same techniques in counseling individuals with disabilities or those who are disadvantaged or have special behavior needs as they would use in counseling anyone else. Some basic principles for successfully providing this important service follow:

- Trust is one of the most important elements in the counseling process.
- People can learn to make logical career choices and decisions.
- To build trust, helpers must be able to genuinely respect, accept, and empathize with the individual.

- Self-concept is one of the most important determinants of career and personal development.
- Individuals can learn new behaviors and extinguish inappropriate ones.
- Significant others influence an individual's behavior and decisions.
- An individual's psychological needs, beliefs, goals, and values are inextricably related to occupational decision making and satisfaction.
- Helpers should use a personalized, humanistic, systematic, and flexible approach in responding to the individual's various characteristics and needs.
- A reciprocal relationship between counselor and client is necessary.
- Each person is a unique individual and may need a different counseling approach.

Major goals of vocational counseling are to help individuals learn about the working world; identify appropriate experiences, courses, and persons who can assist in occupational awareness and exploration activities; choose more specific vocational aptitudes, interests, and needs; determine occupational training areas; and obtain job seeking and securing skills. Counselors should listen to what clients say about their interests, needs, and abilities. However, counselors also should consider the following:

1. Most individuals with special needs generally have fewer work experiences than other persons, and, therefore, their concept of the world of work may be narrower.
2. Many individuals with special learning and/or behavior needs have a long history of failure and rejection and, therefore, may underestimate their potentials and aspirations.
3. Some individuals with special learning and/or behavior needs may have difficulty understanding more complex verbal interchanges and may try to mask the fact that they do not comprehend what is being discussed.
4. Many individuals with cognitive limitations can benefit from shorter but more frequent interactions in which specific assignments are given.
5. Audiovisual equipment, blackboards, role playing, and other nondidactic techniques enhance counseling efforts.

Effective occupational guidance and counseling will provide individuals with special learning and/or behavior needs more than occupational information, testing, and field experience. Occupational guidance and counseling should be a learning-oriented experience that involves an open, personal relationship between a well-trained counselor or special educator and an individual. Counselors should encourage individuals to explore their interests, needs, and abilities by actively listening to and empathizing with their feelings and thoughts. Clients should emerge from this experience with greater self-awareness and confidence in their ability to take responsibility for themselves. Counselors or educators should help clients to learn self-determination skills so that they can make realistic occupational choices and training decisions. Counseling is a process that must be purposely built into the educational program so that it evolves over a period of time and is open to change as students gain new information and experience.

Job Analysis

Job analysis and task analysis for occupational guidance may not seem necessary, but they are effective methods of learning about work, specific jobs, and interest areas. A job analysis is a systematic way of observing jobs to determine what the worker does, how she does it, why she does it, and the skill involved in its performance. Jobs should be analyzed precisely as they presently exist, excluding temporarily assigned tasks. A detailed job description should include all tasks and requirements that contribute to successful performance. Task analysis is the process of breaking a task into smaller steps or skills that are required to complete the task.

Job analysis can become a powerful career awareness and exploration tool for students. When students with special learning and/or behavior needs participate in community-based experiences to various work sites, they should fill out a simple job analysis form, such as the one depicted in Figure 13.1, so that they can become aware of major characteristics and requirements of various jobs. The class and teacher

Job Title _____ DOT Title _____

Name of Firm _____ Code Number _____

Date of Analysis _____ Name of Analyst _____

A. Description of Work Performed _____

_____

_____

B. Job Requirements. Circle number of those required and comment if needed.

1. Adding _____
2. Subtracting _____
3. Multiplying _____
4. Dividing _____
5. Make change _____
6. Use measuring devices _____
7. Read _____
8. Write _____
9. Talk _____
10. Follow instructions _____

11. Use telephone _____
12. Lift, carry, push, pull _____
13. Walk, run, climb, balance _____
14. Stoop, kneel, crouch, crawl _____
15. Stand or sit _____
16. Use hand tools _____
17. Operate machines _____
18. Other _____
19. Other _____
20. Other _____

C. Working Conditions. Circle number that describes the job and comment if needed.

1. Extremely hot _____
2. Extremely cold _____
3. Humid _____
4. Wet _____
5. Dry _____
6. Dusty and dirty _____
7. Noisy _____

8. Good lighting _____
9. Good ventilation _____
10. Tension and pressure _____
11. Distracting conditions _____
12. Hazardous _____
13. Work with others _____
14. Other _____

D. Training Required _____

E. Salary _____

F. Hours Worked _____

G. Good features of the Job _____

_____

H. Poor features of the Job _____

_____

_____

FIGURE 13.1   Example of a Job Analysis Form.

should review each job analysis before students include it in their job information notebook. Students with special learning and/or behavior needs should be encouraged to ask each other questions relative to their separate analyses. Peers or teachers may need to help lower-ability students gather and report the proper information. When students with special learning and/or behavior needs become interested in a specific job, they can begin a task analysis. Once again, students with special learning and/or behavior needs become intimately involved in the task and learn a great deal about the nature of work by themselves and from other class members. In group counseling sessions, the analysis can become a focus of discussion and lively action. Once students with special learning and/or behavior needs have become more conscious and efficient in analyzing jobs, they should be able to use and understand occupational literature and other media. Job and task analysis is an important component of an occupational guidance program and should be part of elementary as well as secondary programs. It complements other career awareness and exploration techniques and is a necessary and worthwhile endeavor for all students.

Simulations of Business and Industry

Establishing a simulated business in or out of school can be a realistic, hands-on experience that can add considerable relevance to both occupational guidance and preparation efforts. Students with special learning and/or behavior needs can assume roles with varying degrees of responsibility so they can get a better perspective of what the job entails.

Career City, developed by the Quincy Public Schools in Illinois, is an innovative example of a simulation. Career City consists of seven small buildings, which are located in the Resource Center of the elementary school. A greenhouse, grocery store, bank, bakery, photography shop, barber and beauty shop, and residential house are depicted in five-by-five-foot structures painted, decorated, and transported by students in special education from the senior high school program. The major objective of Career City is to supplement the classroom curriculum by providing realistic, hands-on career experiences. This learning activity provides elementary school students with an array of career awareness experiences. Students with special learning and/or behavior needs learn to deposit checks in the bank, grow flowers and vegetables in the greenhouse, and use cameras and viewers in the photography lab. Each career has a packet with all the necessary information and equipment that students may need to participate in the many learning activities. Many nonspecial education students also take advantage of this career awareness opportunity. All students seem to have a better understanding of each career after they have participated in the career awareness activities of Career City (Bocke & Price, 1976).

Simulation of an assembly line operation is another example of an activity that can help early elementary students with special learning and/or behavior needs develop career awareness. Students can be provided with information about industry and manufacturing occupations while they experience the importance of cooperation among workers in production efforts and friendly competition and pride in doing quality work. Assembly line workers can visit the class, and field trips can be arranged to certain industries.

At an elementary school in Plainview, Minnesota, students with special learning and/or behavior needs in grades 4 through 6 manage a school store. Their first step in organizing the venture is to gain approval and suggestions from their Career Education Citizen's Advisory Board. The board suggested that students with special learning and/or behavior needs approach local businesses about their plan for a school store, which was wholeheartedly supported. One 6th-grade class was responsible for ordering basic supplies—pencils, crayons, notebook paper, and erasers. A board of directors was elected to set up guidelines for operating the store. The board elected a store manager and personnel director, who developed job assignments and duties, sales people, stock people, and an advertising department. The advertising department consisted of several classes that competed against one another to see who could invent the best advertising gimmicks and promotions. A second venture by the school was a record shop. The school asked several radio stations to save records that were no longer in use. Students with special learning and/or behavior needs made purchases in cash from the record shop or traded used paperback books. A bookstore and travel bureau were other ventures that the school developed (J. Johnson, 1976).

D. Haring (1978) described a successful teacher-designed career education program in an economics class at Scottsdale High School in Arizona. Two hundred seventy-five students formed their own business enterprises that became part of a career education program called Project Work. The students created 89 companies that produced, advertised, and marketed products and provided services for fellow students or community members. Once operation was completed, the company divided the profits in various ways. Some business enterprises were corporations and paid their stockholders. Others were partnerships and sole proprietorships. Students paid appropriate taxes and licensing fees to the student government. Project Work also was conducted at a less sophisticated level in the lower grades. Students felt the project made them more aware of their interests and abilities and improved their attitudes and interest toward school and the teachers.

Business simulations are extremely effective in motivating students to learn academic material, become more knowledgeable about the working world, and develop occupational interests and skills. School personnel can use simulations to integrate their students with special learning and/or behavior needs into business operations and activities with general class students. Only creativity, time, and financial constraints limit the potentials of this technique.

Community-Based Experiences and Speakers

Students with special learning and/or behavior needs should visit a variety of workplaces because direct experience increases the student's comprehension and motivation. Teachers should make community-based experiences a part of the functional curriculum. Community-based experiences should be planned carefully to represent various business establishments in the community. Prior planning with the company should permit the time for students with special learning and/or behavior needs to observe and record pertinent job analysis information and to speak with

some of the people who perform various jobs. The jobs to be viewed should generally be those that the group would most likely be able to assume themselves. Classroom discussions should cover the importance, characteristics, and opportunities associated with each job.

Class speakers are a valuable adjunct to community-based experiences. In some cases, it may be advantageous to have someone from the business speak to the class before a tour to distribute information, show videos, answer questions, identify points of interest, and explain what the students with special learning and/or behavior needs are going to see. In other instances, it may be more beneficial to invite the speaker into the classroom after the visit in the community. Workers should also be invited to such presentations. Former students with special learning and/or behavior needs also can be effective in eliciting the student's interest in and understanding of the industry and its jobs.

Career Information Center and Systems

Career information systems are an important development in occupational resources in recent years. The National Occupational Information Coordinating Committee (NOICC) is a federal interagency committee that promotes the development and use of educational, occupational, and labor market information. NOICC works with a network of state occupational information coordinating committees (SOICCs) that represent state producers and users of occupational information, for example, vocational rehabilitation, employment agencies, job training councils, and economic development agencies. NOICC and the SOICCs have developed and made available occupational information systems, computerized data bases of occupational and educational data, career information delivery systems (CIDSs), and computerized information about occupations and training opportunities. CIDSs are available in about 45 states (McDaniels & Gysbers, 1992). Information on NOICC and SOICC activities can be obtained by contacting NOICC in Washington, DC.

Several commercial career information software systems are presently available for schools. Some of the systems that should be considered for use in working with students with special learning and/or behavior difficulties follows:

- Career Information System (CIS) developed by National CIS, University of Oregon, Eugene, OR 97403
- Coordinate Occupational Information Network (COIN), COIN Career Guidance Products, 3361 Executive Parkway, Suite 302, Toledo, OH 43606
- Guidance Information System (GIS), Houghton-Mifflin Company, Educational Software Division, P.O. Box 683, Hanover, NH 03755
- Kansas Careers, College of Education, Kansas State University, Bluemont Hall, Manhattan, KS 66506

Readers interested in an excellent evaluation of computer-assisted career guidance systems should obtain a copy of the *Journal of Career Development* (Winter 1990 issue).

A career information center can be integral to an occupational guidance delivery system. The center can provide students with special learning and/or behavior needs with a place to gather information about occupations and plan their occupational future with a counselor. This learning and planning should relate to what the student with special learning and/or behavior needs is receiving in classroom transition/career-related activities. The center also should be a place where students with special learning and/or behavior needs can talk with other students about occupations. It should have a sufficient supply of materials so students with special learning and/or behavior needs can find answers to transition/career-related activities. Career information centers can be established at a fairly reasonable cost. Free materials are available from businesses, industries, and various organizations.

The center could provide the following services: career counseling on an individual basis; career seminars; career information to classes; career guidance material; administration and interpretation of aptitude, achievement, and interest tests; financial aid information; military information; information on employment trends, qualifications, and compensation; curriculum planning; resource center for faculty, staff, and parents; and liaison between the school and community, business, and other groups.

Some essential career-related publications, materials, and Internet addresses are: O*Net Online—http://www.onetcenter.org; Occupational Outlook Handbook—http://www.stats.bls.gov; Dictionary of Occupational Titles—http://www.theodora.com; Guide for Occupational Exploration—http://www.wois.org; Encyclopedia of Careers—http://www.metabase.net, a file of brochures on jobs, several regional newspapers, career-related library books, employment opportunity information, and audiovisual materials on interviewing and job-seeking skills. Furniture and equipment should include copying equipment, bulletin boards, overhead projectors, projection screens, a microfiche viewer, conference and work tables, furniture for conversational settings, display racks, bookcases, files, and desks and chairs.

One caution from Patterson and Curl (1992) regarding individuals with disabilities or those with special learning and/or behavior needs is that the career/occupational guidance systems and publications may not adequately reflect the opportunities available with, for example, the modifications or accommodations that can be made for these individuals. With this caution in mind, these materials may be used to expand the options for people with disabilities rather than limiting them.

A computerized job replication computer program developed at the Center on Education and Work, University of Wisconsin-Madison, is one example of an excellent effort to address this need. Their software program helps persons with disabilities explore jobs and identify potential employers by industry and job settings. A five-volume job replication series also is available through the center.

The Missouri Comprehensive Guidance Program

One example of how a comprehensive guidance program can be organized to meet the needs of all students in a school system is the Missouri Comprehensive Guidance Program model, which has undergone many years of developmental work and field testing in Missouri schools and beyond. The program is counselor driven with the assistance of a steering committee and various work groups. As illustrated in Figure 13.2, the model is organized around three major elements: content, organizational framework, and resources.

The first element of this guidance program, *content,* focuses on student competencies categorized into three areas: knowledge of self and others, career planning and exploration, and educational and vocational development. A valuable resource for this component is a resource kit consisting of a wide range of lesson plan type activities that can be used for student instruction in the three areas. The second element, organizational framework, provides the structural framework, programmatic activities, and suggested distribution of counselor time. A program manual is available to provide detailed instructions on program development. The third element, resources, addresses the persons and politics that are needed to support the program. Guidelines for this element also are provided in detail (Starr & Gysbers, 1993).

With the movement toward a greater integration of special education and general education, the Missouri Comprehensive Guidance Program Model provides an excellent vehicle by which students with disabilities and other learning problems can be assimilated into the ongoing guidance services of their schools. Persons interested in obtaining further information on the details of the Missouri model should contact Dr. Norman Gysbers, 310 Noyes Hall, University of Missouri-Columbia, Columbia, MO 65211, or Mr. Marion Starr, Assistant Director, Guidance/Special Needs, Missouri Department of Elementary and Secondary Education, P.O. Box 480, Jefferson City, MO 65101.

Some recommended resources for more extensive information and ideas on counseling and guidance activities for students and program development are the following publications:

- Sitlington, Clark, and Kolstoe (2000), *Transition Education and Services for Adolescents with Disabilities* (3rd ed.)
- McDaniels and Gysbers (1992), *Counseling for Career Development*

- Gysbers and Henderson (1994), *Developing and Managing Your School Guidance Program*

OCCUPATIONAL PREPARATION TECHNIQUES

For too many years, with some exceptions, too many students (including persons with disabilities) with special learning and/or behavior needs, and other disadvantages have been excluded from the mainstream of substantive vocational education. As Benz and Halpern (1993) found in their extensive in-depth follow-up study of former students with disabilities in Nevada and Oregon, the disadvantaged situations that certain subgroups of young adults with disabilities find themselves in after leaving school may have their roots in the discrepancies that occur in high school between the vocational and transitional services they reportedly need and actually receive (1993, p. 209).

Meaningful vocational education opportunities must become available in all schools for all students with special learning and/or behavior needs who desire and want them. Many different approaches and options have been developed over the years so each student can be adequately trained in the vocational area. This section provides some further suggestions and techniques for providing this instruction to students at the various grade levels.

Elementary/Middle School Students

Occupational preparation must begin early, at the elementary level, with appropriate career awareness, exploration, and prevocational activities and experiences that will provide the foundation for the more demanding vocational education programs at the secondary level. However, this is not prevalently implemented. S. C. Moore, Agran, and McSweyn (1990), in their survey of 100 elementary, middle school, and high school special education teachers in Utah, found that very little vocational or related training and

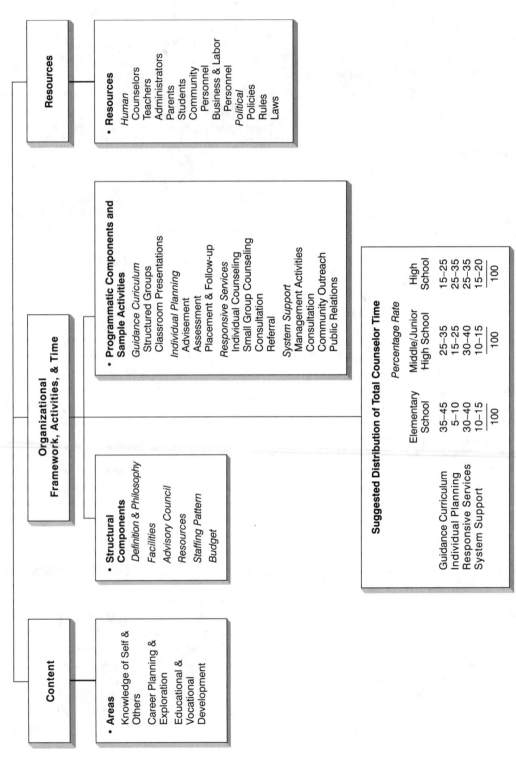

FIGURE 13.2 Missouri Comprehensive Guidance Program elements.

Note: From *Missouri Comprehensive Guidance: A Model for Program Development Implementation and Evaluation* (p. 6) by M. Starr and N. Gysbers, 1993, Jefferson City, MO: Missouri Department of Elementary & Secondary Education. Copyright 1993 by Norman Gysbers. Reprinted by permission.

experiences, such as learning a basic employment vocabulary or viewing different occupations, were provided to younger children, although these were identified as important needs by educational leaders.

The elementary level is an important time to begin the transition/career education process of career awareness and exploration so that students with special learning and/or behavior needs begin to acquire the work personality described in Chapter 3.

Beginning at the elementary level, occupational activities should be designed in a systematic skill-building manner that combines a variety of methods for occupational preparation.

Work Tasks and Projects

Teachers can begin in the occupational preparation aspect of career development by assigning elementary students with special learning and/or behavior needs to a variety of work tasks that include keeping the erasers and blackboards clean, posting and keeping bulletin boards in order, cleaning up and putting away materials, organizing chairs for various classroom activities, cutting out posters and classroom materials, and a host of other prevocational tasks. In addition, students with special learning and/or behavior needs can become involved in various work projects during the year such as making collages, Christmas cards, and decorations; making presents for people in nursing homes; working with wood and learning other crafts; growing, collecting, and identifying plants; preparing stage sets and rehearsing for a class play; decorating Easter eggs; and building model stores and making products out of blocks to sell. Painting also is a particularly effective prevocational activity that helps students with special learning and/or behavior needs build physical-manual skills, work habits and behaviors, and personal-social competencies.

Most of these activities are generally conducted in elementary and middle school programs for all students and should be emphasized even more for students with disabilities or those who have special behavior needs in a purposeful manner. If the teacher emphasizes the relationship between these activities and the working world, students with special learning and/or behavior needs will be able to judge how they

feel about working at various jobs in the community. In this way, educators can plan a purposeful sequence of activities that is related to transition education goals and objectives.

The family needs to be closely informed and involved in each series of prevocational activities for their children with special learning and/or behavior needs and can supplement the school's efforts with work activities in the home. Teachers should encourage parents to work with their children with special learning and/or behavior needs on school projects, both at school and at home, and help these students to pursue specific interests and aptitudes when the school no longer can. Cooperation will help school personnel and family members to become closer and appreciate one another and, in the long run, will enhance the students with special learning and/or behavior needs' transition/career development.

Simulations of Business and Industry

The simulated business approach mentioned in the occupational guidance section also is a specific occupational preparation technique. The students' experiences with Career City and the job analyses they have conducted should help them develop a relatively accurate idea of the job or jobs that they would be suited for within a simulated business. Thus, students can be "hired" to assume various employee roles within Career City. Creation of Career City or a simulated business will take considerable creativity, thought, time, cooperation among disciplines, and probably, money. However, these activities attract and benefit students with special learning and/or behavior needs and involve the school and community in an innovative and effective educational technique. Business and industry can offer technical assistance and materials, and parents and school personnel can use their expertise to help students develop the skills they need to succeed at various jobs within Career City.

On-Campus Training

The school cafeteria, library, gym, district warehouse, and housekeeping, clerical, and groundskeeping departments of schools are all resources that teachers can use in preparing their students with special learning and/or behavior needs for various occupations. Students with special learning and/or behavior needs are generally placed on a work site according to their interest and ability. In many cases, the job functions as a prevocational or career exploration experience. But, if enough supervision and objectivity can be provided at the workplace, these placements also are valuable in helping identify students with special learning and/or behavior needs' interests and training potentials. Care must be taken that students with special learning and/or behavior needs are exposed to all aspects of the job and is not used primarily to do work that no one else wants to do.

In addition, job shadowing, where students with special learning and/or behavior needs observe and follow an employee to learn about a job, and home assignments, which relate to specific occupational tasks, are two other occupational preparation techniques for use at this level. It is never too early to begin helping the student with special learning and/or behavior needs build a work personality.

Secondary-Level Students

Currently, community-based vocational instruction and supported work placements have become more prominent, particularly for students with more severe disabilities or more severe behavior needs. This section discusses several occupational preparation techniques that warrant consideration for use by school personnel at the secondary level for students with both mild and more severe learning disabilities and behavior needs.

Work Experience-Based Transition Education

Work experience-based transition education (WEBTE) is a prominent model of the 1980s that is not particularly visible today. However, its approach to providing students with special learning and/or behavior needs with meaningful career exploration experiences is worthy of adoption with the necessary modifications. In the WEBTE community-based approach, students with special learning and/or behavior needs explore a number of job sites in their community that are developed by a learning coordinator. Students with special learning and/or behavior needs receive hands-on exposure to the world of work but are not paid. These experiences are their first contacts with the world of work before they enter the skill-preparation stage. At the work site, students with special learning and/or behavior needs complete math, English, or other assignments that show how the worker uses each subject content area to complete a specific task. The program has been successful in helping students with special learning and/or behavior needs develop a positive self-concept, explore several occupations at no risk, develop positive work habits and behaviors, develop interests, and help relate academics to the job world.

The state of Iowa has implemented the approach extensively in many schools. Job shadowing is a form of WEBTE, although the process is not as thorough and structured as the WEBTE approach.

Job-Site Career/Vocational Training Programs

Job-site career/vocational training programs provide students with special learning and/or behavior needs with work experience and training in various community businesses and industries. A special educator or vocational educator generally supervises the overall preparation, placement, and supervision of students. Wisniewski, Alper, and Schloss (1991) note there are two major approaches to the on-site training approach: the train-and-place and the place-and-train models. Both models require some degree of preparation for the placement, but in the train-and-place model, the student with special learning and/or behavior needs is expected to have most of the competencies necessary for eventual success. In the place-and-train model, the student with special learning and/or behavior needs is trained on the job, based on a task analysis of the work assignment. Work study and work experience programs could be classified as this type of career/vocational training program. Another term for similar programs is community-based vocational education (CBVE).

Community-based vocational training should begin as early as possible and will depend on the individual student and her level and special behavior needs. Based on the student with special learning and/or behavior needs' vocational assessment and educational background, reasonable personalized decisions should be made regarding appropriate work sites and jobs. Vocational plans should be systematic and must meet the student's special behavior needs. Teachers or counselors must carefully review the work site and have a clear understanding with those individuals with special learning and/or behavior needs with whom the student will interact at the work site. Transition/career development and the work site requirements must be analyzed and structured; therefore, expectations for the student with special learning and/or behavior needs and procedures for reaching these personalized goals must be outlined and discussed with the work supervisors.

"It is important for educators to know that as long as students with disabilities are engaged in vocational exploration, assessment, and training they are considered not employees of the businesses and thus schools and businesses are not violating the provisions of the Fair Labor Standards Act (FLSA) relative to minimum wages, overtime pay, recordkeeping, and child labor. Thus, schools should not hesitate to set up or expand their community-based transition programs."

(Simon, Bourexis, & Norman, 1993)

Many placement personnel believe that the students with special learning and/or behavior needs should receive pay for the work they do on off-campus jobs. Although this is perhaps desirable, students with special learning and/or behavior needs may think that the primary purpose of their working experience is only to earn money. They may select certain work experiences primarily because of the money they can receive rather than the intrinsic exploration and preparation values. If money becomes more important than the value of this work experience, the students with special learning and/or behavior needs will eventually suffer. It might be better to conduct these placements as if the students with special learning and/or behavior needs were taking a vocational/transition education skills-building course. Then if they become proficient and productive after a period of time, monetary benefits can be made available. Teachers should consider this controversial issue when designing a work experience program.

Supported Employment

Supported employment is another training option for secondary and postsecondary programs. It is generally an approach that is used with adults with severe behavior disabilities/needs. An important component of this approach is the ongoing support at the work site by a job coach or employment training specialist, who ensures that the student with special learning and/or behavior needs learns the tasks and receives other services necessary for gaining as much independence as possible. Several models have evolved:

- Individualized Placement Model: On-site training and supports are provided.
- Enclave Model: Six to eight persons receive training and continuous supervision so they can work within a host company, which receives guaranteed productivity at a fixed cost.
- Mobile Crew Model: A group of persons is a member of a business such as a janitorial service that provides contractual services. A specialist provides supervision.
- Benchwork Model: Contract work is secured, and the individuals are taught assembly-like tasks.

In all models, the ultimate goal is training that will lead to competitive employment and an integrated lifestyle as much as possible (Wisniewski et al., 1991). Supported employment was authorized as an appropriate vocational outcome in the Rehabilitation Act Amendments in 1986 and again in 1992.

The supported employment approach is an integrated community-based approach that has been shown to be more effective than a traditional rehabilitation facility or sheltered workshop service, although both of these agencies now generally have a supported employment component as well. Supported employment lends itself well to the current thrust of inclusion, because its focus is on an integrated provision of training and employment for individuals rather than a segregated one.

Rehabilitation Facilities (Community Rehabilitation Centers)

The traditional rehabilitation facility or workshop model has been changing over the years to meet the movement to provide functional assessment and training in the natural setting rather than a more restrictive, protected environment. For some individuals with special learning and/or behavior needs, however, such an in-house service may be a first step in the person with special learning and/or behavior needs' training outside school. Facilities and workshops of this nature are usually well staffed with professionals with vocational/functional evaluation, counseling, vocational education, and job placement training and certification. The facilities are set up as industrial enterprises, either offering subcontract work and/or manufacturing their own products. Thus, the rehabilitation-oriented facility can offer an important option for the vocational training of some students with disabilities and with special learning and/or behavior needs and should be considered an important contributor to their eventual personal, social, and occupational success.

"Imagine schools where the curriculum is so relevant to students' future goals that discipline problems decrease dramatically, teenagers who were never successful in traditional classrooms become focused and excited about learning, and teachers find that their job can, indeed, be fun and rewarding—the way they envisioned it when they chose their profession!"

(Williamson, 1994, p. 11)

Vocational Education

Williamson's (1994) statement, appearing in the March/April issue of *Missouri Schools,* exemplifies what proponents of both transition/career education and

the newly authorized tech prep program believe will result if their programs are implemented throughout the country. With the introduction of the tech prep program, a new vocational education option became available to some students with special learning and/or behavior needs who can benefit from a 2-year college. Tech prep expands vocational education to "combine applied academics with technology training in a way that makes sense to students with special learning and/or behavior needs. It links work experience with career path choice and offers students early exposure to potential employers" (Williamson, 1994, p. 12).

The tech prep concept was introduced originally by Dr. Dale Parnell—a former superintendent, college president, and president of the American Association of Community and Junior Colleges (also a strong spokesperson for the career/transition education movement since the 1970s). Tech prep is intended to address the needs of the "neglected majority," the vast groups of students in the middle quartiles of the secondary school population who fail to develop saleable skills by the time they graduate or leave the high school program. The tech prep program is so similar to the transition/career education concept that it fits perfectly in addressing the occupational career role composing the concept. As one vocational technical school tech prep coordinator has professed, "If Tech Prep is to be really effective in high school, we must start in the upper elementary grades and middle schools to do lots of career awareness so that faculty, parents and students will understand the changes occurring in the workplace" (Kirkpatrick, quoted in Williamson, 1994, p. 13).

All tech prep programs must provide equal access to the full range of technical preparation programs to individuals who are members of special populations, including the development of services appropriate to the needs of such individuals with special learning and/or behavior needs. The impact of tech prep remains to be seen in regard to providing sufficient vocational training opportunities for a significant proportion of students with disabilities and other special behavior needs. However, it seems to hold considerable promise for providing an important mechanism for implementing the intent of the recent school-to-work legislation and the transition/career education approach advocated in this book.

One final program that should be mentioned under the Carl D. Perkins Act of 1998 is the provision for Vocational Education Lighthouse Schools. Secondary schools and area vocational schools can apply for grants to establish and operate high-quality, model vocational programs. Funds may be used to develop and disseminate model approaches for meeting the training needs and career counseling needs of minority, disadvantaged, disabled, and limited English proficiency students. This is just another example of the many mechanisms for educators to use in instituting quality occupational preparation programs for their students.

Postsecondary-Level Students

Many of the services available at the secondary level apply and extend into postsecondary services. The tech prep programs at vocational-technical schools, some community colleges, rehabilitation facilities, and Job Training Partnership Act (JTPA) programs are some of the most prominent services. Special educators need to establish relationships with these agencies so appropriate transitional efforts and follow-along efforts can be provided to ensure the individual with special learning and/or behavior needs' ultimate success.

Examples of Some Vocational Training Materials

Many commercially available materials have been developed to provide educators with useful occupational guidance and skills development tools. A few of these are presented next.

The Employability Enhancement Strategies

The Arkansas Research and Training Center in Vocational Rehabilitation at the University of Arkansas-Fayetteville, has developed assessment and instructional materials that can help educators to better address social/interpersonal skills, vocational choice-making skills, vocational coping skills, and job-seeking skills. Each of their materials is described briefly:

Social/Interpersonal Skills. The Conversation Rating Forms (CRF) measures the student's ability to use specific conversation skills in a role-play situation. Conversation Skills Training (CST) teaches techniques such as the greeting, the opening question, and showing interest.

Vocational Choice-Making Skills. Administered in a structured interview format, the Employability Maturity Interview (EMI) provides a measure of readiness for vocational planning. Individuals with lower readiness scores are involved in the Occupational Choice Strategy (OCS), which teaches problem-solving and decision-making skills in a vocational choice context.

Vocational Coping Skills. Products in the assessment/curriculum tandem that deal with job maintenance include the WPP (Work Personality Profile) (a 58-item behavior rating form), Behavior Management in Work Settings (BMWS), the Work Performance Assessment (WPA) (a 1-hour work simulation measuring student response to common supervisory demands), and Vocational Coping Training (VCT).

Job-Seeking Skills. The Job-Seeking Skills Assessment (JSSA) measures a student's ability to complete a job application and an interview successfully. Skills for each of these tasks are taught in two training packages: Job Application Training (JAT) and Getting Employment Through Interview Training (GET-IT!). These materials can be integrated easily into an occupational curriculum such as LCCE and are valuable tools to help educators implement effective strategies that will prepare students for successful occupational functioning.

Talent Assessment, Inc.

As noted in Chapter 7, Talent Assessment, Inc., has specialized primarily in functional/career assessment materials. However, some of their products also provide important vocational training aspects. The Practical Assessment Exploration System (PAES) places students in a simulated work environment in the classroom, where they engage in a progression of

Curriculum Area	Competency	Subcompetency: The student will be able to:	
OCCUPATIONAL GUIDANCE AND PREPARATION	17. Knowing & Exploring Occupational Possibilities	70. Identify remunerative aspects of work	71. Locate sources of occupational & training information
	18. Selecting & Planning Occupational Choices	76. Make realistic occupational choices	77. Identify requirements of appropriate & available jobs
	19. Exhibiting Appropriate Work Habits & Behaviors	81. Follow directions & observe regulations	82. Recognize importance of attendance & punctuality
	20. Seeking, Securing & Maintaining Employment	88. Search for a job	89. Apply for a job
	21. Exhibiting Sufficient Physical-Manual Skills	94. Demonstrate stamina & endurance	95. Demonstrate satisfactory balance & coordination
	22. Obtaining Specific Occupational Skills		

FIGURE 13.3   Life Centered Career Education Competencies: Occupational Guidance and Preparation Curriculum
Note: From *Life Centered Career Education: A Competency Based Approach* (4th ed., pp. 12–13) by D. E. Brolin, 1993, Arlington, VA: The Council for Exceptional Children. Copyright 1993 by The Council for Exceptional Children. Reprinted by permission.

sequential activities comprising three major areas: business, consumer/home economics, and industrial technology. The components of PAES consist of complete curriculum materials, business activities unit, consumer/home economics unit, manipulatory unit, all data collection forms, computer scoring forms and software, and on-site training. Another product, the Expanding Horizons program, is a satirical program that takes students through the real job world starting with the first job interview to resigning from a job. Seven individual units allow for flexibility by the instructor, who can use the materials for individuals or large groups.

A Day in the Life Program

One particularly interesting and cutting edge computerized software effort to build integrated job skills into secondary programs has been developed at Pennsylvania State University (1993) and is published by Curriculum Associates, Inc. The program, A Day in the Life, is, according to its publisher, "a sophisticated departure from traditional instruction" by building basic skills, life skills, critical thinking, and problem-solving capabilities into five job areas: food services, health, maintenance, retail, and clerical. Learners develop, practice, and apply a variety of literacy skills critical for employability

and job success through job-related, problem-solving activities.

A Day in the Life presents realistic situations illustrating how entry-level employees integrate reading, writing, computation, and critical thinking skills to solve problems and reach goals. Computerized tutorial lessons relate directly to the problem at hand. While the computerware provides literacy instruction, learners also perform actual projects encountered in a day in the life of a worker. The goal is to help the students with special learning and/or behavior needs acquire the basic skills needed for job success.

Many excellent vocational training materials have been developed recently and can be easily identified from the many catalogs and advertisements received by educators. In addition, some of the textbooks that can provide readers with more detailed information on occupational preparation techniques and approaches follow: Rusch (1986), *Competitive Employment Issues and Strategies;* Rusch, Destefano, et al. (1992), *Transition From School to Adult Life: Models, Linkages, and Policies;* Gaylord-Ross (1988), *Vocational Education for Persons with Handicaps* (1988), and the Clark and Kolstoe (1990) text that has been referred to frequently. In addition, two excellent rehabilitation counseling texts for reference on both occupational guidance and preparation techniques are Parker and Szymanski (1992) *Rehabilitation Counseling: Basics and*

72. Identify personal values met through work	73. Identify societal values met through work	74. Classify jobs into occupational categories	75. Investigate local occupational & training opportunities	
78. Identify occupational aptitudes	79. Identify major occupational interests	80. Identify major occupaitonal needs		
83. Recognize importance of supervision	84. Demonstrate knowledge of occupational safety	85. Work with others	86. Meet demands for quality work	87. Work at a satisfactory rate
90. Interview for a job	91. Know know to maintain post-school occupational adjustment	92. Demonstrate knowledge of competitive standards	93. Know how to adjust to changes in employment	
96. Demonstrate manual dexterity	97. Demonstrate sensory discrimination			
There are no specific subcompetencies as they depend on skill being taught				

Beyond, and Roessler and Rubin (1992), *Case Management and Rehabilitation Counseling.*

LCCE MILD CURRICULUM COMPETENCIES

The preceding two chapters focused on many skills critical to independent living. Daily living and personal-social skills are also important for occupational success. In fact, all the competencies of the LCCE Mild Curriculum relate to occupational functioning as well as satisfactory community living, whether in the areas of personal hygiene, communication, independence, or getting around one's community.

In this section, the six LCCE Mild Curriculum occupational skills and their 28 subcompetencies are presented. The competencies and subcompetencies are illustrated in Figure 13.3. The first three competencies involve occupational guidance activities, and the last three relate specifically to occupational preparation. Note that competency 22 does not have specific subcompetencies, because the occupational skill being taught will vary from student to student. Thus, users can write in the subcompetencies for this area when the specific training area has been determined. Activity tips and sample lesson plans from the LCCE competency unit curriculum materials published by the Council for Exceptional Children (Roessler & Brolin, 1992) illustrate the material.

17.0 Knowing and Exploring Occupational Possibilities

Individuals must have a broad perspective of the world of work before they can make satisfying and realistic occupational choices. This competency is closely allied to the career awareness and exploration stages of transition/career education. Students with special learning and/or behavior needs should begin exploring the world of work and specific occupations almost immediately after beginning school. The more that students with special learning and/or behavior needs are aware of the reinforcing values of various jobs, the more likely it is that they will develop motivation and appreciation of the dignity of work and will identify with the occupational world. In conjunction with family and community resources, school personnel must provide an array of awareness and exploration opportunities (i.e., field trips, speakers, literature, summer work, and role-playing) so that occupational possibilities are presented for the students with special learning and/or behavior needs' knowledge and exploration.

A variety of individuals, particularly the student herself, should participate in making the student with special learning and/or behavior needs aware of occupational possibilities. The elementary teacher can relate various subject content matter to job information. She also can elicit the assistance of the students with special learning and/or behavior needs' parents, employers, and employees who work in various settings throughout the community. Many pamphlets and other media can be used. As students with special learning and/or behavior needs progress in their awareness of occupational possibilities, actual exploration of jobs of interest can be offered in school, family, and community settings. Most persons with special learning and/or behavior needs who participate in awareness activities should ideally be involved in helping students with special learning and/or behavior needs explore hands-on experiences and special interest areas. Figure 13.4 illustrates school, family, and community experiences that might be provided to help the student with special learning and/or behavior needs acquire various subcompetencies involved in competency 17, knowing and exploring occupational possibilities. The state employment services (job service), vocational rehabilitation agencies, community colleges, vocational schools, and newspaper ads can be important resources to adult learners. Critical LCCE Mild Curriculum subcompetencies that make up this important competency area are discussed next.

17.70 Identify Remunerative Aspects of Work

In general, elementary students with special learning and/or behavior needs seldom consider the differences among jobs in regard to pay. As students get older and their needs become more clearly defined, this subcompetency takes on added significance. Inherent in this process is the understanding that remuneration often depends on such factors as the demand and supply of workers for the job, community needs for the services or goods provided by the worker, and the skill from training or formal education that students may need to perform the job. Students with special learning and/or behavior needs need to understand why people are paid to work and why there are different pay rates for different jobs. This understanding relates to several of the subcompetencies associated with competency 1, managing personal finances, and can help students with special learning and/or behavior needs to calculate the amount of money they would receive

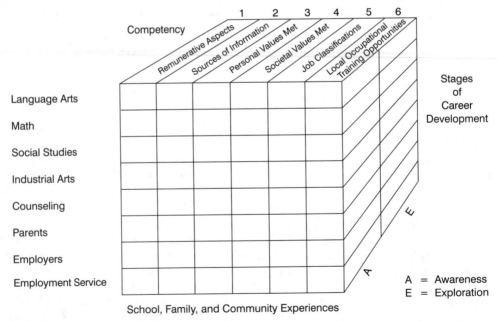

FIGURE 13.4   Examples of Experiences Related to Knowing and Exploring Occupational Possibilities (competency 17).

from engaging in an occupation that interests them and to relate this information to making wise and necessary expenditures and paying taxes. Other functional objectives should include identifying the different kinds of wages (e.g., piece rate or hourly, weekly, or monthly wage) and what personal needs can be met with a salary expected from jobs that interest them.

• • • • • • • • **Activity Tip** • • • • • • • •

Require each student to secure information on one job of interest per week for several weeks each semester. Students should develop and keep a job information sheet. On the left side of a sheet of paper, students should record the name of each job they investigate. The following information is recorded for each job: company, salary, training required, hours worked, and job duties. (This information might be taken from the Job Analysis Form presented in Figure 13.1 if it is used.) Parents can help the student investigate the jobs and complete the sheet. Weekly class discussions cover the jobs that the students have investigated and possible reasons for their salary level. A master list of community jobs can be developed to depict pertinent information relative to remunerative aspects.

17.71 Locate Sources of Occupational and Training Information

Identifying sources of occupational information is closely allied to the previous subcompetency. In addition to the community sources, students with special learning and/or behavior needs should become familiar with such printed information as the *Dictionary of Occupational Titles, Occupational Outlook Handbook,* pamphlets from various businesses and industries, and government announcements. These materials provide a wealth of information that teachers can periodically review, discuss, and make available in the school counselor's office. Another excellent service is provided by commercial publishers who have developed a host of materials in the form of computer-based programs, filmstrips, games, records, cassettes,

and guides that require students with special learning and/or behavior needs to identify the kinds of information available from each source and how they can use these sources to obtain specific information about a particular job.

17.72 Identify Personal Values Met Through Work

Students should learn very early that many personal needs and values can be met by work and that work can become a personally meaningful part of their lives. At the same time, they also must learn that some personal needs and values may have to be gratified through leisure activities and other pursuits. One of the teacher's major goals should be to help students with special learning and/or behavior needs to identify and choose a personally meaningful set of work values that foster their desire to become productive members of society. Values such as a sense of fulfillment, self-sufficiency, personal worth, positive self-concept, success, self-support, acceptance by others, satisfying social relationships, independence, and monetary gratification are examples of needs that students can meet through working. Community-based experiences and classroom visits can give elementary students with special learning and/or behavior needs an opportunity to interact with various types of employed people and can expose them to ways in which these workers meet personal needs and develop values. Students with special learning and/or behavior needs can begin to identify the kind of personal values they presently possess and can visualize how to meet their needs through work.

Group discussions can give students with special learning and/or behavior needs an opportunity to hear how others arrive at their decisions. Parents can discuss the positive aspects of their jobs as well as ways in which they would like to change their jobs (e.g., more responsibility, variety, and physical activity). They should explain how they meet these missing values and needs in their nonoccupational time. Secondary-level students with special learning and/or behavior needs who are on job sites and former students who are employed also can discuss many features of their jobs. Adult learners can identify what personal values they met and didn't meet while working at various jobs. Other functional objectives related to this subcompetency are helping students with special learning and/or behavior needs recognize the importance of work for economic functioning and building self-esteem.

17.73 Identify Societal Values Met Through Work

Students should be introduced to the ways workers affect society. Teaching activities can focus on specific ways individuals from various occupational categories contribute to the betterment of society (e.g., police officers, fire fighters, food service workers, janitors, farmers, computer operators, assembly line workers, clerks, and nurses). Teachers should cover an array of jobs that require various amounts of skill and training. In this way, students with special learning and/or behavior needs can learn that everyone, no matter what he does, contributes meaningfully to society. Weekly community-based experiences, speakers, or class discussions can highlight the social contributions of one or more jobs. Representatives from unions and industries, government, the Chamber of Commerce, and small businesses as well as parents should be extensively involved. Other functional objectives related to this subcompetency are exploring the ways that employees who have different jobs work interdependently and identify the rewards of different occupations.

17.74 Classify Jobs into Occupational Categories

During the elementary years, students with special learning and/or behavior needs should be able to identify the rudiments of major categories of jobs/career paths, particularly those that are relevant to their specific interests. At first, jobs can be classified primarily as white or blue collar, skilled or unskilled, and according to type of work, training, or required education. Students with special learning and/or behavior needs in secondary and adult programs can use information about job and occupational clusters contained in the *Dictionary of Occupational Titles, Occupational Outlook Handbook, Guide for Occupa-*

tional Exploration, and other guides that can add more specifically to learning activities. Teachers should request a representative from the local employment service to explain how students with special learning and/or behavior needs may use major job categories and major criteria. Students with special learning and/or behavior needs should be involved in organizing and participating with employers in a careers day program. Teachers can use bulletin boards, newspapers, and other media to illustrate different occupational systems. A functional objective associated with this subcompetency is to identify education, training, and reimbursement related to various occupational categories.

17.75 Investigate Local Occupational and Training Opportunities

Students should learn about various jobs in their community. After identifying community sources of occupational information, they should secure information from one source for a period of time, write it down, post it on a bulletin board, and present it to the class. The Internet, newspaper advertisements, radio announcements, flyers, and community job surveys are examples of such sources. This exercise enables students with special learning and/or behavior needs to understand and use all community sources of occupational information while learning about jobs and their availability. Students with special learning and/or behavior needs could learn this subcompetency early in the school years. For example, students who are involved in a speech therapy program can conceptualize various community occupations while they learn respective speech sounds. The therapist and teacher can provide a variety of interesting games, role-playing exercises, and other activities that will increase the student's motivation and learning. Close inspection of available jobs can help students with special learning and/or behavior needs to learn more about the working world, job differences, and requirements. Other functional objectives associated with this subcompetency are for students to identify appropriate sources of occupational information and determine appropriate methods of securing and using such information.

The following lesson plan is an example of how three LCCE Mild Curriculum instructional objectives for subcompetency 17.75 can be combined to teach a career awareness lesson. A home/school activity also is included in the lesson plan and addresses the career role of employee.

Lesson Plan 1

17.75.1A:1
17.75.3A:1
17.75.4A:1

LCCE Objective 17.75.1 Select an occupational area and find local employers in the Yellow Pages.

LCCE Objective 17.75.3 Utilize sources of employment information.

LCCE Objective 17.75.4 Locate sources of employment information.

Lesson Objective: Student will identify readily accessible sources of job openings in the local community.

Instructional Resources: Newspaper want ads, local shoppers' newspapers, other sources of local job leads.

Lesson Introduction: Keeping informed of job openings in the community is important. You must know where to get the information you need.

School Activity: **Time: 1 session**

Task:
1. *Advance Preparation:* Collect current sources of information on job leads in the community.
2. Students discuss sources of information about job openings in the community. List their sources on the chalkboard.
3. Present current examples of sources of job lead information, for example, newspaper want ads, openings listed in shoppers' newspapers, company literature, trade magazines, announcements in the business section of the newspaper and listings on Laundromat or restaurant bulletin boards. Pass samples of each source around the class.
4. Small groups review the different sources of information on local job openings. Each group develops a list of five job openings in the community and uses the Yellow Pages to add address and telephone numbers to the job openings listed.
5. Explain the home activity to the students. Have them copy on a sheet of paper the job information sources listed on the chalkboard.

Home/School Activity: **Time: 1 session**

Task:
1. Students share job lead sources with their adult friends and ask them if they know of any other ways to learn of job leads. At the beginning of the next class, students add new job lead sources to the paper they prepared in class.
2. Students share new job lead sources with the class.
3. Volunteers offer to collect examples of the new sources of job lead information and bring them back to the class.
4. Students share new materials with the class when appropriate.

Lesson Plan Evaluation:

Activity: Students will collect information on local job opportunities and interview their adult friends regarding prospects for work.

Criteria: Student will list three ways to learn about local job openings and will list three jobs currently available in the community.

Career Role: Employee

Career Stage: Awareness

Note: From *Life Centered Career Education Competency Units for Occupational Guidance and Preparation* (Vol. 1, p. 145) by R. T. Roessler and D. E. Brolin, 1992, Arlington, VA: The Council for Exceptional Children. Copyright 1992 by The Council for Exceptional Children. Reprinted by permission.

18.0 Selecting and Planning Occupational Choices

With a broad perspective of the working world and the development of a positive set of work values, the student with special learning and/or behavior needs can begin to make preliminary and tentative occupational choices. Although elementary children may promulgate occupational aspirations as part of their career development, teachers should begin serious attempts to identify and direct secondary students with special learning and/or behavior needs toward relevant occupational choices. Many professionals become concerned about encouraging students with special learning and/or behavior needs to make occupational choices too early, believing that these students will be pigeonholed by selecting inappropriate work roles. However, young adolescents with special learning and/or behavior needs who have explored occupational possibilities and have developed personal-social skills are ready to think seriously about their future at about the ninth-grade level. Personalized choices at this stage must be considered subject to change as students with special learning and/or behavior needs mature from further experiences. Making occupational choices gives the students with special learning and/or behavior needs' transition program more significance by revealing that the individual can contribute to society and function as an adult. In the case of adult learners, a considerable period of unemployment or failure may have occurred. Thus, a substantial period of time may pass before students with special learning and/or behavior needs can make an occupational decision.

18.76 Make Realistic Occupational Choices

Experiences from the previous subcompetency will help students with special learning and/or behavior needs discover many jobs that really do not meet their occupational needs, interests, or aptitudes. For those jobs that do, a second level of decisions needs to be made relative to jobs of highest preference. The demand for the occupation, required education and training, and other factors are significant at this level. Students with special learning and/or behavior needs should learn the career ladder that the occupation offers and occupations for which they might qualify. These tentative personalized occupational choices should be based on an analysis of the whole person and should be systematically determined primarily by the students with special learning and/or behavior needs and their parents, employers, and school personnel. Professional guidance and counseling are important for this subcompetency. Another functional objective that should be attempted is for the individual to be able to identify specific work sites where the job of choice is available and to try out the job.

18.77 Identify Requirements of Appropriate and Available Jobs

With a knowledge of sources of occupational information (subcompetency 17.2) and their major occupational needs, interests, and aptitudes, students should be ready to review the specific requirements and characteristics of appropriate and available jobs. Publications such as the *Dictionary of Occupational Titles* should be useful for individual and group sessions. The *Dictionary*, published by the Department of Labor, is a compendium of over 20,000 occupations representing the majority of jobs in the country. These activities can begin seriously during the 10th grade and can become a stimulus for independent job searching and decision making. Vocational assessment adds an important dimension to realistic decision making and planning, as do community resource personnel, who can give an in-depth personal analysis of the job's characteristics. A wide range of commercial games, materials, and packages are available for students. Another objective that should be attempted is to help students identify alternate, related occupations for which they are best qualified.

18.78 Identify Occupational Aptitudes

Use of extensive vocational assessment techniques can help students with special learning and/or behavior needs understand their vocational potentials and specific aptitudes. Before formalized vocational assessment, students with special learning and/or behavior needs will have had some indication of job areas that they are able to learn and perform successfully. Aptitudes or abilities in the following areas should be ascertained: verbal, numerical, spatial, form perception, clerical, motor coordination, finger dexterity, manual dexterity, and mechanical. The General Aptitude Test Battery (GATB) of the U.S. Employment Service is one instrument for identifying the strengths and weaknesses of some students with special learning and/or behavior needs. For others, work sample batteries can be particularly beneficial and provide a better indication of aptitudes than standardized test batteries such as the GATB, which some claim to be discriminating toward minorities relative to its cutoff scores. A substantial number of vocational assessment systems are new on the market and will be discussed in greater detail in the occupational guidance techniques section. Another objective associated with this subcompetency should be to help

the student with special learning and/or behavior needs identify ways of developing needed aptitudes for occupational interests.

18.79 Identify Major Occupational Interests

By 9th or 10th grade, most students should have a basic idea of occupational areas that would interest them. These decisions are related more to what they think they would like to do, for example, "help people by working in a hospital as an aide or orderly," regardless of whether the job meets all or most occupational needs and aptitudes. If the jobs that the student with special learning and/or behavior needs identifies are not within her capability or need structure, she can explore related but more appropriate ones later. What is important is that each individual with special learning and/or behavior needs is beginning to focus on specific occupational areas or jobs based on her knowledge of occupations and self. In some situations, interest inventories can be valuable, but for the most part, interests evolve from experiences and explorations in the workplace. Although occupational interests are unique to each individual, students with special learning and/or behavior needs can learn how others arrived at such decisions by engaging in group interactions. For students who are poor readers or nonreaders, pictorial interest inventories are available. Other objectives that relate to this subcompetency are to help students with special learning and/or behavior needs to identify occupations that permit the pursuit of personal interests and the occupational needs that can be met from these jobs.

18.80 Identify Major Occupational Needs

As students with special learning and/or behavior needs acquire personal-social skills of self-awareness, self-confidence, socially responsible behavior, interpersonal skills, independence, and problem-solving, they should be ready to identify those major occupational needs that are presently part of their work personality. They should be able to determine whether needs such as high pay, independence, achievement, praise, responsibility, authority, use of talents and abilities, advancement, security, social service, variety, and social status are of major importance in their future work life. Group discussions on the topic, supplemented with presentations given by persons working in various occupations, should be provided so that students with special learning and/or behavior needs can make these decisions and other choices related to an appropriate work environment (e.g., outdoor vs. indoor work, sedentary vs. active, urban vs. rural settings). These discussions can serve as a basis for lively and soul-searching inquiry. Teachers also can attempt to have students with special learning and/or behavior needs identify the occupational needs that persons in occupations they are interested in tend to have.

• • • • • • • • **Activity Tip** • • • • • • • •

Have the class construct a list of occupational needs. Ask various members of the class to define and discuss each need. After the students have identified all possible needs, teachers should construct an occupational needs inventory and hand it out to the students. Each student should check which needs he feels are high or low. Each need should be explained again before it is rated. The students should then identify their six most important occupational needs. Students will use this list later when they begin to examine their occupational interests and aptitudes. (The Minnesota Importance Questionnaire is a good instrument to obtain for this activity. Information about it can be obtained from the Department of Psychology at the University of Minnesota.)

19.0 Exhibiting Appropriate Work Habits and Behaviors

Competency 19, exhibiting appropriate work habits and behaviors, transcends the entire educational chain from the early elementary years through adulthood and can be taught by everyone responsible for the individual's career development. Work habits are more than study habits, although both have many similar features. School personnel should emphasize the necessity of developing the work habits and behaviors that all students with special learning and/or behavior needs will need when they begin responsible jobs. At certain times, teachers may simulate working environments in the school setting to illustrate the kinds of expectations employers have of competent workers. Community-based experiences, class speakers, and parents also can play an important role in helping students with special learning and/or behavior needs to develop the subcompetencies of this competency.

19.81 Follow Directions and Observe Regulations

Employers expect their employees to follow directions accurately. These may be given verbally or in writing and will range from very simple one-step directions to those that are complex and require several steps that employees must remember and complete. Gaming and role-playing techniques can be particularly effective in helping students with special learning and/or behavior needs develop these skills. Exercises will need to begin early and be repeated intermittently throughout the grade levels so that all students with special learning and/or behavior needs, especially those who have a lower ability in this area, can learn and retain these skills. After students with special learning and/or behavior needs have learned the lower-order steps, they should gradually learn how to follow more complicated directions. Another objective should be for the student with special learning and/or behavior needs to be able to perform a series of tasks in the home requiring simple-to-complex written instructions.

19.82 Recognize the Importance of Attendance and Punctuality

The classroom situation can be organized to emphasize the importance of attendance and punctuality in the workplace. A classroom time clock is one method that can be used to promote this concept. The student with special learning and/or behavior needs should learn why attendance and punctuality are important to the employer (e.g., loss of production time, business income, and meeting deadlines). Students with special learning and/or behavior needs should learn acceptable and unacceptable reasons for lateness and absenteeism, and what the consequences are in both situations. Once again, employers and workers from various businesses and industries can be effective in presenting their own cases and company policies. Another objective that students should be required to meet is to identify appropriate actions to take if they need to be late or absent from work.

19.83 Recognize the Importance of Supervision

Although accepting supervision is related to previous subcompetencies, it is specific to various methods of supervision that are found in the workplace. Supervision can range from being infrequent and indirect to very frequent and direct. Supervision can be constructive, critical, or unfair. It is important for students with special learning and/or behavior needs to understand the various forms of supervision and how they should react to supervision under different conditions. Role playing is a viable method of presenting students with various situations and types of supervision so they can learn appropriate ways of responding. Role-playing activities can be followed by group discussions that focus on different responses that can help students with special learning and/or behavior needs develop other methods of handling the situation. The teacher also can use various methods of supervising class members and then get reactions to the method. Other objectives that can be attempted for students with special learning and/or behavior needs are for them to observe and discuss supervisory policies in several workplaces and identify various responses that can be used for various types of supervisory practices.

19.84 Demonstrate Knowledge of Occupational Safety

Many employers are afraid to employ people with disabilities or with special learning and/or behavior needs because they believe that these individuals will have more accidents. Thus, teachers should emphasize occupational safety skills to minimize the number of potential accidents that could occur and result in the individuals with special learning and/or behavior needs' dismissal. Videos, community-based experiences, role playing, and class discussions are particularly important in helping students with special learning and/or behavior needs understand potential safety hazards and the necessary precautions they may need to take to avoid unnecessary accidents. Before placement on a community job site, students with special learning and/or behavior needs should be thoroughly prepared to handle all conceivable accidents that could occur at the workplace. This subcompetency should be taught at all levels of the school program so that by the time the students with special learning and/or behavior needs leave school, they are well versed in safety practices. Other objectives associated with this subcompetency should require the student with special learning and/or behavior needs to identify major reasons for practicing safety on the job and potential safety hazards that exist in various types of occupations.

19.85 Work with Others

The inability to get along with co-workers and supervisors is one of the most common reasons people fail on their jobs. Students with special learning and/or behavior needs must learn work expectations, and the school can become a fertile ground for teaching these interactive and cooperative skills. Teachers should create an environment that promotes development of these work skills by encouraging students to practice interacting and cooperating with others. Community-based experiences, role playing, and group discussions also can be used to illustrate and stimulate discussion on reasons for working with others and the individual's importance in cooperative efforts and to help students with special learning and/or behavior needs identify the positive and negative aspects of working together. Another objective might be to simulate actual work environments by developing projects that require students with special learning and/or behavior needs to interact and cooperate with others before they can complete a specific task.

• • • • • • • **Activity Tip** • • • • • • •

Set up an assembly line operation with the assistance of industrial workers from the community. The assembly line operation should be as realistic as possible. Have the workers explain their jobs, particularly as they relate to this competency area. Initiate the work and assess the students with special learning and/or behavior needs on their ability to work with others, accept supervision, and master other subcompetencies related to this competency. Some students with special learning and/or behavior needs may be supervisors or assume other roles associated with this type of work. At the end of the day, the class should discuss the group's performance and future efforts. Rate each student with special learning and/or behavior needs on work habits and behaviors, and provide individual feedback that will increase the students with special learning and/or behavior needs awareness of strong points and areas where they need to improve. (Further discussion and ideas related to this type of activity are provided later in the chapter.)

19.86 Meet Demands for Quality Work

Students with special learning and/or behavior needs will need to know about quality standards for various types of jobs, particularly those that interest them. They should meet such standards on their work assignments, understand when and why such standards are not achieved, and work until they have met standards or until teachers have asserted whether students can perform at that level. Elementary students with special learning and/or behavior needs should strive for quality while they are engaged in projects. Students with special learning and/or behavior needs can be assigned as checkers to ascertain whether work has met the job requirements and can participate in discussions conducted to point out problems. The secondary students with special learning and/or behavior needs' job explorations and try-outs establish the expected criteria that will be used to evaluate their performance. Another objective of this subcompetency should be to have the student with special learning

and/or behavior needs perform simulated work tasks at minimum quality standards.

19.87 Work at a Satisfactory Rate

It is important for students with special learning and/or behavior needs to learn that people are employed to make money for the employer. This requires those students with special learning and/or behavior needs learn how to do work correctly and at a sufficient speed. Teachers should require students with special learning and/or behavior needs to complete certain work activities within a specific period of time so that they form the habit as well as learn the concept. Time standards can be established for various work tasks in and out of the school, and teachers should chart the student with special learning and/or behavior needs' progress until she meets the criterion. Students with special learning and/or behavior needs should participate in establishing reasonable time standards so they can understand how and why time or piece rates are determined. Employers and workers can be useful in conveying the importance of this subcompetency, especially if these skills will help students with special learning and/or behavior needs earn more money. Other objectives associated with this subcompetency should be to help the student with special learning and/or behavior needs identify satisfactory rates required for various jobs of interest and reasons jobs must be performed at certain rates of speed.

The following is a description by Terri Chasteen, a special education teacher in Nixa, Missouri, of how she and her associates are implementing the LCCE approach and using its lesson plans to teach subcompetency 19.87 to her students with special learning and/or behavior needs.

I teach a work-study class consisting of six students who have mild intellectual disabilities, learning disabilities, or behavior disorders. Administrative support in this district has enabled the special education teachers to design two classrooms to meet the curricular needs of these students. One classroom consists of a life skills area with a complete kitchen including a washer and dryer and a living area. Another section of this classroom contains built-in study carrels and a lecture area. The other classroom is a more traditional classroom that includes several work stations such as office skills (filing, binding books, collation, and mailing) and woodworking (gluing, assembling, painting, finishing).

The class is currently working on the Occupational Guidance LCCE Instructional Unit 81, "Following Directions and Observing Regulations." At the beginning of each LCCE unit, the goals and objectives are shared with the students. This enables the students to know what they are expected to gain from the completion of each unit. These objectives are reviewed at the beginning of each lesson. Students are asked to follow directions every day in a variety of different ways. This unit allows them to explore methods to improve their skills in following directions. It also introduces them to the idea that following directions is an important skill not only in their daily routine but also in any of the careers they may choose.

The first lesson was a reflective time when students realized ways they had followed directions in the past. Each student was asked to relate a personal situation. (These students love to talk. The problem was getting them to stop.) Each student was asked to describe a time when she was asked to follow directions and the outcome. Independently, students were asked to write a paragraph describing an experience in following directions, including the outcome and how directions helped them.

The next lesson involved following verbal directions. Problems were discussed in following verbal directions that are vague, lengthy, complex, or hard to understand. Students developed a list of hints that would improve their skills at following verbal directions. A completed list was recorded on the work sheet "Responding to Verbal Instructions" and then placed in their life skills notebooks.

One adaptation I have included while working with the LCCE curriculum was to have the students make a life skills notebook. This notebook consists of information they might need in their future. For example: a resume, lists of information (names, addresses, phone numbers of persons to use as references), and copies of the fact sheets from the LCCE lessons.

The next lesson gave the students an opportunity to practice responding to verbal directions. As a class, the students wrote a dialogue with vague, unclear directions and the listener's appropriate response (i.e., write down directions, ask for clarification, etc.). A videotape was made as the students role-played the dialogue. For additional practice students played the Directions Game.

This game is teacher directed. Each student is asked to complete a list of simple tasks given verbally. Adding one task at a time until a mistake is made continues the game. The winner of the game is the student who can remember and perform the most tasks without making a mistake. This game not only allows the students to practice using the strategies for following directions but also improves short-term memory skills.

The next lesson introduces the second half of the unit, which focuses on following written directions. This was a popular lesson because it allowed the students a chance to practice the skills outside the confines of the classroom. The lesson involved students writing instructions for finding a location on the school grounds, without naming the location. The instructions were then exchanged, and the fun began.

We went beyond the lesson plan and actually took the written instructions and tried to find the location. It was interesting for the students to see for themselves the problems that can occur if the directions are not clear, logical, or in sequential steps. Back in the classroom, students discussed ways to improve writing instructions and the positive aspects of being able to follow well-written directions.

The last objective took several sessions to complete. Students were asked to perform a series of tasks in response to written directions. It was important to overlearn this skill. It was also important to show students the many times in their lives that they are asked to follow directions accurately. The students were asked to collect examples of written directions that would be used in their daily lives in the home, the workplace, and in leisure time. The class then practiced following directions in each of these areas: following a recipe, following written directions to complete an order form, following diagram directions to complete string hand games, and watching a demonstration to make balloon animals. An evaluation of this unit included following three oral and three written directions along with the completion of the work sheet "Comparing Types of Directions."

These students enjoy the learning experiences provided in the LCCE curriculum. The suggested lesson plans are easy to follow and give a variety of activities and ideas that are helpful in planning. It is written in a way that allows the teacher freedom to adapt the lessons to the instructional level of the students. This reduces the students' frustration.

The students also respond well to the many hands-on activities, field trips, and guest speakers.

20.0 Seeking, Securing, and Maintaining Employment

After leaving the formal education system, many students with special learning and/or behavior needs have difficulty seeking, securing, and maintaining employment. Apparently, efforts at teaching this competency have failed to help many students with special learning and/or behavior needs retain this knowledge and ability over time. This is a major downfall of these individuals in the community and is especially unfortunate for those who have been through an extensive educational program. Educators should begin teaching this competency at least by the 10th grade and should continue instructing their students with special learning and/or behavior needs in this area each semester thereafter. Many commercial materials are available for teaching this competency, although professionals may want to develop their own.

20.88 Search for a Job

The ability to develop a logical step-by-step method of searching for a job is a crucial subcompetency. Knowing how to explore sources of information about possible jobs is a beginning. Teachers can help students with special learning and/or behavior needs develop this subcompetency by using bulletin boards to depict the steps that students with special learning and/or behavior needs can take to search for a job and explore various sources of information. Community-based experiences to agencies that help people find jobs, alonng with role playing, games, and guest speakers, also can help students to gain new perspectives in this area. Job descriptions and announcements, advertisements, and commercial materials on job-seeking skills also are available. Other objectives related to this subcompetency include identifying steps involved in searching for a job, researching a specific job, and following through on a job lead.

The following lesson plan from the LCCE Mild Curriculum competency unit manual on occupational guidance and preparation illustrates how subcompetency 20.88 could be addressed at the career exploration stage within the classroom situation. The work sheet accompanying the lesson plan is not included.

Lesson Plan 9   20.88.3E:9

LCCE Objective 20.88.3. Arrange a real or simulated job interview.

Lesson Objective: Student will learn how to contact an employer using appropriate telephone skills.

Instructional Resources: Worksheet Checklist: **Telephoning a Potential Employer**, want ads, "Learner sets" of telephones from telephone company.

Lesson Introduction: Telephone, letter or personal visit may make Employer contacts about job leads. Today's lesson focuses on the telephone contact.

School Activity: **Time: 2 sessions**

Task:
1. Discuss types of employer contacts suggested in want ads, for example, writing or telephoning the employer.
2. Students form pairs and identify three jobs for which they would like more information. Students record the jobs in their Job Lead File for use in Lesson Plan 10.
3. The pairs present their leads and how they would contact the employers to the class.

4. Identify the telephone contact as one way to gather job lead information from an employer. Describe the behaviors for the telephone contact listed on Worksheet Checklist: **Telephoning a Potential Employer**.

5. Demonstrate the worksheet behaviors by playing the role of a job seeker. Ask a student to volunteer to play the role of an employer.
   - Select a job title and employer name.
   - Ask the student to assume the name of the employer and to imagine that he or she has an opening for the selected job title.
   - Ask the student to answer questions as he or she expects the employer would.
   - Role play the 12 worksheet behaviors.

6. Students rate the instructor's performance using the checklist on the worksheet (instructor demonstration).

7. Following the demonstration, stress the following points about how to telephone an employer:
   - Use a telephone in a private, quiet place.
   - Know the information to seek and give.
   - Have pencil and paper ready to record the employer's comments.
   - Use a pleasant tone of voice, be polite in responding and listen carefully.

8. In the second session, groups of four role play the employer contact, taking turns playing the role of job seeker, employer, and observers. The observers should use the worksheet to evaluate the job seeker's performance.

9. Record information on each student's performance as a job seeker as evaluated by the two observers.

Lesson Plan Evaluation:

Activity: Students will practice the employer contact.

Criteria: Student will demonstrate 10 of 12 behaviors required to contact an employer based on information from the observers.

Career Role: Employee

Career Stage: Exploration

Note: From *Life Centered Career Education Competency Units for Occupational Guidance and Preparation* (Vol. 1, pp. 229–230) by R. T. Roessler and D. E. Brolin, 1992, Arlington, VA: The Council for Exceptional Children. Copyright 1992 by The Council for Exceptional Children. Reprinted by permission.

20.89 Apply for a Job

An important objective in vocational programming should be to prepare students with special learning and/or behavior needs to apply for a job. Mastery of this subcompetency is another indicator of the student's ability and independence for vocational functioning. To demonstrate this, the student with special learning and/or behavior needs must become familiar with job application forms and procedures involved in applying for jobs. Beginning in at least the 10th grade, students with special learning and/or behavior needs should learn words that are typically used on application forms and interviews. Students with special learning and/or behavior needs should spend a great deal of time reviewing and completing application forms, learning job vocabulary, role playing, and collecting personal data needed for job applications. Another objective that students with special learning and/or behavior needs should be required to meet is to identify those factors they consider important to them in applying for jobs.

20.90 Interview for a Job

Interviewing skills are inextricably related to the other subcompetencies and should receive careful attention from educators. Employers, workers, and other community resources can help prepare the student with special learning and/or behavior needs for an interview. Students with special learning and/or behavior needs must understand and learn steps involved in securing an interview, what to do and say when requesting an interview on the phone or in person, and how to handle themselves in the actual situation. Role playing, group discussions, videos, speakers and demonstrations, games and commercial materials, videotapes, and other techniques are highly recommended. Other objectives for students with special learning and/or behavior needs should be to complete a simulated job interview in an actual business establishment and practice dressing for and transporting self to job interviews.

20.91 Know How to Maintain Post-School Occupational Adjustment

Occupational adjustment skills are concerned with how former students can resolve potential problems that they may encounter after they have obtained a job. Former students are a fertile source of information that can describe the most significant adjustments that students with special learning and/or behavior needs may need to make in a work environment. Role plays depicting problem areas are a recommended technique that teachers can use to illustrate effective behaviors. Students with special learning and/or behavior needs should keep a notebook of techniques for future use. This subcompetency should be given considerable emphasis during the latter part of the high school program. Another objective for the student with special learning and/or behavior needs would be to identify sources of assistance for programs that students with special learning and/or behavior needs cannot personally resolve.

20.92 Demonstrate Knowledge of Competitive Standards

After students have secured a job, they must perform at the standard expected of other workers. If skills in adjusting to competitive standards are overlooked, former students may lose their jobs because of a mis-

• • • • • • • • **Activity Tip** • • • • • • • •

The students with special learning and/or behavior needs should invite former students back to school to discuss their jobs (or lack of them) and should develop a set of questions relating to post-school adjustment. Discussions should include problems that former students encounter, how they handle those problems, what they feel the students with special behavior needs so as to be successful, and influences that affect their present transition/ career functioning. Later, students with special behavior needs should have the opportunity to observe former students working at their actual jobs. The former students should be encouraged to bring in people who helped them adjust. Some former students may not cooperate in this activity because of their desire to no longer be identified with their past.

• •

understanding of what is expected of workers and how they can advance their position and pay. Employers and workers present this kind of information and conduct on-site visits to various job locations so that students with special learning and/or behavior needs can observe what employers expect of workers at various jobs and how this can be best achieved. Other objectives for students should be to identify jobs of interest and their expected standards and how the individual can achieve improvements.

20.93 Know How to Adjust to Changes in Employment

Most people change jobs about four or five times during their working career. Some people lose their jobs for various employment and nonemployment reasons. Others are promoted or find better positions. Students with special learning and/or behavior needs must learn the factors that determine successful and unsuccessful job adjustment and how to deal with them. Another important objective of this unit of study is to know how to recognize and apply for promotional opportunities. See Chapter 10, pages 273–274, for a career preparation lesson plan designed to help students with special learning and/or behavior needs know how to appropriately resign from a job.

21.0 Exhibiting Sufficient Physical-Manual Skills

Occupations that the majority of individuals with disabilities obtain require physical stamina, endurance, coordination, strength, and dexterity. The jobs available to the many students with disabilities require considerable fine or gross motor dexterity, standing, pulling, pushing, lifting, and carrying abilities. Development of adequate physical-manual skills should begin shortly after they enter school. Teachers can design class activities to promote the use and development of skills that will help students with special learning and/or behavior needs to experience a great deal of personal success, pride, and satisfaction. Thus, a concerted focus needs to be made in this area.

21.94 Demonstrate Stamina and Endurance

Most jobs require a given amount of physical and mental stamina and endurance. The physical education or adapted physical education instructor can assume a significant role in designing special programs to develop the student with special learning and/or behavior needs' skills in this area. Students with special learning and/or behavior needs should chart their progress toward attainment of criterion levels of performance. This type of program can be used at home, where purposeful tasks and responsibilities that relate to other subcompetencies can be designed. Several commercial programs are available for this subcompetency, but these would be unnecessary if the school personnel could develop the resources and activities within and outside of the schools that promote development of these skills. Other objectives that should be incorporated for this subcompetency are to require the student with special learning and/or behavior needs to identify jobs where stamina and endurance are absolutely critical and ways of building these skills to meet individual needs.

21.95 Demonstrate Balance and Coordination

The physical education instructor could assume a major responsibility in evaluating and designing specific individual activities that can improve each student with special learning and/or behavior needs' physical capacities. Teachers may need to consult a registered occupational therapist who can design specific tasks that measure and develop balance and coordination skills in a student with an orthopedic disability. Students with special learning and/or behavior needs should keep a cumulative record of their performance in various activities. This can document progress in terms of functioning level and can help them target new goals. Competitive games and charts may motivate students with special learning and/or behavior needs by drawing attention to the importance of these skills. Other objectives that should be met are to have students with special learning and/or behavior needs identify the relationship between balance and coordination to the working world and to job performance and requirements of various jobs.

21.96 Demonstrate Manual Dexterity

A number of manual dexterity tests may assist people who direct the development of the students with special learning and/or behavior needs' manual dexterity. The Purdue Pegboard (Purdue Research Foundation, 1968), Minnesota Rate of Manipulation Test (Minnesota Employment Stabilization Research Institute, 1969), Wide Range Employment Sample Test (Jastak & Jastak, 1973), and Pennsylvania Bi-Manual Dexterity Test (Roberts, 1945) are examples of standardized instruments for evaluating and developing the student with special learning and/or behavior needs' manual dexterity. Evaluation of students with special learning and/or behavior needs should begin early and continue to serve as a basis for determining what work tasks are within the students with special learning and/or behavior needs' physical capabilities. Other objectives are to help students identify interests in occupations that require a fair degree of manual dexterity and reasons for developing a sufficient degree of dexterity for occupational and community life.

• • • • • • • • **Activity Tip** • • • • • • • •

Use the Purdue Pegboard with another dexterity test to evaluate and motivate students to develop their manual dexterity skills. Individual and group charts can illustrate the students with special learning and/or behavior needs' progress at each testing session. Administer the test in a nonthreatening, gamelike manner and try to challenge students with special behavior needs in an encouraging way. Give students with special learning and/or behavior needs three trials to improve and let them keep the test sheet after you have recorded their right hand, left hand, both hands, and assembly scores. The test should be administered monthly and can be used to plan physical activities that may enhance students' physical-manual skills. (Work samples and other tests may be used in a similar manner.)

• •

21.97 Demonstrate Sensory Discrimination

Many jobs require ability to distinguish sounds, shapes, sizes, and colors. The Talent Assessment Program (TAP; Talent Assessment, no date) is a work sample/task battery that relates sensory discrimination skills to vocational potential. Many teachers also have devised their own methods by using everyday objects. Evaluation of those skills should occur early in the school program. Other objectives are for students with special learning and/or behavior needs to be able to identify the need for sensory discrimination on jobs and the sensory discrimination they many need for jobs that they are interested in.

22.0 Obtaining a Specific Occupational Skill

Many professionals strongly believe that students with special learning and/or behavior needs do not need to leave the formal educational system with a saleable, entry-level occupational skill. Their arguments are that training can be best provided later, that too many other types of learning are necessary, and that secondary students with special learning and/or behavior needs are too young for specific occupational training. Although these arguments may be valid, individuals with disabilities and other behavior difficulties need to acquire a skill before they leave the secondary school for the following reasons:

- Most training facilities beyond the secondary level do not have enough specialists who can effectively meet their needs.
- Many postsecondary programs are unattractive and dehumanizing or too long. Requirements for these programs are often stringent and unnecessary.
- If the student with special learning and/or behavior needs can acquire a specific occupational skill before leaving the secondary school, the student with special learning and/or behavior needs, parents, instructors, employers, and significant others will have more confidence in his ability to learn a saleable skill.
- Training in a specific occupational skill results in development and improvement of other competency areas (e.g., self-confidence, socially responsible behavior, interpersonal skills, independence, problem solving, communication skills, occupational awareness, work habits and behaviors, and physical-manual skills).
- Some individuals with special learning and/or behavior needs may need more intensive training in skills than others.
- Training results in a meaningful curriculum emphasis and makes other instruction relevant and reality based.
- Training provides students with disabilities with an extra advantage over other individuals against whom they will be competing for similar jobs.
- Attainment of an occupational skill can reveal higher-order potentials that students with special learning and/or behavior needs can pursue after the secondary program.
- Training helps eliminate unrealistic occupational choices early enough so students with special

learning and/or behavior needs receive training that is more appropriate to their individual needs and abilities.

Although some students with special learning and/or behavior needs may receive training in post-secondary programs, they should try to obtain a specific occupational skill during the high school years. In addition to the other daily living, personal-social, and occupational skills that are important to the growth of a work personality, students should select a training area that fosters awareness of personal and occupational interests. Selection should be a carefully designed process of career development that is primarily by the student with assistance from parents, instructors, and significant others.

Instruction in daily living curriculum areas may reveal special interests and aptitude for occupations in the clerical, maintenance, personal care, food service, computer, service, recreation and leisure, or transportation fields. Personal-social curriculum areas should reveal the most suitable work environment for the individual (i.e., noisy, calm, pressured, interactive, flexible, restrictive, closely supervised, routine, reinforcing, and impersonal). The occupational curriculum area also should reflect the student with special learning and/or behavior needs' work values, needs, interests, choices, work habits and behaviors, and physical capacities. Thus, in the process of becoming, a work personality emerges and forms to the extent that reasonable training choices can be determined.

LCCE MODERATE CURRICULUM COMPETENCIES

The preceding two chapters focused on many skills critical to successful independent living. Daily living and personal-social skills also are critically important for occupational success. In fact, all the competencies of the LCCE Moderate Curriculum relate to occupational functioning as well as satisfactory community living, whether in the areas of personal hygiene, com-

munication, independence, or getting around one's community.

In this section, the six LCCE Moderate Curriculum occupational skills and their 20 subcompetencies are presented. The competencies and subcompetencies are illustrated in Figure 13.5. The first three competencies involve occupational guidance activities, and the last three relate specifically to occupational preparation. Note that competency 20 does not have specific subcompetencies, because the occupational skill being taught will vary from student to student. Thus, users can write in the subcompetencies for this area when the specific personalized training area has been determined. As each of these is presented in the following discussion, several activity tips are provided. The Council will publish LCCE competency unit curriculum manuals (Loyd & Brolin, in press), similar to the ones already developed for the LCCE Mild Curriculum Program.

....

Most LCCE Mild Curriculum lesson plans from Life Centered Career Education: Competency Units for Occupational Guidance and Preparation Skills *by D. E. Brolin (Arlington, VA: The Council for Exceptional Children, 1992) can be modified for use with the LCCE Moderate Curriculum competencies and subcompetencies.*

....

15.0 Exploring and Locating Occupational Training and Job Placements

Individuals must have a broad perspective of the working world and career paths before they can make satisfying and realistic occupational choices. This competency is closely allied to the career awareness and exploration stages of transition/career education. Students with moderate special learning and/or behavior needs should begin exploring the working world and specific occupations before entering school and certainly after beginning school. The more that students with moderate special learning and/or behavior needs are aware of

Curriculum Area	Competency	Subcompetency: The student will be able to:	
OCCUPATIONAL GUIDANCE AND PREPARATION	15. Making Adequate Decisions	56. Identify rewards of working	57. Locate occupational training and job placement possibilities
	16. Communicating with Others	58. Demonstrate knowledge of occupational interests	59. Demonstrate knowledge of occupational strengths and weaknesses
	17. Knowing & Exploring Occupational Possibilities	63. Apply for occupational training and job placements	64. Interview for occupational training and job placements
	18. Selecting & Planning Occupational Choices	66. Perform work directions and requirements	67. Maintain good attendance and punctuality
	19. Exhibiting Appropriate Work Habits & Behaviors	72. Demonstrate fine motor dexterity in occupational training & job placements	73. Demonstrate gross motor dexterity in occupational training & job placements
	20. Seeking, Securing & Maintaining Employment		

FIGURE 13.5   Life Centered Career Education—Moderate Curriculum: Occupational Guidance and Preparation Skills Competencies

Note. From *Life Centered Career Education: Modified Curriculum for Individuals with Moderate Disabilities* by R. J. Loyd and D. E. Brolin, 1997, Arlington, VA: The Council for Exceptional Children. Copyright 1997 by the Council for Exceptional Children. Reprinted with permission.

the reinforcing values of various jobs, the more likely it is that they will be motivated and develop an appreciation of the dignity of work and will identify with the occupational world. In conjunction with family and community resources, school personnel must provide an array of awareness and exploration opportunities (i.e., community-based teaching experiences, speakers, literature, summer work, and role-playing) so that occupational possibilities are presented for the students with moderate special learning and/or behavior needs' knowledge and exploration.

A variety of individuals, particularly the student herself, should participate in making the moderate student with special learning and/or behavior needs aware of occupational possibilities. The elementary teacher can relate various subjects to career path and specific job information. She also can elicit the assistance of the family members, employers, and employees who work in various settings throughout the community. Many pamphlets and other auditory and visual media can be used. As students with moderate special learning and/or behavior needs progress in their awareness of occupational possibilities, actual exploration of jobs of interest can be offered in the school, family, and community settings. Most persons with moderate special learning and/or behavior needs who participate

in awareness activities should ideally be involved in helping students with these needs explore hands-on experiences and special interest areas. The state employment services (job service), vocational rehabilitation agencies, community colleges, vocational schools, Internet, and newspaper ads also can be important resources to adult learners. Critical LCCE Moderate Curriculum subcompetencies that make up this important competency area are discussed next.

15.56 Identify Rewards of Work

Most elementary students with moderate special learning and/or behavior needs seldom consider the differences among jobs in regard to pay. Their considerations of jobs are probably more closely aligned to that held by a family member, friend, actor, or athlete. And as these students get older and their needs become more clearly defined, this subcompetency takes on added significance. Inherent in this process is the understanding that remuneration often depends on such factors as the demand and supply of workers for the job, community needs for the services or goods provided by the workers, and the skills from training or formal education that students may need to perform the job. Students with moderate special

60. Identify possible and available matching interests and strengths	61. Plan and make realistic occupational training and job placement decisions	62. Develop training plan for occupational choice	
65. Make adjustments to changes in employment status			
68. Respond appropriately to supervision	69. Demonstrate job safety	70. Work cooperatively with others	71. Meet quality and quantity work standards
74. Demonstrate sensory discrimination in occupational training & job placements	75. Demonstrate stamina and endurance		
There are no specific subcompetencies listed here since they depend upon the specific occupational training selected.			

learning and/or behavior needs must understand why people are paid to work and why there are different pay rates for different jobs. This understanding relates to several of the subcompetencies associated with competency 1, managing money. It can help students with these needs calculate the amount of money they would receive from engaging in an occupation that interests them, and it enables them to understand this information and make wise and necessary expenditures. Other functional objectives should include identifying the different wage types (e.g., piece rate or hourly, weekly, or monthly wage) and what personal needs can be met with a salary expected from the jobs that interest them.

Students also should be introduced to the ways workers affect society. Teaching activities can focus on specific ways that individuals from various occupational categories contribute to society (e.g., food service workers, custodians, farmers, computer operators, assembly line workers, and landscaping). Teachers should cover an array of jobs in each of the career paths that require various amounts of skill and training. In this way, students with moderate special learning and/or behavior needs can learn that everyone, no matter what she does, contributes meaningfully to society. Weekly community-based experiences, speakers, or class discussions can highlight the social contributions of one or more jobs. Representatives from unions and industries, the government, Chamber of Commerce, and small businesses as well as parents

should be extensively involved. Other functional objectives related to this subcompetency are exploring the ways that employees who have different jobs work interdependently and identifying the rewards of different occupations.

A final consideration for all students is recognizing whom to request help from and then requesting knowledge about the various jobs in a career path related to students' personalized interest.

• • • • • • • • **Activity Tip** • • • • • • • •
Require each student to secure information on one job of interest per week for several weeks each semester. Students should cut out pictures of the individuals performing that job and paste it onto a poster board. The following information can be pictured for each job: company, salary, training required, hours worked, and job duties. (This information might be taken from the Job Analysis Form presented in Figure 13.1 if it is used.) Family members and teachers can help the student investigate the jobs and complete the poster. Weekly class discussions should cover the jobs that the students have investigated and the possible reasons for their interest in that job. A master list of community jobs can be developed to depict pertinent information relative to remunerative and other important aspects.
• •

15.57 Locate Occupational Training Job Placement Possibilities

Identifying sources of occupational information is closely allied to the previous subcompetency. In addition to the community sources, students with moderate special learning and/or behavior needs should become familiar with such printed information as the *Dictionary of Occupational Titles,* the *Occupational Outlook Handbook,* pamphlets from various businesses and industries, and government announcements. These materials provide a wealth of information that teachers can periodically review, discuss, and make available in the school counselor's office. Another excellent service is provided by commercial publishers who have developed a host of materials in the form of computer-based programs, games, videos, cassettes, and guides that require students with moderate special learning and/or behavior needs to identify the kinds of information available from each source and how they can use these sources to obtain specific information about a particular job in a specific career path.

A final consideration for all students is recognizing whom to request help from in locating occupational training and job placement possibilities.

16.0 Making Occupational Job Placement Choices

With a broad perspective of the working world, the various career paths, and the development of a positive set of work values, the student with moderate special learning and/or behavior needs can begin to make preliminary and tentative occupational choices from the career paths. Although elementary children may promulgate occupational aspirations as part of their career development, teachers should begin serious attempts to identify and direct middle school students with moderate special learning and/or behavior needs toward relevant occupational choices. Many professionals become concerned about encouraging such to make occupational choices too early, believing that these students will be pigeonholed by selecting inappropriate work roles. However, young adolescents with such needs who have explored occupa-

• • • • • • • • **Activity Tip** • • • • • • • •

The students with moderate special learning and/or behavior needs should invite former students back to school to discuss their jobs (or lack of them) and should develop a set of questions relating to postschool adjustment. Discussions should include problems that former students encounter, how they handle those problems, what they feel the students with special behavior needs must have to be successful, and influences that affect their present transition/career functioning. Later, students with special behavior needs should have the opportunity to observe former students working at their actual jobs. The former students should be encouraged to bring in people (reliable alliances) who helped them adjust. Some former students may not cooperate in this activity because of their desire to no longer be identified with their past.

tional possibilities and have developed personal-social skills are ready to think seriously about their future at about the 7th-grade level. Personalized choices at this stage must be considered subject to change as students with moderate special learning and/or behavior needs mature from further community-based experiences. Making occupational choices gives students with moderate special learning and/or behavior needs' transition program more significance by revealing to students that they can contribute to society and function as adults. In the case of adult learners, a considerable period of unemployment or failure may have occurred. Thus, a substantial time period may pass before such can make an occupational decision.

16.58 Demonstrate Knowledge of Occupational Interests

By 6th or 7th grade, most students should have a basic idea of the occupational areas that are of interest to them. These decisions are related more to what they think they would like to do (eg., "help people by working in a hospital as an aide or orderly") regardless of whether the job meets all or most of their occupational needs and aptitudes. If the jobs that the student with moderate special learning and/or behavior needs identifies are not within her capability or need structure, she can explore related but more appropriate ones later. What is important is that each individual with such needs is beginning to focus on specific occupational areas or jobs based on her knowledge of occupations and self. In some situations, reading free pictorial interest inventories can be valuable. But for the most part, interests evolve from community experiences and explorations in the workplace. Although occupational interests are unique to each individual, students with moderate special learning and/or behavior needs can learn how others arrived at such decisions by engaging in group interactions. Other objectives that relate to this subcompetency are to help students with such needs to identify occupations that permit the pursuit of personalized interests and the occupational needs that can be met from these jobs.

A final consideration for all students is recognizing who to request help from and then requesting knowledge about learning about the students' occupational interests.

16.59 Demonstrate Knowledge of Occupational Strengths and Weaknesses

Providing students with moderate special learning and/or behavior needs an opportunity for extensive vocational assessment experiences can help them understand their vocational potentials and specific aptitudes. Before a formalized vocational assessment, these students will have had some indication of the job areas that they are able to learn and perform successfully. Aptitudes or abilities in the following areas should be ascertained: verbal, numerical, spatial, form perception, clerical, motor coordination, finger dexterity, manual dexterity, and mechanical. The General Aptitude Test Battery (GATB) of the U.S. Employment Service is one instrument that can be used for identifying the strengths and weaknesses of some students with moderate special learning and/or behavior needs. For others, commercial or developed work sample batteries can be particularly beneficial and provide a better indication of their aptitudes than standardized test batteries such as the GATB, which some claim to be discriminating toward minorities relative to its cutoff scores. A substantial number of vocational assessment systems are new on the market and will be discussed in greater detail in the occupational guidance techniques section. Another objective associated with this subcompetency should be to help the student with moderate special learning and/or behavior needs identify ways of developing needed aptitudes for occupational interests.

A final consideration for all students is recognizing who to request help from and then requesting knowledge of how to discover personal occupational strengths and weaknesses.

16.60 Identify Possible and Available Matching Interests and Strengths

With the initiation of supplemental financial programs, some people have adopted the attitude that work is not a necessity, which provides a rationale for not working. Students should learn very early that many personal needs and values can be met by work and that work can become a personally meaningful part of their lives. At the same time, they also must learn that some personal needs and values may have to be gratified through leisure activities and other pursuits. One of the teacher's major goals should be to help students with moderate special learning and/or behavior needs to identify and choose a personally meaningful set of work values that fosters their desire to become productive workers in their community. Values such as a sense of fulfillment, self-sufficiency, personal worth, positive self-concept, success, self-support, acceptance by others, satisfaction from social relationships, independence, and monetary gratification are examples of needs that students can meet through working. Community-based experiences and classroom visits can give elementary students with such needs an opportunity to interact with various types of employed people and can expose them to ways in which these workers meet personal needs and develop values. Such students also can begin to identify the kind of personal values they presently possess and can visualize how to meet their needs through work. It may important to elicit the support of numerous agencies to help families and students understand that working holds many key intrinsic benefits than supplemental programs alone.

Group discussions can give students with moderate special learning and/or behavior needs an opportunity to hear how others arrive at their decisions. Parents can discuss the positive aspects of their jobs as well as ways in which they would like to change their jobs (e.g., more responsibility, variety, physical activity). They should explain how they meet these missing values and needs in their nonoccupational time. Secondary-level students with special learning and/or behavior needs who are on job sites and former students who are employed also can discuss many of their job features. Adult learners can identify what personal values they met and didn't meet while working at various jobs. Other functional objectives related to this subcompetency are helping students with special learning and/or behavior needs recognize the importance of work for economic functioning and building self-esteem.

As students with more special learning and/or behavior needs acquire the personal-social skills of self-awareness, self-confidence, socially responsible behavior, interpersonal skills, independence, and problem-solving, they should be ready to identify those major occupational needs that are presently part of their work personality. They also should be able to determine whether needs such as the pay rate, independence, achievement, praise, responsibility, authority, use of aptitudes and abilities, advancement, security, social service, variety, and social status are of major importance in their future work life. Group discussions on the topic, supplemented with presentations given by persons working in various occupations, should be provided so that students with such needs can make these decisions and other choices related to an appropriate work environment (e.g., outdoor versus indoor work, sedentary versus active, urban versus rural settings). These discussions can serve as a basis for lively and soul-searching inquiries. Teachers also can attempt to have such students identify the occupational needs that persons in occupations they are interested in tend to have.

A final consideration for all students is recognizing who to request help from and then requesting knowledge about how to match personalized interests and abilities with various jobs in a career path of interest.

16.61 Plan and Make Realistic Occupational Training and Job Placement Decisions

Experiences from the previous subcompetency will help students with moderate special learning and/or behavior needs to discover many jobs that really do not meet their occupational needs, interests, or aptitudes. For those jobs that do, a second level of decisions must be made relative to the jobs of highest preference. The demand for the occupation, required education and training, and other factors are significant at this level. Students with moderate special learning and/or behavior needs should learn the career ladder that the occupation offers and about other occupations for which they might qualify. These tentative personalized occupational choices should be based on an analysis of the whole person and should be systematically determined primarily by the students and their families, employers, school personnel, and other reliable alliances of their team. Professional guidance and counseling are important for this subcompetency. Another functional objective that should be attempted is for the individual to be able to identify specific work sites where the job of choice is available and to try out the job.

A final consideration for all students is recognizing who to request help from and then requesting assistance in making realistic occupational choices.

16.62 Develop Training Plan for Occupational Choices

An extremely critical part of the elementary education experience for students with moderate learning and/or behavior needs is to be provided career awareness opportunities. Students should learn about various jobs in their community. After identifying community sources of occupational information, they should secure information from one source for a period of time, discuss it with family members and their teacher, post it pictorially on a bulletin board, and present it to the class. The Internet, newspaper advertisements, radio announcements, flyers, and community job surveys are examples of such sources. This exercise enables students to understand and use all community sources of occupational information while learning about jobs and their availability. Students should learn this subcompetency early in their school years. For example, students who are involved in a speech therapy program can conceptualize various community occupations while they learn the respective speech sounds. The therapist and teacher can provide a variety of interesting games, role-playing exercises, and other activities that will increase the student's motivation and learning. Close inspection of available jobs also can help such students to learn more about the working world, job differences, and requirements. Other functional objectives associated with this subcompetency are for students to identify appropriate sources of occupational information and to determine appropriate methods of securing and using such information.

During the elementary years, students with special learning and/or behavior needs should be able to identify the rudiments of major categories of jobs/career paths—particularly those that are relevant to their specific interests. At first, jobs can be classified primarily as white or blue collar, skilled or unskilled, and according to work type, training, or required education. Students with special learning and/or behavior needs in secondary and adult programs can use information about job and occupational clusters contained in the *Dictionary of Occupational Titles, Occupational Outlook Handbook, Guide for Occupational Exploration,* and other guides that can add more specifically to learning activities. Teachers should request a representative from the local employment service to explain how students with special learning and/or behavior needs may use major job categories and criteria. These students should be involved in organizing and participating with employers in a careers day program. Teachers can use bulletin boards, newspapers, and other media to illustrate the different occupational systems. A functional objective associated with this subcompetency is to identify education, training, and reimbursement related to the various occupational categories.

With the knowledge of sources of occupational information (subcompetency 17.2) and their major occupational needs, interests, and aptitudes, students should be ready to review the specific requirements and characteristics of appropriate and available jobs. Publications such as the *Dictionary of Occupational Titles* should be useful for individual and group sessions. The *Dictionary,* published by the Department of Labor, is a compendium of over 20,000 occupations representing the majority of jobs in the country. These activities can be approached seriously during the 8th grade and can become a stimulus for independent job searching and decision making. Vocational assessment adds an important dimension to realistic decision making and planning, as do community resource personnel, who can give an in-depth personal analysis of the job's characteristics. A wide range of commercial games, materials, and packages are available for students with special learning and/or behavior needs. Another objective that should be attempted is to help students with special learning and/or behavior needs identify alternate, related occupations for which they are best qualified.

A final consideration for all students is recognizing who to request help from and then requesting assistance in assembing a training plan for obtaining their personalized occupational choice.

17.0 Applying for and Maintaining Occupational Training and Job Placements

After leaving the formal education system, many students with moderate special learning and/or behavior needs have difficulty seeking, securing, and maintaining competitive employment. Apparently, efforts at teaching this competency have failed to help many students retain this knowledge and ability over time. This is a major downfall for these individuals in the community and is especially unfortunate for those who have been through an extensive educational and transition program such as the LCCE Moderate Curriculum. Educators should begin teaching this competency at least by the 8th grade and should continue instructing their students in this area each semester thereafter. Many commercial materials are available for teaching this competency, although professionals may want to develop their own.

17.63 Apply for Occupational Training and Job Placements

Almost all adults will have to go through the process of applying for a job. This process involves many steps and is difficult for many individuals to do properly. The ability to develop a logical step-by-step method of searching for a job is a crucial subcompetency. Knowing how to explore informational sources about possible jobs is a beginning. Teachers can help students with moderate special learning and/or behavior needs develop this subcompetency by using pictorial bulletin boards to depict the steps that these students can take to search for a job and explore various informational sources. Community-based experiences to agencies that help people find jobs, role playing, games, and guest speakers also can help students to gain new perspectives in this area. Job descriptions and announcements, advertisements, and commercial materials on job-seeking skills also are available. Other objectives related to this subcompetency include identifying the steps involved in searching for a job, researching a specific job, and following through on a job lead.

An important objective in vocational/transitional programming should be to prepare students with moderate special learning and/or behavior needs to apply for a job. Mastery of this subcompetency is another indicator of a student's ability and independence for vocational functioning. To demonstrate this, the student with moderate special learning and/or behavior needs must become familiar with job application forms and procedures involved in applying for jobs. Beginning in at least the 8th grade, students with special learning and/or behavior needs should learn to recognize and read words that are typically used on application forms and interviews. Students with moderate special learning and/or behavior needs should spend a great deal of time reviewing and completing application forms, learning job vocabulary, role playing, and collecting personal data needed

for job applications. Some students with moderate special learning and/or behavior needs may find that a marketing portfolio provides additional resources for demonstrating personalized qualifiations for appropriately applied for jobs. Another objective that students with special learning and/or behavior needs should be required to meet is to identify those factors they consider important to them in applying for jobs.

A final consideration for all students is recognizing who to request help from and then requesting assistance in preparation for applying an appropriate job of interest.

17.64 Interview for Occupational Training and Job Placements

In Chapter 12, the importance of developing adequate communication skills was stressed for success in adult living and working. Students with moderate special learning and/or behavior needs must have sufficient opportunities in their educational programs to develop adequate and augmentative communication skills for use in community living and working. Interviewing skills are inextricably related to the other subcompetencies and should receive careful attention from educators. Employers, workers, and other community resources can help to prepare these students for interviews. Students with such needs must understand and learn the steps involved to secure an interview, what to do and say when requesting an interview on the phone or in person, demonstrate their marketing portfolio, and learn how to handle themselves in the actual situation. Role playing, group discussions, videos, speakers and demonstrations, games and commercial materials, videotapes, and other techniques are highly recommended. Other objectives for students with special learning and/or behavior needs should be to complete a simulated job interview in an actual business establishment and practice dressing for and transporting self to the job interview. Video practice and review also is a good technique for enabling students with moderate special learning and/or behavior needs to review and critique their performance.

A final consideration for all students is recognizing who to request help from and then requesting assistance in preparing for interviews in their personalized occupational choice.

17.65 Make Adjustments to Change in Employment Status

Most people change jobs about four or five times during their working career. Some people lose their jobs for various employment and nonemployment reasons. One major reason for losing a job is not being able to exhibit appropriate personal-social skills in various working situations. Others are promoted or find better positions. Students with moderate special learning and/or behavior needs must learn the factors that determine successful and unsuccessful job adjustment and how to deal with them. Another important objective of this study unit is to know how to recognize and apply for promotional opportunities.

A final consideration for all students is recognizing who to request help from and then requesting assistance when it is necessary to change employment status due to being laid off or searching for a different personalized occupational choice.

18.0 Developing and Maintaining Appropriate Work Skills and Behaviors

Competency 18, developing and maintaining appropriate work skills and behaviors, transcends the entire educational chain from the early elementary years through adulthood and can be taught by everyone responsible for the individual's career development. Work habits are more than study habits, although both have many similar features. School personnel and family members should emphasize the necessity of developing work habits and behaviors that all students with moderate special learning and/or behavior needs will need when they begin responsible jobs. At certain times, teachers may simulate working environments in the school setting to illustrate the kinds of expectations employers have of competent workers. Community-based experiences, class speakers, and family members also can play an important role

in helping students with special learning and/or behavior needs to develop the subcompetencies in this competency.

18.66 Perform Work Directions and Requirements

Following directions accurately and performing the job requirements are the major expectations of employers. These may be given verbally, pictorially, or in writing, and will range from very simple one-step directions to those that are complex and require several steps that employees must remember and complete. Gaming and role-playing techniques can be particularly effective in helping students with moderate special learning and/or behavior needs develop these skills. Exercises will need to begin early and be repeated intermittently throughout all the grade levels so that all students with moderate special learning and/or behavior needs, especially those who have a lower ability in this area, can learn and retain these skills. After students with such needs have learned the lower-order steps, they should gradually learn how to follow more complicated directions. Another objective should be for the student with such needs to be able to perform a series of tasks in the home requiring simple-to-complex written instructions.

A final consideration for all students is recognizing who to request help from and then requesting assistance when they do not understand work directions or requirements.

18.67 Maintain Good Attendance and Punctuality

The classroom situation can be organized to emphasize the importance of attendance and punctuality in the workplace. A classroom clock is one method that can be used to promote this concept. The student with moderate special learning and/or behavior needs should learn why attendance and punctuality are important to the employer (e.g., loss of production time, business income, and meeting deadlines). These students should learn acceptable and unacceptable reasons for lateness and absenteeism, and what the consequences are in both situations. Once again, employers and workers from various businesses and industries can be helpful in presenting their own cases and company policies. Another objective that students should be required to meet is to identify appropriate actions to take if they need to be late or absent from work.

A final consideration for all students is recognizing who to request help from and then requesting assistance in understanding what to do if they must be late or absent from work.

18.68 Respond Appropriately to Supervision

Although accepting supervision is related to previous subcompetencies, it is specific to various supervisory methods that are found in the workplace. Supervision can range from being infrequent and indirect to very frequent and direct. Supervision can be constructive, critical, or unfair. It is important for students with moderate special learning and/or behavior needs to understand the various supervisory forms and how they should react to supervision under different conditions. Role playing is a viable method of presenting students with various situations and types of supervision so they can learn appropriate ways of responding. These role-playing situations can be videotaped. Role-playing activities and reviewing the videotapes can be followed by group discussions that focus on different responses to help students with such needs develop other methods of handling the situation. The teacher also can use various methods of supervising class members and then get their reactions to the methods. Other objectives that can be attempted for students with such needs are for them to observe and discuss supervisory policies in several workplaces and to identify various responses that can be used for various types of supervisory practices.

A final consideration for all students is recognizing who to request help from and then requesting assistance in understanding the employer's supervisory practices.

18.69 Demonstrate Job Safety

Many employers are afraid to employ people with moderate special learning and/or behavior needs because they believe that these individuals will have more accidents. Thus, teachers should emphasize occupational safety skills to minimize the number of potential accidents that could occur and result in the individual's dismissal. Videos, community-based experiences, role playing, and class discussions are particularly important in helping students with such needs understand potential safety hazards and the necessary precautions they may need to take to avoid unnecessary accidents. Before placement on a community job site, these students should be thoroughly prepared to handle all conceivable accidents that could occur in the workplace. This subcompetency should be taught at all levels of the school program so that by the time these students leave school, they are well versed in safety practices. Other objectives associated with this subcompetency should require the student with such needs to identify the major reasons for practicing safety on the job and the potential safety hazards that exist in various occupational settings.

A final consideration for all students is recognizing who to request help from and then requesting assistance when they unsure about the safety procedures at the work site.

18.70 Work Cooperatively with Others

The inability to get along with co-workers and supervisors is one of the most common reasons people fail on their jobs. Students with special learning and/or behavior needs must learn work expectations, and the school can become a fertile ground for teaching these interactive and cooperative skills. Teachers should create an environment that promotes the development of these work skills by encouraging students to practice interacting and cooperating with others. Community-based experiences, role playing, and group discussions also can be used to illustrate and stimulate discussion on reasons for working with others and the individual's importance in cooperative efforts. It also can help such students to identify the positive and negative aspects of working together. Another objective might be to simulate actual work environments by developing projects that require students with special learning and/or behavior needs to interact and cooperate with others before they can complete a specific task.

A final consideration for all students is recognizing who to request help from and then requesting assistance in dealing with personal-social problems at the job site.

18.71 Meet Quality and Quantity Work Standards

Students with moderate special learning and/or behavior needs will need to know about quality standards for various job types, particularly those that interest them. They should meet such standards on their work assignments, understand when and why such standards are not achieved, and work until they have met the standards or until the teachers have ascertained whether students can perform at that particular level. Elementary students with moderate special learning and/or behavior needs should strive for quality while they are engaged in projects. These students can be assigned as checkers to ascertain whether work has met the job requirements and can participate in discussions conducted to point out problems. The secondary students with moderate special learning and/or behavior needs' job explorations and try-outs establish the expected criteria that will be used to evaluate their performance. Another objective of this subcompetency is to have the student with such needs perform simulated work tasks at minimum quality standards.

It is important for students with moderate special learning and/or behavior needs to learn that people are employed to make money for the employer. This requires those students to learn how to do work correctly and at a sufficient speed. Teachers should require such students to complete certain work activities within a specific time period so that they form the habit as well as learn the concept. Time standards can be established for various work tasks in and out of the school, and teachers should chart the student's progress until she meets the criterion. Students should participate in establishing reasonable time standards so that they can understand how and why time or piece rates are determined. Employers and workers can be useful in conveying the importance of this subcompetency, especially if these skills will help students earn more money. Other objectives associated with this subcompetency should be to help the

student to identify satisfactory rates required for various jobs of interest and reasons that jobs must be performed at certain rates of speed.

A final consideration for all students is recognizing whom to request help from and then requesting assistance in determining if they are working at an appropriate pace and producing good quality work.

•••••••• **Activity Tip** ••••••••

Set up an assembly line operation with the assistance of industrial workers from the community. The assembly line operation should be as realistic as possible. Have the workers explain their jobs, particularly as they relate to this competency area. Initiate the work and assess the students with moderate special learning and/or behavior needs on their ability to work with others, accept supervision, and master other subcompetencies related to this competency. Some students may be supervisors or assume other roles associated with this work type. At the end of the day, the class should discuss the group's performance and future efforts. Rate each student on their work habits and behaviors, and provide individual feedback that will increase the students' awareness of their strong points and areas where they need to improve. (Further discussion and ideas related to this type of activity are provided later in the chapter.)

•••••••••••••••••••••••••••••••••••••

19.0 Matching Physical-Manual Skills to Occupational Training and Employment

Occupations that the majority of individuals with disabilities obtain require physical stamina, endurance, coordination, strength, and dexterity. The jobs available to the many students with disabilities require considerable fine or gross motor dexterity, standing, pulling, pushing, lifting, and carrying abilities. Development of adequate physical-manual skills should begin shortly after they enter school. Teachers can design class activities and adapted physical education activities to promote the use and development of skills that will help these students to experience a great deal of personal success, pride, and satisfaction. Thus, a concerted focus must be made in this area.

After students have secured a job, they must perform at the standard expected of other workers. If skills in adjusting to competitive standards are overlooked, former students may lose their jobs because of a misunderstanding of what is expected of workers and how they can advance their position and pay. Employers and workers should present this kind of information and conduct on-site visits to various job locations so that students with special learning and/or behavior needs can observe what employers expect of workers at various jobs and how this can be best achieved. Other objectives for students should be to identify jobs of interest and their expected standards and how the individual can achieve improvements.

19.72 Demonstrate Fine Motor Dexterity in Occupational Training and Job Placements

The physical education or adapted physical education instructor should assume a major responsibility in evaluating and designing specific individual activities that can improve the physical capacities of each student with moderate special learning and/or behavior needs. Teachers may need to consult a registered occupational therapist that can design specific tasks to measure and develop balance and coordination skills in a student with an orthopedic disability. Students with moderate special learning and/or behavior needs should keep a cumulative record of their performance in various activities. This record documents their progress in terms of functioning level and can help them target new goals. Competitive games and charts may motivate students with special learning and/or behavior needs by drawing attention to the importance of these skills. Other objectives that should be met are to have students with moderate special learning and/or behavior needs identify the relationship between balance and coordination in the working world and to job performance and requirements of various jobs.

A final consideration for all students is recognizing who to request help from and then requesting assis-

tance in improving their fine motor dexterity on the work site.

19.73 Demonstrate Gross Motor Dexterity in Occupational Training and Job Placements

A number of manual dexterity tests may assist people who direct the development of the students with moderate special learning and/or behavior needs' manual dexterity. The Purdue Pegboard (Purdue Research Foundation, 1968), Minnesota Rate of Manipulation Test (Minnesota Employment Stabilization Research Institute, 1969), Wide Range Employment Sample Test (Jastak & Jastak, 1973), and Pennsylvania Bi-Manual Dexterity Test (Roberts, 1945) are examples of standardized instruments for evaluating and developing the dexterity of these students. Evaluation of such students should begin early and continue to serve as a basis for determining what work tasks are within their physical capabilities. Other objectives are to help these students identify interests in occupations that require a fair degree of manual dexterity and reasons for developing a sufficient degree of dexterity for occupational and community life.

A final consideration for all students is recognizing who to request help from and then requesting assistance in improving gross motor dexterity on the work site.

19.74 Demonstrate Sensory Discrimination in Occupational Training and Job Placements

Many jobs require the ability to distinguish sounds, shapes, sizes, and colors. The Talent Assessment Program (TAP; Talent Assessment, 1999) is a work sample/task battery that relates sensory discrimination skills to vocational potential. Many teachers also have devised their own methods by using everyday objects. Evaluation of those skills should occur early in the school program. Other objectives for students with moderate special learning and/or behavior needs are to be able to identify the need for sensory discrimination on jobs and the sensory discrimination needed for jobs of interest to the individual.

A final consideration for all students is recognizing who to request help from and then requesting assistance in improving sensory discrimination on the work site.

19.75 Demonstrate Stamina and Endurance

Most jobs require a given amount of physical and mental stamina and endurance. The physical education or adapted physical education instructor can assume a significant role in designing special programs to develop the students with moderate special learning and/or behavior needs' skills in this area. These students should chart their progress toward attainment of the criterion levels of performance. This type of program can be used at home, where purposeful tasks and responsibilities that relate to other subcompetencies can be designed. Several commercial programs are available for this subcompetency, but would be unnecessary if the school personnel could develop the resources and activities within community-based settings to promote development of these skills. Other objectives that should be incorporated in this subcompetency are to require the student with moderate special learning and/or behavior needs to identify jobs where stamina and endurance are absolutely critical and ways of building these skills to meet their individual needs.

A final consideration for all students is recognizing who to request help from and then requesting assistance in improving stamina and endurance on the work site.

20.0 Training and Occupational Choices

Many professionals strongly believe that students with special learning and/or behavior needs do not need to leave the formal educational system with a saleable, entry-level occupational skill. Their arguments are that training can be best provided later, that too many other types of learning are necessary, and

• • • • • • • • **Activity Tip** • • • • • • • •

Have the class construct a list of occupational needs. Ask various class members to define and discuss each need. After the students have identified all possible needs, teachers should construct an occupational needs inventory and hand it out to the students. Each student should check to see if his own needs are high or low. Each need should be explained again before it is rated. The students then should identify their six most important occupational needs. Students will use this list later when they begin to examine their occupational interests and aptitudes. (The Minnesota Importance Questionnaire is a good instrument to obtain for this activity. Information about it can be obtained from the Department of Psychology at the University of Minnesota.)

• • • • • • • • **Activity Tip** • • • • • • • •

Use the Purdue Pegboard with another dexterity test to evaluate and motivate students to develop their manual dexterity skills. Individual and group charts can illustrate the students with special learning and/or behavior needs' progress at each testing session. Administer the test in a nonthreatening, gamelike manner, and try to challenge these students in an encouraging way. Give them three trials to improve and let them keep the test sheet after you have recorded their right hand, left hand, both hands, and assembly scores. The test should be administered monthly and can be used to plan physical activities that may enhance their physical-manual skills. (Work samples and other tests may be used in a similar manner.)

that secondary students with such needs are too young for specific occupational training. Although these arguments may be valid, individuals with disabilities and other special learning and/or behavior difficulties need to acquire a skill before they leave the secondary school for the following reasons:

1. Most training facilities beyond the secondary level do not have enough specialists who can effectively meet their needs.
2. Many postsecondary programs are unattractive and dehumanizing or too long. Requirements for these programs are often stringent and unnecessary.
3. If the student with special learning and/or behavior needs can acquire a specific occupational skill before leaving the secondary school, this student, parents, instructors, employers, and significant others will have more confidence in the student's ability to learn a saleable skill.
4. Training in a specific occupational skill results in development and improvement of other competency areas (e.g., self-confidence, socially responsible behavior, interpersonal skills, independence, problem solving, communication skills, occupational awareness, work habits and behaviors, and physical-manual skills).
5. Some individuals with special learning and/or behavior needs may need more intensive training in skills than others.
6. Training results in a meaningful curriculum emphasis and makes other instruction relevant and reality based.
7. Training provides students with disabilities with an extra advantage over other individuals against whom they will be competing for similar jobs.
8. Attainment of an occupational skill can reveal higher-order potentials that students with special learning and/or behavior needs can pursue after the secondary program.
9. Training helps eliminate unrealistic occupational choices early enough so that students with special learning and/or behavior needs receive training that is more appropriate to their individual needs and abilities.

Although some students with special learning and/or behavior needs may receive training in postsecondary programs, they should try to obtain a specific occupational skill during the high school years. In addition to the other daily living, personal-social, and occupational skills that are important to the growth of a work personality, students should select a training area that fosters awareness of personal and occupational interests. This selection should be a carefully designed process of career development that the student, primarily with assistance from parents, instructors, and significant others, can agree on.

Instruction in daily living curriculum areas may reveal special interests and aptitude for occupations in the clerical, maintenance, personal care, food service, computer, service, recreation and leisure, or transportation fields. Personal-social curriculum areas should reveal the most suitable work environment for the individual (i.e., noisy, calm, pressured, interactive, flexible, restrictive, closely supervised, routine, reinforcing, and impersonal). The occupational curriculum area also should reflect the students with special learning and/or behavior needs' work values, needs, interests, choices, work habits and behaviors, and physical capacities. Thus, in the process of becoming self-determined, a work personality emerges and forms to the extent that reasonable training choices can be determined.

CHAPTER COMMENTARY

Most former students with special learning and/or behavior needs who become employed are in the secondary labor market, which comprises the low-paying, service-oriented jobs with little or no job promotion opportunities. Is this the most to expect from the educational system and the ability level of these students with such needs? We can expect a much better outcome for most of these students if they are better prepared for the demanding requirements of the real world.

Students with special learning and/or behavior needs must have substantial career education and transition services throughout their education program if they are to compete in today's high-tech occupational society. Occupational training models, materials, and techniques have been developed over the years to meet this need. However, the school systems and their personnel must adopt them. The business community seems ready to provide more assistance than ever before, perhaps because they are in even greater need of qualified employees than previously. The Americans with Disabilities Act and School-to-Work Opportunities Act, which instituted work-based tech-prep programs, are good indicators of the window of opportunity that could be available to individuals with disabilities and other behavior difficulties. A change in curriculum and lesson plans at every grade level is now required so that children with special learning and/or behavior needs can learn more about different careers and to link their skills to the world of work.

Teaching the competencies in the occupational guidance and preparation curriculum area will increase the probability that students with special learning and/or behavior needs will select jobs that they can and want to do. People who have successful careers typically can perform the six competencies presented in this chapter. If the instruction begins early enough and the competencies are taught in their entirety, the final result will be employment success for the individual with special learning and/or behavior needs.

. . . .
ACTIVITIES

1. Review the occupational guidance and preparation matrix in Figure 13.3 and then determine what general, vocational, and special education courses would be most appropriate for teaching each of the LCCE Mild Curriculum subcompetencies for your particular students with special behavior needs. Then, identify those LCCE Mild Curriculum subcompetencies/skills in which you would attempt to involve parents. Finally, identify the LCCE Mild Curriculum subcompetencies for which you would include community-based instruction and what community resources you would use to help you teach the LCCE Mild Curriculum subcompetencies.

2. Review the occupational guidance and preparation matrix in Figure 13.5 and then determine what general, vocational, and special education courses would be most appropriate for teaching each of the LCCE Moderate Curriculum subcompetencies for your particular students with special behavior needs. Then, identify those LCCE Moderate Curriculum subcompetencies/skills in which you would attempt to involve parents. Finally, identify the LCCE Moderate Curriculum subcompetencies for which you would include community-based instruction and what community resources you would use to help you teach the LCCE Moderate Curriculum subcompetencies.

3. Develop an instructional objective around one of the LCCE Mild subcompetencies, then write a lesson plan using the LCCE Mild Curriculum format for your students that addresses one of the career stages, instructional settings, and career roles.

4. Develop an instructional objective around one of the LCCE Moderate subcompetencies, then write a lesson plan using the LCCE Moderate Curriculum format for your students that addresses one of the career stages, instructional settings, and career roles.

PART 5

LCCE MILD/MODERATE CURRICULUM IMPLEMENTATION

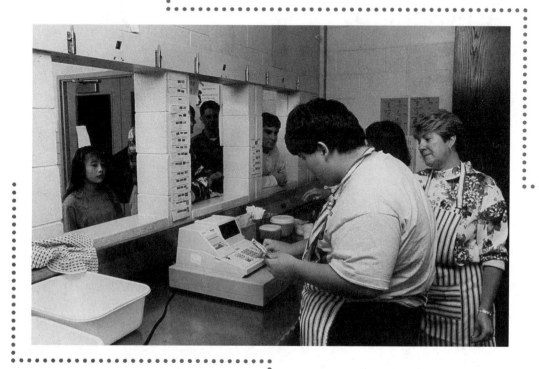

CHAPTER 14

Developing LCCE Mild/
Moderate Curriculum Programs

CHAPTER 15

Critical Transition Issues
and Future Directions

CHAPTER 14

Developing LCCE Mild/Moderate Curriculum Programs

PRELIMINARY QUESTIONS

1. What are some of the major factors that affect the substantial implementation of educational innovations such as functional skills/transition approaches?

2. What significant challenges to educational change can you expect to receive from administrators, teachers, parents, agencies, employers, and students with special learning and/or behavior needs?

3. What 10 major transition barriers would constitute your "Hit Parade"— transition barriers that you believe hinder the implementation of this mandated innovation?

4. What are some of the ways of dealing with these challenges and the transition barriers that the various groups with special learning and/or behavior needs present to functional curriculum change?

5. What is the difference between program development and functional curriculum development? Which one is more typically done?

6. What is a Transition Action Plan (TAP) proposal, and how does it contribute to implementing the transition innovation?

7. Why is transition/career education instruction so important for elementary students with special learning and/or behavior needs, and what should be the focus at this level?

8. How do the goals of secondary education differ from those for elementary and middle school students with special learning and/or behavior needs?

9. How well does the Life Centered Career Education (LCCE) Mild/Moderate Curriculum cover the 14 adult dimensions identified by Missouri LINC as important for transition planning and services?

10. In what type of education settings, with what type of students, and at what education levels is LCCE Mild/Moderate Curriculum being implemented?

OVERVIEW

The overall goals of education, rehabilitation, and transition are to prepare the individual with special learning and/or behavior needs to live and work in society. If individuals with disabilities are to meet these goals, they must develop and integrate the necessary daily living, personal-social, and occupational skills into a rewarding and satisfying lifestyle. This includes learning about personalized interests, needs, abilities, and potential and the realities of a modern world. These understandings can help individuals with special learning and/or behavior needs make appropriate decisions about their four career roles (employment, family, citizen, and recreation/leisure). The implementation of the transition/career education concept should be infused throughout the entire general education curriculum. Thus, if transition/career education is to become a reality for individuals with special learning and/or behavior needs, professionals will need to make changes to implement a meaningful and purposeful transition/career development program.

Until recently, most school systems have provided students with special learning and/or behavior needs with a content-oriented curriculum in which students with special learning and/or behavior needs learn a specific body of knowledge. This approach may not directly suit the individual's needs. Educators should adopt a process-oriented educational philosophy. Process education emphasizes the acquisition of specific skills that are necessary for community living and working and requires professionals to decide on desired outcomes that can be defined in precise, measurable terms. This does not negate the importance of or need for general education. Rather, the program must include both general and career education to maximize the student's career development.

If significant and positive functional changes in general education curriculum are to occur, the program should be carefully planned. It is not easy to convince people to substantially change the teaching, counseling, or services provided to students with special learning and/or behavior needs. They will need to believe in the need to change, be involved in making changes, and be recognized and rewarded for their efforts to change to a more appropriate process. Normalizing the education, rehabilitation, and transition process is an important concept that will need administrative support.

A transition/career development program will most likely succeed if education for all students with special learning and/or behavior needs is directed toward similar goals. This may not always be the case, however, because the curriculum focus for students with special learning and/or behavior needs sometimes differs from the programs planned for their peers. When this occurs, fewer school personnel are involved in the students with special learning and/or behavior needs' education program than if the entire student body were receiving inclusion-oriented transition/career development. We strongly recommend a transition/career development program that encompasses all students within the school system.

"The preparation for transition must be built upon the foundation of career education" (Began, 1990, p. 1). This statement by an educator in a Kansas school reflects the opinion of many school personnel and others throughout this country who are concerned about the future life of individuals with disabilities and those with other special learning and/or behavior needs.

This chapter begins by focusing on the process of functional curriculum change and the many challenges that influence successful change. The following section identifies and discusses several important functional curriculum considerations for instituting a transition/career education approach at the elementary/middle school, secondary, and postsecondary levels. The final section consists of descriptions of several school districts and others that are implementing the LCCE Mild/Moderate Curriculum. Personnel from the schools implementing the LCCE Mild/Moderate Curriculum approaches wrote some of the transition program descriptions in this chapter.

THE PROCESS OF CURRICULUM CHANGE

Transition/career education requires the active participation of the entire school community, parents, and various segments of the community. Interestingly, the current plea for educational reforms, including transition services, calls for cooperative effort and collaboration among these three educative forces. Although education of our young people is everyone's responsibility, collaboration simply has not taken place in this country. Perhaps the message has finally been embraced by more of the American public.

Change does not come easily. As the saying goes, "Everyone's for change, unless they have to do it!" In their two-year federal project, Promoting Collaborative Planning of Career Education for Disabled Students, the Technical Education Research Centers (1980) identified several barriers that prevent collaboration among school personnel and the community from succeeding: time constraints, red tape, communication difficulties, turfdom and ego barriers, reluctance to share "power," disparate organizational goals, and coordination of efforts where typical line authority management techniques cannot be exerted.

Hoyt (1983) points out that before school and community can become true, reliable alliances and succeed, educators, parents, and other members of the community must agree on the purpose of education for our students with special learning and/or behavior needs. They will need to clarify the basic purpose, goals, and objectives of the school if students with learning and/or behavior needs are to have an organized and acceptable system of learning. The question of whom the schools serve must also be answered. Changing general education curricula will not occur unless educators pay considerable attention to these and many other issues. Two major problems are getting the community to accept responsibility and getting the schools to loosen their hold. For members of the community to become involved, they must believe that they will get something in return. The proposal for involvement must make conceptual sense, and educators should be confident that what they propose will work. Otherwise, they will probably never be able to involve the community again.

Significant implementation of any functional curriculum/transition effort depends on several important factors:

- Increased administrative support
- Teacher involvement

CHAPTER OUTLOOK

Mabrey Whetstone is Director of the Division of Special Education Services of the Alabama State Department of Education.

All students with special learning and/or behavior needs deserve high-quality educational/transitional programs provided through functional curricula and learning experiences designed to prepare them for future education, community participation, independent living, meaningful employment, and active citizenship. While the debate about the transformation needed in general and special education continues, national agendas, federal initiatives, state school reform, and statewide testing programs are forcefully directing the curriculum and the focus of instruction. As efforts are made to uniformly apply the same standards to all students with special learning and/or behavior needs, a balance must be struck between the demand for tough, clear standards of academic excellence and the need for functional life skills instruction and integrated educational opportunities. For students of all ages with disabilities, the acquisition of academic skills must be deliberately infused throughout the education program with substantive Life Centered Career Education (LCCE) Mild/Moderate concepts, materials, and experiences. Career education should permeate the entire curriculum and requires competency and subcompetency instruction at all levels in a variety of natural environments. The emphasis on and the direct instruction of these skills (daily living skills, personal-social skills, and occupational

skills), supported by academic skills, will greatly enhance the growth and development essential for students with special learning and/or behavior needs to participate within our rapidly changing and demanding society.

Today we have high expectations for quality individualized programs that will prepare students with disabilities for adult living. No longer acceptable are situation-specific learning, classroom-confined instruction, or totally segregated service delivery. Efforts must be rechanneled to create programs that meet functional curriculum needs of individual students in integrated educational environments within both school and nonschool settings (home, community, employment, and recreational) to facilitate their transition from school to adult life.

Founded on 22 research-based competencies needed for adult living, the LCCE model offers an excellent framework for organizing an effective functional curriculum. In the three curricular content domains, the model addresses the major critical skills all students need for productive living. The model also promotes the concept of infusion into the general curriculum, collaboration and partnership, hands-on experiential learning, instruction in varied integrated environments, informal and formal career/vocational assessment, and the formation of Individualized Education Plan (IEP) goals and objectives for appropriate transition planning. The process described in this chapter provides many ideas for those who will be developing or improving on a comprehensive, ongoing career education approach.

- Coordination of school and agency activities
- Parent/family involvement
- Community opportunities

Roessler (1991a) notes that administrators, specifically the superintendent, must be convinced of the utility of the transition program. Thus, those promoting transition implementation must emphasize such positive outcomes as the large number of students with learning and/or behavior needs who could be served, the fact that current students with learning and/or behavior needs do not possess necessary life skills, and the instructional materials available. In the case of teachers, functional skills implementation depends on such factors as:

- District (superintendent) commitment to the effort
- Building level support (principal, counselors, and curriculum supervisors)
- Staff development opportunities on transition
- Incentives for program adoption (How is this going to affect my students with learning and/or behavior needs?)
- The availability of effective student with learning and/or behavior needs evaluation and instructional materials

In addition, the functional curriculum should be able to link its instructional units to Individualized Education Plan (IEP) objectives, goals in the core curriculum, and graduation requirements.

Solutions to better coordination of school and agency services include getting mandates at the state level by agency and educational leadership so local programs are instituted. Career nights, social events, discussion groups at school and in homes, and home visits are suggested to enhance parent/family involvement. Increased community-based opportunities solutions can be instituted by restructuring the use of existing personnel and giving more emphasis to community living objectives (Roessler, 1991a).

In one state, Missouri, the Excellence in Education Act of 1985 prompted the state to identify learner outcomes for specific subject areas for grades 2 to 10. The resulting core competencies and key skills are used to guide curriculum development in Missouri's school districts. In its publication *Implementing Career Education at the Elementary School Level* (Stephens, 1990), Missouri LINC and the state education agency note that many LCCE Mild/Moderate Curriculum competencies relate directly to the Missouri Comprehensive Guidance Program objectives and Key Skills for Missouri Schools. Their publication provides specific examples of how LCCE Mild/Moderate Curriculum

competencies and subcompetencies can be infused into various subject content matter to meet their guidelines. This publication is available from the Instructional Materials Laboratory, 10 London Hall, University of Missouri-Columbia, MO, 65211.

There are a multitude of reasons why functional curriculum change will present a challenge to those who bravely attempt it. Reformers should be aware of the many challenges that exist from the structure of the education system, the educators, parents, agency personnel, employers, and the students themselves. Figure 14.1 contains a list of challenges that each one of these presents.

Roessler and colleagues (Roessler, 1991a; Roessler, Brolin, & Johnson, 1992; Roessler, Loyd, & Brolin, 1990) have conducted studies of the barriers affecting the implementation of the LCCE Mild/Moderate Curriculum. The studies were conducted with several school district teachers involved in implementing the LCCE Mild/Moderate Curriculum as part of the development and field testing of the assessment and instructional materials being designed by LCCE Mild/Moderate Curriculum staff. This research effort led to the identification of 10 major transition barriers to LCCE Mild/Moderate Curriculum implementation, which Roessler labeled so aptly "Your Hit Parade." The transition barriers are presented in Figure 14.2.

Functional curriculum changers must be ready to address the resistances and barriers to educational change if they expect to succeed. The LCCE Mild/Moderate Curriculum staff developed a strategic and operational planning model for contextual barrier interviews during the early stages of their research to systematically deal with major barriers to implementing transition/career education efforts. Then they developed an instrument called the Barriers Implementation Questionnaire (BIQ), in which staff identify the top barriers and their suggested solutions to each of the major barriers. Through a process of consensus, solutions can be finalized to deal with each one. For example, the following solutions were posed for the perceived barrier of involving parents/families in teaching and reinforcing LCCE Mild/Moderate Curriculum instruction at home and in the community:

Educational System
- Resistance to change
- Institutionalized/bureaucratic nature
- Inflexible, rigid policies/acculturation
- Standard programs
- Limited time for staff development
- Many priorities and pressures
- Schedule
- Graduation requirements
- Transportation costs
- Lack of release time for teachers
- Money for staff and other resources
- Time to do everything needed
- Hiring policies
- School philosophy/purpose of education
- Curriculum emphasis (content) and effectiveness
- Scope and sequencing

Educators
- Their professional orientation
- Resistance to change
- Lack of appropriate training and information
- Attitude
- Trying to meet the needs of diverse students
- Overworked
- Little reward or recognition for extra effort
- Lack of trust
- Lack of support
- Fear of appearing incompetent
- Turfsmanship
- Past failures

Parents
- Limited time to participate
- Inability to carry out activities
- Broken homes
- Mistrust of professionals
- Feel education is school's responsibility
- Too many other responsibilities and problems

- Lack training
- Disinterest
- Hopelessness of future
- Overprotective
- Unrealistic about their child's abilities
- Want their child to be educated like everyone else

Agencies
- Professional rivalries
- Turfsmanship
- Theoretical differences
- Administrative barriers
- Too many clients
- Lack of knowledge and training
- Unclear roles and responsibilities
- Past failures
- Unwillingness to change
- Unwillingness to share
- Fear schools/parents will expect impossible
- Limited funds
- Expect schools to do more

Employers
- Misconceptions
- Difference of opinions
- Learning their language
- Understanding the world of work
- Unclear of their contribution

Students
- Fear of failure and rejection
- Overprotected
- Pressures from parents and others
- Lack of normal experiences
- Learning characteristics
- Unrealistic expectations
- Decision-making problems
- Limited work experience
- Low expectations
- Academic rather than functional skills orientation

FIGURE 14.1 Challenges for curriculum change.

Note: From *Life Centered Career Education: Professional Development activity book* (pp. 364–366) by D. E. Brolin, 1993, Arlington, VA: The Council for Exceptional Children. Copyright 1993 by The Council for Exceptional Children. Reprinted by permission.

---

1. Some parents view education of their children as the responsibility of the schools.
2. Some teachers are reluctant to change existing materials.
3. Schools lack specialized personnel (job developers, job coaches).
4. Community work sites are limited.
5. School and agency personnel are unaware of each others' contributions.
6. No money, personnel, and time for school/agency collaboration.
7. An overemphasis on basic education at the expense of career education.
8. Little time to develop and coordinate LCCE parent involvement.
9. Administrators lack knowledge of LCCE.
10. Teachers and parents are unaware of agency services.

FIGURE 14.2   Your Hit Parade: Top 10 barriers to LCCE implementation.
Note: From "Your Hit Parade" in *LCCE/Employability Enhancement Project* by R. Roessler, 1991, Columbia: University of Missouri-Columbia. Copyright 1991 by D. E. Brolin. Reprinted by permission.

- Increase the number of occasions that bring parents/family members and the school together, such as career nights, social events, home visits, and parent information packets.
- Develop a board-approved parent-compliance contract specifying the type and amount of parental participation required in the student with learning and/or behavior needs' program.
- Have groups of parents meet at regularly scheduled intervals to discuss students with learning and/or behavior needs' progress.
- Conduct transition/rehabilitation training programs that teach parents/family members how to contribute to the school's LCCE Mild/Moderate Curriculum efforts (Roessler, 1991a).

"Effective educational programs don't just happen. A sound philosophical base and an effective planning process are necessary."

(Gysbers, quoted in
Kokaska & Brolin, 1985, p. 253)

There is no simple recipe as to how transition/career education can be structured in a preschool-to-postsecondary program. But the important point is that educators swing into action and start by developing a Transition Action Plan (TAP). One example of such a plan is presented in Figure 14.3, which illustrates the preliminary TAP developed by a LCCE Mild Curriculum Committee of the Grand Rapids, Michigan, Public Schools for one of their schools interested in implementing LCCE Mild/Moderate Curriculum. The reader should keep in mind that every school situation is different and that what works in one community will not necessarily succeed in another.

In the next section, more specific functional curriculum considerations are discussed in relation to elementary, secondary, and postsecondary programs and within the four curriculum areas of functional academic, daily living, personal-social, and occupational skills.

CURRICULUM CONSIDERATIONS

Much has been written about functional curriculum change and development. As Dever (1989) has pointed out, however, most functional instruction development efforts in the last 20 years have been program development for individuals rather than

SPECIAL EDUCATION PROGRAMS AND SERVICES

West Middle School
615 Turner N.W.
Grand Rapids, MI 49504
(616) 771-3300

Classroom Services
Psychological Services
Social Work Services
Teacher Consultant Services
Speech and Language Services

LCCE ACTION PLAN PROPOSAL

Name(s):   LCCE Curriculum Committee   School: Central

A. LCCE MILD/MODERATE CURRICULUM ADOPTION

1. We believe the major transition objectives of the educational program for students with special learning and/or behavior needs are based on the following three major domains of the LCCE Mild/Moderate Curriculum program:
   a.   personal/social skills
   b.   independent living skills
   c.   occupational skills

2. We believe our school/district needs to change its focus for these students with special learning and/or behavior needs because:
   a.   students with special learning and/or behavior needs are unprepared to function in society
   b.   students with special learning and/or behavior needs are dropping out of school
   c.   current curriculum does not meet needs
   d.   need to teach students with special learning and/or behavior needs to cope with a changing society

3. We propose the adoption of the Life-Centered Career Education (LCCE) Mild/Moderate Curriculum:
   a.   to provide a "road map" to adult living and working (transition)
   b.   to build self concept
   c.   to keep students motivated and in school

4. LCCE Mild/Moderate Curriculum approach (explanation of LCCE):
   a.   identifies "real life" needs for our students with special learning and/or behavior needs
   b.   offers a vehicle to transition a student to adult community postsecondary education and/or employment and community living
   c.   allows for the infusion of these competencies into current curriculum
   d.   provides consistent programming between all schools
   e.   allows students with special learning and/or behavior needs to become aware of their community resources and services
   f.   students with special learning and/or behavior needs can see an end to a means (scope and sequence)

FIGURE 14.3   LCCE Transition Plan (TAP) Grand Rapids, Michigan.

Note. From Grand Rapids, Michigan, Public Schools, West Middle School. Reprinted by permission.

(continues)

B. CURRICULUM MODIFICATIONS/CHANGES NEEDED FOR LCCE MILD/MODERATE CURRICULUM IMPLEMENTATION

1. Curriculum Modification Changes
   a. Correlate the graduation standards with the LCCE Mild/Moderate Curriculum
   b. Conduct functional testing all incoming 8th, 9th, and 10th graders with knowledge batteries (students with mild learning and/or behavior needs) and PKB for students with more severe learning and/or behavior needs
   c. Develop LCCE Mild/Moderate Curriculum Map—identification of the LCCE Mild/Moderate Curriculum competencies and subcompetencies into which content areas they will be infused.
   d. Develop a list of the LCCE Mild/Moderate competencies and objectives for IEP/ITP goals and objective

2. Administrative Changes
   a. Building Principals become knowledgeable about development of the LCCE Mild/Moderate Curriculum Transition Program
   b. Counselors will be knowledgeable about functional curriculum and implications for students with special learning and/or behavior needs' postsecondary and/or employment needs

3. Staff Changes (e.g., how can LCCE be used when special education teachers are being used as tutors instead of teaching functional skills or assisting general education teachers to infuse the LCCE Mild/Moderate Curriculum into their content areas?)
   a. Grand Rapids Public Schools Special Education Teachers will be designated as LCCE Specialists to enlist the support of general education teachers in order to help general education infuse the LCCE Mild/Moderate Curriculum competencies and subcompetencies into their content areas as appropriate to enrich the functional curriculum of the school district.

4. Parent Involvement
   a. Transition Planning
   b. Orientation (parent)

5. Community Involvement
   a. Establish partnerships/agreements with local business and industry
   b. Establish interagency agreements with community agencies
   c. Establish partnership program with universities in area
   d. LCCE Mild/Moderate Curriculum Implementation Barriers/Solutions
   e. Adoption by Board of Education/Superintendent/Provide Presentation outlining the needs and benefits of providing an appropriate transition program using the LCCE Mild/Moderate Curriculum Program
   f. Acceptance by Special Education
   g. Teachers/Provide Inservice
   h. Acceptance by General Education Teachers/Provide Inservice
   i. Acceptance by Special Education students/Implement Peer Buddies Program with students without disabilities

FIGURE 14.3   Continued.

C. STEPS TO IMPLEMENT LCCE AND TIMELINES

Steps/Timeline

1.	Present LCCE Mild/Moderate Curriculum Presentation to Board of Education and Superintendent	4/1/01
2.	Present LCCE Mild/Moderate Curriculum Transition training to administrators, teachers, and staff	5/1/01
3.	Correlate the LCCE Mild/Moderate Curriculum Competencies with local and state curriculum standards	8/1/01
4.	Complete LCCE Curriculum Map and transition curriculum materials review	9/1/01
5.	Present LCCE Mild/Moderate Curriculum training to parents	9/15/01
6.	Administer LCCE Knowledge Batteries to students with mild learning and/or behavior needs	10/1/01
7.	Administer LCCE PKBs to students with more severe learning and/or behavior needs	10/1/01
8.	Organize course objectives to be part of IEP/ITP	11/1/01
9.	Provide follow-up training	12/1/01
10.	Evaluate the program implementation and meet with administration and superintendent	3/01/02

FIGURE 14.3 Continued.

functional curriculum development per se. The difference between the two is that a program is what is taught to a specific learner with special learning and/or behavior needs over a specific period of time, whereas a functional curriculum is a statement of what anyone would have to learn to reach a transitional goal. Dever noted that there is widespread confusion on this matter and that most program development guides have been labeled as curricula, which may account for the lack of functional curriculum development in recent years (1989, p. 395). He identified the LCCE Mild Curriculum as one of the few that meets this criterion. Others (Sabornie & deBettencourt, 1997; Cummings & Maddux, 1987) rated the LCCE Mild Curriculum as the most comprehensive and efficacious for delivering transition/career education to students with special learning and/or behavior needs.

Roger and David Johnson of the University of Minnesota have promoted and studied the application of a cooperative learning approach (R. T. Johnson & Johnson, 1982; R. T. Johnson & Johnson 1983; R. T. Johnson, Johnson, & Rynders, 1981; Nevin, Johnson, & Johnson, 1982). For several years, they have investigated procedures that general education classroom teachers can use to ensure successful inclusion/integration. General educators should maintain the following three assumptions:

1. It is unnecessary and unrealistic to ask general education classroom teachers to become experts in special education because special education expertise is already in the school.
2. Any instructional strategy implemented in the general education classroom to facilitate the integration of students with disabilities should

benefit the education of all students, not just those with special learning and/or behavior needs.

3. The first priority of inclusion is to build positive relationships among students with and without special learning and/or behavior needs.

Johnson and Johnson believe that when students with special learning and/or behavior needs are liked, accepted, and chosen as friends, inclusion/integration has a positive influence on the lives of all students. They state that just placing a student in a classroom and providing her with her own individualistic learning experiences is not effective inclusion. Inclusion/integration must involve the student with special learning and/or behavior needs participating in the instructional activities, even though the student does not learn all of the information presented in the instructional activities. Their studies have revealed that students with special learning and/or behavior needs who have been placed in cooperative learning environments have higher self-esteem, interact more, feel more accepted by teachers and other students, achieve more, and behave more appropriately in the classroom than those students with special learning and/or behavior needs who have been placed in competitive and individualistic instructional systems. The transition/career education approach lends itself nicely to the cooperative learning model.

Through the process of conducting transition in-service workshops and developing a transition ac-

tion plan (TAP) for the school, the partnership between all possible school personnel, in addition to family and community representatives, can become established. An example of a transition action plan written by one school district was presented in Figure 14.3.

As indicated in earlier chapters, transition/career education transcends the entire curriculum and requires competency and subcompetency instruction at all levels. Functional curriculum emphasis will vary from school to school and student to student, depending on the school's resources, philosophy, and preparedness. Based on our experience, transition/career education instruction in academic, daily living, occupational, and personal-social skills follows the breakdown over the kindergarten-to-adult curriculum period, as depicted in Figure 14.4.

Each if these curriculum areas is next discussed in relation to elementary, secondary, and postsecondary programming.

Elementary/Middle School Programming

It is essential that transition/career education be instituted substantially at the elementary level. Functional skills, self-knowledge, and knowledge of the world of

FIGURE 14.4 Suggested curriculum for career development at various grade levels.

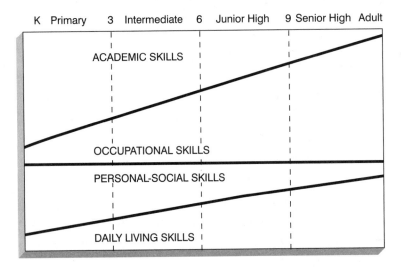

work need to be taught at this level so the students with special learning and/or behavior needs can function at a much higher degree in the secondary grades. What is taught in a transition/career education program is compatible with the skills required for transition services; thus, it is a vital component of the entire transition process. At the elementary level, infusing career awareness and exploration can build the foundation for transition growth activities into the variety of existing subjects being taught. Thus, students with special learning and/or behavior needs acquire basic daily living, personal-social, and occupational skills at a rudimentary level.

The importance of a transition/career education emphasis beginning at the elementary level has been outlined in the position paper of the Council for Exceptional Children (CEC) Division on Career Development alluded to in an earlier chapter (G. M. Clark et al., 1991), which offered five critical principles relative to this need:

1. Education for career development and transition is for individuals with disabilities at all ages.
2. Career development is a process begun at birth that continues throughout life.
3. Early career development is essential for making satisfactory choices later.
4. Significant gaps or periods of neglect in any area of basic human development affects career development and the transition from one stage of life to another.
5. Career development is responsive to intervention and programming, when the programming involves direct instruction for individual needs.

G. M. Clark et al. noted that "it is unrealistic to expect satisfactory career development and transition education outcomes when intervention is delayed until students reach high school" and that

each student's IEP should go beyond basic academic skills to provide for instruction and guidance as needed for:

- Developing age-appropriate functioning in independent daily living tasks, including knowledge and skills needed at home, at school, and in the community;

- Developing positive values and attitudes and age-appropriate behaviors for participating confidently in the home, at school, and in the community;
- Establishing and maintaining positive, age-appropriate interpersonal relationships in the home, at school, and in the community; and
- Developing awareness of occupational alternatives, orientation to the realities of the work world, and achieving age-appropriate, gross and fine motor skills. (1991, pp. 117—118)

This strong position taken by national leaders reflects the pressing need for educators at the elementary and middle school levels to make the necessary modifications for a more substantial transition/career education approach. Some guidelines for each of the four major curriculum areas constituting the approach described in this book are presented next.

Functional Academic Skills Instruction

During the elementary years, students with special learning and/or behavior needs must learn functional academic skills such as reading, writing, and arithmetic. This must be the primary emphasis during these years because academic skills lay the foundation for subsequent learning of the daily living and occupational skills needed for community living and working.

Daily Living Skills Instruction

Several subcompetencies can be taught during the elementary years in addition to basic academic skills. Daily living skills include identifying money and making correct change; managing money; making wise expenditures; using a vending machine; maintaining a living environment; dressing appropriately; developing grooming and hygiene skills; developing eating skills; understanding local laws and government; practicing basic first aid; participating in basic leisure and recreational group activities; and understanding traffic laws and safety practices, which are subcompetencies that these students with special learning and/or behavior needs can learn or can begin to learn.

Personal-Social Skills Instruction

The elementary years are particularly important for developing adequate personal-social skills. The preschool years of life are vital to personality development. Children with disabilities, in particular, are vulnerable to the attitudes and behaviors of others toward them, which, in many instances, may be manifested by ridicule, hostility, rejection, or physical abuse. Thus, they must learn how to handle these negative behaviors and should discover enough about themselves so that they feel they are worthwhile people. This functional area needs much more attention if these students with special learning and/or behavior needs are going to benefit from educational efforts and attain optimal transition/career development. All seven competencies of the LCCE Mild Curriculum and their subcompetencies along with the six competencies of the LCCE Moderate Curriculum and their subcompetencies should become part of the instructional/ transitional program at the elementary level. All school personnel teaching these students with special learning and/or behavior needs should include personal-social development as part of transition instruction.

Occupational Skills

Transition/career education highlights the need for elementary programs to provide much more attention to the students with special learning and/or behavior needs' occupational development at this level. Young children with special learning and/or behavior needs are interested in the world of work and actively seek to find out what their parents and significant others do to make a living. Educators should emphasize many of the following "work personality" building subcompetencies in this curriculum area during the student's elementary years: work attitudes and values; remunerative aspects of working; work habits (ability to follow directions, work with others, accept supervision, maintain good attendance and punctuality, achieve quality and quantity performance, follow safety procedures); and physical-manual skills (balance, coordination, dexterity, stamina).

Secondary Programming

Until recently, educators have perceived the secondary level as the point at which transitional efforts should begin. As noted earlier in this book, however, these perceptions have changed, and it is now generally accepted that substantial efforts at the elementary level are needed if the students with special learning and/or behavior needs are to gain the necessary functional skills by the time they leave the secondary program. At the secondary level, educators can concentrate on more extensive career exploration and preparation (skill-building) experiences if the elementary and middle school programs have done their part in providing substantive career awareness and exploration opportunities and preparation. The position paper by the Division on Career Development and Transition noted:

> The goals of secondary education are not the same as for elementary and middle school education. Basic skills are assumed for a majority of secondary students and the goal is to move them to higher levels of performance to prepare them for postsecondary education demands or for advanced levels of skills needed for employment (G. M. Clark et al., 1994).

Some guidelines for instruction in the four major functional curriculum areas are presented next.

Academic Skills

At the junior high school level, a decrease in teaching academic skills should begin, although much of this instruction can be directed to teaching specific functional daily living and occupational skills. Of course, this will vary with the student with special learning and/or behavior needs and her potential and personalized needs for academic skills instruction which can partly be determined by reviewing annually the student's age 25 projection. At this age, however, students with special learning and/or behavior needs begin questioning the relative value of what they are learning compared to what they will do later in their adult life of working and community living.

Daily Living Skills

At the junior high level, a much greater emphasis on functional daily living skills should occur. Learning about banking and credit facilities, home maintenance, adequate housing, use of basic appliances and tools, physical fitness, nutrition and weight control practices, marriage and child care practices, meal planning, preparation and purchasing, traffic rules, and use of various means of transportation are subcompetencies that can begin to be learned and perhaps acquired by the time students with special learning and/or behavior needs enter high school.

At the senior high school level, the student with special learning and/or behavior needs should have learned the subcompetencies that were taught earlier and also those that have not yet been taught or emphasized. Learning how to keep financial records, calculate and pay taxes, maintain a home interior, prevent and treat common illnesses, respond to questioning by the law, plan vacations, and drive a car are higher-order subcompetencies that some students may never learn adequately. Students unable to learn certain competencies or subcompetencies will need to know how they can ask for and receive assistance, perform an alternative skill, or partially participate in the functional skill. For example, a student may not be able to drive a car but can learn to access available transportation resources (i.e., public transportation, taxis, become a paid or nonpaid passenger, ask family members or friends, etc.).

Personal-Social Skills

If educators attempt to help students with special learning and/or behavior needs develop personal-social skills during the elementary years, emphasis on these subcompetencies may be decreased during the secondary programs. This is not meant to de-emphasize the importance of personal-social skills. Rather, we mean to imply that if educators help students learn enough about themselves, develop self-confidence, demonstrate self-determination, and display socially responsible behavior, the need to learn other personal-social skills may be reduced. On the other hand, certain students with special learning and/or behavior needs who

have not acquired these skills will need to spend a substantial amount of time in this functional area. All school personnel and guidance and counseling persons should use their special expertise to help students with special learning and/or behavior needs overcome unusually deficient behaviors. Rehabilitation counselors also can offer work adjustment services in a rehabilitation or employment setting to help young adults with special learning and/or behavior needs acquire the personal-social skills needed for transition/career development.

Occupational Skills

As the student with special learning and/or behavior needs progresses through the educational system, the occupational emphasis needs to become even greater. At the junior high school level, students with special learning and/or behavior needs should be exposed to industrial arts, home economics, trade and industrial technology, and other vocational subjects so they can develop prevocational skills and motivations. Career exploration experiences in the community become important, and the opportunity to try out various jobs in the classroom and community (besides in the home) will enhance the student with special learning and/or behavior needs' self-concept as a productive member of society. Educators should initiate occupational guidance activities, such as those discussed in Chapter 13, to assist students with special learning and/or behavior needs in career development and decision-making skills.

During the high school years, occupational skills should form at least half of the functional curriculum for most students with special learning and/or behavior needs. A Career Information and Assessment Center will help students with special learning and/or behavior needs learn more about jobs, specific vocational aptitudes and interests, and job-seeking skills and procedures. Such a center should be open at any time for the student with special learning and/or behavior needs, teacher, parent, and community representative and should be integral to students' weekly functional program. Vocational education coursework, work or job samples, on-the-job work experiences in the community, and other activities of this nature should be provided. The entire school faculty should work toward the goal of helping students with special learning and/or behavior needs prepare for adult community living and working requirements and economic, social, and personal fulfillment.

Postsecondary Level

Many students with special learning and/or behavior needs will not acquire a sufficient level of competence in functional skills to make the successful transition from the secondary program to postsecondary learning/training experiences and/or work, community living, and participation. Thus, further opportunities to acquire the competencies needed for adult adjustment must be provided. Vocational-technical schools, community colleges, rehabilitation programs, Job Training and Partnership Act (JTPA) programs, and other specialized centers are important contributors in the transition process and in the ultimate success or failure of individuals with special learning and/or behavior needs. Each of these agencies could adopt a functional skills focus, such as LCCE Mild/Moderate Curriculum, and work closely with the secondary programs to provide a consistent continuum of transition services for students who need further training.

Academic Functional Skills

Adult transition programs need to assess the extent to which the individual with special learning and/or behavior needs has acquired the academic skills needed for community living and working. For the latter, the emphasis should be on those functional academic skills needed for job goals. Variance in the number of functional academic skills that the individual with special learning and/or behavior needs learns depends on the quality of public school services.

Daily Living Skills

Adult programs should provide transition training for individuals with special learning and/or behavior needs who have not acquired these subcompetencies

but have the potential to acquire these skills. This needs to be carefully and systematically discerned.

Personal-Social Skills

Individual and group counseling services are generally an important service provided by adult programs. Thus, individuals with special learning and/or behavior needs who have deficiencies in this area should be given ample opportunity to learn the necessary personal-social skills for personal and vocational functioning. This functional area has been the most problematic to adults with special learning and/or behavior needs attempting to successfully live and work in their community.

Occupational Skills

The major emphasis of most postsecondary programs is vocational training. These agencies are well equipped to help individuals with special learning and/or behavior needs acquire all five competencies that comprise the occupational guidance and preparation of both the LCCE Mild and Moderate Curriculum programs. Most of these agencies have more extensive functional vocational assessment and training materials and work closely with community employers for on-site vocational training and eventual job placement.

The purpose of transition planning is not only for eventual employment but also for all other major aspects of adult functioning. Missouri LINC (Stephens, 1992) identified 14 important adult functional dimensions that must be addressed in transition planning if students with special learning and/or behavior needs are to become independent and successful: career planning, employment options, postsecondary education, financial assistance/income support, community participation, advocacy/legal services, transportation, recreation/leisure, self-advocacy, insurance, socialization/friends, personal management, living arrangements, and medical services. The LCCE Mild/Moderate Curriculum covers most of these areas, which can provide a good foundation for the Individualized Transition Plan (ITP), as illustrated in Figure 14.5.

Adult Role Dimensions (Missouri LINC)	LCCE Competencies																					
	Daily Living									Personal–Social							Occupational					
	1	2	3	4	5	6	7	8	9	10	11	12	13	14	15	16	17	18	19	20	21	22
Career Planning Options										●							●	●				
Employment Options																	●	●				
Postsecondary Training																			●		●	●
Financial Assistance/Income Support	●																					
Community Participation							●	●	●													
Advocacy/Legal Services																						
Leisure/Recreation								●														
Transportation									●													
Self-Advocacy											●	●	●	●	●	●				●		
Socialization/Friends												●	●									
Personal Management	●	●	●	●	●	●																
Living Arrangements		●																				
Medical																						
Insurance																						
Other																						

FIGURE 14.5 Correlation of LCCE Competencies to Missouri LINC's Transition Dimension.

435

In summary, functional curricula, such as LCCE Mild/Moderate Curricula, provide educators with a comprehensive scope and sequence approach from elementary to postsecondary programs. Such an approach defines the major goals of the educational and transitional program; discerns what should be taught at each level; provides a checks and balances system so students with special learning and/or behavior needs are continually assessed for their learning needs relative to functional skills; and results in a common language and understanding among educators at all levels as to the purpose of the entire education process for their students with special learning and/or behavior needs. In the process, the students with special learning and/or behavior needs, their parents, and the community will also understand the focus and purpose of the entire transition program and the expected final result.

LIFE CENTERED CAREER EDUCATION MILD/ MODERATE PROGRAMS

In previous editions of this book, several school districts that had implemented LCCE Mild Curriculum were described. These included Pine Plains Central School District No. 1, Pine Plains, New York; Holly Hill Junior High School, Holly Hill, Florida; Oakland County Schools, Pontiac, Michigan; Leavenworth Special Education Cooperative, Leavenworth, Kansas; Huron Residential Services for Youth, Inc., Ann Arbor, Michigan; and Gault Junior High School, Tacoma, Washington, which is now a middle school. For this edition, only Gault was contacted regarding its status in providing students with the LCCE Curriculum approach. JoAnn Balmer, the teacher, now retired, who provided the previous information, reported that although her school may not be following the LCCE Curriculum approach to the letter, the district as a whole has adopted an integrated functional curriculum approach in all school levels of special and regular education. Thus, the information about Gault Middle School has been retained.

The LCCE Mild Curriculum is being implemented in hundreds of school districts as well as countries such as Taiwan. In states such as Alabama and North Dakota, the state agency has been particularly supportive of the curriculum and has strongly recommended its implementation. Mabrey Whetstone, the Chapter Outlook author for this chapter, has been instrumental in designating LCCE Mild Curriculum as a relevant functional skills curriculum for Alabama and has secured the LCCE Mild Curriculum materials and provided training for all districts receptive to its implementation. Chapter 3 mentioned the incorporation of the LCCE Mild Curriculum in one of the North Dakota curriculum guides.

THE LCCE MILD/ MODERATE CURRICULUM IMPLEMENTATION PROCESS

The implementation of any innovation requires extensive planning, support, and efforts from the entire school and community resources. IDEA 1990's mandate of addressing transition in students with special learning and/or behavior needs established the need for schools and communities to develop programs to provide transition programming for these students. The LCCE Mild/Moderate Curriculum Training Manual (Loyd & Brolin, 2002) includes the steps for developing a transition action plan (TAP). The LCCE TAP is a systematic approach to developing a transition program addressing the functional needs and transition mandates outlined in IDEA 1990 and IDEA 1997. All innovations require a discernible planning component and support from the LEA's Board of Education and superintendent.

Although many education innovations have been introduced, most have a short-lived existence. Several major barriers to innovation implementation and sustainability have been identified in the professional literature. The following list identifies some of the most common barriers to transition programming implementation and sustainability: lack of administrative support, failure to gain teacher support, lack of financial support, personnel change, lack of training, and failure to gain community support and inter-agency agreements. Resolution of many transition programming barriers have been identified in the Grand Rapids, Michigan LCCE TAP in Figure 14.3.

LCCE Transition Action Plan (TAP) Development

The LCCE Mild/Moderate Curriculum Training Manual (Loyd & Brolin, 2002) includes a component outlining the steps for developing an LCCE Mild/Moderate Curriculum TAP. The following steps are included in the LCCE Mild/Moderate Curriculum TAP that provide the activities necessary to implement this transition program in the district:

LCCE Transition Action Plan Steps

A. LCCE MILD/MODERATE CURRICULUM ADOPTION

This section of the TAP provides the rationale for adopting the LCCE Mild/Moderate Curriculum program in the district. Examples of why a need exists to ensure that students with special learning and/or behavior needs are provided the functional skills to make the successful transition from school to postsecondary training and/or employment and community living are given. This section also introduces the LCCE Mild/Moderate Curriculum as a substantive functional program that addresses students with special learning and/or behavior needs' transition outcomes. Expected results of the LCCE Mild/Moderate Curriculum program implementation are also included in this section. This section provides the value of this program to justify its need for implementation so as to gain Board of Education and superintendent support and approval.

B. CURRICULUM MODIFICATIONS/ CHANGES NEEDED FOR LCCE MILD/ MODERATE CURRICULUM IMPLEMENTATION

The second section outlines the following activities needed to correlate the LCCE Mild/Moderate Curriculum with the existing curriculum and

district and state standards. In this section, activities are described for infusing the LCCE Mild/Moderate Curriculum competencies into the general education content areas. Other areas in this section of TAP include addressing administrative needs; staffing changes; involving parents/family members; involving community business and industry; involving community agencies; and implementation and sustainability barriers and solutions.

Curriculum Modification Activities

1. Correlate the graduation standards with the LCCE Mild/Moderate Curriculum
2. Conduct functional testing of all incoming 8th, 9th, and 10th graders with knowledge batteries (students with mild learning and/or behavior needs) and PKB for students with more severe learning and/or behavior needs
3. Develop LCCE Mild/Moderate Curriculum Map—identification of the LCCE Mild/Moderate Curriculum competencies and sub-competencies into which content areas they will be infused
4. Develop a list of the LCCE Mild/Moderate competencies and objectives for IEP/ITP goals and objectives

Administrative Changes/Needs

1. Building principals provided LCCE Mild/Moderate Curriculum Transition Program training
2. Counselors and content area coordinators provided LCCE Mild/Moderate Curriculum Transition Program training. Specifically, knowledge about functional curriculum and implications for students with special learning and/or behavior needs' postsecondary and/or employment needs

Staff Changes

1. Selecting a Transition Program Coordinator
2. Providing LCCE Mild/Moderate Curriculum program training to teachers and other support personnel
3. Designating LCCE specialists for each building (K-12)

Parent/Family Members' Involvement

1. Provide transition training to parents/family members

Community Business and Industry Involvement

1. Provide transition training to business and industry personnel
2. Establish partnerships/agreements with local business and industry

Community Agency Involvement

1. Provide transition training to community agency personnel
2. Establish interagency agreements with community agencies
3. Establish partnership program with universities in area

LCCE Mild/Moderate Curriculum Implementation Barriers/Solutions

1. Identify possible barriers to implementation and sustainability

C. STEPS TO IMPLEMENT LCCE AND TIMELINES

This section of the TAP identifies the steps to be taken by the district to implement and sustain the LCCE Mild/Moderate Curriculum program. Timelines for meeting the implementation and sustainability activities are identified and conducted. Finally, this section describes the LCCE Mild/Moderate Curriculum Transition program evaluation.

EXAMPLES OF LCCE MILD/ MODERATE PROGRAMS

This section presents a description of some of the efforts to implement the LCCE Mild/Moderate Curriculum program in some school districts throughout the country. Many of these LCCE Mild/Moderate Curriculum programs have been in existence and sustained their implementation since the introduction of the LCCE Curriculum approach in the late seventies. Additional information on LCCE Curriculum approach implementation success and sustainability will be provided later in this chapter. The success and popularity of this functional curriculum is evident by the fact that LCCE Mild/Moderate Curriculum materials are being used in every state.

School personnel have provided some of this information directly to the author; the remainder has been extracted from materials published by the schools themselves.

Gault Middle School, Tacoma, Washington*

Junior high students with special learning and/or behavior needs can be the worst in the world and the best in the universe. The students with special learning and/or behavior needs at Gault are earthy, sometimes rude, and socially unskilled; however, once they have established a trusting relationship, they are caring, thoughtful, and accepting of their teachers and peers.

Gault is a school with a declining enrollment; most of the students with special learning and/or behavior needs are underachievers who have obtained the lowest CTBS scores in the district. The general education staff is skilled and makes every effort to work effectively under difficult circumstances. They expressed a need for support personnel and alternatives so they could cope with the unique population at Gault. Resource students were especially in need of alternatives that would defeat the failure cycle. The low self-concept among students with special learning and/or behavior needs blocked the achievement of their potential.

When the staff decided that "the way it has always been" was not enough and that changes were necessary, they sought alternative methods that would resolve the problems. They scrutinized traditional instruction-drill-homework models in search of the answer. A closer look at the situation revealed the following ideas:

---

*Information was provided by JoAnn N. Balmer, who was a teacher at Gault Junior High School, Tacoma School District, Tacoma, Washington. (Gault Junior High Scool is now Gault Middle School.)

1. Traditionally, resource students with special learning and/or behavior needs have been over-individualized. Every student with special learning and/or behavior needs worked in a corner on her own level, memorizing and completing extensive homework assignments without behavioral incidents; but none of the students with special learning and/or behavior needs could get along in a group setting. Anger in the form of verbal and physical abuse toward peers and supervisors and inability to share or work together on a project was the rule rather than the exception. This environment was not conducive to optimal learning, so the structure of the classroom was changed to a group process format.

2. Students with special learning and/or behavior needs could not apply their knowledge. Every student with special learning and/or behavior needs had been drilled on fractions and decimals, but none of them could double a recipe or make correct change. Every student with special learning and/or behavior needs was able to add, subtract, multiply, and divide, but if they were required to apply this information, most students with special learning and/or behavior needs drew a complete blank. Using math and English to solve problems in life was impossible. Memorizing facts in social studies and science was confusing because most students with special learning and/or behavior needs could not remember what they learned.

3. Students with special learning and/or behavior needs had difficulty understanding cause-and-effect relationships. The use of reason by the teacher in the form of communication, values clarification, and positive reinforcement was the key toward building desired students with special learning and/or behavior needs' self-control. Skill building was necessary in dealing with peer-adult conflict if self-defeating behavior was to be erased from the students with special learning and/or behavior needs' repertoire. The students with special learning and/or behavior needs responded positively to a "soft glove" over a "hard-nosed" approach. Such an approach helped them move in the direction of a trusting relationship with the supervisor. At the onset of the semester, the students were informed that there would be no E's or "hacks;" their performance in the class would be re-viewed bimonthly and their behavior would be discussed with the class group when necessary. They were told that we all care about each other because each individual is important (1) as a person, (2) for his contribution to the learning environment, and (3) to the group as a whole. Individual conferences and parent-student conferences were held as needed for the IEP process and when general goal evaluation seemed appropriate. The teacher's behavior was also open for discussion. The class had a democratic structure.

4. The learning resource center atmosphere should be a supportive, trusting, and interesting environment where students with special learning and/or behavior needs can find themselves and be themselves. At Gault, pencils, paper, and emotional support were available to each student with special learning and/or behavior needs at all times through the day. A snack was in the cupboard if the student was hungry (better attention and work comes from a full stomach).

5. School is the job of the student with special learning and/or behavior needs. Most of the students with special learning and/or behavior needs lacked work skills, realistic employment goals, and employed role models in their community. Attendance, punctuality, task completion, appropriate behavior toward supervisors and peers, good grooming, acceptance of constructive criticism, and willingness to attempt all assigned jobs were used to help students develop work skills. Students set three types of employment goals: (1) overshoot ("I want to be an attorney, and if I can't read or write, my secretary will do all that stuff for me"); (2) middle hugger ("Who needs a job? I have welfare"); and (3) undershoot ("I don't know what I will do because I can't do anything anyway"). Self-awareness and self-analysis had to be a major force in the functional curriculum. It was never expected that junior high students would know exactly what they wanted to do, but the students with special learning and/or behavior needs needed to set some goals if they were to start thinking about work and make the association between school and future work. Exploration of the job clusters and the functional academic, physical, and personality strengths needed in each area were infused into the transition program. After two months of on-the-job study and

a teacher who had a career/vocational background, career infusion was the logical model to follow. The major categories of the LCCE Mild/Moderate Curriculum competencies and their incorporation into the general and resource curriculum are outlined in Table 14.1.

North St. Francois County R-I, Bonne Terre-Desloge, Missouri*

The LCCE Mild/Moderate Curriculum has proven to be a valuable instrument that has enabled our School to Employment Transition Program to flourish, and, most importantly, our students to succeed.

For years, our parents of students in special education have been concerned about their children. One of their major concerns was whether or not their sons or daughters were going to make it on their own and become productive members of society. Unfortunately, we in education have discussed our students' weaknesses and limitations with their parents, told them how far behind their children were to their peers, and that they were having difficulty in their classes. This made parents feel even more concerned.

Numerous times, parents have said to me, "When I am gone, what is going to happen to my son or daughter?"

Now, with the LCCE Mild/Moderate Curriculum, parents can see that we are helping our students with special learning and/or behavior needs learn skills to become independent and lead productive lives.

It means so much more to our parents to tell them that their sons and daughters can do things such as write checks, fill out job applications, buy and care for their clothing, and get along well with others than it does to tell them that the student with special learning and/or behavior needs' math is on the fourth-grade level or reading is on the third-grade level.

Our parents feel relieved and happy. Someone is addressing the real needs of their children so that they can become independent and successful.

I believe that the LCCE Mild/Moderate Curriculum program has helped bring our families closer together. Parents and their sons/daughters with special learning and/or behavior needs are working on LCCE competencies at home. My students with special learning and/or behavior needs often share positive learning experiences they have at home with LCCE Mild/Moderate Curriculum projects or lessons. Students' and parents' self-esteem has also been elevated. Family members are often asked to be guest speakers or helpers for our LCCE Mild/Moderate Curriculum lessons. This has helped our parents feel respected, as well as proud of their accomplishments. Our students with special learning and/or behavior needs are also proud of their parents, brothers, sisters, or other relatives for teaching and sharing with our class.

Because of these positive experiences, I believe our students with special learning and/or behavior needs and their parents are now taking a more active role in the development and participation of IEP/ITPs.

Our students with special learning and/or behavior needs are excited about LCCE Curriculum materials, because most of them for the first time in their lives can see that what they are learning directly helps them in their daily lives and in the future. Classes now seem more meaningful to them. They no longer feel compared with their peers but now perceive the ability to acquire a skill to be used in life as an adult.

When our students with special learning and/or behavior needs can perform many of the LCCE Mild/Moderate Curriculum skills they need to function day to day, they develop confidence, and when they have control of their environment rather than the environment controlling them, they feel more confident and better about themselves.

*This information was provided by Pat Burch, Special Education Teacher/Transition Coordinator, North St. Francois County R-1 Public Schools in Bonne Terre-Desloge, Missouri, who has used the LCCE Curriculum with her students for many years.

TABLE 14.1   Life Centered Career Education Competencies and Instructional Areas at Gault Junior High School

Competency Category	Instructional Area
1. Managing personal finances	*Math* Identifying coins and making change Verifying a bargain Writing and keeping a budget Writing checks: keeping and balancing a checkbook Understanding payroll deductions, income tax, social security Recognizing a bargain: reading and verifying advertisements
2. Selecting and managing a home	*Basic skills* (contact), *health* Decorating and maintaining the classroom Making basic home repairs Cooking and planning balanced meals Eating proper foods and controlling weight Understanding vitamins and minerals for basic health
3. Caring for personal needs	*Basic skills* (contact) *health, physical education* (contact) Developing hygiene and grooming skills Understanding the need for physical activity (health and weight control) Learning rules for common games as a participator and spectator Learning first-aid skills Obtaining knowledge of common illness and when to seek medical attention Obtaining knowledge of over-the-counter and prescribed medication
4. Raising children and meeting marriage responsibilities	*Health* Babysitting Learning home and school safety practices Identifying marriage responsibilities and appropriate dating behavior
5. Buying, preparing, and consuming food	*Math, basic skills* (contact) Developing table manners Planning and preparing nutritious meals on a budget Obtaining knowledge of the supermarket (sales, impulse buying, selection of a market, advertising) Storing food and using leftovers Recognizing the importance of kitchen cleanliness
6. Buying and caring for clothing	*Basic skills* (contact) *English, math* Reading and following label directions Using a washer and dryer (using settings, soap, bleach, fabric softener) Ironing Selecting clothes (choosing colors, styles, and bargains) Mending Sorting clothing for laundry

(continues)

TABLE 14.1 Continued.

Competency Category	Instructional Area
7. Exhibiting responsible citizenship	*Social studies* Understanding school government (student, administrative structure, school board function) Registering to vote and fulfilling responsibilities Understanding city, county, state, and national government function, and responsibility and service to constituents Understanding personal rights as a citizen Developing awareness of world problems and issues (malnutrition, conflict, nuclear proliferation) Gaining knowledge of the political process Mapping, charting, and reading graphs Developing basic knowledge of U.S. history (events, people)
8. Utilizing recreational facilities and engaging in leisure	*Physical education* (contact), *health* Developing knowledge of community recreational facilities (contact person, eligibility requirements, cost) Understanding need for recreation Understanding spectator sports
9. Getting around the community	*Math, English* Reading transportation schedules Developing awareness of requirements and responsibilities of being a licensed driver of a car, motorcycle Obtaining knowledge of insurance Reading maps Understanding the function of the police traffic division Planning a trip (cost of ticket, gas, miles per gallon) Developing awareness of bicycle safety practices
10. Achieving self-awareness	*Health, physical education* (contact), *English, social studies* Identifying values and emotions Identifying conflict and coping with stress Expressing feelings (anger, joy) Understanding and experiencing group interaction Developing awareness of body and its interaction in space
11. Acquiring self-confidence	*Health, social studies, English, math* Analyzing levels of competency performance and engaging in self-analysis Understanding potential level(s) of performance Developing awareness of strengths and weaknesses Developing awareness and understanding of personal behaviors Coping and identifying with conflict and ability to identify ownership of the problem Accepting praise and criticism Accepting teasing Listening actively to others

TABLE 14.1   Continued.

Competency Category	Instructional Area
11. (continued)	Analyzing and providing feedback to others Recognizing stress and when to seek assistance
12. Achieving socially responsible behavior	*All contact and resource classes* Developing acceptable field trip, assembly, and speaker behavior Knowing strengths and weaknesses and developing an active plan to build on strengths and correct or accept weaknesses Understanding behavior in various situations (school, home, job) Recognizing the rights of self and others, the evils of assault, vandalism, abuse Recognizing a feeling of self in the world of school, family and future employment Expressing realistic ambitions and hopes for the near and far future Understanding school as his or her job
13. Maintaining adequate interpersonal skills	*All contact and resource classes* Developing ability to define, acquire, and maintain friendship Identifying different levels of friendship and acquaintanceship Understanding dating behavior Clarifying personal values in heterosexual relationships Establishing and maintaining close relationships Developing awareness of strengths and weaknesses in self-organization on a variety of tasks (class, social, family) Developing ability to listen, ask questions, and respond appropriately Gathering facts and setting realistic goals
14. Achieving independence	*All contact and resource classes* Completing assigned responsibilities (see 13)
15. Making adequate decisions	*All contact and resource classes* Gathering facts, discussing alternatives, and reaching conclusions Understanding the need for goals in a variety of situations Becoming aware of the concept of cause and effect Accepting consequences for personal actions Seeking out the assistance of advisor, counselor, etc., when a need for problem solving arises
16. Communicating adequately with others	*All contact and resource classes* Recognizing and appropriately responding to emergency situations Realizing the need for academic abilities (reading, writing) to fulfill future goals Understanding the need for commercial types of communication in our daily lives (newspapers, TV, magazines)

(continues)

TABLE 14.1   Continued .

Competency Category	Instructional Area
16. (continued)	Developing knowledge of the psychology of advertising Completing forms
17. Knowing and exploring occupational possibilities	*All resource classes* Understanding the need for value such as self-concept, acceptance of others, independence, self-sufficiency Realizing and meeting the responsibility of completing assignments, making up assignments after an absence Realizing the advantages of work Obtaining knowledge on career clusters and the requirements of each Developing knowledge of unions, community industries Developing knowledge of steps in seeking employment and/or training
18. Selecting and planning occupational choices	*All resource classes* Obtaining knowledge of various types of jobs Identifying job categories Identifying appropriate types of work (outdoor vs. indoor) Identifying strengths and abilities (verbal, numerical, coordination, mechanical) Identifying possibilities for entry level jobs (first part-time job)
19. Exhibiting appropriate work habits and behaviors	*All contact and resource classes* Following written and verbal instructions Understanding the team concept (following and leading) Developing ability to take turns Developing ability to agree or disagree appropriately Developing awareness of the importance of attendance, punctuality, quality of work, and productivity
20. Exhibiting sufficient physical-manual skills	*Physical education* (contact), *health* Realizing the importance of exercise and diet to physical well-being Understanding and fulfilling a need for physical activity for optimal success toward future work and community living

Searching for a job is always somewhat frightening, but can you imagine how much more difficult it would be if you did not have the skills necessary to communicate in a job interview? Some of our students with special learning and/or behavior needs thought it was so frightening they wouldn't even attempt to find a job; as with many things in life, many students with special learning and/or behavior needs found that when given a chance to practice and to experience the situation in a controlled setting, the actual situation isn't that frightening. What our students with special learning and/or behavior needs were afraid of was the unknown, and once it is known, their fears are alleviated. The LCCE Mild/Moderate Curriculum program provides our students with special learning and/or behavior needs a means to take advantage of these opportunities.

Teachers at North St. Francois County are excited about the LCCE Mild/Moderate Curriculum program. Nationwide, there is often a high turnover rate of teachers in special education because, given the traditional educational model, special teachers aren't always quite sure how much they are helping the student. Grade levels may have increased somewhat, but what difference did that make in the student's life? With the LCCE Mild/Moderate Curriculum program, the teacher can see exactly how the students with special learning and/or behavior needs' level of independence is increased. They know students with special learning and/or behavior needs are being prepared for the future and know exactly what students with special learning and/or behavior needs need to focus on to prepare for living on their own as an adult.

Our teachers feel good about students with special learning and/or behavior needs' successes and what they are doing to get their students ready for the adult world of community living and working.

General education faculty members in our school respect our LCCE Mild/Moderate Curriculum program. They can see the practical aspects that are offered through the LCCE Mild/Moderate Curriculum program and can easily understand that a transition program is needed to prepare our students with special learning and/or behavior needs for the future. They see that the effort and time spent are very productive. General education teachers are incorporating LCCE Curriculum objectives into their general education content classes for our mainstream students with special learning and/or behavior needs. The LCCE Mild/Moderate Curriculum goals and objectives are clear to everyone; our special education/transition program has more credibility because success can be measured. Our LCCE Mild/Moderate Curriculum program has helped bring respect to special education staff and students with special learning and/or behavior needs.

The community also benefits from our LCCE Mild/Moderate Curriculum program. Formerly, students with special learning and/or behavior needs were leaving special classes unprepared for the world and subsequently had to rely on their families for support. These students with special learning and/or behavior needs are now being employed and living independently. They hold jobs, provide services in the community, pay taxes, and do not rely on tax-supported programs for their livelihood.

Businesses in our community are providing employment opportunities for our students with special learning and/or behavior needs. Community agencies and employers are opening their doors for community-based experiences and as guest speakers.

Administrators and staff are proud of our students with special learning and/or behavior needs. They often take an active role in our LCCE Mild/Moderate Curriculum activities and share our accomplishments with others in the community.

Our LCCE Mild/Moderate Curriculum program definitely enables the students with special learning and/or behavior needs, their parents, the community, and teachers to work together for a common goal, to ensure a successful transition from student to independent adult, family member, citizen, and employee.

Birmingham, Alabama*

The LCCE Mild/Moderate functional curriculum has been used exclusively in the Supported Vocational Training Program within the Jefferson County School System in Birmingham, Alabama, since 1987. The Supported Vocational Training Program (SVT) is a community-based work experience model based on the principles of supported employment within a vocational education setting. Supported Vocational Training has as its foundation a required functional curriculum taught primarily by special education teachers.

Students with special learning and/or behavior needs served by the Supported Vocational Training Program are in grades 9 to 12. Some are in comprehensive high school settings. Others are in area vocational centers. All students with special learning and/or behavior needs who participate in SVT and the LCCE Mild/Moderate Curriculum are students with disabilities. The majority of these students have mild-to-moderate disabilities in the area of limited intellectual functioning paired with secondary disabling

---

*This information was provided by Beverly Lavender, Transition Coordinator, Jefferson County Schools, Birmingham, Alabama.

conditions. Exclusively, all students with special learning and/or behavior needs receive either a vocational diploma or certificates of completion rather than high school diplomas upon graduation from high school.

Simultaneously, students with special learning and/or behavior needs receive classroom instruction in the LCCE Mild/Moderate Curriculum domains of daily living skills, personal social skills, and occupational guidance and preparation skills, as well as employability skills training by the SVT training staff. Students with special learning and/or behavior needs are given Form A of the LCCE Knowledge Assessment Battery in the fall. Performance Assessment Batteries are given on individual competencies as these units are taught throughout the school year, SVT staff use all domains of the LCCE Mild/Moderate Curriculum, especially the occupational guidance and preparation domain as an infused functional curriculum resource for their employability skills classes. SVT staff, which consist of a special education-funded work instructor and a vocational education-funded transition coordinator/job developer/job coach, provide situational work assessments (in lieu of traditional functional vocational evaluation methods), unpaid work instruction/experience, part-time paid work experience, and long-term career job placement services.

Jefferson County Schools, as our functional curriculum, have officially adopted the LCCE Mild/Moderate functional curriculum for students with disabilities. Within the Vocational Education Department, the home economics teachers are using the LCCE Mild/Moderate Curriculum instructional units to provide alternative activities/instruction for students with disabilities within their home economics course of study. All facets of the LCCE Mild/Moderate Curriculum infuse beautifully into our home economics curriculum. All general education home economics teachers have access to the LCCE Mild/Moderate instructional units through our transition coordinator in the Vocational Education Department. A very high percentage of our students with disabilities elect home economics in the sixth, seventh, and eighth grades.

At Minor High School, the Supported Vocational Training Program has been merged with a consultative special/transition education model. General education content instructors provide English, math, science, and social studies instruction to students with disabilities. These instructors are using the LCCE Mild/Moderate Curriculum instructional units as a resource/supplement to their traditional academic curriculum. Functional courses also are being offered on the master schedule with titles including LCCE math, LCCE English, LCCE science, LCCE social studies, and LCCE health at Minor High School and Gardendale High School.

As more general education vocational education instructors become familiar with the LCCE Mild/Moderate Curriculum instructional units, more of our trades and industrial education instructors are using the LCCE Mild/Moderate Curriculum units to enrich their required employability skills modules.

Wayne and Kent Counties, Michigan (The Wayne State University Project)*

In Michigan, the LCCE Mild/Moderate Curriculum has been the focus of a large number of school districts, particularly in Utica, Muskegon, and the metropolitan Detroit-Wayne County and the Grand Rapids-Kent County areas. A major project directed by Dr. Sharon Field at Wayne State University was conducted from 1991 to 1994 to build a culturally relevant, community-referenced functional curriculum in Michigan, using the LCCE Mild/Moderate Curriculum. Eight school districts worked closely with the Wayne State University staff. In Kent County, the school districts were Grand Rapids, Lowell, Rockford, and Wyoming. In Wayne County they were Dearborn, Inkster, River Rouge, and Wyandotte. Staff from each of these schools worked extensively with project staff to field test and modify the LCCE Curriculum framework, lesson plans, and assessments for the culturally diverse students in their settings. This required sensitizing both the curriculum and the

---

*This information was provided by Linda Ortman, Transition Specialist, Grand Rapids, Michigan.

people using it to the cultural, ethnic, religious, and racial diversity represented in each school district. The result has been a substantive implementation of LCCE Mild/Moderate in most of these districts.

In the Inkster School District, which has predominantly African-American students, the LCCE Mild/Moderate Curriculum is being used with the high school's special education students. Teachers have noted that LCCE Mild/Moderate Curriculum "has helped make a difference. Teachers have definitely seen a change in student behavior, attendance, and overall attitude toward learning" (*The Sounding Board*, 1994, p. 12). Some of the students with special learning and/or behavior needs involved in the curriculum the Kent County school districts have expressed these opinions:

> Nina (age 16): It's interesting. It teaches you different things you need to know for your life.... Now, we are going to Burger King on Monday, Tuesday, and Wednesday. We work and learn how Burger King works. It teaches us how to get along with others.
> Todd (age 19): We work as a team. Before, I didn't get out in the community.
> Michele (age 17): I think it's made a difference. It's really easier to understand. Like how to clean— it's really doing it. We clean sinks, sweep and mop the floor, and wipe off the tables. When we learned about what tools to use, it was mostly paper work, but [we need] real activities, later.
> Matt (age 17): I think it is excellent. We are learning to wash clothes, and what to clean with. When I get my own house, I'll know what to do with my money—how to budget. (Martinez, 1993, p. 11)

As an offshoot of the Wayne State Project, the Kent Transition Center (KTC) in Grand Rapids, in cooperation with the local school districts in the Kent Intermediate School District, has developed a transition implementation model using the LCCE Mild/Moderate Curriculum as a central focus. Figure 14.6 illustrates how the LCCE Curriculum competencies span the range of all seven-program outcomes that have been determined as critical for transitioning their students as responsible citizens and competitive employees.

Other Schools and Districts

In Colorado, two particularly noteworthy efforts should be mentioned. The Aurora Public Schools, Aurora, Colorado, Department of Special Education modified their district-adopted general education curriculum by using the LCCE Moderate Curriculum for moderate needs students to serve as a functional scope and sequence for their elementary students. Staff are using the 75 LCCE Moderate Curriculum subcompetencies within the specified courses that each should be taught, the materials needed, suggested time allotment, and several community learning experiences for delivering the instruction. The Colorado School for the Blind and Deaf also has adopted the LCCE Mild/Moderate Curriculum and has made several presentations around the country describing their implementation efforts.

The use of the LCCE Mild/Moderate Curriculum model for elementary students at Cordley Elementary School in Lawrence, Kansas, was reported in Teaching *Exceptional Children* by J. Beck et al. (1994), who established a set of functional skills and student objectives based on the LCCE Mild/Moderate competencies and subcompetencies. They note that many of the functional skills contained in the LCCE Mild/Moderate Curriculum are taught in the general education curriculum for elementary and secondary students without disabilities. Thus, when general education and special education teachers collaborate to plan age-appropriate lessons, the LCCE Mild/Moderate functional skills are incorporated into the lessons and units. A strong community-based instruction and inclusion focus has been instituted for the elementary students, which includes those with mental retardation.

In Missouri, several school districts have implemented the LCCE Mild/Moderate Curriculum approach. The Nixa R-II School District in Nixa, Missouri is using the LCCE Moderate Curriculum as their functional curriculum for elementary students with special needs to provide an organized and coordinated method of curricular presentation. The LCCE Mild Curriculum is currently being used in four special education classes at the secondary level

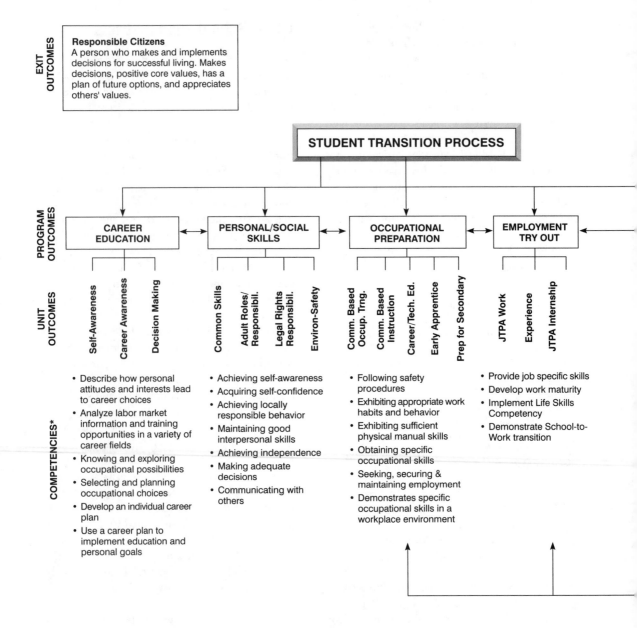

FIGURE 14.6   Kent Transition Implementation Model.
Note: From Kent County transition implementation model. Copyright by Kent Transition Center, Grand Rapids, Michigan. Reprinted by permission.

and also in the general education consumer math class. This class, designed as a-class-within-a-class (special/general education team-taught) format, fo-cuses on providing students with special learning and/or behavior needs a more realistic experience of being a consumer. The rationale for the development

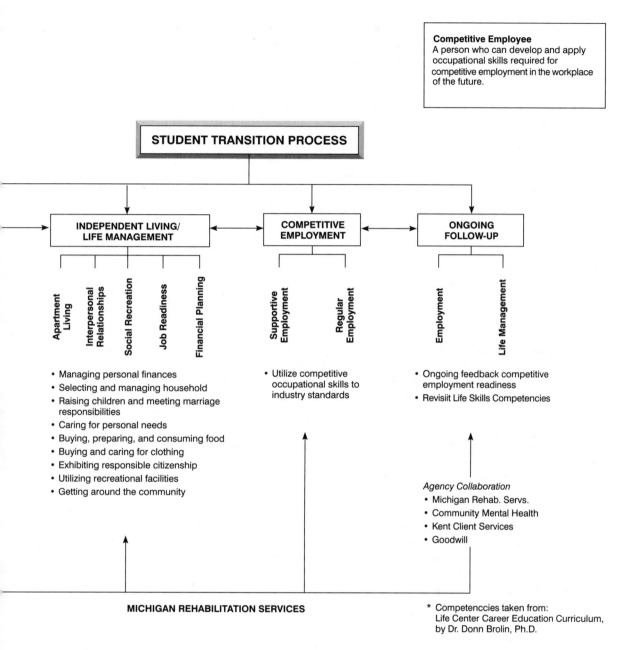

Competitive Employee
A person who can develop and apply occupational skills required for competitive employment in the workplace of the future.

STUDENT TRANSITION PROCESS

INDEPENDENT LIVING/ LIFE MANAGEMENT

- Apartment Living
- Interpersonal Relationships
- Social Recreation
- Job Readiness
- Financial Planning

- Managing personal finances
- Selecting and managing household
- Raising children and meeting marriage responsibilities
- Caring for personal needs
- Buying, preparing, and consuming food
- Buying and caring for clothing
- Exhibiting responsible citizenship
- Utilizing recreational facilities
- Getting around the community

COMPETITIVE EMPLOYMENT

- Supportive Employment
- Regular Employment

- Utilize competitive occupational skills to industry standards

ONGOING FOLLOW-UP

- Employment
- Life Management

- Ongoing feedback competitive employment readiness
- Revisiit Life Skills Competencies

Agency Collaboration
- Michigan Rehab. Servs.
- Community Mental Health
- Kent Client Services
- Goodwill

MICHIGAN REHABILITATION SERVICES

* Competenccies taken from:
Life Center Career Education Curriculum, by Dr. Donn Brolin, Ph.D.

of this class was concern about the students with special learning and/or behavior needs' retaining consumer math skills for later use. To meet these needs, the course was designed for students with special learning and/or behavior needs who may have difficulty succeeding in the more traditional consumer math class. Students apply for jobs in the microsociety of the classroom, use a time clock, are paid based on hours worked, and are responsible for maintaining a checking account. Students with special learning and/or behavior needs can select to be employed as a judge, reporter, insurance adjuster, bank teller, maintenance worker, or other entry-level positions. Many of the LCCE Mild/Moderate Curriculum competencies fit naturally into the course outline. (Information provided by Terri Chasteen, Special Education Teacher, Nixa, Missouri.)

The Aurora R-VIII Schools, in the Aurora, Missouri, Special Education Department, decided to use LCCE Mild/Moderate Curriculum goals as a format for writing transition goals and objectives for their ITPs. Their staff wrote more specific measurable objectives for each LCCE Moderate Curriculum competency area so each could be taught in the primary grades. The staff adopted the LCCE Mild/Moderate Curriculum because of its flexibility and because its framework helps staff ensure that each student with special learning and/or behavior needs is given the opportunity to develop the functional skills that will lead to successful adult community post-secondary training, employment, and living. They note that the LCCE Mild/Moderate Curriculum aids them in determining if there are gaps in the students with special learning and/or behavior needs' transition program or if duplications are occurring as the students with special learning and/or behavior needs move from one level to another. In the implementation process, the specific objectives for each LCCE Mild/Moderate subcompetency are infused into many functional areas (i.e., math, reading, language arts, social skills, speech/language, and daily living skills). A star is noted beside each IEP/ITP goal and objective that is part of the students with special learning and/or behavior needs' transition program. The LCCE Mild/Moderate matrixes or grids illustrating the 22 Mild/20 Moderate competencies and 97 Mild/75 Moderate subcompetencies is placed in the students with special learning and/or behavior needs' ITP folder as a reference for needed instructional efforts.

The Grundy County R-IX Schools, in Trenton, Missouri, have instituted a substantial LCCE Mild/Moderate Curriculum implementation effort in their schools. For example, at their Adams Middle School, LCCE Mild/Moderate Curriculum competencies have been infused into both general and special education classrooms. General education teachers have found LCCE Mild/Moderate Curriculum competencies/subcompetencies to add variety and enrich the standard curriculum. Many key functional skills (mentioned in an earlier section) are taught through enrichment objectives that are found in the LCCE Mild/Moderate Curriculum program. Special educators have found their students with special learning and/or behavior needs to be more motivated because they can see how the instruction is related to life outside the classroom. For example, a unit entitled "We're Growing a Future" used many of the LCCE Mild Curriculum objectives for this Earth Week activity. The functional personal-social domain is viewed as particularly important for these students with special learning and/or behavior needs to ensure acquisition for use in community living and working as adults. Their LCCE Mild/Moderate Curriculum program is considered to provide a format for providing direction to their students. Parents are receptive to this functional approach because they can understand the need to teach these critical competencies to their children. IEP/ITPs are more meaningful to all concerned. (Information supplied by Dorothy Hanes and Louise Reasoner, regular and special education class teachers, Trenton, Missouri.)

The Missouri School for the Blind in St. Louis has adapted the LCCE Mild/Moderate Curriculum for their students with visual impairments and blindness. They found that the LCCE Mild Curriculum needed only minimal modifications. They correlated the LCCE Mild Curriculum objectives to their existing courses to make the infusion process easier to track when implemented. They also added some additional objectives to meet the needs of their students with special learning and/or behavior needs.

Many other school districts in Missouri (e.g., Booneville, Marshall, Higginsville, Joplin, North Kansas City, Camdenton, Chillicothe, St. Charles, St. Louis, and Hermann) have various degrees of LCCE Mild/Moderate curriculum instruction infused into their programs. In Minnesota, numerous school districts in both urban and rural areas have implemented the LCCE Mild/Moderate Curriculum program at various levels and degrees. Some of these are located in Albany, Brainerd, Crookston, Paynesville, St. Cloud, St. Paul, and many other districts throughout the state.

Taiwan: An International Perspective

Several years ago, Donn Brolin spent considerable time with two Taiwanese professors from the National Changhua University of Education, Dr. Tianway Sheu and Dr. Tair-Jye Chou, who came to the University of Missouri in Columbia to learn the intricacies of the LCCE Mild/Moderate Curriculum system. Afterward, Drs. Sheu and Chou returned to their country to translate much the LCCE Curriculum materials into Chinese in preparation of a substantial implementation effort. The LCCE Mild Curriculum has become quite popular in the special schools of Taiwan, and presently the professors are re-editing the materials to implement the LCCE Moderate Curriculum program for students with more severe cognitive disabilities from 1st to 12th grade. Considerable research activity also has built into their efforts to assess the impact of the approach with Chinese students (Sheu & Chou, personal communication, 1994).

Several other countries have been using the LCCE Mild/Moderate Curriculum program to enhance their functional and transition efforts for students with special learning and/or behavior needs. Israel and Canada have numerous schools that have modified the LCCE Mild/Moderate Curriculum program to be appropriate for their students with special learning and/or behavior needs. At the annual International Council for Exceptional Children conference, the authors have been informed of the use of the LCCE Mild/Moderate Curriculum program. Many Canadian educators have requested LCCE staff to include Canadian currency in the LCCE Curriculum instructional materials.

CHAPTER COMMENTARY

As the examples presented in the preceeding section indicate, the LCCE Mild/Moderate Curriculum is being used at all levels and in many different educational settings. A particular strength of its curriculum model is its applicability for inclusive settings and general education students. This and other curricula such as those identified in Chapter 2 are available to assist school districts in conceptualizing and instituting the necessary functional skills efforts needed for students with special learning and/or behavior needs in their communities.

Functional skills curricula to enhance the career development and transition success for all students, including those requiring special education services, must begin at the elementary level. This is the conclusion reached by most experts in the field. It is not difficult to integrate transition/career education concepts and materials into the ongoing developmental curriculum if educators are trained to do it. In fact, most will endorse this approach at this level. If an appropriate scope and sequence of functional/career education instruction and experiences are implemented into the K–12+ programs of a school district, students with special learning and/or behavior needs will leave the educational system either prepared to function independently and obtain satisfactory employment or prepared to benefit from various postsecondary services opportunities.

The transition/career education approach does not denigrate the need for a solid basic academic and enrichment skills focus to our educational efforts. Rather, it holds the promise for enriching it even more and providing a more functional, realistic, and practical component that will motivate students with special learning and/or behavior needs to see the importance of all subject matter, to attain higher levels of academic achievement, to stay in school, and to attain successful adult outcomes. Educators should be sanguine about the potential that combining conventional methods with a substantive functional skills/career development holds for delivering a complete and relevant educational/transitional program for their students with special learning and/or behavior needs.

ACTIVITIES

1. Based on your understanding of the transition/ career development process and important functional skills needing to be learned, identify the functional/career education objectives/changes that you believe must be instituted at the elementary, middle school/junior high, senior high,

and postsecondary levels for your students with special learning and/or behavior needs to develop an adequate work personality so they have the attitudes, behaviors, and skills needed to succeed after school.

2. Identify how you would counteract the resistances that you would most likely encounter from various groups that are needed to support these transitional efforts.

Educational System
- Resistance to change
- Institutionalized/bureaucratic nature
- Inflexible, rigid policies/acculturation
- Standard programs
- Limited time for staff development
- Many priorities and pressures
- Schedule
- Graduation requirements
- Transportation costs
- Lack of release time for teachers
- Money for staff and other resources
- Time to do everything needed
- Hiring policies
- School philosophy/purpose of education
- Curriculum emphasis (content) and effectiveness
- Scope and sequencing

Educators
- Their professional orientation
- Resistance to change
- Lack of appropriate training and information
- Attitude
- Trying to meet the needs of diverse students
- Overworked
- Little reward or recognition for extra effort
- Lack of trust
- Lack of support
- Fear of appearing incompetent
- Turfsmanship
- Past failures

Parents
- Limited time to participate
- Inability to carry out activities
- Broken homes
- Mistrust of professionals
- Feel education is school's responsibility
- Too many other responsibilities and problems
- Lack of training
- Disinterest
- Hopelessness of future
- Overprotective
- Unrealistic about their child's abilities
- Want his or her child to be educated like everyone else

Agencies
- Professional rivalries
- Turfsmanship
- Theoretical differences
- Administrative barriers
- Too many clients
- Lack of knowledge and training
- Unclear roles and responsibilities
- Past failures
- Unwillingness to change
- Unwillingness to share
- Fear schools/parents will expect impossible
- Limited funds
- Expect schools to do more

Employers
- Misconceptions
- Differences of opinion
- Learning their language
- Understanding the working world
- Unclear of their contribution

Students
- Fear of failure and rejection
- Overprotected
- Pressures from parents and others
- Lack of normal experiences
- Learning characteristics
- Unrealistic expectations
- Decision-making problems
- Limited work experience
- Low expectations
- Academic, rather than functional skills, orientation

CHAPTER 15

Critical Transition Issues and Future Directions

PRELIMINARY QUESTIONS

1. What are some of the major issues related to implementing a career development/functional skills approach for students with special learning and/or behavior needs?
2. What is meant by "old wine in new bottles" relative to new educational concepts or terms?
3. What are some of the problems and needs that impede implementing the transition/career education approach?
4. Why is the educational establishment so difficult to change?
5. Explain the terms *machine bureaucracy, professional bureaucracy,* and *adhocracy* and how they relate to educational change.
6. What is meant by the saying, "The more things change, the more they stay the same!"?
7. What has research uncovered regarding the practice of Individualized Education Program (IEP) development?
8. How can all students be accommodated into the mainstream when it has so many problems handling the diversity it already has?
9. What solutions would you recommend to overcome the many barriers to educational change?
10. What do we know about best practices and the postschool outcome of students with special learning and/or behavior needs undertaking transition programs?

OVERVIEW

Throughout this text we have referred to the fact that important functional curricular changes are difficult to implement because of the numerous forces that can impede all efforts to improve the educational system—the bureaucracy, boards of education, and some administrators, teachers, other school personnel, families, agencies, employers, and even some students with special learning and/or behavior needs themselves.

Almost 10 years has elapsed and even more significant, we have entered into a new millennium since the last edition of this textbook. In that edition, major issues and future directions relative to the transition/career education concept were identified and discussed as we moved toward the twenty-first century. What has been the response by society to what is being advocated in this book—a transition/functional curriculum approach? Are students with special learning and/or behavior needs now acquiring the functional skills needed to make a successful transition from school to post-secondary training and/or working and community living? Has significant change occurred in the past 10 years to improve the transition outcome and quality of life of students in the thousands of school districts throughout this country who present special learning and/or behavior needs?

In this chapter, because there is a need to continue discussion of many of the same issues discussed in the previous edition, some are still being posed. The chapter does not intend to cover all critical issues pertaining to the transitional curriculum needs of students with special learning and/or behavior needs. Rather, it focuses on those related to the topic of this book and assesses the progress since the turn of the century. After the discussion of major issues, some problems and possible solutions to the major issues and problems are presented. The contributions to this final chapter by a close colleague and friend, Dr. Michael Bullis, who has made significant contributions to the development of the transition/career education concept for several decades, is greatly appreciated and valued.

MAJOR CRITICAL TRANSITION ISSUES

Many critical issues inextricably have an impact on innovation changes and implementation efforts in a school district. Inclusion, funding, scheduling, grading, providing sufficient community-based instruction, the awarding of diplomas, and the transformation of special education personnel to a consultative role are examples. Although these are important issues, this section focuses on those that are particularly relevant to the career education

CHAPTER OUTLOOK

Dr. Michael Bullis *is a Professor in Special Education at the University of Oregon's College of Education. Dr. Bullis is a prolific writer and researcher in the fields of Rehabilitation and Special Education.*

Ironically, in thinking about what I should say in this foreword, I found myself reflecting back 20 years to my doctoral training at the University of Oregon, where much of my profesional identity was forged. In that training, two central themes were burned into my cortex through instruction, hard work, and example from the many outstanding professionals with whom I was fortunate to study and know. These themes are as follows.

- *Our field is based in a larger social context that we must understand as those social forces will influence our professional activities to some greater or lesser degree.* In the space of just more than a decade, the term and contemporary usage of "Transition" was coined, computers are as common as cars, our economy has grown unstable, children bring guns to school to shoot other students and teachers, and as I write this our country stands on the precipice of a war in the Middle East. What will these changes mean for our practice and field? Moreover, understanding these forces goes far beyond the limited field of education and the four walls of the school building, extending into the broader realm of social science.
- *We should have a blazing contempt for mediocrity and a healthy skepticism for claims that seem too good to be true.* Our professional activities, in some way, affect the lives of the people with special needs we have chosen to serve and the development of those growing

numbers of young professionals entering our field (well, younger than me, anyway). What we do as educators, researchers, service providers, and policymakers in special education, rehabilitation, and transition is too important to base in prevailing political correctness and the current "intervention of the month." Further, we should be grand in our goals and conservative in our conclusions.

Another idea that I came to appreciate was driven home through the many mind-bending discussions I had with Dr. Philip Browning, then the director of my doctoral training program and now the Chair of Rehabilitation and Special Education at Auburn University. Phil impressed upon me how important it was in building a research agenda to try to anticipate where the field would be 10 years in the future and then to atriculate that vision before others. This idea is fully congruent with my task in this brief narrative.

Now, do I *really* know what the future will bring? If I *really* knew, I would have retired a long time ago, lived wealthy and happy on a tropical island, learned to hit pitch shots that fly impossibly high and land with precision, and tie perfectly colored flies that catch a trout on every cast. Nevertheless, I will try to make some prognostications that make sense to me.

A fact of modern life is that children and adolescents who are of school age have been exposed to an incredible bombardment of information from television, movies, music, and the Internet. Needless to say, not all of this exposure has had a positive influence on the development of adolescents. This exposure, coupled with soaring divorce rates, a decline in the American family's disposable income, and a concomitant explosion in daily living costs, has led to a marked increase of high-risk behaviors exhibited by girls and boys aged 12 to 17 years. Conservative estimates indicate that one out of four adolescents will be, or are, at risk to drop out of school, commit criminal acts, abuse alcohol and/or drugs, or engage in dangerous serial sexual relationships (Donovan & Jessor, 1985; Dryfoos, 1990). Further, among this high-risk group it is probable that a fair number of adolescents do not—for whatever reasons—have a special education label and thus do not receive transition services, despite their clear needs for such instruction (Bullis, Yovanoff, Mueller, & Havel, 2002).

Realistically, no one intervention—however powerful it may be—is likely to be effective with the majority of the young people who may be, or who at least should be (far more than we will admit will drop out of school before receiving transition services) in transition programs. When we approach the challenge of working with today's students, we must remember these facts and that we have access to these young people for only a short time and our interventions are understandably, and unfortunately, short-term as well. A fair portion of our work should, then, be focused on building service networks for these young people that extend beyond the school walls and into the community. Also, given the magnitude of the multiple problems many young people face, we must conceptualize our interventions in terms of months and perhaps years, not in weeks and days.

Today's society has grown much more complex than in previous times—as have family-wage jobs. No longer can an adolescent drop out of school and be reasonably assured of finding a fairly high-paying job that does not require sophisticated academic skills. Those jobs that are available to adolescents without requisite academic skills tend to be dead-end, without hope of earning a reasonable wage and achieving the American Dream. A challenge we must address relates to developing creative ways to teach the skills needed in today's

job market to learners who may have difficulty grasping basic academic concepts.

In a related vein, it is generally acknowledged that competitive work experience is a critical component of transition programs for adolescents with special needs. However, every time I speak in various parts of the country on this topic, someone in the audience never fails to state emphatically that there is no way that his or her administrator will let either them or their students out of school to find community-based work or to work. It seems to me that this fundamental stumbling block must be, and can be, addressed. Moreover, as our economy descends further into the toilet and jobs become more and more scarce, what type of employment opportunities will be available for our students? How can we entice employers to work with our programs and give our kids a chance to work?

Finally, in the 20 years I have worked in our field—in fact, working in our field before it had its current name of Transition—I have grown increasingly discouraged with the lack of science on which to base our practice. As the past Co-Editor of *Career Development for Exceptional Individuals*, an editorial board member on other journals related to our field, and a grant proposal reviewer at the state and national levels, I am concerned about the paucity of research—especially high-quality research, whether it is qualitative or quantitative—that is produced on transition issues. I tell our doctoral students regularly that schools are horrible places to conduct rigorous research as the practical constraints of public education in many ways runs contrary to scientific procedures (e.g., random assignment to treatment or control conditions). These difficulties do not, however, excuse us from the charge to develop and implement creative procedures and ways to study transition practices.

We *must* carefully study much of what we hear others talk about, what is written in journals, and many of the good ideas presented in this book. Once we are sure that an idea(s) in question, in fact, has enough merit to implement with adolescents and young adults with disabilities, we *must* work to streamline those practices into their leanest and most powerful form. I have come to believe that it is a relatively simple thing to create a complicated intervention based on external funds, and with a mass of graduate students and other professionals extraneous to the typical educational setting. True brilliance lays in creating simple, pragmatic, and yet powerful interventions that can be sustained over time without folks such as me.

To end, I want to admit that all I *really* know is that in the transition field there are a lot of good people working as hard as they can to help some of the most vulnerable adolescents in our society to achieve at their maximum potential. Good luck in the years to come—I can't wait to see what type of future you help to create.

References

Bullis, M., Yovanoff, P., Mueller, G., & Havel, E. (2002). Life on the "outs"—Examination of the facility-to-community transition of incarcerated adolescents. *Exceptional Children, 69,* 7–22.

Donovan, J., & Jessor, R. (1985). Structure of problem behavior in adolescence and young adulthood. *Journal of Consulting and Clinical Psychology, 53,* 890–904.

Dryfoos, J. (1990). *Adolescents at risk.* New York: Oxford University Press.

approach advocated in this book. Some of the major transition issues have been identified and discussed by Sitlington, Clark, and Kolstoe (1990) and will be briefly reviewed in this text.

Critical Transition Issues Identified by Sitlington, Clark, and Kolstoe

In their excellent text entitled, *Transition Education and Services for Adolescents with Disabilities* (2000), Sitlington, Clark, and Kolstoe pose four important issues they believe should be addressed in planning for the successful implementation of transitional and functional curriculum programming for students with special learning and/or behavior needs. Each of these is identified next with Sitlington, Clark, and Kolstoe's opinion of each issue.

• *Issue #1: Life-skills education and the inclusive education movement are often seen as two different approaches.* Ensure that all students, including those with special learning and/or behavior needs, are provided an education that prepares them to leave school and participate in post-secondary education and/or employment, and community living while attaining an acceptable quality of life with or without support. More educators today than ever before believe that all students with special learning and/or behavior needs benefit and should participate in general education classrooms if it is determined to be the least restrictive environment (LRE). Thus, there is no difference in practice as long as the LRE is decided upon by the student and her IEP/ITP committtee.

Many students need exposure to life-skills education to permit successful adult adjustment. The LCCE Mild/Moderate Curriculum TAP and/or district's transition program must ensure that all service delivery options include appropriate life-skills instructional activities, including the general education content areas at the secondary level. What is most important is deciding how much life-skills instruction should be based on personalized program development for students with special learning and/or behavior needs. Specifically, the student will direct the IEP/ITP by providing her interests and needs and then participate collaboratively with the team to set appropriate educational/transitional program goals.

• *Issue #2: The assessment of the transition education needs of individuals with disabilities and their involvement in statewide and district-wide assessment programs is often left to chance.* Although these are two separate assessment issues as they pertain to the overall program for students with special learning and/or behavior needs, they do help in the overall planning toward age projections. As provided in IDEA 1997, students along with the IEP/ITP team may decide that participation in the state-wide or district-wide assessments is not appropriate. This does not exempt students from exit exams, as IDEA requires that these students are provided with a more functional transitional assessment prior to leaving school. Life-skills performance portfolios are an example of how many districts are meeting this provision. These students would normally be receiving a high degree of life-skills already. Students with mild learning and/or behavior needs are required to take the tests with or without modifications and accommodations. Many states require students to pass this assessment to receive the general education diploma. Other states have developed an occupational diploma for students who cannot pass this test but complete a functional/vocational curriculum program. Thus, a relationship of these two types of assessment are dependent on the student with special and/or learning needs' personalized program.

- *Issue #3: Minimum competency testing and standards may adversely affect the graduation type of exit document of students with disabilities.* The response in issue #2 addressed the exit document concern. For years, districts have been in a quandary regarding the most normalized approach for indicating completion of the school program. With the advent of the occupational diploma, some districts now offer three options, the regular diploma and a special education completion of the IEP/ITP program as the other traditionally provided exit documents. This issue is more relevant today as IDEA 1997 has promoted inclusion of students with disabilities. The secondary period of education is a critical period for acquiring the functional skills and behaviors needed for successful adult community and vocational adjustment. Every general education and/or special education course these students take at the high school level must enhance their transition development. For most students, this will require certain specialized courses (general or special education) to focus on the functional curriculum areas that will most ap-

propriately prepare them for their successful transition. If districts do not infuse these functional skills into all courses and expect them to meet the same competency standards, the dropout rate will, in our opinion, escalate even more and set back the many gains made by the special education field in the past 30 years. This is not meant to imply that special education students should continue to be segregated, rather that district transition programs must ensure that there is a high correlation between state standards and functional curricula programs (i.e., Clark & Kolstoe, "School-Based Career Development and Transition Education Model," [1990]; Brolin & Loyd, "LCCE Mild/Moderate Curriculum Program," [1997]; Cronin & Patton, "Domains of Adulthood," [1993]). Some districts have correlated their state standards with life-skills curricula goals, thus allowing students with special learning and/or behavior needs to receive competencies that will permit student success on the competency tests, attaining necessary life-skills and to receive the standard diploma. Again, what is most critical is to have the student with special learning and/or behavior needs lead her IEP/ITP committee in developing an appropriate personalized program.

- *Issue #4: Transition education and services are still an add-on in many IEPs.* Although IDEA 1997 mandates that all students with special learning and/or behavior needs age 14 years and older need to address transition interests and needs in the IEP/ITP, many districts are not including appropriate transition goals/objectives. Several explanations for this lack of attention to appropriate IEP/ITP transition goals may be: (1) many districts do not have a scope and sequenced special education curriculum; (2) many districts have an infused/ functional curriculum within the general education curriculum; and (3) the student and her IEP/ITP committee not having functional transition assessment information to assist in developing appropriate transition education and services. We recommend that districts establish transition plans (ITP) to assist them in developing transition education and services. This would help ensure that appropriate transition goals are included in students with special learning and/or behavior needs' IEP/ITPs.

- *Issue #5: Formal training in self-determination is often not provided.* Many students with learning and/or behavior needs leave school without the critical skills to engage in self-determination activities. Self-determination activities include the ability to: manage personal affairs; set and achieve appropriate goals; and regulate behavior independently. Although the importance of providing self-determination instruction has become an ever-increasingly reported component of transition programs for students with special learning and/or behavior needs, many districts have not infused self-determination programs into the general education or special education curricula. An integral part of self-determination is the ability to make good decisions without being coerced by family or other support services. It is our belief that self-determination is one of the most critical skills students with special learning and/or behavior needs should acquire for achieving the successful adult outcomes of attending post-secondary training, gaining and retaining employment, and living in the community with an adequate quality of life. For students with more severe learning and/or behavior needs whose rights have been transferred to an advocacy source, they should be given every opportunity to participate in all decisions regarding their quality of life activities and services.

"Having seen one full cycle of transition interest and having researched previous cycles, I am struck with a gnawing thought that some of the youth of today may be no better off—and possibly less better off—than their counterparts were 15 years ago."

(Szymanski, 1994, p. 402)

Transition Issues Identified in the Previous Edition

In the previous edition of this book, several issues were presented that are critical to the successful im-

plementation of a transition/career education approach that could provide a mechanism for functional skills instruction and transition services. Those that are particularly important today are revisited in the following discussion.

Transition Definitions

Our field is expert in reinventing the wheel and in renaming previous terms and concepts—"old wine in new bottles," so to speak. Over the years, for example, the definitions of several disabilities have been changed, some governmental agencies have changed their names, and several professional organizations have done likewise. Some might wonder if our field suffers from an identity crisis!

Career education was the popular educational reform term during the invigorating decade of the 1970s and into the 1980s. But new federal bureaucrats and politicians establish their own vernacular and abnegate those of their predecessors. Thus, more recent terms such as *transition, self-determination,* and *inclusion* came into vogue and were promoted in the 1990s and into the 2000s. Early in this new century, we will probably need to be prepared to welcome newer buzz words from those who dictate the language and direction of the field educating students with special learning and/or behavior needs.

"The more things change, the more they stay the same!"

(Roessler, Shearin, & Williams, 1993)

Whatever term we use (career education, transition, life skills, functional skills, vocational education, inclusion, quality of life education, self-determination, work-based learning), we are talking essentially, and hopefully, about the same major educational goal, namely, preparing students with special learning and/or behavior needs to successfully live, interact, and work in their community.

The term *transition* reflects this major educational goal because it affirms the commitment to emphasizing preparation for both employment and unpaid productive work activities that one must be able to perform in the home, in community service activities, and in avocational pursuits. Transition/career education reflects this text's educational focus—to help every student with special learning and/or behavior needs acquire a satisfactory career and lifestyle. Unlike the outcome-oriented terms such as quality of life, vocational education, and self-determination, transition/career education is a more specifically focused educational intervention to prepare students with special learning and/or behavior needs for a successful transition, quality of life, and to be self-determined, independent individuals. And, it includes inclusion requiring the active involvement of general educators, not just vocational or special educators.

Transition/career education is generally viewed in one of three ways:

1. As an expansion of vocational education
2. As preparation to function in all adult roles
3. As preparation for all the various career roles, settings, and events in which productive work activity occurs for individuals with special learning and/or behavior needs which helps them to become a totally functioning person.

The latter view was adopted by the Council for Exceptional Children's (CEC), Division of Career Development and Transition which issued a policy paper (Halpern, 1994) with the following life adjustment, work-focused definition of transition education:

Transition refers to a change in status from behaving primarily as a student to assuming emergent adult roles in the community. These roles include employment, participating in post-secondary education, maintaining a home, becoming appropriately involved in the community, and experiencing satisfactory personal and social relationships. The process of enhancing transition involves the participation and coordination of school programs, adult agency services, and natural supports within the community. The foundations for transition should be laid during the elementary and middle school years, guided by the broad concept of career development. Transition planning should begin no later than age 14, and students should be encouraged, to the full extent of their capabilities, to assume a max-

imum amount of responsibility, to the full extent of their capabilities, to assume a maximum amount of responsibility for such planning. (p. 117)

A life-centered, work-oriented view has been adopted by the Life Centered Career Education (LCCE) Mild/Moderate Curriculum because of its focus on preparing students with special learning and/or behavior needs for both the paid and the many unpaid work activities responsible adults must perform in home, civic, and avocational endeavors. An important concept inherent in this view is that, during periods of unemployment, individuals with special learning and/or behavior needs can still feel that they are worthwhile contributors to their family and community by engaging in productive work activities in the home, doing volunteer and other community work, and being involved in hobbies and other productive avocational activities.

The New Millennium of Change. Transition/career education concepts have become embodied in conceptualizations of these current terms—*inclusion, functional skills, life skills,* and *self-determination*—and even the more broadened view of vocational education. Halpern (1993) suggests a term that has been bandied about for many years, "quality of life," as appropriate for a conceptual framework for evaluating transition outcomes and three domains: physical and material well-being, performance of adult roles, and personal fulfillment.

Thanks to the bureaucracy, the field is at no loss for inventing new terms and priorities! What is needed is for educational leaders and decision makers to move up to the next step and provide the field with specific guidelines, directions, and methods for implementing what they profess.

Instructional Delivery

Many issues or questions relate to the instructional delivery of the transition/career education approach. Some of the critical issues are the following:

1. *Should transition/career education be a separate program or infused into the general education curriculum?*

Many educators view transition/career education as a separate course that should be taught for 1 hour each day during students with special learning and/or behavior needs' day. Another more appropriate view of the transition concept is that it should be infused throughout the K-12 curriculum and that all school personnel should modify their course content to incorporate some level of transition/career education. Although it is probably easier to develop a separate course, the most preferable way is the more ubiquitous infusion of its concepts and materials into school, home, and community settings.

2. *What functional/life skills need to be taught?*

This book has provided some direction to this question by presenting several functional curriculums and resources. In the case of the LCCE Mild/Moderate Curriculum, its 22/20 competencies have been adopted by many school districts throughout the country. Some school districts have expanded the list of competencies or subcompetencies, depending on the nature of their students with special learning and/or behavior needs and their own situation. The important point is that most of these functional skills have been identified, and many are already being addressed, to varying degrees, in the general and special education curricula. It is each school district's responsibility to make decisions about how they will meet transition needs. Today, with the grave concern about the many societal problems—crime, violence, drugs, sex education/life-style, sexually transmitted diseases, and acquired immune deficiency syndrome (AIDS)—these topics will need even greater attention this century than in the past.

3. *How much of the curriculum will need to be devoted to functional life skills?*

Considerable time will need to be allocated to teaching these functional skills if students with special learning and/or behavior needs are to really learn and retain them. This will be no easy task with the many pressures to meet so many educational needs in today's society. To adopt the transition/career education approach, functional skills instruction needs to be infused into all existing content courses, home assignments, and community settings. Transition/career education will need to be a very significant and pervasive part of what is taught. The transition/career education approach will enhance the assimilation and achievement of all students with special learning and/or behavior needs in inclusion classes because its instruction is related to the real world and practical experiences. It is important to remember that much of what is being promoted as necessary for students with special learning and/or behavior needs' transition/career development is already being taught to varying degrees.

Can functional skills instruction be adequately provided only in inclusive settings?

4. *Does transition/career education aid or hinder inclusion efforts?*

Transition/career education can propitiously enhance the integration of students with special learning and/or behavior needs into general education classes. Most students with special learning and/or behavior needs learn best when the instruction is related to the real world and there are hands-on experiences. An important selling point to general educators is that transition/career education can be integrated into all content area classes and for all students. Thus, transition/career education is one vehicle for successful inclusion. Although inclusion is very important, a variety of out-of-school ecological environments will still be needed to provide students with all of the instruction and experiences needed for adult adjustment preparation.

5. *What should be done with current courses, materials, and teaching approaches?*

Transition/career education requires all educators to take a hard look at what they are doing and how their content area courses can be modified, materials added or eliminated, and some other teaching methods added to make them more functional. However, it does not call for a wholesale abandonment of present practices. Rather, transition/career education adds greater relevance to the basic skills curriculum and requires a more democratic environment. Transition/career education is not the only education students with special learning and/or behavior needs should receive; however, it should be a very significant component of the entire basic curriculum. School districts must develop more systematic and comprehensive transition action plans (TAP) so that all content area courses, materials, and instruction can be presented in an effective scope and sequence.

The New Millennium of Change—Whose Responsibility?   Evidence indicates that many general educators are changing standard teaching practices to inject more interesting and real-life content and activities into their courses, including more community-based experiences. For example, all four national finalists for the Teacher of the Year award interviewed on one of the national news telecasts in January 1994 cited the incorporation of what we have described as transition/career education as the highlight of their innovative practice, when asked why they thought they were nominated for the award. Other recent TV programs and magazine articles have cited transition/career education activities that are happening in many school districts as innovative school programs and practices in this country. The transition/career education approach has become a highly desirable practice in many of the more outstanding schools that have parted from the standard method of educating children with special learning and/or behavior needs. The recently passed School-to-Work Opportunities Act is a good example of the impact of the transition/career education approach.

"How can inclusion so dramatically incorporate an increase in diversity when it has such obvious difficulty accommodating the student diversity it already has?"

(Fuchs & Fuchs, 1994, p. 302)

Although many general educators still view transition/career education as a separate course, progressive educators have infused or integrated its concepts and materials into their academic-oriented curriculum. There still needs to be a greater emphasis to view transition/career education as an integrated component within the basic skills curriculum and its courses. There has been some positive movement in this direction in the past 35 years, but more work needs to be done.

The increased transition movement toward inclusion will still require an appropriate program of services for students with special learning and/or behavior needs. But, as Fuchs and Fuchs (1994)

noted, there are real concerns about how this can be done. The transition/career education approach is one vehicle for meeting this need. Thus, transition/career education should be viewed as one of the most important contributors to the inclusion effort.

Transition/Career Education Responsibility

Who is responsible for teaching and promoting transition/career education? The transition/career education approach and the IEP and Individualized Transition Plan (ITP) clearly specify a shared responsibility for the student with special learning and/or behavior needs' education. With the continually changing role of the special educator as a resource and support specialist, more attention can be directed to reliable alliances (i.e., family, employer, agency, and community-based experiences) to enhance the shared responsibility and needs of students with special learning and/or behavior needs. As more students with special learning and/or behavior needs are served in the general education classroom, special educators can enrich the student's transitional educational experience by helping the general education teachers institute transition/career education concepts and materials and community resources that will benefit all other class members.

"What kind of relationship do we want teachers to have with each other—isolationist and territorial or collaborative?"

(F. Smith, 1989, p. 358)

Both general and special education teachers are responsible for this transition effort. But unfortunately, teacher collaboration is not a common practice. In most schools, all general and special education teachers work alone, planning and preparing their lessons and materials alone, struggling to solve their instructional, curricular, and management problems (Inger, 1993). If real transitional education progress is to occur, it is obvious that a collaborative atmosphere must be established.

A transition curriculum mapping approach, using a school's transition specialist and curriculum team and/or other personnel, is one method of determining who, where, and when the various functional skills can be taught. This functional approach does require, as described earlier, a collaborative effort between school personnel and the student's family, community resources, and various employers in contributing to the students' learning the functional skills.

The New Millennium of Change—Reliable Alliances/Partnerships. Many general education teachers still do not seem to view it as their responsibility to meet the transition/career development needs of their students with special learning and/or behavior needs. Although this attitude should change, teacher preservice and inservice institutions are not encouraging general education teachers to engage in this needed transformation. In numerous school districts, however, substantial collegial relationships are developing. The emergence of collaborative teams, co-teaching, and the use of cooperative learning and community-based instruction strategies are starting to overcome these barriers. In our experience, if general education teachers understand the importance of the student with special learning and/or behavior needs' being in her class and has the support from special education to provide appropriate instruction, integration will become more successful and a reality. But, if the student with special learning and/or behavior needs is placed into general education without substantive and meaningful goals, little success will be experienced by the student with special learning and/or behavior needs, the general education teacher, and her students. *Transition/career education, especially for students with special learning needs, makes sense to most general education teachers because they can see the realistic goals that are being set for each student even those with special learning and/or behavior needs.* And, in the process, other students in the class also benefit. With the movement toward a more unified educational system, rather than the two disengaged systems of the past, the transition/career education approach offers a vehicle for such an integrated effort.

Reliable Alliances/Partnerships

How can parents/family members, employers, and agencies be more involved in the transition experience? This question has plagued all general and spe-

cial educators for the last century. Although some parents/family members will never cooperate with the school, many others, when approached properly, understand the goals of the transitional educational efforts for their child with special learning and/or behavior needs and how they can participate. Community employers are recognizing more than ever their responsibility to schools. But they must be first approached with benefits to the students with special learning and behavior needs and, like the parents, must understand the overall goals of the educational program for the students and how they fit in. The involvement of various community agencies is also important. However, schools must realize these agencies have limited funds, personnel, and resources and often heavy caseloads. Thus, they expect the school to provide the students with substantial preparation for personal independence and employment if they are to help those who will need further assistance and training after leaving the educational system.

The New Millennium of Change—Personnel Preparation. Substantial progress has been made in developing important partnerships between schools and their community in many school districts throughout the country. As noted in earlier chapters, this is particularly true with the business community, although not as remarkably in the case of the education sector. The dramatic increase in the involvement of business and industry with school personnel in recent years is a very encouraging development. In the case of agency involvement, Szymanski (1994) warns that the requirement in the Individuals with Disabilities Education Act (IDEA) of 1997 for multiagency involvement in planning and services can serve as both a blessing and a curse. Although there is a greater likelihood students with special learning and/or behavior needs will not fall through the cracks as frequently, she cautions that these requirements may threaten to decrease family and individual students with special learning and/or behavior needs' control of the transition process.

The experts have written much about this topic, and considerable progress is still needed. The supported employment movement has perhaps made the most significant progress in forming close reliable alliances with the business community. However, closer agency and family partnerships still need considerable improvement. School personnel can do much to encourage the establishment of reliable alliances with students with special learning and/or behavior needs and their advocates.

Personnel Preparation

Previous editions of this book recommended colleges and universities to teach transition/career education concepts to all types of educators. We also asked what constitutes an effective delivery system, how it would be carried out, and who would do the transition training. Because LEA staff development is so critical to make significant changes, we suggested that local school districts take the initiative to train their own staff to implement transition programming. And, we recommended that state and local administrators needed to convince university teacher trainers to incorporate transition training in their personnel preparation programs.

The New Millennium of Change.   Some transition progress has been made, but universities are really slow to change. Some university educators, most notably those belonging to the CEC Division on Career Development and Transition (DCDT), are teaching transition/career education concepts and materials. Other educators, mainly those with vocational education backgrounds, are promoting vocational education concepts and materials relative to transition. There is no uniform consensus among university personnel as to the best specific approach; therefore, they teach what they want to teach. In many cases, this is similar to the transition/career education approach advocated in this textbook. One example of a university that is responding to the need is Auburn University, which has initiated a secondary special education teacher training program that incorporates many of the major components of transition/career education and transition: functional assessment and curricula, vocational and community preparation, self-determination and family involvement, and interagency collaboration (Browning & Dunn, 1994).

There still seems to be considerable reluctance by school districts to train their staff to use university personnel to provide in-service training on transition/career education. As noted in Chapter 3, an in-service/staff development training package with videotapes is available to school districts that want to train their own personnel on the LCCE Mild/Moderate Curriculum. Funds for the development of these products were provided by the U.S. Office of Special Education Programs (OSEP), Division of Personnel Preparation, which has assumed an important role in promoting the initiation of both in-service and preservice training programs to prepare various types of professionals for transition programs. The agency has distributed funds for special projects and university teacher training programs to several universities committed to training their students in the transition area.

SOME PROBLEMS AND NEEDS

This section addresses some of the problems and needs that are important to implementing the transition/career education/functional life-skills approach. Undoubtedly, many other problems exist and could be cited. Described next are some of those that are especially important to the focus of this book.

Everyone is for change—if they don't have to do it!

Attitudinal Barriers

What is the greatest obstacle to implementing the transition/career education approach advocated in this book? The answer is, unfortunately, attitudes. Everyone is for change, as long as they are the ones who don't need to change. Remember the old adage, "We have met the enemy and they are . . . us"? This continues to be the greatest barrier to meeting the transition/career development/life-skills needs of the students in American schools who will not go on to college to become atomic scientists, physicians, lawyers, teachers, CEOs, and the like. It is evident to almost everyone that these students with special learning and/or behavior needs should have a practical, functionally oriented curriculum approach so they learn the skills and behaviors to be successfully employed and perform the activities of daily living that will allow them to manage their own personal affairs and have meaningful relationships. Some teachers must abandon the fantasy that job satisfaction comes only by working with the brighter students in the academic and enrichment areas.

The attitudes of and legendary lack of cooperation among many professional disciplines and agencies also present a serious problem to transition efforts by the schools. Despite the 1990 mandates that many of these agencies must interface and work with their local school districts, many shirk their responsibility to the school, which results in ineffective cooperative arrangements. Common among some caseworkers are the attitude that it is the school's responsibility to prepare the student with special learning and/or behavior needs until graduation or dropout time and the complaint that they already have too many clients to serve. Many community agencies even refuse to cooperate with each other. Too many seem more ready to defend their existence and protect their reputation rather than reflect concern for the people they serve.

Some postsecondary agencies that should provide education and training services refuse to accommodate persons with disabilities, as the law mandates, and exclude them as "ineligible" for their services without due justification. There continues to be a need to expose and monitor those community agencies that are uncooperative and that fail to provide the services they are responsible for in meeting the needs of the student with special learning and/or behavior needs. Thankfully, there are many outstanding and committed agencies and caseworkers who have provided invaluable assistance and on whom the schools can depend.

The Educational Establishment

It is a well-known fact that American public schools, with a few exceptions, are notorious for their ability to resist change and innovation. Too many continue to perpetuate the mystique that basic academic skills instruction should be the primary criteria of a mean-

ingful education and that all students with special learning and/or behavior needs will miraculously be transformed into successfully functioning citizens and employees of their community. And, as Mellard and Clark found in their National Study of High School Programs for Handicapped Youth in Transition (1992), too many directors of special education and superintendents give first priority to their school's organization and administration, not the important elements of a quality program.

Despite all the hue and cry for reform, we are still faced with the tremendous challenge of changing the establishment.

In his thought-provoking book entitled *Behind Special Education* (1991), Skrtic paints a dismal picture of the rigid structure existing in American schools and in special education itself. Dr. Skrtic introduces two terms that he says are important for understanding the structure and functioning of school organizations, *machine bureaucracy* and *professional bureaucracy*, and a third term *advocacy*, which is important to understanding special education and educational restructuring. Workers in a machine bureaucracy are tightly coupled links in a chain, each doing one part of a job. Workers in a professional bureaucracy are loosely coupled, doing their own thing such as teaching. Schools are conceptualized, managed, and governed like machine bureaucracies, forcing teachers and other professionals to function in an environment that is structurally nonadaptable at the classroom level and to offer standard programs, which many students with special learning and/or behavior needs (including disabilities) simply cannot fit into successfully.

The adhocracy, according to Skrtic (1991), is premised on the principle of innovation, that is, problem-solving, rather than standardization. Adhocracy uses creative effort to find novel solutions. Skrtic believes that special education itself is not a rationally conceived and coordinated system of services because it is uncoupled from the basic operation of the school, as well as from other transition needs programs. He notes that a basic problem with the special education legislation is that it attempts to force an adhocratic value orientation (i.e., engaging in creative effort to find a novel solution) on a professional bureaucracy by treating it as if it were a machine bureaucracy. (p. 184)

[In the process] schools appear to be complying with its procedural requirements because of the adoption of practices that, although they may be well intended and in some respects actually may result in positive outcomes, serve largely to symbolize (e.g., IEPs and resource rooms) and ceremonialize (e.g., IEP staffings and mainstreaming) compliance with the letter of the law rather than conformance with its spirit. (p. 188)

Skrtic's (1991) analysis of the educational system's bureaucracy and why we have such a difficult time meeting students' transition needs is an important contribution and insight to those who are attempting implementation efforts. We must understand the system in which we are operating and its suppressing factors to best make the changes possible. It is difficult to do justice to Skrtic's fine presentation on the topic; therefore, interested readers should secure his publication for a more accurate, in-depth understanding of his analysis of this problem.

Societal Adjustment Barriers

The follow-up data revealing the high rate of dropouts, unemployment, social and emotional deficiencies, and family problems that students with special learning and behavior needs encounter in their school and postschool lives has been available for years. Researchers and experts in the transition field have been repeating in the literature what has been known and persisted for many decades—simply, that life after school for most students with special learning and/or behavior needs is usually a disaster. And, although some school districts have concerned and committed personnel who want to change, they are often outnumbered by those who do not. Consequently, nothing changes regarding transition changes. This is a very discouraging dilemma because the losers in the process are the students with special learning and/or behavior needs, the family, and society.

The educational system, its boards of education, and its educators cannot be completely blamed as the only culprits to instituting a more mechanical approach. Resistance also is mounted by many parents, agencies, employers, and the students with special learning and behavior needs themselves who also have the primary stake in what is offered in the school's curriculum. In Chapter 14, many of the challenges that must be faced in making the necessary changes were identified and discussed.

Schools need an action plan to begin the change process.

A change to a more functional curriculum approach, for all students, including those with special learning and/or behavior needs, will only occur when the major stakeholders in a community's educational system decide that the major purpose of their efforts is to prepare their students with special learning and/or behavior needs for successful community and adult functioning and back it up with a definitive plan of action (such as the one presented in the previous chapter) that will institute a transition/career development curriculum that will realistically lead to this goal. Such a functional curriculum must be developed by an influential group such as a district-wide curriculum committee or Transition Action Plan (TAP) with substantial and meaningful input from various community representatives, parents, and students. The school district will need either to begin from scratch to design such a transition system or to secure one, such as the LCCE Mild/Moderate Curriculum, that is already available and can be adapted and modified for its purposes.

The preceding discussion is intended to convey that changing curriculum is not an easy matter; in fact, it is a very complex phenomenon that will not occur serendipitously.

The Individualized Education Plan

The IEP is the means by which each student is supposed to be ensured a personalized appropriate education. It is a legal mechanism with specific content requirements, designated developers, and as discussed previously, it must now include transition services that will enable students with disabilities to better ensure their future adult adjustment needs, that is, integrated employment, vocational training, postsecondary education, adult service linkages, independent living, and community participation (NICHCY, 1993; Wehman, 1992). However, in too many instances, IEP/ITPs are not being developed and carried out as intended by the federal legislation (Smith, 1990). Roessler, Shearin, and Williams (1993) identified several serious problems based on their literature review of the practice of IEP/ITP development:

- Student assessments either fail to identify students with special learning and/or learning needs or, if they do, assessments are too infrequently the basis for goals in the IEP/ITP.
- IEP/ITPs do not reflect input from a variety of perspectives (multiple disciplines) regarding the students with special learning and behavior needs.
- Parents/family members are not involved in the IEP/ITP process.
- IEP/ITPs have serious procedural deficiencies.
- IEP/ITPs reflect a narrow range of goals and subobjectives that rarely include plans for achieving adult outcomes.

Regarding the latter problem, Roessler et al. (1993) noted a study by Lynch and Beare (1990), which found only 4% of IEP/ITP objectives to be what can be considered functional skills (domestic, community, hygiene, recreation/leisure, and vocational), whereas 86% of the objectives were academic and behavioral management goals. Other studies (e.g., Epstein, Patton, Polloway, & Foley, 1992) have reported similar results. This again reveals the critical need to change policies and practices if students with special learning and/or behavior needs are to gain the behaviors and skills needed for successful adult functioning. Otherwise, as the authors note, "The more things change, the more they stay the same!"

Most IEPs do not contain functional skills/career education objectives for transition planning and services.

The fact that most IEP/ITPs do not contain functional skills/career education objectives for transition planning and services is a serious indictment on the current educational system. Most schools are not responding to the requirements of the federal (IDEA 1997) and state laws, the competency needs of students with special learning and behavior needs, and—what is considered critical by many parent groups, organizations, and leaders in the field—the instructional needs that must be provided in the learning environments. Why is this not being monitored appropriately by state educational agencies and those responsible for ensuring these students with special learning and behavior needs an appropriate education as mandated by our federal and state laws?

Personnel Preparation Barriers

Most teacher training programs have been unresponsive to the transition/career education/functional skill area. In many institutions of higher education, one faculty member may be given this responsibility, while the remainder teach traditional academic, disability, and behavioral courses to perpetuate the conventional, categorical approach. In several instances, little interface with the general education program is maintained, despite the current thrust toward inclusive education for students with disabilities. Local and state educational agencies will need to work more closely with institutions of higher education if the approach advocated in this book is to be achieved. Teachers need to be oriented and trained in the transition/career education/functional skill area during their preservice education if they are expected to be receptive and feel knowledgeable enough to institute the approach in their courses later. This will not require an unreasonable amount of time and energy. There is no curricular reason why this not occurring in teacher preparation programs. All teacher education programs should include a transition program component in individual course or infused into the entire course content.

FUTURE DIRECTIONS

One should probably never be so presumptuous (or preposterous) as to think that we have all the answers to the age-old problem of making changes in our educational system. At the same time, one who is advocating such a change must be able to provide some suggestions for future directions to those who intend to engage in this frustrating but challenging and rewarding venture. If so, the following major recommendations are presented by us to help provide future directions toward solving transition issues and problems presented in general.

Start with the Top Administrators

Administrators at the state and local level have been employed to develop and ensure that the highest quality and most relevant educational/transitional services are made available to students with special learning and/or behavior needs under their jurisdiction. Most school administrators are committed to this goal. Those who are not need to be exposed and replaced by competent, committed professionals who will work diligently with all school staff to make the changes that are necessary for the benefit of the students with special learning and behavior needs.

Transition specialists and others have the responsibility to convey to administration the needs of their students with special learning and/or behavior needs to help plan for their transition resolution. This will be a challenge because as Skrtic (1991) has noted,

> Professional behavior in schools is governed more by institutionalized, cultural norms than it is by rational, knowledge-based actions designed to improve instructional effectiveness. Things are done in certain ways simply because they have always been done that way. . . . [S]tandard programs are passed on from one generation of teachers to another within an institutionalized context . . . [and] students whose needs fall

outside of the standard programs must be forced into them, or out of the classroom—a situation compounded by the rational-technical approach to school management. (1991, pp. 176, 178)

A more proactive stance by laypeople and professionals who want to change the transition system must be undertaken in the future. *Parents who are movers and shakers should be used by educators to convince administrators to change policies and practices.* Administrators are more likely to be responsive to angry (but reasonable) parents of students than their own personnel. Teachers must not be reluctant to involve them in the transition change process when a mountain needs to be moved.

Figure 15.1 contains suggestions offered a few years ago to educational leaders as important actions for state and local educational agencies to adopt in ensuring a meaningful transition/career development effort in their states and local communities. These actions are as important today as they were yesterday. Thus, they are presented to help readers make the changes advocated in this book.

Adopt a Comprehensive Functional Curriculum Model

Schools across the country need to come to grips with how they can offer their students who have a special learning and/or behavior need a functional skills/career development curriculum and how it can be infused into the school's ongoing basic skills curriculum. Too many schools interpret the transition mandate as primarily an arrangement of services from other agencies and fail to recognize its functional skills/career development curriculum requirements.

Comprehensive functional skill curricula that are built on a solid theoretical basis and that have been field tested regarding the utility of their conceptual framework and curriculum materials are badly needed in school districts. A logical functional scope and sequence must be established so teachers at the middle school/junior high levels know what transitional/career development experiences and instruction their students received earlier to avoid duplication. Then,

The State Education Agency

1. Identify transition as a priority in state plan.
2. Clarify the concept of transition in position paper and/or state guide that promotes a functional curriculum.
3. Designate a state transition coordinator.
4. In-service state staff on transition so they can provide proper guidance to LEAs.
5. Provide enough monies for LEAs to devise programs and train staff.
6. Develop opperational interagency linkages.
7. Promote transition in university training programs and make available to provide technical assistance.
8. Emphasize the need for substantial/meaningful transition objectives in the IEP.
9. Clarify the role of special education teachers in LEA.
10. Conduct informative follow-up studies to discern program needs for transition leading to curriculum.
11. Devise meaningful methods for encouraging parent involvement.
12. Devise means by which meaningful partnerships with business and industry can be instituted in LEAs.
13. Provide a hotline/information center for LEAs.
14. Provide continuing technical assistance and funding to LEAs that implement meaningful transition programs.
15. Recognize LEAs that develop effective transition programs—model schools.
16. Provide direction to LEAs on how community-based instruction, including transportation/scheduling issues can be managed.

The Local Education Agency

1. Designate transition coordinators in schools.
2. Develop transition teams.
3. Clarify roles including resource teaching.
4. Provide funds for staff development training.
5. Provide time for developing the program.
6. Give relief from other duties.
7. Provide personnel with enough information.
8. Give staff opportunity to decide to do transition.
9. Clarify the purpose of education-expected outcomes.
10. Identify a functional curriculum/framework on which they can build a comprehensive transition program.
11. Decide on a definition/conceptualization of transition—narrow or comprehensive?
12. Develop meaningful partners and support from parents and employers.
13. Develop K-12 scope and sequence for transitional efforts.
14. Develop meaningful interagency relationships.
15. Provide rewards and incentives to implementors.
16. Don't be seen as only a special education initiative.

FIGURE 15.1   Transition: What is education's role?

Note: From *Life Centered Career Education: Trainer's Manual and Professional Development Activity Book* (3rd ed., p. 294) by D. E. Brolin, 1993, Arlington, VA: The Council for Exceptional Children. Copyright 1993 by The Council for Exceptional Children. Reprinted by permission.

they can build on prior learning to enhance the students' transition/career development and prepare them for a high school level program.

Inclusive education advocates generally support a process approach rather than the conventional basic skills curriculum and its predefined knowledge-base focus. One of the problems with the basic skills curriculum is that teachers feel obligated to teach it, and the students with special learning and behavior needs must learn it. However, when including students, general education teachers are presented with a diversity of students who require a different set of activities and materials. Inclusion therefore requires greater transition planning and effort among general and special education teachers and in the process segregates the students within the mainstream and reduces social interaction (Fuchs & Fuchs, 1994).

> Curriculum and instruction are the foundation of restructuring education. Highly focused academic curricula with objectives and attainment targets tied to specific grade levels are not forgiving of students who may learn at a different pace or may learn differently. Inflexible instructional approaches wrongly assume that all students can be successful in one approach. Schools or school districts are therefore faced with making decisions regarding how the diverse learners can be best taught, while maintaining high expectations for students within a balanced curriculum. (McLaughlin & Warren, 1992, p. 59)

The options, as these writers point out, are either a unified curriculum or separate or alternative curricula. For some students, this may be a separate alternative/functional curriculum, but for most students, this should be a parallel curricular approach in which a systematic modification of the regular curricula is conducted so the students with special learning and/or behavior needs can be guided by the same personalized transition learning outcomes that have been identified by the state or local district for all students.

Although the inclusion advocates must be commended for their deep commitment and concern about the placement of students with disabilities into general education, the total educational needs of these students with special learning and/or behavior needs must be considered. Unless dramatic changes occur in the general education curriculum, many important career development/functional skills instructional needs and experiences will never be provided, and continued dropouts and failure will result. Future curricular efforts must be directed to a total functional educational effort rather than primarily an academic placement focus.

Educational reform approaches such as the LCCE Mild/Moderate Curriculum, the Clark-Kolstoe model, the Dever model, the Cronin-Patton Top Down model, and 20/20 Analysis (Reynolds et al., 1993), which presents a noncategorical alternative to traditional approaches of educating students with special learning and/or behavior needs, can be used to deliver a comprehensive functional skills curriculum. In the process, students with special learning and/or behavior needs should receive the personalized attention they require for learning and a greater emphasis on learning the actual, real-life skills needed to function as a productive citizen of their community.

Establish an Accountability System

The abysmal results of the transition follow-up studies on the adult adjustment of former students receiving special education services have been mentioned several times throughout this book. The statistics never seem to change yet the educational/transitional process goes on in practically the same manner, despite the constant rhetoric for transition reform and change. Well-designed follow-up studies of former students are important in identifying curriculum deficiencies so the need for functional curriculum changes are substantiated and accepted by the educational community. But, as J. R. Johnson and Rusch have found in their review of transition research, "little empirical evidence exists to support relationships between identified best-practices and post-school outcomes" (1993, p. 13).

Several researchers have noted that most of the accountability by schools has been in relation to compliance with and responding to the federal regulations and not with program content, quality, effectiveness, and certain service-delivery costs (D. R. Johnson et al., 1993; Mellard & Clark, 1992; Skrtic, 1991). Management and accountability systems such as the one described by D. R. Johnson et al. (1993), the Transition Information and Planning System (TIPS), are important for gathering in-school follow-along and postschool follow-up data on each student for better transition program planning. Such data can be analyzed in relation to the school services received, student and family characteristics, student achievement, community contextual factors, and later-life outcomes (D. R. Johnson et al., 1993).

In the near future, much more accountability of the transitional system will be required. Two efforts that are underway to help school districts implement more functional skill-oriented curricula are the work of Halpern and colleagues, who have developed a Community Transition Team Model (CTTM) and a project by The National Center on Educational Outcomes (NCEO) at the University of Minnesota. The Oregon CTTM is a systems change approach to improving secondary special education and transition programs at the local community level (Halpern, Benz, & Lindstrom, 1991). Several materials and a computerized management system have been developed to assist in the implementation of the model. The NCEO project staff are working with state departments of education, national policy-making groups, and others to develop indicators of educational outcomes of students (Ysseldyke, Thurlow, & Gilman, 1993). A conceptual model of domains and outcomes has been devised that contains many of the competencies similar to those in the LCCE Mild/Moderate Curriculum model with the exception of occupational skills, which does not appear to be addressed.

It is surprising that school districts conduct so little follow-up transition activity of their former students with special learning and behavior needs. It is almost as if they don't want to find out what has happened to their former students! Many special educators, at the high school level, often know their students' outcome because they informally keep tabs on them, especially in small communities. However,

an organized data collection system as recommended by Johnson and colleagues is practically nonexistent in the majority of schools. Again, those responsible for this lackadaisical effort should be admonished.

Improve the IEP/ITP Content

Earlier in this chapter, the problems that Roessler and his colleagues (1993) found in their study of IEPs/ITPs were reported. They further noted that assessments based on a transition/career education curriculum facilitate the inclusion of a greater variety of goals and objectives in the IEP/ITP. By using the LCCE Mild Knowledge and Performance Batteries and the LCCE Moderate PKBs and PABs, they believe the team can better select instructional goals that will better ensure the students with special learning and behavior needs' preparation for transition services and adult roles.

A renewed effort to ensure that IEPs/ITPs contain a more substantive functional skills instructional component will be instituted in the near future. If the transition/career education approach to enhance functional skills instruction and transition services is to occur meaningfully, considerable changes in the current IEP content must be initiated. Several schools are now required to write ITPs, which is one step in the right direction.

One of the things that teachers can do to improve the content of the IEP/ITPs is to develop instructional goals and objectives that will achieve the following:

- Help develop the work personality.
- Promote self-awareness and positive self-concepts.
- Stress independence and self-determination.
- Raise expectations.
- Use young adult projection
- Develop reliable alliances/partnerships
- Promote educational activities in the home and community.
- Relate the labor market needs.
- Use more community resources.
- Increase the amount of career education activities.
- Use more cooperative learning.

- Incorporate ongoing career assessment with instruction.
- Keep in mind the purpose of education.

In Chapter 7, a method for implementing a substantive IEP/ITP approach using the LCCE Mild/Moderate Curriculum framework was presented. Many schools have recognized the usefulness of the LCCE Mild/Moderate Curriulum competency-based approach to the TAP mandate and have used the competencies and subcompetencies as core elements of their efforts. Several others have used the LCCE Mild/Moderate Curriculum approach as their standards based program.

CHAPTER COMMENTARY

Without question, this is a propitious time to implement what is being advocated in this book—a transition/career education/functional skills approach that will better equip students in American schools to make a successful transition from school to adult functioning. Unlike those students who are college bound, most students with special learning and/or behavior needs will not receive the postsecondary education that will ultimately lead them to obtain a well-paying job, acquire acceptable social skills and friendships, and become productive members of their home and community. For too many, their postsecondary education may be acquired in rehabilitation or correctional programs. Thus, it is more critical than ever for elementary and secondary schools to assume greater transition responsibility for providing both a solid basic academic and a functional skills education for students with special learning and behavior needs to enhance their chances for employment and productive living opportunities.

Individuals with special learning and/or behavior needs or those who have disabilities or who are disadvantaged are a greatly underused resource in our society because the educational system, for the most part, has not prepared them to develop and realize their potentials. The result is that the majority end up getting, at best, the secondary labor market jobs that are low paying and lead nowhere. In addition, a disproportionate number of these students with special learning and/or behavior needs get in trouble with the law, end up on welfare, or experience other unfortunate life circumstances. These tragedies do not have to happen, at least for the vast majority.

The injection of a substantial transition/career education/functional skills curricular approach in the kindergarten-to-postsecondary basic education curriculum will help to significantly correct the deficiencies in those school districts that have not adequately restructured their programs. Although transition/career education is certainly not a panacea by itself, it is one important future direction that must be earnestly undertaken in our current educational restructuring that is underway in the 2000s.

Let's reverse the disheartening adage noted earlier by Roessler and his associates (1993), "the more things change, the more they stay the same." Let's finally institute the significant changes that have been identified for years as critically needed for all students with special learning and/or behavior needs. We have the methods and the materials to help almost every student to become a worthwhile, self-determined, productive, and independent functioning individual who can have a decent quality of life. *Now, we must meet this challenge rather than talk about it.* Our students are depending on us. It is now up to YOU.

ACTIVITIES

1. Develop a transition action plan (TAP) to present to your administration that will provide the impetus for starting the process of implementing a substantial career education curricular approach in your district.
2. Besides the content contained in your transition action plan (TAP), prepare a compelling presentation to your administration that will convince them to strongly support the action plan you propose. Good luck! (*Note:* An action plan outline is presented in Appendix H.)

Appendix A

Cooperative Agreement Between the Department of Education and the Division of Rehabilitation Services, State of West Virginia

●●●

PREAMBLE

This agreement is designed to improve the cooperative and collaborative efforts between the Department of Education (hereinafter "Education") and the Division of Rehabilitation Services (hereinafter "Rehabilitation"), for the purpose of more effective and efficient service delivery to individuals with disabilities of our state. This cooperative agreement shall ensure that each student with disabilities in the state who needs special education, vocational education, and/or vocational rehabilitation services is promptly identified, and the appropriate services including transition services and modifications, when necessary, are made available to the individual. As used in this document, Education refers specifically to vocational education and special education programs.

DETERMINATION OF AGENCY RESPONSIBILITY

The education and vocational training of students ages 3 to 21 who have not graduated and who have

been identified as disabled are the responsibility of Education. Special education programs shall continue to be provided to those students who are at least 21 years old and receiving special education services prior to September 1, 1991, until the end of the school year in which they became 23 years of age. Students ages 14 to 21 who have not graduated and who desire vocational training will have equal access to secondary vocational training, provided reasonable accommodation or modification can be made. In addition, the training must be: (1) realistic in light of actual or anticipated opportunities for gainful employment or supported employment; and, (2) must be suited to the individual's needs, interest, and ability to benefit from such training.

Individuals with disabilities shall have equal access to services that are normally provided by public schools for non-disabled individuals (e.g., adult education or continuing education programs), provided that reasonable accommodation or modification can be made. The adult training programs must be realistic in light of actual or anticipated opportunities for gainful or supported employment and suited to the individual's needs, interests, and ability to benefit from such training.

For students ages 16 to 21 who have left school by way of graduation and/or have exited the school sys-

Note. From *TRIAD Telecommunications Project: Transition Manual* by I. D. Cook and M. T. Urbanic, 1990, Institute: West Virginia Graduate College. Copyright 1990 by West Virginia Graduate College. Adapted by permission.

tem, the responsibility of vocational services rests with Rehabilitation.

Rehabilitation will provide services that are legally the responsibility of Rehabilitation for those students who are approaching or are of working age and are determined by Rehabilitation to be eligible for services.

Eligibility for Rehabilitation services is based on:

1. The documented presence of a physical or mental disability, which for the individual constitutes or results in a substantial handicap to employment; and,
2. A reasonable expectation that rehabilitation services can benefit the individual in terms of employability.

Each agency will cooperate to provide referral, support, and assistance to the agency with responsibility for services. Each agency will participate in the planning of transition services for individuals with disabilities.

STUDENT/CLIENT REFERRAL

The agency first making contact with the individual applicant assumes responsibility to initiate procedures, provide appropriate services, or make referral to the other agency.

INDIVIDUAL EDUCATION PROGRAM/ INDIVIDUALIZED WRITTEN REHABILITATION PROGRAM

Education is responsible for providing special education and related services appropriate for each eligible student enrolled in the school system. At the earliest time that a student is identified at an age potentially

eligible for rehabilitation services, it is important that Education and Rehabilitation work together on determining what, when, and how services are to be provided. At the time of the development of the Four Year Education Plan, students covered by Section 504 can be identified and referred for appropriate services. Since the Individualized Education Program (IEP), which focuses on educational goals, and the Individual Written Rehabilitation Program (IWRP), which focuses on vocational goals, have components in common, it is agreed that an essential step for cooperative planning for secondary school youth is the joint development of an IEP/IWRP. Therefore, when support responsibilities are anticipated, the IEP and/or IWRP will be developed cooperatively and the individual's program components (vocational training, vocational goals, objectives, services, timelines, etc.) and fiscal responsibilities will be specified.

SERVICES

The agency that has responsibility for providing services shall make available appropriate services for the individual. An individual with disabilities may refuse the services from the agency. However, another agency is not obligated to duplicate the services being offered by the responsible agency. (A detailed listing of services and responsible agencies is contained in the Service Responsibility Chart that follows.)

COORDINATED PLANNING

Each agency shall operate in accordance with its respective laws (P.L. 101–476, the Individuals with Disabilities Education Act; P.L. 101–302, the Carl D. Perkins Vocational Applied Technology Education Act; and Vocational Rehabilitation Act of 1973 as amended), regulations, and state plan. Education and Rehabilitation agree jointly to plan and develop appropriate areas of their respective state plan.

CONFIDENTIALITY OF INFORMATION

Personnel employed by Education and Rehabilitation and assigned to cooperatively provide services to students with disabilities will have appropriate access to confidential information within the boundaries of the legal constraints of each agency to expedite the provision of vocational services.

LIAISON COMMITTEE

It is agreed that Education (special education and vocational education) and Rehabilitation each shall appoint at least one representative to a liaison committee, which shall meet at least quarterly (February, May, August, and November). The liaison committee shall assist in:

1. the exchange and dissemination of information;
2. coordination of each agency's state plan;
3. provision of necessary inservice training between staff of the agencies;
4. utilization of training facilities for students/clients of the agencies;
5. identification of ideas needing additional cooperative planning and action; and,
6. planning for transitional services.

LOCAL AGREEMENTS

The education and vocational preparation of an individual with disabilities to his/her fullest potential is a complex process requiring numerous services from different agencies. The establishment of interagency agreements promotes the effective, efficient, and economical provision of services. Each agency will encourage and provide assistance toward the establishment of a similar statement of cooperation between the local educational agencies and local Rehabilitation offices throughout the state.

It is recommended that at the local level, Education (special education and vocational education) and Rehabilitation establish a local liaison committee to meet quarterly. The liaison committee shall assist in:

1. planning for transition services;
2. provision of the necessary inservice training between staff of the agencies;
3. identification of areas needing additional cooperation; and,
4. coordination of local project plans, if applicable.

Communication between agency representatives and the sharing of pertinent educational, vocational, programmatic, and diagnostic information is necessary for cooperative planning. Upon the duly approved cooperative agreement between Rehabilitation and the local educational agency, certified rehabilitation counselors assigned as agents to the school system become an integral part of the educational process.

ARTICULATION

The State Rehabilitation Center, an approved NCAA special option facility, will accept educational diploma credits from all local educational agencies for joint clients served at the Center. Likewise, all local educational agencies will reciprocate in the acceptance of educational diploma credits for joint clients served at the Rehabilitation Center who are returning to local educational agencies for further services. This articulation procedure will be implemented by the joint development of a Four Year Education Plan, IEP, and/or IWRP.

AGREED TO

_____   _____
President   DATE
State Board of Education and
State Board of Rehabilitation

_____   _____
State Superintendent of Schools   DATE

_____   _____
Director   DATE
Division of Rehabilitation Services

7/13/90

Appendix B
List of Professional Organizations

Organization and Address	Publications	Features
Alexander Graham Bell Association for the Deaf 3417 Volta Place, NW Washington, DC 20007-2778 (202) 337-5220	*Volta Review* *Newsounds*	Follows philosophy of mainstreaming deaf children emphasizing oral-deaf education. Provides information services for parents and professionals. Sponsors children's rights advocacy network. Offers financial aid programs for oral hearing impaired people.
American Association on Mental Retardation (AAMR) 1719 Kalorama Road, NW Washington DC 20009-2683 (202) 387-1968 (800) 424-3688	*American Journal on Mental Retardation* *Mental Retardation News & Notes*	Interdisciplinary team of professionals and concerned individuals in the field. Holds national and regional meetings and provides information on latest research and practices.
American Council on Rural Special Education (ACRES) University of Utah 221 Milton Bennion Hall Salt Lake City, UT 84112 (801) 585-5659	*Ruralink* *Rural Special Education Quarterly*	Dedicated to the interests of individuals with disabilities living in rural areas. Provides job referral service, conferences, monographs, and other resources.
American Deafness and Rehabilitation Association (ADARA) P.O. Box 251554 Little Rock, AR 72225 (501) 868-8850 Fax (501) 868-8812	*Journal of the American Deafness and Rehabilitation Association* *The ADARA Update*	Network of professionals and community persons. Holds forums, conferences, and workshops. Provides information on referral service about careers, university programs, and job opportunities.
American Foundation for the Blind (AFB) 15 West 16th Street New York, NY 10011 (212) 620-2155	*Journal of Visual Impairment and Blindness* *AFB News*	Provides information and consultation in education, rehabilitation, employment, and special products.
American Printing House for the Blind, Inc. 1839 Frankfort Avenue P.O. Box 6085 Louisville, KY 40206-0085 (502) 895-2405 (800) 223-1839	*APH Slate*	Provides reading materials: books in braille and large type; and recorded form, educational aids, tools, and supplies.
Boy Scouts of America 1325 West Walnut Hill Lane Irving, TX 75015-7079 (214) 580-2430	*Boys Life* *Scouting Magazine*	Develops and promotes the Learning for Life Program, which is being implemented in elementary schools across the country and includes attention to students with special needs.

Organization and Address	Publications	Features
Center for Minority Special Education (CMSE) P.O. Box 6107 Hampton, VA 23668		Provides technical assistance for research and documentation proposals in special education, rehabilitation, and related services.
Clearinghouse on Disability Information Office of Special Education and Rehabilitative Services (OSERS) U.S. Department of Education Room 3132, Switzer Building 330 C Street, SW Washington, DC 20202-2524 (202) 205-8241	*OSERS News in Print*	Provides information on federal funding, federal legislation, and federal programs serving people with disabilities.
Council for Exceptional Children (CEC) 1110 North Glebe Road, Suite 300 Arlington, VA 22201-5704 (703) 620-3660 (888) 232-7733	*Exceptional Children Teaching Exceptional Children CEC Today*	Dedicated to advancing the quality of education for exceptional children and improving the conditions under which special educators work. Has 17 special interest divisions, e.g., Council for Children with Behavioral Disorders, Division on Developmental Disabilities.
Division on Career Development and Transition Council for Exceptional Children (CEC) 1110 North Glebe Road, Suite 300 Arlington, VA 22201-5704 (703) 620-3660 (888) 232-7733	*Career Development for Exceptional Individuals, DCD Network*	A division of the Council for Exceptional Children that addresses and promotes the career development needs of all types of exceptional students.
Epilepsy Foundation of America 4351 Garden City Drive Landover, MD 20785 (301) 459-3700 (800) 332-1000	*Epilepsy USA*	Provides technical, referral, and research information services. Works with Congress and government agencies to advance the interests of people with epilepsy.
National Association of the Deaf (NAD) 814 Thayer Avenue Silver Spring, MD 20910 (301) 587-1788	*Broadcaster Deaf American*	Provides and publishes information on deafness and hearing loss. Serves as an advocate and legal consultant for this disability group. Holds regional workshops and youth programs.
National Association of the Physically Handicapped, Inc. Bethesda Scarlott Oaks, #GA 4 440 Lafayette Avenue Cincinnati, OH 45220-1073	*NAPH National Newsletter*	Works to advance the social, economic, and physical welfare of the physically disabled. Advocates and supports legislation that benefits people with disabilities.
National Association of Protection and Advocacy Systems (NAPAS) 900 Second Street, NE, Suite 211 Washington, DC 20002 (202) 408-9514 (202) 408-9521 (TDD)		Membership association of the directors of Protection and Advocacy Systems for Persons with Developmental Disabilities and for Persons with Mental Illness and the Client Assistance Program. Provides technical assistance and training for members and staffs. Monitors congressional and federal agency activities related to disability issues and oversight administration.

Organization and Address	Publications	Features
National Association of Vocational Education Special Needs Personnel (NAVESNP) c/o American Vocational Association (AVA) 1410 King Street Alexandria, VA 22314 (703) 683-3111 (800) 892-2274	*The NAVESNP Journal*	Membership organization of secondary and post-vocational professionals concerned with the education of disadvantaged students and students with disabilities or other special needs. Five regional divisions provide information consultancy to consumers.
National Center of Youth with Disabilities (NCYD) Adolescent Health Program University of Minnesota Box 721–UMHC Harvard Street at East River Road Minneapolis, MN 55455 (612) 626-2825 (800) 333-6293	*Cydline Reviews* *Connections*	Serves as a technical assistance and information resource center focusing on adolescents with chronic illness and disability and issues that surround their transition to adult life. On-line computerized database provides information on current research, model programs, training and educational materials, federal and state law, and legislation.
National Center for Learning Disabilities 99 Park Avenue, 6th Floor New York, NY 10016 (212) 687-7211	*THEIR WORLD* *NCLD Newsletter*	Provides information and referrals about special education programs and products to parents and professionals.
National Clearinghouse for Professions in Special Education Information Center c/o Council for Exceptional Children 1110 North Glebe Road, Suite 300, Arlington, VA 22201 (703) 264-9475 (703) 624-9946 (TTD)		Collects, synthesizes, and disseminates information on career opportunities, personnel supply and demand, and personnel preparation programs for increasing the supply of qualified professionals serving individuals with disabilities. It provides information, technical assistance, and linkages to promote local, state, and national efforts to collect useful information in these areas.
National Council on Disability U.S. Department of Education 800 Independence Avenue, SW, Suite 814 Washington, DC 20591 (202) 267-3846 (202) 267-3232 (TDD)	*FOCUS*	An independent federal agency of 15 members appointed by the President and confirmed by the Senate. Addresses, analyzes, and makes recommendations on issues of public policy that affect people with disabilities.
National Easter Seal Society 70 East Lake Street Chicago, IL 60601-5907 (312) 726-6200 (800) 221-6827	*Washington Watch Line*	A nonprofit community-based health agency dedicated to increasing the independence of people with disabilities. Offers a wide range of services, research, and programs to assist adults and children with disabilities and their families.

Organization and Address	Publications	Features
National Federation of the Blind (NFB) 1800 Johnson Street Baltimore, MD 21230 (301) 659-9314	*The Braille Monitor* *Future Reflections*	Provides information, resources, scholarships, and referral services for people with visual impairment.
National Information Center for Children and Youth with Disabilities (NICHCY) P.O. Box 1492 Washington, DC 20013 (703) 893-6061 (800) 999-5599	*NICHCY News Digest* *Transition Summary*	Information and referral clearinghouse for families and professionals concerned with disability issues and children and youth ages 22 and under.
National Organization on Disability 910 16th Street, NW, Suite 600 Washington, DC 20006 (202) 293-5960 (800) 248-2253	*NOD Report*	Works to improve attitudes toward people with disabilities, expand educational and employment opportunities, eliminate physical barriers, increase participation in religious, cultural, and recreational activities.
National Parent Network on Disabilities 1600 Prince Street, Suite 115 Alexandria, VA 22314-2836 (703) 684-6763		Provides legislative representation, reference, and referrals. Holds national and regional conferences. Is involved in materials development and distribution. Has a database linking parents to local, state, regional, national, and/or international services.
National Rehabilitation Association 633 S. Washington Street Alexandria, VA 22314 (703) 836-0850	*Journal of Rehabilitation*	Involved in advocacy, legislative design, and the development of education and training programs for people with disabilities.
National Spinal Cord Injury Association 600 W. Cummings Park, Suite 2000 Woburn, MA 01801 (617) 935-2722 (800) 962-9629		Provides information to injured individuals, families, health care professionals, and other agencies. Holds conventions and seminars.
President's Committee on Employment of People with Disabilities 1331 F Street, NW Washington, DC 20004-1107 (202) 376-6200	*Tips and Trends* *Worklife*	Provides information, referral, and assistance concerning employment and people with disabilities. Holds conferences, seminars, and workshops on issues concerning employment.
TASH: The Association for Persons with Severe Handicaps 11201 Greenwood Avenue N Seattle, WA 98133 (206) 361-8870 (206) 361-0113 (TDD)	*TASH Newsletter* *DC Update*	Dedicated to improving the living, learning, and working environments of people with severe disabilities. Offers information and referral services.

Organization and Address	Publications	Features
Technical Assistance for Special Populations Program (TASPP)	*TASPP Bulletin* *TASPP Brief*	Assists in improving vocational education programs for youth and adults with special needs.
The Arc 500 E. Border Street, 3rd Floor Arlington, TX 76010 (817) 640-0204 (800) 433-5255	*The Arc Today*	Trains volunteers to work with mentally challenged people, develops models in areas of education, training, and residence, and furthers employment opportunities.
United Cerebral Palsy Association 1522 K Street, NW, Suite 1112 Washington, DC 20005 (202) 842-1266 (800) 872-5827	*UCP News* *Word From Washington*	Involved in research and advocacy. Provides services ranging from preschool to adult work programs.

Appendix C
LCCE Performance Test 17

FORM A: EXAMINER

Knowing and Exploring Occupational Possibilities (Occupational Guidance and Preparation)

Materials for Duplication

Test Question 1:   Occupational Remuneration
Test Question 2:   Job Information
Test Question 3:   Values from a Job
Test Question 4:   Job Categories
Test Question 5:   Investigate Job Opportunities
Want Ads Sheet
Score Sheet

Materials Needed

Telephone directories.

Directions

This test can be given in approximately one class period. Answers may be written or given orally, but care must be taken so other students do not overhear responses. Some directions and vocabulary used in this test may be too advanced for some students and may require further explanation. This test assesses the students' ability to:

1. identify remunerative aspects of work
2. locate sources of occupational and training information
3. identify personal values met through work
4. classify jobs into occupational categories
5. investigate local occupational and training opportunities

Scoring Procedures

If the test has previously been administered to the student, circle the number of times on the score sheet.

Examples of appropriate responses are provided on the score sheet for items that may have several acceptable answers. Some questions may have only one acceptable response.

For questions requiring demonstrations or role playing, the examiner must make a judgment about scoring. Further guidelines are presented below.

Written Responses   On the score sheet, circle the example(s) the student has identified. If the student gives an example that seems appropriate but is not listed on the score sheet, record that response on the line provided. Then record the student's score.

Oral Responses   For test questions to which the student responded orally rather than in writing, record the student's response on the score sheet and score the response.

Observed Responses   For test questions requiring the student to perform by demonstrating or role playing, record the response immediately after the response is made. If the task is not performed appropriately, note the reason for the point loss on the line provided.

Each question, including the subquestions, is worth up to 2 points. A student must attain a total score of 8–10 for mastery. Record the final score on the Student Competency Assessment Record (SCAR).

Note. From *Life Centered Career Education: Competency Assessment Performance Batteries,* by D. E. Brolin, 1992, Arlington, VA: The Council for Exceptional Children. Copyright 1992 by The Council for Exceptional Children. Reprinted by permission.

Allow students to respond to each request before reading the next task.

Question 1: Occupational Remuneration
(Group Administration)

To the Examiner: Students are to provide explanations for differences in occupational remuneration and why people take lower paying jobs. Also, students are to answer a question concerning types of reductions to paychecks. Distribute Test Question 1.

Read to Students: Look at Test Question 1 and read along with me. People get paid different amounts of money depending on the kind of job they have. Lawyers and doctors make more money than dishwashers and food servers. (a) Give one reason why this is so. (b) Explain why people take lower paying jobs when others pay so much better. (c) When thinking of how much money you're going to make at a job, you must also consider what reductions will be made to your paycheck before you get it. An example of a reduction is money taken out for your retirement plan. List two other possible reductions there may be to a person's paycheck.

Question 2: Job Information
(Group Administration)

To the Examiner: Students are to use telephone directories to list four local sources (other than school) of occupational information. Distribute Test Question 2 and telephone directories.

Read to Students: Look at Test Question 2 and read along with me. There are many different places you can go to get information about jobs. Using the phone book, find four places in your town or area, other than school, where you could go to find information about jobs or careers and write the four places on the lines provided.

Question 3: Values from a Job
(Group Administration)

To the Examiner: Students are to identify personal values met through work. Distribute Test Question 3.

Read to Students: Look at Test Question 3 and read along with me. There are many personal values, or rewards, that a person can get from a job. Why do you think bus drivers work as bus drivers? Besides money, what is another reward each of the following employees get from his or her work?

Question 4: Job Categories
(Group Administration)

To the Examiner: Students are to demonstrate the ability to classify jobs into occupational categories. Distribute Test Question 4 and give a simple explanation of each of the four jobs listed on the Test Question.

Read to Students: Look at Test Question 4 and read along with me. Different jobs fit into different categories. Some of these different categories include jobs that require more education or less education, and a lot of sitting or a lot of moving around. (Briefly explain each of the jobs listed below.) Now that I have explained the four jobs listed below, you should be able to see how each of the four jobs fits in a different square. Match the jobs with the job categories given above the squares, and write that job in the correct square.

Question 5: Investigate Job Opportunities
(Group Administration)

To the Examiner: Students are to demonstrate the ability to investigate occupational opportunities. Distribute Test Question 5 and the Want Ads Sheet.

Read to Students: Look at Test Question 5 and read along with me. There are two job descriptions listed below. Using the Want Ads Sheet, pick the job ads that would relate to the two job descriptions listed. Write four ad numbers (not the telephone numbers) for each job in the spaces provided. The first job listed is food service/kitchen worker. This is a worker who performs duties related to preparation or delivery of food or to the upkeep of kitchen work areas and equipment. The second job listed is truck driver. This is a worker who drives a truck to transport materials, merchandise, equipment, or people.

LCCE PERFORMANCE TEST 17—Form A
Knowing and Exploring Occupational Possibilities
Score Sheet

Student _____ School _____

Examiner _____ Date _____ Previous Admins. **1 2 3 4 5**

Question	Possible Points		Examples of Appropriate Responses	Score
Occupational Remuneration				
1	.5	a.	.5 pt. for an appropriate response: More education, more training, greater skill, higher demand.	_____
	.5	b.	.5 pt. for an appropriate response: Don't want to change location, not something they would enjoy doing, too difficult a job, happy with current work situation, don't want to leave family or friends, don't have the skills or training, can't afford to get training.	_____
	1	c.	.5 pt. for an appropriate response: Federal income tax, state income tax, Social Security, donations, parking fees.	_____
Job Information				
2	2		.5 pt. for an appropriate response: Library, employment service, Chamber of Commerce, career center, placement center, various private employment agencies, vocational-technical schools.	_____

Values from a Job

3   .5   a.   .5 pt. for an appropriate response:
                                Meet people, see new places, responsibility.

_____   _____

           .5   b.   .5 pt. for an appropriate response:
                                Be creative, work with hands, personal
                                satisfaction.

_____   _____

           .5   c.   .5 pt. for an appropriate response:
                                Meet people, move around, help people.

_____   _____

           .5   d.   .5 pt. for an appropriate response:
                                Meet people, move around, help people.

_____   _____

Job Categories

4   2   .5 pt. for each correct response:
                              a. Pilot
                              b. Receptionist
                              c. Emergency Room Doctor
                              d. Fire Fighter

_____   _____

Investigate Job Opportunities

5   2   2 pts. for correctly listing eight jobs.
                              1 pt. for correctly listing at least four jobs:
                              Food Service Worker—2, 9, 12, 14
                              Truck Driver—4, 5, 8, 13

_____   _____

                              TOTAL POSSIBLE POINTS   10
                              Needed for Mastery   8

                              Student's Total   _____

LCCE PERFORMANCE TEST 17—Form A

Test Question 1: Occupational Remuneration

Name _____ Date _____

People get paid different amounts of money depending on the kinds of jobs they have. Lawyers and doctors make more money than dishwashers and food servers.

a. Give one reason why this is so.

_____

b. Explain why people take lower paying jobs when others pay so much better.

_____

c. When thinking of how much money you're going to make at a job, you must also consider what reductions will be made to your paycheck before you get it. An example of a reduction is money taken out for your retirement plan. List two other possible reductions there may be to a person's paycheck.

1. _____

2. _____

LCCE PERFORMANCE TEST 17—Form A
Test Question 2: Job Information

Name _____ Date _____

There are many different places you can go to get information about jobs. Using the phone book, find four places in your town or area, other than school, where you could go to find information about jobs or careers and write the four places on the lines provided.

1. _____

2. _____

3. _____

4. _____

LCCE PERFORMANCE TEST 17—Form A
Test Question 3: Personal Values from a Job

Name _____ Date _____

There are many personal values, or rewards, that a person can get from a job. Why do you think bus drivers work as bus drivers? Besides money, what is another reward each of the following employees get from his or her work?

a. Bus driver _____

_____

b. Carpenter _____

_____

c. Janitor _____

_____

d. Hotel maid _____

_____

LCCE PERFORMANCE TEST 17—Form A

Test Question 4:   Job Categories

Name——————————————————————— Date ———————————————

Different jobs fit into different categories. Some of these different categories include jobs that require more education or less education, and a lot of sitting or a lot of moving around. Now that I have explained the four jobs listed below, you should be able to see how each of the four jobs fits in a different square. Match the jobs with the job categories given above the squares, and write that job in the correct square.

Jobs:
   Emergency Room Doctor
   Fire Fighter
   Receptionist
   Pilot

a. More Education
and
Sitting

b. Less Education
and
Sitting

c.   More Education
and
Moving Around

d. Less Education
and
Moving Around

LCCE PERFORMANCE TEST 17—Form A

Test Question 5: Investigate Job Opportunities

Name _____ Date _____

There are two job descriptions listed below. Using the Want Ads Sheet, pick the job ads that would relate to each of the two job descriptions listed. Write four ad numbers (not the telephone numbers) for each job in the spaces provided.

Job 1:   Food Service/Kitchen Worker

Description: A worker who performs duties related to preparation or delivery of food or to the upkeep of kitchen work areas and equipment.

Ad numbers:

1. _____
2. _____
3. _____
4. _____

Job 2:   Truck Driver

Description: A worker who drives a truck to transport materials, merchandise, equipment, or people.

Ad numbers:

1. _____
2. _____
3. _____
4. _____

Name _____ Date _____

WANT ADS

Hospital Aide–
Must be able to push carts of medicine through hallways. Must be able to lift 25 lbs. or more. Duties: Assisting hospital personnel with patient care. For more information call:
447-2293
1

Dishwasher needed at Lindy's. All shifts available. Part-time or full-time. $5/hr. Call:
937-2569
2

Needed – Carpenter to finish recording studio. Roughing has been done. Need custom cases, cabinets, and other recording essentials. If experienced call:
750-3738
3

Person to drive beef truck for Binghamm's Foods, Inc. Must have grade 2 license with experience. For more info call:
339-2700
4

Delivery person needed immediately! Will drive truck of produce from market to store. Must be able to lift 50 lbs. or more. Good pay and benefits. Truck provided. Call:
773-2653
5

Builder needed to do deck and patio work. 3 mos. trial then steady pay and benefits. Upward mobility in new company possible. Inquire:
953-9927
6

Nurse's Helper –
Courteous, hard working person needed to help nurse care for elderly gentleman. Good pay. Long hours. Interested? Call:
328-4785
7

Open-road transport operator needed to drive 18 wheel rig from Marshall Junction to 14 points of destination. Excellent pay. Day and night shifts available. Loading and unloading required. Interested? Call:
769-2783
8

Chef needed to cook appetizers at Loi's. Must be ACS member and have 2 yrs experience. Excellent remuneration. Call:
937-4672
9

Skilled toy maker needed to craft toys from raw wood stock. Experience preferred. Bring sample of work. Call Chris at Santa's Helpers, Inc.
895-2203
10

Patient Care Attendant –
Westside Geriatric Unit looking for nurse's aides and custodial personnel. Morning, evening, and night shifts available. Call for more information:
945-2600
11

Busboy needed at Tim's Family Restaurant. $4.25/hr Evenings:
435-7567
12

Truck Driver –
Needed for delivering tires from local distributor across country. Good pay. Will drive in team of 2. For more information call Bob at:
256-4895
13

Mess cook for boys' dorm needed immediately. Experience cooking large portions. Salary and benefits. Apply to Western Central Eastern College:
893-1452
14

Craftsman position open at Ferguson's Clocks and Cabinets. Need carpenter experienced at working with differing hardwoods to run molding operations. Pay is $17.50/hr. Call:
225-9090
15

Nurse's Aides –
5 nurse's aides are needed immediately for new burn unit at Mercy Hospital. Experience working with people preferred. Inquiries to Janet at:
335-0478
16

Appendix D
Functional Assessment Resources

• •

Catalogs are available from the following organizations, which contain information on functional assessment inventories, standardized tests, basic skills assessment instruments, transition assessment batteries, and work sample systems.

American Guidance Service
Publisher's Building
Circle Pines, MN 55014–1796
(900) 328-2560

Arkansas Research & Training Center in Vocational
Rehabilitation Publications Department
P.O. Box 1358
Hot Springs, AR 71902
(501) 624-4411 Ext. 316

The Council for Exceptional Children
1110 North Glebe Road, Suite 300
Arlington, VA 22201–5704

CTB/McGraw-Hill
2500 Garden Road
Monterey, CA 93940
(800) 538-9547

Curriculum Associates TM, Inc.
5 Esquire Road
N. Billerica, MA 01862-2589

J. E. Stewart
18518 Kenlake Place Northeast
Seattle, WA 98155
(206) 486-4510

Materials Development Center
Stout Vocational Rehabilitation Institute
University of Wisconsin-Stout
Menomonie, WI 54751
(715) 232-1342

McCarron-Dial Systems, Inc.
P.O. Box 45628
Dallas, TX 75245
(214) 247-5945

Supported Employment Technical Assistance Project
B 125 West Fee Hall
Michigan State University
E. Lansing, MI 48824-1316
(517) 355-0166

TALENT ASSESSMENT, INC.
P.O. Box 5087
Jacksonville, FL 32247
(800) 634-1472
(800) 225-0248

VALPAR International Corporation
P.O. Box 5767
Tucson, AZ 85703-5767
(800) 528-7070

Virginia Commonwealth University
Rehabilitation Research and Training Center
VCU Box 2011
Richmond, VA 23284–0001
Attn: Resource Dissemination
(804) 257-1851

Appendix E

LCCE Resources Available from the Council for Exceptional Children

● ●

Life Centered Career Education:
A Competency Based Approach
Fifth Edition
Donn E. Brolin
The guide contains the most current set of transitional objectives and units for the 97 LCCE subcompetencies. Includes the Competency Rating Scale and IEP Forms with transition components.
No. P180F. 1997. 180 pp.
ISBN 0–86586–241–9. Price $28

Life Centered Career Education:
Modified Curriculum for
Individuals with Moderate Disabilities
Robert J. Loyd & Donn E. Brolin
The guide contains the most current set of transitional objectives and units for the 75 LCCE Moderate subcompetencies. Includes the Competency Rating Scale and IEP Forms with transition components.
No. P5194. 1997. 106 pp.
ISBN 0–86586-293-1. Price $26

Life Centered Career Education: The Complete
Curriculum and Assessment Package
Includes over 1,100 lesson plans covering Daily Living Skills, Personal-Social Skills, and Occupational Skills; Knowledge Batteries (10 copies of each of two alternative forms); Performance Batteries; Administration Manuals; and Technical Report.
No. P371. 1992. Price $980

LCCE: Daily Living Skills
Donn E. Brolin
Includes 472 lesson plans covering personal finances, household management, personal needs,

family responsibilities, food preparation, citizenship responsibilities, and leisure.
No. P367. 1992. 1,556 pp. Three loose-leaf binders.
ISBN 0–86586–224–9. Price $400

LCCE: Personal-Social Skills
Donn E. Brolin
Provides 370 lesson plans for developing self-awareness, self-confidence, socially responsible behavior, good interpersonal skills, independence, decision-making, and communication skills.
No. P368. 1992. 1,348 pp. Three loose-leaf binders.
ISBN 0–86586–225–7. Price $400

LCCE: Occupational Guidance and Preparation
Richard T. Roessler and Donn E. Brolin
Includes 286 lesson plans to help students explore occupational possibilities; make occupational choices; develop appropriate work habits; seek, secure, and maintain employment; exhibit sufficient physical/manual skills; and obtain specific occupational competencies.
No. P369. 1992. 670 pp. Two loose-leaf binders.
ISBN 0–86586–226–5. Price $300

LCCE: Competency Assessment
Knowledge Batteries
Available in parallel forms, each Knowledge Battery consists of 200 multiple-choice questions that cover the first 20 competencies. Primarily a screening instrument, the Knowledge Batteries were designed to pinpoint specific competency deficiencies. Package includes an Administration Manual, a Technical Report, and samples of each

form of the test. Also included are two introductory sets of 10 Knowledge Batteries, Forms A and B, to use with students.
No. P370K. 1992. 152 pp.
ISBN 0–86586–239–7. Price $125

LCCE: Competency Assessment Performance Batteries

The Performance Batteries consist of two alternative forms for each of the 21 competency units. Items are primarily performance-based and should be administered to students before and after instructional units have been taught. Performance Batteries are administered individually or to small groups of students. Test materials must be reproduced as needed. Performance Batteries are packaged in a loose-leaf binder along with an Administration Manual.
No. P370P. 1992. 675 pp.
ISBN 0–86586–240–0. Price $225

Additional Sets of Knowledge Batteries

Packages of 10 tests may be ordered separately to be used by students. Students may answer questions directly in the test booklets by circling the correct choice or may use a standard machine-scorable form. Knowledge Batteries may not be reproduced.
LCCE: Knowledge Battery Form A (10 per package)
No. P372. $50

LCCE: Knowledge Battery Form B

(10 per package)
No. P373. $50

Life Centered Career Education: The Training Package

Donn E. Brolin
Includes:
• Ten Videotapes
• Trainer's Manual
• Professional Development Activity Book
• LCCE: A Competency Based Approach
No. M5000. 1993. Package Price $975

Ten Videotapes

Session 1:   The Need to Change and the Law (23:38 min) No. M5001
Session 2:   The LCCE Curriculum (K–12) (49:36 min) No. M5002
Session 3:   Assessing Functional Skills (57:48 min) No. M5003
Session 4:   Teaching Daily Living Skills (58:41 min) No. M5004
Session 5:   Teaching Personal Social Skills (58:26 min) No. M5005
Session 6:   Teaching Occupational Skills (58:82 min) No. M5006
Session 7:   Selection, Modification, and Development of Instructional Materials (Part 1) (29:10 min) Involving Parents in Functional Curriculum (Part 2) (27:29 min) No. M5007
Session 8:   Involving Business and Industry (Part 1) (28:32 min) Interagency Collaboration (Part 2) (30:30 min) No. M5008
Session 9:   Curriculum Modification and Change (56:27 min) No. M5009
Session 10: Individualized Transition Planning and Implementation (62:37 min) No. M5010

Tapes may be ordered separately by Stock Number. Price $100 each

Life Centered Career Education: Trainer's Manual, Third Edition and Professional Development Activity Book

Donn E. Brolin
This two-volume set of training materials includes a 96-page third edition of the Trainer's Manual and a 458-page Activity Book designed for use by all participants who are in training.

Trainer's Manual

These training materials provide approximately 30 hours of LCCE in-service training and are de-

signed to support the video presentations. Orientation and directions for conducting each session are outlined in the Trainer's Manual.
No. M5011. 1993. Price $70

Activity Book

Designed for use by all participants in the training program. Each session includes objectives, key concepts from that session's video, session activities, note-taking pages, resource materials, and assignments for the next session. The Activity Book is packaged in a loose-leaf binder.
No. M5013. 1993. Price $40

Prices may change without notice. Please call (703) 620-3660 to confirm prices and shipping charges. LCCE On-site Training is also available from CEC. For more information about LCCE workshops and academies call (703) 620–3660.

The Council for Exceptional Children
1110 North Glebe Road
Suite 300
Arlington, VA 22201
(703) 620-3660 (Voice)
(703) 264-9494 (FAX)
(703) 264-9446 (TTY)

Materials Correlated to the LCCE Competencies/Subcompetencies and List of Publishers

• •

MATERIALS CORRELATED TO THE LCCE COMPETENCIES/ SUBCOMPETENCIES

Competency 1: Managing Personal Finances

Subcompetency 5, 6

Banking Language and Credit Language. Globe Fearon.

These situation-specific work texts give the students the vocabulary associated with banking and credit.

Reading Level: 3.0
Interest Level: 3–12/ABE/ESL

Subcompetency 1–6

Working Makes Sense. Globe Fearon.

Students acquire and practice skills using fractions, percents, and amounts over $100—while learning about employment, banking, and budgeting. Automated teller machines, check endorsement, bank statements, and employee benefits are introduced.

Reading Level: 3.0
Interest Level: 6–12/ABE/ESL

Subcompetency 2

Using Dollars and Sense. Globe Fearon.

Provides consumer-oriented exercises on estimating, using supermarket shelf labels, averaging prices, find-ing errors on receipts, as well as weights and measures and making change.

Reading Level: 3.0
Interest Level: 3–12/ABE/ESL

Subcompetency 1–6

Living in the Real World. EBSCO.

This program is designed to teach students how to manage money, balance checkbooks, and deal with unexpected outcomes.

Level: Junior-Senior High School

Subcompetency 1–6

Real-Life Math (Stuart Swartz). Pro-Ed.

This program is designed to teach students to deal with personal money management and business transactions. Spirit masters, posters, and audiocassettes accompany the teacher's manual.

Level: Junior-Senior High School

Subcompetency 2

Consumer Skills for Teenagers and Consumer Skills for Living on Your Own. Quercus.

Students learn to prioritize needs and budget with specific amounts.

Reading Level: 2.5–2.6

Subcompetency 1–6

Mathematics for Consumers. AGS.

This text extends basic math skills through their application to important everyday situations such as paying taxes, buying food, banking, etc. Student workbook, blackline masters, teacher's manual, and teacher's resource binder accompany the text.

Interest Level: Grades 8–12; adult

Subcompetency 1–6

Practical Math. Fearon.

The text reinforces basic life skills such as the importance of math competence in money management, banking, career choices, everyday living, and more. The classroom resource binder includes blackline masters and work sheets.

Reading Level: Below 4
Interest Level: 7–12; adult

Subcompetency 1–6

Reading for Survival in Today's Society. Scott Foresman.

This text helps students develop functional reading skills with practical readings such as electric bills, consumer information, recipes, and more.

Reading Levels: Volume I, Grades 6–9; Volume II, Grades 8–12

Subcompetency 3

Building Life Skills Text. Lakeshore Learning Materials.

This text, accompanied by a teacher's guide and activity book, teaches students life management skills such as budgeting, health, nutrition, how to shop for food, and more.

Reading Level: 5.0–7.0

Subcompetency 3

Lifeschool. Pacemaker Learning Materials.

This multilevel program is designed to help the teacher meet the basic skills needs for hard-to-reach students. The binder contains 10 modules with lessons, worksheets, and more, which focus on money, housing, groceries, clothing, and more.

Reading Level: Grades 3.5–4.5

Subcompetency 1–6

Math for Everyday Living. Lakeshore Reading Materials.

This microcomputer software—Apple II Family—teaches students to become wise money managers. The program includes lesson disks, backup disks, and reproducible activity sheets.

Reading Level: Grades 3.5–4.5

Subcompetency 1–6

Everyday Consumer English. Lakeshore Reading Materials.

Lessons that introduce students to making a budget, using banking services, shopping at the supermarket, and leasing an apartment. Also incorporate comprehension questions, grammar exercises, and vocabulary and spelling activities.

Reading Level: Grades 4.5–6.0

Subcompetency 1–6

Math for Successful Living. Gameco Industries, Inc.

This microcomputer software includes five programs, which focus on time cards and paychecks, managing a checking account, budgeting, buying on credit, and shopping strategies.

Level: Grades 7–12

Subcompetency 1–2

Learning Through Reading Series. Book I. Wallet War (N. Bowling, I. D. Cook, & D. Salyers). Science Research Associates.

The *Wallet War* is a part of a series designed to teach students practical life skills while supporting reading skills. The text teaches students how to use food stamps and money wisely. A criterion-referenced pre-post-test, audiotape, and teacher's guide accompany Book I.

Level: Junior-Senior High School

Competency 2: Selecting and Managing a Household

Subcompetency 9, 10

Buying with Sense. Globe Fearon.

High-interest format lets students put math skills to use while following an about-to-be married couple through the process of buying everything they need to set up a home.

Reading Level: 4.0
Interest Level: 6–12/ABE/ESL

Subcompetency 9

Lifeschool. Pacemaker Learning Series.

(See Competency 1 for description.)
Reading Level: Grades 3.5–4.5

Subcompetency 12–13, 15–16

Health. The Pacemaker Curriculum. Globe Fearon.

This practical text covers both physical and mental health. Systems of the body, safety, and urgent topics such as alcohol, drugs, sexuality, and AIDS are addressed. Covers materials required for GED testing.

Reading Level: Below 4.0
Interest Level: 6–12/ABE/ESL

Subcompetency 13, 14

Good Grooming for Guys and Good Grooming for Girls. Globe Fearon.

These two books show how grooming makes a difference in teens' lives.
Reading Level: 4.0–6.0
Interest Level: 6–12

Subcompetency 13, 16

Self-Help Skills Kit. EBSCO.

Fourteen goal areas, including grooming, dressing, and personal safety are covered. A teacher's guide accompanies the kit.
Level: Early childhood–elementary

Subcompetency 13

Personal Care Skills. Pro-Ed.

This program is designed to provide individualized instruction in daily living skills that enable students to be more independent while fostering increased self-esteem. The complete program includes *A Manual of Basic Teaching Strategy*, 13 training manuals, and a tape cassette.

Level: Elementary

Subcompetency 12, 15

Take Care of Yourself. Quercus.

This text includes objectives that cover health vocabulary, distinguishing self-help conditions from those requiring a doctor's care and developing a plan for basic body care involving diet, rest, and exercise.
Reading Level: 2.3

Subcompetency 12

Nutrition Mission. Good Apple.

Reproducibles teach the five basic food groups essential to good health.
Level: Pregrade 2

Subcompetency 12

Building Life Skills Text. Lakeshore Learning Materials.

(See Competency 1 for description.)

Reading Level: 5.0–7.0

Subcompetency 12

Keeping Fit. Janus.

Presents the physical and emotional health benefits of regular exercise.

Reading Level: 3.5–4.0
Interest Level: 6–12/ABE

Subcompetency 12–13, 15

Looking Good. Janus.

This step-by-step guide to good grooming motivates students to take responsibility for their own health, appearance, and self-esteem.

Reading Level: 3.5–4.0
Interest Level: 6–12/ABE

Subcompetency 12–13, 15

Decisions for Health. Steck Vaughn.

This program covers interests of developing mature student—nutrition, hygiene, safety, and more. Black-line masters are included with the teacher's guide.

Grade Level: 7–12
Reading Level: 3–4

Subcompetency 12, 16

I Am Amazing. AGS.

This program promotes health, safety, and self-esteem. It includes an activity manual, cards, game boards, posters, and an audiocassette.

Level: Preschool–K.

Subcompetency 15

Help! Janus.

Prepares students to handle 10 common minor medical emergencies including electrical shocks and burns.

Reading Level: 2.3–3.0
Interest Level: 6–12

Subcompetency 13, 14

Learning Through Reading Series. Book 2. Cleaning Up Your Act (N. Bowling, I. D. Cook, & D. Salyers). Science Research Associates.

Cleaning Up Your Act is a part of a series designed to teach practical life skills while supporting reading skills. Book 2 teaches personal hygiene and its social implications. A criterion-referenced pre-post-test, audiotape, and teacher's guide accompany Book 2.

Subcompetency 16

Let's Learn About Safety. Good Apple.

Safety education activities, take-home games, home/school materials, and parent information sheets are provided.

Level: Pregrade 2

Competency 4: Raising Children and Meeting Marriage Responsibilities

Subcompetency 17–19

Interpersonal Relations. Globe Fearon.

This module contains information about problem solving, family planning, pregnancy, baby care, aging, and death and dying.

Reading Level: 1.0–4.0
Interest Level: 9–12/ABE/ESL

Subcompetency 17–18

Building Life Skills Text. Lakeshore Learning Material.

Students learn how to care for children, among other things.

Reading Level: 5.0–7.0

Competency 5: Buying, Preparing, and Consuming Food

Subcompetency 20–25

Functional Work Series. Grocery Words. EBSCO.

This computer software program teaches students 100 words needed to read and write grocery lists and to find items in a grocery store.

Level: Ages 10–adult

Subcompetency 20–25

Functional Word Series. Fast Food. EBSCO.

This computer software program teaches students 100 words that will help them order a meal from a fast-food or restaurant menu.

Level: Ages 10–adult

Subcompetency 24

Self-Help Skills Kit. EBSCO.

This kit includes goals for teaching eating, drinking, and more.

Level: Early childhood–elementary

Subcompetency 25

Basic Home Economics. AGS.

This text helps prepare secondary level students for an adulthood of successful independent living. Written for low-level readers, it focuses on the practical application of consumerism, housing, food, nutrition, and more. A teacher's guide, activities, and blackline mas-

ters of tests and reinforcement exercises accompany the text.

Level: 8–12; adult

Subcompetency 24

Eating Skills Game. Attainment Company.

A programming guide and workbooks accompany this game, which teaches good table manners.

Subcompetency 20

Learning Through Reading Series (N. Bowling, I. D. Cook, & D. Salyers). Book I. Wallet War. Science Research Associates.

(See Competency 1 for description.)

Level: Junior–Senior High School

Subcompetency 20

Building Life Skills Text. Lakeshore Learning Materials.

(See Competency 1 for description.)

Reading Level: 5.0–7.0

Subcompetency 20

Comparison Shopping. Hartley Coursework.

Grocery shopping is the focus of this computer software game: the student "goes" to the grocery store with a list of things to buy. The learner takes into account unit price, value, and coupons.

Level: 4–8.

Subcompetency 24–25

The Foods We Eat. Steck-Vaughn.

This activity module helps students recognize, name, and classify foods from all five food groups and encourages them to choose foods that create healthy meals.

Level: Grades K–2

Subcompetency 20

The Supermarket Program. Steck-Vaughn.

This program enhances and strengthens essential language skills while teaching students about health, nutrition, money, and more.

Level: Grades 1–5

Subcompetency 20, 25

Kitchen Math. Gameco Industries, Inc.

This set of 40 work sheets provides practice in applying basic math to shopping, meal planning, and other kitchen-related activities.

Level: Grades 4–12

Competency 6: Buying and Caring for Clothing

Subcompetency 26

Doing Home Laundry. Pro-Ed.

This is a program developed to increase independence in the home and training for employment in a laundry hotel, etc.

Level: Elementary–High School

Subcompetency 27

Building Life Skills. Lakeshore Learning Materials.
(See Competency 1 for description.)

Reading Level: Grades 3.5–4.5

Competency 7: Exhibiting Responsible Citizenship

Subcompetency 29–32

Our Government in Action. Government at Work. It's Our Government. Globe Fearon.

This series of texts is relevant and involving; it demonstrates the role of government and civics in students' everyday lives. The teacher's guide provides teaching suggestions, answer keys, and easily duplicated Work Master sheets.

Reading Level: 2.5–4.0
Interest Level: 6–12/ABE/ESL

Competency 8: Utilizing Recreational Facilities and Engaging in Leisure Time

Subcompetency 33–37

Keeping Fit (2nd Ed.). Globe Fearon.

The physical and emotional health benefits of regular exercise are presented. The personal fitness goals of each character in the story provide incentives and strategies students can use.

Reading Level: 3.5–4.0
Interest Level: 6–12/ABE

Subcompetency 33–37

Reading Schedules. Globe Fearon.

This work text covers different kinds of schedules and how to read them: how to understand abbreviations on calendars, bus schedules, class schedules, and movie/TV listings.

Reading Level: 2.0–3.5
Interest Level: 6–12/ABE

Subcompetency 33–36

Learning Through Reading Series. Book 3. A Night on the Town (N. Bowling, I. D. Cook, & D. Salyers). Science Research Associates.

A Night on the Town is a part of a series designed to teach practical skills while supporting reading skills. Book 3 teaches students how to organize and plan future events. A criterion-referenced pre-post-test, audiotape, and teacher's guide accompany this book.

Level: Junior–Senior High School

Competency 9: Getting Around the Community

Subcompetency 38–41

Keys to Responsible Driving. Lakeshore Reading Materials.

This microcomputer software—Apple II Family—lets students experience what it is like to be behind the wheel. It includes two disks, backup disks, teacher's guide, and users' guide.

Reading Level: Grades 4.0–5.0

Subcompetency 38–40

Getting Around Cities and Towns. Globe Fearon.

These work texts build confidence by showing how to get around one's neighborhood, then progress to more complex skills such as reading building directories, street maps, bus routes, and more.

Reading Level: 2.0–3.5
Interest Level: 6–12/ABE

Subcompetency 39–40

Finding Your Way. Globe Fearon.

These two work texts teach special needs students to find their way around their neighborhood and city.

Reading Level: 2.6
Interest Level: 3–9/ABE

Subcompetency 39–40

Taking a Trip. Fearon.

This work text prepares students for independent out-of-town travel.

Reading Level: 3.2
Interest Level: 4–12/ABE/ESL

Competency 10: Achieving Self-Awareness

Subcompetency 42–45

Janus Job Planner. Janus.

Self-scoring inventories of work interests, values, attitudes, working conditions, self-esteem, and more are the focus of this career-planning tool.

Reading Level: 2.5–4.0

Subcompetency 42–45

Self-Help Skills Kit. EBSCO.

This kit includes goal areas for teaching self-awareness, social speaking, and more.

Level: Early Childhood–Elementary

Competency 11: Acquiring Self-Confidence

Subcompetency 46–50

Feelings. Belonging. Caring. Loving. Relating. Good Apple.

The open-ended activities in this series of books are designed for the students to improve their own self-concepts while developing a better understanding of themselves and others.

Level: Grades 2–8

Subcompetency 46–50

Self-Esteem Library. Wieser Educational, Inc.

This series is designed to raise the level of self-esteem in teens.

Reading Level: 4.0–6.0

Subcompetency 46, 50

Discovering Self-Confidence. Globe Fearon.

Shows students how to develop the self-confidence to reach their goals and have the strength to say "no" to peer pressure on drugs and alcohol.

Reading Level: 4.0–6.0
Interest Level: 6–12

Competency 12: Achieving Socially Responsible Behavior

Subcompetency 51–53, 55

Lifeschool 2000: Government and Law and Community Resources. Globe Fearon.

These modules contain lessons about traffic laws, accidents, taxes, consumer rights, citizenship, and immigration law and provide up-to-date information about social welfare programs, emergency services, crime prevention, and others.

Reading Level: 1.0–4.0
Interest Level: 9–12/ABE/ESL

Subcompetency 51–55

All About You Game. Attainment.

A programming guide and a workbook are included with this game, which provides a lively format to discuss personal issues and interpersonal skills, such as how to be more independent, thoughtful, respecting of the rights of others, and how to deal with peer pressure.

Level: Junior–Senior High School

Subcompetency 51–55

Work Behavior Training Program. EBSCO.

This social skills training program for the workplace provides a structured approach to job-related training to help students learn what's expected of them on the job.

Level: Junior–Senior High School

Subcompetency 51–55

Learning Through Reading Series. Book 3. A Night on the Town (N. Bowling, I. D. Cook, & D. Salyers).

(See Competency 8 for description.)
Level: Junior–Senior High School

Subcompetency 52

Following Directions. Lawrence Productions.

This computer software program encourages students to improve their ability to follow directions.

Level: Secondary

Competency 13: Maintaining Good Interpersonal Skills

Subcompetency 56–58

DUSO: Developing Understanding of Self and Others. AGS.

This program is designed to develop social skills, listening skills, a positive self-image, and an appreciation of individual strengths. The materials include a teacher's guide, puppets, activity cards, audiocassettes, blackline masters, and more.

Levels: DUSO I, K–Grade 2; DUSO II, Grades 3–4

Subcompetency 56–58

The Walker Social Skills Curriculum. Pro-Ed.

The Accepts Program: A Curriculum for Children's Effective Peer and Teacher Skills.

This program, designed to be used by regular and special education teachers, cognitively teaches social skills as subject matter content.

Level: K–6

The ACCESS Program: Adolescent Curriculum for Communication and Effective Social Skills.

This program, designed for use by regular and special education teachers, teaches peer-to-peer skills, skills for relating to adults, and self-management skills. The materials for these programs include a program guide, videotape, and study guide.

Level: Middle–High School

Subcompetency 56–58

Lifeschool: Occupations and Interpersonal Skills. Globe Fearon.

One half of this multilevel program focuses on relating to others, and the other half focuses on specific employment skills. The 10 self-pacing modules consist of work sheets, activities, teacher's guide, and more.

Reading Level: Grades 2.0–4.5

Subcompetency 56–58

Conversation and Friendship Skills. Lakeshore Educational Inc.

This module includes skill books, workbooks, comic books, practice cards, and blackline masters.

Interest Level: 6–12

Competency 14: Achieving Independence

Subcompetency 59–61

Don't Get Fired. Janus.

Thirteen stories portray young employees who jeopardize their jobs by inappropriate behaviors.

Reading Level: 2.5–4.0

Subcompetency 59–61

Read On! Write On! Series. Globe Fearon.

As students progress through the sequential series, they develop thinking, communication, and socialization skills while examining their own values.

Reading Level: 2.5–4.0
Interest Level: 6–12

Competency 15: Making Adequate Decisions

Subcompetency 62–66

Get Hired. Janus.

Thirteen shortcuts to landing a job are presented in a way students can appreciate and quickly use.

Reading Level: 2.5–4.0
Interest Level: 6–12/ABE/ESL

Subcompetency 62–66

Choosing. Good Apple.

This book helps students in determining choices and more through activities that can be integrated into language, writing, and social studies content areas of the curriculum.

Level: Grades 3–8

Subcompetency 64–66

Problem Solving for Job Success Series. Lakeshore Reading Materials.

This workbook series develops students' decision-making skills and teaches strategies for coping with everyday problems on the job.

Reading Level: Grades 5.0–6.5

Competency 16: Communicating with Others

Subcompetency 68–69

Pacemaker Communication Series. Globe Fearon.

These three work texts help students develop communication and socialization skills.

Reading Level: 2.8
Interest Level: 5–12/ABE/ESL

Subcompetency 67–69

Discovering Self-Expression and Communication. Rosen Publishing Group

This book discusses the dangers of keeping feelings bottled up and teaches students how to express themselves. The eight chapters include Communication, The Message, Nonverbal Communication, The Language of Personal Power, and Listening.

Reading Level: 4.0–6.0
Interest Level: 6–12

Subcompetency 67–69

Communicating. Good Apple.

The open-ended activities in this unit are designed for the students to improve their own self-concepts while developing a better understanding of themselves and others.

Level: Grades 3–8

Subcompetency 67–69

Communication Skills Module. EBSCO.

This module is made up of three interactive components including a teletrainer, telephone skills cassettes, and a simple English curriculum. The materials provide realistic instruction that students need to get along on the job, at home, in school, and anywhere else. The telephone trainer may be used to train anyone to use TDD machines to communicate with the hearing impaired.

Level: Ungraded.

Competency 17: Knowing and Exploring Occupational Possibilities

Subcompetency 70–75

Janus Job Planner. Janus.

(See Competency 10 for description.)
Reading Level: 2.5–4.0

Get Hired. Janus.

(See Competency 15 for description.)
Reading Level: 2.5–4.0
Interest Level: 6–12/ABE/ESL

Subcompetency 70–75

Learning Through Reading Series. Book 4. Serious Business (N. Bowling, I. D. Cook, & D. Salyers). Science Research Associates.

Serious Business is part of a series designed to teach practical skills while supporting reading skills. This book teaches what skills are required for getting and keeping a job. A criterion-referenced pre-post-test, audiotape, and teacher's guide accompany Book 4.

Level: Junior–Senior High School

Competency 18: Selecting and Planning Occupational Choices

Subcompetency 70–75

Janus Job Planner. Janus.

(See Competency 10 for description.)
Reading Level: 2.5–4.0/ABC/ESL
Interest Level: 6–12/ABE/ESL

Subcompetency 76–77

The Job Box. Lakeshore Reading Materials.

A set of 56 books and teacher's guide cover seven occupational clusters and are designed to give students realistic information about opportunities available to them.

Reading Level: Grades 3.0–4.0

Subcompetency 77

Community Helpers. Steck Vaughn.

This activity module teaches children about job duties of people they encounter every day.

Level: K–2

Competency 19: Exhibiting Appropriate Work Habits and Behaviors

Subcompetency 81–87

Learning Through Reading Series. Book 5. The Pay Off (N. Bowling, I. D. Cook, & D. Salyers). Science Research Associates.

The Pay Off is a part of a series designed to teach students practical life skills while supporting reading skills. *The Pay-Off* teaches students the responsibilities and benefits of being a good employee. A criterion-referenced pre-post-test, audiotape, and teacher's guide accompany Book 5.

Level: Junior–Senior High School

Subcompetency 81–87

Time Incentive Program. EBSCO.

This program is designed to teach punctuality, improve workplace skills, increase accuracy and rate of work, evaluate production, and help ensure job security. The materials include a card rack, time cards, job cards, and instructional guide.

Level: Junior–Senior High School

Subcompetency 81–87

Worktales. Globe Fearon.

This series dramatizes workplace issues such as job stress, sexism, safety, assertiveness, substance abuse, and coping with layoff. A curriculum guide and reproducible activity sheets accompany the series.

Reading Level: 1.8–2.9
Interest Level: 9–12/ABE/ESL

Subcompetency 81–87

Workplace Skills Game. Attainment Co.

This game looks at relationships with co-workers and supervisors, work behaviors, attendance, punctuality, and more.

Level: Junior–Senior High School

Subcompetency 81–87

Social Skills on the Job. AGS.

The materials include a videotape, teacher's guide, blackline masters, and computer disks. The varied interactive materials teach skills that provide a bridge between school and the workplace.

Level: Ages 15 and up

Subcompetency 81–87

Don't Get Fired. Janus.

(See Competency 14 for description.)
Level: Reading Level 2.5–4.0

Subcompetency 81–87

Good Work Habits. AGS.

This workbook is designed to teach 12 good work habits using a story format.

Reading Level: 4.0
Interest Level: 9–12; adult

Subcompetency 81–83, 85

Working I (6 videos) and Working II (2 videos). James Stanfield Publishing Co.

These eight videos illustrate behaviors and attitudes important to getting and keeping a job and developing effective interactions with both supervisors and co-workers.

Level: Junior–Senior High School

Subcompetency 81–87

English for the World of Work. AGS.

This program provides training for the world of work, including seeking, securing, and holding a job. The materials include a teacher's guide, student workbook, blackline masters, and a teacher's resource binder.

Interest Level: 8–12; adult

Subcompetency 81

Following Directions. Lawrence Productions.

(See Competency 12 for description.)

Level: Secondary

Subcompetency 82, 85

Work Habits. Lawrence Productions.

This high-interest, low-vocabulary computer software program is a part of the Job Success Series. It deals with cooperation, attitude, attendance, and more.

Level: Secondary

Subcompetency 81–87

Your Personal Habits. Lawrence Productions.

This high-interest, low-vocabulary computer software program is a part of the Job Success series. It deals

with appropriate work habits and behaviors and a variety of jobs.

Level: Secondary

Subcompetency 81–86

Working. I. James Stanfield Publishing Co.

This series of videotapes and the teacher's guide help students learn behaviors and attitudes important to getting and keeping a job. Good grooming habits, punctuality, accepting criticism, conforming to schedules, and other important points are covered.

Level: Junior–Senior High School

Competency 20: Seeking, Securing, and Maintaining a Job

Subcompetency 88–93

The following series of books helps students meet the challenges of the working world (Globe Fearon, Publisher).

Attitudes for Work

Reading Level: 2.7
Interest Level: 6–12/ABE

Finding a Job

Reading Level: 3.0
Interest Level: 6–12/ABE

Keeping a Job

Reading Level: 3.0
Interest Level: 6–12/ABE/ESL

How to Look Good to an Employer

Reading Level: 5.0–6.0
Interest Level: 6–12/ABE

Careers: Exploration and Decisions

Reading Level: 5.0–6.0
Interest Level: 6–12/ABE

Get That Job

Reading Level: 12.2
Interest Level: 6–12

The Way to Work

Reading Level: 2.2
Interest Level: 6–12

Subcompetency 88–93

Occupational Notebook Program (I. D. Cook). Opportunities for Learning.

This is a complete program dealing with the practical skills and basic knowledge required to find and hold a job. A realistic appraisal of personal strengths and weaknesses, techniques for locating jobs, what employers look for and expect from their employees, practice in filling out application forms, interview techniques, using transportation, and communication are included. This program is adaptable to the needs of all students, regular or special needs. The materials include a student notebook and teacher's guide.

Level: Junior–Senior High School

Subcompetency 89–90

Get the Job. Quercus.

This is a skill-oriented text relating to completing applications, such as Social Security card and job applications, and job interviewing.

Reading Level: 2.2

Subcompetency 90

Workplace Simulation. EBSCO.

This is a hands-on program that incorporates all aspects of a job from the interviewing process to evaluating the completed job.

Level: Junior–Senior High School

Subcompetency 90

Get Hired. Janus.

(See Competency 15 for description.)

Reading Level: 2.5–4.0
Interest Level: 6–12/ABE/ESL

Subcompetency 89

Job Application File. Janus.

Student practice on large-size components of typical application.

Reading Level: 2.5–4.0

Subcompetency 90

Job Interview Practice PAK. Janus.

This practice PAK contains materials to create role-play simulations for 30 different jobs.

Reading Level: 2.0–4.0
Interest Level: 8–adult

Subcompetency 88–93

English for the World of Work. Wieser Educational, Inc.

Actual working situations are used in an easy-to-read format that teaches proper English language skills. The text develops communication skills essential for obtaining, keeping, and advancing in a job and is accompanied by student workbooks, blackline masters, and teacher's manual.

Reading Level: 3.7

Subcompetency 90

Job Interview. Janus.

Students are introduced to the basics of interviewing.

Reading Level: 2.5–4.0

Competency 21: Exhibiting Sufficient Physical-Manual Skills

Subcompetency 94

Keeping Fit. Janus.

Presents the physical and emotional health benefits of regular exercise.

Reading Level: 3.5–4.0
Interest Level: 6–12/ABE

Subcompetency 94–97

Take Care of Yourself. Globe Fearon.

Supports important objectives for lifetime health including body systems and immunization.

Reading Level: 2.3–3.0
Interest Level: 6–12

LISTING OF PUBLISHERS

Allyn & Bacon, Inc.
7 Wells Avenue
Newton, MA 02159

AGS
American Guidance Service
4201 Woodland Road
P.O. Box 99
Circle Pines, MN 55014–1796

Attainment Company
P.O. Box 930160
Verona, WI 53593–0160

EBSCO Curriculum Materials
Division of EBSCO Industries, Inc.
Box 11542
Birmingham, AL 35202–1542

Curriculum Associates, Inc.
5 Esquire Road
N. Billerica, MA 01862–2589

Fearon Publishers
500 Harbor Blvd.
Belmont, CA 94002

Gamco Industries, Inc.
P.O. Box 310R
Big Spring, TX 79721–1911

Globe Fearon
4350 Equity Drive
P.O. Box 2649
Columbus, OH 43216

Good Apple
1204 Buchanan St.
Box 299
Carthage, IL 62321–0299

Hartley Courseware
133 Bridge St.
Demondale, MI 48821

James Stanfield Publishing Co.
Drawer CEC
P.O. Box 41058
Santa Barbara, CA 93140

Janus Book Publishers, Inc.
2501 Industrial Parkway W
Haywood, CA 94545

Lakeshore Learning Materials
2695 E. Dominquez St.
P.O. Box 6261
Carson, CA 90749

Love Publishing Company
1777 S. Bellaire Street
Denver, CO 80222

Opportunities for Learning
20417 Nordhoss St.
Chatsworth, CA 91311

Pro-Ed
5341 Industrial Oaks Boulevard
Austin, TX 78735

Quercus
Simon & Schuster School Group
4343 Equity Drive
P.O. Box 2649
Columbus, OH 43216

The Rosen Publishing Group
29 East 21st Street
New York, NY 10010

Saddleback Educational, Inc.
3505 Cadillac Avenue
Building F–9
Costa Mesa, CA 92626

Scott Foresman, A Division of Harper
Lifelong Learning Books
1900 East Lake Avenue
Glenview, IL 60025–9881

Science Research Associates/McGraw-Hill
220 East Danieldale Road
DeSoto, TX 75115-2490

Steck-Vaughn Co.
P.O. Box 26015
Austin, TX 78755

Weiser Educational, Inc.
30085 Commercio, Department 594
Rancho Santa Margarita, CA 92688

Blank Lesson Plan Outline

· ·

_____

LCCE Objective:

Lesson Objective:

Instructional Resources:

Lesson Introduction:

School Activity: Time:

Task:

   1.

   2.

   3.

   4.

Community/School Activity: Time:

Task:

   1.

   2.

   3.

Home/School Activity: Time:

Task:

   1.

   2.

   3

Lesson Plan Evaluation:

Activity:

Criterion:

Career Role:

Career Stage:

Appendix H
LCCE Transition Action Plan Proposal

• •

Name _____

School/Location _____

A.   LCCE Mild/Moderate Curriculum Adoption

1.   The major objectives and outcomes of our educational programs should be

    a. _____

    b. _____

    c. _____

    d. _____

    e. _____

2.   We need to integrate a functional curriculum into our overall educational programs because

    a. _____

    b. _____

    c. _____

    d. _____

    e. _____

3.   We propose the adoption of the Life Centered Career Education (LCCE) curriculum, which (description of)

_____

_____

_____

_____

_____

_____

4. LCCE is being recommended for adoption because it:

_____

_____

_____

_____

_____

_____

B. Curriculum Modifications/Changes Needed for LCCE Implementation
   Mild/Moderate Curriculum Implementation

1. Curriculum Modification Changes

   a. _____

   b. _____

   c. _____

   d. _____

   e. _____

2. Administrative/Policy Changes

   a. _____

   b. _____

   c. _____

   d. _____

   e. _____

3. Staff Changes

   a. _____

   b. _____

   c. _____

   d. _____

   e. _____

4. Parent Involvement Needs and Strategies

   a. _____

   b. _____

   c. _____

   d. _____

5. Community Involvement Needs and Strategies

    a. _____

    b. _____

    c. _____

    d. _____

6. LCCE Mild/Moderate Curriculum Implementation Barriers/Solutions

    a. _____

    b. _____

    c. _____

    d. _____

    e. _____

C. STEPS TO IMPLEMENT LCCE AND TIME LINES

	Steps	Time Line
1.	_____	_____
2.	_____	_____
3.	_____	_____
4.	_____	_____
5.	_____	_____
6.	_____	_____
7.	_____	_____
8.	_____	_____
9.	_____	_____
10.	_____	_____

D. Final Comments/Recommendations—support for staff

Date: _____

By: _____

_____

_____

_____

Transition/Career Development Websites

Internet Resources for Special Children

http://www.irsc.org
http://www.hood.edu/seri

Very Special Arts

http://www.vsarts.org

The Council for Exceptional Children (CEC)

http://www.cec.sped.org

The Association of Severe Handicaps (TASH website)

http://www.tash.org

Individual Education Plans

http://www.IEPengine.com
http://www.classplus.com/classplus

Parents/Families Information

http://www.pacers.org
http://www.kidsource.com
http://www.edlaw.net

Speech, Language, and Hearing Association

http://www.asha.org

Learning Disabilities

http://www.ldonline.com

Mental Retardation

http://www.aamr.com
http://www.thearc.org

American Print House for Blind

http://www.aph.com

National Organization for the Deaf

http://www.nad.org

United Cerebral Palsy Association

http://www.ucpa.org

Spina Bifida Organization

http://www.sbaa.org

Muscular Dystrophy Organization

http://mdausa.org

Brain Injury Organization

http://www.biausa.org

Epilespy Foundation of America

http://www.efa.org

American Diabetes Association

http://www.diabetes.org

Autism Society of America

http://www.autism-society.org

Attention Deficit/Hyperactivity Disorders

http://www.chadd.org
http://www.ldanatl.org

National Association for Gifted Children

http://www.nagc.org

Multicultural Information

http://www.ernie.wmht.org
http://www.Tesol.org

Teaching Organization

http://www.nea.org
http://www.aft.org

National Clearinghouse on Child Abuse and Neglect

http://www.calib.com

Department of Special Education

http://www.osers.edu

Pro-Ed Publishing

http://www.proedinc.com

American Council on Education; information on GED

http://www.acenet.edu

American Disabilities Act

http://www.usdoj.gov/crt/ada

Individuals with Disabilities Education Act 1997

http://www.ed.gov/offices/OSERS/IDEA/index/html
http://www.ideapractices.org

National Information Center for Children and Youth with Disabilities

http://www.nichy.org

Educational Resource Information Center (ERIC) system

http://www.askeric.org

Kids on the Block

http://www.kotb.com

Assistive Technology for the Disabled

http://www.closingthegap.com
http://www.cast.org
http://www.ataccess.org
http://www.abledata.com

At-risk Student

http://www.ed.ove/offices/OERI/At-risk
http://www.dropoutprevention.org
http://www.safeyouth.org

Career-related publications, materials

O*Net Online
    http://www.onetcenter.org
Occupational Outlook Handbook
    http://www .stats.bls.gov
Dictionary of Occupational Titles
    http://www .theodora.com
Guide for Occupational Exploration
    http://www .wois.org.
Encyclopedia of Careers
    http://www.metabase.net.

References

Agran, M., Snow, K., & Swaner, J. (1999). A survey of secondary level teachers' opinions on community-based instruction and inclusive education. *Journal of the Association for Persons with Severe Handicaps, 24*(1), 58–62.

Alberg, J., Petry, C., & Eller, S. (1994). *The social skills planning guide.* Longmont, CA: Sopris West.

American Vocational Association. (1990). *The AVA guide to the Carl D. Perkins Vocational and Applied Technology Education Act of 1990.* Alexandria, VA: Author.

The Arc. (1991). *The Americans with Disabilities Act at work.* Arlington, TX: Author.

Banks, J. (1992). A comment on "teacher perceptions of the regular education initiative." *Exceptional Children, 58*(6), 564.

Beck, J., Broers, J., Hogue, E., Shipstead, J., & Knowlton, E. (1994). Strategies for functional community-based instruction and inclusion for children with mental retardation. *Teaching Exceptional Children, 26*(2), 44–48.

Beck, S. L. (1988). Career education for students with handicaps. *Monograph 3*(3), 2–8.

Began, W. (1990). LCCE teacher's perspective. *The Career Educator,* The University of Missouri-Columbia, *3*(3), 2–3.

Bellamy, G. T. (1985). Transition progress: Comments on Hasazi, Gordon, and Roe. *Exceptional Children, 51*(6), 474–477.

Benz, M. R., & Halpern, A. S. (1993). Vocational and transition services needed and received by students with disabilities during their last year of high school. *Career Development for Exceptional Individuals, 16*(2), 197–211.

Bereiter, C. (1985). The changing face of educational disadvantagement. *Phi Delta Kappan, 66*(8), 538–554.

Bigge, J. (1988). *Curriculum based instruction.* Mountain View, CA: Mayfield Publishing.

Bloom, L. A., Perlmutter, J., & Burrell, L. (1999). The general educator: Applying constructivism to inclusive classrooms. *Intervention in School and Clinic, 34*(3), 132–136.

Board of Education, Sacramento City Unified School District v. Rachel Holland, Div. S-90–1171–DFL Order.

Bocke, J., & Price, D. (1976). Experiential approach for the exceptional adolescent. *Thresholds in Secondary Education, 2*(3), 12–13.

Brigance, A. H. (1999). *The Employability skills inventory.* Billerica, MA: Curriculum Associates.

Brolin, D. E. (1978). *Life centered career education: A competency-based approach.* Arlington, VA: The Council for Exceptional Children.

Brolin, D. E. (1983a). Career education: Where do we go from here? *Career Development for Exceptional Individuals, 6,* 3–14.

Brolin, D. E. (1983b). *Life centered career education: A competency-based approach* (2nd ed.). Arlington, VA: The Council for Exceptional Children.

Brolin, D. E. (1989). *Life centered career education: A competency-based approach* (3rd ed.). Arlington, VA: The Council for Exceptional Children.

Brolin, D. E. (1992a). *Life centered career education: Competency assessment knowledge battery.* Arlington, VA: The Council for Exceptional Children.

Brolin, D. E. (1992b). *Life centered career education: Competency assessment performance battery.* Arlington, VA: The Council for Exceptional Children.

Brolin, D. E. (1992c). *Life centered career education: Daily living skills.* Arlington, VA: The Council for Exceptional Children.

Brolin, D. E. (1992d). *Life centered career education: Personal-social skills.* Arlington, VA: The Council for Exceptional Children.

Brolin, D. E. (1993). *Life centered career education: Professional development activity book.* Arlington, VA: The Council for Exceptional Children.

Brolin, D. E. (1997). *Life centered career education: A competency-based approach* (5th ed.). Arlington, VA: The Council for Exceptional Children.

Brolin, D. E., Cook, I. S., & O'Keefe, S. (1994). Going the distance with life centered career education. *Rural Special Education Quarterly, 13*(1), 64–67.

Brolin, D. E., & Schatzman, B. (1989). Lifelong career development. In D. E. Berkell & J. M. Brown (Eds.), *Transition from school to work for persons with disabilities.* New York: Longman.

Brolin, D. E., & Wehmeyer, M. L. (1995). *Life centered career education: Self-determination scale.* Arlington, VA: The Council for Exceptional Children.

Brophy, J. (1986). Research linking teacher behavior to student achievement: Potential implications for instruction of Chapter 1 students. In B. I. Williams, P. A. Richmond, & B. J. Mason (Eds.), *Designs for compensatory education: Conference proceedings and papers* (pp. 121–179). Washington, DC: Research and Evaluation Associates.

Brown v. Board of Education of Topeka Kansas, 347 U.S. 483 (1954).

Brown, C., Browning, P., & Dunn, C. (1992). *Secondary special education programs in Alabama: A statewide study.* Auburn, AL: A Program for the Study on Disability, Department of Rehabilitation and Special Education, Auburn University.

Browning, P. (1994). Self-determination: An essential ingredient in transition. In P. Browning (Ed.), *Transition III in Alabama: A profile of commitment* (pp. 93–105). Auburn, AL: Auburn University.

Browning, P., & Brechin, C. (1993). Assessment in transition: A functional definition and collaborative program for practice. *Vocational Evaluation and Work Adjustment Bulletin, 26,* 123–127.

Browning, P., & Dunn, C. (1994). Auburn University's teacher preparation program with an emphasis at the secondary level. In P. Browning (Ed.), *Transition III in Alabama: A profile of commitment* (pp. 76–91). Auburn, AL: Auburn University.

Browning, P., Dunn, C., & Brown, C. (1993). School to community transition for youth with disabilities. In R. C. Eaves & P. J. McLaughlin (Eds.), *Recent advances in special education and rehabilitation* (pp. 193–209). Boston: Andover Medical Publishers.

Bullis, M., Bull, B., Johnson, B., & Peters, D. (1994). Young adults who are hearing impaired and deaf in a transition study: Did they and their parents supply similar data? *Exceptional Children, 60*(4), 323–333.

Bullis, M., & Gaylord-Ross, R. (1991). *Moving on: Transitions for youth with behavior disorders.* Arlington, VA: The Council for Exceptional Children.

Bullis, M., Moran, T., Benz, M. R., Todis, B., & Johnson, M. D. (2002). Description and evaluation of the ARIES project achieving rehabilitation, individualized education, and employment success for adolescents with emotional disturbance. *Career Development of Exceptional Individuals, 25*(1), 41–58.

Bush, G. (1991). *America 2000: An education strategy.* Washington, DC: U.S. Department of Education.

Byrnes, M. (1990). The regular education initiative debate: A view from the field. *Exceptional Children, 56*(4), 345–349.

Campbell, L. W., Todd, M., & O'Rourke, E. (1971). *Work-study handbook for educable mentally retarded minors enrolled in high school programs in California public schools.* Sacramento, CA: California State Department of Education.

Carpignano, J., & Bigge, J. (1983). Teaching basic thinking skills. In J. Bigge (Ed.), *Curriculum based instruction* (pp. 187–232). Mountain View, CA: Mayfield Publishing.

Carter, J., & Sugai, G. (1989). Social skills curriculum analysis. *Teaching Exceptional Children, 22*(1), 36–39.

Chadsey-Rusch, J., Rusch, F. R., & Phelps, L. A. (1988). Epilogue: Analysis and syntheses of transition issues. In D. E. Berkell & J. M. Brown (Eds.), *Transition from school to work for persons with disabilities* (pp. 227–241). New York: Longman.

Clark, D. H. (1993). Meeting special needs— business and education: A partnership that works. *The Journal for Vocational Special Needs Education, 15*(2), 31–35.

Clark, G. M. (1979). *Career education for the handicapped child in the elementary classroom.* Denver, CO: Love Publishing.

Clark, G. M. (1991). *Functional curriculum and its place in the regular education initiative.* Paper presented at the seventh International Conference of the Division on Career Development, Kansas City, MO.

Clark, G. M. (1994). Is a functional curriculum approach compatible with an inclusive education model? *Teaching Exceptional Children, 26*(2), 36–39.

Clark, G. M. (1998). Assessment for transition planning: Transition series. Austin, TX: Pro-Ed.

Clark, G. M., Carlson, B. C., Fisher, S., Cook, I. D., & D'Alonzo, B. J. (1991). Career development for students with disabilities in elementary schools: A position statement of the Division on Career Development. *Career Development for Exceptional Individuals, 14,* 109–120.

Clark, G. M., Field, S., Patton, J. R., Brolin, D. E., & Sitlington, P. L. (1994). *Life skills instruction: A necessary component for all students with disabilities: A position statement of the Division on Career Development and Transition.* Arlington, VA: The Council for Exceptional Children, The Division on Career Development and Transition.

Clark, G. M., & Kolstoe, O. P. (1990). *Career development and transition education for adolescents with disabilities.* Boston: Allyn & Bacon.

Clark, G. M., & Kolstoe, O. P. (1995). *Career development and transition education for adolescents with disabilities* (2nd ed.). Boston: Allyn & Bacon.

Clark, G. M., & White, W. J. (1980). *Career education for the handicapped: Current perspectives for teachers.* Boothwyn, PA: Education Resources Center.

Cook, I. D. (1974). *Materials handbook.* Institute, WV: West Virginia College of Graduate Studies.

Cook, I. D. (1979). *Curriculum methods and materials for the handicapped in career/vocational education: Part 4. Developing learning activities.* Institute, WV: West Virginia Graduate College.

Cook, I. D. (1987). *Occupational notebook program, teacher's guide.* Chatsworth, CA: Opportunities for Learning.

Cook, I. D. (1993). *Task analysis of matching materials to characteristics of the learner. The LCCE profes-sional development affinity book.* Institute, WV: West Virginia Graduate College.

Cook, I. D., & Thurman-Urbanic, M. (1990). *Transition manual: TRIAD telecommunications project.* Institute, WV: West Virginia Graduate College.

Council for Exceptional Children. (1976). Official actions of the delegate assembly at the 54th annual international convention. *Exceptional Children, 43*(1), 41–45.

Council for Exceptional Children. (1978). *Position paper on career education.* Arlington, VA: Author.

Council for Exceptional Children. (1992). *Life centered career education: Professional development activity book.* Arlington, VA: Author.

Council for Exceptional Children. (1993). Policy on inclusive schools and community settings. Adopted by the CEC delegate assembly, 1993. *Teaching Exceptional Children Supplement, 25*(4), 3–6.

Council for Exceptional Children. (1994). *Policy manual.* Arlington, VA: Author.

Council for Exceptional Children, Division on Career Development and Transition. (1994, Fall). Life Skills Instruction: A Necessary Component for All Students with Disabilities: A position statement of the Division on Career Development and Transition. Clark, G. M., Field, S., Patton, J. R., Brolin, D. E., & Sitlington, P. L., *Career Development for Exceptional Individuals, 17*(2), 125–134.

Council for Exceptional Children, Division on Mental Retardation and Developmental Disabilities. (1992). *Position paper.* Arlington, VA: Author.

Council for Exceptional Children, Division on Mental Retardation and Developmental Disabilities. (1994). MRDD position paper: Dealing with secondary curricula and policy issues for students with MR/DD. *MRDD Express, 4*(3), 3–4.

Crewe, N. M., Athelstan, G. T., & University of Minnesota. (1984). *Functional assessment inventory manual.* Menomonie, WI: University of Wisconsin-Stout, Materials Development Center.

Cronin, M. E., & Patton, J. R. (1993). *Life skills instruction for all students with special needs: A practical guide for integrating real-life content into the curriculum.* Austin, TX: Pro-Ed.

Cummings, R. W., & Maddux, C. D. (1987). *Career and vocational education for the mildly handicapped.* Springfield, IL: Thomas.

Cutler, B. C. (1993). *You, your child, and special education.* Baltimore: Paul H. Brookes.

D'Alonzo, B. J., & Geordano, G. (1994). Strategies for developing rural transition programs. *Rural Special Education Quarterly, 13*(1), 37–45.

Darley, J. M., & Latane, B. (1968). When will people help in a crisis? *Psychology Today, 2*(7), 54–57, 70–71.

Davis, D. E. (1988). *My friends and me.* Circle Pines, MN: American Guidance Service.

Davis, S. (1992). *Report card to the nation on inclusion in education of students with mental retardation.* Arlington, TX: The Arc.

Davis, S. (1993). *A status report to the nation on inclusion in employment of people with mental retardation.* Arlington, TX: The Arc.

Davis, S., & Wehmeyer, M. L. (1991). *Ten steps to independence: Promoting self-determination in the home.* Arlington, TX: The Arc.

Davis, W. E. (1989). The regular education initiative debate: Its promises and problems. *Exceptional Children, 55*(5), 440–446.

deBettencourt, L. U., & Zigmond, N. (1990). The learning disabled secondary school dropout: What teachers should know. What teachers can do. *Teacher Education and Special Education, 13*(1), 17–20.

Denny, M. R. (1966). Theoretical analysis and its application to training the mentally retarded. In N. R. Ellis (Ed.), *International review of research in mental retardation: Vol. 2.* New York: Academic Press.

Design for ability. (1994). *Workwell, 1,* 28–31.

DeStefano, L., Linn, R., & Markward, M. (1987). *Review of student assessment instruments and practices in use in secondary/transition projects.* University of Illinois at Urbana-Champaign: Secondary Transition Intervention Effectiveness Institute.

Dever, R. B. (1988). *Community living skills: A taxonomy.* Washington, DC: American Association on Mental Retardation.

Dever, R. B. (1989). A taxonomy of community living skills. *Exceptional Children, 55*(5), 395–404.

Diana v. State Board of Education of California, C-70 37 RFP (District Court of Northern California, 1970).

Dictionary of Occupational Titles (4th ed.). (1977). Washington, DC: U.S. Government Printing Office.

Didley, D. R. (1987, October 29–30). *Transition: New challenge for special education* (pp. 1–13). Paper presented at the Annual Conference of the Association for the Severely Handicapped, Chicago, IL.

Dunn, L. M. (1968). Special education for the mildly retarded: Is much of it justifiable? *Exceptional Children, 35,* 5–22.

Egelston-Dodd, J., & DeCaro, J. (1982). National project on career education: Description and impact report. *Career Development for Exceptional Individuals, 5,* 87–97.

Elksnin, N., & Elksnin, L. K. (1991). Facilitating the vocational success of students with mild handicaps. *The Journal for Vocational Special Needs Education, 13*(2), 5–11.

Ellis, N. R. (1970). Memory processes in retardates and normals. In N. R. Ellis (Ed.), *International review of research in mental retardation: Vol. 4.* New York: Academic Press.

Elrod, F., & Gilliland, M. (1991–1992). A call for neo-progressivism in educating economically disadvantaged children with disabilities: A curricular example. *National Forum of Special Education Journal, 2*(2), 19–27.

Encyclopedia of Associations (26th ed.). (1992). Detroit, MI: Gale Research.

Epstein, M., Patton, J., Polloway, E., & Foley, R. (1992). Educational services for students with behavior disorders: A review of individualized education programs. *Teacher Education and Special Education, 15,* 41–48.

Equal Employment Opportunity Commission. (1991, July 26). Part 1630—Regulations to implement the equal employment provisions of the Americans with Disabilities Act. *Federal Register, 56*(144), 35726–35753.

Everson, J. M., & McNulty, K. (1992). Interagency teams: Building local transition programs through parental and professional partnerships. In F. R. Rusch, L. Destefano, J. Chadsey-Rusch, L. A. Phelps, & E. Szymanski (Eds.), *Transition from school to adult life: Models, linkages, and policy* (pp. 341–351). Sycamore, IL: Sycamore Publishing.

Field, S. (1996). Self-determination instructional strategies for youth with learning disabilities. *Journal of Learning Disabilities, 29,* 40–52.

Field, S., & Hoffman, A. (1994). Development of a model for self-determination. *Career Development for Exceptional Individuals, 17*(2), 159–169.

Field, S., LeRoy, B., & Rivera, S. (1994). Meeting functional curriculum needs in middle school general education classrooms. *Teaching Exceptional Children, 26*(2), 40–43.

Fisher, M. A., & Zeaman, D. (1973). Attention/retention theory of retardate discrimination learning. In N. R. Ellis (Ed.), *International review of research in mental retardation: Vol. 6.* New York: Academic Press.

Flaxman, E., & Inger, M. (1991). Parents and schooling in the 1990s. *The ERIC Review, 1*(3), 2–6.

Frank, A. R., & Sitlington, P. L. (1993). Graduates with mental disabilities: The story three years later. *Education and Training in Mental Retardation, 28*(1), 30–37.

Fuchs, D., & Fuchs, L. S. (1994). Inclusive schools movement and the radicalization of special education reform. *Exceptional Children, 60*(4), 294–309.

Gaylord-Ross, R. (Ed.). (1988). *Vocational education for persons with handicaps.* Mountain View, CA: Mayfield Publishing.

Gearhart, B. G. (1985). *Learning disabilities: Educational strategies.* St. Louis, MO: Times Mirror/ Mosby College Publishing.

Gemmel, S. J., & Peterson, M. (1989). Supported employment and provision of on-going support services: A pilot project. *Career Development for Exceptional Individuals, 12*(2), 123–128.

Gibbs, J. (1987). *Tribes: A process for social development and cooperative learning.* Santa Rosa, CA: Center Source Publications.

Gilhool, T. K. (1973). Education: An inalienable right. *Exceptional Children, 39,* 597–609.

Gillet, P. (1980). Career education in special elementary education program. *Teaching Exceptional Children, 13*(1), 17–21.

Gilliam, J. E., & Coleman, M. C. (1981). Who influences IEP decisions? *Exceptional Children, 47,* 642–644.

Gloeckler, L. C. (1993). Systems change and transition services for secondary youth with disabilities. *OSERS News in Print, 6*(6), 6–12.

Goals 2000: Educate America Act, 20 U.S.C. § 5801 (1994).

Goldstein, A. P. (1988). *The prepare curriculum: Teaching prosocial competencies.* Champaign, IL: Research Press.

Goldstein, A. P., Sprafkin, R. P., Gershaw, N. J., & Klein, P. (1980). *Skillstreaming the adolescent.* Champaign, IL: Research Press.

Graubard, P. S. (1973). Children with behavioral disabilities. In L. M. Dunn (Ed.), *Exceptional children in the schools.* New York: Holt, Rinehart & Winston.

Greenan, J. P. (1986). Curriculum and assessment in generalizable skills instruction. *The Journal for Vocational Special Needs Education, 9*(1), 3–10.

Gysbers, N. C., & Henderson, P. (1994). *Developing and managing your school guidance program* (2nd ed.). Alexandria, VA: American Counseling Association.

Hagner, D., & Daning, R. (1993). Opening lines: How job developers talk to employers. *Career Development for Exceptional Individuals, 16*(2), 123–134.

Hahn, A., Danzberger, J., & Lefkowitz, B. (1987). *Dropouts in America: Enough is known for action.* Washington, DC: Institute for Educational Leadership.

Halloran, W. D. (1993). Transition services requirement: Issues, implications, challenge. In P. Browning (Ed.), *Transition II in Alabama: A profile of commitment* (pp. 1–15). Auburn, AL: Auburn University.

Halpern, A. S. (1985). Transition: A look at the foundations. *Exceptional Children, 51*(6), 479–486.

Halpern, A. S. (1992). Transition: Old wine in new bottles. *Exceptional Children, 58*(3), 202–211.

Halpern, A. S. (1993). Quality of life as a conceptual framework for evaluating transition outcomes. *Exceptional Children, 59*(6), 486–498.

Halpern, A. S. (1994). The transition of youth with disabilities to adult life: A position statement of the Division on Career Development and Transition, the Council for Exceptional Children. *Career Development for Exceptional Individuals, 17,* 115–124.

Halpern, A. S., Benz, M., & Lindstrom, L. (1991). *A systems change approach to improving secondary special education and transition programs at the local community level.* Unpublished manuscript, University of Oregon, Eugene.

Halpern, A. S., Dorenz, B., & Benz, M. R. (1993). Job experiences of students with disabilities during their last two years in school. *Career Development for Exceptional Individuals, 16*(1), 63–73.

Halpern, A. S., & Fuhrer, M. J. (1984). *Functional assessment in rehabilitation.* Baltimore: Paul H. Brookes.

Halpern, A. S., Irvin, L., & Landman, J. T. (1979). *Tests for everyday living.* Monterey, CA: CTB/McGraw-Hill.

Halpern, A. S., Lehmann, J., Irvin, L., & Heiry, T. (1982). *Contemporary assessment: For mentally retarded adolescents and adults.* Baltimore: University Park Press.

Halpern, A. S., Raffeld, P., Irvin, L. K., Link, R., & Munkres, A. (1985). *Social and prevocational information battery.* Monterey, CA: CTB/McGraw-Hill.

Haring, D. (1978, January 1–3). *Learn and earn with project work.* Paper presented at the meeting of the Career Education Workshop, St. Louis, MO.

Haring, N. G. (1982). *Exceptional children and youth.* Upper Saddle River, NJ: Merrill/Prentice Hall.

Harrington, T., & O'Shea, A. (Eds.). (1984). *Guide to occupational exploration* (2nd ed.). Circle Pines, MN: American Guidance Service.

Hauser, S. (1993, November/December). How Herman Miller put the ADA into action. *FM Journal,* 25–27.

Hazel, J. S., Schumacher, J. B., Sherman, J. A., & Sheldon-Wildgen, R. (1981). *Asset: A social skills program.* Champaign, IL: Research Press.

Heal, L. W., Copher, J. I., DeStephano, L., & Rusch, F. R. (1989). A comparison of successful and unsuccessful placements of secondary students with mental handicaps into competitive employment. *Career Development for Exceptional Individuals, 12*(2), 167–177.

Hendrick Hudson School District v. Rowley, No. 80–1002 (1986).

Heskett, J. (1993). Inclusive education for the disabled. *Missouri Innovations in Special Education, 21*(2), 1–2, 8.

Higgins, A., Fowler, S. A., & Chandler, L. K. (1988). Planning school transitions: Family and professional collaboration. *Journal of the Division for Early Childhood, 12*(2), 108–115.

Hobson v. Hansen, 393 U.S. 801 (1968).

Horne, R. L. (1991). The education of children and youth with special needs: What do the laws say? *NICHCY News Digest, 1*(1), 1–15.

House Report No. 101–544, 10 (1990).

Hoyt, K. B. (1975). *An introduction to career education. A policy paper of the U.S. Department of Education.* Washington, DC: U.S. Office of Education.

Hoyt, K. B. (1976). Community resources for career education. *Monographs on career education.* Washington, DC: U.S. Office of Education.

Hoyt, K. B. (1980). *Career education for persons with visual handicaps.* Paper presented at the Helen Keller Centennial Conference, Boston, MA.

Hoyt, K. B. (1982). Federal and state participation in career education: Past, present, and future. *Journal of Career Education, 9*(1), 5–15.

Hoyt, K. B. (1983, June). *How to fix the public's schools in eight not-so-easy steps.* Working paper. Council of State Planning Agencies, National Governors Association.

Hoyt, K. B. (1987). Trends in career education: Implications for the future. In *Career education in transition: Trends and implications for the future* (pp. 5–35). Columbus, OH: ERIC Clearinghouse on Adult, Career, and Vocational Education.

Hoyt, K. B. (1993). Reaction to the three solutions for transition from school to employment. *Youth Policy, 15*(6 & 7), 36.

Hull, D. (1992, March). Tech prep: Practical application for America's work force. *School Shop/Technical Directions,* 17–19.

Iannacone, C. J., Wienke, W. D., & Cosden, M. A. (1992 December-January). Social skills instruction in secondary schools: Factors affecting its implementation. *The High School Journal,* 111–118.

Inger, M. (1993). Teacher collaboration in secondary schools. *Centerfocus, 2,* 1–4.

Jackson, D. A., Jackson, N. F., Bennett, M. L., Bynum, D. M., & Faryna, E. (1991). *Learning to get along: Social effectiveness training for people with development disabilities.* Champaign, IL: Research Press.

Jackson, N. F., Jackson, D. A., & Monroe, C. (1983). *Getting along with others.* Champaign, IL: Research Press.

Jastak, J., & Jastak, S. (1973). *Wide range employment sample test.* Wilmington, DE: Jastak Associates.

Jenkins, J. R., & Pious, C. G. (1991). Full inclusion and the REI: A reply to Thousand and Villa. *Exceptional Children, 56*(6), 562–564.

Jenkins, J. R., Pious, C. G., & Jewell, M. (1990). Special education and the regular education initiative: Basic assumptions. *Exceptional Children, 56*(6), 479–491.

Johnson, D., Bruininks, R. H., & Thurlow, M. L. (1987). Meeting the challenge of transition service planning through improved interagency cooperation. *Exceptional Children, 53*(6), 530–533.

Johnson, D. R., Thompson, S. J., Sinclair, M. F., Krantz, G. C., Evelo, S., Stolte, K., & Thompson, J. R. (1993). Considerations in the design and follow-up and follow-along systems for improving transition programs and services. *Career Development for Exceptional Individuals, 16*(2), 225–238.

Johnson, J. (1976, March 4–5). *School stores: A vital part of your career education program.* Paper presented at the meeting of the Career Education Workshop, St. Louis, MO.

Johnson, J. R., & Rusch, F. R. (1993). Secondary special education and transition services: Identification and recommendations for future research and demonstration. *Career Development for Exceptional Individuals, 16*(1), 1–18.

Johnson, R. T., & Johnson, D. W. (1982). Effects of cooperative and competitive learning experiences on interpersonal attraction between handicapped and nonhandicapped students. *Journal of Social Psychology, 116,* 211–219.

Johnson, R. T., & Johnson, D. W. (1983). Effects of cooperative, competitive, and individualistic learning experiences on social development. *Exceptional Children, 49,* 323–329.

Johnson, R. T., Johnson, D. W., & Rynders, J. (1981). Effect of cooperative, competitive, and individualistic learning experiences on self-esteem of handicapped and nonhandicapped students. *Journal of Psychology, 108,* 31–34.

Kaufman, J. M. (1985). *Characteristics of children's behavior disorders* (3rd ed.). Upper Saddle River, NJ: Merrill/Prentice Hall.

Kaufman, J. M., Kameenui, E. J., Birman, B., & Danielson, L. (1990). Special education and the process of change: Victim or master of educational reform? *Exceptional Children, 57*(2), 109–115.

Killilea, M. (1960). *Karen.* New York: Dell.

Kirk, S. A., & Gallagher, J. J. (1989). *Educating exceptional children.* Boston: Houghton Mifflin.

Kohler, P. D. (1993). Best practices in transition: Substantiated or implied? *Career Development for Exceptional Individuals, 16,* 107–121.

Kohler, P. D. (1994). *A conceptual model of effective transition practices.* Champaign, IL: University of Illinois, Transition Research Institute.

Kohler, P. D., DeStefano, F., Wermuth, T., Grayson, T., & McGinty, S. (1994). An analysis of exemplary transition programs: How and why are they selected? *Career Development for Exceptional Individuals, 17,* 187–202.

Kokaska, C. J., & Brolin, D. E. (1985). *Career education for handicapped individuals* (2nd ed.). Upper Saddle River, NJ: Merrill/Prentice Hall.

Kolstoe, O. P. (1976). Developing career awareness: The foundation of a career education program. In G. B. Blackburn (Ed.), *Colloquium series on career education for handicapped adolescents.* West Lafayette, IN: Purdue University.

Langone, J. (1990). *Teaching students with mild and moderate learning problems.* Boston: Allyn & Bacon.

Larson, C. (1981). *EBCE state of Iowa dissemination model for MD and LD students.* Fort Dodge, IA: Iowa Central Community College.

Lewis, R. B., & Doorlag, D. H. (2003). *Teaching students in the general education classroom* (6th ed.). Upper Saddle River, NJ: Merrill/Prentice Hall.

Lichtenstein, S. (1993). Transition from school to adulthood: Case studies of adults with learning disabilities who dropped out of school. *Exceptional Children, 59*(4), 336–347.

Lindsey, J. D. (1993). *Computers and exceptional individuals* (2nd ed.). Austin, TX: Pro-Ed.

Linkenhoker, D., & McCarron, L. (1983). *Adaptive behavior: The street survival skills questionnaire.* Dallas, TX: Common Market Press.

Linthicum, E., Cole, J. T., & D'Alonzo, B. J. (1991). Employment and the Americans with Disabilities Act of 1990. *Career Development for Exceptional Individuals, 14*(1), 1–13.

Lippman, L., & Goldberg, I. (1973). *Right to education: Anatomy of the Pennsylvania case and its implications for exceptional children.* New York: Teachers College Press, Columbia University.

Loyd, R. J., & Brolin, D. E. (1989). Parents'/family members' involvement and training in the LCCE curriculum program. In R. J. Loyd & D. E. Brolin, *Life centered career education: Trainer's manual.* Arlington, VA: The Council for Exceptional Children.

Loyd, R. J., & Brolin, D. E. (1997). *Life centered career education: Modified curriculum for individuals with moderate disabilities.* Arlington, VA: The Council for Exceptional Children.

Loyd, R. J., & Brolin, D. E. (2002). *Life centered career education: Mild/moderate curriculum training manual.* Arlington, VA: The Council for Exceptional Children.

Loyd, R. J., & Brolin, D. E. (in press). *The LCCE Moderate Curriculum Competency Rating Scale-M (CRS-M).* Arlington, VA: The Council for Exceptional Children.

Loyd, R. J., & Brolin, D. E. (in press). *The LCCE Moderate Performance Assessment Battery: LCCE-M PAB.* Arlington, VA: The Council for Exceptional Children.

Loyd, R. J., and Brolin, D. E. (in press). *The LCCE Moderate Pictorial Knowledge Battery: LCCE-M PKB.* Arlington, VA: The Council for Exceptional Children.

Luftig, R. L. (1987). *Teaching the mentally retarded student.* Boston: Allyn & Bacon.

Lynch, E., & Beare, P. (1990). The quality of IEP objectives and their relevance to instruction for students with mental retardation and behavioral disorders. *Remedial and Special Education, 11,* 48–55.

Martinez, L. (1993, Spring). Enhancing community and cultural relevance of high school curriculum. *Inclusive Communities Newsletter.* Detroit, MI: Developmental Disabilities Institute, Wayne State University.

Mastropieri, M. A., & Scruggs, T. E. (2000). *The inclusive classroom: Strategies for effective instruction.* Upper Saddle River, NJ: Merrill/Prentice Hall.

McDaniels, C., & Gysbers, N. C. (1992). *Counseling for career development.* San Francisco: Jossey-Bass.

McFadden, D. L., & Burke, E. P. (1991). Developmental disabilities and the new paradigm: Directions for the 1990s. *Mental Retardation, 29,* iii–vi.

McLaughlin, M. J., & Warren, S. H. (1992). *Issues and options in restructuring schools and special education programs.* College Park, MD: University of Maryland and Westat, Inc.

Mellard, D. F., & Clark, G. M. (1992). *National high school project. Vol. 2: A quantitative description of comprehensive services and practices for students with disabilities. Final report.* Grant No. G008530217, OSERS Department of Special Education. Lawrence, KS: University of Kansas.

Mercer, C. D. (1983). *Students with learning disabilities* (2nd ed.). Upper Saddle River, NJ: Merrill/Prentice Hall.

Mercer, C. D., & Mercer, A. R. (2001). *Teaching students with learning problems* (6th ed.). Upper Saddle River, NJ: Merrill/Prentice Hall.

Mercer, C. D., & Snell, M. E. (1977). *Learning theory research in mental retardation.* Upper Saddle River, NJ: Merrill/Prentice Hall.

Meyen, E. L. (1990). *Exceptional children in today's school.* Denver, CO: Love Publishing.

Mills v. Board of Education in the District of Columbia, 348 F. Supp. 866 D.D.C. (1972).

Minnesota Department of Education. (1990). Outcome-based education gives teachers chance for a larger role in planning. *Education Update, 25*(1), 1.

Minnesota Employment Stabilization Research Institute. (1969). *Minnesota rate of manipulation test.* Circle Pines, NM: American Guidance Service.

Missouri Department of Elementary and Secondary Education. (1992). *A proposal to implement outcome-based graduation in Missouri high schools.* Jefferson City, MO: Author.

Missouri LINC. (1992). *Legislation regarding special populations.* Columbia, MO: University of Missouri-Columbia.

Mithaug, D. E., Mar, D. K., & Stewart, J. E. (1978). *Prevocational assessment and curriculum guide.* Seattle, WA: J. E. Stewart.

Moon, S., Goodall, P., Barcus, M., & Brooke, V. (1986). *The supported work model of competitive employment for citizens with severe handicaps: A guide for job trainers.* (rev. ed.). Richmond, VA: Virginia Commonwealth University, Rehabilitation Research and Training Center.

Moore, E. J., & Gysbers, N. C. (1972). Career development: A new focus. *Educational Leadership, 30,* 1–8.

Moore, S. C., Agran, M., & McSweyn, C. A. (1990). Career education: Are we starting early enough? *Career Development for Exceptional Individuals, 13*(2), 129–134.

Murphy, J. (1991). The educational reform movement of the 1980s: A comprehensive analysis. In J. Murphy (Ed.), *The educational reform movement of the 1980s: Perspective and cases.* Berkeley, CA: McCutchan.

National Association for Industry-Education Cooperation. (1993, June-July). *Newsletter.*

National Center for Educational Outcomes. (1993). NCEO finds states active in "outcomes" efforts. *Outcomes, 2*(2), 2.

National Commission on Excellence in Education. (1983). *A nation at risk.* Washington, DC: U.S. Government Printing Office.

National Education Association, Educational Policies Commission. (1938). *The purposes of education in American democracy.* Washington, DC: Author.

National Education Association, Educational Policies Commission. (1952). *Education for all American youth: A further look.* Washington, DC: Author.

National Information Center for Children and Youth with Disabilities (1997). The IDEA amendments of 1997. *NICHCY News Digest, 26,* 1–38.

National Organization on Disability and Business Week salute the members of the Disability 2000 Council. (1993, December 27). *Business Week,* 13–19.

Naylor, M. (1985). *Role of vocational education in transition services for handicapped youth.* Washington, DC: National Institute of Education.

Neil, S. B. (1977). Clearing the air in career education. *American Education, 13*(2), 6–9, 13.

Neubert, D. A., & Tilson, G. R. (1987). The critical stage of transition: A challenge and an opportunity. *The Journal of Vocational Special Needs Education, 13,* 3–7.

Nevin, A., Johnson, D. W., & Johnson, R. (1982). Effects of groups and individual contingencies on academic performance and social relations of special needs students. *Journal of Social Psychology, 116,* 41–49.

NICHCY. (1993). Transition services in the IEP. *NICHCY Transition Summary, 3*(1), 1–20.

Nihira, K., Leland, H., & Lambert, N. (1993). *AAMD adaptive behavior scale* (residential and school 2nd ed.). Austin, TX: Pro-Ed.

North Dakota Department of Public Instruction. (1990). *Special education in North Dakota: Guide*

II—*Educational programming for students with mild and moderate mental retardation.* Bismarck, ND: Author.

Nugent, G., & Stone, C. (1981). Think it through: An interactive videodisk for the hearing impaired. In *Proceedings of the Johns Hopkins first national search for applications of personal computing to the handicapped* (pp. 49–51). Los Angeles: IIEE Computer Society Press.

Oberti v. Board of Education of the Borough of Clementon School District, C.A. No. 91–2818, D.N.J. (1992).

O'Leary, E. (1989). *A study to identify educational outcome for secondary mildly handicapped students from public high school programs as perceived by parents, employers, and educators.* Unpublished dissertation, University of Illinois, Champaign-Urbana.

Parker, R. (1991a). *The OASIS-2 aptitude survey—2.* Austin, TX: Pro-Ed.

Parker, R. (1991b). *The OASIS-2 interest schedule—2.* Austin, TX: Pro-Ed.

Parker, R. M., & Szymanski, E. M. (1992). *Rehabilitation counseling: Basics and beyond* (2nd ed.). Austin, TX: Pro-Ed.

Patterson, J. B., & Curl, R. M. (1992). Using occupational and labor market information in transition services. In F. R. Rusch et al. (Eds.), *Transition from school to adult life: Models, linkages, and policies* (pp. 353–369). Sycamore: IL: Sycamore Publishing.

Pennsylvania Association for Retarded Children v. Commonwealth of Pennsylvania. 334, F. Supp. 1257, E.D.Ua. (1971).

Pennsylvania State University Institute for the Study of Adult Literacy. (1993). *A day in the life.* North Billerica, MA: Curriculum Associates.

Phelps, L. A. (1976). *Instructional development for special needs learners: An inservice resource guide.* Urbana, IL: Department of Vocational and Technical Education, University of Illinois.

Phelps, L. A., & Maddy-Bernstein, C. (1992). Developing effective partnerships for special populations: The challenge of partnerships and alliances. *The Journal for Vocational Special Needs Education, 14*(2 & 3), 33–36.

Polloway, E. A., & Patton, J. R. (1993). *Strategies for teaching learners with special needs* (5th ed.). Upper Saddle River, NJ: Merrill/Prentice Hall.

Polloway, E. A., Patton, J. R., Payne, J. S., & Payne, R. A. (1989). *Strategies for teaching learners with special needs* (4th ed.). Upper Saddle River, NJ: Merrill/Prentice Hall.

The President's Committee on Employment of People with Disabilities. (1987). *Disabled Americans at work.* Washington, DC: U.S. Government Printing Office.

The President's Committee on Employment of People with Disabilities. (1993, October). *Energize America—Employ Ability.* Washington, DC: U.S. Government Printing Office.

The President's Committee on Employment of the Handicapped. (1977, September). *Newsletter.* Washington, DC: U.S. Government Printing Office.

The President's Panel on Mental Retardation. (1963). *Report to the President: A proposed program for national action to combat mental retardation.* Washington, DC: U.S. Government Printing Office.

Purdue Research Foundation. (1968). *Purdue pegboard.* Chicago: Science Research Associates.

Revell, G. (1993, Winter). PL 102–569: The Rehabilitation Act Amendments of 1992. *Virginia Commonwealth Newsletter.*

Reynolds, M. C., & Birch, J. W. (1982). *Teaching exceptional children in America's schools.* Arlington, VA: The Council for Exceptional Children.

Reynolds, M. C., Zetlin, A. G., & Wang, M. C. (1993). 20/20 analysis: Taking a close look at the margins. *Exceptional Children, 59*(4), 294–300.

Roberts, J. R. (1945). *Pennsylvania bi-manual work sample.* Circle Pines, MN: American Guidance Service.

Roessler, R. T. (1991a). A problem-solving approach to implementing career education. *Career Development for Exceptional Individuals, 14*(2), 59–66.

Roessler, R. T. (1991b). *Your hit parade.* Columbia, MO: University of Missouri-Columbia, LCCE/Employability Enhancement Project.

Roessler, R. T., & Brolin, D. E. (1992). *LCCE competency units for occupational guidance and prepa-*

ration. Arlington, VA: The Council for Exceptional Children.

Roessler, R. T., Brolin, D. E., & Johnson, J. M. (1992). Barriers to the implementation of career education for special education. *Journal of Career Development, 18*(4), 271–282.

Roessler, R. T., Loyd, R. J., & Brolin, D. E. (1990). Implementing life centered career education: Contextual barriers and implementation recommendations. *Academic Therapy, 25*(4), 523–533.

Roessler, R. T., & Rubin, S. E. (1992). *Case management and rehabilitation counseling.* Austin, TX: Pro-Ed.

Roessler, R. T., Shearin, A. A., & Williams, E. R. (1993). *From 94–142 to 101–476: The more things change the more they stay the same.* Fayetteville, AR: University of Arkansas.

Rose, E., Friend, M., & Farnum, M. (1988). Transition planning for mildly handicapped students: The secondary school counselor's role. *The School Counselor, 52,* 275–293.

Rusch, F. R. (Ed.). (1986). *Competitive employment issues and strategies.* Baltimore: Paul H. Brookes.

Rusch, F. R, & Chadsey, J. G. (1998). *Beyond high school: Transition from school to work.* Boston: Wadsworth Publishing Company.

Rusch, F. R., Destefano, L., Chadsey-Rusch, J., Phelps, L. A., & Szymanski, E. (Eds.). (1992). *Transition from school to adult life: Models, linkages, and policy.* Sycamore, IL: Sycamore Publishing.

Rusch, F. R., Kohler, P. D., & Hughes, C. (1992). An analysis of OSERS-sponsored secondary special education and transitional services research. *Career Education for Exceptional Individuals, 15,* 121–143.

Rusch, F. R., Schutz, R. P., Mithaug, D. E., Stewart, J. E., & Mar, D. K. (1982). *Vocational assessment and curriculum guide.* Seattle, WA: J. E. Stewart.

Rylance, B. J. (1997). Predictors of high school graduation or dropping out for youths with severe emotional disturbances. *Behavior Disturbances, 23,* 5–7.

Sabornie, E. J., & deBettencourt, L. U. (1997). *Teaching students with mild disabilities at the secondary level.* Upper Saddle River, NJ: Merrill/Prentice Hall.

Salvia, J., & Ysseldyke, J. E. (1998). *Assessment* (7th edition). Boston: Houghton Mifflin.

Schloss, P. J., Smith, M. A., & Schloss, C. N. (1990). *Instructional methods for adolescents with learning and behavior problems.* Boston: Allyn & Bacon.

Schrag, J., & Burnette, J. (1994). Inclusive schools. *Teaching Exceptional Children, 26*(3), 64–68.

Schumacher, J. B., Hazel, J. S., & Pederson, C. S. (1988). *Social skills for daily living.* Circle Pines, MN: American Guidance Service.

Semmel, M. I., Abernathy, T. V., Butera, G., & Lesar, S. (1991). Teacher perceptions of the regular education initiative. *Exceptional Children, 58*(1), 9–23.

Shanker, A. (1994). Push to integrate all disabled kids in regular classes is destructive. *Associated Press.* Author.

Shapiro, J. P., Bowermaster, D., & Loeb, P. (1993, December 13). Separate and unequal. *U.S. News & World Report,* pp. 46–50, 54–56, 60.

Simon, M., Bourexis, P., & Norman, M. (1993, Winter). Labor, education departments team for smooth transition. *Counterpoint,* 14–15.

Sinclair, M. F., & Christenson, S. L. (1992). Home-school collaboration: A building block of empowerment. *IMPACT—Feature Issue on Family Empowerment, 5*(2), 12–13.

Sinclair, M. F., Christenson, S. L., Evelo, D. L., & Hurley, C. M. (1998). Dropout prevention for youth with disabilities: Efficacy of a sustained school engagement procedure. *Exceptional Children, 65*(1), 7–21.

Singer, G. H. S., & Powers, L. C. (1993). Contributing to resilience in families: An overview. In G. H. S. Singer & L. C. Powers (Eds.), *Families, disability and empowerment: Active coping skills and strategies for family interventions* (pp. 1–25). Baltimore: Paul H. Brookes.

Sitlington, P. L. (1991). Curriculum-based assessment—What does it mean? *The Career Educator, 4*(1), 1–2.

Sitlington, P. L., Brolin, D. E., Clark, G. M., & Vacanti, J. M. (1985). Career/vocational assessment in the public school setting: The position of the

Division on Career Development. *Career Development for Exceptional Individuals, 8*(1), 3–6.

Sitlington, P. L., Clark, G. M., & Kolstoe, O. P. (2000). *Transition education and services for adolescents with disabilities* (3rd. ed.). Needham, MA: Allyn & Bacon.

Sitlington, P. L., & Frank, A. R. (1993). *Iowa statewide follow-up study: Adult adjustment of individuals with learning disabilities three vs. one year out of school.* Des Moines, IA: Iowa Department of Education.

Sitlington, P. L., & Frank, A. R. (1998). *Follow-up studies in transition.* Austin, TX: Pro-Ed.

Sitlington, P. L., Frank, A. R., & Carson, R. (1991). Adult adjustment among high school graduates with mild disabilities. *Exceptional Children, 59*(3), 221–233.

Sitlington, P. L., Frank, A. R., & Cooper, L. (1989). *Iowa statewide follow-up study: Adult adjustment of individuals with learning disabilities one year after leaving school.* Des Moines, IA: Iowa Department of Education.

Sitlington, P. L., Neubert, D. A., Begun, W., Lombard, R. C., & Leconte, P. J. (1996). *Access for success: Handbook on transition assessment.* Arlington, VA: The Council for Exceptional Children.

Skrtic, T. M. (1991). *Behind special education: A critical analysis of professional culture and school organization.* Denver, CO: Love Publishing.

Smith, C., & Rojewski, J. (1993). School-to-work transition: Alternatives for educational reform. *Youth & Society, 25,* 222–250.

Smith, F. (1989, January). Overselling literacy. *Phi Delta Kappan,* 353–359.

Smith, S. (1990). Individualized Education Programs (IEPs) in special education. From intent to acquiescence. *Exceptional Children, 57*(1), 6–14.

Smith, T. E. C., & Hilton, A. (1994). Program design for students with mental retardation. *Education and Training in Mental Retardation and Developmental Disabilities, 29*(1), 3–8.

Sonnenschein, P. (1981). Parents and professionals: An uneasy relationship. *Teaching Exceptional Children, 14,* 62–65.

The Sounding Board, 1(3), 1994. School District of the City of Inkster, MI.

Sparrow, S. S., Balla, D. A., & Cicchetti, D. V. (1985). *Vineland adaptive behavior scales.* Circle Pines, MN: American Guidance Service.

Spitz, H. H. (1973). Consolidating facts into the schematized learning and memory system of educable retardates. In N. R. Ellis (Ed.), *International review of research in mental retardation: Vol. 6.* New York: Academic Press.

Starr, M., & Gysbers, N. (1993). *Missouri comprehensive guidance: A model for program development, implementation, and evaluation.* Jefferson City, MO: Missouri Department of Elementary and Secondary Education.

Steelcase, Inc. (no date). *Employee handbook.* Grand Rapids, MI: Author.

Steelcase, Inc. (no date). *Workwell Magazine, 1,* 28. Grand Rapids, MI: Author.

Steele, P., Burrows, R., Kiburz, P., & Sitlington, P. (1990). *An interagency venture: Transitioning for people with moderate and severe disabilities.* Des Moines, IA: Iowa Department of Education.

Stephens, A. (1992). Life after high school: The purpose of transition planning. *Missouri Lincletter, 14*(4), 1–4.

Stephens, A. (Ed.). (1990). *Implementing career education at the elementary school level.* Columbia, MO: University of Missouri-Columbia, Missouri LINC.

Stephens, T. M. (1978). *Social skills in the classroom.* Columbus, OH: Cedars Press.

Stodden, R. A., Ianacone, R. N., Boone, R. M., & Bisconer, W. W. (1987). *Curriculum-based vocational assessment: A guide for addressing youth with special needs.* Honolulu, HI: Centre Publications International Education Corporation.

Supported Employment Technical Assistance Project. (1989). *Traumatic brain injury: Supplemental manual (employment training specialist series).* Lansing, MI: Michigan State University.

Swisher, J., & Clark, G. M. (1991). Curriculum-based vocational assessment of students with special needs at the middle school/junior high school levels. *The Journal for Vocational Special Needs Education, 13*(3), 9–14.

Swisher, J., & Clark, G. M. (1991). *Practical Arts Evaluation System (PAES)*. Jacksonville, FL: Talent Assessment.

Szymanski, E. M. (1994). Transition: Life-span and life-space considerations for empowerment. *Exceptional Children, 60*(5), 402–410.

Talent Assessment. (no date). *The talent assessment program*. Jacksonville, FL: Author.

Technical Education Research Centers. (1983). *Promoting collaborative planning of career education for disabled students*. Cambridge, MA: Author.

Thomas, S. W. (1992). Vocational assessment and the ADA: Issues and approaches for the rehabilitation professional. In Directions in Rehabilitation (Ed.), *Understanding the Americans with Disabilities Act* (pp. 4.3–4.16). New York: The Hatherleigh Co., Ltd.

Thousand, J. S., & Villa, R. A. (1991). A futuristic view of the REI: A response to Jenkins, Pious, and Jewell. *Exceptional Children, 57*(6), 556–562.

Tindall, L. W. (1992). Business linkages. In F. R. Rusch, L. Destefano, J. Chadsey-Rusch, L. A. Phelps, & E. Szymanski (Eds.), *Transition from school to adult life: Models, linkages, and policy* (pp. 319–339). Sycamore: IL: Sycamore Publishing.

Turnbull, A. P., & Turnbull, H. R. (1978). *Parents speak out: Views from the other side of the two-way mirror*. Upper Saddle River, NJ: Merrill/Prentice Hall.

Turnbull, A. P., Strickland, B. B., & Brantley, J. C. (1982). *Developing and implementing individualized education programs* (2nd ed.). Upper Saddle River, NJ: Merrill/Prentice Hall.

Turnbull, A. P., & Turnbull, H. R. (2001). *Families, professionals, and exceptionality: Collaborating for empowerment* (4th ed.). Upper Saddle River, NJ: Merrill/Prentice Hall.

U.S. Department of Education. (1991). *America 2000: An education strategy*. Washington, DC: Author.

U.S. Department of Education. (1994). *Goals 2000: A world-class education for every child*. Washington, DC: Author.

U.S. Department of Education. (1999). *To assure the free appropriate education of all children with disabilities: Twenty-first annual report to Congress on the implementation of the Individuals with Disabilities Education Act*. Washington, DC: Author.

U.S. Department of Education. (2001). *To assure the free appropriate education of all children with disabilities: Twenty-third annual report to Congress on the implementation of the Individuals with Disabilities Education Act*. Washington, DC: Author.

U.S. Department of Education, Office of Special Education and Rehabilitative Services. (1992). *Summary of existing legislation affecting people with disabilities*. Washington, DC: Author.

U.S. Department of Education, Office of Special Education Programs. (1992). *Fourteenth annual report to Congress on the implementation of the Individuals with Disabilities Education Act*. Washington, DC: Author.

U.S. Department of Education, Office of Special Education Programs. (1993). *Fifteenth annual report to Congress on the implementation of the Individuals with Disabilities Education Act*. Washington, DC: Author.

U.S. House of Representatives. (1990). Report No. 101–544, 10.

U.S. House of Representatives. (1993). Report No. 103–378.

VALPAR International. (1986). *Prevocational readiness battery—VALPAR 17*. Tucson, AZ: VALPAR International Corporation.

Vanderbilt/Minnesota Social Interaction Project. (1993). *Play time/social time: Organizing your classroom to build interaction skills*. Tucson, AZ: Communication Skill Builders.

Wagner, M. (1991). Sticking it out: Secondary school completion. In M. Wagner, L. Newman, R. D'Amico, E. D. Joy, P. Butler-Nalin, C. Marder, & R. Cox (Eds.), *Youth with disabilities: How are they doing? The first comprehensive report from the National Longitudinal Transition Study of Special Education Students*. Menlo Park, CA: SRI International.

Wagner, M., D'Amico, R., Marder, C., Newman, L., & Blackorley, J. (1992). *What happens next? Trends in post-school outcomes of youth with disabilities*. Menlo Park, CA: SRI International.

Wagner, M., Newman, L., D'Amico, R., Joy, E. D., & Blackorley, J. (Eds.). (1991). *Youth with disabilities: How are they doing? The first comprehensive report from the National Longitudinal Transition Study of Special Education Students.* Menlo Park, CA: SRI International.

Waksman, S., & Messmer, C. L. (1985). *Waksman social skills curriculum (AIEP Education).* Portland, OR: ASIEP.

Walker, H., & Sylvester, R. (1991). Where is school along the path to prison? *Educational Leadership, 49,* 14–16.

Walker, H. M., Todis, B., Holmes, D., & Horton, G. (1988). *The ACCESS program: Adolescent curriculum for communication and effective social skills.* Austin, TX: Pro-Ed.

Walker, H. M., Todis, B., Holmes, D., & Horton, G. (1988). *The Walker social skills curriculum: The ACCESS program.* Austin, TX: Pro-Ed.

Ward, M. J. (1991). Self-determination re-visited: Going beyond expectations. *Transition Summary, National Information Center for Children and Youth with Handicaps, 7,* 2–4, 12.

Ward, M. J. (1992). Introduction to secondary special education and transition issues. In F. R. Rusch, L. Destefano, J. Chadsey-Rusch, L. A. Phelps, & E. Szymanski (Eds.), *Transition from school to adult life: Models, linkages, and policy* (pp. 387–389). Sycamore, IL: Sycamore Publishing.

Ward, M. J., & Halloran, W. D. (1993). Transition issues for the 1990s. *OSERS News in Print, 6*(6), 4–5.

Ward, M. J., & Halloran, W. D. (1989). Transition to uncertainty: Status of many school learners with severe disabilities. *Career Development for Exceptional Individuals, 12*(12), 71–81.

Warger, C. L. (1991, December). Peer tutoring: When working together is better than working alone. *Research and Resources on Special Education, 30.* ERIC Clearinghouse on Handicapped and Gifted Children.

Wehman, P. (1981). *Competitive employment: New horizons for severely disabled individuals.* Baltimore: Paul W. Brookes.

Wehman, P. (1992). *Life beyond the classroom.* Baltimore: Paul H. Brookes.

Wehman, P. (2001). *Life beyond the classroom: Transition strategies for young people with disabilities* (3rd ed.). Baltimore: Paul H. Brookes.

Wehman, P., & Hill, J. W. (1985). *Competitive employment for persons with mental retardation.* Richmond, VA: Virginia Commonwealth University.

Wehman, P., Moon, S., Everson, J. M., & Barcus, J. M. (1988). *Transition from school to work.* Baltimore: Paul H. Brookes.

Wehman, P., Parent, W., Wood, W., Talbert, C. M., Jasper, C., Miller, S., Marchant, J., & Walker, R. (1989). From school to competitive employment for young adults with mental retardation: Transition in practice. *Career Development for Exceptional Individuals, 12*(2), 97–105.

Wehmeyer, M. L. (1992). Self-determination and the education of students with mental retardation. *Education and Training in Mental Retardation, 27,* 303–314.

Wehmeyer, M. L. (1993). *Life centered career education: Self-determination scale.* Arlington, VA: The Council for Exceptional Children.

Wehmeyer, M. L. (2001). Self-determination and transition. In P. Wehman (Ed.), *Life beyond the classroom: Transition strategies for young people with disabilities* (3rd ed., pp 35–60). Baltimore: Paul H. Brookes.

Wehmeyer, M. L., Agran, M., & Hughes, C. (1998). *Teaching self-determination to students with disabilities: Basic skills for successful transition.* Baltimore: Paul H. Brookes.

Wehmeyer, M. L., Agran, M., & Hughes, C. (2001). *Teaching self-determination to students with disabilities: Basic skills for successful transition.* Baltimore: Paul H. Brookes.

Wehmeyer, M. L., Kelchner, K., & Richards, S. (1993). *Individual and environmental factors related to the self-determination of adults with mental retardation.* Arlington, TX: The Arc.

Weisenstein, G. R., & Elrod, G. F. (1987). Transition services for adolescent individuals with mild mental retardation. In R. N. Ianacone & R. Stodden (Eds.), *Transition issues and directions.* Arlington, VA: The Council for Exceptional Children, Division on Mental Retardation.

West, L. L., Corbey, A., Stephens, A., Jones, B., Miller, R. J., & Wircenski, S. (1992). *Integrating transition planning into the IEP process.* Arlington, VA: The Council for Exceptional Children.

Whetstone, M. (1993). IDEAS and transition: Outcomes and answers. In P. Browning (Ed.), *Transition II in Alabama: A profile of commitment.* Auburn, AL: Auburn University.

Wickwire, P. N. (1993). America at school and work in the 1990s: Career education—An opportunity. *Youth Policy, 15*(6 & 7), 16–23.

Wilka, J., & Rudrud, E. H. (1992). School transition to employment partnership (STEP): Employability curriculum. *The Journal of Vocational Special Needs Education, 15*(1), 9–13.

Will, M. (1984a). Let us pause and reflect—but not too long. *Exceptional Children, 51,* 11–16.

Will, M. (1984b). *OSERS programming for transition of youth with disabilities: Bridges from school to working life.* Washington, DC: Office of Special Education and Rehabilitative Services, U.S. Department of Education, Office of Information for the Handicapped.

Williamson, P. (1994). Tech prep ... The win/win program. *Missouri Schools, 60*(2), 11–14.

Winters, K. (1993). *Building bridges from school to work: A background paper for the Goals 2000—Educate America satellite town meeting.* Washington, DC: Office of Policy and Planning, Vocational and Adult Education.

Wisniewski, L. A., Alper, S., & Schloss, P. (1991). Work-experience and work-study programs for students with special needs: Quality indicators of transition services. *Career Development for Exceptional Individuals, 14*(1), 43–58.

Wolfensberger, W. (1972). *The principle of normalization in human services.* Toronto, Canada: National Institute on Mental Retardation, York University Campus.

Wood, M. M. (1986). *Developmental therapy in the classroom.* Austin, TX: Pro-Ed.

Wright, T. J., & Leung, P. (1993). *Meeting the unique needs of minorities with disabilities: A report to the President and Congress.* Washington, DC: National Council on Disability.

Ysseldyke, J. E., Algozzine, B., & Thurlow, M. L. (1992). *Critical issues in special education* (2nd ed.). Boston: Houghton Mifflin.

Ysseldyke, J. E., Thurlow, M. L., & Gilman, C. J. (1993). *Educational outcomes and indicators for students completing school.* Minneapolis, MN: College of Education, National Center on Educational Outcomes.

Zadny, J. J., & James, L. F. (1976). Another view on placement: State of the art 1976. *Studies in Placement Monograph No. 1.* Portland, OR: School of Social Work, Portland State University.

Zeaman, D., & House, B. J. (1963). The roles of attention in retardate discrimination learning. In N. R. Ellis (Ed.), *Handbook of mental deficiency.* New York: McGraw-Hill.

Zigler, E. (1966). Mental retardation: Current issues and approaches. In L. Hoffman & M. Hoffman (Eds.), *Review of child development research, 2.* New York: Russell Sage Foundation.

Zigmond, N., & Thornton, H. S. (1985). Follow-up of post-secondary aged LD graduates and dropouts. *Learning Disabilities Research, 1*(1), 50–55.

Name Index

Subject Index

• •

Note: Boldface numbers indicate illustrations and tables.